CONTEMPORARY ISSUES IN CURRICULUM

FIFTH EDITION

ALLAN C. ORNSTEIN
St. John's University

EDWARD F. PAJAK
Johns Hopkins University

STACEY B. ORNSTEIN
New York University

Boston Columbus Indianapolis New York San Francisco Upper Saddle River
Amsterdam Cape Town Dubai London Madrid Milan Munich Paris Montreal Toronto
Delhi Mexico City Sao Paulo Sydney Hong Kong Seoul Singapore Taipei Tokyo

Vice President and Editor in Chief: Jeffery W. Johnston
Executive Editor and Publisher: Stephen D. Dragin
Vice President, Director of Marketing: Quinn Perkson
Marketing Manager: Christopher Barry
Senior Managing Editor: Pamela D. Bennett
Senior Project Manager: Mary Harlan
Project Manager: Susan Hannahs
Senior Art Director: Jayne Conte
Cover Designer: Suzanne Duda
Cover Art: Getty Images, Inc.
Full-Service Project Management: Niraj Bhatt, Aptara®, Inc.
Composition: Aptara®, Inc.
Text and Cover Printer/Bindery: Courier/Stoughton
Text Font: Palatino

Library of Congress Cataloging-in-Publication Data

Contemporary issues in curriculum / [edited by] Allan C. Ornstein, Edward F. Pajak, Stacey B. Ornstein. —5th ed.
p. cm.
ISBN-13: 978-0-13-509447-1
ISBN-10: 0-13-509447-X
1. Education—Curricula—United States. 2. Curriculum planning—United States.
I. Ornstein, Allan C. II. Pajak, Edward III. Ornstein, Stacey B.
LB1570.C813 2011
375.001—dc22

2009053894

10 9 8 7 6 5 4 3 2

www.pearsonhighered.com

ISBN-10: 0-13-509447-X
ISBN-13: 978-0-13-509447-1

Contributors

Benjamin S. Bloom, Emeritus, University of Chicago
Ronald S. Brandt, Association for Supervision and Curriculum Development
Ted Britton, WestEd's National Center for Improving Science Education
Evans Clinchy, Northeastern University
Arthur L. Costa, Emeritus, California State University, Sacramento
Larry Cuban, Emeritus, Stanford University
Linda Darling-Hammond, Stanford University
Daniel L. Duke, University of Virginia
Howard Gardner, Harvard Graduate School of Education
Tom Gasner, University of Wisconsin, Whitewater
Geneva Gay, University of Washington
Carl D. Glickman, Emeritus, University of Georgia
Maxine Greene, Emeritus, Teachers College, Columbia University
Andy Hargreaves, Lynch School of Education, Boston College
Harold Hodgkinson, Center for Demographic Policy, Washington, D.C.
Lawrence Kohlberg, Emeritus, Harvard University
Alfie Kohn, Author and Lecturer on Education and Human Behavior
Frank Levy, Massachusetts Institute of Technology
Todd I. Lubart, Yale University
Veronica Boix Mansilla, Harvard Graduate School of Education
Frank Masci, Johns Hopkins University
Laura McCloskey, Stanford University
Peter McLaren, University of California, Los Angeles
Richard J. Murnane, Harvard Graduate School of Education
Nel Noddings, Stanford University
Jeannie S. Oakes, University of California, Los Angeles
Allan C. Ornstein, St. John's University
Jason Ornstein, Consultant for United States Army and Homeland Security
Edward F. Pajak, Johns Hopkins University
Parker J. Palmer, American Association for Higher Education
David Perkins, Harvard Graduate School of Education
Stanley Pogrow, San Francisco State University
James Popham, Emeritus, University of California, Los Angeles
Phillip C. Schlechty, Schlechty Center for Leadership in School Reform, Louisville, KY
Thomas J. Sergiovanni, Trinity University
Dennis Shirley, Lynch School of Education, Boston College
Nancy Faust Sizer, Francis W. Parker Charter School, Massachusetts
Theodore R. Sizer, Coalition of Essential Schools, California
Robert J. Sternberg, Yale University
Elaine Stotko, Johns Hopkins University
Ralph W. Tyler, Center for Advanced Study in the Behavioral Sciences, California
Herbert J. Walberg, Emeritus, University of Illinois, Chicago
Harry K. Wong, Author and Lecturer on Teacher Success and Retention

CONTRIBUTORS

Benjamin S. Bloom, Emeritus, University of Chicago
Ronald S. Brandt, Association for Supervision and Curriculum Development
Ted Britton, WestEd's National Center for Improving Science Education
Evans Clinchy, Northeastern University
Arthur L. Costa, Emeritus, California State University, Sacramento
Larry Cuban, Emeritus, Stanford University
Linda Darling-Hammond, Stanford University
Daniel L. Duke, University of Virginia
Howard Gardner, Harvard Graduate School of Education
Tom Ganser, University of Wisconsin, Whitewater
Geneva Gay, University of Washington
Carl D. Glickman, Emeritus, University of Georgia
Maxine Greene, Emeritus, Teachers College, Columbia University
Andy Hargreaves, Lynch School of Education, Boston College
Harold Hodgkinson, Center for Demographic Policy, Washington, D.C.
Lawrence Kohlberg, Emeritus, Harvard University
Alfie Kohn, Author and Lecturer on Education and Human Behavior
Frank Levy, Massachusetts Institute of Technology
Todd I. Lubart, Yale University
Veronica Boix Mansilla, Harvard Graduate School of Education
Frank Mauro, Johns Hopkins University
Laura McCloskey, Stanford University
Peter McLaren, University of California, Los Angeles
Richard J. Murnane, Harvard Graduate School of Education
Nel Noddings, Stanford University
Jeannie S. Oakes, University of California, Los Angeles
Allan C. Ornstein, St. John's University
Jason Ornstein, Consultant for United States Army and Homeland Security
Edward F. Pajak, Johns Hopkins University
Parker J. Palmer, American Association for Higher Education
David Perkins, Harvard Graduate School of Education
Stanley Pogrow, San Francisco State University
James Popham, Emeritus, University of California, Los Angeles
Phillip C. Schlechty, Schlechty Center for Leadership in School Reform, Louisville, KY
Thomas J. Sergiovanni, Trinity University
Dennis Shirley, Lynch School of Education, Boston College
Nancy Faust Sizer, Francis W. Parker Charter School, Massachusetts
Theodore R. Sizer, Coalition of Essential Schools, California
Robert J. Sternberg, Yale University
Elaine Stotko, Johns Hopkins University
Ralph W. Tyler, Center for Advanced Study in the Behavioral Sciences, California
Herbert J. Walberg, Emeritus, University of Illinois, Chicago
Harry K. Wong, Author and Lecturer on Teacher Success and Retention

Contents

Preface

This fifth edition of *Contemporary Issues in Curriculum* is a book for students or school leaders studying the disciplines of curriculum, instruction, supervision, administration, and teacher education. It is written for those who are exploring the issues that have the potential to influence the implementation, planning, and evaluation of curriculum at all levels of learning. The articles reflect emergent trends in the field of curriculum.

NEW TO THIS EDITION

In an effort to improve and streamline the new edition, the editors have added 10 new chapters and deleted 15, thus reducing the number of chapters from 40 to a more manageable 35. As in earlier editions, the overall intent of the editors was to focus on well-known contributors in the field of curriculum and to select articles that were easy to read and that simultaneously offered an in-depth perspective on a subject or issue important to curriculum. In deciding to delete or add chapters, the editors considered two factors: (1) Whether the original article had become dated or irrelevant to the changing trends in schools and/or society and (2) whether the original piece was either too lengthy or difficult to fully understand. Then, the purpose was to incorporate new chapters that students and instructors would find relevant to the field of curriculum and their own personal situations. The criteria for selection of the new chapters were

- The new articles are meant to interest those who are preparing for a teaching career as well as experienced educators concerned with education issues and policies.
- The chapters are valuable for use in introductory courses in curriculum and in a variety of upper-level and graduate education courses.
- The new authors (as in the case of previous editions) are well known in the field of curriculum and/or related domains—philosophy, teaching, learning, instruction, supervision, and policy. To be sure, the best authors in all fields of social science and education have a distinctive message.
- The authors chosen represent various ideological viewpoints. In some cases, such as the chapters by Schlechty, Darling-Hammond/McCloskey, and Ornstein/Ornstein, the facts put into evidence represent a political position like that of an attorney advocating a case before a jury.
- The story and issues in the new chapters are well defined and coherent and offer a comprehensive body of information on various educational trends and curriculum issues. They are written in a way that engages readers or takes sides in some political or philosophical struggle.
- The articles selected are intended to be controversial to encourage critical thinking and are organized to give the reader ready access to important ideas and issues that affect education in general and curriculum in particular.
- Although the notions of currency and relevancy filtered through the selection process, it is essential to understand that our pasts are our present, and there are no single timelines, no specific historical periods, separate from another time period. Another factor was duration, that the articles selected would have a time value of at least 5 years into the future.

- The editors are particularly concerned about traditional issues related to teaching and learning, as well as contemporary issues such as global, multicultural, and egalitarian perspectives. Given this bias, the greatest amount of change took place in the section on curriculum and policy.
- Finally, it is naïve to believe that more education stories on the front page of any newspaper or on CNN will change the course of schools or radically alter the curriculum. Nevertheless, the authors chosen tend to have the wind behind their backs and a broad frame of reference for understanding the important problems and trends affecting the present and future in education, as well as the field of curriculum.

ORGANIZATION OF THE TEXT

This book is divided into six parts: philosophy, teaching, learning, instruction, supervision, and policy. Each part consists of five or six chapters and is preceded by an introduction that provides a brief overview of the articles and focuses the reader's attention on the issues to be discussed. Each chapter begins with a set of focusing questions and ends with several discussion questions. A pro–con chart that explores views on both sides of a current controversial curricular concern and a case study problem appear at the end of each part. These instructional features help the reader integrate the content and the issues of the book. Instructors may wish to use these features as the bases for class discussion or essay assignments.

To ensure that the breadth and depth of viewpoints in the field are represented, we have included articles that portray current trends and illustrate the dynamism within the field. The readings present views that reflect traditionally held beliefs as well as other perspectives that might be considered more controversial in nature. Students and practitioners should have an opportunity to investigate the breadth of issues that are affecting curriculum and be able to access such information in a single source. Readers are encouraged to examine and debate these issues, formulate their own ideas regarding the issues affecting the field of curriculum, and decide what direction that field should take.

In Part I, the Schlechty chapter is new. No additions were made for Part II. The Mansilla/Gardner piece was added for Part III. In the next part, the Costa and Pogrow chapters are new. There are two new pieces in Part V, by Popham and Duke. As for the sixth part, the four new chapters are by Hargreaves/Shirley, Darling-Hammond/McClosky, Cuban, and Ornstein/Ornstein.

We acknowledge with gratitude the many authors who granted us permission to reprint their work. Allan Ornstein expresses love for Esther, his wife, and especially his children, Joel, Stacey, and Jason, and advises them to always take the high road in life. Edward Pajak thanks Diane, his wife, and children, Alexandra and Zachary, for their encouragement and support. Stacey Ornstein dedicates this book to her family and thanks them for their continuous support in all her endeavors.

We thank the following reviewers for their helpful suggestions: Jane S. Cardi, West Virginia University; Mary C. Clement, Berry College; Jacquelyn Culpepper, Mercer College; and Sandra Mahoney, University of the Pacific. Finally, Monica Hudock is acknowledged for her assistance in assembling the book.

PART ONE

Curriculum and Philosophy

How does philosophy influence the curriculum? To what extent does the curriculum reflect personal beliefs and societal ways? How do different conceptions of curriculum affect schooling and student achievement? In what way has curriculum been a catalyst in empowering certain segments of society while disenfranchising others?

In Chapter 1, Allan Ornstein considers how philosophy guides the organization of the curriculum. He explores how beliefs about the purposes of education are reflected in the subject matter and the process of teaching and learning. In the second chapter, Ronald Brandt and Ralph Tyler present a rationale for establishing educational goals. They identify the sources that they believe should be considered before articulating goals, as well as how goals should be used in planning learning activities.

In Chapter 3, Peter McLaren pays tribute to the memory of Paulo Freire, who was one of the first philosophers to write about education in terms of politics, globalism, and liberation. McLaren outlines Freire's life and teachings, his influence on North American critical theory, and his unique emphasis on the power of love. Next, Maxine Greene reminds us of the essential role that arts experiences play in helping students develop esthetic awareness. She explains why encounters with the arts are likely to enrich students' learning experiences. She also discusses why experience with the arts is critical to combating the delivery of prescriptive curricula and developing students' metacognitive strategies. In Chapter 5, Phillip C. Schlechty questions policy makers' disdain for local school boards and their single-minded focus on test scores. He suggests that local communities should be more involved in identifying standards for what students should know and are able to do than members of the bureaucratic elite. Active local involvement in education reform, he believes, holds the potential to transform schools and revitalize communities as well.

CHAPTER 1

Philosophy as a Basis for Curriculum Decisions

ALLAN C. ORNSTEIN

FOCUSING QUESTIONS

1. How does philosophy guide the organization and implementation of curriculum?
2. What are the sources of knowledge that shape a person's philosophy of curriculum?
3. What are the sources of knowledge that shape your philosophical view of curriculum?
4. How do the aims, means, and ends of education differ?
5. What is the major philosophical issue that must be determined before we can define a philosophy of curriculum?
6. What are the four major educational philosophies that have influenced curriculum in the United States?
7. What is your philosophy of curriculum?

Philosophic issues always have had and still do have an impact on schools and society. Contemporary society and its schools are changing fundamentally and rapidly, much more so than in the past. There is a special urgency that dictates continuous appraisal and reappraisal of the role of schools, and calls for a philosophy of education. Without philosophy, educators are directionless in the whats and hows of organizing and implementing what we are trying to achieve. In short, our philosophy of education influences, and to a large extent determines, our educational decisions, choices, and alternatives.

PHILOSOPHY AND CURRICULUM

Philosophy provides educators, especially curriculum specialists, with a framework for organizing schools and classrooms. It helps them answer questions about what the school's purpose is, what subjects are of value, how students learn, and what methods and materials to use. Philosophy provides them with a framework for broad issues and tasks, such as determining the goals of education, subject content and its organization, the process of teaching and learning, and, in general, what experiences and activities to stress in schools and classrooms. It also provides educators with a basis for making such decisions as what workbooks, textbooks, or other cognitive and noncognitive activities to utilize and how to utilize them, what and how much homework to assign, how to test students and how to use the test results, and what courses or subject matter to emphasize.

The importance of philosophy in determining curriculum decisions is expressed well by the classic statement of Thomas Hopkins (1941): "Philosophy has entered into every important decision that has ever been made about curriculum and teaching in the past and will continue to be the basis of every important decision in the future. . . . There is rarely a moment in a school day when a teacher is not confronted with occasions where philosophy is a vital part of action." Hopkins' statement reminds us of how important philosophy is to all aspects of curriculum decisions, whether it operates overtly or covertly. Indeed, almost all elements of curriculum are based on philosophy. As John Goodlad (1979b) points out, philosophy is the beginning point in curriculum decision making and is the basis for all subsequent decisions regarding curriculum. Philosophy becomes the criterion for determining the aims, means, and ends of curriculum. The aims are statements of value, based on philosophical beliefs; the means represent processes and methods, which reflect philosophical choices; and the ends connote the facts, concepts, and principles of the knowledge or behavior learned—what is felt to be important to learning.

Smith, Stanley, and Shores (1957) also put great emphasis on the role of philosophy in developing curriculum, asserting it is essential when formulating and justifying educational purposes, selecting and organizing knowledge, formulating basic procedures and activities, and dealing with verbal traps (what we see versus what is read). Curriculum theorists, they point out, often fail to recognize both how important philosophy is to developing curriculum and how it influences aspects of curriculum.

Philosophy and the Curriculum Specialist

The philosophy of curriculum specialists reflects their life experiences, common sense, social and economic background, education, and general beliefs about people. An individual's philosophy evolves and continues to evolve as long as there is personal growth, development, and learning from experience. Philosophy is a description, explanation, and evaluation of the world as seen from personal perspective, or through what some social scientists call "social lenses."

Curriculum specialists can turn to many sources of knowledge, but no matter how many sources they draw on or how many authorities they listen to, their decisions are shaped by all the experiences that have affected them and the social groups with which they identify. These decisions are based on values, attitudes, and beliefs that they have developed, involving their knowledge and interpretation of causes, events, and their consequences. Philosophy determines principles for guiding action.

No one can be totally objective in a cultural or social setting, but curriculum specialists can broaden their base of knowledge and experiences by trying to understand other people's sense of values and by analyzing problems from various perspectives. They can also try to modify their own critical analyses and points of view by learning from their experiences and those of others. Curriculum specialists who are unwilling to modify their points of view, or compromise philosophical positions when school officials or their colleagues espouse another philosophy, are at risk of causing conflict and disrupting the school. Ronald Doll (1986) puts it this way: "Conflict among curriculum planners occurs when persons . . . hold positions along a continuum of [different] beliefs and . . . persuasions." The conflict may become so intense that "curriculum study grinds to a halt." Most of the time, the differences can be reconciled "temporarily in deference to the demands of a temporary, immediate task." However, Doll further explains that "teachers and administrators who are clearly divided in philosophy can seldom work together in close proximity for long periods of time."

The more mature and understanding and the less personally threatened and ego-involved individuals are, the more capable they are of reexamining or modifying their philosophy, or at least of being willing to appreciate other points of view. It is important for curriculum specialists to regard their attitudes and beliefs as tentative—as subject to reexamination whenever facts or trends challenge them. Equally dangerous for curriculum specialists is the opposite—indecision or lack of any philosophy, which can be reflected in attempts to avoid commitment to a set of values. A measure of positive conviction is essential to prudent action. Having a personal philosophy that is tentative or subject to modification does not lead to lack of conviction or disorganized behavior. Curriculum specialists can arrive at their conclusions on the best evidence available, and they then can change when better evidence surfaces.

Philosophy as a Curriculum Source

The function of philosophy can be conceived as either the base for the starting point in curriculum development or an interdependent function of other functions in curriculum development. John Dewey (1916) represents the first school of thought by contending that "philosophy may . . . be defined as the general theory of education," and that "the business of philosophy is to provide [the framework] for the aims and methods" of schools. For Dewey, philosophy provides a generalized meaning to our lives and a way of thinking, "an explicit formulation of the . . . mental and moral attitudes in respect to the difficulties of contemporary social life." Philosophy is not only a starting point for schools; it is also crucial for all curriculum activities. For as Dewey adds, "Education is the laboratory in which philosophic distinctions become concrete and are tested."

Highly influenced by Dewey, Ralph Tyler's (1949) framework of curriculum includes philosophy as only one of five criteria commonly used for selecting educational purposes. The relationship between philosophy and the other criteria—studies of learners, studies of contemporary life, suggestions from subject specialists, and the psychology of learning—is the basis for determining the school's purposes. Although philosophy is not the starting point in Tyler's curriculum, but rather interacts on an equal basis with the other criteria, he does seem to place more importance on philosophy for developing educational purposes. Tyler (1949) writes, "The educational and social philosophy to which the school is committed can serve as the first screen for developing the social program." He concludes that "philosophy attempts to define the nature of the good life and a good society," and that the "educational philosophies in a democratic society are likely to emphasize strongly democratic values in schools."

There can be no serious discussion about philosophy until we embrace the question of what is education. When we agree on what education is, we can ask what the school's purpose is. We can then pursue philosophy, aims, and goals of curriculum. According to Goodlad (1979b), the school's first responsibility is to the social order, what he calls the "nation-state," but in our society the sense of individual growth and potential is paramount. This duality—society versus the individual—has been a major philosophical issue in Western society for centuries and was a very important issue in Dewey's works. As

Dewey (1916) claimed, we not only wish "to make [good] citizens and workers" but also ultimately want "to make human beings who will live life to the fullest."

The compromise of the duality between national allegiance and individual fulfillment is a noble aim that should guide all curriculum specialists—from the means to the ends. When many individuals grow and prosper, then society flourishes. The original question set forth by Goodlad can be answered: Education is growth and the focal point for the individual as well as society; it is a never-ending process of life, and the more refined the guiding philosophy the better the quality of the educational process.

In considering the influence of philosophic thought on curriculum, several classification schemes are possible; therefore, no superiority is claimed for the categories used in the tables here. The clusters of ideas are those that often evolve openly or unwittingly during curriculum planning.

Four major educational philosophies have influenced curriculum in the United States: Perennialism, Essentialism, Progressivism, and Reconstructionism. Table 1.1 provides an overview of these education philosophies and how they affect curriculum, instruction, and teaching. Teachers and administrators should compare the content of the categories with their own philosophical "lens" in terms of how they view curriculum and how other views of curriculum and related instructional and teaching issues may disagree.

Another way of interpreting philosophy and its effect on curriculum is to analyze philosophy in terms of polarity. The danger of this method is to simplify it in terms of a dichotomy, not to recognize that there are overlaps and shifts. Table 1.2 illustrates philosophy in terms of traditional and contemporary categories. The traditional philosophy, as shown, tends to overlap with Perennialism and Essentialism. Contemporary philosophy tends to coincide with Progressivism and Reconstructionism.

Table 1.2 shows that traditional philosophy focuses on the past, emphasizes fixed and absolute values, and glorifies our cultural heritage. Contemporary philosophy emphasizes the present and future and views events as changeable and relative; for the latter, nothing can be preserved forever, for despite any attempt, change is inevitable. The traditionalists wish to train the mind, emphasize subject matter, and fill the learner with knowledge and information. Those who ascribe to contemporary philosophies are more concerned with problem solving and emphasize student interests and needs. Whereas subject matter is considered important for its own sake, according to traditionalists, certain subjects are more important than others. For contemporary educators, subject matter is considered a medium for teaching skills and attitudes, and most subjects have similar value. According to the traditionalists, the teacher is an authority in subject matter, who dominates the lesson with explanations and lectures. For the contemporary proponent, the teacher is a guide for learning, as well as an agent for change; students and teachers often are engaged in dialogue.

In terms of social issues and society, traditionalists view education as a means of providing direction, control, and restraint, while their counterparts focus on individual expression and freedom from authority. Citizenship is linked to cognitive development for the traditional educator, and it is linked to moral and social development for the contemporary educator. Knowledge and the disciplines prepare students for freedom, according to the traditional view, but it is direct experience in democratic living and political/social action which prepares students for freedom, according to the contemporary ideal. Traditionalists believe in excellence, and contemporary educators favor equality. The traditional view of education maintains that group values come first, where cooperative and conforming behaviors are important

Table 1.1 Overview of Educational Philosophies

	Philosophical Base	*Instructional Objective*	*Knowledge*	*Role of Teacher*	*Curriculum Focus*	*Related Curriculum Trends*
Perennialism	Realism	To educate the rational person; to cultivate the intellect	Focus on past and permanent studies; mastery of facts and timeless knowledge	Teacher helps students think rationally; based on Socratic method and oral exposition; explicit teaching of traditional values	Classical subjects; literary analysis; constant curriculum	Great books; *Paideia* proposal
Essentialism	Idealism, Realism	To promote the intellectual growth of the individual; to educate the competent person	Essential skills and academic subjects; mastery of concepts and principles of subject matter	Teacher is authority in his or her field; explicit teaching of traditional values	Essential skills (three Rs) and essential subjects (English, arithmetic, science, history, and foreign language)	Back to basics; excellence in education
Progressivism	Pragmatism	To promote democratic, social living	Knowledge leads to growth and development; a living-learning process; focus on active and interesting learning	Teacher is a guide for problem solving and scientific inquiry	Based on students' interests; involves the application of human problems and affairs; inter-disciplinary subject matter; activities and projects	Relevant curriculum; humanistic education; alternative and free schooling
Reconstructionism	Pragmatism	To improve and reconstruct society; education for change and social reform	Skills and subjects needed to identify and ameliorate problems of society; learning is active and concerned with contemporary and future society	Teacher serves as an agent of change and reform; acts as a project director and research leader; helps students become aware of problems confronting humankind	Emphasis on social sciences and social research methods; examination of social, economic, and political problems; focus on present and future trends as well as national and international issues	Equality of education; cultural pluralism; international education; futurism

Source: Allan C. Ornstein and Francis P. Hunkins, *Curriculum: Foundations, Principles, and Theory,* 3rd ed. (Boston: Allyn and Bacon, 1998), p. 56.

Table 1.2 Overview of Traditional and Contemporary Philosophies

Philosophical Consideration	*Traditional Philosophy*	*Contemporary Philosophy*
Educational philosophy	Perennialism, Essentialism	Progressivism, Reconstructionism
Direction in time	Superiority of past; education for preserving past	Education is growth; reconstruction of present experiences; changing society; concern for future and shaping it
Values	Fixed, absolute, objective, and/or universal	Changeable, subjective, and/or relative
Educational process	Education is viewed as instruction; mind is disciplined and filled with knowledge	Education is viewed as creative self-learning; active process in which learner reconstructs knowledge
Intellectual emphasis	To train or discipline the mind; emphasis on subject matter	To engage in problem-solving activities and social activities; emphasis on student interests and needs
Worth of subject matter	Subject matter for its own importance; certain subjects are better than others for training the mind	Subject matter is a medium for teaching skills, attitudes, and intellectual processes; all subjects have similar value for problem-solving activities
Curriculum content	Curriculum is composed of three Rs, as well as liberal studies or essential academic subjects	Curriculum is composed of three Rs, as well as skills and concepts in arts, sciences, and vocational studies
Learning	Emphasis on cognitive learning; learning is acquiring knowledge and/or competency in disciplines	Emphasis on whole child; learning is giving meaning to experiences and/or active involvement in reform
Grouping	Homogeneous grouping and teaching of students by ability	Heterogeneous grouping and integration of students by ability (as well as race, sex, and class)
Teacher	Teacher is an authority on subject matter; teacher plans activities; teacher supplies knowledge to student; teacher talks, dominates lesson; Socratic method	Teacher is a guide for inquiry and change agent; teacher and students plan activities; students learn on their own independent of the teacher; teacher-student dialogue; student initiates much of the discussion and activities
Social roles	Education involves direction, control, and restraint; group (family, community, church, nation, etc.) always comes first	Education involves individual expression; individual comes first
Citizenship	Cognitive and moral development leads to good citizenship	Personal and social development leads to good citizenship
Freedom and democracy	Acceptance of one's fate, conformity, and compliance with authority; knowledge and discipline prepare students for freedom	Emphasis on creativeness, nonconformity, and self-actualization; direct experiences in democratic living and political/social action prepare students for freedom
Excellence vs. equality	Excellence in education; education as far as human potential permits; academic rewards and jobs based on merit	Equality of education; education which permits more than one chance and more than an equal chance to disadvantaged groups; education and employment sectors consider unequal abilities of individuals and put some restraints on achieving individuals so that different outcomes and group scores, if any, are reduced
Society	Emphasis on group values; acceptance of norms of and roles in society; cooperative and conforming behavior; importance of society; individual restricted by custom and tradition of society	Emphasis on individual growth and development; belief in individual with ability to modify, even reconstruct, the social environment; independent and self-realizing, fully functioning behavior; importance of person; full opportunity to develop one's own potential

for the good of society. Contemporary educators assert that what is good for the individual should come first, and they believe in the individual modifying and perhaps reconstructing society.

The Curriculum Specialist at Work

Philosophy gives meaning to our decisions and actions. In the absence of a philosophy, educators are vulnerable to externally imposed prescriptions, to fads and frills, to authoritarian schemes, and to other "isms." Dewey (1916) was so convinced of the importance of philosophy that he viewed it as the all-encompassing aspect of the educational process—as necessary for "forming fundamental dispositions, intellectual and emotional, toward nature and fellow man." If this conclusion is accepted, it becomes evident that many aspects of a curriculum, if not most of the educational processes in school, are developed from a philosophy. Even if it is believed that Dewey's point is an overstatement, the pervasiveness of philosophy in determining views of reality, the values and knowledge that are worthwhile, and the decisions to be made about education and curriculum should still be recognized.

Very few schools adopt a single philosophy; in practice, most schools combine various philosophies. Moreover, the author's position is that no single philosophy, old or new, should serve as the exclusive guide for making decisions about schools or about the curriculum. All philosophical groups want the same things of education—that is, they wish to improve the educational process, to enhance the achievement of the learner, to produce better and more productive citizens, and to improve society. Because of their different views of reality, values, and knowledge, however, they find it difficult to agree on how to achieve these ends.

What we need to do, as curricularists, is to search for the middle ground, a highly elusive and abstract concept, in which there is no extreme emphasis on subject matter or student, cognitive development or sociopsychological development, excellence or equality. What we need is a prudent school philosophy, one that is politically and economically feasible, that serves the needs of students and society. Implicit in this view of education is that too much emphasis on any one philosophy may do harm and cause conflict. How much one philosophy is emphasized, under the guise of reform (or for whatever reason), is critical because no one society can give itself over to extreme "isms" or political views and still remain a democracy. The kind of society that evolves is in part reflected in the education system, which is influenced by the philosophy that is eventually defined and developed.

CONCLUSION

In the final analysis, curriculum specialists must understand that they are continuously faced with curriculum decisions, and that philosophy is important in determining these decisions. Unfortunately, few school people test their notions of curriculum against their school's statement of philosophy. According to Brandt and Tyler (1983), it is not uncommon to find teachers and administrators developing elaborate lists of behavioral objectives with little or no consideration to the overall philosophy of the school. Curriculum workers need to provide assistance in developing and designing school practices that coincide with the philosophy of the school and community. Teaching, learning, and curriculum are all interwoven in school practices and should reflect a school's and a community's philosophy.

REFERENCES

Brandt, R. S., & Tyler, R. W. (1983). "Goals and Objectives." In F. W. English, ed., *Fundamental Curriculum Decisions.* Alexandria, VA: Association for Supervision and Curriculum Development.

Dewey, J. (1916). *Democracy and Education.* New York: Macmillan, pp. 383–384.

Doll, R. C. (1986). *Curriculum Improvement: Decision-making and Process,* 6th ed. Boston: Allyn and Bacon, p. 30.

Goodlad, J. I. (1979a). *Curriculum Inquiry.* New York: McGraw-Hill.

Goodlad, J. I. (1979b). *What Schools Are For.* Bloomington, IN: Phi Delta Kappa Educational Foundation.

Goodlad, J. I. (1984). *A Place Called School.* New York: McGraw-Hill.

Hopkins, L. T. (1941). *Interaction: The Democratic Process.* Boston: D. C. Heath, pp. 198–200.

Smith, B. O., Stanley, W. O., & Shores, J. H. (1957). *Fundamentals of Curriculum Development,* rev. ed. New York: Worldbook.

Tyler, R. W. (1949). *Basic Principles of Curriculum and Instruction.* Chicago: University of Chicago Press, pp. 33–34.

DISCUSSION QUESTIONS

1. Which philosophical approach reflects your beliefs about (a) the school's purpose, (b) what subjects are of value, (c) how students learn, and (d) the process of teaching and learning?
2. What curriculum focus would the perennialists and essentialists recommend for our increasingly diverse school-age population?
3. What curriculum would the progressivists and reconstructionists select for a multicultural student population?
4. Should curriculum workers adopt a single philosophy to guide their practices? Why? Why not?
5. Which philosophy is most relevant to contemporary education? Why?

CHAPTER 2

Goals and Objectives

RONALD S. BRANDT
RALPH W. TYLER

FOCUSING QUESTIONS

1. Why is it important to establish goals for student learning?
2. How do goals and objectives differ?
3. What are three types of goals?
4. What are the factors that should be considered in developing educational goals?
5. What is the relationship between goals and learning activities?
6. In what ways are curriculum goals integral to the process of evaluation?
7. What types of goals should be addressed by schools?

Whether planning for one classroom or many, curriculum developers must have a clear idea of what they expect students to learn. Establishing goals is an important and necessary step because there are many desirable things students could learn—more than schools have time to teach them—so schools should spend valuable instructional time only on high-priority learnings.

Another reason for clarifying goals is that schools must be able to resist pressures from various sources. Some of the things schools are asked to teach are untrue, would hinder students' development, or would help make them narrow, bigoted persons. Some would focus students' learning so narrowly it would reduce, rather than increase, their life options.

FORMS OF GOALS AND OBJECTIVES

Statements of intent appear in different forms, and words such as goals, objectives, aims, ends, outcomes, and purposes are often used interchangeably. Some people find it useful to think of goals as long-term aims to be achieved eventually and objectives as specific learning students are to acquire as a result of current instruction.

Planners in the Portland, Oregon, area schools say these distinctions are not clear enough to meet organizational planning requirements. They use "goal" to mean any desired outcome of a program, regardless of its specificity, and "objective" only in connection with *program change objectives,* which are defined as statements of intent to change program elements in specified ways. Doherty and Peters (1981) say this distinction avoids confusion and is consistent with the philosophy of "management by objectives."

They refer to three types of goals: instructional, support, and management. Educational goals are defined as learnings to be acquired; support goals as services to be rendered; and management goals as functions of management, such as planning, operating, and evaluating. Such a goal structure permits evaluation to focus on measures of learning acquired (educational outcomes), measures of quantity and quality of service delivery (support outcomes), and measures of quality and effectiveness of management functions (management outcomes).

The Tri-County Goal Development Project, which has published 14 volumes containing over 25,000 goal statements,[1] is concerned only with *educational goals.* For these collections, the following distinctions are made within the general category of "goals":

System level goals (set for the school district by the board of education)
Program level goals (set by curriculum personnel in each subject field)
Course level goals (set by groups of teachers for each subject or unit of instruction)
Instructional level goals (set by individual teachers for daily planning)

Examples of this outcome hierarchy are shown in Figure 2.1.

What distinguishes this system of terminology from others is its recognition that a learning outcome has the same essential character at all levels of planning (hence the appropriateness of a single term, goal, to describe it) and that the level of generality used to represent learning varies with the planning requirements at each level of school organization. The degree of generality chosen for planning at each level is, of course, a matter of judgment; there is no "correct" level but only a sense of appropriateness to purpose.

Teachers, curriculum specialists, and university consultants who write and review course goals use the following guidelines (Doherty & Peters, 1980, pp. 26–27):

1. Is the stated educational outcome potentially significant?
2. Does the goal begin with "The student knows . . ." if it is a knowledge goal and "The student is able to . . ." if it is a process goal?
3. Is the goal stated in language that is sufficiently clear, concise, and appropriate? (Can it be stated in simpler language and/or fewer words?)
4. Can learning experiences be thought of that would lead to the goal's achievement?
5. Do curricular options exist for the goal's achievement? (Methodology should not be a part of the learning outcome statement.)

System Goal:	The student knows and is able to apply basic scientific and technological processes.
Program Goal:	The student is able to use the conventional language, instruments, and operations of science.
Course Goal:	The student is able to classify organisms according to their conventional taxonomic categories.
Instructional Goal:	The student is able to correctly classify cuttings from the following trees as needleleaf, hemlock, pine, spruce, fir, larch, cypress, redwood, and cedar.

FIGURE 2.1 Examples of Goals at Each Level of Planning

6. Does the goal clearly contribute to the attainment of one or more of the program goals in its subject area?
7. Can the goal be identified with the approximate level of student development?
8. Can criteria for evaluating the goal be identified?

Curriculum developers need to decide the types and definitions of goals most useful to them and to users of their materials. Some authors advise avoiding vagueness by using highly specific language.[2] Mager (1962) and other writers insist that words denoting observable behaviors, such as "construct" and "identify," should be used in place of words like "understand" and "appreciate." Others reject this approach, claiming that behavioral objectives "are in no way adequate for conceptualizing most of our most cherished educational aspirations" (Eisner, 1979, p. 101). Unfortunately this dispute has developed into a debate about behavioral objectives rather than dialogue over the kinds of behavior appropriate for a humane and civilized person.

The debate is partly semantic and partly conceptual. To some persons the word "behavior" carries the meaning of an observable act, like the movement of the fingers in typing. To them, behavioral objectives refer only to overt behavior. Others use the term "behavior" to emphasize the active nature of the learner. They want to emphasize that learners are not passive receptacles but living, reasoning persons. In this sense, behavior refers to all kinds of human reactions.

For example, a detailed set of "behavioral goals" was prepared by French and others (1957). Organized under the major headings of "self-realization," "face-to-face relationships," and "membership in large organizations," *Behavioral Goals of General Education in High School* includes aims such as "Shows growing ability to appreciate and apply good standards of performance and artistic principles." These are expanded by illustrative behaviors such as "Appreciates good workmanship and design in commercial products."

The other aspect of the debate over behavioral objectives arises from focusing on limited kinds of learning, such as training factory workers to perform specific tasks. The term "conditioning" is commonly used for the learning of behaviors initiated by clear stimuli and calling for automatic, fixed responses. Most driving behavior, for example, consists of conditioned responses to traffic lights, to the approach of other cars and pedestrians, and to the sensations a driver receives from the car's movements. Conditioning is a necessary and important type of learning.

In some situations, though, an automatic response is inappropriate. A more complex model of learning compatible with development of responsible persons in a changing society conceives of the learner as actively seeking meaning. This implies understanding and conscious pursuit of one's goals. The rewards of such learning include the satisfaction of coping with problems successfully.

Planning curriculum for self-directed learning requires goals that are not directly observable: ways of thinking, understanding of concepts and principles, broadening and deepening of interests, changing of attitudes, developing satisfying emotional responses to aesthetic experiences, and the like.

Even these goals, however, should use terms with clearly defined meanings. Saying that a student should "understand the concept of freedom" is far too broad and ambiguous, both because the meaning of the term "concept" is not sufficiently agreed on among educators and because concept words such as "freedom" have too great a range of possible informational loadings to ensure similar interpretation from teacher to teacher. If used at all, such a statement would be at the program level and would require increasingly specific elaboration at the course and lesson plan levels.

Some educators find it useful to refer to a particular type of goal as a *competency.* Used in the early 1970s in connection with Oregon's effort to relate high school instruction to daily life (Oregon State Board, 1972), the term "minimum competency" has become identified with state and district testing programs designed to ensure that students have a minimum level of basic skills before being promoted or graduated. Spady (1978) and other advocates of performance-based education point out that competency involves more than "capacities" such as the ability to read and calculate; it should refer to *application* of school-learned skills in situations outside of school.

One definition of competency is the ability to perform a set of related tasks with a high degree of skill. The concept is especially useful in vocational education, where a particular competency can be broken down through task analysis into its component skills so that teachers and curriculum planners have both a broad statement of expected performance and an array of skills specific enough to be taught and measured (Chalupsky & others, 1981).

CONSIDERATIONS IN CHOOSING GOALS

Educational goals should reflect three important factors: the nature of organized knowledge, the nature of society, and the nature of learners (Tyler, 1949). An obvious source is the nature of organized fields of study. Schools teach music, chemistry, and algebra because these fields have been developed through centuries of painstaking inquiry. Each academic discipline has its own concepts, principles, and processes. It would be unthinkable to neglect passing on to future generations this priceless heritage and these tools for continued learning.

Another factor affecting school goals is the nature of society. For example, the goals of education in the United States are quite different from those in Russia. In the United States, we stress individuality, competition, creativity, and freedom to choose government officials. Russian schools teach loyalty to the state and subordination of one's individuality to the welfare of the collective. One result is that most U.S. schools offer a great many electives, while the curriculum in Russian schools consists mostly of required subjects. For example, all students in Russia must study advanced mathematics and science to serve their technologically advanced nation (Wirszup, 1981).

U.S. schools have assumed, explicitly or implicitly, many goals related to the nature of society. For example, schools offer drug education, sex education, driver education, and other programs because of concerns about the values and behavior of youth and adults. Schools teach visual literacy because of the influence of television, consumer education because our economic system offers so many choices, and energy education because of the shortage of natural resources.

A goal statement by Ehrenberg and Ehrenberg (1978) specifically recognizes the expectations of society. Their model for curriculum development begins with a statement of "ends sought": "It is intended that as a result of participating in the K–12 educational program students will consistently and effectively take *intelligent, ethical action:* (1) to accomplish the tasks society legitimately expects of all its members, and (2) to establish and pursue worthwhile goals of their own choosing."

The curriculum development process outlined by the Ehrenbergs involves preparing a complete rationale for the ends-sought statement and then defining, for example, areas of societal expectations. The work of the curriculum developer consists of defining a framework of "criterion tasks," all either derived from expectations of society or necessary to pursue individual goals. These tasks, at various levels of pupil development, become the focus of day-to-day instruction. In this way, all curriculum is directly related to school system goals.

A third consideration in choosing goals, sometimes overlooked, is the nature of learners. For example, because Lawrence Kohlberg (1980) found that children pass through a series of stages in their moral development, he believes schools should adopt the goal of raising students' levels of moral reasoning. Sternberg (1981) and other "information processing" psychologists believe that intelligence is, partly at least, a set of strategies and skills that can be learned. Their research suggests, according to Sternberg, that schools can and should set a goal of improving students' intellectual performance.

Recognizing that students often have little interest in knowledge for its own sake or in adult applications of that knowledge, some educators believe goals not only should be based on what we know about students, but should come from students themselves. Many alternative schools emphasize this source of goals more than conventional schools typically do (Raywid, 1981).

While knowledge, society, and learners are all legitimate considerations, the three are sometimes in conflict. For example, many of the products of the curriculum reform movement of the 1960s had goals based almost exclusively on the nature of knowledge. The emphasis of curriculum developers was on the "structure of the disciplines" (Bruner, 1960). Goals of some curriculums failed to fully reflect the nature of society and students, so teachers either refused to use them or gave up after trying them for a year or two (Stake & Easley, 1978).

In the 1970s, educators and the general public reacted against this discipline-centered emphasis by stressing practical activities drawn from daily life. Schools were urged to teach students how to balance a checkbook, how to choose economical purchases, how to complete a job application, and how to read a traffic ticket. Career education enthusiasts, not content with the reasonable idea that education should help prepare students for satisfying careers, claimed that *all* education should be career-related in some way.

Conflicts of this sort between the academic and the practical are persistent and unavoidable, but curriculum developers err if they emphasize only one source of goals and ignore the others. If noneducators are preoccupied with only one factor, educational leaders have a responsibility to stress the importance of the others and to insist on balance.

SCOPE OF THE SCHOOL'S RESPONSIBILITY

There have been many attempts to define the general aims of schools and school programs, including the well-known Cardinal Principles listed by a national commission in 1918. The seven goals in that report—health, fundamental processes, worthy home membership, vocation, civic education, worthy use of leisure, and ethical character—encompass nearly every aspect of human existence, and most goal statements written since that time have been equally comprehensive.

Some authors contend that schools are mistaken to assume such broad aims. Martin (1980) argued that intellectual development and citizenship are the only goals for which schools should have primary responsibility and that other institutions should be mainly responsible for such goals as worthy home membership. He proposed that schools undertake a new role of coordinating educational efforts of all community agencies.

Paul (1982) reported that in three different communities large numbers of teachers, students, and parents agreed on a limited set of goals confined mostly to basic skills. Paul contended that schools often confuse the issue when involving citizens in setting goals because they ask what students should learn rather than what schools should teach. Goal surveys conducted by her organization showed, she said, that adults want young people to develop many qualities for which they do not expect schools to be responsible.

Undeniably, the aims and activities of U.S. schools are multiple and diverse. They not only teach toothbrushing, crafts, religion, care of animals, advertising, cooking, automobile repair, philosophy, hunting, and chess; they also provide health and food services to children, conduct parent education classes, and offer a variety of programs for the elderly. Periodic review of these obligations is clearly in order. However, in trying to delimit their mission, schools must not minimize concern for qualities that, though hard to define and develop, distinguish educated persons from the less educated.

A carefully refined statement of goals of schooling in the United States was developed by Goodlad (1979) and his colleagues in connection with their Study of Schooling. Deliberately derived from an analysis of hundreds of goal statements adopted by school districts and state departments of education so as to reflect accurately the currently declared aims of U.S. education, the list comprises 65 goals in 12 categories, including "intellectual development," "self-concept," and "moral and ethical character."

An equally broad set of goals is used in Pennsylvania's Educational Quality Assessment, which includes questions intended to measure such elusive aims as "understanding others" and "self-esteem." School districts must give the tests at least once every five years as part of a plan to make schools accountable for the 12 state-adopted goals (Seiverling, 1980). An adaptation of the Pennsylvania goals was used by the ASCD Committee on Research and Theory (1980) in connection with their plan for *Measuring and Attaining the Goals of Education.*

In many cases, schools contribute modestly or not at all to helping students become loving parents and considerate neighbors. In other cases, school experiences may have lasting effects on values, attitudes, and behavior. We believe school goals should include such aims as "interpersonal relations" and "autonomy," as well as "intellectual development" and "basic skills" (Goodlad, 1979), although the goal statement should specifically recognize that most goals are not the exclusive domain of schools but are a shared responsibility with other institutions.

ESTABLISHING LOCAL GOALS

It is usually helpful to begin identification of goals by listing all the promising possibilities from various sources. Consider contemporary *society.* What things could one's students learn that would help them meet current demands and take advantage of future opportunities? General data about modern society may be found in studies of economic, political, and social conditions. Data directly relevant to the lives of one's students will usually require local studies, which can be made by older students, parents, and other local people.

Consider the *background of the students:* their previous experiences, things they have already learned, their interests and needs—that is, the gaps between desired ways of thinking, feeling, and acting and their present ways. This information should be specific to one's own students, although generalized studies of the development of children and youth in our culture will suggest what to look for.

Consider the potential of the various *subject fields.* What things could one's students learn about their world and themselves from the sciences, history, literature, and so on? What can mathematics provide as a resource for their lives? Visual arts? Music? Each new generation is likely to find new possibilities in these growing fields of knowledge and human expression.

In the effort to identify possible goals, don't be unduly concerned about the form in which you state these "things to be learned." For example, you may find a possibility in "Learn new ways of expressing emotions through various experiences provided in literature," and another in "Understand how animal ecologies are disturbed and the consequences of the disturbance." These are in different forms and at different levels of generality, but at this stage the purpose is only to consider carefully all the promising possibilities. Later, those selected as most important and appropriate for one's students can be refined and restated in common form so as to guide curriculum developers in designing learning experiences. At that point, it will probably be helpful to standardize terms and definitions. At early stages, however, curriculum developers should use terminology familiar and understandable to teachers, principals, parents, and citizens rather than insisting on distinctions that others may have difficulty remembering and using.

The comprehensive list of possible outcomes should be carefully scrutinized to sift out those that appear to be of minor importance or in conflict with the school's educational philosophy. The list should also be examined in the light of the apparent prospects for one's students being able to learn these things in school. For example, we know that things once learned are usually forgotten unless there are continuing opportunities to use them. So one criterion for retaining a goal is that students will have opportunities in and out of school to think, feel, and act as expected. We also know that learning of habits requires continuous practice with few errors, so work and study habits should be selected as goals only if they are to be emphasized consistently in school work.

This procedure for identifying what students are to be helped to learn is designed to prevent a common weakness in curriculum development: selection of goals that are obsolete or irrelevant, inappropriate for students' current levels of development, not in keeping with sound scholarship, not in harmony with America's democratic philosophy, or for which the school cannot provide the necessary learning conditions.

A common practice when planning curriculum is to refer to published taxonomies (Bloom & others, 1956; Krathwohl & others, 1964). Taxonomies can be useful for their original purpose—classifying goals already formulated—but they do not resolve the issue of the relevance of any particular goal to contemporary society or to one's own students. The Bloom and Krathwohl taxonomies are organized in terms of what the authors conceive to be higher or lower levels, but higher ones are not always more important or even necessary. In typewriting, for example, so-called higher mental processes interfere with the speed and accuracy of typing.

A similar caution applies to uncritically taking goals from curriculum materials of other school systems. The fact that educators in Scarsdale or some other district chose certain goals is not in itself evidence that they are appropriate for your students.

Development of general goals for a school system should be a lengthy process with opportunities for students, parents, and others to participate. This can be done, for example, by sponsoring "town meetings," by publishing draft statements of goals in local newspapers with an invitation to respond, and by holding and publicizing hearings on goals sponsored by the board of education.

A factor that complicates the matter is that some sources of goals are simply not subject to a majority vote. Knowledge—whether about physics, poetry, or welding—is the province of specialists. Educators sometimes know more about the nature of children and the learning process than many other adults in the community. Nevertheless, in a democracy there is no higher authority than the people, so the people must be involved in deciding what public schools are to teach.

Most general goals, because they are so broad and because they deal with major categories of human experience, are acceptable to most people. Few will quarrel with a goal such as "Know about human beings, their environments and their achievements, past and present." The problem in developing a general goal statement is usually not to decide which goals are proper and which are not, but to select among many possibilities those which are most important, are at the proper level of generality, and are at least partially the responsibility of schools.

While general goals are not usually controversial, more specific ones can be. For example, parents might not quarrel with "Understand and follow practices associated with good health," but some would reject "Describe two effective and two ineffective methods of birth control." Thus, parents and other citizens should be involved in formulating course and program goals as well as general system goals.

USING GOALS TO PLAN LEARNING ACTIVITIES

To some extent, well-stated goals imply the kinds of learning activities that would be appropriate for achieving them. For example, if an instructional goal is "Solve word problems requiring estimation involving use of simple fractions such as ½, ¼, ⅔," students would have to practice estimating solutions to practical problems as well as learning to calculate using fractions. In many instances, however, knowing the goal does not automatically help an educator know how to teach it. For example, to enable students to "understand and appreciate significant human achievements," one teacher might have students read about outstanding scientists of the 19th century, supplement the readings with several lectures, and give a multiple-choice examination. Another teacher might decide to divide students into groups and have each group prepare a presentation to the class about a great scientist using demonstrations, dramatic skits, and so on. Forging the link between goals and other steps in curriculum development requires professional knowledge, experience, and imagination.

A factor that distorts what might appear to be a straightforward relationship between goals and activities is that every instructional activity has multiple goals. The goal-setting process is sometimes seen as a one-to-one relationship between various levels of goals and levels of school activity. For example, the mission of a local school system might be to "Offer all students equitable opportunities for a basic education plus some opportunities to develop individual talents and interests." "Basic education" would be defined to include "Communicate effectively by reading, writing, speaking, observing, and listening." A middle school in that district might have a goal such as "Read and understand nonfiction at a level of the average article in *Reader's Digest*" or, more specifically, "Students will be able to distinguish between expressions of fact and opinion in writing."

While similar chains of related goals are basic to sound curriculum planning, developers should never assume that such simplicity fully represents the reality of schools. When a teacher is engaged in teaching reading, he or she must also be conscious of and teach toward other goals: thinking ability, knowledge of human achievements, relationships with others, positive self-concept, and so on.

Not only must teachers address several officially adopted "outside" goals all at once; they must cope with "inside" goals as well. Although Goodlad (1979) uses declared goals to remind educators and the public what schools are said to be for, he cautions that the ends-means model doesn't do justice to the educational process and offers, as an alternative, an ecological perspective. Insisting that school activities should "be viewed for their intrinsic value, quite apart from their linkage or lack of linkage to stated ends" (p. 76), he points out that in addition to "goals that have been set outside of the system for the system" there are also goals inside the system—"students' goals, teachers' goals, principals' goals, and so on—and . . . these goals are not necessarily compatible" (p. 77).

The message to curriculum developers is that although "outside" goals and objectives are fundamental to educational planning, the relationship between purposes and practices is more complex than it may seem.

USING GOALS IN CURRICULUM EVALUATION

Some writers argue that specific objectives are essential in order to design suitable evaluation plans and write valid test items. The work of the National Assessment of Educational Progress shows, however, that even evaluators may not require objectives written in highly technical language.[3] National Assessment objectives do not contain stipulations of conditions or performance standards; in fact, they are expected to meet just two criteria: clarity and importance. The educators, citizens, and subject matter experts who review the objectives are asked, "Do you understand what this objective means? How important is it that students learn this in school?" Objectives are often considered clear and important even though they are stated briefly and simply. When the objectives have been identified, National Assessment staff members or consultants develop exercises designed to be operational definitions of the intended outcomes. Conditions, standards of performance, and so on are specified for the exercises, not for the objectives.

Setting goals is difficult because it requires assembling and weighing all the factors to be considered in selecting the relatively few but important goals that can be attained with the limited time and resources available to schools. The demands and opportunities of society, the needs of students, the resources of scholarship, the values of democracy, and the conditions needed for effective learning must all be considered.

A common error is the failure to distinguish purposes appropriate for the school from those attainable largely through experiences in the home and community. The school can reinforce the family in helping children develop punctuality, dependability, self-discipline, and other important habits. The school can be and usually is a community in which children and adults respect each other, treat each other fairly, and cooperate. But the primary task for which public schools were established is to enlarge students' vision and experience by helping them learn to draw upon the resources of scholarship, thus overcoming the limitations of direct experience and the narrow confines of a local environment. Students can learn to use sources of knowledge that are more accurate and reliable than folklore and superstition. They can participate vicariously through literature and the arts with peoples whose lives are both similar to and different from those they have known. The school is the only institution whose primary purpose is enabling students to explore these scholarly fields and to learn to use them as resources in their own lives. Great emphasis should be given to goals of this sort.

Goals are frequently not stated at the appropriate degree of generality–specificity for each level of educational responsibility. Goals promulgated by state education authorities should not be too specific because of the wide variation in conditions among districts in the state. State goals should furnish general guidance for the kinds and areas of learning for which schools are responsible in that state. The school district should furnish more detailed guidance by identifying goals that fall between the general aims listed by the state and those appropriate to the local school. School goals should be adapted to the background of students and the needs and resources of the neighborhood, especially the educational role the parents can assume. The goals of each teacher should be designed to attain the goals of the school. The test of whether a goal is stated at the appropriate degree of generality–specificity is its clarity and helpfulness in guiding the educational activities necessary at that level of responsibility.

CONCLUSION

When states list specific skills as goals and develop statewide testing programs to measure them, they may overlook a significant part of what schools should teach: understanding, analysis, and problem solving. If students are taught only to follow prescribed rules, they will be unable to deal with varied situations. Another common limitation of such lists is their neglect of affective components, such as finding satisfaction in reading and developing the habit of reading to learn.

The form and wording of goals and objectives should be appropriate for the way they are to be used. For clarity, we have generally used the term "goal" for all statements of intended learning outcomes regardless of their degree of specificity, but we recognize that no one formula is best for all situations. The criteria for judging goals and objectives are their usefulness in communicating educational purposes and their helpfulness to teachers in planning educational activities.

ENDNOTES

1. Available from Commercial-Educational Distributing Service, P.O. Box 4791, Portland, OR 97208.
2. Collections of "measurable objectives" may be purchased from Instructional Objectives Exchange, Box 24095-M, Los Angeles, CA 90024-0095.
3. National Assessment has developed objectives for a number of subject areas, including art, citizenship, career and a occupational development, literature, mathematics, music, reading, science, social studies, and writing. Because they have been carefully written and thoroughly reviewed, the objectives and accompanying exercises are a helpful resource for local curriculum developers, although they are designed only for assessment, not for curriculum planning.

REFERENCES

ASCD Committee on Research and Theory, Wilbur B. Brookover, Chairman. (1980). *Measuring and Attaining the Goals of Education.* Alexandria, VA: Association for Supervision and Curriculum Development.

Bloom, Benjamin S. (Ed.). (1956). *Taxonomy of Educational Objectives: The Classification of Educational Goals. Handbook I: Cognitive Domain.* New York: David McKay.

Bruner, Jerome. (1960). *The Process of Education.* Cambridge, MA: Harvard University.

Chalupsky, Albert B., Phillips-Jones, Linda, & Danoff, Malcolm N. (1981). "Competency Measurement in Vocational Education: A Review of the State of the Art." Prepared by American Institute for Research. Washington, DC: Office of Vocational and Adult Education, U.S. Department of Education.

Commission on the Reorganization of Secondary Education, U.S. Office of Education. (1918). *Cardinal Principles of Secondary Education.* Washington, DC: Government Printing Office.

Doherty, Victor W., & Peters, Linda B. (1980). *Introduction to K–12 Course Goals for Educational Planning and Evaluation*, 3rd ed. Portland, OR: Commercial-Educational Distributing Services.

Doherty, Victor W., & Peters, Linda B. (1981, May). "Goals and Objectives in Educational Planning and Evaluation." *Educational Leadership* 38: 606.

Ehrenberg, Sydelle D., & Ehrenberg, Lyle, M. (1978). *A Strategy for Curriculum Design—The ICI Model.* Miami: Institute for Curriculum and Instruction.

Eisner, Eliot W. (1979). *The Educational Imagination.* New York: Macmillan.

French, Will. (1957). *Behavioral Goals of General Education in High School.* New York: Russell Sage Foundation.

Goodlad, John I. (1979). *What Schools Are For?* Bloomington, IN: Phi Delta Kappa.

Kohlberg, Lawrence. (1980, October). "Moral Education: A Response to Thomas Sobol." *Educational Leadership* 38: 19–23.

Krathwohl, David R., & others. (1964). *Taxonomy of Educational Objectives: The Classification of Educational Goals, Handbook II: Affective Domain.* New York: David McKay Company, Inc.

Mager, R.F. (1962). *Preparing Instructional Objectives.* Palo Alto, CA: Fearon Publishers.

Martin, John Henry. (1980, January). "Reconsidering the Goals of High School Education." *Educational Leadership* 37: 278–285.

Oregon State Board of Education. (1972). "Minimum State Requirements Standards for Graduation from High School." Salem, Oregon.

Paul, Regina. (1982, January). "Are You Out on a Limb?" *Educational Leadership* 39: 260–264.

Raywid, Mary Anne. (1981, April). "The First Decade of Public School Alternatives." *Phi Delta Kappan* 62: 551–554.

Seiverling, Richard F. (Ed.). (1980). *Educational Quality Assessment: Getting Out the EQA Results.* Harrisburg, PA: Pennsylvania Department of Education.

Spady, William G. (1978, October). "The Concept and Implications of Competency-Based Education." *Educational Leadership* 36: 16–22.

Stake, R.E., & Easley, J.A., Jr. (1978). *Case Studies in Science Education.* 2 vols. Washington, DC: U.S. Government Printing Office.

Sternberg, Robert J. (1981, October). "Intelligence as Thinking and Learning Skills." *Educational Leadership* 39: 18–20.

Tyler, Ralph W. (1949). *Basic Principles of Curriculum and Instruction.* 1974 ed. Chicago: University of Chicago Press.

Wirszup, Izaak. (1981, February). "The Soviet Challenge." *Educational Leadership* 38: 358–360.

DISCUSSION QUESTIONS

1. What should the goals of contemporary education be?
2. Should the goals of education be the same for all students?
3. What is the best method for defining goals: by behavioral objectives or by competencies?
4. Who should assume responsibility for determining educational goals: the federal government, the state board of education, local school districts, building principals, or the faculty at each school? Why?
5. What is the best criterion for judging goals and objectives?

CHAPTER 3

A Pedagogy of Possibility

PETER McLAREN

FOCUSING QUESTIONS

1. What is critical pedagogy?
2. Are teaching and curriculum guided by political ideology?
3. How are literacy and freedom related?
4. Does education always liberate?
5. Does love have a place in education?

> [W]hat I have been proposing from my political convictions, my philosophical convictions, is a profound respect for the total autonomy of the educator. What I have been proposing is a profound respect for the cultural identity of students—a cultural identity that implies respect for the language of the other, the color of the other, the gender of the other, the class of the other, the sexual orientation of the other, the intellectual capacity of the other; that implies the ability to stimulate the creativity of the other. But these things take place in a social and historical context and not in pure air. These things take place in history and I, Paulo Freire, am not the owner of history.
>
> —Paulo Freire, 1997a, pp. 307–308

Paulo Freire was one of the first internationally recognized educational thinkers who fully appreciated the relationship among education, politics, imperialism, and liberation. Generally considered the inaugural philosopher of critical pedagogy, Freire was able to effectively recast pedagogy on a global basis in the direction of a radical politics of historical struggle, a direction that he expanded into a lifetime project. Long before his death on May 2, 1997, Freire had acquired a mythic stature among progressive educators, social workers, and theologians as well as scholars and researchers from numerous disciplinary traditions, for fomenting interest in the ways that education can serve as a vehicle for social and economic transformation. What is now termed "a politics of liberation" is a topic of pivotal significance among educational activists throughout the globe and one to which

Freire had made important and pioneering contributions.

FREIRE'S PHILOSOPHY OF PEDAGOGY: A PREFERENTIAL OPTION FOR THE POOR

Freire's life vehemently unveils the imprints of a life lived within the margins of power and prestige. Because his work was centered around the issue of social and political change, Freire has always been considered controversial, especially by educational establishments in Europe and North America. While he is recognized as one of the most significant philosophers of liberation and a pioneer in critical literacy and critical pedagogy, his work continues to be taken up mostly by educators working outside of the educational mainstream. The marginal status of Freire's followers is undoubtedly due to the fact that Freire believed educational change must be accompanied by significant changes in the social and political structure in which education takes place. It is a position most educators would find politically untenable or hopelessly utopian. It is certainly a position that threatens the interests of those already well served by the dominant culture.

Freire believed that the ongoing production of the social world through dialogue occurs in dialectical interplay with the structural features of society such as its social relations of production, cultural formations, and institutional arrangements. In the process of becoming literate—a process Freire referred to as "praxis"—meaning circulates, is acted upon, and is revised, resulting in political interpretation, sense-making, and will formation. The outcome of this intersubjectivity produced through praxis is never fully predetermined.

A staunch critic of neo-liberalism, Freire perceived a major ideological tension to be situated in the ability of people to retain a concept of the political beyond a consumer identity constructed from the panoply of market logics. Further, the sociality and the discourses of daily life cannot be a priori defined as excluding the realm of politics.

Freire's personal contact with Brazilian peasants early in his life profoundly shaped his assent to popular revolts against economic exploitation in Latin America, Africa, and elsewhere. Given the basic contradictions facing a social order encapsulated in the exploitation of the vast majority of Brazilian society, the task or mission of Freire centered on the transformation of the relations of the production of social wealth (together with the ideological-political levels). Yet such an attempt to establish a new social order underwritten by a just system of appropriation and distribution of social wealth was to relegate Freire to the ranks of educators considered to be subversive to the state. For Freire, the very protocols of literacy and the act of "coming to know" must themselves be transformed in order to make a prominent place for issues of social justice and the struggle for emancipation. Freire taught that in order for the oppressed to materialize their self-activity as a revolutionary force, they must develop a collective consciousness of their own constitution or formation as a subaltern class, as well as an ethos of solidarity and interdependence. For Freire, a pedagogy of critical literacy becomes the primary vehicle for the development of "critical consciousness" among the poor, leading to a process of exploration and creative effort that conjoins deep personal meaning and common purpose. Literacy, for Freire, becomes the common "process" of participation open to all individuals. The problem of "critical consciousness" cannot be posed in abstraction from the significant historical contexts in which knowledge is produced, engaged, and appropriated.

Freire lamented the brute reality that witnessed the oppressed always living as the detachable appendages of other people's dreams and desires. It seemed to Freire that the dreams of the poor were always dreamt for them by distant others who were removed from the daily struggles of the working class and were either unable or unwilling to recognize the dreams that burned in the habitats of their hearts. Based on a recognition of the cultural underpinnings of folk traditions and the importance of the collective construction of knowledge, Freire's pedagogical project created a vivid new vocabulary of concern for the oppressed, and uncoiled a new and powerful political terminology that enabled the oppressed to analyze their location within the privileging hierarchy of capitalist society and engage in attempts to dislocate themselves from existing cycles of social reproduction. Literacy programs developed by Freire and his colleagues for disempowered peasants are now employed in countries all over the world. By linking the categories of history, politics, economics, and class to the concepts of culture and power, Freire managed to develop both a language of critique and a language of hope that work conjointly and dialectically and which have proven successful in helping generations of disenfranchised peoples to liberate themselves.

Freire recognized that there is no way of representing the consciousness of the oppressed that escapes the founding assumptions of the culture and society in which the teacher of a cultural worker is implicated (Freire, 1973, 1978, 1985, 1993a, 1993b, 1998a; Freire & Macedo, 1987). Long before postmodernists brought us their version of "identity politics," Freire understood that the subjectivities of the oppressed are to be considered heterogeneous and ideologically pertuse and cannot be represented extratextually—that is, outside of the discursive embeddedness of the educator's own founding value and epistemological assumptions (McLaren & Leonard, 1993).

Freire understood that as the oppressed take more control of their own history, they assimilate more rapidly into society, but on their own terms. He warrants the reputation as a preeminent critical educationalist in the way that he was able to foreground the means by which *the pedagogical* (the localized pedagogical encounter between teacher and student) is implicated in *the political* (the social relations of production within the global capitalist economy). Whereas mainstream educators often decapitate the social context from the self and thereby cauterize the dialectical movement between them, Freire stresses the dialectical motion between the subject and object, the self and the social, and human agency and social structure.

Educators who work within a Freirean-inspired critical pedagogy are indebted to Freire's philosophical insights more than to his commentaries on teaching methodologies (Taylor, 1993). Freire's working vocabulary of philosophical concepts enables the world of the oppressed to become visible, to inscribe itself as a text to be engaged and understood by the oppressed and non-oppressed alike. Freire's work does not reduce the world to a text but rather stipulates the conditions for the possibility of various competing and conflicting discourses, or ways of making sense out of lived experiences. Freire interrogates the catachresis of value by urging educators to identify the aporias within their own philosophies of teaching and daily life (1998a, 1998b).

In all of Freire's teachings, the concept of truth becomes vitiatingly unwound as the truth becomes linked to one's emplacement in the reigning narratives *about* truth. Of course, Freire's own work can be used against itself in this regard, and interpreted as an epiphenomenon of the narratives that create the textual effects of his own work. Freire would have encouraged readers to scrutinize and critique the ideology of his work in the same manner that he encouraged them to interrogate other texts.

FREIRE'S INFLUENCE ON NORTH AMERICAN CRITICAL PEDAGOGY

Discovering that pedagogy existed largely in pathological conditions, Freire sought to advance new approaches to teaching and learning, carefully avoiding those "banking" varieties that separated mind from body, thought from action, and social critique from transformative praxis. Often accompanied by Dewey's (1916) approaches to teaching and learning as well as those, like Habermas (1979, 1987), that stress communicative competency and non-distorted forms of communication, critical pedagogy constitutes a set of practices that uncovers the ways in which the process of schooling represses the contingency of its own selection of values and the means through which educational goals are subtended by macrostructures of power and privilege. For Freire, pedagogy has as much to do with the teachable heart as the teachable mind, and as much to do with efforts to change the world as it does with rethinking the categories that we use to analyze our current condition within history. In this way, Freire has pushed the debate over pedagogy out of familiar well-worn grooves. In essence, Freire's work is about hope. He writes: "Hope is a natural, possible, and necessary impetus in the context of our unfinishedness . . . without it, instead of history we would have pure determinism" (1998b, p. 69).

Freire's work has unarguably been the driving force behind North American efforts at developing critical pedagogy. Critical pedagogy is a way of thinking about, negotiating, and transforming the relationship among classroom teaching, the production of knowledge, the institutional structures of the school, and the social and material relations of the wider community, society, and nation-state (McLaren, 1993, 1997a; McLaren & Lankshear, 1994). Developed by progressive teachers attempting to eliminate inequalities on the basis of social class, it has also sparked a wide array of anti-sexist, anti-racist, and anti-homophobic classroom-based curricula and policy initiatives. Freirean-inspired critical pedagogies in North America have grown out of a number of theoretical developments such as Latin American philosophies of liberation (McLaren, 1993); critical literacy (Macedo, 1994; Lankshear & McLaren, 1993); the sociology of knowledge (Giroux & McLaren, 1989; McLaren, 1995; Fine, 1991); the Frankfurt school of critical theory (Giroux, 1983; McLaren & Giarelli, 1995); adult education (Hall, 1998); feminist theory (Weiler, 1988; Gore, 1993; Lather, 1991; Ellsworth, 1989); bilingual and bicultural education (Moraes, 1996; Darder, 1991; Wink, 1997; Cummins, 1989); teacher education (McLaren, 1993) and neo-Marxist cultural criticism (McLaren, 1997b). In more recent years, it has been taken up by educators influenced by debates over postmodernism and poststructuralism (Kincheloe, 1993; Kanpol, 1992; Aronowitz & Giroux, 1991; Giroux & McLaren, 1989; McLaren, 1995); cultural studies (Giroux & McLaren, 1994; Kincheloe, 1993; Giroux, Lankshear, McLaren, & Peters, 1996); and multiculturalism (Sleeter & McLaren, 1995; McLaren, 1997c; Kincheloe & Steinberg, 1997; Sleeter & Grant, 1988; Leistyna, 1999; McCarthy, 1988). For Freire, schools are places where, as part of civil society, spaces of uncoerced interaction can be created.

Yet even with such a divergent array of influences, at the level of classroom life, Freirean pedagogy is often erroneously perceived as synonymous with whole language instruction, adult literacy programs, and new "constructivist" approaches to teaching and learning based on Vygotsky's work. Not all such programs are necessarily Freirean, but they need to be judged in relation to the contextual specificity of their philosophy, their praxis, and their ethos of critical responsiveness with respect to bringing about a more just and humane social order. Lankshear and McLaren (1993, pp. 43–44) have summarized six learning principles from Freire's work which are intended to provide teachers with pivotal points of reference in the development of their pedagogical practices:

1. The world must be approached as an object to be understood and known by the efforts of learners themselves. Moreover, their acts of knowing are to be stimulated and grounded in their own being, experiences, needs, circumstances, and destinies.
2. The historical and cultural world must be approached as a created, transformable reality which, like humans themselves, is constantly in the process of being shaped and made by human deed in accordance with ideological representations of reality.
3. Learners must learn how to actively make connections between their own lived conditions and being and the making of reality that has occurred to date.
4. They must consider the possibility for "new makings" of reality, the new possibilities for *being* that emerge from new makings, and become committed to shaping a new enabling and regenerative history. New makings are a collective, shared, social enterprise in which the voices of all participants must be heard.
5. In the literacy phase, learners come to see the importance of print for this shared project. By achieving print competence within the process of bringing their experience and meanings to bear on the world in active construction and reconstruction (of lived relations and practice), learners will actually *experience* their own potency in the very act of understanding what it means to be a human subject. In the post-literacy phase, the basis for action is print-assisted exploration of generative *themes.* Addressing the theme of "Western culture" as conceived by people like Hirsh and reified in prevailing curricula and pedagogies, and seeking to transcend this conception . . . involves exactly the kind of praxis Freire intends.
6. Learners must come to understand how the myths of dominant discourses are, precisely, myths which oppress and marginalize them—but which can be transcended through transformative action.

While critics often decry Freire's educational approach for its idealist vision of social transformation, its supporters, including Freire, have complained that critical pedagogy has often been domesticated and reduced to student-directed learning approaches devoid of social critique.

Once considered by the faint-hearted guardians of the American dream as a term of opprobrium, critical pedagogy has become so completely psychologized, so liberally humanized, so technologized, and so conceptually postmodernized that its current relationship to broader liberation struggles and to Freire's stress on revolutionary class struggle seems severely attenuated if not fatally terminated. Because Freire believed that the challenge of transforming schools should be directed at overcoming socioeconomic injustice linked to the political and economic structures of society, any attempt at school reform that claims to be inspired by Freire—but that is only concerned with social patterns of representation, interpretation, or communication, and that does not connect these patterns to redistributive measures and structures that reinforce such patterns—exempts itself from the most important insights of Freire's work. Freire's approach stipulates a trenchant understanding of patterns of distribution and redistribution in order to transform—and not just interpret—the underlying economic structures that produce relations of exploitation. Freire was also concerned with practicing a politics of diversity and self-affirmation—in short, a cultural politics—not as a mere end-in-itself but in relation to a larger politics of liberation and social justice. Consequently, a Freirean pedagogy of liberation is totalizing without being dominating in that it always attends dialectically to the specific or local "act of knowing" as a political process that takes place in the larger conflictual arena of capitalist relations of exploitation, an arena where large groups of people palpably and undeniably suffer needless privations and pain due to alienation and poverty. Thus, a pedagogy of the oppressed involves not only a redistribution of material resources, but also a struggle over cultural meanings in relation to the multiple social locations of students and teachers and their position within the global division of labor.

Has Freire's name become a floating signifier to be attached adventitiously to any chosen referent within the multi-stranded terrain of progressive education? To a certain extent, this has already happened. Liberal progressives are drawn to Freire's humanism; Marxists and neo-Marxists are drawn to his revolutionary praxis and his history of working with revolutionary political regimes; left liberals are drawn to his critical utopianism; and even conservatives begrudgingly respect his stress on ethics. No doubt his work will be domesticated by his followers—as selected aspects of his corpus are appropriated uncritically and decontextualized from his larger political project of struggling for the realization of a truly socialist democracy—in order to make a more comfortable fit with various conflicting political agendas. Consequently, it is important to read Freire in the context of his entire corpus of works, from *Pedagogy of the Oppressed* (1993b) to his reflection on this early work, *Pedagogy of Hope* (1994), and to his *Pedagogy of Freedom* (1998b).

FREIREAN PEDAGOGY: ITS SHORTCOMINGS

Those who have an important stake in the meaning of Freire's life and work will continue to disagree over how his politics and pedagogy should be interpreted. The assertive generality of Freire's formulations of and pronouncements on pedagogy can be highly frustrating, in that they index important concerns but do not fully provide the necessary theoretical basis for positing more progressive and programmatic alternatives to the theories and perspectives that he is criticizing. For instance, few accounts are provided as to how teachers are to move from critical thought to critical practice. Yet Freire's weakness is also a source of his strength and marks the durability of his thought. It is precisely his refusal to spell out alternative solutions that enables his work to be "reinvented" in the contexts in which his readers find themselves, thereby enjoying a contextually specific "translation" across geographic, geopolitical, and cultural borders. It also grants to Freire's corpus of works a universal character, as they are able to retain their heuristic potency (much like the works of Marx) such that they can be conscripted by educators to criticize and to counterpoint pedagogical practices worldwide. In fact, Freire urged his readers to reinvent him in the context of their local struggles. What could be retained in every instance of this reinvention process is Freire's constant and unstoppable ethics of solidarity and an unrepentant utopianism. Freire writes that "the progressive educator must always be moving out on his or her own, continually reinventing me and reinventing what it means to be democratic in his or her own specific cultural and historical context" (1997a, p. 308).

Some have assigned to Freire's work the Archimedian conceit of the idealist utopian view of society. But such a criticism risks overlooking the practical utility of Freirean pedagogy, especially when one considers the success of the literacy campaigns that relied heavily on his work. Freire seizes on the occult presence of seeds of redemption at the center of a world gone mad. Yet his politics of liberation resists subsumption under a codified set of universal principles; rather it animates a set of ethical imperatives that together serve as a precipitate of our answering the call of the other who is suffering from a heavy heart and an empty stomach. Such imperatives do not mark a naive utopian faith in the future; rather, they presage a form of active, irreverent, and uncompromising hope in the possibilities of the present.

The legacy of racism left by the New World European oppressor—that Blacks and Latino/as are simply a species of inferior invertebrates—was harshly condemned but never systematically analyzed by Freire. And while Freire was a vociferous critic of racism and sexism, he did not, as Kathleen Weiler (1996) points out, sufficiently problematize his conceptualization of liberation and the oppressed in terms of his own male experience.

From the perspective of North American critical pedagogy, Freire's politics of liberation partakes of its own political inertia consequent in the limited range of narratives out of which he constructs his praxis of hope and transformation. For instance, Freire failed to articulate fully his position on Christianity (Elias, 1994) and the male bias in his literacy method (Taylor, 1993). Freire rarely addressed the ways in which oppression on the bases of ethnicity, class, and sexual orientation are intermingled. As a number of North American critics have pointed out, Freire failed to fully engage the issue of white male privilege (Ladson-Billings, 1997) or the interest and agency of African Americans apart from a wider movement of emancipatory practices (Murrell, 1997). When Freire did address this issue, he often retreated into mystical abstractions, thereby discounting the deep significance of patriarchy as a practice of oppression (Weiler, 1996). Yet these lacunae should in no way diminish the genius, courage, and compassion of Freire's work.

The modality of theoretical envisioning deployed by Freire is decidedly modernist but, as I have argued elsewhere (McLaren, 1997c), some trappings of postmodernist discourses are immanent—yet barely registered—in Freire's peripatetic articulation of human agency. Social theory identified as "postmodern" runs the serious risk of ignoring the brute reality that working people the world over share a common subjection to a capitalist exploitation. The violent realities of the global economy are often dissipated within postmodern social theories. On the other hand, pedagogies of liberation such as Freire's, underwritten by modernist Marxian discourses, often seriously ignore issues of race, gender, and sexual orientation. Freire was aware of these omissions (Freire, 1997b, 1998a, 1998b) and had begun to address them with a passionate conviction in his most recent work. Despite the fact that deconstructionists such as Stuart Parker (1997) have revealed much of the work of the critical educational tradition—exemplified by the work of Freire—to be located within modernist assumptions of teacher autonomy, assumptions that essentially serve as "devices of enchantment" which can be deconstructed as discursive fictions, Freire's work holds vital importance. Freire's contribution remains signal not for its methodology of literacy alone but in the final instance for its ability to create a pedagogy of practical consciousness that presages critical action (Taylor, 1993). Freire's primary achievement remains that of his role as the "Vagabond of the Obvious," a term which he often used to describe his pedagogical role. The shortcomings of Freire's work constitute more than minor rhetorical fallout to be sure, but as Freire's aforementioned critics also acknowledge, they should not detract from Freire's central importance as a foundational educational thinker, a philosopher who ranks among the most important educators of this century or any other.

Bearing witness to enduring imbalances of power on a global level—the worldwide problem of overcapacity, the random destruction by unregulated markets accompanying the new bargain-basement capitalism, the imposition of exchange values upon all productions of value, the creation of a uniform culture of pure consumption, or Wal-Martization of global culture, the vampirism of Western carpetbaggers sucking the lifeblood from the open veins of South America, opportunistic politicians, assaults on diasporic cultures, and a new wave of xenophobia—have brought about a serious political inertia within the United States left in general and the educational left in particular. The logic of privatization and free trade—where social labor is the means and measure of value and surplus social labor lies at the heart of profit—now shapes the very fabric of our lifeworld. The logic of transnational capitalism now flagrantly guides educational policy and practice to such an extent that one could say without exaggeration that education has been reduced to a subsector of the economy. To the extent that the future of education is intimately connected to the ability of teachers to become more critically self-reflective in analyzing ways in which their own lives and those of their students have been inscribed by enchaining discursive practices and material social relations supporting powerful elite groups at the expense of the majority of the population, Freire's work is indispensable to the progressive evolution of educational thought. Of course, the continuing advancement of critical pedagogy and Freirean praxis cannot be divorced from the crisis of the late bourgeois world whose greatest symptom includes the logic of consumption as a regulating democratic ideal. Freire was always a revolutionary and as such never abandoned the dream of a radical transformation of the world. Freire writes:

> My rebellion against every kind of discrimination, from the most explicit and crying to the most covert and hypocritical, which is no less offensive and immoral, has been with me from my childhood. Since as far back as I can remember, I have reacted almost instinctively against any word, deed, or sign of racial discrimination, or, for that matter, discrimination against the poor, which quite a bit later, I came to define as class discrimination. (1994, p. 144)

As Freire's future hagiographers wrestle in the educational arena over what represents the "real" Freire and his legacy, Freire's work will continue to be felt in the lives of those who knew him and who loved him. Just as importantly, his work will continue to influence generations of educators, scholars, and activists around the world.

Freire acknowledged that decolonization was a project that knows no endpoint, no final closure. It is a lifetime struggle that requires counterintuitive insight, honesty, compassion, and a willingness to brush one's personal history against the grain of "naive consciousness" or common-sense understanding. After engaging the legacy of revolutionary struggles of the oppressed that has been bequeathed to us by Freire, it remains impossible to conceive of pedagogical practice evacuated of social critique. Freire has left stratified deposits of pedagogical insight upon which future developments of progressive education can be built. There is still reason to hope for a cooperative pedagogical venture among those who support a Freirean class-based pedagogical struggle, feminist pedagogy, or a pedagogy informed by queer theory and politics, that may lead to a revival of serious educational thinking in which the category of liberation may continue to have and to make meaning. The internationalization of the market and its border-crossing dimensions strongly suggests that in order to halt the continuing assaults of the market on human subjectivity, cultural workers must create alliances across national borders.

THE POWER OF LOVE

What sets Freire apart from most other leftist educators in this era of cynical reason is his unashamed stress on the importance and power of love. Love, he claims, is the most crucial characteristic of dialogue and the constitutive force animating all pedagogies of liberation:

> Dialogue cannot exist, however, in the absence of a profound love for the world and for people. The naming of the world, which is

> an act of creation and re-creation, is not possible if it is not infused with love. Love is, at the same time, the foundation of dialogue and dialogue itself. It is thus necessarily the task of responsible Subjects and cannot exist in a relation of domination. Domination reveals the pathology of love: sadism in the dominator and masochism in the dominated. Because love is an act of courage, not of fear, love is commitment to others. No matter where the oppressed are found, the act of love is commitment to their cause—the cause of liberation. And this commitment, because it is loving, is dialogical. As an act of bravery, love cannot be sentimental: as an act of freedom, it must not serve as a pretext for manipulation. It must generate other acts of freedom; otherwise, it is not love. Only by abolishing the situation of oppression is it possible to restore the love which that situation made impossible. If I do not love the world—if I do not love life—if I do not love people—I cannot enter into dialogue. (1993b, pp. 70–71)

For Freire, love always stipulates a political project since a love for humankind that remains disconnected from politics does a profound disservice to its object. It is possible to love only by virtue of the presence of others. A love that does not liberate feeds off its object like worms on a corpse. Its narcissism destroys the other by turning the other into itself; it transforms the other into inert matter that it uses to fertilize its own image. Here the act of love becomes the act of self-love, as the subject becomes its own object, consuming itself in an orgy of necrophilia. Whereas authentic love opens up the self to the Other, narcissistic love culminates in a self-dissolving spiral by refusing the Other who stands at the door of self-understanding. Only when the Other is encountered behind the door can the self find its authentic eyes, ears, and voice in the art of dialogic, reciprocal understanding.

Love both embodies struggle and pushes it beyond its source. In Freirean terms, revolutionary love is always pointed in the direction of commitment and fidelity to a global project of emancipation. This commitment is sustained by preventing nihilism and despair from imposing their own life-denying inevitability in times of social strife and cultural turmoil. Anchored in narratives of transgression and dissent, love becomes the foundation of hope. In this way, love can never be reduced to personal declarations or pronouncements but exists always in asymmetrical relations of anxiety and resolve, interdependence and singularity. Love, in this Freirean sense, becomes the oxygen of revolution, nourishing the blood of historical memory. It is through reciprocal dialogue that love is able to serve as a form of testimony to those who have struggled and suffered before us, and whose spirit of struggle had survived efforts to extinguish it and remove it from the archives of human achievement. Refusing to embrace the Orphic lyre or the crown of thorns, Freirean pedagogy faces the intractable forces of capitalist domination with a bittersweet optimism. Freire understood that while we often abandon hope, we are never abandoned by hope. This is because hope is forever engraved in the human heart and inspires us to reach beyond the carnal limits of our species being.

The Freirean agent works silently but steadfastly in the margins of culture and the interstices of collapsing public sectors, away from the power-charged arenas of public spectacles of accusation and blame regarding what is wrong with our schools. Freirean educators do not conceive of their work as an antidote to today's sociocultural ills and the declining level of ambition with respect to contemporary society's commitment to democracy. Rather, their efforts are patiently directed at creating counter-hegemonic sites of political struggle, radically alternative epistemological frameworks, and adversarial interpretations and cultural practices, as well as advocacy domains for disenfranchised groups.

Freirean pedagogy is vitally important for contemporary educators to revisit, to build upon, and to reinvent in the contextual specificity of today's sociopolitical context with its traumatizing inequalities. Like Freire, we need to restore to liberation its rightful place as the central project of education.

ENDNOTE

1. Peter McLaren is a professor of education at the Graduate School of Education and Information Studies, University of California, Los Angeles. He specializes in critical pedagogy, critical theory, and critical ethnography. He is an Associate of the Paulo Freire Institute, São Paulo, Brazil.

This paper is part of a larger text delivered at the Annual Convention of the American Educational Research Association, San Diego, April, 1998.

REFERENCES

Aronowitz, S., & Giroux, H. A. (1991). *Postmodern Education*. Minneapolis, MN: University of Minnesota Press.

Cummins, J. (1989). *Empowering Minority Students*. Sacramento, CA: California Association for Bilingual Education.

Darder, A. (1991). *Culture and Power in the Classroom: A Critical Foundation for Bicultural Education*. Westport, CT: Bergin and Garvey.

Dewey, J. (1916). *Democracy and Education*. New York: Macmillan Company.

Elias, J. (1994). *Paulo Freire: Pedagogue of Revolution*. Melbourne, FL: Krieger Publishing Company.

Ellsworth, E. (1989). "Why Doesn't This Feel Empowering? Working through the Repressive Myths of Critical Pedagogy." *Harvard Educational Review, 59*(5): 297–324.

Fine, M. (1991). *Framing Dropouts*. Albany, NY: State University of New York Press.

Freire, P. (1973). *Education for Critical Consciousness*. New York: Seabury Press.

Freire, P. (1978). *Pedagogy in Process. The Letters to Guinea Bissau*. New York: Seabury Press.

Freire, P. (1985). *The Politics of Education: Culture, Power, and Liberation*. South Hadley, MA: Bergin & Garvey.

Freire, P. (1993a). *Pedagogy of the City*. New York: Continuum.

Freire, P. (1993b). *Pedagogy of the Oppressed*. New York: Continuum.

Freire, P. (1994). *Pedagogy of Hope: Reliving Pedagogy of the Oppressed*. New York: Continuum.

Freire, P. (1997a). "A Response." In P. Freire, J. W. Fraser, D. Macedo, T. McKinnon, & W. T. Stokes (Eds.), *Mentoring the Member: A Critical Dialogue with Paulo Freire* (pp. 303–329). New York: Peter Lang Publishers.

Freire, P. (1997b). *Teachers as Cultural Workers: Letters to Those Who Dare to Teach*. (D. Macedo, K. Koike, & A. Oliviera, Trans.). Boulder, CO: Westview Press.

Freire, P. (1998a). *Pedagogy of the Heart*. New York: Continuum.

Freire, P. (1998b). *Pedagogy of Freedom: Ethics, Democracy, and Civic Courage*. Boulder, CO: Rowman and Littlefield Publishers, Inc.

Freire, P., & Macedo, D. (1987). *Literacy: Reading the Word and the World*. South Hadley, MA: Bergin & Garvey.

Giroux, H. A. (1983). *Theory and Resistance in Education: A Pedagogy for the Opposition*. South Hadley, MA: Bergin & Garvey.

Giroux, H. A., Lankshear, C., McLaren, P., & Peters, M. (1996). *Counternarratives: Cultural Studies and Critical Pedagogies in the Postmodern Spaces*. London and New York: Routledge.

Giroux, H., & McLaren, P. (Eds.). (1989). *Critical Pedagogy, the State, and Cultural Struggle*. Albany, NY: State University of New York Press.

Giroux, H., & McLaren, P. (Eds.). (1994). *Between Borders: Pedagogy and the Politics of Cultural Studies*. New York and London: Routledge.

Gore, J. (1993). *The Struggle for Pedagogies: Critical and Feminist Discourses as Regimes of Truth*. New York: Routledge.

Habermas, J. (1979). *Communication and the Evolution of Society*. (T. McCarthy, Trans.) Boston: Beacon Press.

Habermas, J. (1987). *The Theory of Communicative Action: Vol. 2, Lifeworld and System: A Critique of Functionalist Reason*. (T. McCarthy, Trans.) Boston: Beacon Press.

Hall, B. (1998). " 'Please Don't Bother the Canaries': Paulo Freire and the International Council for Adult Education." *Convergence, xxxi*(1–2): 95–103.

Kanpol, B. (1992). *Towards a Theory and Practice of Teacher Cultural Politics: Continuing the Postmodern Debate.* Norwood, NJ: Ablex Publications.

Kincheloe, J. (1993). *Toward a Critical Politics of Teacher Thinking: Mapping the Postmodern.* South Hadley, MA: Bergin and Garvey.

Kincheloe, J., & Steinberg, S. (1997). *Changing Multiculturalism.* Buckingham/Philadelphia: Open University Press.

Ladson-Billings, G. (1997). "I Know Why This Doesn't Feel Empowering: A Critical *Race* Analysis of Critical Pedagogy." In P. Freire, J. W. Fraser, D. Macedo, T. McKinnon, & W. T. Stokes (Eds.), *Mentoring the Mentor* (pp. 127–141). New York: Peter Lang Publishers.

Lankshear, C., & McLaren, P. (Eds.). (1993). Introduction. In C. Lankshear & P. McLaren (Eds.), *Critical Literacy: Politics, Praxis, and the Postmodern* (pp. 1–56). Albany, NY: State University of New York Press.

Lather, P. (1991). *Getting Smart: Feminist Research and Pedagogy within the Postmodern.* New York and London: Routledge.

Leistyna, P. (1999). *Presence of Mind: Education and the Politics of Deception.* Boulder, CO: Westview Press.

Macedo, D. (1994). *Literacies of Power.* Boulder, CO: Westview Press.

McCarthy, C. (1988). "Rethinking Liberal and Radical Perspectives on Racial Inequality in Schooling: Making the Case for Nonsynchrony." *Harvard Educational Review, 58*(3): 265–279.

McLaren, P. (1993). *Life in Schools: An Introduction to Critical Pedagogy in the Social Foundations of Education.* White Plains, NY: Longman, Inc.

McLaren, P. (1995). *Critical Pedagogy and Predatory Culture.* New York and London: Routledge.

McLaren, P. (1997a). "La Lucha Continua: Freire, Boal and the Challenge of History. To My Brothers and Sisters in Struggle." *Researcher, 1*(2): 5–10.

McLaren, P. (1997b). "Freirean Pedagogy: The Challenge of Postmodernism and the Politics of Race." In P. Freire, J. W. Fraser, D. Macedo, T. McKinnon, & W. T. Stokes (Eds.), *Mentoring the Mentor* (pp. 99–125). New York: Peter Lang Publishers.

McLaren, P. (1997c). *Revolutionary Multiculturalism: Pedagogies of Dissent for the New Millenium.* Boulder, CO: Westview Press.

McLaren, P., & Giarelli, J. (Eds.). (1995). *Critical Theory and Educational Research.* Albany, NY: State University of New York Press.

McLaren, P., & Lankshear, C. (Eds.). (1994). *Politics of Liberation: Paths from Freire.* New York and London: Routledge.

McLaren, P., & Leonard, P. (Eds.). (1993). *Paulo Freire: A Critical Encounter.* New York and London: Routledge.

Moraes, M. (1996). *Bilingual Education: A Dialogue with the Bahktin Circle.* Albany, NY: State University of New York Press.

Murrell, P., Jr. (1997). "Digging Again the Family Wells: A Freirean Literacy Framework as Emancipatory Pedagogy for African-American Children." In P. Freire, J. W. Fraser, D. Macedo, T. McKinnon, & W. T. Stokes (Eds.), *Mentoring the Mentor* (pp. 19–58). New York: Peter Lang Publishers.

Parker, S. (1997). *Reflective Teaching in the Postmodern World: A Manifesto for Education in Postmodernity.* Buckingham and Philadelphia: Open University Press.

Sleeter, C., & Grant, C. (1988). *Making Choices for Multicultural Education: Five Approaches to Race, Class, and Gender.* Columbus, OH: Merrill Publishing.

Sleeter, C., & McLaren, P. (Eds.). (1995). *Multicultural Education, Critical Pedagogy, and the Politics of Difference.* Albany, NY: State University of New York Press.

Taylor, P. (1993). *The Texts of Paulo Freire.* Buckingham and Philadelphia: Open University Press.

Weiler, K. (1988). *Women Teaching for Change: Gender, Class and Power.* South Hadley, MA: Bergin & Garvey.

Weiler, K. (1996). "Myths of Paulo Freire." *Educational Theory 46*(3): 353–371.

Wink, J. (1997). *Critical Pedagogy: Notes from the Real World.* White Plains, NY: Longman Publishers.

DISCUSSION QUESTIONS

1. How does critical pedagogy differ from ordinary teaching?
2. Should teaching and curriculum be guided by political ideology? Must they be?
3. How is literacy the cornerstone of freedom?
4. What would an emancipatory curriculum look like? How would it be taught?
5. What should be the place of love in education?

CHAPTER 4

Art and Imagination: Overcoming a Desperate Stasis

MAXINE GREENE

FOCUSING QUESTIONS

1. What are the existential contexts of education?
2. How do encounters with the arts influence student engagement in learning?
3. How might experience with the arts affect student (a) imagination, (b) construction of reality, and (c) depth of perspective?
4. What is the relationship between individual freedom and learning?
5. What are the contradictory goals of education?
6. What is the relationship between encounters with the arts and the goals of education?

The existential contexts of education reach far beyond what is conceived of in Goals 2000. They have to do with the human condition in these often desolate days, and in some ways they make the notions of world-class achievement, benchmarks, and the rest seem superficial and limited, if not absurd. They extend beyond the appalling actualities of family breakdown, homelessness, violence, and the "savage inequalities" described by Jonathan Kozol, although social injustice has an existential dimension.

Like their elders, children and young persons inhabit a world of fearful moral uncertainty—a world in which it appears that almost nothing can be done to reduce suffering, contain massacres, and protect human rights. The faces of refugee children in search of their mothers, of teenage girls repeatedly raped by soldiers, of rootless people staring at the charred remains of churches and libraries may strike some of us as little more than a "virtual reality." Those who persist in looking feel numbed and, reminded over and over of helplessness, are persuaded to look away.

It has been said that Pablo Picasso's paintings of "weeping women" have become the icons of our time.[1] They have replaced the statues of men on horseback and men in battle; they overshadow the emblems of what once seemed worth fighting for, perhaps dying for. When even the young confront images of loss and death, as most of us are bound to do today, "it is important that everything we love be summed up into something unforgettably beautiful."[2] This suggests one of the roles of the arts. To see sketch after sketch of women holding dead babies, as Picasso has forced us to do, is to become aware of a tragic deficiency in the fabric of life. If we know enough to make those paintings the objects of our experience, to encounter them against the background of our lives, we are likely to strain toward conceptions of a better order of things, in which there will be no more wars that make women weep like that, no more bombs to murder innocent children. We are likely, in rebelling against such horror, to summon up images of smiling mothers and lovely children, metaphors for what *ought* to be.

Clearly, this is not the only role of the arts, although encounters with them frequently do move us to want to restore some kind of order, to repair, and to heal. Participatory involvement with the many forms of art does enable us, at the very least, to *see* more in our experience, to *hear* more on normally unheard frequencies, to *become conscious* of what daily routines, habits, and conventions have obscured.

We might think of what Pecola Breedlove in *The Bluest Eye* has made us realize about the metanarrative implicit in the Dick and Jane basal readers or in the cultural artifact called Shirley Temple, who made so many invisible children yearn desperately to have blue eyes.[3] We might recall the revelations discovered by so many through an involvement with *Schindler's List*. We might try to retrieve the physical consciousness of unutterable grief aroused in us by Martha Graham's dance "Lamentation," with only feet and hands visible outside draped fabric—and agony expressed through stress lines on the cloth. To see more, to hear more. By such experiences, we are not only lurched out of the familiar and the taken for granted, but we may also discover new avenues for action. We may experience a sudden sense of new possibilities and thus new beginnings.

The prevailing cynicism with regard to values and the feelings of resignation it breeds cannot help but create an atmosphere in the schools that is at odds with the unpredictability associated with the experience of art. The neglect of the arts by those who identified the goals of Goals 2000 was consistent with the focus on the manageable, the predictable, and the measurable. There have been efforts to include the arts in the official statements of goals, but the arguments mustered in their favor are of a piece with the arguments for education geared toward economic competitiveness, technological mastery, and the rest. They have also helped support the dominant arguments for the development of "higher-level skills," academic achievement, standards, and preparation for the workplace.

The danger afflicting both teachers and students because of such emphases is, in part, the danger of feeling locked into existing circumstances defined by others. Young people find themselves described as "human resources," rather than as persons who are centers of choice and evaluation. It is suggested that young people are to be molded in the service of technology and the market, no matter who they are. Yet, as many are now realizing, great numbers of our young people will find themselves unable to locate satisfying jobs, and the very notion of "all the children" and even of human resources carries with it deceptions of all kinds. Perhaps it is no wonder that the dominant mood in many classrooms is one of passive reception.

Umberto Eco, the Italian critic of popular culture, writes about the desperate need to introduce a critical dimension into such reception. Where media and messages are concerned, it is far more important, he says, to focus on the point of reception than on the point of transmission. Finding a threat in "the universal of technological communication" and in situations where "the medium is the message," he calls seriously for a return to individual resistance. "To the anonymous divinity of Technological Communication, our answer could be: 'Not thy, but *our* will be done.'"[4]

The kind of resistance Eco has in mind can best be evoked when imagination is released. But, as we well know, the bombardment of images identified with "Technological Communication" frequently has the effect of freezing imaginative thinking. Instead of freeing audiences to look at things as if they could be otherwise, present-day media impose predigested frameworks on their audiences. Dreams are caught in the meshes of the salable; the alternative to gloom or feelings of pointlessness is consumerist acquisition. For Mary Warnock, imagination is identified with the belief that "there is more in our experience of the world than can possibly meet the unreflecting eye."[5] It tells us that experience always holds more than we can predict. But Warnock knows that acknowledging the existence of undiscovered vistas and perspectives requires reflectiveness. The passive, apathetic person is all too likely to be unresponsive to ideas of the unreal, as if, the merely possible. He or she becomes the one who bars the arts as frivolous, mere frills, irrelevant to learning in the postindustrial world.

It is my conviction that informed engagements with the several arts would be the most likely way to release the imaginative capacity and give it play. However, this does not happen automatically or "naturally." We have all witnessed the surface contacts with paintings when groups of tourists hasten through museums. Without time spent, without tutoring, and without dialogue regarding the arts, people merely seek the right labels. They look for the artists' names. There are those who watch a ballet for the story, not for the movement or the music; they wait for Giselle to go mad or for Sleeping Beauty to be awakened or for the white swan to return.

Mere exposure to a work of art is not sufficient to occasion an aesthetic experience. There must be conscious participation in a work, a going out of energy, an ability to notice what is there to be noticed in the play, the poem, the quartet. "Knowing about," even in the most formal, academic manner, is entirely different from creating an unreal world imaginatively and entering it perceptually, affectively, and cognitively. To introduce people to such engagement is to strike a delicate balance between helping learners to pay heed—to attend to shapes, patterns, sounds, rhythms, figures of speech, contours, lines, and so on—and freeing them to perceive particular works as meaningful. Indeed, the inability to control what is discovered as meaningful makes many traditional educators uneasy and strikes them as being at odds with conceptions of a norm, even with notions of appropriate "cultural literacy." This uneasiness may well be at the root of certain administrators' current preoccupation with national standards.

However, if we are to provide occasions for significant encounters with works of art, we have to combat standardization and what Hannah Arendt called "thoughtlessness" on the part of all those involved. What she meant by thoughtlessness was "the heedless recklessness or hopeless confusion or complacent repetition of 'truths' which have become trivial and empty."[6] There is something in that statement that recalls what John Dewey described as a "social pathology"—a condition that still seems to afflict us today. Dewey wrote that it manifests itself "in querulousness, in impotent drifting, in uneasy snatching at distractions, in idealization of the long established, in a facile optimism assumed as a cloak."[7] Concerned about "sloppiness, superficiality, and recourse to sensations as a substitute for ideas," Dewey made the point that "thinking deprived of its normal course takes refuge in academic specialism."[8]

For Arendt, the remedy for this condition is "to think what we are doing." She had in mind developing a self-reflectiveness that originates in situated life, the life of persons open to one another in their distinctive locations and engaging one another in dialogue. Provoked by the spectacle of the Nazi Adolf Eichmann, Arendt warned against "clichés, stock phrases, adherence to conventional, standardized codes of expression and conduct," which have, she said, "the socially recognized function of protecting us against reality, that is, against the claim on our thinking attention that all events and facts make by virtue of their existence."[9] She was not calling for a new intellectualism or for a new concentration on "higher-order skills." She was asking for a way of seeking clarity and authenticity in the face of thoughtlessness, and it seems to me that we might ask much the same thing if we are committed to the release of the imagination and truly wish to open the young to the arts.

Thoughtfulness in this sense is necessary if we are to resist the messages of the media in the fashion Eco suggests, and it is difficult to think of young imaginations being freed without learners finding out how to take a critical and thoughtful approach to the illusory or fabricated "realities" presented to them by the media. To be thoughtful about what we are doing is to be conscious of ourselves struggling to make meanings, to make critical sense of what authoritative others are offering as objectively "real."

I find a metaphor for the reification of experience in the plague as it is confronted in Albert Camus' novel. The pestilence that struck the town of Oran (submerged as it was in habit and "doing business") thrust most of the inhabitants into resignation, isolation, or despair. Gradually revealing itself as inexorable and incurable, the plague froze people in place; it was simply *there.* At first Dr. Rieux fights the plague for the most abstract of reasons: because it is his job. Only later, when the unspeakable tragedies he witnesses make him actually think about what he is doing, does he reconceive his practice and his struggle and talk about not wanting to be complicit with the pestilence. By then he has met Tarrou, who is trying to be a "saint without God" and who has the wit and, yes, the imagination to organize people into sanitary squads to fight the plague and make it the moral concern of all.

Tarrou has the imagination too to find in the plague a metaphor for indifference or distancing or (we might say) thoughtlessness. Everyone carries the microbe, he tells his friend; it is only natural. He means what Hannah Arendt meant—and Dewey and Eco and all the others who resist a lack of concern. He has in mind evasions of complex problems, the embrace of facile formulations of the human predicament, the reliance on conventional solutions—all those factors I would say stand in the way of imaginative thinking and engagement with the arts. "All the rest," says Tarrou, "health, integrity, purity (if you like)—is a product of the human will, of a vigilance that must never falter." He means, of course, that we (and those who are our students) must be given opportunities to choose to be persons of integrity, persons who care.

Tarrou has a deep suspicion of turgid language that obscures the actualities of things, that too often substitutes abstract constructions for concrete particulars. This is one of the modes of the thoughtlessness Arendt was urging us to fight. She, too, wanted to use "plain, clear-cut language." She wanted to urge people, as does Tarrou, to attend to what is around them, "to stop and think." I am trying to affirm that this kind of awareness, this openness to the world, is what allows for the consciousness of alternative possibilities and thus for a willingness to risk encounters with the "weeping women," with Euripides' *Medea,* with *Moby Dick,* with Balanchine's (and, yes, the Scripture's) *Prodigal Son,* with Mahler's *Songs of the Earth.*

Another novel that enables its readers to envisage what stands in the way of imagination is Christa Wolf's *Accident: A Day's News.* It moves me to clarify my own response to the technical and the abstract. I turn to it not in order to add to my knowledge or to find some buried truth, but because it makes me see, over the course of time, what I might never have seen in my own lived world.

The power the book holds for me may be because it has to do with the accident at Chernobyl, as experienced by a woman writer, who is also a mother and grandmother. She is preoccupied by her brother's brain surgery, taking place on the same day, and by the consequences of the nuclear accident for her grandchildren and for children around the world. She spends no time wondering about her own response to such a crisis; her preoccupation is with others—those she loves and the unknown ones whom she cannot for a moment forget. It is particularly interesting, within the context of an ethic of care, to contain for a moment within our own experience the thoughts of a frightened young mother, the narrator's daughter, picturing what it means to pour away thousands of liters of milk for fear of poisoning children while "children on the other side of the earth are perishing for lack of those foods."

The narrator wants to change the conversation and asks her daughter to "tell me something else, preferably about the children." Whereupon she hears that "the little one had pranced about the kitchen, a wing nut on his thumb, his hand held high. Me Punch. Me Punch. I was thrilled by the image."[10] Only a moment before, another sequence of pictures had come into her mind and caused her to

> admire the way in which everything fits together with a sleepwalker's precision: the desire of most people for a comfortable life, their tendency to believe the speakers on raised platforms and the men in white coats; the addiction to harmony and the fear of contradiction of the many seem to correspond to the arrogance and hunger for power, the dedication to profit, unscrupulous inquisitiveness, and self-infatuation of the few. So what was it that didn't add up in this equation?[11]

This passage seems to me to suggest the kind of questioning and, yes, the kind of picturing that may well be barred by the preoccupation with "world-class achievement" and by the focus on human resources that permeate Goals 2000.

But it does not have to be so. Cognitive adventuring and inquiry are much more likely to be provoked by the narrator's question about "this equation" than by the best of curriculum frameworks or by the most responsible and "authentic" assessment. To set the imagination moving in response to a text such as Wolf's may well be to confront learners with a demand to choose in a fundamental way between a desire for harmony with its easy answers and a commitment to the risky search for alternative possibilities.

Wolf's narrator, almost as if she were one of Picasso's weeping women, looks at the blue sky and, quoting some nameless source, says, "Aghast, the mothers search the sky for the inventions of learned men."[12] Like others to whom I have referred, she begins pondering the language and the difficulty of breaking through such terms as "half-life," "cesium," and "cloud" when "polluted rain" is so much more direct. Once again, the experience of the literary work may help us feel the need to break through the mystification of technology and the language to which it has given rise.

The narrator feels the need to battle the disengagement that often goes with knowing and speaking. When she ponders the motives of those who thought up the procedures for the "peaceful utilization of nuclear energy," she recalls a youthful protest against a power plant and the rebukes and reprimands directed at the protesters for their skepticism with regard to a scientific utopia. And then she lists the activities that the men of science and technology presumably do not pursue and would probably consider a waste of time if they were forced to:

> Changing a baby's diapers. Cooking, shopping with a child on one's arm or in the baby carriage. Doing the laundry, hanging it up to dry, taking it down, folding it, ironing it, darning it. Sweeping the floor, mopping it, polishing it, vacuuming it. Dusting. Sewing. Knitting. Crocheting. Embroidering. Doing the dishes. Taking care of a sick child. Thinking up stories to tell. Singing songs. And how many of these activities do I myself consider a waste of time?[13]

Reading this passage and posing a new set of questions, we cannot but consider the role of such concrete images in classroom conversation and in our efforts to awaken persons to talk about what ought to be. The narrator believes that the "expanding monstrous technological creation" may be a substitute for life for many people. She is quite aware of the benevolent aspects of technology: her brother, after all, is having advanced neurosurgery (which he does survive). But she is thinking, as we might well do in the schools, about the consequences of technological expansion for the ones we love. Her thinking may remind us of how important it is to keep alive images of "everything we love." I want to believe that by doing so we may be able to create classroom atmospheres that once again encourage individuals to have hope.

This brings me back to my argument for the arts, so unconscionably neglected in the talk swirling around Goals 2000. It is important to make the point that the events that make up aesthetic experiences are events that occur within and by means of the transactions with our environment that situate us in time and space. Some say that participatory encounters with paintings, dances, stories, and the rest enable us to recapture a lost spontaneity. By breaking through the frames of presuppositions and conventions, we may be enabled to reconnect ourselves with the processes of becoming who we are. By reflecting on our life histories, we may be able to gain some perspective on the men in white coats, even on our own desires to withdraw from complexity and to embrace a predictable harmony. By becoming aware of ourselves as questioners, as makers of meaning, as persons engaged in constructing and reconstructing realities with those around us, we may be able to communicate to students the notion that reality depends on perspective, that its construction is never complete, and that there is always more. I am reminded of Paul Cézanne's several renderings of Mont St. Victoire and of his way of suggesting that it must be viewed from several angles if its reality is to be apprehended.

Cézanne made much of the insertion of the body into his landscapes, and that itself may suggest a dimension of experience with which to ground our thinking and the thinking of those we teach. There are some who suggest that, of all the arts, dance confronts most directly the question of what it means to be human. Arnold Berleant writes that

> in establishing a human realm through movement, the dancer, with the participating audience, engages in the basic act out of which arise both all experience and our human constructions of the world. . . . [That basic act] stands as the direct denial of that most pernicious of all dualisms, the division of body and consciousness. In dance, thought is primed at the point of action. This is not the reflection of the contemplative mind but rather intellect poised in the body, not the deliberate consideration of alternative courses but thought in process, intimately responding to and guiding the actively engaged body.[14]

The focus is on process and practice; the skill in the making is embodied in the object made. In addition, dance provides occasions for the emergence of the integrated self. Surely, this ought to be taken into account in our peculiarly technical and academic time.

Some of what Berleant says relates as well to painting, if painting is viewed as an orientation in time and space of the physical body—of both perceiver and creator. If we take a participatory stance, we may enter a landscape or a room or an open street. Different modes of perception are asked of us, of course, by different artists, but that ought to mean a widening of sensitivity with regard to perceived form, color, and space. Jean-Paul Sartre, writing about painting, made a point that is significant for anyone concerned about the role of art and the awakening of imagination:

> The work is never limited to the painted, sculpted or narrated object. Just as one perceives things only against the background of the world, so the objects represented by art appear against the back-ground of the universe. . . . [T]he creative act aims at a total renewal of the world. Each painting, each book, is a recovery of the totality of being. Each of them presents this totality to the freedom of the spectator. For this is quite the final goal of art: to recover this world by giving it to be seen as it is, but as if it had its source in human freedom.[15]

In this passage Sartre suggests the many ways in which classroom encounters with the arts can move the young to imagine, to extend, and to renew. And surely nothing can be more important than finding the source of learning not in extrinsic demands, but in human freedom.

All this is directly related to developing what is today described as the active learner, here conceived as one awakened to pursue meaning. There are, of course, two contradictory tendencies in education today: one has to do with shaping malleable young people to serve the needs of technology in a postindustrial society; the other has to do with educating young people to grow and to become different, to find their individual voices, and to participate in a community in the making. Encounters with the arts nurture and sometimes provoke the growth of individuals who reach out to one another as they seek clearings in their experience and try to live more ardently in the world. If the significance of the arts for growth, inventiveness, and problem solving is recognized at last, a desperate stasis may be overcome, and people may come to recognize the need for new raids on what T. S. Eliot called the "inarticulate."

I choose to end this extended reflection on art and imagination with some words from "Elegy in Joy," by Muriel Rukeyser:

> Out of our life the living eyes
> See peace in our own image made,
> Able to give only what we can give:
> Bearing two days like midnight. "Live,"
> The moment offers: the night requires
> Promise effort love and praise.
>
> Now there are no maps and no magicians.
> No prophets but the young prophet, the sense
> of the world.
> The gift of our time, the world to be discovered.
> All the continents giving off their several lights,
> the one sea, and the air. And all things glow.[16]

These words offer life; they offer hope; they offer the prospect of discovery; they offer light. By resisting the tyranny of the technical, we may yet make them our pedagogic creed.

ENDNOTES

1. Judi Freeman, *Picasso and the Weeping Women* (Los Angeles: Los Angeles Museum of Art, 1994).
2. Michel Leiris. "Faire-part," in E. C. Oppler, ed., *Picasso's Guernica* (New York: Norton, 1988), p. 201.
3. Toni Morrison, *The Bluest Eye* (New York: Washington Square Press, 1970), p. 19.
4. Richard Kearney, *The Wake of Imagination* (Minneapolis: University of Minnesota Press, 1988), p. 382.
5. Mary Warnock, *Imagination* (Berkeley: University of California Press, 1978), p. 202.
6. Hannah - Arendt, *The Human Condition* (Chicago: University of Chicago Press, 1958), p. 5.
7. John Dewey, *The Public and Its Problems* (Athens, OH: Swallow Press, 1954), p. 170.

8. Ibid., p. 168.
9. Hannah Arendt, *Thinking: Vol. II, The Life of the Mind* (New York: Harcourt Brace Jovanovich, 1978), p. 4.
10. Christa Wolf, *Accident: A Day's News* (New York: Farrar, Straus & Giroux, 1989), p. 17.
11. Ibid.
12. Ibid., p. 27.
13. Ibid., p. 31.
14. Arnold Berleant, *Art and Engagement* (Philadelphia: Temple University Press, 1991), p. 167.
15. Jean-Paul Sartre, *Literature and Existentialism* (New York: Citadel Press, 1949), p. 57.
16. Muriel Rukeyser, "Tenth Elegy: An Elegy in Joy," in idem. *Out in Silence: Selected Poems* (Evanston, IL: TriQuarterly Books, 1992), p. 104.

DISCUSSION QUESTIONS

1. What are the implications of understanding the existential contexts of education and educational goals?
2. Why does inclusion of the arts in the school curriculum continue to be a topic of debate among many educators?
3. Why is mere exposure to a work of art insufficient for stimulating an aesthetic experience?
4. How does a neglect of the arts in school experiences affect students?
5. How might repeated significant encounters with the arts be used to combat standardization?

CHAPTER 5

No Community Left Behind

PHILLIP C. SCHLECHTY

FOCUSING QUESTIONS:

1. Describe the history of increased federal involvement in public education.
2. What is the community building function of public schools?
3. How can schools be transformed?
4. What are accountability and equity and how does the author suggest addressing these concerns?
5. How can virtual schools offer choice to students and families?
6. What role do families and communities play in public schools?

If control of the local schools were returned to their communities, Mr. Schlechty believes, the results would be twofold. Communities would unite around the common cause of setting expectations for the schools, and the schools would improve to meet those expectations.

The debate over the reauthorization of No Child Left Behind (NCLB) generally overlooks—or looks past—what may be the most fundamental flaw in that legislation. As the law is now written, decisions regarding what the young should know and be able to do are removed from the hands of parents and local community leaders and turned over to officials and experts located far from the schoolhouse door. Removing the debate over such an important matter from the reach of citizens at the local level—and denying them the right to act on the results of their debates—destroys one of the greatest resources the nation has in the struggle to maintain a sense of community in an increasingly globalized and impersonal world.[1]

Good schools require strong communities to support them. It is time state legislators and members of Congress awakened to the fact that the best chance we have of significantly improving the quality of education received by most Americans is to revitalize the idea of local control of schools. Rather than entrusting the future of education to bureaucrats at the state and federal levels, regardless of how "expert" these bureaucrats may be, we must give our attention to building trustworthy local communities. I will argue that placing local communities at the center of the debate over standards is the best way to build such trustworthy communities. It is also the best way to create great schools in every community.

APPLEBEE'S AMERICA

In a recent book titled *Applebee's America*, the authors observe that many politicians and religious leaders are discovering that two of the most important motivators for many Americans are the quest for community and the desire to be associated with a cause that is greater than themselves.[2] Americans are tired of sloganeering. They no longer respond well to bureaucratic jargon and symbols. Rather, Americans respond to leaders who appeal to "gut values" that have to do with their sense of belonging and their ability to contribute to the greater good.

This suggests that American citizens will be increasingly unlikely to respond to leaders who are fixated on such instrumental concerns as test scores or who speak of students as products to be shaped to meet the needs of multinational corporations. Rather, Americans will want leaders who link school improvement efforts to the development of children as human beings and to the quality of community life. Instead of thinking and talking about test scores, they will want to be involved in discussions about what children need to know and should be able to do, and they will want to know, as well, that the results of these discussions can and will make a difference in what goes on in their schools.

The unfortunate fact is that, as things now stand, many local school boards are barriers to community involvement in the life of schools, just as state and federal agencies are.[3] Rather than seeking ways to reform the mechanisms of local control and causing school boards to operate differently, policy makers use the dysfunctional nature of many school boards as a convenient rationale for removing the control of schools from local communities. The fact is that legislation like NCLB results in part from the disdain some members of the policy elite have for ordinary citizens and from the belief these elites harbor that they know better than ordinary citizens what children need to know and be able to do. Thus, in a very real sense, the failure of the systems through which the sentiments of local communities can be developed and expressed is being used as a cover for taking away from local communities the right to express these sentiments in any meaningful way.

If it happens that local citizens are not sufficiently informed about education to make decisions about what children should learn in school, taking power away from the citizens is not the answer. The answer is to provide them with the education *they* need.

Moreover, if properly framed, the debates over what schools should teach and what standards should prevail could serve as a primary means by which communities could become educated about the condition of education. It is through such education that *trustworthy* communities might be created and defined. It is through such discussions that the common ground that binds communities together could be discovered.

Building schools into the fabric of community life by involving schools in the building of communities, as well as involving communities in establishing standards for their schools, will satisfy both the needs of adults and the needs of children. Indeed, given globalization of the economy and the revolutions that are occurring in the way information is transmitted, processed, and communicated, if we do not move quickly to build a sense of community among us at the same time that we dramatically improve our schools, then the blessings that the information revolution promises can quickly turn into a hell that even Orwell could not describe.

Absent the kind of communitywide conversations needed to define standards for schools and absent meaningful local input into the way those standards are to be assessed, the community-building potential of schools can never be exploited. If there was ever a time when community-building institutions were critical to the life of this nation, that time is now. The community-building conversations public schools might create cannot occur if conversations about standards take place only among experts and a few selected committee members in offices far from local school districts. These conversations almost certainly will not occur at all if schools are made into the government agencies they are fast becoming under current policy.

COMMITMENT AND COMPLIANCE

The issue of where standards should be established is more than a community-building issue. It is a quality issue as well. If standards are to inspire excellence as opposed to minimum compliance, then the standards must have intrinsic value in the context where they are being applied.

With regard to schooling, this means parents and teachers, as well as other concerned citizens, must understand the standards well enough to embrace them and to know when they are being met and when they are not. Such understanding and commitment can only be gained when parents, teachers, and community leaders are involved—and feel they are involved—in the development of standards and in the enforcement of standards. Indeed, the fact that standards must be enforced from the outside through threats of punishment and promises of reward is prima facie evidence that the standards being used to assess student performance are not personally compelling to teachers or to students.

If standards are to be compelling, they must be based on values that are cherished by those to whom they are applied. In addition, they must be assessed by means that are credible to those to whom they apply. Standards are not likely to compel action when single tests become substitutes for a standard, even if the standard itself is compelling.

When a test score becomes a proxy for a standard, then the problem is no longer framed by the standard; it is framed by the test. The goal becomes beating the test rather than educating children. As I heard one superintendent say, "We know why so many schools are not meeting the standard. Too many students are marking the wrong answers. All we have to do is figure out some way to get them to mark more right answers." Although this comment was made in jest, it contains more than a bit of truth about the way some school leaders are approaching the need to make sufficient progress each year to satisfy the standards set by the states that are operating as proxies for the federal government.

THE EROSION OF LOCAL CONTROL

One of the most dramatic changes that has occurred over the course of my career, which began in the late 1950s, has to do with the willingness of the U.S. Congress to exert control over the operation of local schools. Prior to the launching of Sputnik I in 1957, many members of Congress would become almost apoplectic at the mere mention of the prospect of federal intervention in the life of local schools. As Stewart McClure, chief clerk of the Senate Committee on Labor, Education, and Public Welfare at the time Sputnik was launched, recalled, whenever the idea of federal intervention in the life of local schools came up, some members of Congress would "get white and scream and wave their hands in the air about the *horrible* prospects of this vicious, cold hand of federal bureaucracy being laid upon these pristine, splendid local schools that knew better than anyone what needed to be done, and so forth and so forth."[4]

It is difficult to imagine federal legislators in the 1950s being willing to advance the idea that Congress had any business meddling in the way teachers were paid or specifying the frequency with which tests had to be given. Today, such proposals and actions are commonplace—so commonplace that the propriety of federal control by state proxies is not even seriously debated. Rather, criticisms fasten on the technical aspects by which federal control is exercised (e.g., how many tests are enough tests?) and the absence of adequate funding to support the mandates that are enacted. Only a few have had the temerity to suggest that NCLB is simply wrongheaded.[5]

For the first few years after Sputnik, confidence in the notion that federal aid did not necessarily translate into federal control seemed to be well grounded. The National Defense Education Act (1958), for example, specifically prohibited the federal government from providing any form of direction, supervision, or control over curriculum, programs of instruction, or administration of personnel in any educational institution. Similarly, when the National Science Foundation became involved in curriculum development, its officials were very careful to insist that the agency offer "grants" to private providers rather than contracts. (As a recipient of many of these grants, I was well aware of this distinction and the significance the leaders of NSF attached to it.)

The turning point in making federal intervention into local educational matters legitimate was the Elementary and Secondary Education Act (ESEA) of 1965. Unlike previous federal education legislation, ESEA was based on the assumption that the spending clause of the U.S. Constitution entitled Congress to behave more aggressively toward local schools than had traditionally been the case.

The spending clause, along with the commerce clause, had been used quite effectively by New Deal legislators to bypass 10th Amendment prohibitions in many areas of civic life that had, theretofore, been exempt from federal control. Since 1965, these precedents have been applied increasingly to education, until the 10th Amendment is becoming as irrelevant in education as it is in many other areas of civic life.

NCLB is nothing more or less than the latest reauthorization of this 1965 legislation, which is once again up for renewal. Unfortunately, the present round of legislation does not seem likely to reverse the trend that began in 1965. Indeed, even as I write this and no doubt as you read it, congressional committees and their expert advisors are busy crafting even more regulations than existed in the version of ESEA that has come to be known as NCLB. Only a few legislators have had the courage to suggest that the problem may be that the federal government has no business regulating the operation of local schools in the first place, and few of the education lobbying groups have taken this position. Apparently, federal government control of local schools is acceptable to some professional educators as long as that control is exercised in ways that serve the interests of their particular professional group. Our children and our nation deserve better, and our traditions demand better.[6]

THE COMMUNITY-BUILDING FUNCTION OF PUBLIC SCHOOLS

Make no mistake. I am not opposed to federal involvement in public education or to federal aid to education. What I am opposed to is federal *control* of local schools. Indeed, I would prefer less state control. What I am in favor of is maximum participation by local citizens in determining the direction their schools should take and the ends their schools should serve. What I want is schools that help *build* communities as well as serve them. I want the schools to have more meaning in the life of communities than do government agencies such as the postal service. Schools are, or should be, cultural institutions that define communities and signify how members of a community see themselves and their collective futures.

The needs of business for a "world-class work force" and the needs of colleges for "qualified students" are important and must be satisfied. These needs are more likely to be met, however, if the needs of students, parents, and communities are served well first. What is good for children, parents, and local communities is good for American business and higher education. (Whether or not one should add "vice versa" to this statement, as Charles Wilson, the former CEO of General Motors, once did when making a similar claim, depends on the social sensitivity and civic orientation of American business and of our institutions of higher education.)

Business leaders who would help the schools improve must surely understand that one of the reasons many American businesses get into trouble is that they place the needs of stockholders and management above the needs and values of customers or the welfare of their employees. In business terms, students and parents are the first-line customers of schools. Students are not products and parents are not stockholders or even stakeholders. Students and parents are—or should be—the focal point of school activity.

Businesses and institutions of higher learning are stakeholders in and have rightful claims on the public schools. The biggest stakeholders, however, are our posterity and our democratic way of life. To respond well to the needs of these stakeholders, the schools must ensure that all children are well educated and fully prepared to participate in and benefit from a vital democratic social order. And that goal is more likely to be achieved if the public schools attend to their real business: providing engaging intellectual experiences for students that result in their learning what they need to know to lead full and satisfying lives in a democracy that is threatening to overwhelm its citizens with information. This means that schools must provide all students with experiences that engage them in vital intellectual pursuits—experiences that require them to discipline their minds and from which they learn those things necessary to be able to distinguish sense from nonsense.

Certainly, preparing our students for their role in our democracy means that all students should learn to read and write. It also means all students need to have what Aristotle referred to as an "educational acquaintance" with the academic disciplines. More than that, all students need to develop an appreciation for the culture they inherit and the attitudes and dispositions it takes to fully participate in a democratic life—tolerance for diverse opinions, willingness to listen to and hear others, the ability to think critically and creatively, an expansiveness of views, a feeling of hope for the future, and a sense of charity toward others. These are things that do not show up on a test, but they are probably more important for students and society than many things that do appear on tests.

Unfortunately, federal intervention in schools and overbearing state intervention distract the attention of teachers from the needs of students and the needs of the communities in which schools are located. This top-down pressure results in fastening the attention of teachers and principals on meeting the requirements imposed by a bureaucratically oriented policy community concerned more with producing measurable results than with producing profound outcomes.

THE NEED FOR SCHOOL TRANSFORMATION

The fundamental problem with our schools is that they are bureaucratic in form. So long as they retain this form, they cannot accomplish what we want them to accomplish.

Schools, especially urban schools, were bureaucratic long before state legislators and members of Congress became assertive regarding their role as arbiters of the educational tastes of all citizens. Unfortunately, all that the present reform movement is doing is relocating bureaucratic authority from the local level to the state and federal levels. The schools are being reformed, but they are certainly not being *trans*formed.

Rational authority and expert authority—rather than the moral authority of the community and its leaders (including its educational leaders)—continue to dominate decisions about schooling. If schools are to be based in moral authority derived from community consent and consensus, then what we need are schools that follow Peter Senge's model for learning organizations. According to Senge, learning organizations are organizations where people continually expand their capacity to create the results they truly desire, where new and expansive patterns of thinking are nurtured, where collective aspiration is set free, and where people are continually learning to see the whole together.[7]

Creativity, expansiveness, and collective will are typical of a learning organization. Learning organizations manifest a sense of community because they are based on shared commitments and common beliefs. They are based on trust and mutual respect and assume a common commitment to excellence and shared standards by which excellence is judged.

Bureaucracies, on the other hand, are segmented systems that are held together by rationalized rules and clear sets of sanctions in support of those rules. Unlike learning organizations, in which standards are used to set direction and inspire action, bureaucracies rely on standards and their enforcement as the primary means of exercising organizational power and ensuring compliance. Bureaucracies seek to ensure minimums. Learning organizations seek to promote optimal performance.

Organizational theorists have recognized for many years that bureaucratic accountability measures are more likely to increase estrangement and sabotage than they are to drive performance to increasingly higher levels, especially when the standards are applied in the mindless way that many government bureaucrats are prone to apply them. Indeed, when standards are imposed by bureaucratic superiors, those most affected by the standards—in this case teachers and students—are likely to comply only to the point necessary to avoid punishment.

Today's state and federal efforts to improve schools are based on the assumption that standards imposed from outside a system can inspire excellence within a system even as they ensure that performance does not fall below some minimum level. As organizational theorists have also known for a long time, this assumption reflects a mistaken view of human motivation. If the auditing process associated with enforcing standards becomes too onerous and if the anxiety produced becomes too high, the presence of externally imposed standards will almost ensure mediocrity—even in places where there once was a commitment to excellence.

Given the direction that NCLB has set, I am convinced that the best we can hope for is that eventually all children will have equal access to a mediocre education. Those who want excellence will need to look outside the public schools. Surely that is not what state legislators and members of Congress intend, nor is it what our society and our economy demand. And it is decidedly not what all our children deserve.

INCENTIVES FOR TRANSFORMATION: A FEW RECOMMENDATIONS

The answer to the problems that vex our schools is to provide federal incentives to local school districts to transform their schools into learning organizations charged with the obligation to provide each student with the kind of education a discerning community expects and demands. To ensure accountability, local districts should be given incentives and support to develop ways of making the performance of the schools transparent enough to give the citizens of the community a sound basis for judging whether they are getting what they expect from their schools. The federal government might also provide incentives to local school districts to link their school improvement efforts to efforts to build and maintain a sense of community around the schools, for schools that have no community to serve cannot serve students very well.

What might these recommendations look like in practice? Here is a proposal:

- The federal government should move toward a pattern of block grants rather than categorical funding based on narrowly defined contracts. The National Defense Education Act of 1958 might serve as a reference point.
- Block grants should be specifically targeted toward encouraging local initiatives that address issues like those addressed by NCLB: making the performance of schools and school districts more transparent and understandable to citizens in the local community, addressing equity concerns, and facing up to issues that have to do with the distribution of resources and talent.
- States could be required to develop state plans for making the use of these funds transparent to all citizens in the state and also for making transparent the impact of these funds on the performance of schools and the achievement of students. (The federal government would play no role in approving these plans. The only role of the federal government would be to ensure that such plans exist and have been made transparent to the citizenry.)
- The type of accountability plan local communities adopt should be left up to the local school board, with the stipulation that each district would conduct an annual survey of all citizens regarding their level of satisfaction with the performance of the schools, as well as with the quantity and quality of the information regarding school performance.
- Federal funds could be provided for the specific purpose of supporting community efforts to establish standards for school and student performance and for creating assessment systems consistent with these standards.
- In support of the idea of market-driven accountability (discussed below) and as a source of technical assistance to local school districts, the federal government should provide sufficient funding to each state to create a virtual high school capable of providing by electronic means a comprehensive curriculum to any high school student in the state, as well as offering supplemental educational opportunities for elementary-age children. (The Florida Virtual High School might be used as a model for such an effort.)

Accountability and equity. Two of the primary concerns of NCLB are accountability and equity. These concerns are legitimate and should not go unaddressed. Here is how I would propose addressing these issues:

- To receive federal block grants, states could require that local school districts be prepared to present on an annual basis evidence that 1) parents are satisfied that they are well informed regarding the performance of their own children and have a reasonable basis for comparing it with that of other children in the district; 2) parents have a basis for comparing the graduates of their schools with the graduates of other schools in the state and nation; and 3) local taxpayers are satisfied with the way the schools are operating and have adequate information to judge the schools' performance.

- The state could audit the processes by which taxpayer and parent satisfaction data are collected and made public and then make the results of these audits available to the local media. The standards applied in the audit would be those standards commonly applied to studies of public opinion and surveys of attitudes. (If legislators want more standardization than this process can accommodate, it would probably do no great harm to empower the state to conduct these surveys on an annual basis and return the results to the community.)
- Targeted block grants would be made available to local school districts to help them develop the capacity to meet the expectations outlined above.
- Targeted block grants would be made available for local school districts to develop responses to any evidence of achievement gaps between identifiable groups. These funds would also be used to support reports to the community showing how and where funds have been expended, as well as the intended and actual impact of those expenditures.
- States would be expected to develop academic standards that all graduates of local schools would meet. States would also develop a means of auditing a sample of graduates to determine whether or not they do, in fact, meet the standards. The results of this audit would be widely publicized.
- School improvement funds would be made available through block grants, and the targets of these grants would be clearly specified. The law would make it clear that the local school district is obliged to present evidence that the funds provided are being used to serve the population identified and that data on the effects of the expenditure are systematically collected and made public. However, there would be no predetermined evaluation plan; rather, the state would specify standards for an evaluation plan to which local communities would need to respond.

CHOICE

I am sympathetic to the view that market forces can serve as powerful tools to help make organizations accountable. However, I do not believe that privatization is the only way to bring market forces to bear on local school leaders. Another way is for the state to create competing modes of delivering education that are available statewide. Parents and students would then be able to choose alternatives if they are dissatisfied with what their local community has to offer.

Nor is choice among existing public schools the only option. For example, the state of Florida has created a virtual school that provides students with an alternative means of meeting the requirements for a high school diploma offered by their local school districts. Some state-run virtual schools suffer from the same pathologies that afflict many other state bureaucracies, but others, like the Florida Virtual School, possess many qualities that characterize a learning organization.

Assuming my assessment of the Florida Virtual School is accurate, there is no reason that a similar school could not be established in every state (with help from federal funding). Such a school could serve as an accessible choice for any student or parent who found the local school offerings unacceptable. This virtual school alternative has many advantages, especially when viewed as part of an accountability system attached to a statewide school improvement effort. Here are some of the potential advantages of the virtual school option:

- Any student in the state could enroll in courses offered by the virtual school at no additional cost to parents or students. Whether or not the virtual school would be empowered to offer diplomas would be a matter left up to the state. (The Florida Virtual School does not offer diplomas.)

- If the state chose to do so, local school districts might be charged for virtual courses taken by students enrolled in the local school unless these courses were taken as a part of a formal partnership between the local school and the virtual school. The aim here would be to encourage underperforming schools to take advantage of the opportunities such partnerships might provide to increase access to technical assistance in the use of digital learning opportunities to improve schools.
- The virtual school can be made subject to the same transparency requirements that are applied to locally run public schools. (Private schools, especially parochial schools, are often exempt from such state mandates, even when they receive voucher payments.)
- School choice is really not a viable option in many smaller school districts because population density does not make it possible to support a brick-and-mortar alternative school. Moreover, commuting to a school in another district can often present students with insurmountable obstacles in terms of time and money. Virtual schooling can be delivered at any time and in any place, and the funding to make the needed hardware available would be considerably less than the cost of new school buildings.[8]
- Partnering relationships between the state virtual schools and local schools would offer the possibility of creating truly blended schools and could improve local schools without destroying them and without having the state engaging in a non-voluntary "takeover."
- Home-schooling families could be given access to the services of the state-run virtual school. Indeed, the state, using the standards it sets for high school graduation for students in local schools, might empower the state virtual school to grant diplomas to home-school students as long as the state virtual school is subject to the same auditing process that applies to local school districts.
- The number of students opting out of local schools and pursuing their studies through the state-sponsored alternative could be published in the annual report of each local school district. It would be up to the citizens of the local community to attach meaning to these numbers and to determine whether they were indicative of a problem with the schools or simply a matter of the idiosyncratic preferences of a few families.

CLOSING COMMENTS

Clearly, we need schools that are much different from the ones we now have. However, this does not mean that schools need to be made into more efficient bureaucracies or governmental agencies. Rather than becoming reformed bureaucracies, schools need to be transformed into vital community institutions capable of engaging the hearts and the minds of students, parents, and others who are seeking connections with their community. Schools should not only serve the educational needs of students but also become focal points for building community among the increasing number of Americans who are seeking association with a cause that will unite rather than divide.

It is time to retrieve our schools from the bureaucrats who would transform them into just one more government agency that provides minimum performance. It is time to reinvent our schools as vital centers of community life and places around which the culturally diverse society that typifies America can be united in a common cause bigger than any of us.

ENDNOTES

1. Though he says it differently, David Mathews makes a similar point in his excellent book *Reclaiming Public Education by Reclaiming Our*

Democracy (Dayton: Kettering Foundation Press, 2006).

2. Douglas B. Sosnik, Matthew J. Dowd, and Ron Fournier, *Applebee's America: How Successful Political, Business, and Religious Leaders Connect with the New American Community* (New York: Simon & Schuster, 2006).

3. The argument I am making here is in many ways similar to the argument David Mathews presents in *Reclaiming Public Education by Reclaiming Our Democracy*. The main difference is that I believe that the best way to reclaim our democracy is by reclaiming the public schools. Indeed, it is my view that the public schools are the last best hope we have of creating the kind of communities we need to ensure the continuation of our democratic way of life, and thus it is essential that school leaders—especially school boards—assume the role of community builders rather than representatives of the factions and groups that now divide our communities.

4. Stewart E. McClure, chief clerk, Senate Committee on Labor, Education and Public Welfare, "1949–1973 Oral History Interviews," Senate Historical Office, Washington, D.C., January 1983, pp. 110–11. Available at www.senate.gov. Google the title.

5. This point is also made by Neal McCluskey and Andrew Coulson in a recent op-ed piece that appeared in the *Louisville Courier Journal* under the headline "The Failures of No Child Left Behind." This article appeared after I had drafted this piece, but it was gratifying to find support for what I am asserting. See Neal McCluskey and Andrew J. Coulson, "The Failures of No Child Left Behind: A Report by the Cato Institute," *Louisville Courier Journal*, 13 September 2007, p. A-11.

6. See, for example, Joel Packer, "The NEA Supports Substantial Overhaul, Not Repeal, of NCLB," *Phi Delta Kappan*, December 2007, pp. 265–69.

7. Peter Senge, *The Fifth Discipline: The Art and Practice of the Learning Organization* (New York: Doubleday Currency, 1990), p. 3.

8. So much of the attention of education policy makers is focused on solving the problems of large urban districts (those with more than 100,000 students) that it is sometimes overlooked that nearly two-thirds of all students attend schools in districts with fewer than 25,000 students (K-12) and that nearly one-third attend schools in districts with fewer than 5,000 students. School choice has much less meaning in a small town in South Dakota than it might have in inner-city Chicago.

DISCUSSION QUESTIONS:

1. The author agues return of local control would unite communities and improve expectations. Do you agree with this argument? Explain.
2. Since the authorization of No Child Left Behind (NCLB), do you believe it is possible to return to more local control of public education?
3. The author discusses choice in addition to privatization. What role, if any, do you believe charter schools play in school reform?
4. What is the difference between school reform and school transformation? Are they mutually exclusive? Is one better than the other? Explain.
5. Is it possible to have nationwide accountability and more local control? Explain.

PRO-CON CHART 1

Should the schools introduce a values-centered curriculum for all students?

PRO	CON
1. There are certain basic core values that educators involved in curriculum development should be able to agree on.	**1.** Values are not objective or neutral. Therefore, educators involved in curriculum development cannot easily agree on them.
2. The classroom is a place in which students can define what values are and share a diversity of viewpoints.	**2.** Engaging students in discussion will lead to peer pressure and indoctrination.
3. Students should be able to explore their values in a classroom setting.	**3.** Unstated teacher attitudes may impinge upon students' ability to identify their own preferences.
4. Valuing is part of citizenship education, and therefore, schools have a responsibility to teach valuing.	**4.** Values are not part of civic education. Moreover, values education is the responsibility of the home, not the school.
5. Students need to learn to express themselves forthrightly and to make choices without fear of condemnation.	**5.** There is no assurance that the teacher can model values, much less provide appropriate instructional activities that will promote these behaviors.

CASE STUDY 1

A Clash Concerning the Arts Curriculum

Andrea Brown had recently been hired as the assistant principal in charge of curriculum at the Newberry Elementary School. Brown, an advocate for arts education, had a humanistic orientation to curriculum. The principal, Al Sigel, had an essentialist view of the curriculum. Adhering to a back to basics focus, Sigel felt that math, science, and computer education should be emphasized and that arts courses were frivolous.

The state code and the school's educational manuals indicated that all students were required to receive 40 minutes of music, art, and dance per week. Without discussing his intentions with Brown or eliciting faculty reactions, Sigel distributed a memo to the staff at the first faculty meeting of the school year indicating that music, art, and dance courses were to be eliminated from the academic schedule as specific courses and that teachers should integrate these subjects into social studies and English. The extra class time was to be equally distributed to provide additional math, science, and computer education classes.

Upon learning about this decision, several parents approached Brown and asked that she assist them in getting the arts classes placed back into the schedule. Brown felt an ethical and educational obligation to address the parents' concern. While cognizant of the legal implications, she also believed the arts were an essential curriculum component. She pondered how she might approach this situation.

Assume that you are the assistant principal. Consider the circumstances described in the case. How would you propose to handle the parents' concerns?

Consider also the implications of taking one of the following actions in response to the parents' request:

1. Confront the principal and cite the state- and school-mandated requirements concerning course time allocations.
2. Resign from the position and state that she and Sigel had irresolvable differences regarding their philosophical orientation to curriculum.
3. Take the curriculum-related concerns to the district superintendent in charge of instruction.
4. Present an inservice workshop to the teaching staff about the intrinsic and utilitarian values of an arts education.
5. Lead a coalition of concerned parents and ask for a meeting with the principal.

PART TWO

Curriculum and Teaching

What are the trends that influence student success and teachers' selection of instructional approaches? What methods are most appropriate for teaching a diverse population of learners? How do teachers' identities, teacher thinking, practical knowledge, and teacher effectiveness affect the ways in which teachers deliver the curriculum?

In Chapter 6, Nel Noddings explains why caring for oneself and others is an important outcome of education and how curriculum can be chosen to develop the inner growth of students. She proposes that schools should become communities of caring, where care becomes a major purpose that guides school policy, as well as the individual and collective practices of teachers. Next, Parker Palmer describes three origins of difficulties that teachers face: the enormous scope and ever-changing nature of subject matter, the complexity of students as real human beings, and the fact that the best teaching emerges from who the teacher is as a person. Taking time to listen to the teacher who resides within oneself, he proposes, is a better guide to practice than the latest instructional techniques.

In Chapter 8, Allan Ornstein raises the question of whether teaching should be considered an art or a science. His discussion of this issue provides a framework for a proposal to reconceptualize teaching and its study in a way that would place greater emphasis on matters of moral and humanistic importance. Next, Herbert Walberg provides a comprehensive review of research on the effects of various methods of teaching. He summarizes what is known about the psychological elements of teaching, the various patterns that individual teachers can implement in their classrooms, the more complex systems of instruction that require special planning and resources, and effective instructional methods for specific content areas and populations of students.

In Chapter 10, Edward Pajak, Elaine Stotko, and Frank Masci suggest that support for new teachers should respect and nurture and build on their preferred styles of teaching. Four styles are identified—knowing, caring, inspiring, and inventing—and suggestions for a new and powerful way to differentiate support for beginning teachers are offered. In the last chapter in Part Two, Linda Darling-Hammond documents the importance of qualified teachers for student achievement and describes four factors that research has shown help to reduce teacher attrition. A number of practical steps that leaders can take to retain good teachers are described.

CHAPTER 6

Teaching Themes of Care

NEL NODDINGS

FOCUSING QUESTIONS

1. How is caring an essential part of teaching?
2. Why is it important to teach children to care?
3. How can caring be incorporated into the curriculum?
4. Are some subject areas more suited for teaching themes of care?
5. What might a curriculum that included themes of caring look like and how would it be implemented?

Some educators today—and I include myself among them—would like to see a complete reorganization of the school curriculum. We would like to give a central place to the questions and issues that lie at the core of human existence. One possibility would be to organize the curriculum around themes of care—caring for self, for intimate others, for strangers and global others, for the natural world and its nonhuman creatures, for the human-made world, and for ideas.[1]

A realistic assessment of schooling in the present political climate makes it clear that such a plan is not likely to be implemented. However, we can use the rich vocabulary of care in educational planning and introduce themes of care into regular subject-matter classes. Here, I will first give a brief rationale for teaching themes of care; second, I will suggest ways of choosing and organizing such themes; and, finally, I'll say a bit about the structures required to support such teaching.

WHY TEACH CARING?

In an age when violence among schoolchildren is at an unprecedented level, when children are bearing children with little knowledge of how to care for them, when the society and even the schools often concentrate on materialistic messages, it may be unnecessary to argue that we should care more genuinely for our children and teach them to care. However, many otherwise reasonable people seem to believe that our educational problems consist largely of low scores on achievement tests. My contention is, first, that we should want more from our educational efforts than adequate academic achievement and, second, that we will not achieve even that meager success unless our children believe that they themselves are cared for and learn to care for others.

There is much to be gained, both academically and humanly, by including themes of care in our curriculum. First, such inclusion may well expand our students' cultural literacy. For example, as we discuss in math classes, the attempts of great mathematicians to prove the existence of God or to reconcile a God who is all good with the reality of evil in the world, students will hear names, ideas, and words that are not part of the standard curriculum. Although such incidental learning cannot replace the systematic and sequential learning required by those who plan careers in mathematically oriented fields, it can be powerful in expanding students' cultural horizons and in inspiring further study.

Second, themes of care help us to connect the standard subjects. The use of literature in mathematics classes, of history in science classes, and of art and music in all classes can give students a feeling of the wholeness in their education. After all, why should they seriously study five different subjects if their teachers, who are educated people, only seem to know and appreciate one?

Third, themes of care connect our students and our subjects to great existential questions. What is the meaning of life? Are there gods? How should I live?

Fourth, sharing such themes can connect us person-to-person. When teachers discuss themes of care, they may become real persons to their students and so enable them to construct new knowledge. Martin Buber put it this way:

> Trust, trust in the world, because this human being exists—that is the most inward achievement of the relation in education. Because this human being exists, meaninglessness, however hard pressed you are by it, cannot be the real truth. Because this human being exists, in the darkness the light lies hidden, in fear salvation, and in the callousness of one's fellowman the great love.[2]

Finally, I should emphasize that caring is not just a warm, fuzzy feeling that makes people kind and likable. Caring implies a continuous search for competence. When we care, we want to do our very best for the objects of our care. To have as our educational goal the production of caring, competent, loving, and lovable people is not anti-intellectual. Rather, it demonstrates respect for the full range of human talents. Not all human beings are good at or interested in mathematics, science, or British literature. But all humans can be helped to lead lives of deep concern for others, for the natural world and its creatures, and for the preservation of the human-made world. They can be led to develop the skills and knowledge necessary to make positive contributions, regardless of the occupation they may choose.

CHOOSING AND ORGANIZING THEMES OF CARE

Care is conveyed in many ways. At the institutional level, schools can be organized to provide continuity and support for relationships of care and trust.[3] At the individual level, parents and teachers show their caring through characteristic forms of attention: by cooperating in children's activities, by sharing their own dreams and doubts, and by providing carefully for the steady growth of the children in their charge. Personal manifestations of care are probably more important in children's lives than any particular curriculum or pattern of pedagogy.

However, curriculum can be selected with caring in mind. That is, educators can manifest their care in the choice of curriculum, and appropriately chosen curriculum can contribute to the growth of children as carers. Within each large domain of care, many topics are suitable for thematic units: in the domain of "caring for self," for example, we might consider life stages, spiritual growth, and what it means to develop an admirable character; in exploring the topic of caring for intimate others, we might include units on love, friendship, and parenting; under the theme of caring for strangers and global others, we might study war, poverty, and tolerance; in addressing the idea of caring for the human-made world, we might encourage competence with the machines that surround us and a real appreciation for the marvels of technology. Many other examples exist. Furthermore, there are at least two different ways to approach the development of such themes: units can be constructed by interdisciplinary teams, or themes can be identified by individual teachers and addressed periodically throughout a year's or semester's work.

The interdisciplinary approach is familiar in core programs, and such programs are becoming more and more popular at the middle school level. One key to a successful interdisciplinary unit is the degree of genuinely enthusiastic support it receives from the teachers involved. Too often, arbitrary or artificial groupings are formed, and teachers are forced to make contributions that they themselves do not value highly. For example, math and science teachers are sometimes automatically lumped together, and rich humanistic possibilities may be lost. If I, as a math teacher, want to include historical, biographical, and literary topics in my math lessons, I might prefer to work with English and social studies teachers. Thus, it is important to involve teachers in the initial selection of broad areas for themes, as well as in their implementation.

Such interdisciplinary arrangements also work well at the college level. I recently received a copy of the syllabus for a college course titled "The Search for Meaning," which was co-taught by an economist, a university chaplain, and a psychiatrist.[4] The course is interdisciplinary, intellectually rich, and aimed squarely at the central questions of life.

At the high school level, where students desperately need to engage in the study and practice of caring, it is harder to form interdisciplinary teams. A conflict arises as teachers acknowledge the intensity of the subject-matter preparation their students need for further education. Good teachers often wish there were time in the day to co-teach unconventional topics of great importance, and they even admit that their students are not getting what they need for full personal development. But they feel constrained by the requirements of a highly competitive world and the structures of schooling established by that world.

Is there a way out of this conflict? Imaginative, like-minded teachers might agree to emphasize a particular theme in their separate classes. Such themes as war, poverty, crime, racism, or sexism can be addressed in almost every subject area. The teachers should agree on some core ideas related to caring that will be discussed in all classes, but beyond the central commitment to address themes of care, the topics can be handled in whatever way seems suitable in a given subject.

Consider, for example, what a mathematics class might contribute to a unit on crime. Statistical information might be gathered on the location and number of crimes, on rates for various kinds of crime, on the ages of offenders, and on the cost to society; graphs and charts could be constructed. Data on changes in crime rates could be assembled. Intriguing questions could be asked: Were property crime rates lower when penalties were more severe—when, for example, even children were hanged as thieves? What does an average criminal case cost by way of lawyers' fees, police investigation, and court processing? Does it cost more to house a youth in a detention center or in an elite private school?

None of this would have to occupy a full period every day. The regular sequential work of the math class could go on at a slightly reduced rate (e.g., fewer textbook exercises as homework), and the work on crime could proceed in the form of interdisciplinary projects over a considerable period of time. Most important would be the continual reminder in all classes that the topic is part of a larger theme of caring for strangers and fellow citizens. It takes only a few minutes to talk about what it means to live in safety, to trust one's neighbors, to feel secure in greeting strangers. Students should be told that metal detectors and security guards were not part of their parents' school lives, and they should be encouraged to hope for a safer and more open future. Notice the words I've used in this paragraph: caring, trust, safety, strangers, hope. Each could be used as an organizing theme for another unit of study.

English and social studies teachers would obviously have much to contribute to a unit on crime. For example, students might read *Oliver Twist,* and they might also study and discuss the social conditions that seemed to promote crime in 19th-century England. Do similar conditions exist in our country today? The selection of materials could include both classic works and modern stories and films. Students might even be introduced to some of the mystery stories that adults read so avidly on airplanes and beaches, and teachers should be engaged in lively discussion about the comparative value of the various stories.

Science teachers might find that a unit on crime would enrich their teaching of evolution. They could bring up the topic of social Darwinism, which played such a strong role in social policy during the late 19th and early 20th centuries. To what degree are criminal tendencies inherited? Should children be tested for the genetic defects that are suspected of predisposing some people to crime? Are females less competent than males in moral reasoning? (Why did some scientists and philosophers think this was true?) Why do males commit so many more violent acts than females?

Teachers of the arts can also be involved. A unit on crime might provide a wonderful opportunity to critique "gangsta rap" and other currently popular forms of music. Students might profitably learn how the control of art contributed to national criminality during the Nazi era. These are ideas that pop into my mind. Far more various and far richer ideas will come from teachers who specialize in these subjects.

There are risks, of course, in undertaking any unit of study that focuses on matters of controversy or deep existential concern, and teachers should anticipate these risks. What if students want to compare the incomes of teachers and cocaine dealers? What if they point to contemporary personalities from politics, entertainment, business, or sports who seem to escape the law and profit from what seems to be criminal behavior? My own inclination would be to allow free discussion of these cases and to be prepared to counteract them with powerful stories of honesty, compassion, moderation, and charity.

An even more difficult problem may arise. Suppose a student discloses his or her own criminal activities? Fear of this sort of occurrence may send teachers scurrying for safer topics. But, in fact, any instructional method that uses narrative forms or encourages personal expression runs this risk. For example, students of English as a second language who write proudly about their own hard lives and new hopes may disclose that their parents are illegal immigrants. A girl may write passages that lead her teacher to suspect sexual abuse. A boy may brag about objects he has "ripped off." Clearly, as we use these powerful methods that encourage students to initiate discussion and share their experiences, we must reflect on the ethical issues involved, consider appropriate responses to such issues, and prepare teachers to handle them responsibly.

Caring teachers must help students make wise decisions about what information they will share about themselves. On the one hand, teachers want their students to express themselves, and they want their students to trust in and consult them. On the other hand, teachers have an obligation to protect immature students from making disclosures that they might later regret. There is a deep ethical problem here. Too often educators assume that only religious fundamentalists and right-wing extremists object to the discussion of emotionally and morally charged issues. In reality, there is a real danger of intrusiveness and lack of respect in methods that fail to recognize the vulnerability of students. Therefore, as teachers plan units and lessons on moral issues, they should anticipate the tough problems that may arise. I am arguing here that it is morally irresponsible to simply ignore existential questions and themes of care; we must attend to them. But it is equally irresponsible to approach these deep concerns without caution and careful preparation.

So far, I have discussed two ways of organizing interdisciplinary units on themes of care. In one, teachers actually teach together in teams; in the other, teachers agree on a theme and a central focus on care, but they do what they can, when they can, in their own classrooms. A variation on this second way—which is also open to teachers who have to work alone—is to choose several themes and weave them into regular course material over an entire semester or year. The particular themes will depend on the interests and preparation of each teacher.

For example, if I were teaching high school mathematics today, I would use religious/existential questions as a pervasive theme because the biographies of mathematicians are filled with accounts of their speculations on matters of God, other dimensions, and the infinite—and because these topics fascinate me. There are so many wonderful stories to be told: Descartes' proof of the existence of God, Pascal's famous wager, Plato's world of forms, Newton's attempt to verify biblical chronology, Leibniz's detailed theodicy, current attempts to describe a divine domain in terms of metasystems, and mystical speculations on the infinite.[5] Some of these stories can be told as rich "asides" in five minutes or less. Others might occupy the better part of several class periods.

Other mathematics teachers might use an interest in architecture and design, art, music, or machinery as continuing themes in the domain of "caring for the human-made world." Still others might introduce the mathematics of living things. The possibilities are endless. In choosing and pursuing these themes, teachers should be aware that they are both helping their students learn to care and demonstrating their own caring by sharing interests that go well beyond the demands of textbook pedagogy.

Still another way to introduce themes of care into regular classrooms is to be prepared to respond spontaneously to events that occur in the school or in the neighborhood. Older teachers have one advantage in this area: they probably have a greater store of experience and stories on which to draw. However, younger teachers have the advantage of being closer to their students' lives and experiences; they are more likely to be familiar with the music, films, and sports figures that interest their students. All teachers should be prepared to respond to the needs of students who are suffering from the death of friends, conflicts between groups of students, pressure to use drugs or to engage in sex, and other troubles so rampant in the lives of today's children. Too often schools rely on experts—"grief counselors" and the like—when what children really need is the continuing compassion and presence of adults who represent constancy and care in their lives. Artificially separating the emotional, academic, and moral care of children into tasks for specially designated experts contributes to the fragmentation of life in schools.

Of course, I do not mean to imply that experts are unnecessary, nor do I mean to suggest that some matters should not be reserved for parents or psychologists. But our society has gone too far in compartmentalizing the care of its children. When we ask whose job it is to teach children how to care, an appropriate initial response is "Everyone's." Having accepted universal responsibility, we can then ask about the special contributions and limitations of various individuals and groups.

SUPPORTING STRUCTURES

What kind of schools and teacher preparation are required, if themes of care are to be taught effectively? First, and most important, care must be taken seriously as a major purpose of schools; that is, educators must recognize that caring for students is fundamental in teaching and that developing people with a strong capacity for care is a major objective of responsible education. Schools properly pursue many other objectives—developing artistic talent, promoting multicultural understanding, diversifying curriculum to meet the academic and vocational needs of all students, forging connections with community agencies and parents, and so on. Schools cannot be single-purpose institutions. Indeed, many of us would argue that it is logically and practically impossible to achieve that single academic purpose if other purposes are not recognized and accepted. This contention is confirmed in the success stories of several inner-city schools.[6]

Once it is recognized that school is a place in which students are cared for and learn to care, that recognition should be powerful in guiding policy. In the late 1950s, schools in the United States, under the guidance of James Conant and others, placed the curriculum at the top of the educational priority list. Because the nation's leaders wanted schools to provide high-powered courses in mathematics and science, it was recommended that small high schools be replaced by efficient larger structures complete with sophisticated laboratories and specialist teachers. Economies of scale were anticipated, but the main argument for consolidation and regionalization centered on the curriculum. All over the country, small schools were closed, and students were herded into larger facilities with "more offerings." We did not think carefully about schools as communities and about what might be lost as we pursued a curriculum-driven ideal.

Today many educators are calling for smaller schools and more family-like groupings. These are good proposals, but teachers, parents, and students should be engaged in continuing discussion about what they are trying to achieve through the new arrangements. For example, if test scores do not immediately rise, participants should be courageous in explaining that test scores were not the main object of the changes. Most of us who argue for caring in schools are intuitively quite sure that children in such settings will in fact become more competent learners. But, if they cannot prove their academic competence in a prescribed period of time, should we give up on caring and on teaching them to care? That would be foolish. There is more to life and learning than the academic proficiency demonstrated by test scores.

In addition to steadfastness of purpose, schools must consider continuity of people and place. If we are concerned with caring and community, then we must make it possible for students and teachers to stay together for several years so that mutual trust can develop and students can feel a sense of belonging in their "schoolhome."[7]

More than one scheme of organization can satisfy the need for continuity. Elementary school children can stay with the same teacher for several years, or they can work with a stable team of specialist teachers for several years. In the latter arrangement, there may be program advantages; that is, children taught by subject-matter experts who get to know them well over an extended period of time may learn more about the particular subjects. At the high school level, the same specialist teachers might work with students throughout their years in high school. Or, as Theodore Sizer has suggested, one teacher might teach two subjects to a group of 30 students rather than one subject to 60 students, thereby reducing the number of different adults with whom students interact each day.[8] In all the suggested arrangements, placements should be made by mutual consent whenever possible. Teachers and students who hate or distrust one another should not be forced to stay together.

A policy of keeping students and teachers together for several years supports caring in two essential ways: it provides time for the development of caring relations, and it makes teaching themes of care more feasible. When trust has been established, teacher and students can discuss matters that would be hard for a group of strangers to approach, and classmates learn to support one another in sensitive situations.

The structural changes suggested here are not expensive. If a high school teacher must teach five classes a day, it costs no more for three of these classes to be composed of continuing students than for all five classes to comprise new students—i.e., strangers. The recommended changes come directly out of a clear-headed assessment of our major aims and purposes. We failed to suggest them earlier because we had other, too limited, goals in mind.

I have made one set of structural changes sound easy, and I do believe that they are easily made. But the curricular and pedagogical changes that are required may be more difficult. High school textbooks rarely contain the kinds of supplementary material I have described, and teachers are not formally prepared to incorporate such material. Too often, even the people we regard as strongly prepared in a liberal arts major are unprepared to discuss the history of their subject, its relation to other subjects, the biographies of its great figures, its connections to the great existential questions, and the ethical responsibilities of those who work in that discipline. To teach themes of care in an academically effective way, teachers will have to engage in projects of self-education.

At present, neither liberal arts departments nor schools of education pay much attention to connecting academic subjects with themes of care. For example, biology students may learn something of the anatomy and physiology of mammals but nothing at all about the care of living animals; they may never be asked to consider the moral issues involved in the annual euthanasia of millions of pets. Mathematics students may learn to solve quadratic equations but never study what it means to live in a mathematicized world. In enlightened history classes, students may learn something about the problems of racism and colonialism but never hear anything about the evolution of childhood, the contributions of women in both domestic and public caregiving, or the connection between the feminization of caregiving and public policy. A liberal education that neglects matters that are central to a fully human life hardly warrants the name,[9] and a professional education that confines itself to technique does nothing to close the gaps in liberal education.

The greatest structural obstacle, however, may simply be legitimizing the inclusion of themes of care in the curriculum. Teachers in the early grades have long included such themes as a regular part of their work, and middle school educators are becoming more sensitive to developmental needs involving care. But secondary schools, where violence, apathy, and alienation are most evident, do little to develop the capacity to care. Today, even elementary teachers complain that the pressure to produce high test scores inhibits the work they regard as central to their mission: the development of caring and competent people. Therefore, it would seem that the most fundamental change required is one of attitude. Teachers can be very special people in the lives of children, and it should be legitimate for them to spend time developing relations of trust, talking with students about problems that are central to their lives, and guiding them toward greater sensitivity and competence across all the domains of care.

ENDNOTES

1. For the theoretical argument, see Nel Noddings, *The Challenge to Care in Schools* (New York: Teachers College Press, 1992); for a practical example and rich documentation, see Sharon Quint, *Schooling Homeless Children* (New York: Teachers College Press, 1994).
2. Martin Buber, *Between Man and Man* (New York: Macmillan, 1965), p. 98.
3. Noddings, *The Challenge to Care in Schools.*
4. See Thomas H. Naylor, William H. Willimon, and Magdalena R. Naylor, *The Search for Meaning* (Nashville, TN: Abingdon Press, 1994).
5. Nel Noddings, *Educating for Intelligent Belief and Unbelief* (New York: Teachers College Press, 1993).
6. See Deborah Meier, "How Our Schools Could Be," *Phi Delta Kappan,* January 1995, pp. 369–373; Quint, *Schooling Homeless Children.*
7. See Jane Roland Martin, *The Schoolhome: Rethinking Schools for Changing Families* (Cambridge, MA: Harvard University Press, 1992).
8. Theodore Sizer, *Horace's Compromise: The Dilemma of the American High School* (Boston: Houghton Mifflin, 1984).
9. See Bruce Wilshire, *The Moral Collapse of the University* (Albany: State University of New York Press, 1990).

DISCUSSION QUESTIONS

1. Is teaching themes of care a legitimate responsibility for schools?
2. What are some advantages of an interdisciplinary unit on caring?
3. What might be some obstacles to implementing a curriculum that included themes of care?
4. What arguments would be useful for convincing a school board that themes of caring should be included in the curriculum?
5. What steps would you take as curriculum director to implement themes of caring in classrooms districtwide?

CHAPTER 7

The Heart of a Teacher

Parker J. Palmer

FOCUSING QUESTIONS

1. Is teaching an occupation or is it a vocation?
2. Does it matter who a teacher is as a person? Why?
3. What are the qualities of a great teacher?
4. Why do some teachers eventually become disillusioned and cynical?
5. How might teacher colleagues support each other's efforts to become great teachers?

WE TEACH WHO WE ARE

I am a teacher at heart, and there are moments in the classroom when I can hardly hold the joy. When my students and I discover uncharted territory to explore, when the pathway out of a thicket opens up before us, when our experience is illumined by the lightning-life of the mind—then teaching is the finest work I know.

But at other moments, the classroom is so lifeless or painful or confused—and I am so powerless to do anything about it—that my claim to be a teacher seems a transparent sham. Then the enemy is everywhere: in those students from some alien planet, in that subject I thought I knew, and in the personal pathology that keeps me earning my living this way. What a fool I was to imagine that I had mastered this occult art—harder to divine than tea leaves and impossible for mortals to do even passably well!

The tangles of teaching have three important sources. The first two are commonplace, but the third, and most fundamental, is rarely given its due. First, the subjects we teach are as large and complex as life, so our knowledge of them is always flawed and partial. No matter how we devote ourselves to reading and research, teaching requires a command of content that always eludes our grasp. Second, the students we teach are larger than life and even more complex. To see them clearly and see them whole, and respond to them wisely in the moment, requires a fusion of Freud and Solomon that few of us achieve.

If students and subjects accounted for all the complexities of teaching, our standard ways of coping would do—keep up with our fields as best we can, and learn enough techniques to stay ahead of the student psyche. But there is another reason for these complexities: we teach who we are.

Teaching, like any truly human activity, emerges from one's inwardness, for better or worse. As I teach, I project the condition of my soul onto my students, my subject, and our way of being together. The entanglements I experience in the classroom are often no more or less than the convolutions of my inner life. Viewed from this angle, teaching holds a mirror to the soul. If I am willing to look in that mirror, and not run from what I see, I have a chance to gain self–knowledge—and knowing myself is as crucial to good teaching as knowing my students and my subject.

In fact, knowing my students and my subject depends heavily on self-knowledge. When I do not know myself, I cannot know who my students are. I will see them through a glass darkly, in the shadows of my unexamined life—and when I cannot see them clearly, I cannot teach them well. When I do not know myself, I cannot know my subject—not at the deepest levels of embodied, personal meaning. I will know it only abstractly, from a distance, a congeries of concepts as far removed from the world as I am from personal truth.

We need to open a new frontier in our exploration of good teaching: the inner landscape of a teacher's life. To chart that landscape fully, three important paths must be taken—intellectual, emotional, and spiritual—and none can be ignored. Reduce teaching to intellect and it becomes a cold abstraction; reduce it to emotions and it becomes narcissistic; reduce it to the spiritual and it loses its anchor to the world. Intellect, emotion, and spirit depend on each other for wholeness. They are interwoven in the human self and in education at its best, and we need to interweave them in our pedagogical discourse as well.

By intellectual I mean the way we think about teaching and learning—the form and content of our concepts of how people know and learn, of the nature of our students and our subjects. By emotional, I mean the way we and our students feel as we teach and learn—feelings that can either enlarge or diminish the exchange between us. By spiritual, I mean the diverse ways we answer the heart's longing to be connected with the largeness of life—a longing that animates love and work, especially the work called teaching.

TEACHING BEYOND TECHNIQUE

After three decades of trying to learn my craft, every class comes down to this: my students and I, face to face, engaged in an ancient and exacting exchange called education. The techniques I have mastered do not disappear, but neither do they suffice. Face to face with my students, only one resource is at my immediate command: my identity, my selfhood, my sense of this "I" who teaches—without which I have no sense of the "Thou" who learns.

Here is a secret hidden in plain sight: good teaching cannot be reduced to technique; good teaching comes from the identity and integrity of the teacher. In every class I teach, my ability to connect with my students, and to connect them with the subject, depends less on the methods I use than on the degree to which I know and trust my selfhood—and am willing to make it available and vulnerable in the service of learning.

My evidence for this claim comes, in part, from years of asking students to tell me about their good teachers. As I listen to those stories, it becomes impossible to claim that all good teachers use similar techniques: some lecture non-stop and others speak very little, some stay close to their material and others loose the imagination, some teach with the carrot and others with the stick.

But in every story I have heard, good teachers share one trait: a strong sense of personal identity infuses their work. "Dr. A is really there when she teaches," a student tells me, or "Mr. B has such enthusiasm for his subject," or "You can tell that this is really Prof. C's life."

One student I heard about said she could not describe her good teachers because they were so different from each other. But she could describe her bad teachers because they were all the same: "Their words float somewhere in front of their faces, like the balloon speech in cartoons." With one remarkable image she said it all. Bad teachers distance themselves from the subject they are teaching—and, in the process, from their students.

Good teachers join self, subject, and students in the fabric of life because they teach from an integral and undivided self; they manifest in their own lives, and evoke in their students, a "capacity for connectedness." They are able to weave a complex web of connections between themselves, their subjects, and their students, so that students can learn to weave a world for themselves. The methods used by these weavers vary widely: lectures, Socratic dialogues, laboratory experiments, collaborative problem-solving, creative chaos. The connections made by good teachers are held not in their methods but in their hearts—meaning heart in its ancient sense, the place where intellect and emotion and spirit and will converge in the human self.

If good teaching cannot be reduced to technique, I no longer need to suffer the pain of having my peculiar gift as a teacher crammed into the Procrustean bed of someone else's method and the standards prescribed by it. That pain is felt throughout education today as we insist upon the method *du jour*—leaving people who teach differently feeling devalued, forcing them to measure up to norms not their own.

I will never forget one professor who, moments before I was to start a workshop on teaching, unloaded years of pent-up workshop animus on me: "I am an organic chemist. Are you going to spend the next two days telling me that I am supposed to teach organic chemistry through role-playing?" His wry question was not only related to his distinctive discipline but also to his distinctive self: we must find an approach to teaching that respects the diversity of teachers as well as disciplines, which methodological reductionism fails to do.

The capacity for connectedness manifests itself in diverse and wondrous ways—as many ways as there are forms of personal identity. Two great teachers stand out from my own undergraduate experience. They differed radically from each other in technique, but both were gifted at connecting students, teacher, and subject in a community of learning.

One of those teachers assigned a lot of reading in her course on methods of social research and, when we gathered around the seminar table on the first day, said, "Any comments or questions?" She had the courage to wait out our stupefied (and stupefying) silence, minute after minute after minute, gazing around the table with a benign look on her face—and then, after the passage of a small eternity, to rise, pick up her books, and say, as she walked toward the door, "Class dismissed."

This scenario more or less repeated itself a second time, but by the third time we met, our high SAT scores had kicked in, and we realized that the big dollars we were paying for this education would be wasted if we did not get with the program. So we started doing the reading, making comments, asking questions—and our teacher proved herself to be a brilliant interlocutor, co-researcher, and guide in the midst of confusions, a "weaver" of connectedness in her own interactive and inimitable way.

My other great mentor taught the history of social thought. He did not know the meaning of silence and he was awkward at interaction; he lectured incessantly while we sat in rows and took notes. Indeed, he became so engaged with his material that he was often impatient with our questions. But his classes were nonetheless permeated with a sense of connectedness and community.

How did he manage this alchemy? Partly by giving lectures that went far beyond presenting the data of social theory into staging the drama of social thought. He told stories from the lives of great thinkers as well as explaining their ideas; we could almost see Karl Marx, sitting alone in the British Museum Library, writing *Das Kapital.* Through active imagination we were brought into community with the thinker himself, and with the personal and social conditions that stimulated his thought.

But the drama of my mentor's lectures went farther still. He would make a strong Marxist statement, and we would transcribe it in our notebooks as if it were holy writ. Then a puzzled look would pass over his face. He would pause, step to one side, turn, and look back at the space he had just exited—and argue with his own statement from an Hegelian point of view! This was not an artificial device but a genuine expression of the intellectual drama that continually occupied this teacher's mind and heart.

"Drama" does not mean histrionics, of course, and remembering that fact can help us name a form of connectedness that is palpable and powerful without being overtly interactive, or even face to face. When I go to the theater, I sometimes feel strongly connected to the action, as if my own life were being portrayed on stage. But I have no desire to raise my hand and respond to the line just spoken, or run up the aisle, jump onto the stage, and join in the action. Sitting in the audience, I am already on stage "in person," connected in an inward and invisible way that we rarely credit as the powerful form of community that it is. With a good drama, I do not need overt interaction to be "in community" with those characters and their lives.

I used to wonder how my mentor, who was so awkward in his face-to-face relations with students, managed to simulate community so well. Now I understand: he was in community without us! Who needs 20-year-olds from the suburbs when you are hanging out constantly with the likes of Marx and Hegel, Durkheim, Weber and Troeltsch? This is "community" of the highest sort—this capacity for connectedness that allows one to converse with the dead, to speak and listen in an invisible network of relationships that enlarges one's world and enriches one's life. (We should praise, not deride, First Ladies who "talk" with Eleanor Roosevelt; the ability to learn from wise but long-gone souls is nothing less than a classic mark of a liberal education!)

Yet my great professor, though he communed more intimately with the great figures of social thought than with the people close at hand, cared deeply about his students. The passion with which he lectured was not only for his subject, but for us to know his subject. He wanted us to meet and learn from the constant companions of his intellect and imagination, and he made those introductions in a way that was deeply integral to his own nature. He brought us into a form of community that did not require small numbers of students sitting in a circle and learning through dialogue.

These two great teachers were polar opposites in substance and in style. But both created the connectedness, the community, that is essential to teaching and learning. They did so by trusting and teaching from true self, from the identity and integrity that is the source of all good work—and by employing quite different techniques that allowed them to reveal rather than conceal who they were.

Their genius as teachers, and their profound gifts to me, would have been diminished and destroyed had their practice been forced into the Procrustean bed of the method of the moment. The proper place for technique is not to subdue subjectivity, not to mask and distance the self from the work, but—as one grows in self-knowledge—to help bring forth and amplify the gifts of self on which good work depends.

TEACHING AND TRUE SELF

The claim that good teaching comes from the identity and integrity of the teacher might sound like a truism, and a pious one at that: good teaching comes from good people. But by "identity" and "integrity" I do not mean only our noble features, or the good deeds we do, or the brave faces we wear to conceal our confusions and complexities. Identity and integrity have as much to do with our shadows and limits, our wounds and fears, as with our strengths and potentials.

By identity I mean an evolving nexus where all the forces that constitute my life converge in the mystery of self: my genetic makeup, the nature of the man and woman who gave me life, the culture in which I was raised, people who have sustained me and people who have done me harm, the good and ill I have done to others and to myself, the experience of love and suffering—and much, much more. In the midst of that complex field, identity is a moving intersection of the inner and outer forces that make me who I am, converging in the irreducible mystery of being human.

By integrity I mean whatever wholeness I am able to find within that nexus as its vectors form and re-form the pattern of my life. Integrity requires that I discern what is integral to my selfhood, what fits and what does not—and that I choose life-giving ways of relating to the forces that converge within me: do I welcome them or fear them, embrace them or reject them, move with them or against them? By choosing integrity, I become more whole, but wholeness does not mean perfection. It means becoming more real by acknowledging the whole of who I am.

Identity and integrity are not the granite from which fictional heroes are hewn. They are subtle dimensions of the complex, demanding, and lifelong process of self-discovery. Identity lies in the intersection of the diverse forces that make up my life, and integrity lies in relating to those forces in ways that bring me wholeness and life rather than fragmentation and death.

Those are my definitions—but try as I may to refine them, they always come out too pat. Identity and integrity can never be fully named or known by anyone, including the person who bears them. They constitute that familiar strangeness we take with us to the grave, elusive realities that can be caught only occasionally out of the corner of the eye.

Stories are the best way to portray realities of this sort, so here is a tale of two teachers—a tale based on people I have known, whose lives tell me more about the subtleties of identity and integrity than any theory could.

Alan and Eric were born into two different families of skilled craftspeople, rural folk with little formal schooling but gifted in the manual arts. Both boys evinced this gift from childhood onward, and as each grew in skill at working with his hands, each developed a sense of self in which the pride of craft was key.

The two shared another gift as well: both excelled in school and became the first in their working-class families to go to college. Both did well as undergraduates, both were admitted to graduate school, both earned doctorates, and both chose academic careers.

But here their paths diverged. Though the gift of craft was central in both men's sense of self, Alan was able to weave that gift into his academic vocation, while the fabric of Eric's life unraveled early on.

Catapulted from his rural community into an elite private college at age 18, Eric suffered severe culture shock—and never overcame it. He was insecure with fellow students and, later, with academic colleagues who came from backgrounds he saw as more "cultured" than his own. He learned to speak and act like an intellectual, but he always felt fraudulent among people who were, in his eyes, to the manor born.

But insecurity neither altered Eric's course nor drew him into self-reflection. Instead, he bullied his way into professional life on the theory that the best defense is a good offense. He made pronouncements rather than probes. He listened for weaknesses rather than strengths in what other people said. He argued with anyone about anything—and responded with veiled contempt to whatever was said in return.

In the classroom, Eric was critical and judgmental, quick to put down the "stupid question," adept at trapping students with trick questions of his own, then merciless in mocking wrong answers. He seemed driven by a need to inflict upon his students the same wound that academic life had inflicted upon him—the wound of being embarrassed by some essential part of one's self.

But when Eric went home to his workbench and lost himself in craft, he found himself as well. He became warm and welcoming, at home in the world and glad to extend hospitality to others. Reconnected with his roots, centered in his true self, he was able to reclaim a quiet and confident core—which he quickly lost as soon as he returned to campus.

Alan's is a different story. His leap from countryside to campus did not induce culture shock, in part because he attended a land-grant university where many students had backgrounds much like his own. He was not driven to hide his gift, but was able to honor and transform it by turning it toward things academic: he brought to his study, and later to his teaching and research, the same sense of craft that his ancestors had brought to their work with metal and wood.

Watching Alan teach, you felt that you were watching a craftsman at work—and if you knew his history, you understood that this feeling was more than metaphor. In his lectures, every move Alan made was informed by attention to detail and respect for the materials at hand; he connected ideas with the precision of dovetail joinery and finished the job with a polished summary.

But the power of Alan's teaching went well beyond crafted performance. His students knew that Alan would extend himself with great generosity to any of them who wanted to become an apprentice in his field, just as the elders in his own family had extended themselves to help young Alan grow in his original craft.

Alan taught from an undivided self—the integral state of being that is central to good teaching. In the undivided self, every major thread of one's life experience is honored, creating a weave of such coherence and strength that it can hold students and subject as well as self. Such a self, inwardly integrated, is able to make the outward connections on which good teaching depends.

But Eric failed to weave the central strand of his identity into his academic vocation. His was a self divided, engaged in a civil war. He projected that inner warfare onto the outer world, and his teaching devolved into combat instead of craft. The divided self will always distance itself from others, and may even try to destroy them, to defend its fragile identity.

If Eric had not been alienated as an undergraduate—or if his alienation had led to self-reflection instead of self-defense—it is possible that he, like Alan, could have found integrity in his academic vocation, could have woven the major strands of his identity into his work. But part of the mystery of selfhood is the fact that one size does not fit all: what is integral to one person lacks integrity for another. Throughout his life, there were persistent clues that academia was not a life-giving choice for Eric, not a context in which his true self could emerge healthy and whole, not a vocation integral to his unique nature.

The self is not infinitely elastic—it has potentials and it has limits. If the work we do lacks integrity for us, then we, the work, and the people we do it with will suffer. Alan's self was enlarged by his academic vocation, and the work he did was a joy to behold. Eric's self was diminished by his encounter with academia, and choosing a different vocation might have been his only way to recover integrity lost.

WHEN TEACHERS LOSE HEART

As good teachers weave the fabric that joins them with students and subjects, the heart is the loom on which the threads are tied: the tension is held, the shuttle flies, and the fabric is stretched tight. Small wonder, then, that teaching tugs at the heart, opens the heart, even breaks the heart—and the more one loves teaching, the more heartbreaking it can be.

We became teachers for reasons of the heart, animated by a passion for some subject and for helping people to learn. But many of us lose heart as the years of teaching go by. How can we take heart in teaching once more, so we can do what good teachers always do—give heart to our students? The courage to teach is the courage to keep one's heart open in those very moments when the heart is asked to hold more than it is able, so that teacher and students and subject can be woven into the fabric of community that learning and living require.

There are no techniques for reclaiming our hearts, for keeping our hearts open. Indeed, the heart does not seek "fixes" but insight and understanding. When we lose heart, we need an understanding of our condition that will liberate us from that condition, a diagnosis that will lead us toward new ways of being in the classroom simply by telling the truth about who, and how, we are. Truth, not technique, is what heals and empowers the heart.

We lose heart, in part, because teaching is a daily exercise in vulnerability. I need not reveal personal secrets to feel naked in front of a class. I need only parse a sentence or work a proof on the board while my students doze off or pass notes. No matter how technical or abstract my subject may be, the things I teach are things I care about—and what I care about helps define my selfhood.

Unlike many professions, teaching is always done at the dangerous intersection of personal and public life. A good therapist must work in a personal way, but never publicly: the therapist who reveals as much as a client's name is derelict. A good trial lawyer must work in a public forum, but unswayed by personal opinion: the lawyer who allows his or her feelings about a client's guilt to weaken the client's defense is guilty of malpractice.

But a good teacher must stand where personal and public meet, dealing with the thundering flow of traffic at an intersection where "weaving a web of connectedness" feels more like crossing a freeway on foot. As we try to connect ourselves and our subjects with our students, we make ourselves, as well as our subjects, vulnerable to indifference, judgment, ridicule.

To reduce our vulnerability, we disconnect from students, from subjects, and even from ourselves. We build a wall between inner truth and outer performance, and we play-act the teacher's part. Our words, spoken at remove from our hearts, become "the balloon speech in cartoons," and we become caricatures of ourselves. We distance ourselves from students and subject to minimize the danger—forgetting that distance makes life more dangerous still by isolating the self.

This self-protective split of personhood from practice is encouraged by an academic culture that distrusts personal truth. Though the academy claims to value multiple modes of knowing, it honors only one—an "objective" way of knowing that takes us into the "real" world by taking us "out of ourselves."

In this culture, objective facts are regarded as pure while subjective feelings are suspect and sullied. In this culture, the self is not a source to be tapped but a danger to be suppressed, not a potential to be fulfilled but an obstacle to be overcome. In this culture, the pathology of speech disconnected from self is regarded, and rewarded, as a virtue.

If my sketch of the academic bias against selfhood seems overdone, here is a story from my own teaching experience. I assigned my students a series of brief analytical essays involving themes in the texts we were going to be reading. Then I assigned a parallel series of autobiographical sketches, related to those themes, so my students could see connections between the textbook concepts and their own lives.

After the first class, a student spoke to me: "In those autobiographical essays you asked us to write, is it okay to use the word 'I'?"

I did not know whether to laugh or cry—but I knew that my response would have considerable impact on a young man who had just opened himself to ridicule. I told him that not only could he use the word "I," but I hoped he would use it freely and often. Then I asked what had led to his question.

"I'm a history major," he said, "and each time I use 'I' in a paper, they knock off half a grade."

The academic bias against subjectivity not only forces our students to write poorly ("It is believed . . ." instead of "I believe . . ."); it deforms their thinking about themselves and their world. In a single stroke, we delude our students into believing that bad prose turns opinions into facts and we alienate them from their own inner lives.

Faculty often complain that students have no regard for the gifts of insight and understanding that are the true payoff of education—they care only about short-term outcomes in the "real" world: "Will this major get me a job?" "How will this assignment be useful in 'real' life?"

But those are not the questions deep in our students' hearts. They are merely the questions they have been taught to ask, not only by tuition-paying parents who want their children to be employable, but by an academic culture that distrusts and devalues inner reality. Of course our students are cynical about the inner outcomes of education: we teach them that the subjective self is irrelevant and even unreal.

The foundation of any culture lies in the way it answers the question "Where do reality and power reside?" For some cultures the answer is the gods; for some it is nature; for some it is tradition. In our culture, the answer is clear: reality and power reside in the external world of objects and events, and in the sciences that study that world, while the inner realm of "heart" is a romantic fantasy—an escape from harsh realities perhaps, but surely not a source of leverage over "the real world."

We are obsessed with manipulating externals because we believe that they will give us some power over reality and win us some freedom from its constraints. Mesmerized by a technology that seems to do just that, we dismiss the inward world. We turn every question we face into an objective problem to be solved—and we believe that for every objective problem there is some sort of technical fix.

That is why, we train doctors to repair the body but not to honor the spirit; clergy to be CEOs but not spiritual guides; teachers to master techniques but not to engage their students' hearts—or their own. That is why, our students are cynical about the efficacy of an education that transforms the inner landscape of their lives: when academic culture dismisses inner truth and pays homage only to the objective world, students as well as teachers lose heart.

LISTENING TO THE TEACHER WITHIN

Recovering the heart to teach requires us to reclaim our relationship with the teacher within. This teacher is one whom we knew when we were children but lost touch with as we grew into adulthood, a teacher who continually invites me to honor my true self—not my ego or expectations or image or role, but the self I am when all the externals are stripped away.

By inner teacher, I do not mean "conscience" or "superego," moral arbiter or internalized judge. In fact, conscience, as it is commonly understood, can get us into deep vocational trouble. When we listen primarily for what we "ought" to be doing with our lives, we may find ourselves hounded by external expectations that can distort our identity and integrity. There is much that I "ought" to be doing by some abstract moral calculus. But is it my vocation? Am I gifted and called to do it? Is this particular "ought" a place of intersection between my inner self and the outer world, or is it someone else's image of how my life should look?

When I follow only the oughts, I may find myself doing work that is ethically laudable but that is not mine to do. A vocation that is not mine, no matter how externally valued, does violence to the self—in the precise sense that it violates my identity and integrity on behalf of some abstract norm. When I violate myself, I invariably end up violating the people I work with. How many teachers inflict their own pain on their students—the pain that comes from doing a work that never was, or no longer is, their true work?

The teacher within is not the voice of conscience but of identity and integrity. It speaks not of what ought to be, but of what is real for us, of what is true. It says things like, "This is what fits you and this is what doesn't." "This is who you are and this is who you are not." "This is what gives you life and this is what kills your spirit—or makes you wish you were dead." The teacher within stands guard at the gate of selfhood, warding off whatever insults our integrity and welcoming whatever affirms it. The voice of the inward teacher reminds me of my potentials and limits as I negotiate the force field of my life.

I realize that the idea of a "teacher within" strikes some academics as a romantic fantasy, but I cannot fathom why. If there is no such reality in our lives, centuries of Western discourse about the aims of education become so much lip-flapping. In classical understanding, education is the attempt to "lead out" from within the self a core of wisdom that has the power to resist falsehood and live in the light of truth, not by external norms but by reasoned and reflective self-determination. The inward teacher is the living core of our lives that is addressed and evoked by any education worthy of the name.

Perhaps the idea is unpopular because it compels us to look at two of the most difficult truths about teaching. The first is that what we teach will never "take" unless it connects with the inward, living core of our students' lives, with our students' inward teachers.

We can, and do, make education an exclusively outward enterprise, forcing students to memorize and repeat facts without ever appealing to their inner truth—and we get predictable results: many students never want to read a challenging book or think a creative thought once they get out of school. The kind of teaching that transforms people does not happen if the student's inward teacher is ignored.

The second truth is even more daunting: we can speak to the teacher within our students only when we are on speaking terms with the teacher within ourselves.

The student who said that her bad teachers spoke like cartoon characters was describing teachers who have grown deaf to their inner guide, who have so thoroughly separated inner truth from outer actions that they have lost touch with a sense of self. Deep speaks to deep, and when we have not sounded our own depths, we cannot sound the depths of our students' lives.

How does one attend to the voice of the teacher within? I have no particular methods to suggest, other than the familiar ones: solitude and silence, meditative reading and walking in the woods, keeping a journal, finding a friend who will simply listen. I merely propose that we need to learn as many ways as we can of "talking to ourselves."

That phrase, of course, is one we normally use to name a symptom of mental imbalance—a clear sign of how our culture regards the idea of an inner voice! But people who learn to talk to themselves may soon delight in the discovery that the teacher within is the sanest conversation partner they have ever had.

We need to find every possible way to listen to that voice and take its counsel seriously, not only for the sake of our work, but for the sake of our own health. If someone in the outer world is trying to tell us something important and we ignore his or her presence, that person either gives up and stops speaking or becomes more and more violent in attempting to get our attention.

Similarly, if we do not respond to the voice of the inward teacher, it will either stop speaking or become violent: I am convinced that some forms of depression, of which I have personal experience, are induced by a long-ignored inner teacher trying desperately to get us to listen by threatening to destroy us. When we honor that voice with simple attention, it responds by speaking more gently and engaging us in a life-giving conversation of the soul.

That conversation does not have to reach conclusions in order to be of value: we do not need to emerge from "talking to ourselves" with clear goals, objectives, and plans. Measuring the value of inner dialogue by its practical outcomes is like measuring the value of a friendship by the number of problems that are solved when friends get together.

Conversation among friends has its own rewards: in the presence of our friends we have the simple joy of feeling at ease, at home, trusted and able to trust. We attend to the inner teacher not to get fixed but to befriend the deeper self, to cultivate a sense of identity and integrity that allows us to feel at home wherever we are.

Listening to the inner teacher also offers an answer to one of the most basic questions teachers face: how can I develop the authority to teach, the capacity to stand my ground in the midst of the complex forces of both the classroom and my own life?

In a culture of objectification and technique we often confuse authority with power, but the two are not the same. Power works from the outside in, but authority works from the inside out. We are mistaken when we seek "authority" outside ourselves, in sources ranging from the subtle skills of group process to that less-than-subtle method of social control called grading. This view of teaching turns the teacher into the cop on the corner, trying to keep things moving amicably and by consent, but always having recourse to the coercive power of the law.

External tools of power have occasional utility in teaching, but they are no substitute for authority, the authority that comes from the teacher's inner life. The clue is in the word itself, which has "author" at its core. Authority is granted to people who are perceived as "authoring" their own words, their own actions, their own lives, rather than playing a scripted role at great remove from their own hearts. When teachers depend on the coercive powers of law or technique, they have no authority at all.

I am painfully aware of the times in my own teaching when I lose touch with my inner teacher, and therefore, with my own authority. In those times, I try to gain power by barricading myself behind the podium and my status while wielding the threat of grades. But when my teaching is authorized by the teacher within me, I need neither weapons nor armor to teach.

Authority comes as I reclaim my identity and integrity, remembering my selfhood and my sense of vocation. Then teaching can come from the depths of my own truth—and the truth that is within my students has a chance to respond in kind.

INSTITUTIONS AND THE HUMAN HEART

My concern for the "inner landscape" of teaching may seem indulgent, even irrelevant, at a time when many teachers are struggling simply to survive. Wouldn't it be more practical, I am sometimes asked, to offer tips, tricks, and techniques for staying alive in the classroom, things that ordinary teachers can use in everyday life?

I have worked with countless teachers, and many of them have confirmed my own experience: as important as methods may be, the most practical thing we can achieve in any kind of work is insight into what is happening inside us as we do it. The more familiar we are with our inner terrain, the more surefooted our teaching—and living—becomes.

I have heard that in the training of therapists, which involves much practical technique, there is a saying: "Technique is what you use until the therapist arrives." Good methods can help a therapist find a way into the client's dilemma, but good therapy does not begin until the real-life therapist joins with the real life of the client.

Technique is what teachers use until the real teacher arrives, and we need to find as many ways as possible to help that teacher show up. But if we want to develop the identity and integrity that good teaching requires, we must do something alien to academic culture: we must talk to each other about our inner lives—risky stuff in a profession that fears the personal and seeks safety in the technical, the distant, the abstract.

I was reminded of that fear recently as I listened to a group of faculty argue about what to do when students share personal experiences in class—experiences that are related to the themes of the course, but that some professors regard as "more suited to a therapy session than to a college classroom."

The house soon divided along predictable lines. On one side were the scholars, insisting that the subject is primary and must never be compromised for the sake of the students' lives. On the other side were the student-centered folks, insisting that the lives of students must always come first even if it means that the subject gets short-changed. The more vigorously these camps promoted their polarized ideas, the more antagonistic they became—and the less they learned about pedagogy or about themselves.

The gap between these views seems unbridgeable—until we understand what creates it. At bottom, these professors were not debating teaching techniques. They were revealing the diversity of identity and integrity among themselves, saying, in various ways, "Here are my own limits and potentials when it comes to dealing with the relation between the subject and my students' lives."

If we stopped lobbing pedagogical points at each other and spoke about who we are as teachers, a remarkable thing might happen: identity and integrity might grow within us and among us, instead of hardening as they do when we defend our fixed positions from the foxholes of the pedagogy wars.

But telling the truth about ourselves with colleagues in the workplace is an enterprise fraught with danger, against which we have erected formidable taboos. We fear making ourselves vulnerable in the midst of competitive people and politics that could easily turn against us, and we claim the inalienable right to separate the "personal" and the "professional" into airtight compartments (even though everyone knows the two are inseparably intertwined). So we keep the workplace conversation objective and external, finding it safer to talk about technique than about selfhood.

Indeed, the story I most often hear from faculty (and other professionals) is that the institutions in which they work are the heart's worst enemy. In this story, institutions continually try to diminish the human heart in order to consolidate their own power, and the individual is left with a discouraging choice: to distance one's self from the institution and its mission and sink into deepening cynicism (an occupational hazard of academic life) or to maintain eternal vigilance against institutional invasion and fight for one's life when it comes.

Taking the conversation of colleagues into the deep places where we might grow in self-knowledge for the sake of our professional practice will not be an easy, or popular, task. But it is a task that leaders of every educational institution must take up if they wish to strengthen their institution's capacity to pursue the educational mission. How can schools educate students if they fail to support the teacher's inner life? To educate is to guide students on an inner journey toward more truthful ways of seeing and being in the world. How can schools perform their mission without encouraging the guides to scout out that inner terrain?

Now that this century of objectification and manipulation by technique has drawn to a close, we are experiencing an exhaustion of institutional resourcefulness at the very time when the problems that our institutions must address grow deeper and more demanding. Just as 20th-century medicine, famous for its externalized fixes for disease, has found itself required to reach deeper for the psychological and spiritual dimensions of healing, so 20th-century education must open up a new frontier in teaching and learning—the frontier of the teacher's inner life.

How this might be done is a subject I have explored in earlier essays,[1,2] so I will not repeat myself here. In "Good Talk about Good Teaching," I examined some of the key elements necessary for an institution to host noncompulsory, non-invasive opportunities for faculty to help themselves and each other grow inwardly as teachers. In "Divided No More," I explored things we can do on our own when institutions are resistant or hostile to the inner agenda.

Our task is to create enough safe spaces and trusting relationships within the academic workplace—hedged about by appropriate structural protections—that more of us will be able to tell the truth about our own struggles and joys as teachers in ways that befriend the soul and give it room to grow. Not all spaces can be safe, not all relationships trustworthy, but we can surely develop more of them than we now have so that an increase of honesty and healing can happen within us and among us—for our own sake, the sake of our teaching, and the sake of our students.

Honesty and healing sometimes happen quite simply, thanks to the alchemical powers of the human soul. When I, with 30 years of teaching experience, speak openly about the fact that I still approach each new class with trepidation, younger faculty tell me that this makes their own fears seem more natural—and thus easier to transcend—and a rich dialogue about the teacher's selfhood often ensues. We do not discuss techniques for "fear management," if such exist. Instead, we meet as fellow travelers and offer encouragement to each other in this demanding but deeply rewarding journey across the inner landscape of education—calling each other back to the identity and integrity that animate all good work, not least the work called teaching.

ENDNOTES

1. Parker J. Palmer, "Good Talk about Good Teaching: Improving Teaching Through Conversation and Community," *Change Magazine*, November/December, 1993, pp. 8–13. A revised version appears as Chapter VI in *The Courage to Teach*.
2. Parker J. Palmer, "Divided No More: A Movement Approach to Educational Reform," Change Magazine, March/April, 1992, pp. 10–17. A revised version appears as Chapter VII in *The Courage to Teach*.

REFERENCE

Palmer, P. J. (1998). *The Courage to Teach: Exploring the Inner Landscape of a Teacher's Life*. San Francisco: Jossey-Bass.

DISCUSSION QUESTIONS

1. Have you ever personally known any great teachers? What made them great teachers?
2. In what ways have you been profoundly influenced by teachers you have encountered?
3. Do all great teachers have certain qualities in common?
4. What does Palmer mean when he talks about listening to the "inner teacher"?
5. What are some implications of Palmer's ideas for curriculum? For professional development?

CHAPTER 8

Critical Issues in Teaching

ALLAN C. ORNSTEIN

FOCUSING QUESTIONS

1. In what ways may teaching be considered to be a science?
2. In what ways may teaching be considered to be an art?
3. How are teachers portrayed in the popular media?
4. How much influence do teachers have in making the world a better place?
5. How should schools and teachers address the horrors of 20th-century violence?

This chapter will briefly examine the issue of whether teaching is a science or an art; it is an issue that has gained attention among teachers of teachers and their students. This issue is also used as a springboard to introduce the second part of the piece: how we can improve teaching by emphasizing humanistic and moral issues, as well as the need for reconceptualizing the nature of teaching. In the second part of the chapter, the discussion will extend beyond the traditional themes of teaching. The content will most likely upset some readers, and still others may find it far too emotional or argumentative. I do believe, however, that when a critic or commentator attempts to rethink, reevaluate, or reconceptualize a field of study, a subject, or a domain that is rooted in tradition, a certain amount of resistance and criticism will surface and reflect the reader's thoughts.

This chapter is based on portions of the author's book *Teaching and Schooling in America: Prior and Post 9-11* (Boston: Allyn and Bacon, 2003). The book is concerned with life and death, good and evil, peace and war, education and miseducation, traditional and progressive education, equality and inequality. It starts with the ancient Greeks and Romans and ends with post 9-11 society, including American, Chinese, Indian, and Arabic cultures.

THE SCIENCE VERSUS THE ART OF TEACHING

We cannot agree on whether teaching is a science or an art. Some readers may say that this is a hopeless dichotomy, similar to that of theory versus practice, because the real world rarely consists of neat packages and either–or situations. N. L. Gage uses this distinction between *teaching as a science* and *as an art* to describe the elements of predictability in teaching and what constitutes good teaching. A science of teaching, he contends, "implies that good teaching will some day be attainable by closely following vigorous laws that yield high predictability and control." Teaching is more than a science, he observes, because it also involves "artistic judgment about the best ways to teach." When teaching leaves the laboratory or textbook and goes face to face with students, "the opportunity for artistry expands enormously."[1] No science can prescribe successfully at all the twists and turns as teaching unfolds or as teachers respond with judgment, insight, or sensitivity to promote learning. These are expressions of art that depart from the rules and principles of science.

Is such a limited scientific basis of teaching even worthwhile to consider? Yes, but the practitioner must learn as a teacher to draw not only from his or her professional knowledge (which is grounded in *scientific principles*), but also from a set of personal experiences and resources (sometimes called *craft knowledge*) that is uniquely defined and exhibited by the teacher's own personality and "gut" reaction to classroom events that unfold (which form the basis for the *art* of teaching). For Philip Jackson, the hunches, judgments, and insights of the teacher, as he or she responds spontaneously to events in the classroom, are as important as, and perhaps even more important than, the science of teaching.[2] The routine activities of the classroom, the social patterns and dynamics among students, and the accommodations and compromises between students and teachers are much more important than any theory about teaching, because it is the everyday routines and relationships that determine the processes and outcomes of teaching.

To some extent, the act of teaching must be considered intuitive and interactive, not prescriptive or predictable. According to Elliot Eisner, teaching is based primarily on feelings and artistry, not scientific rules. In an age of science and technology, there is a special need to consider teaching as an art and craft. Eisner condemns the scientific movement in psychology, especially behaviorism, and the scientific movement in education, especially school management, as reducing the teaching act to trivial specifications. He regards teaching as a "poetic metaphor" more suited to satisfying the soul than to informing the head, more concerned with the whole than with a set of discrete skills or stimuli. Our role as teachers, he claims, should not be that of a "puppeteer," an "engineer," or a manager; rather, it is "to orchestrate the dialogue [as the conductor of a symphony] moving from one side of the room to the other."[3]

The idea is to perceive patterns in motion, to improvise within the classroom, and to avoid the mechanical or prescribed rules. The need is to act human, to display feelings to affirm and value our students. The idea is to be able to smile, clap, and laugh with your students while you teach them. Sadly, many teachers lack the self-confidence to openly express their emotions, feelings, or real personality.

Louis Rubin has a similar view of teaching: that effectiveness and artistry go hand in hand. The interplay of students and teacher is crucial and cannot be predetermined with carefully devised strategies. Confronted with everyday problems that cannot be easily predicted, the teacher must rely on intuition and on "insight acquired through long experience."[4] Rubin refers to such terms as "with-it-ness," "instructional judgments," "quick cognitive leaps," and "informal guesses" to explain the difference between the effective teacher and the ineffective teacher. Recognizing the limits to rationality, he claims that for the artistic teacher a "feel for what is right often is more productive than prolonged analysis." In the final analysis, Rubin compares the teacher's pedagogy with the "artist's colors, poet's words, sculptor's clay, and musician's notes,"[5] in my view all of which need a certain amount of artistic judgment to get the right mix, medium, or blend.

Other researchers are more extreme in their analysis of teaching solely as an art, providing romantic accounts and tales of successful teaching and teaching strategies, described in language that could hardly be taken for social science research. They consider the act of teaching akin to drama, an esthetic and kinesthetic endeavor, and feel that those who wish to teach should audition in a teaching studio and be trained as performing artists. Good teaching is likened to good theater, and a good teacher is likened to a good actor.[6]

Seymour Sarason describes the teacher as a performing artist. Like an actor, conductor, or artist, the teacher attempts to *instruct* and *move* the audience.[7] More significantly, this author maintains that the actor, artist, or teacher attempts to *transform* the audience in terms of thinking and instilling new ideas. By transforming the audience, we alter the person's outlook toward objects or ideas. Revolutionary thought, I maintain, is built on poetry, music, art, movies, and speeches. And, ultimately, it is the esthetics, ideas, and values (the art, music, food, customs, laws, and thoughts) that define who we are. Hence, it is teachers in the broadest sense, including actors, artists, poets, writers, and of course parents, who make the difference for society.

Given the metaphor of the *performing artist,* a certain amount of talent or innate ability is needed to be effective, along with sufficient rehearsal and caring behavior. But knowledge or understanding of the audience is also needed. *Mr. Holland's Opus* makes the point. The teacher was unsuccessful in the beginning of the movie, despite his knowledge of music, compassion, and desire to give the students his "all." In the remaining part of the movie, however, through some "magical" awakening, he redefined his methods (science of teaching) and acting (art of teaching), with the result that the audience (students) became interested and learned to appreciate good music. Mr. Holland originally thought the problem was in the minds of the audience. Not until he realized that it was the other way around, that it was his attitude that needed to be improved, was he successful.[8]

In *The King and I,* the British teacher, Anna, was successful from the outset, despite cultural differences and the gender inequalities of the society (Siam). Not only was she caring and compassionate, but she also understood her students. She was able to adapt to their needs, interests, and abilities—and affirm their individuality. The song "Getting to Know You" makes the point. She reminded some of us of the school teachers we knew when we were kids—the loving and joyful teacher in Sylvia Ashton-Warner's *Teacher,* written some 40 years ago, or a combination of the author's two favorite elementary school teachers whom he remembers fondly and dedicated one of his books to: Mrs. Katz, "a warm, friendly, and understanding teacher," and Mrs. Schwartz, "a tough, nurturing school marm who drilled the facts and enforced the rules."[9]

Both movies underscore the need for teachers to understand students and for good teachers to connect with the audience. Through either previous learning (*pedagogical knowledge*) or practical experience (*craft knowledge*), the teacher must know how students think and feel. A certain amount of training helps one to understand students, but it is only a starting point. A successful teacher first understands and accepts himself or herself, then understands and accepts others. Arthur

Jersild summed it up some 50 years ago: "self understanding requires something quite different from the methods . . . and skills of know-how . . . emphasized in education [courses]." Planning, role playing, and all the other methods and techniques—what we call scientific principles—are helpful, but what is also needed "is a more personal kind of searching, which will enable the teacher to identify his own concerns and to share the concerns of his students."[10] Thus, teaching is not just an academic or cognitive enterprise; it involves people and an affective (feelings, attitudes, and emotions) or artistic component that has little to do with pedagogical or scientific knowledge.

The more we consider teaching as an art, packed with emotions, feelings, and excitement, the more difficult it is to derive rules or generalizations. If teaching is more an art than a science, then principles and practices cannot be easily codified or developed in the classroom or easily learned by others. Hence, there is little reason to offer instructional method courses in education. If, however, teaching is more of a science, or at least partly a science, then pedagogy is predictable to that extent; it can be observed and measured with some accuracy, and the research can be applied to the practice of teaching (as a physician applies scientific knowledge to the practice of medicine) and also learned in a college classroom or on the job.

But a word of caution is needed. The more we rely on artistic interpretations or on old stories and accounts about teachers, the more we fall victim to fantasy, wit, and romantic rhetoric, and the more we depend on hearsay and conjecture, rather than on social science or objective data, in evaluating teacher competency. On the other hand, the more we rely on the scientific interpretations of teaching, the more we overlook those commonsense and spontaneous processes of teaching, and the sounds, smells, and visual flavor of the classroom. The more scientific we are in our approach to teaching, the more we ignore what we cannot accommodate to our empirical assumptions or principles. What sometimes occurs, according to Eisner, is that the educationally significant but difficult to measure or observe is replaced by what is insignificant but comparatively easy to measure or observe.[11]

It is necessary to blend artistic impressions and relevant stories about teaching, because good teaching involves emotions and feeling, with the objectivity of observations and measurements and the precision of language. There is nothing wrong with considering good teaching to be an art, but we must also consider it to lend itself to a prescriptive science or practice. If it does not, then there is little assurance that prospective teachers can be trained to be teachers—told what to do, how to instruct students, how to manage students, and so forth—and educators will be extremely vulnerable to public criticism and to people outside the profession telling them how and what to teach.

True knowledge of teaching is achieved by practice and experience in the classroom. According to some observers, the beliefs, values, and norms—that is, the knowledge—that teachers come to have the most faith in and use most frequently to guide their teaching are those consistent with traditions that have "worked" in the classroom. Although it seems to be more everyday and common sense–based than highly specialized and theoretical, the process still includes the receiving and using of data that can be partially planned and scientifically analyzed. But we assume that there are still professional and technical skills that can be taught to teachers and designed and developed in advance with underlying scientific principles and research-based data. Some of us would refer to this as *pedagogical knowledge* or *craft knowledge* as opposed to subject-matter or content-based knowledge.

Indeed, the real value of scientific procedures may not be realized in terms of research or theoretical generalizations that can be translated into practice. Research may have limited potential for teachers, but it can help them to become aware of the problems and needs of students. Scientific generalizations and theories may not always be applicable to specific teaching situations, but such propositions can help in the formulation of a reliable and valid base for teaching in classrooms. Scientific ideas can serve as a starting point for the discussion and analysis of the art of teaching.

RECONCEPTUALIZING TEACHING

To argue that good teaching boils down to a set of prescriptive behaviors, methods, or proficiency levels, that teachers must follow a "new" research-based teaching plan or evaluation system, or that decisions about teacher accountability can be assessed in terms of students passing a multiple-choice test is to miss the human aspect of teaching, the real *stuff* of what teaching is all about.

Stress on assessment and evaluation systems illustrates that behaviorism has won at the expense of humanistic psychology. Put in different terms, the ideas of Thorndike and Watson have prevailed over the ideas of Dewey and Kilpatrick. It also suggests that school administrators, policy makers, and researchers would rather focus on the *science* of teaching—behaviors and outcomes that can be observed, counted, or measured—than on the *art* of teaching with its humanistic and hard-to-measure variables.

Robert Linn contends that assessment of teachers and students can be easily mandated, implemented, and reported and thus have wide appeal under the guise of "reform." Although these assessment systems are supposed to improve education, they don't necessarily do so.[12] Real reform is complex and costly (for example, reducing class size, raising teacher salaries, introducing special reading programs, extending the school day and year), and it takes time before the results are evident. People such as politicians and business leaders, who seem to be leading this latest wave of reform, want a quick, easy, and cheap fix. Thus, they will always opt for assessment because it is simple and inexpensive to implement. It creates heightened media visibility, the feeling that something is being done, and the Hawthorne effect or novelty tends to elevate short-term gains. This assessment focus (which is a form of behaviorism) also provides a rationale for teacher education programs, because it suggests that we can identify good teaching. Yet it is questionable, given our current knowledge of teaching and teacher education and the importance of personality, whether new teachers can be properly prepared in terms of both academic rigor and practical reality.

For those in the business of preparing teachers, there is the need to provide a research base and rationale showing that teachers who enroll and complete a teacher education program are more likely to be effective teachers than those who lack such training. The fact that there are several alternative certification programs for teachers in more than 40 states, through which nearly 5 percent (as high as 16 percent in Texas and 22 percent in New Jersey) of the nationwide teaching force entered teaching,[13] makes teachers of teachers (professors of education) take notice and try to demonstrate that their teacher preparation programs work and that they can prepare effective teachers. Indeed, there is a need to identify teacher behaviors and methods that work under certain conditions, leading many educators to favor behaviorism (or prescriptive ideas and specific tasks) and assessment systems (closed-ended, tiny, measurable variables) that correlate teaching and learning.

Being able to describe detailed methods of teaching and how and why teachers do what they do should improve the performance of teachers. But all the new research hardly tells the whole story of teaching—what leads to teacher effectiveness and student learning. Being able to describe teachers' thinking or decision making and analyzing their stories and reflective practices suggest that we understand and can improve teaching. The new research on teaching, with its stories, biographies, reflective practices, and qualitative methods, provides a platform and publication outlet for researchers. It promotes their expertise (which in turn continues to separate them from practitioners) and permits them to continue to subordinate teaching to research. It also provides a new paradigm for analyzing teaching, because the old models (teacher styles, teacher characteristics, teacher effectiveness, etc.) have become exhausted and repetitive. The issues and questions related to the new paradigm create new educational wars and controversy between traditional and nontraditional researchers, between quantitative and qualitative advocates. It is questionable, however, whether this new knowledge base about teaching really improves teaching and learning or leads to substantial and sustained improvement.

The Need for Humanistic Teaching

The focus of teacher research should be on the learner, not on the teacher; on the feelings and attitudes of the student, not on knowledge and information (because feelings and attitudes will eventually determine what knowledge and information are sought after and acquired); and on the long-term development and growth of the students, not on short-term objectives or specific teacher tasks. But if teachers spend more time with the learners' feelings and attitudes, as well as on social and personal growth, teachers may be penalized when cognitive student outcomes (little pieces of information) on high-stake tests are correlated with their behaviors and methods in class.

Students need to be encouraged and nurtured by their teachers, especially when they are young. They are too dependent on approval from significant adults—first their parents, then their teachers. Parents and teachers need to help young children and adolescents to establish a source for self-esteem by focusing on their strengths, supporting them, discouraging negative self-talk, and helping them to take control of their lives with their own culture and values.

People (including young people) with high self-esteem achieve at high levels, and the more one achieves, the better one feels about oneself. The opposite is also true: Students who fail to master the subject matter get down on themselves and eventually give up. Students with low self-esteem give up quickly. In short, student self-esteem and achievement are directly related. If we can nurture students' self-esteem, almost everything else will fall into place, including achievement scores and academic outcomes. Regardless of how smart or talented a child, if he or she has personal problems, cognition will be detrimentally affected.

This builds a strong argument for creating successful experiences for students to help them to feel good about themselves. The long-term benefits are obvious: The more students learn to like themselves, the more they will achieve; and the more they achieve, the more they will like themselves. But this takes time, involves a lot of nurturing, and does not show up on a standardized test within a semester or school year; moreover, it does not help the teacher who is being evaluated by a content- or test-driven school administrator who is looking for results now. It certainly does not benefit the teacher who is being evaluated for how many times he or she attended departmental meetings, whether the shades in the classroom were even, or whether his or her instructional objectives were clearly stated.

It is obvious that certain behaviors contribute to good teaching. The trouble is that there is little agreement on exactly what behaviors or methods are most important. There are some teachers who gain theoretical knowledge of "what works," but are unable to put the ideas into practice. Some teachers with similar preparation act effortlessly in the classroom and others consider teaching a chore. All this suggests that teaching cannot be described in terms of a checklist or a precise model. It also suggests that teaching is a humanistic activity that deals with people (not tiny behaviors or competencies) and how people (teachers and students) develop and behave in a variety of classroom and school settings.

Although the research on teacher effectiveness provides a vocabulary and system for improving our insight into good teaching, there is a danger that this research may lead to some of us becoming too rigid in our view of teaching. Following only one teacher model or evaluation system can lead to too much emphasis on specific behaviors that can be easily measured or prescribed in advance, at the expense of ignoring humanistic behaviors, such as esthetic appreciation, emotions, values, and moral responsibility, that cannot be easily measured or prescribed in advance.

Although some educators recognize that humanistic factors influence teaching, we continue to define most teacher behaviors in terms of behaviorist and cognitive factors. Most teacher evaluation instruments tend to de-emphasize the human side of teaching because it is difficult to measure. In an attempt to be scientific, to predict and control behavior and to assess group patterns, we sometimes lose sight of the attitudes of teachers and their relations with students.

In providing feedback and evaluation for teachers, many factors need to be considered so that the advice or information does not fall on deaf ears. Teachers appreciate feedback processes whereby they can improve their teaching as long as the processes are honest and professionally planned and administered, as long as teachers are permitted to make mistakes, and as long as more than one model of effectiveness is considered so that they can adapt recommended behaviors and methods to fit their own personality and philosophy of teaching.

Teachers must be permitted to incorporate specific teacher behaviors and methods according to their own unique personalities and philosophies, to pick and choose from a wide range of research and theory, and to discard other teacher behaviors that conflict with their own style without the fear of being considered ineffective. Many school districts, and even state departments of education, have developed evaluation instruments and salary plans based exclusively on prescriptive and product-oriented behaviors. Even worse, teachers who do not exhibit these behaviors are often penalized or labeled as "marginal" or "incompetent."[14] There is danger that many more school districts and states will continue to jump on this bandwagon and make decisions based on prescriptive teacher research, without recognizing or giving credibility to other teacher behaviors or methods that might be humanistic because they deal with feelings, emotions, and personal connections with people—what some educators label as fuzzy or vague criteria.

Humanistic Teaching

In the early 20th century, humanistic principles of teaching and learning were envisioned in the theories of progressive education: in the *child-centered* lab school directed by John Dewey at the University of Chicago from 1896 to 1904; the *play-centered* methods and materials introduced by Maria Montessori, which were designed to develop the practical, sensor, and formal skills of prekindergarten and kindergarten slum children of Italy starting in 1908; and the *activity-centered* practices of William Kilpatrick, who in the 1920s and 1930s urged that elementary teachers organize classrooms around social activities, group enterprises, and group projects and allow children to say what they think.

All these progressive theories were highly humanistic and stressed the child's interests, individuality, and creativity—in short, the child's freedom to develop naturally, free from teacher domination and the weight of rote learning. But progressivism failed because, in the view of Lawrence Cremin, there were not enough good teachers to implement progressive thought in classrooms and schools.[15] To be sure, it is much easier to stress knowledge, rote learning, and right answers than it is to teach about ideas, to consider the interests and needs of students, and to give them freedom to explore and interact with each other without teacher constraints.

By the end of the 20th century, the humanistic teacher was depicted by William Glasser's "positive" and "supportive" teacher who could manage students without coercion and teach without failure.[16] It was also illustrated by Robert Fried's "passionate" teacher and Vito Perrone's "teacher with a heart"—teachers who live to teach young children and refuse to submit to apathy or criticism that may infect the school in which they work.[17] These teachers are dedicated and caring, they actively engage students in their classrooms, and they affirm their identities. The students do not have to ask whether their teacher is interested in them, thinks of them, or knows their interests or concerns. The answer is definitely yes.

The humanistic teacher is also portrayed by Theodore Sizer's mythical teacher called "Horace," who is dedicated and enjoys teaching, treats learning as a humane enterprise, inspires his students to learn, and encourages them to develop their powers of thought, taste, and character.[18] Yet the system forces Horace to make a number of compromises in planning, teaching, and grading, which he knows that, if we lived in an ideal world (with more than 24 hours in a day), he would not make. Horace is a trooper; he hides his frustration. Critics of teachers don't really want to hear him or face facts; they don't even know what it is like to teach. Sizer simply states, "Most jobs in the real world have a gap between what would be nice and what is possible. One adjusts."[19] Hence, most caring, dedicated teachers are forced to make some compromises, take some shortcuts, and make some accommodations. As long as no one gets upset and no one complains, the system permits a chasm between rhetoric (the rosy picture) and reality (slow burnout).

There is also the humanistic element in Nel Noddings' ideal teacher, who focuses on the nurturing of "competent, caring, loving, and lovable persons." To that end, she describes teaching as a caring profession in which teachers should convey to students the caring way of thinking about one's self, siblings, strangers, animals, plants, and the physical environment. She stresses the affective aspect of teaching: the need to focus on the child's strengths and interests, the need for an individualized curriculum built around the child's abilities and needs.[20] Caring, according to Noddings, cannot be achieved by a formula or checklist. It calls for different behaviors for different situations, from tenderness to tough love. Good teaching, like good parenting, requires continuous effort, trusting relationships, and continuity of purpose—the purpose of caring, appreciating human connections, and respecting people and ideas from a historical, multicultural, and diverse perspective.[21]

Actually, the humanistic teacher is someone who highlights the personal and social dimension in teaching and learning, as opposed to the behavioral, scientific, or technological aspects. We might argue that everything that the teacher does is "human" and the expression "humanistic teaching" is a cliché. However, I would use the term in a loose sense to describe the teacher who emphasizes the arts as opposed to the sciences and people instead of numbers. Although the teacher understands the value of many subjects, including the sciences and social sciences, he or she feels that there is the need for students to understand certain *ideas* and *values,* some rooted in 3,000 years or more of philosophy, literature, art, music, theater, and the like. Without certain agreed-on content, our heritage would crumble and we would be at the mercy of chance and ignorance; moreover, our education enterprise would be subject to the whim and fancy of local fringe groups.

Humanistic education, according to Jacques Barzun, the elegant and eloquent writer on history and humanism, leads to a form of knowledge that helps us to deal with the nature of life, but it does not guarantee a more gracious or noble life:

> The humanities will not sort out the world's evils and were never meant to cure [our] troubles. . . . They will not heal diseased minds or broken hearts any more than they will foster political democracy or settle international disputes.

The humanities (and, if I may add, the humanistic teacher) "have meaning," according to Barzun, "because of the inhumanity of life; what they depict is strife and disaster"[22]; and, if I may add, by example, they help us to deal with the human condition and provide guidelines for moral behavior, good taste, and the improvement of civilization.

On a schoolwide level, the author would argue that humanism (what Fried calls "passion," Perrone calls "heart," Sizer calls "dedication," Noddings calls "caring," and Barzun calls "the well-rounded person") means eliminating homogeneous grouping and the labeling and tracking of students and reducing competitive grading. It means that we eliminate the notion that everyone should go to college since it creates frustration, anger, and unrealistic expectations among large numbers of children and youth. According to Paul Goodman, it requires that society find viable occupational options for noncollege graduates and jobs that have decent salaries, respect, and social status.[23] It suggests, according to John Gardner, that we recognize various forms of excellence—the excellent teacher, the excellent artist, the excellent plumber, and the excellent bus driver; otherwise, we create a myopic view of talent and a subsequent tension that will threaten a democratic society.[24] It also means that we appreciate and nurture different student abilities, aptitudes, and skills, what Howard Gardner calls "multiple intelligences."[25]

Humanistic versus Nonhumanistic Thought

If we fail to adapt a more caring and compassionate view of teaching and schooling, then we fall victim to excessive competiveness and materialism—and eventually to class differences that will divide society into dominant and subordinate groups. Pursuant to neo-Marxist and radical postmodern thinking, we create a permanent underclass who live in "squalid" (Kozol's word), "dehumanizing" (Freire's word), and "colonialized" (Giroux's and McClain's word) conditions. The outcome is a society in which a disproportionate number of low-achieving students and poor, minority, and special needs children are locked into future low-end jobs, unemployment, or what Oscar Lewis, some 40 years ago, referred to as the "culture of poverty," whereby poverty is transferred from generation to generation.[26] In short, a new subordinate group, the have-nots, is construed as dumb, lazy, and de-skilled by a school system and society that encourage competitiveness and judge people on different characteristics and different outcomes.

This human situation is tolerated by the majority of the populace because egalitarianism, social justice, and human dignity are wrongly conceived or ignored. Our prejudices become ingrained in our thinking because they become institutionalized by society. Moreover, we come to rely on "scientific objectivity" to excuse or defend educational and social practices that generate and then perpetuate these dominant–subordinate conditions. There should be no room in this country, or in any society that claims to be civilized, for second-class citizenship, or even for people who think of themselves as second-class citizens. There have been enough second-class citizens in the world.

Down through the ages, the vast majority of humans have been barbarians, slaves, serfs, peasants, and extremely poor and uneducated. Almost one half to one percent of the population—the monarchs and nobility, popes and cardinals, military leaders and generals, czars, capitalists, and the like—have possessed more than 50 percent of the wealth and resources existing within their particular period of history. Even today, 1.2 billion people (or 20 percent of the world's population) live on less than one dollar a day, and 50 percent of the developing countries' 4.5 billion population live on less than two dollars a day, the greatest percentages being in South Asia, sub-Saharan Africa, and Latin America.[27] These poor people live under squalid conditions that very few of us, except for a few scholars and human rights workers, fully comprehend or care to know about. But it is this poverty and hopelessness in developing countries, and the resulting difference in quality of life and culture, that leads to deep and lasting hatred toward the more prosperous Western World and a form of madness in which people don't care if they die or are blown to pieces.

Too many people in this country and other countries have been forced to give up their identities, to move from their world to another world, to assimilate: to pass for white, Christian, or "straight." No one should have to pretend her or his whole life; to live in a closet; to disown her or his family, ethnic group, or religion—never to return to her or his people. Of course, we can argue that ethnocentrism and religious zeal are also sources of the worst atrocities. True believers come in all shapes, stripes, and ideologies, and there has been a steady oversupply of lawless opportunists and willing executioners, no matter how low their position in the chain of command may be, who take pleasure in the destruction and annihilation of other people.

Some readers may consider the above interpretation as an attempt to instill neo-Marxist, postmodern, or illusory rhetoric in the discussion, but the author contends that lack of humanism and moral teaching has resulted in lack of conscience and caring throughout the ages and throughout the globe. The outcomes are similar for all time: human suffering, oppression, fanaticism, and wholesale slaughter of human life under a political or religious ideology that mocks the individual and is suffused with hatred, brute force, and terrorism. It represents the exploitive and dark side of the human psyche, inflicted on humans by humans for centuries, from the treatment of Roman gladiators, African slaves, and European peasantry to the burning of witches and hanging of blacks and gays in the United States. Of course, the Japanese atrocities in Nanking, the Holocaust in Europe, the purges of Stalin and Mao, and the killing fields of Pol Pot are the darkest pages of history, totally irrational and extreme forms of evil that cannot be fully understood with only words. Narratives from victims, photographs, and films must become part of the discourse for us to fully comprehend the extent of this rampant barbarism and blasphemy. Blaming today's generation for another generation's sins is not the answer, but learning from old injustices and immorality is valuable so that we do not repeat history, so that we become a more civil and compassionate society.

Remembering the Dead

All of us have lived most of our lives in the 20th century, and all the lost souls who no longer exist because of mankind's cruelty and hatred must be remembered. Most of the voices and faces we never knew; therefore, it is easy to become detached from their demise and to treat them as an abstract statistic. In fact, the larger the number of dead, thousands or millions, the easier it is to become detached by adding zeros (because the mind is unable to fathom the reality and enormity of the deed) unless the individual or his or her loved ones were part of the cruel nature of history. Among the dead, some were famous for something and are in our encyclopedias, but the vast majority have been forgotten and funneled into anonymity and nothingness. All they can hope is for the poet, painter, or musician to make use of them through pen, canvas, or lyrics in order for the living to gain understanding. In this connection, it is for the teacher to educate the next generation—to make use of these forgotten and transitory people, to help them to return among the living just for a brief moment, to explain the order of magnitude of lost lives and a counting system that involves five, six, or seven zeros.

As educators who grew up in the 20th century, we must now educate students of the 21st century that the most cruel and vile acts against humanity were committed in the 20th century, much worse than the attacks on the World Trade Center, which I mention because some of us have lost loved ones or known people who died. Despite its educated populace, the most heinous deeds were committed in the last century, which produced the most efficient machines to kill the most people. And, after being surrounded by mass murder, rape, and pillage, we become detached from these violent and deathward-leaning acts; we deal with these encounters by abstracting and anatomizing them through a variety of academic subjects and topics. We keep them under lock and key so that our young children and students have almost no real knowledge of Nanking, the Holocaust, Stalin's or Mao's purges, the killing fields, or more recently Kosovo and Rwanda. Even at home—Antietam (4,000+ dead), Gettysburg (50,000+), Pearl Harbor (2,300), and now the World Trade Center (2,900)—the dead are forgotten, as if they never existed, except by some individual who buried a loved one.

As teachers, we must make sense of our past through our philosophy, history, literature, art, poetry, and music. We are required to ask our students to think about the true believers and zealots and the willing oppressors and opportunists who have ravaged the earth. We must pay homage to the millions who perished in the wars and witch hunts, the purges and extermination camps of the 20th century. We must hear their voices, see their faces, and understand their final thoughts of life in the midst of background screams, muzzled groans, and sad goodbyes—and then the stench of death—to fully comprehend the barbaric deeds of humanity, and how many more times throughout all time that evil has prevailed over good.

Indeed, I am reminded of an old soldier, a World War II veteran, discussing the Battle of the Bulge (275,000 dead). He could not remember how he celebrated his last birthday or why he just opened the refrigerator, but he could vividly recount the conditions of the battlefield as if it had been yesterday: gray foreboding clouds, the snow-covered grass, the cold nipping at his toes and fingers, the rubble of the dead around him, the eyes of the enemy and the tatter of machine guns in front, the smell of fuel oil and ashes of annihilation mixed in the countryside air.

In detail, he could still recall the names of the fallen dead on his left side and right side, the last words and groans of his doomed comrades; but soon the old soldier would die along with his memories. For that moment, there was nothing impersonal or abstract about the slaughter—the excruciating combat, the lost voices and faces, the sense of madness around him.

We must try to provide, as part of the teaching role, some reassurance to our students that good can prevail over evil, that morality can topple immorality. Although we should not be weighed down by the past, we must remember all the nameless and voiceless people who suffered and died a senseless or terrible death before their time and keep the specter and memory of the nations, tribes, and political and religious zealots that committed the acts of violence against these victims. We must fight off fading memories and amnesia so that we have a chance to prevent, or at least reduce, the worst natures in us, the resulting blasphemy and evil that have characterized so many of the inhabitants of the last century.

As teachers, we should inspire our students and help them to deal with the nature of life and society; this is one of our most important professional roles. Yet it ought to come as no surprise that we rarely connect with our students in this way. Is it because we lack passion, a sense of history or loyalty to an ideal, or merely shy from moral messages? I think that it is all these, and thus we fail the memory of the people of the last century and previous centuries who died unjustly.

As teachers, we often fail in our role to elaborate on the agony of our history, that the need to reduce the ruthlessness and atrocities of humans rests with us. All the people who are alive today are connected to the past like a cloud that sweeps through the constellations and eventually disappears. Among the thinkers of society, and especially among our writers, poets, and artists, as well as our teachers, there should be a thirst for knowledge that remembers the dead and then goes beyond the borders of the dead to elaborate on life and improve society.

Students' Learning Opportunities

Edward Pajak questions whether teaching children about evil is likely to make them virtuous. Introducing students to this kind of "content" before they are emotionally mature and intellectually sophisticated may have exactly the opposite effect of what is intended.[28] There is a human tendency to identify with the aggressor and those in power, to laugh at or ridicule the victim. Like many adults, young children may not have the intellectual or emotional capacity to process horrifying information in a clear and sophisticated manner. Premature and excessive emphasis on the dark side of history and society informs unsophisticated students about which groups represent "legitimate" targets for hate.

But we cannot protect the new generation from the chambers of horrors that have characterized most of our history. We cannot continue to allow only a little darkness to spill out in our classrooms, to keep the horrors hemmed in by limiting the dark side of human behavior to a few sentences or paragraphs in a textbook or a few comments in class. However, I would rely on Piaget's principles of cognition, that the child's formal mental operations (or advanced stage of cognition) develop between ages 11 and 15, whereby the adolescent is capable of analyzing ideas, engaging in abstract operations, and clarifying values. Even before the age of 11, the concepts of right and wrong, fairness, and basic democratic laws and principles are understood. Similarly, Piaget's theory of moral development, along with Kohlberg's notion of moral reasoning and moral ideology, suggests that teens can understand the principles of ethics, contractual obligations, conscience, and justice. There is some variation, of course, which has to do with the student's family, religion, and cultural background, due to biases and prejudices that develop outside the school. But this is exactly what the teacher has to overcome; it is part of the teacher's role.

Let me put it in a different way: Blind hatred, erroneous claims of superiority, and ideological fanaticism, by which the individual is drowned out by the mass, made impotent, then dehumanized and/or slaughtered, represent the ugly side of humanity. They can be depicted as the opposite of the music of Bach; the art of Michelangelo; the stories of Cervantes and Shakespeare; the philosophy of Kant, Locke, and Rousseau; the poems of Robert Frost, Emily Dickinson, and Lao-Tzu; and the spiritual messages of Muhammad, Buddha, and Gandhi. Teachers, in the past, have emphasized the good side of humanity. I urge that both sides need to be explored. By ignoring the ugly side of civilization, teachers unwittingly create a void among future generations—a lack of humanity, compassion, and moral constraint.

The ideals of right and wrong, justice and goodness are rooted in Western morality, Greek and Judeo-Christian ideas, as well as Eastern philosophy and religious thought, and should be incorporated into the curriculum. Education without concern for certain universal and humanistic truths, values, and ways of behaving hinders the moral fiber of society. Taken to the next step, it leads to man's natural aggression, based on biological and animal instincts. Freud would say this means that the *id* has gained the upper hand over the *super ego* (personal and social conscience). In the worst case scenario, it suggests the rise of Nieztche's "superman" complex and the subsequent rationale for racism, imperialism, colonialism, religious fanaticism, and militarism, accompanied by the death of hundreds of millions of people (50 million people alone in World War II) and the destruction of hundreds of nation-states and racial, ethnic, or religious groups, since Rome was built and Christ preached the gospel. With moral constraints, man's aggressive instincts are played out in board rooms and on Wall Street, as well as on high school, college, and professional football fields and wrestling arenas; on Saturday and Sunday mornings on suburban pee-wee soccer fields and on big-city asphalt basketball courts; and daily among us older "folks" (Bush's term) who commit road rage on American highways and byways—what most of us would call socially acceptable behavior or wink at and write off as a little extreme.

But the teaching of knowledge without morality leads to extreme competitiveness, human stratification, and survival of the fittest. Put in different words, unchecked emphasis on performance through which the same students always "win" and another group always "loses"; or the elitist notion that the right of a student to an education persists only as far as his or her intellectual capabilities; or the labeling, categorizing, and tracking of students and noting of differences among people (smart, dumb; superior, inferior) suggest a school system and a society that encourage, and even foster, all the wrong "isms"—colonialism, imperialism, fascism, and racism. In fact, almost all militant and imperialist societies stress their own efficiency and superiority over other societies—nothing more than excuses and theories for explaining man's inhumanity to man. Even worse, this type of thinking and behavior is often derived from and supported by "scientific explanations," laws, religious theology, or political ideology—doctrines created by people to suppress other people.

Moral and Civic Virtues

Teaching and schooling should be committed to a higher purpose, a humanistic–moral purpose designed not only to enhance academic grades but also for personal and social responsibility. It should be built around people and community, around respecting, caring for, and having compassion toward others. It means that teachers in the classroom deal with social and moral issues, with the human condition and good and evil. It means that students be encouraged to ask "why," as opposed to being encouraged to give the "right" answer. The question should start with family conversation, but must be nurtured in school during the formative years of learning so that a sense of social and moral consciousness is developed. But precisely on this score, our teachers and schools register a disturbing deficit, originally because it was thought to tread on the spiritual domain and now because there is little time to inquire about and discuss important ideas and issues, because the curriculum is test driven by trivia items of knowledge and short-answer outcomes.

According to one social critic, "why?" is the existential question that every individual must be permitted to ask and must receive an appropriate and meaningful answer to from those in power or who mete out justice. If the question is denied, then the individual has no basic rights.[29] It is the purest form of totalitarianism in which the individual is trivialized, as in the Roman empire, where the ruling classes' main amusement was watching humans being eaten by animals or fighting each other to the death; in the cattle cars to the concentration camps of Auschwitz and Maidenek, where the individual was reduced to a serial number and human remains were often retrofitted into soap products, lamp shades, and gold rings; and in the Serbian ethnic cleansing and rape of Bosnia and Kosovo and the cleansing and rape of Rwanda.

How many of us can locate Rwanda on the map? Does anyone among us know where Auschwitz and Maidenek are located? How many among us, except for a few elderly statesmen, scholars, and descendants of the victims, care? Given the "luxury of late birth" and "geographical distance," who among us are expected to do more than cite a few numbers or statements to put the horrors of humanity into some context or understanding? Who cares about the sufferings of all the folk groups, tribes, and nations since we came out of the caves? How many of us know the names of one or two people who died in Nanking, at Pearl Harbor, in the Holocaust, at Juno or Utah beach, in the killing fields of Cambodia, or in Croatia or Kosovo? Can we cite one name that appears on the Arch of Triumph or the Vietnam Memorial? Who can recall or ever knew the name of the pilot (Paul Tibbots) who dropped the A-bomb on Hiroshima—what his thoughts were as he approached the target or after the carnage and cloud of dust? Who among us care to know or can explain what happened or why it happened that more than 100 million soldiers and civilians died in war (or related civilian activities) in the last century in what I would call the most ruthless century—consisting of the most vile deeds and crimes against people? How do we weigh the smug claims of Western technology and industry with the millions who died beside railroad tracks and in battle trenches?

Well, we all die—no kidding—but many of us die when we are not ready to die, without any maps or charts of the journey. Modern philosophy, history, and literature have sanitized these deaths. We have more details (dates, names, and places) than we can process, so those who were murdered, raped, gassed, and executed have been generalized into nonindividuals. The lucky ones were cared for by people who rarely knew anything about their history, knew nothing about who they were, and sometimes did not even know their names. It is an old story, repeated several times in different places and periods of history, yet it must be examined by teachers and students so that there is a better chance of preventing, or at least reducing, this common madness in society.

And Americans are not innocent, given our inhuman and criminal treatment of Native Americans and black Americans—that is, the near extermination and remaining dismemberment of an entire Indian civilization over a 50-year period under the banner of westward expansion and the subhuman treatment of blacks during 100 years of slavery, followed by the exclusion of blacks from American society during the Post-Reconstruction and Jim Crow era (keenly illustrated by white and black toilets and segregated schools and housing and other public facilities).

We all know when injustices are being perpetrated, but we often do not act or want to deal with them. Throughout the ages, man has deceived himself by remaining indifferent or looking the other way in the midst of the worst atrocities and crimes, connoting a human flaw or moral fault in our character. Periodically, a nation or ethnic group has to pay a heavy price and be held accountable for its actions or inactions. Although the past has taught us how not to act, we periodically fall from civilized to uncivilized practices because our dark side checkmates our good side (the music of Bach, the plays of Shakespeare), because of our aggressive and competitive nature to beat the next person. As long as we have bread on our table and sufficient clothes on our back, we often remain silent, look the other way, or become true believers—in effect, blinded by our own inaction to the vile deeds of others.

Moral practices start with the family and continue with the church and community, but teachers must play an active role if ours is to be a more compassionate, caring, and just society. As teachers, we need to encourage open debate concerning the thorniest issues of the present and past, welcome-discussions without ad hominem attacks or stereotypes, and build a sense of community (what the French call *civisme*) and character. We are forced to flee from our comfortable classroom niches, go beyond facts, raise thoughtful questions that stem from meaningful readings, and transcend the cognitive domain into the moral universe. We must promote this type of teaching for all grade levels.

Our readings in school should have a moral flavor to encourage discussion, thinking, and ultimately the transformation of the learner. Even at the primary grade level, reading must not be wasted by assigning "See Spot Run" or "A Sunday Trip to Granny"; rather the emphasis should be on folktales and stories, such as "Jack and the Beanstalk," "Rumpelstiltskin," "Seasons," and "The Mouse and the Wizard," from all parts of the world.

The relationships among history, literary criticism, and philosophy raise many questions about human conditions and civilizations. These ideas express the nature of humanity and society, considered by some to be part of the Great Books, Junior Great Books, or Great Ideas programs. Call it what you want, these readings deal with moral conscience and historical consciousness, and this is what students should be reading.

The idea is for the teacher to capture the students' imaginations, to have them explore ideas and issues, support arguments, and draw conclusions—what some of us might call *critical thinking*. At the same time, students need to examine, analyze, and interpret morally laden books to help them understand the evil or dark side of humans—what happens when morality is dethroned for greed, hatred, or some god or ideology; when excellence or efficiency is pushed to an extreme in which *all* trains are expected to run on time and all soldiers are expected to follow orders and die for the glory of some god, the nation, or the ego of old politicians.

There is need to balance the scales of justice and face the truth when history is rewritten for religious or nationalistic reasons or for apologies and excuses that what happened was historically inevitable or historically justifiable; or when "those people" were different from us, backward and uneducated; or when "they" had too much power and money—whatever hocus-pocus rationale is used to distort the truth and alter beliefs. Teachers must decide what is important in the curriculum, what has been omitted and what has been included for discussion. Often big-city teachers are rendered impotent in this professional role, and the curriculum is imposed on them from the central office by a few bureaucrats (former teachers and principals) who eventually lose touch with the community, classroom reality, and the needs of students. Regardless of our politics and idiosyncratic judgments, as professionals we need to become more involved in curriculum development and decide how the content in class achieves a balanced portrait of the past and present, of other people and nations. We need to take positions—moral positions appropriate for a changing society and diverse society, a society that is willing to face and deal with its problems. Students must be encouraged by their teachers to raise questions, take positions, and act morally responsible. To some extent, it is a position set forth by old reconstructionists such as John Dewey, George Counts, and Ted Brameld.

The writer, poet, musician, and teacher need to summon the shades of the past to fight off anonymity and amnesia. Through selected readings or even through film (for students who are unable to read fluently), we need to restore our fading and faltering memories, to show that the dead who were taken before it was their time to die did not die in vain. A war memorial is not the answer. It may serve political or nationalistic interests and raise the specter (genre) of jingoism, but it cannot convey the moral lessons of the past. It can evoke tears and stimulate pride, but it cannot lead to critical and analytical thought to clarify arguments, to explain and defend concepts and ideas, and to maintain purposeful and critical discussion.

The writer, poet, musician, and teacher must remember the people who lived and died. As teachers, we must capture the agony and lessons of history as well as the goodness of humanity through our philosophy, history, literature, music, and art. We must retain the vestiges of the lost world, where people died a terrible death as victims of war, poverty, nationalism, racism, or religious fanaticism, and try to make sense of all the senseless crimes that people are capable of committing.

The people who shaped my world and your world, for the greater part, no longer exist. We have twenty-five or thirty years as teachers to make an imprint on the next generation, to remember the millions who are not in the encyclopedias and who no longer exist, to pass on their thoughts and deeds to the next generations. As teachers, the necessity of our work requires that we understand what is at stake: improving and enriching society by making the next generation care about what is morally right and motivating students to accomplish great things that exhibit the good side of what is human.

Moving from literature and philosophy to active teaching and learning means that students be encouraged and rewarded for moral and community action, for helping others and volunteering their time and service. It means that character development and civic service receive the same attention and recognition that we give to A students and star quarterbacks. It calls for special assemblies, special scholarships, and special staff development programs that promote character development, the desire to help others, and the expectation of social and civic involvement. It means that we give character development—helping and caring for others, contributing and giving back to the school and community—as much attention as we give academics and sports in school.

I am not talking about a special course or program to meet some "service-learning" requirement, but rather a school ethos or a common philosophy that teachers and administrators support. The idea must permeate the entire school and be expected and required for all students. One or two teachers attempting to teach moral responsibility or civic participation cannot effect long-term change; it takes a team effort and schoolwide policy. It demands nothing less than a reconceptualization of the roles, expectations, and activities of students and teachers involved in the life of schools and communities. The idea flows back to the early philosophy and cardinal principles of progressive education of the 1910s and 1920s and the old core curriculum of the 1930s and 1940s, which promoted the study of moral and social issues, social responsibility, and civic education and youth service for the community and nation.

It also means that we consider the basic elementary school, conceived by Ernest Boyer and the Carnegie Foundation, that focuses on the child and community, where schools are kept small so that people work together and feel connected and empowered; it means that the school provides emotional and social support for children, beyond academics, to focus on the whole child and to teach the importance of values, ethics, and moral responsibility.[30] It suggests that a moral and civil society is a requirement for democracy to work, as so keenly described 150 years ago in Alex de Tocqueville's classic treatise *Democracy in America;* it means that we teach the importance of connecting with nature and the ecology of our planet, to preserve our resources and ensure our future. It requires that we bring competitiveness and social cohesion, excellence and equality, as well as material wealth and poverty, into harmony—not an easy task, like squaring a circle. Finally, we need to look into the future: The bomb is an eclipse, but the products of technology and the biological sciences—from medicines and foods to better babies (altering the DNA of generations to come) and extending life (by eliminating or adding genes or inserting computer chips)—offer new ways to play god and leave us with many moral issues to ponder.

FINAL WORDS

A few final and personal notes to the reader. We have shared some reflective moments together, maybe as long as an hour, and perhaps some of these thoughts will last. All of us are filled with memories of people who lived and died, and all of us can personally identify with our own racial, ethnic, or religious group that has suffered from the ruthless behavior of others. All of us who perceive ourselves as members of a minority group understand the notions of subordination and suffering. We experience our own transitoriness and mortality every day as we read in the news or see on television the acts of violence committed by people toward other people.

The wisdom of the Bible and the virtues of religious leaders provide me with little comfort or hope, because the people who should know better and preach hope are often burdened by their own biases, prejudices, and ill-feelings toward other people who summon up different interpretations of the past and present. Although the clergy can be construed as teachers, their mission and agenda center around ideology, and their methods historically have been used to promote this way of thinking. The sword and fire, or worse, are the same methods adopted by modern-day totalitarian nations.

As I take hold of my pen and describe a cruel and sad world—flawed by its own stupidity, hatred, and crimes, a host of isms—I provide the idea for teachers to speculate about their own roles and what education is all about or should be about. I hope that a deep sense of human guilt and teacher triumph of consciousness of humanity will help future citizens of the world be more responsible in terms of character and compassion. Indeed, it is the teacher's role to keep revisiting history, to fight off amnesia and to become a spokesperson for the dead, and thus to improve the human condition. It is a professional role rarely, if ever, described in the education literature in such a blunt way; it is an idea worth considering, in a world where the United States is at the zenith of its power, but would rather hide from the evils of the world.

Finally, I am reminded of an old saying that was popular when, in the words of Billy Joel, "I wore a younger man's clothes" (in my case, cutoff shorts and roman sandals): "We don't know what World War III will be fought with, but World War IV will be fought with rocks."[31] I am reminded of the mundane words of last goodbyes—"I love you," "I will wait for you in heaven," "Tell her I will forever miss her." I am reminded of Carl Sandburg's *Grass*—all the wars, all the dead, and all the grass that keeps growing; then I think of James Joyce's *The Dead,* describing the demise of the ordinary people, "falling faintly through the universe."

On a more personal level, I am reminded of Yevgeni Yevtushenko, who saw himself and his ancestors "persecuted, spat on, and slandered" for centuries in Europe. It culminated in his homeland, Mother Russia, with the death of tens of thousands in Belostok (the most violent pogrom) and hundreds of thousands at Babi Yar (a mass murder, mass grave). "Like one long soundless scream . . . I'm every old man executed here/ As I am every child murdered./ Rest the victims' bones." So few people seem to care, so few seem to remember. Yet, because of the long roads and caravans traveled by my ancestors, I recall that so many people in so many lands, since ancient Egypt and Rome, have been thrown back by the boot, the sword, and the law—by a soldier, crusader, king, or despot. I have no need to hear false excuses or false proclamations in the name of hatred, stupidity, or herd behavior. I have no patience or pity for fools, zealots, and tyrants who strip people of their dignity and then put them to death. Even worse, I fear those in power who are given to genocidal impulses and are bent on reducing whole villages to rubble and destroying whole cultures and civilizations to nothing more than a line or two in some morally toned poems like "The Waste Land" or "Babi Yar." I can only take some limited comfort in John Donne's holy sonnet "Death, be not proud": "we wake eternally, and Death shall be no more."

I am reminded of all the English teachers trying to teach these poems, and also trying to teach the *Iliad, King Lear, Gulliver's Travels,* and *The Death of Ivan Illych,* the best that has been thought and said in our culture. Then I am reminded of all the bored students, squirming and sweating in their seats, dozing and doodling, watching the clock tick by tick, and missing the bittersweet phrases and opportunity to reflect on ways ordinary and tragic.

I long for a simpler day: *Little House on the Prairie, Leave It to Beaver, Gilligan's Island,* and *Ozzie and Harriet.* But the clock cannot be turned back. In another instant, I recall Mickey and Minnie and Uncle Miltie; Huey, Louie, and Dewey; Captain Video, Captain Kangaroo, and Howdy Doody; "Here's to You, Mrs. Robinson"; Marilyn and Jolt'n Joe. Has anyone seen my childhood heroes—Jackie, Pee Wee, and Duke? Can you tell me where? They're all gone, especially John, Bobby, and Martin, but remembered in history books.

I can also recall playing catch with Dad and stickball in the schoolyard with Jack and Larry. Then there were Mrs. Katz, Mrs. Schwartz, and Miss Hess from P.S. 42 Queens; Mr. Faulkner, Mr. Tietz, and Miss Gussow from Far Rockaway High School. All my favorite teachers are gone, too, but I thought it would be the right thing to do, in the dearness of remembering a simpler period and vanishing era, to recall the names of teachers, largely forgotten, who taught for 25 to 30 years and made a difference to thousands of kids from my generation. All of you can cherish the names of other teachers who made a difference in your lives—and all of you can ponder the larger role of teaching in the changing world that we live in.

ENDNOTES

1. N. L. Gage, *The Scientific Basis of the Art of Teaching* (New York: Teachers College Press, Columbia University, 1978), pp. 15, 17.
2. Philip Jackson, *Life in Classrooms,* 2nd ed. (New York: Teachers College Press, 1990).
3. Elliot W. Eisner, "The Art and Craft of Teachers," *Educational Researcher* (April 1983), p. 8. Also see Elliot W. Eisner, *The Kind of Schools We Need* (Portsmouth, NH: Heinemann, 1998).
4. Louis J. Rubin, *Artistry of Teaching* (New York: Random House, 1985), p. 61.
5. Ibid., pp. 60, 69.
6. Jonathan Cohen, *Educating Minds and Hearts* (New York: Teachers College Press, Columbia University, 1999); Robert Fried, *The Passionate Teacher* (Boston: Beacon Press, 1995).
7. Seymore B. Sarason, *Teaching as a Performing Art* (New York: Teachers College Press, Columbia University, 1999).
8. Ibid.
9. Sylvia Ashton-Warner, *Teacher* (New York: Simon and Schuster, 1964); Allan C. Ornstein, *Strategies for Effective Teaching,* 2nd ed. (Dubuque, IA: Brown and Benchmark, 1995), dedication page.

10. Arthur Jersild, *When Teachers Face Themselves* (New York: Teachers College Press, Columbia University, 1955), p. 3.
11. Elliot W. Eisner, "The Promise and Perils of Alternative Forms of Data Representation," *Educational Researcher* (August–September 1997), pp. 4–11.
12. Robert L. Linn, "Assessment and Accountability," *Educational Researcher* (March 2000), pp. 4–15.
13. Abbey Goodnough, "Regents Create a New Path to Teaching," *New York Times*, July 15, 2000, pp. B4, B7.
14. Allan C. Ornstein, "Beyond Effective Teaching," in A. C. Ornstein, ed., *Teaching: Theory into Practice* (Boston: Allyn and Bacon, 1995), pp. 273–291.
15. Lawrence A. Cremin, *The Transformation of the School* (New York: Random House, 1961).
16. William Glasser, *Schools Without Failure* (New York: Harper & Row, 1969); Glasser, *The Quality School* (New York: HarperCollins, 1990).
17. Robert Fried, *The Passionate Teacher;* Vito Perrone, *Teacher with a Heart* (New York: Teachers College Press, 1998).
18. Theodore R. Sizer, *Horace's Compromise* (Boston: Houghton Mifflin, 1985).
19. Ibid., p. 20.
20. Nel Noddings, *The Challenge to Care in Schools* (New York: Teachers College Press, Columbia University, 1992).
21. Ibid.
22. Jacques Barzun, *Teachers in America*, rev. ed. (Lanham, MD: University Press of America, 1972).
23. Paul Goodman, *Compulsory Mis-Education* (New York: Horizon Press, 1964).
24. John Gardner, *Excellence: Can We Be Equal Too?* (New York: Harper & Row, 1962).
25. Howard Gardner, *Frames of Mind: The Theory of Multiple Intelligences* (New York: Basic Books, 1983).
26. Oscar Lewis, "The Culture of Poverty," *Scientific American* (October 1996), pp. 19–25.
27. "Poverty and Globalization," Center for Global Studies Conference, St. John's University, April 26, 2001. Based on 1998 World Bank Data.
28. Comments made by Edward Pajak to the author, September 6, 2001.
29. Fritz Stern, "The Importance of 'Why'," *World Policy Journal* (Spring 2000), pp. 1–8.
30. Ernest L. Boyer, "The Basic School: Focusing on the Child," *Elementary Principal* (January 1994), pp. 29–32.
31. Francis X. Clines, "A New Form of Grieving," *New York Times*, September 16, 2001, Sect. 4, p. 3.

DISCUSSION QUESTIONS

1. How would you defend the claim that teaching should be considered an art?
2. How would you defend the claim that teaching should be considered a science?
3. What qualities does the author think are most important for a teacher to possess?
4. What are the benefits of having teachers focus their instruction on the dark side of human nature? What are the drawbacks?
5. Who should decide which topics are legitimate for students to learn about? How should such decisions be made?

CHAPTER 9

Productive Teachers: Assessing the Knowledge Base

HERBERT J. WALBERG

FOCUSING QUESTIONS

1. What are the components of teaching that emphasize what teachers do?
2. What does the behavioral model emphasize concerning cues, engagement, correctives, and reinforcement?
3. How do explicit teaching and comprehension teaching differ?
4. What is open education?
5. How do programmed instruction, mastery learning, adaptive instruction, and computer-assisted instruction differ in terms of planning and instructional components?
6. How do the aims of accelerated programs, ability grouping, whole-group instruction, and cooperative learning programs differ?
7. What approaches and goals are emphasized by microteaching and inservice education?

Some teaching techniques have remarkable effects on learning, while others confer only trivial advantages or even hinder the learning process. Over the past decade, there has been an explosion of research activity centering on the question of what constitutes effective teaching. Ten years ago, several psychologists observed signs of a "quiet revolution" in educational research. Five years later, nearly 3,000 studies of effective teaching techniques existed. By 1987, an Australian/U.S. team was able to assess 134 reviews of 7,827 field studies and several large-scale U.S. and international surveys of learning.[1]

Here, I will give an overview of the findings to date on elementary and secondary school students and will evaluate the more recent and definitive reviews of research on teaching and instruction. Surveying the vast literature on the effects of various instructional methods allows us to consider the advantages and disadvantages of different techniques—including some effective ones that are no longer popular.

I will begin by considering the effects of the psychological elements of teaching, and I will discuss methods and patterns of teaching that a single teacher can accomplish without unusual arrangements or equipment. Then I will turn to systems of instruction that require special planning, student grouping, and materials. Next I will describe effects that are unique to particular methods of teaching reading, writing, science, and mathematics. Finally, I will discuss special students and techniques for dealing with them and the effects of particular types of training on teachers. It is important to bear in mind that, when we try to apply in our own classrooms the methods we have read about, we may attain results that are half—or twice—as good as the average estimates reported below. Our success will depend not only on careful implementation but also on our purposes. The best saw swung as a hammer does little good.

PSYCHOLOGICAL ELEMENTS

A little history will help us understand the evolution of psychological research on teaching. Even though educators require balance, psychologists have often emphasized thought, feeling, or behavior at the expense of the other two components of the psyche. Today, thinking or cognition is sovereign in psychology, but half a century ago behaviorists insisted on specific operational definitions (and they continue to do so). In particular, Yale psychologists John Dollard and Neal Miller, stimulated by E. L. Thorndike and B. F. Skinner, wrote about cues, responses, and positive reinforcement, especially in psychotherapy. Later Miller and Dollard isolated three components of teaching—cues, engagement, and reinforcement—that are similar to the elements of input, process, and output in physiology.[2] Their influential work led researchers to consider what teachers *do* instead of focusing on their age, experience, certification, college degrees, or other factors not directly connected to what their students learn.[3]

The behavioral model emphasized (1) the quality of the instructional cues impinging on the learner, (2) the learner's active engagement, and (3) the reinforcements or rewards that encourage continuing effort over time. Benjamin Bloom recognized, however, that in cycles of cues and effort learners may fail the first time or even repeatedly. Thus they may practice incorrect behavior, and so they cannot be reinforced. Therefore, he emphasized feedback to correct errors and frequent testing to check progress. Inspired by John Carroll's model of school learning, Bloom also emphasized engaged learning time and stressed that some learners require much more time than others.[4]

The effects of cues, engagement, reinforcement, and corrective feedback on student learning are enormous.[5] The research demonstrating these effects has been unusually rigorous and well-controlled. Even though the research was conducted in school classes, the investigators helped to ensure precise timing and deployment of the elements and relied on short-term studies, which usually lasted less than a month. Similar effects are difficult to sustain for long time periods.

Cues

As operationalized, cues show students what is to be learned and explain how to learn it. Their quality depends on the clarity, salience, and meaningfulness of explanations and directions provided by the teacher, the instructional materials, or both. Ideally, as the learners gain confidence, the salience and number of cues can be reduced.

Engagement

The extent to which students actively and persistently participate in learning until appropriate responses are firmly entrenched in their repertoires is known as engagement. Such participation can be indexed by the extent to which the teacher engages students in overt or covert activity. A high degree of engagement is indicated by an absence of irrelevant behavior and by concentration on tasks, enthusiastic contributions to group discussion, and lengthy study.

Corrective Feedback

Corrective feedback remedies errors in oral or written responses. Ideally, students should waste little time on incorrect responses, and teachers should detect difficulties rapidly and then remedy them by reteaching or using alternative methods. When necessary, teachers should also provide students with additional time for practice.

Reinforcement

The immense effort elicited by athletics, games, and other cooperative and competitive activities illustrates the power of immediate and direct reinforcement and shows that some endeavors are intrinsically rewarding. By comparison, classroom reinforcement may seem crass or jejune. The usual classroom reinforcers are acknowledgment of correctness and social approval, typically expressed by praise or a smile. More unusual reinforcers include providing contingent activity—for example, initiating a music lesson or other enjoyable activity as a reward for 90 percent correctness on a math test. Other reinforcers are tokens or check marks that are accumulated for discrete accomplishments and that can be exchanged for tangible reinforcers such as cookies, trinkets, or toys.

In special education programs, students have been reinforced not only for academic achievement but also for minutes spent on reading, for attempts to learn, and for the accuracy with which they perform tasks. Margo Mastropieri and Thomas Scruggs have shown that results can be impressive when the environment can be rigorously controlled and when teachers can accurately gear reinforcement to performance, as in programs for unruly or emotionally disturbed students. Improved behavior and achievement, however, may fail to extend past the period of reinforcement or beyond the special environment.[6]

Educators ordinarily confine reinforcement to marks, grades, and awards because they must assume that students work for such intangible, long-term goals as pleasing parents, furthering their education, achieving success in later life, and the intrinsic satisfaction of learning itself. Even so, when corrective feedback and reinforcement are clear, rapid, and appropriate, they can powerfully affect learning by efficiently signaling students what to do next. In ordinary classrooms, then, the chief value of reinforcement is informational rather than motivational.

METHODS OF TEACHING

The psychological elements just discussed undergird many teaching methods and the design of most instructional media. Techniques to improve the affective or informational content of cues, engagement, correctives, and reinforcement have shown a wide range of effects.

Cues

Advance organizers are brief overviews that relate new concepts or terms to previous learning. They are effective if they connect new learning and old. Those delivered by the teacher or graphically illustrated in texts work best.

Adjunct questions alert students to key questions that should be answered—particularly in texts. They work best when questions are repeated on posttests, and they work moderately well when posttest questions are similar or related to the adjuncts. As we might expect, however, adjunct questions divert attention from incidental material that might otherwise be learned.

Goal setting suggests specific objectives, guidelines, methods, or standards for learning that can be spelled out explicitly. Like the use of adjunct questions, goal setting sacrifices incidental for intended learning.

Learning hierarchies assume that instruction can be made more efficient if the facts, skills, or ideas that logically or psychologically precede others are presented first. Teaching and instructional media sequenced in this way appear to be slightly more effective. However, learners may adapt themselves to apparently ill-sequenced material, and it may even be advantageous to learn to do so, since human life, as Franz Kafka showed, may depart from logic.

Pretests are benchmarks for determining how much students learn under various methods of teaching. Psychologists have found, however, that pretests can have positive cuing effects if they show students what will be emphasized in instruction and on posttests.

Several principles follow from surveying the effects of these methods. To concentrate learning on essential points and to save time (as would be appropriate in training), remove elaborations and extraneous oral and written prose. To focus learners on selected questions or to teach them to find answers in elaborated prose, use adjunct questions and goal setting. To encourage the acquisition of as much undifferentiated material as possible, as in college lecture courses, assign big blocks of text and test students on randomly selected points.

Although the means of producing certain results may seem clear, reaching a consensus on educational purposes may be difficult. Clarity at the start saves time and helps learners to see things the teacher's way, but it limits individual autonomy and deep personal insights. Zen masters ask novices about the sound of one hand clapping and wait a decade or two for an answer. Hiroshi Azuma and Robert Hess find that Japanese mothers use more indirection and vagueness in teaching their young children than do assertive American mothers, and I have observed Japanese science teachers asking questions and leaving them long unresolved. Do the Japanese cultivate initiative and perseverance by these methods?

Engagement

High expectations transmit teachers' standards of learning and performance. They may function both as cues and as incentives for students to put extended effort and perseverance into learning.

Frequent tests increase learning by stimulating greater effort and providing intermittent feedback. However, the effects of tests on performance are larger for quizzes than for final examinations.

Questioning also appears to work by promoting engagement and may encourage deeper thinking—as in Plato's accounts of Socrates. Questioning has bigger effects in science than in other subjects. Mary Budd Rowe and Kenneth Tobin have shown that *wait time*—allowing students several seconds to reflect rather than the usual .9 of a second—leads to longer and better answers.

Correctives and Reinforcement

Corrective feedback remedies errors by reteaching, either with the same or with a different method. This practice has moderate effects that are somewhat higher in science—perhaps because learning science often involves more conceptualizing while learning other subjects may allow more memorizing.

Homework by itself constructively extends engaged learning time. Correctives and reinforcement in the form of grades and comments on homework raise its effects dramatically.

Praise has a small positive effect. For young or disturbed children, praise may lack the power of the tangible reinforcers used in psychological experiments. For students who are able to see ahead, grades and personal standards maybe more powerful reinforcers than momentary encouragement. Moreover, praise may be under- or oversupplied; it may appear demeaning or sardonic; and it may pale in comparison with the disincentives to academic achievement afforded by youth culture in the form of cars, clothing, dating, and athletics.

None of this is to say that encouragement, incentives, and good classroom morale should be abandoned; honey may indeed be better than vinegar. Yet, as cognitive psychologists point out, the main classroom value of reinforcement may lie in its capacity to inform the student about progress rather than in its power to reward.

PATTERNS OF TEACHING

As explained above, methods of teaching enact or combine more fundamental psychological elements. By further extension, *patterns* of teaching integrate elements and methods of teaching. The process of determining these more inclusive formulations was another step in the evolution of psychological research on education. Behavioral research evolved in the 1950s from psychological laboratories to short-term, controlled classroom experiments on one element at a time. In the 1970s, educational researchers tried to find patterns of effective practices from observations of ordinary teaching.

Thus behaviorists traded educational realism for theoretical parsimony and scientific rigor; later psychologists preferred realism until their insights could be experimentally confirmed. Fortunately, the results of both approaches appear to converge. Moreover, it seems possible to incorporate the work of cognitive psychologists of the 1980s into an enlarged understanding of teaching.

Explicit Teaching

Explicit teaching can be viewed as traditional or conventional whole-group teaching done well. Since most teaching has changed little in the last three-quarters of a century and may not change substantially in the near future,[7] it is worth knowing how to make the usual practice most productive. Since it has evolved from ordinary practice, explicit teaching seems natural to carry out and does not disrupt conventional institutions and expectations. Furthermore, it can incorporate many previously discussed elements and methods.

Systematic research was initiated in the early 1960s by N. L. Gage, Donald Medley, and others who employed "process–product" investigations of the association between what teachers do and how much their students learn. Jere Brophy, Carolyn Evertson, Thomas Good, and Jane Stallings later contributed substantially to this effort. Walter Doyle, Penelope Peterson, and Lee Shulman put the results into a psychological context. Barak Rosenshine has periodically reviewed the research, and Gage and Margaret Needels recently measured the results and pointed out their implications.

The various contributors to the knowledge base do not completely agree about the essential components of explicit teaching, and they refer to it by different names, such as process–product, direct, active, and effective teaching. The researchers weigh their own results heavily, but Rosenshine, a longstanding and comprehensive reviewer, has taken an eagle's-eye view of the results.[8]

In his early reviews of the correlational studies, Rosenshine discussed the traits of effective teachers, including clarity, task orientation, enthusiasm, and flexibility, as well as their tendency to structure their presentations and occasionally to use student ideas. From later observational and control-group research, Rosenshine identified six phased functions of explicit teaching: (1) daily review, checking of homework, and reteaching if necessary; (2) rapid presentation of new content and skills in small steps; (3) guided student practice with close monitoring by teachers; (4) corrective feedback and instructional reinforcement; (5) independent practice in seatwork and homework, with a success rate of more than 90 percent; and (6) weekly and monthly review.

Comprehension Teaching

The heirs of Aristotle and of the Anglo-American tradition of Bacon, Locke, Thorndike, and Skinner objected to philosophical "armchair" opinions; mid-century behaviorists, particularly John Watson, constructively insisted on hard empirical data about learning. But they also saw the child's mind as a blank tablet and seemed to encourage active teaching and passive acquisition of isolated facts. Reacting to such atomism and to William James' "bucket" metaphor, cognitive psychologists in the early 1980s revived research on student-centered learning and "higher mental processes," in the tradition of Plato, Socrates, Kant, Rousseau, Dewey, Freud, and Piaget. In American hands, however, this European tradition has sometimes led to vacuity and permissiveness, as in the extremes of the "progressive education" movement of the 1930s.

Oddly, the Russian psychologist Lev Vygotsky hit on an influential compromise: emphasizing the two-way nature of teaching, he identified a "zone of proximal development," which extends from what learners can do independently to the maximum that they can do with the teacher's help.[9] Accordingly, teachers should set up "scaffolding" for building knowledge and then remove it when it becomes unnecessary. In mathematics, for example, the teacher can give prompts and examples, foster independent use, and then withdraw support. This approach is similar to the "prompting" and "fading" of the behavioral cues, and it seems commonsensical. It has revived interest in granting some autonomy to students.

During the 1980s, cognitive research on teaching sought ways to encourage self-monitoring, self-teaching, or "metacognition" to foster independence. Skills were seen as important, but the learner's monitoring and management of them had priority, as though the explicit teaching functions of planning, allocating time, and reviewing were partly transferred to the learner.

For example, David Pearson outlined three phases: (1) modeling, in which the teacher exhibits the desired behavior; (2) guided practice, in which students perform with help from the teacher; and (3) application, in which students perform independently of the teacher—steps that correspond to explicit teaching functions. Anne Marie Palincsar and Anne Brown described a program of "reciprocal teaching" that fosters comprehension by having students take turns in leading dialogues on pertinent features of a text. By assuming the kind of planning and executive control ordinarily exercised by teachers, students learn planning, structuring, and self-management. Perhaps that is why, tutors learn from teaching and why we say that to learn something well, one should teach it.

Comprehension teaching encourages students to measure their progress toward explicit goals. If necessary, they can reallocate their time to different activities. In this way, self-awareness, personal control, and positive self-evaluation can be increased.[10]

LEARNER AUTONOMY IN SCIENCE

The National Science Foundation sponsored many studies of student inquiry and autonomy that showed that giving students opportunities to manipulate science materials, to contract with teachers about what to learn, to inquire on their own, and to engage in activity-based curricula all had substantial positive effects. Group- and self-direction, however, had smaller positive effects, and pass/fail and self-grading had small negative effects. Methods of providing greater learner autonomy may also work well in subjects other than science, as in the more radical approach that I discuss next.

OPEN EDUCATION

In the late 1960s, open educators expanded autonomy in the primary grades by enabling students to join teachers in planning educational purposes, means, and evaluation. In contrast to teacher- and textbook-centered education, open education gave students a voice in deciding what to learn—even to the point of writing their own texts to share with one another. Open educators tried to foster cooperation, critical thinking, constructive attitudes, and self-directed lifelong learning. They revived the spirit of the New England town meeting, Thoreau's self-reliance, Emerson's transcendentalism, and Dewey's progressivism. Their ideas also resonate with the "client-centered" psychotherapy of Carl Rogers, which emphasizes the "unconditional worth" of the person.

Rose Giaconia and Larry Hedges' synthesis of 153 studies showed that open education had worthwhile effects on creativity, independence, cooperation, attitudes toward teachers and schools, mental ability, psychological adjustment, and curiosity. Students in open programs had less motivation for grade grubbing, but they differed little from other students in actual achievement, self-concept, and anxiety.

However, Giaconia and Hedges also found that the open programs that were more effective in producing the positive outcomes with regard to attitudes, creativity, and self-concept sacrificed some academic achievement on standardized tests. These programs emphasized the role of the child in learning and the use of individualized instruction, manipulative materials, and diagnostic rather than norm-referenced evaluation. However, they did not include three other components thought by some to be essential to open programs: multi-age grouping, open space, and team teaching.

Giaconia and Hedges speculated that children in the most extreme open programs may do somewhat less well on conventional achievement tests because they have little experience with them. At any rate, it appears that open classrooms enhance several nonstandard outcomes without detracting from academic achievement unless they are radically extreme.[11]

INSTRUCTIONAL SYSTEMS

All the techniques discussed thus far can be planned and executed by a single teacher. They may entail some extra effort, encouragement, or training, but they do not call for unusual preparation or materials. In contrast, instructional systems require special arrangements and planning, and they often combine several components of instruction. Moreover, they tend to emphasize the adaptation of instruction to individual students rather than the adaptation of students to a fixed pattern of teaching. A little history will aid our understanding of current instructional systems.

Programmed Instruction

Developed in the 1950s, programmed instruction presents a series of "frames," each one of which conveys an item of information and requires a student response. *Linear programs* present a graduated series of frames that require such small increments in knowledge that learning steps may be nearly errorless and may be continuously reinforced by progression to the next frame. Able students proceed quickly under these conditions.

Branched programs direct students back for reteaching when necessary, to the side for correctives, and ahead when they already know parts of the material. The ideas of continuous progress and branching influenced later developers, who tried to optimize learning by individualization, mastery learning, and adaptive instruction.

Individualization adapts instruction to individual needs by applying variations in speed or branching and by using booklets, worksheets, coaching, and the like. Perhaps because they have been vaguely defined and poorly operationalized, individualized programs have had small effects. Other systems (discussed below) appear more effective for adapting instruction to the needs of individual learners.

Mastery Learning

Combining the psychological elements of instruction with suitable amounts of time, mastery learning employs formative tests to allocate time and to guide reinforcement and corrective feedback. In the most definitive synthesis of research on mastery learning, James Kulik and Chen-Lin Kulik reported substantial positive effects. Mastery programs that yielded larger effects established a criterion of 95 percent to 100 percent mastery and required repeated testing to mastery before allowing students to proceed to additional units (which yielded gigantic effects of one standard deviation). Mastery learning yielded larger effects with less-able students and reduced the difference between their performance and that of abler groups.

The success of mastery learning is attributable to several factors. The Kuliks, for example, found that when control groups were provided feedback from quizzes, the mastery groups' advantage was smaller. As Bloom pointed out, mastery learning takes additional time; the Kuliks found that mastery learning required a median of 16 percent (and up to 97 percent) more time than conventional instruction. The seven studies that provided equal time for mastery and control groups showed only a small advantage for mastery learning on standardized tests. However, the advantage was moderate on experimenter-made, criterion-referenced tests for nine equal-time studies. These results illustrate the separate contributions to mastery learning of cuing, feedback, and time.

Mastery learning yielded larger effects in studies of less than a month's duration than in those lasting more than four months. Retention probably declines sharply no matter what the educational method, but the decline can be more confidently noted with regard to mastery learning since it has been more extensively studied than other methods.

Bloom and his students have reported larger effects than has Robert Slavin, who reviewed their work. Thomas Guskey and S. L. Gates, for example, reported an average effect size of .78 estimated from 38 studies of elementary and secondary students. In response to Slavin, Lorin Anderson and Robert Burns pointed out two reasons for larger effects in some studies, especially those under Bloom's supervision. Bloom has been more interested in what is possible than in what is likely; he has sought to find the limits of learning. His students, moreover, have conducted tightly controlled experiments over time periods of less than a semester or less than a year.[12]

Adaptive Instruction

Developed by Margaret Wang and others, adaptive instruction combines elements of mastery learning, cooperative learning, open education, tutoring, computer-assisted instruction, and comprehension teaching into a complex system whose aim is to tailor instruction to the needs of individuals and small groups. Managerial functions—including such activities as planning, allocating time, delegating tasks to aides and students, and quality control—are carried out by a master teacher. Adaptive instruction is a comprehensive program for the whole school day rather than a single method that requires simple integration into one subject or into a single teacher's repertoire. Its effects on achievement are substantial, but its broader effects are probably underestimated, since adaptive instruction aims at diverse ends—including student autonomy, intrinsic motivation, and teacher and student choice—which are poorly reflected by the usual outcome measures.

COMPUTER-ASSISTED INSTRUCTION

Ours is an electronic age, and computers have already had a substantial impact on learning. With the costs of hardware declining and with software becoming increasingly sophisticated, we may hope for still greater effects as computers are better integrated into school programs.

Computers show the greatest advantage for handicapped students—probably because they are more adaptive to their special needs than teachers might be. Computers may also be more patient, discreet, nonjudgmental, or even encouraging about progress. Perhaps for the same reasons, computers generally have bigger effects in elementary schools than in high schools or colleges.

Another explanation for the disparate results is also plausible. Elementary schools provide less tracking and fewer differentiated courses for homogeneous groups. Computers may be better adapted to larger within-class differences among elementary students because they allow them to proceed at their own pace without engaging in invidious comparisons.

Simulations and games, with or without computer implementation, require active, specific responses from learners and may strike a balance between vicarious book learning and the dynamic, complicated, and competitive "real world." The interactiveness, speed, intensity, movement, color, and sound of computers add interest and information to academic learning. Unless geared to educational purposes, however, computer games can also waste time.

STUDENT GROUPING

Teaching students what they already know and teaching them what they are yet incapable of learning are equally wasteful practices and may even be harmful to motivation. For this reason, traditional whole-class teaching of heterogeneous groups can present serious difficulties—a problem that is often unacknowledged in our egalitarian age. Outside of universities, however, most educators recognize that it is difficult to teach arithmetic and trigonometry at the same time. (Even some English professors might balk at teaching phonics and deconstructionism simultaneously.) If we want to teach students as much as possible rather than to make them all alike, we need to consider how they are grouped and try to help the full range of students.

Acceleration

Accelerated programs identify talented youth (often in mathematics and science) and group them together or with older students. Such programs provide counseling, encouragement, contact with accomplished adults, grade skipping, summer school, and the compression of the standard curriculum into fewer years. The effects are huge in elementary schools, substantial in junior high schools, and moderate in senior high schools. The smaller effects at more advanced levels may be attributable to the smaller advantage of acceleration over the tracking and differentiated course selection practiced in high schools.

The effects of acceleration on educational attitudes, vocational plans, participation in school activities, popularity, psychological adjustment, and character ratings have been mixed and often insignificant. These outcomes may not be systematically affected in either direction.

Ability Grouping

Students are placed in ability groups according to achievement, intelligence test scores, personal insights, and subjective opinions. In high school, ability grouping leaves deficient and average students unaffected, but it has beneficial effects on talented students and on attitudes toward the subject matter. In elementary school, the grouping of students with similar reading achievement but from different grades yields substantial effects. Within-class grouping in mathematics yields worthwhile effects, but generalized ability grouping does not.

Tutoring

Because it gears instruction to individual or small-group needs, tutoring is highly beneficial to both tutors and tutees. It yields particularly large effects in mathematics—perhaps because of the subject's well-defined scope and organization.

In whole-group instruction, teachers may ordinarily focus on average or deficient students to ensure that they master the lessons. When talented students are freed from repetition and slow progression, they can proceed quickly. Grouping may work best when students are accurately grouped according to their specific subject-matter needs rather than according to I.Q., demeanor, or other irrelevant characteristics.

Well-defined subject matter and student grouping may be among the chief reasons why Japanese students lead the world in academic achievement: the curriculum is explicit, rigorous, and nationally uniform. In primary schools, weaker students, with maternal help, study harder and longer to keep up with these explicit requirements. Subject-matter tests are administered to screen students for "lower" and "upper" secondary schools and for universities of various gradations of rigor and prestige. Each such screening determines occupational, marital, and other adult prospects; long-term adult rewards thus reinforce educational effort.[13]

SOCIAL ENVIRONMENT

Cooperative learning programs delegate some control of the pacing and methods of learning to groups of between two and six students, who work together and sometimes compete with other groups within classes. Such programs are successful for several reasons. They provide relief from the excessive teacher/student interaction of whole-group teaching, they free time for the interactive engagement of students, and they present opportunities for targeted cues, engagement, correctives, and reinforcement. As in comprehension teaching, the acts of tutoring and teaching may encourage students to think for themselves about the organization of subject matter and the productive allocation of time.

Many correlational studies suggest that *classroom morale* is associated with achievement gains, with greater interest in subject matter, and with the worthy outcome of voluntary participation in nonrequired subject-related activities. Morale is assessed by asking students to agree or disagree with such statements as "Most of the students know one another well" and "The class members know the purpose of the lessons."

Students who perceive the atmosphere as friendly, satisfying, focused on goals, and challenging and who feel that the classroom has the required materials tend to learn more. Those who perceive the atmosphere as fostering student cliques, disorganization, apathy, favoritism, and friction learn less. The research on morale, though plausible, lacks the specificity and causal confidence of the controlled experiments on directly alterable methods.

READING EFFECTS

Comprehension teaching, because it may extend to several subjects in elementary school, has already been discussed as a pattern of teaching. Several other methods have substantial effects on reading achievement.

Adaptive speed training involves principles that are similar to those of comprehension training. Students learn to vary their pace and the depth of their reflection according to the difficulty of the material and their reading purposes.

Reading methods vary widely, but their largest effects seem to occur when teachers are systematically trained, almost irrespective of particularities of method. Phonics or "word-attack" approaches, however, have a moderate advantage over guessing and "whole-word" approaches in the teaching of beginning reading—perhaps because early misconceptions are avoided. Phonics may also reduce the need for excessive reteaching and correctives.

Pictures in the text can be very helpful, although they add to the cost of a book and occupy space that could otherwise be used for prose. In order of their effectiveness, several types of pictures can be distinguished. Transformative pictures recode information into concrete and memorable form, relate information in a well-organized context, and provide links for systematic retrieval. Interpretive pictures, like advance organizers, make the text comprehensible by relating abstract terms to concrete ones and by connecting the unfamiliar and difficult to previously acquired knowledge. Organizational pictures, including maps and diagrams, show the coherence of objects or events in space and time. Representational pictures are photos or other concrete representations of what is discussed in the text. Decorative pictures present (possibly irrelevant or conflicting) information that is incidental to intended learning (although decoration may add interest if not information).

Pictures can provide vivid imagery and metaphors that facilitate memory, show what is important to learn, and intensify the effects of prose. Pictures may sometimes allow students to bypass the text, but memorable, well-written prose may obviate pictures.[14]

WRITING EFFECTS

Sixty well-designed studies of methods of teaching writing compared 72 experimental groups with control groups. The methods below are presented in the order of their effectiveness.

The *inquiry method* requires students to find and state specific details that convey personal experience vividly, to examine sets of data to develop and support explanatory generalizations, or to analyze situations that present ethical problems and arguments.

Scales are criteria or specific questions that students can apply to their own and others' writing to improve it.

Sentence combining shows students how to build complex sentences from simpler ones.

Models are presentations of good pieces of writing to serve as exemplars for students.

Free writing allows students to write about whatever occurs to them.

Grammar and mechanics include sentence parsing and the analysis of parts of speech.

SCIENCE EFFECTS

Introduced in response to the launch of *Sputnik I*, the "new" science curricula, sponsored by the National Science Foundation, yielded substantial effects on learning. They efficiently added value by producing superior learning on tests of their intended outcomes and on tests of general subject-matter goals. The new curricula also yielded effects ranging from small to substantial on such often-unmeasured outcomes as creativity, problem solving, scientific attitudes and skills, logical thinking, and achievement in nonscience subject matter.

Perhaps these advantages are attributable to the combined efforts of teachers, psychologists, and scientists, who collaborated to ensure that the curricula would be based on modern content and would foster effective teaching practices. The scientists may have been able to generate enthusiasm for teaching scientific methods, for laboratory work, and for other reforms.

The new science curricula worked well in improving achievement and other outcomes. Ironically, they are often forgotten today, despite the fact that, by international standards, U.S. students score poorly in mathematics and science.

Inquiry Teaching. Often practiced in Japan, this method requires students to formulate hypotheses, reason about their credibility, and design experiments to test their validity. Inquiry teaching yields substantial effects, particularly on the understanding of scientific processes.

Audiotutorials. These are tape-recorded instructions for using laboratory equipment, manipulatives, and readings for topical lessons or whole courses. This simple approach yields somewhat better results than conventional instruction, allows independent learning, and has the further advantage of individual pacing—allowing students to pursue special topics or to take courses on their own.

Original Source Papers. This method derives from the Great Books approach of the late Robert Maynard Hutchins, former president of the University of Chicago, and his colleague Mortimer Adler. They saw more value in reading Plato or Newton than in resorting to predigested textbook accounts. The use of original sources in teaching trades breadth for depth in the belief that it is better to know a few ideas of transcending importance than to learn many unconnected bits of soon-forgotten information. Advocates of this approach have shown that such knowledge can be acquired by studying and discussing original scientific papers of historical or scientific significance.

Other methods of teaching science have effects that are near zero—that is, close to the effects of traditional methods of teaching. They include team teaching, departmentalized elementary programs, and media-based instruction. The equal results for media methods, however, suggest that choices can be based on cost and convenience. Since television programs and films can be broadcast, they can provide equally effective education in different and widespread locations (even in different parts of the world by satellite). Moreover, students today can interact online with teachers and fellow students who are far away.

There are some successful precedents for the use of media-based instruction. For a decade, the Chicago community colleges provided dozens of mainly one-way television courses to hundreds of thousands of students, who did most of their studying at home but participated in discussion and testing sessions at several sites in the metropolitan area. The best lecturers, media specialists, and test constructors could be employed, and tapes of the courses could be rebroadcast repeatedly.

In several Third World countries that are gaining in achievement and school enrollments, ministries of education make efficient and successful use of such low-cost, effective "distance education" for remote elementary and secondary schools.

The Oklahoma and Minnesota state departments of education apparently lead the nation in providing small high schools in rural areas with specialized television teachers and interactive courses in advanced science, mathematics, foreign language, and other subjects.

MATHEMATICS EFFECTS

In the heyday of its Education Directorate, the National Science Foundation sponsored considerable research not only on science but also on mathematics. Some worthwhile effects were found.

Manipulative Materials

The use of Cuisenaire rods, balance beams, counting sticks, and measuring scales allows students to engage directly in learning instead of passively following abstract presentations by the teacher. Students can handle the materials, see the relation of abstract ideas and concrete embodiments, and check hypothesized answers by quick empirical testing without having to wait for quiz results or feedback from the teacher. This method apparently results in enormous effects.

Problem Solving

In mathematics teaching, a focus on problem solving yields worthwhile effects. Such an approach requires comprehension of terms and their application to varied examples. It may motivate students by showing them the application of mathematical ideas to "real-world" questions.

New Math

The so-called new math produced beneficial results, although it was not as successful as the new science curricula. Both reforms probably gained their learning advantages partly by testing what they taught.

SPECIAL POPULATIONS AND TECHNIQUES

We can also gain insights from programs that lie outside the usual scope of elementary and secondary classrooms.

Early Intervention

Programs of early intervention include educational, psychological, and therapeutic components for handicapped, at-risk, and disadvantaged children from the ages of one month to 5½ years. Studies of these programs found that the large, immediate effects of these programs declined rapidly and disappeared after three years.

Preschool Programs

Preschool programs also showed initial learning effects that were not sustained. It appears that young children can learn more than is normally assumed, but, like other learners, they can also forget. The key to sustained gains may be sustained programs and effective families—not one-shot approaches.

Programs for the Handicapped

Students classified as mentally retarded, emotionally disturbed, or learning disabled have been subjects in research that has several important implications. When they serve as tutors of one another and of younger students, handicapped students can learn well—a finding similar to those in comprehension-monitoring and tutoring studies of nonhandicapped children. Moreover, handicapped students are often spuriously classified, and we may underestimate their capacities.

Mainstreaming

Studies show that mildly to moderately handicapped students can prosper in regular classes and thereby avoid the invidious "labeling" that is often based on misclassification.

Psycholinguistic Training

Providing psycholinguistic training to special needs students yields positive effects. This approach consists of testing and remedying specific deficits in language skills.

Patient Education

Educating patients about diseases and treatments can affect mortality, morbidity, and lengths of illness and hospitalization. In studies of the acquisition of knowledge regarding drug usage for hypertension, diabetes, and other chronic conditions, one-to-one and group counseling (with or without instructional material) produced greater effects than providing instruction through labels on bottles or package inserts for patients.

Labels, special containers, memory aids, and behavior modification were successful in minimizing later errors in drug usage. The most efficacious educational principles were specification of intentions, relevance to the needs of the learner, provision of personal answers to questions, reinforcement and feedback on progress, facilitation of correct dosage (e.g., the use of unit-dose containers), and instructional and treatment regimens suited to personal convenience (e.g., prescribing drugs for administration at mealtimes).

In-Service Training of Physicians

Such training shows large effects on doctors' knowledge and on their classroom or laboratory performance but only moderate effects on the outcomes of treating actual patients. Knowledge and performance, even in practical training, may help, but they hardly guarantee successful application in practice. Can an accomplished mathematician handle the intricacies of federal income tax?

Panaceas and Shortcuts

At the request of the U.S. Army, the National Academy of Sciences evaluated exotic techniques for enhancing learning and performance that are described in popular psychology (and presumably are being exploited in California and Russia).[15] However, little or no evidence was found for the efficacy of learning during sleep; for mental practice of motor skills; for "integration" of left and right hemispheres of the brain; for parapsychological techniques; for biofeedback; for extrasensory perception, mental telepathy, and "mind over matter" exercises; or for "neurolinguistic programming," in which instructors identify the students' modes of learning and mimic the students' behaviors as they teach.

The Greeks found no royal road to geometry; even kings, if they desired mastery, had to sweat over Euclid's elements. Perhaps brain research will eventually yield a magic elixir or a panacea, but for proof of its existence educators should insist on hard data in refereed scientific journals.

EFFECTS ON TEACHERS

Programs to help teachers in their work have had substantial effects—notwithstanding complaints about typical in-service training sessions. Do physicians complain about the medical care they get?

Microteaching

Developed at Stanford University in the 1960s, microteaching is a behavioral approach for pre-service and in-service training that has substantial effects. It employs the explanation and modeling of selected teaching techniques; televised practice with small groups of students; discussion, correctives, and reinforcement while watching playback; and recycling through subsequent practice and playback sessions with new groups of students.

In-Service Education

In-service training for teachers also proves to have substantial effects. Somewhat like the case of in-service training of physicians, the biggest effects are on the teacher's knowledge, but effects on classroom behavior and student achievement are also notable.

For in-service training, authoritative planning and execution seem to work best; informal coaching by itself seems ineffective. Allowing the instructor to be responsible for the design and teaching of the sessions works better than relying on presentations by teachers and group discussions. The best techniques are observation and classroom practices, video/audio feedback, and practice.

The most effective training combines lectures, modeling, practice, and coaching. The size of the training group, ranging from one to more than 60, makes no detectable difference.

Some apparent effects may be attributable to the selectivity of the program rather than to its superior efficacy. For example, federal-, state-, and university-sponsored programs appear more effective than locally initiated programs. Competitive selection of participants and the granting of college credit apparently work better as incentives than extra pay, renewal of certification, or no incentives. Independent study seems to have larger effects than workshops, courses, minicourses, and institutes.

CONCLUSION

Psychological research provides first-order estimates of the effects of instructional means on educational ends under various conditions. But some instructional practices may be costly—not in terms of dollars but in terms of new or complicated arrangements that may be difficult for some teachers and districts to adopt. Thus estimates of effects are only one basis for decision making. We need to consider the productivity or value of effects in relation to total costs, including the time and energies of educators and students.

Knowledge from the field of psychology alone is not sufficient to prescribe practices, since different means bring about different ends. Educators must decide whether the learning effort is to be directed by teachers, by students, or by the curriculum. They must choose among a range of facts and concepts, breadth and depth, short- and long-term ends, academic knowledge and knowledge that has direct application in the real world, equal opportunity and equal results. They must decide which aspect of Plato's triumvirate of thinking, feeling, and acting will take precedence. Once these choices are made, educators can turn to the researchers' estimates of effects as one basis for determining the most productive practices.

ENDNOTES

1. Herbert J. Walberg, Diane Schiller, and Geneva D. Haertel, "The Quiet Revolution in Educational Research," *Phi Delta Kappan*, November 1979, pp. 179–183; Herbert J. Walberg, "Improving the Productivity of America's Schools," *Educational Leadership*, vol. 41, 1984, pp. 19–27; and Barry J. Fraser, Herbert J. Walberg, Wayne W. Welch, and John A. Hattie, "Syntheses of Educational Productivity Research," *International Journal of Educational Research*, vol. 11, 1987, pp. 73–145.
2. Neal Miller and John Dollard, *Social Learning and Imitation* (New Haven, CT: Yale University Press, 1941); and John Dollard and Neal Miller, *Personality and Psychotherapy* (New York: McGraw-Hill, 1950).
3. Eric A. Hanushek, "Throwing Money at Schools," *Journal of Policy Analysis and Management*, vol. 1, 1981, pp. 19–41; and Herbert J. Walberg and William F. Fowler, "Expenditure and Size Efficiencies of Public School Districts," *Educational Researcher*, vol. 16, 1987, pp. 515–526.
4. Benjamin S. Bloom, *Human Characteristics and School Learning* (New York: McGraw-Hill, 1976); and John B. Carroll, "A Model of School Learning," *Teachers College Record*, vol. 64, 1963, pp. 723–733.
5. The effects are expressed as differences between experimental and control groups in units of standard deviations. For further details and references, see my chapter in Merlin C. Wittrock, ed., *Handbook of Research on Teaching* (New York: Macmillan, 1986).
6. Margo A. Mastropieri and Thomas E. Scruggs, *Effective Instruction for Special Education* (Boston: Little, Brown, 1987).
7. John Hoetker and William P. Ahlbrand, "The Persistence of the Recitation," *American Educational Research Journal*, vol. 6, 1969, pp. 145–167.
8. For a full account of most views, see Penelope L. Peterson and Herbert J. Walberg, eds., *Research on Teaching* (Berkeley, CA: McCutchan, 1979); and Wittrock, op. cit.
9. Lev Vygotsky, *Mind in Society* (Cambridge, MA: Harvard University Press, 1978).

10. Anne Marie Palincsar and Anne Brown, "Reciprocal Teaching of Comprehension-Fostering and Comprehension-Monitoring Activities," *Cognition and Instruction*, vol. 1, 1984, pp. 117–176; David Pearson, "Reading Comprehension Instruction: Six Necessary Steps," *Reading Teacher*, vol. 38, 1985, pp. 724–738; and Paul R. Pintrich et al., "Instructional Psychology," *Annual Review of Psychology*, vol. 37, 1986, pp. 611–651.

11. Rose M. Giaconia and Larry V. Hedges, "Identifying Features on Effective Open Education," *Review of Educational Research*, vol. 52, 1982, pp. 579–602.

12. James A. Kulik and Chen-Lin Kulik, "Mastery Testing and Student Learning," *Journal of Educational Technology Systems*, vol. 15, 1986, pp. 325–345; Lorin W. Anderson and Robert B. Burns, "Values, Evidence, and Mastery Learning," *Review of Educational Research*, vol. 57, 1988, pp. 215–223; Thomas R. Guskey and S. L. Gates, "Synthesis of Research on the Effects of Mastery Learning in Elementary and Secondary Classrooms," *Educational Leadership*, May 1986, pp. 73–80; and Robert E. Slavin, "Mastery Learning Reconsidered," *Review of Educational Research*, vol. 57, 1988, pp. 175–213.

13. Herbert J. Walberg, "What Can We Learn from Japanese Education?," *The World and I*, March 1988, pp. 661–665.

14. Joel R. Levin, Gary J. Anglin, and Russell N. Carney, "On Empirically Validating Functions of Pictures in Prose," in D. M. Willows and H. A. Houghton, eds., *The Psychology of Illustration* (New York: Springer-Verlag, 1987).

15. Daniel Druckman and John A. Swets, eds., *Enhancing Human Performance* (Washington, DC: National Academy Press, 1988).

DISCUSSION QUESTIONS

1. How can teachers use or improve cues, engagement, correctives, and reinforcement to facilitate student achievement?
2. How do explicit teaching and comprehension teaching differ in terms of methods and elements?
3. Consider the advantages and disadvantages of open education. Is open education appropriate for all educational settings and students? Why? Why not?
4. How can knowledge from the field of psychology be used to guide curriculum development?
5. In what ways have programs and techniques developed for special populations influenced elementary and secondary curriculum development?

CHAPTER 10

Honoring Diverse Styles of Beginning Teachers

EDWARD F. PAJAK
ELAINE STOTKO
FRANK MASCI

FOCUSING QUESTIONS

1. How would you describe a teacher's style of teaching?
2. How does teacher style differ from teacher characteristics? Teacher behavior? Teacher effectiveness?
3. How is a teacher's style influenced by his or her educational philosophy?
4. How would you describe a teacher's cycle of learning?
5. How does a teacher's professional learning differ from problem solving? Critical thinking? Transfer of learning?
6. What kind of supervisor would you prefer to have observing and mentoring your teaching?

Schools today face the responsibility of guaranteeing high-quality instruction for every student, while simultaneously having to recruit and retain unprecedented numbers of new and second-career teachers. This dual challenge is achievable, we believe, only by supporting teachers in ways that are compatible with how they most naturally learn and teach. In other words, those educators who provide support to new teachers should strive to work with them in the same way that teachers are expected to work with students—by recognizing and celebrating a diversity of styles and responding to differences in ways that enhance learning for everyone.

The standards movement in education has set for itself the admirable goal of high expectations for all students. Because students differ in their styles of learning, experienced teachers recognize the importance of providing alternative paths for achieving these agreed-upon outcomes. Similarly, the time has come for us to realize that new teachers do not all learn or teach the same way. Talk to several new teachers about why they are teachers, what teaching means to them, how they know when they are successful, and what gives them the most satisfaction, and you'll discover that some teachers place great emphasis on imparting knowledge to students, while others stress the importance of helping students discover knowledge for themselves. Some teachers believe in getting actively involved in their students' lives, while others prefer to maintain a more distanced professional relationship. Some teachers dedicate themselves to social change and justice for all students, while others concentrate their efforts on individual students who show promise of becoming leaders of their generation.

These different perspectives of teaching reflect various experiences or styles of teaching—inventing, knowing, caring, and inspiring—that highlight differences in how individuals perceive and process information (Pajak, 2003). When *inventing* teachers talk about teaching, for example, they tend to emphasize the importance of "having students solve problems" and of "seeing students apply their learning to real situations." *Knowing* teachers are more likely to focus on "helping kids learn content" and to believe they are successful when they "see students mastering the subject matter." *Caring* teachers often say that "providing opportunities for student growth" is most important, and they define success in terms of "building a classroom community." Finally, *inspiring* teachers tend to view teaching as "an opportunity to shape the future" and derive satisfaction from "seeing students make independent decisions."

These four ways of experiencing teaching are clearly evident in the literature on education. The *inventing* perspective is expressed, for example, in the scholarship of Jean Piaget and Hilda Taba; advocacy for the *knowing* viewpoint may be found in the writings of Benjamin Bloom and Mortimer Adler; the importance of the *caring* attitude is explained to us by Nel Noddings and Parker Palmer; and the *inspiring* stance is articulated in the work of Paulo Freire and Maxine Greene. The four styles can also be seen in depictions of teachers in popular culture. Jaime Escalante, in the movie *Stand and Deliver,* is an example of an *inventing* teacher. Marva Collins in the made-for-TV movie *The Marva Collins Story,* represents a *knowing* teacher. Roberta Guaspari, in the film *Music of the Heart,* depicts a *caring* teacher, and LouAnne Johnson, in *Dangerous Minds,* an *inspiring* teacher.

A TEACHER-PROOF TEACHER?

Why do different teacher styles matter? Forty or more years ago, during the Cold War and post-Sputnik era, some experts in education tried to develop what has been termed the "teacher-proof curriculum," in the belief that if instruction and curriculum were controlled to a sufficient degree, teachers would be forced into teaching only what was prescribed by the experts. Today, we fear, the inflexible enforcement of standards for teaching is moving us toward a "teacher-proof teacher," one who is standardized to the point of being unable to think independently or to act on personal convictions. Yet, we know from the study of teaching styles that real teachers are more complex, as the following vignettes demonstrate.

Inventing

Students in Ken Garry's eleventh-grade world history class have come to expect the unexpected. Still, on one memorable day at the beginning of the Russian history unit, even they were surprised to see a somewhat disheveled, unshaven Mr. Garry enter the room. They were certainly not prepared for what happened next. He took out a razor and began to shave. Then he posed a series of questions, beginning with "What did my shaving have to do with an event in Russian history?" A very lively discussion ensued around the fact that Peter the Great, in one of his efforts to westernize the country, ordered his nobles, the Boyars, to shave off their flowing beards. The students were likely not only to remember this event but, as a result of the discussion, to place it within the larger context of the modernization of Russia.

Knowing

To an observer entering Pam Gilbert's twelfth-grade English classroom, it is immediately apparent that each student has a clear idea of her expectations. Daily objectives are posted; each student is given a detailed agenda of what is to be covered during the lesson; and posters that describe rules, submission requirements for papers, and assignment deadlines are prominent throughout the room. Ms. Gilbert's lesson plans reveal that instruction is largely teacher-directed and focused on the learning of factual information and key concepts. Group work is also part of her instructional strategy; she typically assigns students to groups, giving each student a specific responsibility within the group. The classroom climate is one of efficiency and purpose.

Caring

Gloria Silverman loves children, and her eighth-grade mathematics students, if pressed, would admit to affection for her as well. They would cite her keen interest in their lives, her close contact with their parents (they might even give grudging appreciation for this), and her willingness to "go the extra mile" to help them understand the sometimes bewildering intricacies of the rudiments of algebra. Surprisingly large numbers of students attend her daily lunchtime help sessions and are grateful for her tenacious insistence on learning the subject matter, always couched in an almost parental concern for their well-being.

Inspiring

Second graders, at the very beginning of their educational experience, certainly represent a wealth of untapped possibility. They are impressionable and usually very eager to please. No one realizes this more and capitalizes on it better than their teacher, Joanna Chakitis. To describe her classroom environment as a wonderland is an understatement. The walls are covered with colorful and stimulating instructional materials, stations for work on individualized assignments, and job charts for student helpers. Even the ceiling contains examples of student work. The students in Ms. Chakitis's class are the beneficiaries of exceptionally creative and innovative teaching practices that are carefully designed to promote their growth and development.

SUPPORTING NEW TEACHERS

Beginning teachers often find themselves facing expectations and advice from university supervisors, mentor teachers, peer coaches, principals, and district office supervisors. How should support systems for new teachers that are provided by universities and schools respond to these diverse teaching styles? Our fundamental principle is simple, yet powerful. Those who provide support to new teachers—mentors, peer coaches, university supervisors, and principals—should make a deliberate effort to honor and legitimate perspectives and practices that differ from their own preferred styles of perceiving and judging reality. The starting point for helping new teachers succeed, in other words, should be the development of the teacher's preferred style. Once that style has been successfully developed, of course, the teacher should be encouraged to expand his or her repertoire of strategies and perspectives.

Teaching is much more than simply a job. For a great many people, teaching is a way of living their lives. Teaching is closely connected, in other words, to how teachers view themselves as people. Indeed, what teachers do in their classrooms is tightly wrapped up with, and difficult to separate from, their very identities. Support systems and mentoring practices that conflict with the teacher's identity and core values are, at the very least, useless and, at the worst, destructive.

Although any one of the experiences of teaching—*inventing, knowing, caring, inspiring*—can be a useful guide to practice, it is only a starting point. All of these paths must be traced if a teacher is to become truly effective. Supervisors (i.e., mentors, coaches, principals) are expected to ensure that new teachers know their subject matter and can teach, but in reality the support that new teachers need is much more complicated. An effective mentor is able to support the new teacher's personal and emotional needs and to help the teacher become an inquiring professional and reflective practitioner.

Each student that a teacher meets in the classroom requires different things at different times—explanations and reliable ways of thinking, high standards and understanding, nurturing care and emotional support, inspiration and values—and a teacher ought to be able to provide them all. Similarly, those who support beginning teachers should be able to offer differentiated support as well. Unfortunately, classroom observations and evaluations in most school systems rely on instruments or standards that favor only the organized and businesslike demeanor of the knowing teacher. The innovation, creativity, and democratic goals of caring, inventing, and inspiring teachers are usually de-emphasized or even implicitly discouraged.

Adult learning theorist David Kolb (1984) identified four types of learners that roughly correspond to the teaching styles described here. Most people develop preferences for a particular style of learning, he believes, as a result of events in their lives, personality differences, environmental circumstances, and education. No one style is necessarily better or worse than another, he insists. The important thing is to recognize that differences among learners do exist. His model portrays people as dynamic learners and problem solvers who constantly respond to their environments by engaging in new experiences, reflecting on these experiences from various perspectives, creating understandings and generalizations, and applying these understandings to their lives and to their work (Sims & Sims, 1995). Bernice McCarthy (1982, 1990) has long advocated linking Kolb's work to our understanding of teaching and learning.

Integrating the wisdom of three great educators—John Dewey, Jean Piaget, and Kurt Lewin—Kolb (1984) proposes a recurring cycle of learning that includes four phases. Teacher development can be understood as a recurring cycle of growth that begins with (a) concrete experience, followed by (b) empathic reflection, (c) construction of meaning, and (d) active experimentation. As teachers progress through the learning cycle, they complement their initial teaching style with functions that have lain dormant. Integrating the styles allows them to recognize and enact a wider range of choices and decisions when facing new situations. These phases of learning are best pursued with the support of a mentor, a clinical coach, or a team of colleagues. The descriptions of the four phases of learning, which appear below, are followed by an example of a clinical coach, Ms. Jeanette Greene, engaged in the process of observing and conferring with Gloria Silverman, the caring teacher described previously.

The Phases

1. The *concrete experience* phase of learning requires the clinical coach to actively engage the teacher in problem solving. Concrete data concerning teacher and

student behavior and their relationship to curriculum, standards, objectives, methods, materials, or classroom artifacts are considered. A key question for the teacher during this phase is "How well am I really doing?"

2. During the *empathic reflection* phase of learning, the coach displays and models empathy. Multiple perspectives are considered for the purpose of gaining insight into the subjective experience of students who inhabit the teacher's classroom. A question for the teacher to answer during this phase is "What is going on here for everyone involved, both for myself and for the students?"
3. In the *construction of meaning* phase of learning, the clinical coach encourages the teacher to raise theoretical and ethical issues, form generalizations, and propose hypotheses concerning cause and effect relationships. The central question for the teacher during this phase is "What does all this mean?"
4. Finally, during the *active experimentation* phase of learning, the coach steps back and empowers the teacher to take action. What has been learned is applied to practical problems in the classroom, accompanied by the collection of new data. The question for the teacher that guides this phase of the cycle is "How can I do things better?" (Pajak, 2003)

The key to applying these phases of learning is to help teachers enter the cycle at the phase that comes most naturally to them. When working with a caring teacher, for example, the mentor or coach should pay special attention to developing trust and a positive climate that will contribute to collaboration and mutual learning. Beginning a conversation that asks a caring teacher to empathically reflect on the experience of his or her students in the classroom will both be nonthreatening and serve to engage the teacher in the learning cycle.

The Example

Jeanette Greene, as clinical coach, has done her homework. The day prior to her observation of Gloria Silverman, who exhibits a caring style of teaching, she scheduled a brief meeting for them to discuss the plan for the lesson. Having this conversation in advance demonstrates to Gloria that Jeanette respects her as a person and initiates the learning cycle by getting Gloria to focus on her teaching. The meeting also provides an opportunity for Jeanette to learn about the strategies that Gloria intends to use and how they relate to the purposes of the lesson.

The next day, Jeanette observes Gloria, recording a descriptive narrative of what is said and done by both the teacher and students, including some notes describing the feeling-tone within the classroom. Following the observation, Jeanette conducts an analysis of the data, looking for connections between observed events and student learning that will reinforce good practices, as well as patterns that relate to the interpersonal climate in the classroom. Later in the day, Jeanette meets with Gloria for the post-observation conference. For purposes of this example, we will assume that Gloria's lesson was generally positive, but there were several issues that Jeanette felt needed attention.

The first part of the conference, which corresponds to the *concrete experience* phase of learning, would be concerned chiefly with the data—in this case, a detailed discussion of the lesson that was observed. Jeanette would show Gloria the descriptive narrative she recorded along with specific events and patterns that relate to student learning and interpersonal behavior.

As Jeanette shifts to the *empathic reflection* phase, she needs to remember that caring teachers can be very sensitive and have their feelings easily hurt. While offering generous praise for positive aspects of the lesson, Jeanette should also tactfully introduce the areas of concern and even offer some concrete suggestions for Gloria to try. Since the major question of this phase is "What is going on here for everyone involved, both the teacher and the students?" Jeanette can tap into Gloria's intense concern for her students and ask how her actions directly affect them as she encourages Gloria to expand her teaching repertoire.

Jeanette can begin the *construction of meaning* phase of learning by restating the major issues and by inviting Gloria to propose some strategies for modifying her instruction that are consistent with her personal values and beliefs about teaching and learning. Either Jeanette or Gloria might also propose concepts or theoretical perspectives that place their conversation within a broader framework. Again, by keeping the focus on the enhanced learning of Gloria's students, Jeanette honors Gloria's caring style, while facilitating her movement through the adult learning cycle.

The *active experimentation* phase of learning necessitates Gloria's implementing the recommendations collaboratively developed in the post-observation conference. Gloria's major motivation to carry out the recommendations should be in response to the questions "How can I do things better?" and "How can I become a better teacher?" Jeanette will work with Gloria to determine the focus of a subsequent observation to be conducted after Gloria has had time to try out some of the strategies identified. She will then establish with Gloria an appropriate time for the subsequent observation and follow-up conference to discuss Gloria's degree of success in implementing these innovations.

The intention is to gently nudge teachers out of their comfort zones and change their behavior by exposing them to alternative learning environments during each of the four phases (Rainey & Kolb, 1995). When Jeanette works with an inspiring teacher such as Joanna Chakitis, *construction of meaning* would be the starting point for discussion. In this case, Jeanette could begin with a conversation about personal values and beliefs about teaching and its purposes, and then encourage Joanna to move along to *active experimentation* by posing hypotheses about specific relationships between her behavior and student outcomes (How can I do things better?), with an eye toward the *concrete experience* phase (How well am I really doing?), which then would lead to *empathic* reflection.

When embedded in the reality of classroom experience, alternative learning environments structured around the four phases can allow teachers to take greater responsibility for their own professional growth and gradually develop a full range of teaching styles. Teams of teachers might be organized in a school according to their style preferences, perhaps by grade level or subject area, where they read and share instructional materials to more finely hone their natural abilities. Individual teachers could rotate through different teams as they gain fluency with different styles, or entire teams could explore different learning environments together over a period of time. The purpose of such teams is not to "track" teachers, but to create within a school "a cooperative human community that cherishes and utilizes individual uniqueness" (Kolb, 1984, p. 62). An awareness and appreciation of different styles can be helpful, for example, for improving communication, resolving conflicts amicably, selecting team members, and identifying mediators and as a framework for professional development.

MATCHING MENTORS AND TEACHERS

Honoring different teaching styles is not a technique to be used from time to time, but instead an entirely new way of thinking about support. At best, we typically offer teachers a "take it or leave it" form of support, because we have a natural tendency to want teachers to teach their classes the way we would if we were the teacher. But if a beginning teacher is forced to adopt a style of thinking and teaching by someone who is unsympathetic or inflexible, the beginning teacher is likely to become frustrated and discouraged and may never attain his or her full potential.

In an ideal world, every beginning teacher would be matched with a supervisor who shared his or her style, at least initially, to enhance communication and minimize frustration. Another workable strategy, however, may be to select clinical coaches who are knowledgeable about and sensitive to different teaching styles and who are comfortable allowing new teachers to teach to their strengths, while still understanding when and how to help the new teacher move out of his or her comfort zone and into an exploration of other styles.

Rather than advocating a particular way of behaving or thinking, this new form of support facilitates learning by modeling alternative behaviors and patterns of thinking. At each phase of the learning cycle, the supervisor or mentor becomes a clinical coach who is (a) a colleague who models and supports conscious awareness of the personal experience of teaching, (b) an empathic listener and sounding board who facilitates an understanding of the effect that teaching has on students, (c) a knowledgeable resource who helps interpret subjective and objective information to arrive at moral and conceptual meaning, and (d) a coach who empowers teachers toward action planning and hypothesis testing.

Attending to teacher differences requires flexibility and an environment that includes mutual respect, safety, shared responsibility for learning, and an emphasis on personal growth. Such change requires the clinical coach to meet teachers where they are and then build on their strengths, rather than relying on a remedial mentality. At a minimum, clinical coaches should:

- Reflect on their own beliefs about learning, teaching, and support.
- Assess and reflect on the needs of the new teacher as learner.
- Be sensitive to preferences for perceiving and processing information, on the part of both the teacher and the coach.
- Develop and use a variety of communication strategies.
- Develop and use a range of supervisory approaches.
- Clarify the roles of supervisor and teacher.
- Begin building an inclusive community of learners that welcomes diverse learning styles and preferences.

It is true that schools are not structured for individualized supervision, but then neither are classrooms designed for individualized instruction. Honoring diverse teaching styles is worth the extra effort, we believe, because it gives teachers greater choice and voice, which contributes to the coherence of their individual goals for professional development, is consistent with other reforms and classroom activities with which teachers are already involved, and can help build a schoolwide learning community that respects differences.

REFERENCES

Kolb, D. A. (1984). *Experiential Learning*. Englewood Cliffs, NJ: Prentice Hall.

McCarthy, B. (1982). "Improving Staff Development through CBAM and 4MAT." *Educational Leadership*, *40*(1): 20–25.

McCarthy, B. (1990). "Using the 4MAT System to Bring Learning Styles to Schools." *Educational Leadership*, *48*(2): 31–37.

Pajak, E. (2003). *Honoring Diverse Teaching Styles: A Guide for Supervisors*. Alexandria, VA: Association for Supervision and Curriculum Development.

Rainey, M. A., & Kolb, D. A. (1995). "Using Experiential Learning Theory and Learning Styles in Diversity Education." In, R. R. Sims & S. J. Sims (Eds.), *The Importance of Learning Styles*. Westport, CT: Greenwood Press.

Sims, R. R., & Sims, S. J. (1995). *The Importance of Learning Styles*. Westport, CT: Greenwood Press.

DISCUSSION QUESTIONS

1. Which best describes your own teaching style: knowing, caring, inventing, or inspiring? Why?
2. Do you agree with the authors' assessment that certain education policies are attempting to move us toward a "teacher-proof teacher"?
3. What advantages and drawbacks exist in having a variety of teaching styles represented in a school?
4. Which of the four styles of teaching identified in this chapter is most popular today? Which is most often disregarded or overlooked?
5. When you were a beginning teacher, would a system of support that honored your preferred teaching style have been helpful to you?

CHAPTER 11

Keeping Good Teachers: Why It Matters, What Leaders Can Do

LINDA DARLING-HAMMOND

FOCUSING QUESTIONS

1. How can a comfortable learning/teaching environment be created?
2. Why is teacher attrition such a large problem?
3. How can qualified teachers be encouraged to continue teaching?
4. What types of programs may be instituted to help fight teacher attrition?
5. What are some of the reasons teachers leave the profession? Change schools?

> How teachers are paid was a part of it, but overwhelmingly the things that would destroy the morale of teachers who wanted to leave were the working conditions . . . working in poor facilities, having to pay for supplies, and so on.
>
> —A Los Angeles teacher talking about a high-turnover school

> The first-grade classroom in which I found myself five years ago had some two dozen ancient and tattered books, an incomplete curriculum, and a collection of outdated content standards. But I later came to thrive in my profession because of the preparation I received in my credential program: the practice I received developing appropriate curriculum; exposure to a wide range of learning theories; training in working with non-English-speaking students and children labeled "at risk."
>
> It is the big things, though, that continue to sustain me as a professional and give me the courage to remain and grow: my understanding of the importance of asking questions about my own practice, the collegial relationships, and my belief in my responsibility to my students and to the institution of public education.
>
> —A California teacher from a strong urban teacher education program

What keeps some people in teaching while others give up? What can we do to increase the holding power of the teaching profession and to create a stable, expert teaching force in all kinds of districts? Some of the answers to these questions are predictable; others are surprising. The way schools hire and the way they use their resources can make a major difference.

Keeping good teachers should be one of the most important agenda items for any school leader. Substantial research evidence suggests that well-prepared, capable teachers have the largest impact on student learning (see Darling-Hammond, 2000b; Wilson, Floden, & Ferrini-Mundy, 2001). Effective teachers constitute a valuable human resource for schools—one that needs to be treasured and supported.

THE CHALLENGE OF TEACHER ATTRITION

The No Child Left Behind Act's requirement that schools staff all classrooms with "highly qualified teachers" creates a major challenge, especially for schools in inner-city and poor rural areas. The problem does not lie in the numbers of teachers available; we produce many more qualified teachers than we hire. The hard part is *keeping* the teachers we prepare.

The uphill climb to staff our schools with qualified teachers becomes steeper when teachers leave in large numbers. Since the early 1990s, the annual number of exits from teaching has surpassed the number of entrants by an increasing amount (Figure 11.1), putting pressure on the nation's hiring systems. Less than 20 percent of this attrition is due to retirement (Henke, Chen, & Geis, 2000; Ingersoll, 2001).

Steep attrition in the first few years of teaching is a longstanding problem. About one-third of new teachers leave the profession within five years. Rates of attrition from individual schools and districts include these leavers, plus movers who go from one school or district to another. Taken together, leavers and movers particularly affect schools that serve poor and minority

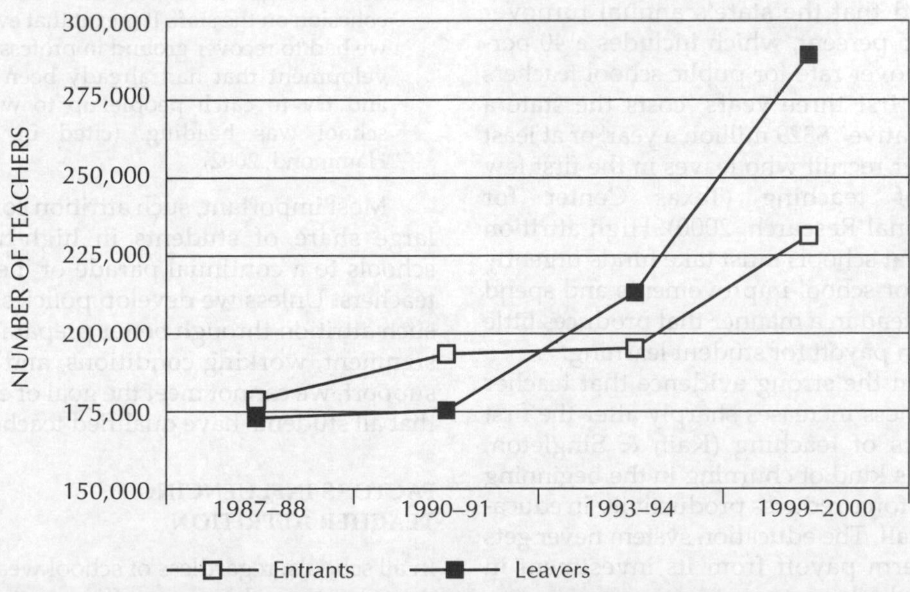

FIGURE 11.1 Trends in Teacher Entry and Attrition, 1987–2000
Source: Adapted from Ingersoll (2001).

students. Teacher turnover is 50 percent higher in high-poverty than in low-poverty schools (Ingersoll, 2001), and new teachers in urban districts exit or transfer at higher rates than their suburban counterparts do (Hanushek, Kain, & Rivkin, 1999).

High-poverty schools suffer higher rates of attrition for many reasons. Salary plays a part: Teachers in schools serving the largest concentrations of low-income students earn, at the top of the scale, one-third less than those in higher-income schools (National Center for Education Statistics [NCES], 1997). They also face fewer resources, poorer working conditions, and the stress of working with many students and families who have a wide range of needs. In addition, more teachers in these schools are underprepared and unsupported, factors that strongly influence attrition (Darling-Hammond, 2000a).

THE HEAVY COSTS OF ATTRITION

Early attrition from teaching bears enormous costs. A recent study in Texas, for example, estimated that the state's annual turnover rate of 15 percent, which includes a 40 percent turnover rate for public school teachers in their first three years, costs the state a "conservative" $329 million a year, or at least $8,000 per recruit who leaves in the first few years of teaching (Texas Center for Educational Research, 2000). High attrition means that schools must take funds urgently needed for school improvements and spend them instead in a manner that produces little long-term payoff for student learning.

Given the strong evidence that teacher effectiveness increases sharply after the first few years of teaching (Kain & Singleton, 1996), this kind of churning in the beginning teaching force reduces productivity in education overall. The education system never gets a long-term payoff from its investment in novices who leave.

In addition, large concentrations of underprepared teachers create a drain on schools' financial and human resources. In a startling number of urban schools across the United States, a large share of teachers are inexperienced, underqualified, or both. One recent estimate indicates that more than 20 percent of schools in California have more than 20 percent of their staffs teaching without credentials. These inexperienced teachers are assigned almost exclusively to low-income schools serving students of color (Shields et al., 2001).

Such schools must continually pour money into recruitment efforts and professional support for these new teachers. Other teachers, including those who serve as mentors, are stretched thin and feel overburdened by the needs of their colleagues in addition to those of their students. Schools squander scarce resources trying to reteach the basics each year to teachers who come in with few tools and leave before they become skilled (Carroll, Reichardt, & Guarino, 2000). As a principal in one such school noted,

> Having that many new teachers on the staff at any given time meant that there was less of a knowledge base. . . . It meant there was less cohesion on the staff. It meant that every year, we had to recover ground in professional development that had already been covered and try to catch people up to where the school was heading. (cited in Darling-Hammond, 2002)

Most important, such attrition consigns a large share of students in high-turnover schools to a continual parade of ineffective teachers. Unless we develop policies to stem such attrition through better preparation, assignment, working conditions, and mentor support, we cannot meet the goal of ensuring that all students have qualified teachers.

FACTORS INFLUENCING TEACHER ATTRITION

In all schools, regardless of school wealth, student demographics, or staffing patterns, the most important resource for continuing improvement is the knowledge and skill of the school's best prepared and most committed teachers. Four major factors strongly influence whether and when teachers leave specific schools or the education profession entirely: salaries, working conditions, preparation, and mentoring support in the early years.

Salaries

Even though teachers are more altruistically motivated than are some other workers, teaching must compete with other occupations for talented college and university graduates each year. To attract its share of these graduates and to offer sufficient incentives for professional preparation, the teaching profession must be competitive in terms of wages and working conditions.

Unfortunately, teacher salaries are relatively low. Overall, teacher salaries are about 20 percent below the salaries of other professionals with comparable education and training. Data from the Bureau of Labor Statistics show that in 2001, the average teacher salary ($44,040) ranked below that of registered nurses ($48,240), accountants/auditors ($50,700), dental hygienists ($56,770), and computer programmers ($71,130) (National Commission on Teaching and America's Future [NCTAF], 2003).

Teachers are more likely to quit when they work in districts that offer lower wages and when their salaries are low relative to alternative wage opportunities, especially teachers in such high-demand fields as math and science (Brewer, 1996; Mont & Rees, 1996; Murnane & Olsen, 1990; Theobald & Gritz, 1996). Salary differences seem to matter more at the start of the teaching career (Gritz & Theobald, 1996; Hanushek et al., 1999), whereas experienced teachers appear to place more importance on working conditions (Loeb & Page, 2000).

Working Conditions

Surveys of teachers have long shown that working conditions play a major role in teachers' decisions to switch schools or leave the profession. Teachers' feelings about administrative support, resources for teaching, and teacher input into decision making are strongly related to their plans to stay in teaching and to their reasons for leaving (Darling-Hammond, 2000a; Ingersoll, 2001, 2002). High- and low-wealth schools differ greatly, on average, in the support that they give teachers. Teachers in more advantaged communities experience easier working conditions, including smaller class sizes and pupil loads and greater influence over school decisions (NCES, 1997).

The high attrition of teachers from schools serving lower-income or lower-achieving students appears to be substantially influenced by the poorer working conditions typically found in those schools. For example, a survey of California teachers (Harris, 2002) found that teachers in high-minority, low-income schools report significantly worse working conditions, including poorer facilities, less access to textbooks and supplies, fewer administrative supports, and larger class sizes. Further, teachers surveyed were significantly more likely to say that they planned to leave the school soon if the working conditions were poor.

An analysis of these California data found that serious turnover problems at the school level were influenced most by working conditions, ranging from large class sizes and poor facilities to multitrack, year-round schedules and low administrative support (Loeb, Darling-Hammond, & Luczak, 2003). Together with salaries, these factors far outweighed the demographic characteristics of students in predicting turnover at the school level. This finding suggests that working conditions should be one target for policies aimed at retaining qualified teachers in high-need schools.

Teacher Preparation

A growing body of evidence indicates that teachers who lack adequate initial preparation are more likely to leave the profession. A recent National Center for Education Statistics report found that 29 percent of new teachers who had not had any student teaching experience left within five years, compared with only 15 percent of those who had done student teaching as part of a teacher education program (Henke et al., 2000). The same study found that 49 percent of uncertified entrants left within five years, compared with only 14 percent of certified entrants. In California, the state standards board found that 40 percent of emergency-permit teachers left the profession within a year, and two-thirds never received a credential (Darling-Hammond, 2002).

In Massachusetts, nearly half of all recruits from the Massachusetts Institute for New Teachers program had left within three years (Fowler, 2002), and in Houston, Texas, the attrition rate averaged 80 percent after two years for Teach for America recruits (Raymond, Fletcher, & Luque, 2001).

Other research evidence suggests that the more training prospective teachers receive, the more likely they are to stay. For example, a longitudinal study of 11 programs found that those who graduate from five-year teacher education programs enter and stay in teaching at much higher rates than do four-year teacher education graduates from the same institutions (Andrew & Schwab, 1995). These longer, redesigned programs provide a major in a disciplinary field, as well as intensive pedagogical training and long-term student teaching. As Figure 11.2 shows, both four-year and five-year teacher education graduates enter and stay in teaching positions at higher rates than do teachers hired through alternative programs that give them only a few weeks of training (Darling-Hammond, 2000a).

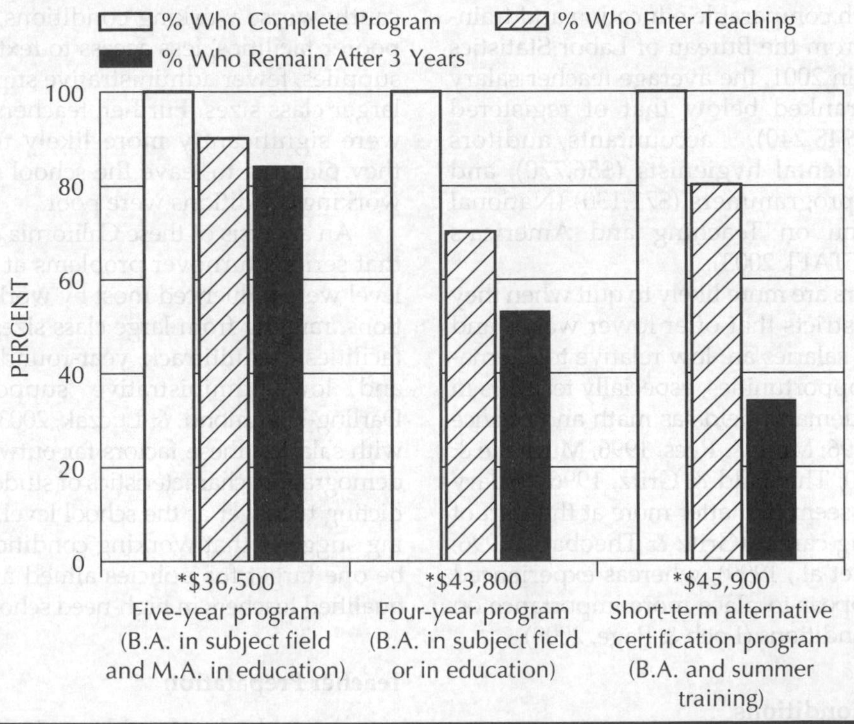

FIGURE 11.2 Average Retention Rates for Different Pathways into Teaching

*Estimated cost per third-year teacher.

Source: Darling-Hammond (2000a).

Taking into account the costs to states, universities, and school districts for preparation, recruitment, induction, and replacement due to attrition, the actual cost of preparing a career teacher in the more intensive five-year programs is actually less than the cost of preparing a greater number of teachers in short-term programs of only a few weeks' duration. Graduates of extended five-year programs also report higher levels of satisfaction with their preparation and receive higher ratings from principals and colleagues.

In 2000, new teachers who had received training in specific aspects of teaching (for example, selection and use of instructional materials, child psychology, and learning theory), who experienced practice teaching, and who received feedback on their teaching left the profession at rates one-half as great as those who had no training in these areas (NCTAF, 2003). Similarly, first-year teachers who felt that they were well prepared for teaching were much more likely to plan to stay in teaching than those who felt poorly prepared. On such items as preparation in planning lessons, using a range of instructional methods, and assessing students, two-thirds of those reporting strong preparation intended to stay, compared with only one-third of those reporting weak preparation (see Figure 11.3). In these studies and others, graduates of teacher education programs felt significantly better prepared

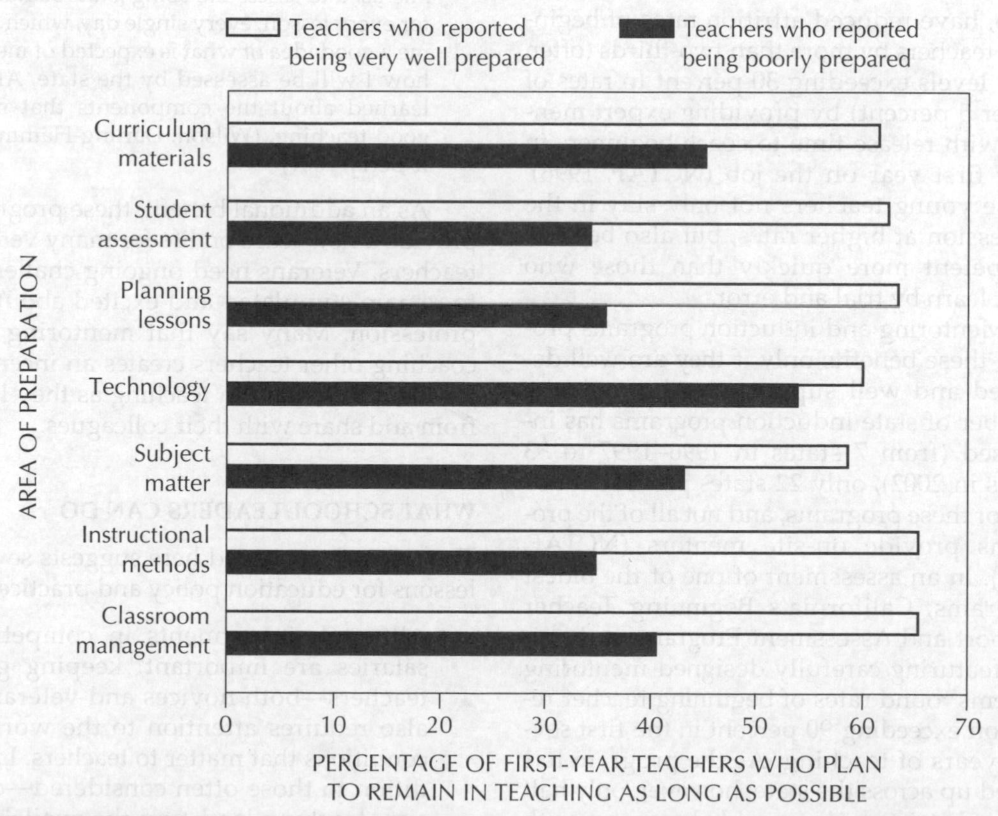

FIGURE 11.3 Effects of Preparedness on Beginning Teachers' Plans to Stay in Teaching

Source: Unpublished tabulations from Schools and Staffing Surveys, Teacher Questionnair, 1999–2000.

and more efficacious, and they planned to stay in teaching longer than did those entering through alternative routes or with no training (Darling-Hammond, Chung, & Frelow, 2002; NCTAF, 2003).

Mentoring Support

Schools can enhance the beneficial effects of strong initial preparation with strong induction and mentoring in the first years of teaching. A number of studies have found that well-designed mentoring programs raise retention rates for new teachers by improving their attitudes, feelings of efficacy, and instructional skills.

Such districts as Rochester, New York, and Cincinnati, Columbus, and Toledo, Ohio, have reduced attrition rates of beginning teachers by more than two-thirds (often from levels exceeding 30 percent to rates of under 5 percent) by providing expert mentors with release time to coach beginners in their first year on the job (NCTAF, 1996). These young teachers not only stay in the profession at higher rates, but also become competent more quickly than those who must learn by trial and error.

Mentoring and induction programs produce these benefits only if they are well designed and well supported. Although the number of state induction programs has increased (from 7 states in 1996–1997 to 33 states in 2002), only 22 states provide funding for these programs, and not all of the programs provide on-site mentors (NCTAF, 2003). In an assessment of one of the oldest programs, California's Beginning Teacher Support and Assessment Program, early pilots featuring carefully designed mentoring systems found rates of beginning teacher retention exceeding 90 percent in the first several years of teaching. As the program has scaled up across the state, however, only half of the districts have provided mentors with time to coach novices in their classrooms (Shields et al., 2001).

Most effective are state induction programs that are tied to high-quality preparation. In Connecticut, for example, districts that hire beginning teachers must provide them with mentors who have received training in the state's teaching standards and its portfolio assessment system, which were introduced as part of reforms during the 1990s. These reforms also raised salaries and standards for teachers and created an assessment of teaching for professional licensure modeled after that of the National Board for Professional Teaching Standards. A beginning teacher noted of this connected system,

> One of the things that helped me a lot is that my cooperating teacher last year is a state assessor and she used to do live assessments. . . . She used to assess me using [state standards] for every lesson, every single day, which gave me a good idea of what is expected of me and how I will be assessed by the state. Also, I learned about the components that make good teaching. (Wilson, Darling-Hammond, & Berry, 2001)

As an additional benefit, these programs provide a new lease on life for many veteran teachers. Veterans need ongoing challenges to remain stimulated and excited about the profession. Many say that mentoring and coaching other teachers creates an incentive for them to remain in teaching as they learn from and share with their colleagues.

WHAT SCHOOL LEADERS CAN DO

The research reviewed here suggests several lessons for education policy and practice:

- Although investments in competitive salaries are important, keeping good teachers—both novices and veterans—also requires attention to the working conditions that matter to teachers. In addition to those often considered—class size, teaching load, and the availability of materials—key conditions include teacher participation in decision making, strong and supportive instructional leadership from principals, and collegial learning opportunities.

- Seeking out and hiring better-prepared teachers has many payoffs and savings in the long run in terms of both lower attrition and higher levels of competence.
- When the high costs of attrition are calculated, many of the strategic investments needed to keep good teachers—such as providing mentoring for beginners and creating ongoing learning and leadership challenges for veterans—actually pay for themselves to a large degree.

School systems can create a magnetic effect when they make it clear that they are committed to finding, keeping, and supporting good teachers. In urban centers, just as in suburban and rural areas, good teachers gravitate to schools where they know they will be appreciated and supported in their work. These teachers become a magnet for others who seek environments in which they can learn from their colleagues and create success for their students. Great school leaders create nurturing school environments in which accomplished teaching can flourish and grow.

REFERENCES

Andrew, M., & Schwab, R. L. (1995). "Has Reform in Teacher Education Influenced Teacher Performance? An Outcome Assessment of Graduates of Eleven Teacher Education Programs." *Action in Teacher Education, 17:* 43–53.

Brewer, D. J. (1996). "Career Paths and Quit Decisions: Evidence from Teaching." *Journal of Labor Economics, 14(2):* 313–339.

Carroll, S., Reichardt, R., & Guarino, C. (2000). *The Distribution of Teachers among California's School Districts and Schools.* Santa Monica, CA: RAND.

Darling-Hammond, L. (2000a). *Solving the Dilemmas of Teacher Supply, Demand, and Quality.* New York: National Commission on Teaching and America's Future.

Darling-Hammond, L. (2000b). "Teacher Quality and Student Achievement: A Review of State Policy Evidence." *Educational Policy Analysis Archives, 8*(1) [Online journal]. Available: http://epaa.asu.edu/epaa/v8n1

Darling-Hammond, L. (2002). *Access to Quality Teaching: An Analysis of Inequality in California's Public Schools.* Stanford, CA: Stanford University.

Darling-Hammond, L., Chung, R., & Frelow, F. (2002). "Variation in Teacher Preparation: How Well Do Different Pathways Prepare Teachers to Teach?" *Journal of Teacher Education, 53*(4): 286–302.

Fowler, C. (2002). "Fast Track . . . Slow Going? Education Policy Clearinghouse Research Brief, Vol. 2, Issue 1 [Online]. Available: www.edpolicy.org/publications/documents/updatev2i1.pdf

Gritz, R. M., & Theobald, N. D. (1996). "The Effects of School District Spending Priorities on Length of Stay in Teaching." *Journal of Human Resources, 31*(3): 477–512.

Hanushek, E. A., Kain, J. F., & Rivkin, S. G. (1999). "Do Higher Salaries Buy Better Teachers?" Working Paper No. 7082. Cambridge, MA: National Bureau of Economic Research.

Harris, P. (2002). *Survey of California Teachers.* Rochester, NY: Peter Harris Research Group.

Henke, R., Chen, X., & Geis, S. (2000). *Progress through the Teacher Pipeline: 1992–1993 College Graduates and Elementary/Secondary School Teaching as of 1997.* Washington, DC: National Center for Education Statistics, U.S. Department of Education.

Ingersoll, R. M. (2001). "Teacher Turnover and Teacher Shortages: An Organizational Analysis." *American Educational Research Journal, 38*(3): 499–534.

Ingersoll, R. M. (2002). *Out-of-Field Teaching, Educational Inequality, and the Organization of Schools: An Exploratory Analysis.* Seattle, WA: Center for the Study of Teaching and Policy, University of Washington.

Kain, J. F., & Singleton, K. (1996, May/June). "Equality of Educational Opportunity Revisited." *New England Economic Review,* 87–111.

Loeb, S., Darling-Hammond, L., & Luczak, J. (2003). *Teacher Turnover: The Role of Working Conditions and Salaries in Recruiting and Retaining Teachers.* Stanford, CA: Stanford University School of Education.

Loeb, S., & Page, M. (2000). "Examining the Link between Teacher Wages and Student Outcomes." *Review of Economics and Statistics, 82*(3): 393–408.

Mont, D., & Rees, D. I. (1996). "The Influence of Classroom Characteristics on High School Teacher Turnover." *Economic Inquiry, 34:* 152–167.

Murnane, R. J., & Olsen, R. J. (1990). "The Effects of Salaries and Opportunity Costs on Length of Stay in Teaching: Evidence from North Carolina." *The Journal of Human Resources, 25*(1): 106–124.

National Center for Education Statistics (NCES). (1997). *America's Teachers: Profile of a Profession, 1993–1994.* Washington, DC: U.S. Department of Education.

National Commission on Teaching and America's Future (NCTAF). (1996). *What Matters Most: Teaching for America's Future.* New York: Author.

National Commission on Teaching and America's Future (NCTAF). (2003). *No Dream Denied: A Pledge to America's Children.* New York: Author.

Raymond, M., Fletcher, S., & Luque, J. (2001). *Teach for America: An Evaluation of Teacher Differences and Student Outcomes in Houston, Texas.* Stanford, CA: Center for Research on Educational Outcomes, The Hoover Institution, Stanford University.

Shields, P. M., Humphrey, D. C., Wechsler, M. E., Riel, L. M., Tiffany-Morales, J., Woodworth, K., Youg, V. M., & Price, T. (2001). *The Status of the Teaching Profession, 2001.* Santa Cruz, CA: The Center for the Future of Teaching and Learning.

Texas Center for Educational Research. (2000). *The Cost of Teacher Turnover.* Austin, TX: Texas State Board for Teacher Certification.

Theobald, N. D., & Gritz, R. M. (1996). "The Effects of School District Spending Priorities on the Exit Paths of Beginning Teachers Leaving the District." *Economics of Education Review, 15*(1): 11–22.

Wilson, S., Darling-Hammond, L., & Berry, B. (2001). *A Case of Successful Teaching Policy: Connecticut's Long-Term Efforts to Improve Teaching and Learning.* Seattle, WA: Center for the Study of Teaching and Policy, University of Washington.

Wilson, S., Floden, R., & Ferrini-Mundy, J. (2001). *Teacher Preparation Research: Current Knowledge, Gaps, and Recommendations.* Seattle, WA: University of Washington, Center for the Study of Teaching and Policy.

DISCUSSION QUESTIONS

1. What were the reasons that you became a teacher?
2. What are the reasons that you remain in the profession?
3. Have you ever seriously thought about leaving the classroom? Why or why not?
4. Which do you think would do most to improve teachers' effectiveness: higher salaries, better working conditions, better preparation, or better mentoring?
5. Which do you think would make the least difference?

PRO-CON CHART 2

Should teachers be held accountable for their teaching?

PRO	CON
1. Teaching should be guided by clear objectives and outcomes.	**1.** Many factors influence teaching and learning that have little to do with measurable objectives and outcomes.
2. Students have a right to receive a quality education, whereby professionals are held accountable for their behavior.	**2.** Educational accountability is a cooperative responsibility of students, teachers, parents, and taxpayers.
3. Accountability will encourage teachers to uphold high standards for instruction.	**3.** Teachers can provide instruction but they cannot force students to learn.
4. Feedback from accountability evaluation measures will provide teachers with information about their instructional strengths and weaknesses.	**4.** Mandating accountability will demoralize teachers and reduce their professional status.
5. Accountability will provide standards that are derived through consensual agreement and will offer objective assessment.	**5.** There will always be disagreement on who is accountable, for what, and to whom.

CASE STUDY 2

School District Proposes Evaluations by Students

Kamhi County School District in West Suburb had proposed to vote on implementing a change to their current teacher evaluation procedures. The proposed change would permit junior high students to participate in the evaluation process of their teachers, beginning in the spring. As a way of gathering feedback, all thirty principals were asked to complete an anonymous three-part survey. In Parts One and Two, the principals were asked to cite the advantages and disadvantages of this proposed change. In Part Three, they were asked to provide a plan that outlined how they would implement this approach in their building site if it were enacted.

While reading the survey responses, Marilyn Lauter, assistant superintendent for instruction, noticed two items, unsigned letters from both a student and a teacher, that caught her attention. The student argued that because students are consumers of teachers' services, they should have a right to have their voices heard. The teacher's letter expressed complete opposition to the proposed change, citing that students lacked the maturity to provide feedback. The teacher's letter also stated that such a change would advocate the philosophy and teaching styles of certain administrators, thereby limiting the teacher's voice. Furthermore, the letter stated that if the district voted to enact this change as policy, the teachers would probably strike. Lauter was feeling very uncomfortable with both letters, but also knew that more discussion was needed before any policy change should be taken to a vote.

Discuss the issues raised by the student and the teacher and consider the following questions:

1. Should junior high students be involved in the evaluation of their teachers? Why? Why not?
2. If you were the assistant superintendent for instruction, how would you handle this situation?
3. What other approaches might have been used to elicit feedback from the teachers, parents, and students concerning the proposed policy change to the teacher evaluation process?
4. In what ways might students' evaluations of teachers affect their instruction or your own instruction?
5. What evidence does research provide about the ability of junior high students to evaluate teachers?
6. How might teachers and parents in your school district react to this proposed policy change in teacher evaluation procedures?

PART THREE

Curriculum and Learning

What is the relationship between learning and curriculum? What role does active participation play in student achievement? To what extent are higher-order thinking, creativity, and moral education emphasized in curriculum delivery? How has standardized testing influenced student confidence? What is the role of character education in students' learning experiences?

In Chapter 12, Theodore R. Sizer and Nancy Faust Sizer argue that moral or character education is an intellectual endeavor that must allow students opportunities to act and think. Students should be encouraged to deal with important and relevant ideas, even when the outcome of their grappling with difficult situations is uncertain.

Next, Robert Sternberg and Todd Lubart discuss the factors that characterize creative thinking. The authors describe the type of instruction that fosters creative thinking. They suggest that students should be given more responsibility for selecting the type of problems that they investigate, rather than relying on teacher-constructed problems. In Chapter 14, Lawrence Kohlberg describes how moral education promotes the aims of education. He compares the cognitive-developmental approach with other approaches to moral education. Alfie Kohn then presents a critical analysis of the limitations of current character education program strategies. He describes why divergent approaches would exemplify a program different from traditional approaches to moral development. The author suggests ways that reflection can be used to enhance students' moral growth.

In Chapter 16, Jeannie Oakes explains how the policy of tracking has affected student outcomes. She explores the reasons that the practice of tracking persists and explains how educators, despite evidence to the contrary, tend to justify the practice of tracking as being beneficial for students. Through actual case studies, Oakes examines the relationship among the practice of tracking, in-school segregation, and educational opportunity. In the final chapter in Part Three.

Veronica Boix Mansilla and Howard Gardner call on teachers to teach the distinct ways of thinking that are represented in the various disciplines, rather than simply requiring students to simply memorized fact, formulas, and figures. Practical suggestions for stimulating student thinking in the classroom are offered.

CHAPTER 12

Grappling

THEODORE R. SIZER
NANCY FAUST SIZER

FOCUSING QUESTIONS

1. Why should teachers be concerned with moral or character education?
2. How can teachers involve students more actively in their learning?
3. Why is it important for students to think deeply about what they learn?
4. What are the characteristics of a demanding curriculum?
5. What role should values play in student learning?

School is a frustration for Carl. He just can't see the good it does him. Even more, he can't see the good he does it. In social studies, the teacher tells him which U.S. presidents were the greatest. At least she also tells him exactly why. His parents say he should be grateful for that; they only got to memorize the list, never to hear the explanations so it's more interesting to think about. Still, he'd like to have the chance to tell her why he thinks a president who manages to avoid a war is as good as one who leads a nation in a war.

In math, he's told that there is one right answer and one way to get to that right answer. In English, he's told that the music lyrics he dotes on are inferior poetry. Even when he is asked to write, he's told how many paragraphs he should use to get his ideas across to "the reader." Which reader? Wouldn't it matter who he or she was?

And when his teacher takes his class to the computer room only to find a substitute there who doesn't know how to run the new machines, Carl is not allowed to read the computer manual so that he can help to get the class started. He tries to argue that he's done this before at home and even at school and that he and his classmates need the time in the lab if they are to finish their projects. But he gets a little too near to rudeness, and the teacher, visibly upset, cuts him off. "I don't know what's happened to kids these days," she says to us as she turns the class back toward her classroom to wait out the period. "They're so irresponsible."

In fact, this last situation requires some deeper consideration. There is, of course, no guarantee that Carl could have figured out how to run the new machines and thus saved the time for his classmates and his teacher. It's hard to predict how much time his grappling would have taken or what its outcome would have been. The problem could have been "solved" on a superficial level, or it might have needed a lot more work. Carl's energy might have given out; he might even have damaged the equipment. Nor is there any excuse for the rudeness that those who know more than others about technology or any other subjects often display.

Still, Carl had been treated as if he were an empty vessel, as if his skills and his opinions were of no value to those around him. In the computer room, he was told that there was nothing that he or anyone else could do. Instead, they were all to go back to their classroom and act as if nothing had happened. The result was an intellectual and a moral vacuum.

Why does an intellectual vacuum so often lead to a moral one as well? Schools exist for children, but children are often seen as the school's clients, as its powerless people. They are told that they are in school not because of what they know but because of what they don't know. All over the world, powerless people lose the instinct to help, because they are so often rebuffed. Yet, even if he had ultimately been unsuccessful, struggling with the computer manual would have been a good use of Carl's mind. He would have been fulfilling the real purpose of schooling: to equip himself to be of use both to himself and to others. He would have used what he already knew to reach out and learn more about how computers work. And he would have put himself on the line in a good cause.

Putting oneself on the line may be valuable, but it invites the kind of criticism that is rarely applied to the young. Raising the young is exquisitely tricky business. A fifty-ish father grumped to us about his daughter who was just graduating from high school. The young woman had announced to her parents that she was determined to become a writer. "A writer?" her dad snorted to us. "What would she write about? She doesn't know anything."

The young woman was full of passion. She liked to string words out, playing with them. She wrote exclusively about her own world, casting it as a revelation. She labored hard in English courses and had had several intense pieces published in the school's literary magazine. She had skimmed over her other courses, doing only the minimum. Nonetheless, she was an honors student. She surely would get a book award at graduation and deservedly so.

And yet her dad had a telling point. Behind his daughter's enthusiasms was glibness. Her skill was admirable, and her joy in the application of that skill was palpable. Her ability to describe her own thoughts and feelings was unusual. But the young woman did not even know that she knew relatively little, that there was important knowledge that required a broader context than her own life.

The father, caught in the practical demands of earning a living and tired of years of teenage hubris, is understandably cautious. But if he is smart, he will keep his concerns to himself. The energy, even the presumption, of the young writer should not be reined in just because so much of it is based on self-absorption and naiveté. Instead, in taking herself seriously and wanting to write for an ever-widening audience, she will be motivated to take an increased interest in the ways of the world. Time will tell.

In case after case, this is how we have seen growing up work. A student's hope and sense of agency are often dependent on her belief that there is something she can do that is valued by others. Not just other kids, but adults as well. And not empty "self-esteem building activities," but the outcome of her best efforts, in which she has real confidence. From that point on, talent intertwines constantly with content, as the student challenges herself to perform at higher levels for a broader audience.

And so it is with learning the habits of civil behavior. The skills are important. Showing restraint. Being willing to listen. Having empathy. Feeling responsible for something and some people beyond oneself and one's personal coterie of friends. Being nice. Getting along in one's daily interactions.

But there must be more. Most interactions in life are complex; more than talent and good habits are needed to address them well. Few are mastered by merely applying a slogan such as "Just say no." Context is critical if not crucial. The thoughts and resultant actions of, say, a Polish-German day laborer working near Auschwitz in 1944, a person who sees the full trains come and the empty trains go, might be appreciably different from the conclusions about the Holocaust reached by an outraged American teenager sitting in an unthreatened high school classroom 50 years later. It will help the teenager to absorb the complexity of the situation if he can reflect as if from the shoes of the laborer, not necessarily to agree, but to empathize and to understand. In this Second World War moment there is powerful stuff: the particulars of a situation, in necessarily exquisite and painful detail. That stuff, if well and carefully considered, provides the perspective that is ultimately the heart of truly moral decisions. Educators call this content.

The habits of civil behavior can do much to bring safety to a school's halls. But the meanings of civil behavior are much tougher to present. They transcend one's immediate environment. When fully and painstakingly constructed, they provide a distant mirror, the meaning of one's immediate condition viewed against a sweep of human and environmental experience, past and present.

One has to grapple with those meanings. If not, "behavior" is reduced to glib catchwords that provoke little more than periodic puffs of self-righteousness. A curriculum rich in content will teach young people that important matters of sensitive living have everything to do with hard, substantive, and often agonizingly painful thought. The students will write plays or stories or imagined memoirs that will help them to get at the considerations inside that hypothetical day laborer's head.

Grappling is necessarily a balancing act. One tries to do what one has never done before and so learns more about what one wants to do. The reader's sense of his own power is built up by letting him try to understand the computer manual so the class can go forward. The writer's humility and appreciation of context are built up by asking her to take on another's complex identity before she tries to write about it. Each task is doable, but difficult; each requires that the student put him- or herself firmly on the line.

The first step in creating such a demanding curriculum is to believe that it can be done. Wise schoolpeople and parents should not underestimate the power that they can find in young minds, bodies, and hearts. Recently the newspapers reported that an 11-year-old took her younger cousin on a three-hour drive in the family car, crossing state lines, navigating effectively, looking for an uncle but settling for an aunt. Everyone who commented on the incident remarked on how naughty these children were, how neglectful was the mother who had left them and the keys in the car while she went to an exercise salon, how unobservant was the gas station attendant who sold them gas without noticing how young they were. No one wondered at the sheer competence lurking like a shadow underneath the youngsters' foolishness.

We're selling our children short when we believe that grappling is beyond them. In fact, most of them are engaging in dilemmas of intense seriousness while we're looking the other way. Most teenagers have watched one or another substance be abused, heard adults who are important to them treat each other harshly, and wondered why so many are poor in a rich country. Many have been mugged figuratively and some literally. The teenage mother or caregiver has been a fixture for centuries. Most modern wars have been fought (albeit neither started nor led) by teenage males. To treat adolescents as delicate flowers unable to act and think is a costly pretense, as patronizing as it is wasteful. Young people can do things, and they do do things now. Older folk should accept that fact and labor hard to provide the perspective that can affect, in a principled manner, the way that young people inform those actions that, willy-nilly, they will take.

Adolescents are no different from the rest of us. They resist mandates issued from on high, and most of them won't be forced into good habits. But they are willing to talk about moral choices, and they can decide that some courses of action are better than others. In fact, they are eager to formulate opinions on these matters, as long as they are trusted to take their time and examine their assumptions as carefully as they can. They can do this in school, by considering examples—some literary, some historical, some scientific—that are interesting and nuanced and in which a human must choose between possible actions. When they work it all through in a variety of assignments, they learn much about literature and history and about the human condition and the multiple ways in which it might develop. All of this considering is what helps the teenager to deepen his or her understanding of values and thus to construct a personal moral code. This last and most private step in the process is the most important one. Finally, the test of a good school is how its students behave when no one is looking, how they are in the mall as well as in the school's classrooms and corridors.

Most teachers are fond of the word "engagement," because it means that the students are really taking an interest in the work that the teacher has designed for them. Grappling, however, goes one step further. It presumes that the student has something to add to the story. Either hypothetically or actually, the student is asked to offer his or her input.

The input may be in the form of added information. High school students who are analyzing the racial and ethnic disagreements in their city may be asked to research immigration patterns, previous political relationships, or a number of other factors in order to get a clearer picture of what is in the minds of those who are involved in contemporary problems. The resultant information can be scrutinized carefully by their classmates, by their teacher, and by outside groups, both for the way it was gathered and for what it means. If it was gathered in the traditional ways of research, it can reinforce habits that are basically good ones: honesty, freedom from bias, the use of orderly procedures, and so forth. If it was gathered in unconventional ways, such as through chats with one's highly prejudiced uncle, those ways can be analyzed and even justified, at least on certain grounds. Once gathered, the research can be presented in graphs and photographs, essays and statistics, with much discussion of the way each format contributes to an overall understanding of the situation.

The students' input may also be in the form of opinion. Most high school students spend a lot of time considering such matters as pushing and shoving or even more violent activities and whether they are dangerous or are an inevitable part of life. They think about deterrence: when and how much a threatened punishment keeps them from doing something. They think about authority and about what its best and worst uses ought to be. They think about ethnicity and about how much it influences a person's overall approach to things. They question the religion that has been important to their family, the grandmother who believes that they ought to write thank-you notes, and the teacher who takes offense at sloppy work. They are at an unsettled time in their lives, while the many different thoughts they are having start to form themselves into opinions that they may keep all their lives.

We should be grateful for their confusion: it is part of life to think for oneself, and nature needs that little blip between generations. We can learn to live with and even harness (though that may be a "bad word" and suggest a "restrictive" concept) the energy of teenagers. The thoughts that are roiling around in the students' heads should be invited out and put to work. They should be applied to schoolwork, the better to develop and grow in the sunlight, the better to be made subject to others' questions.

Schoolwork is about violence and deterrence and authority and tradition and behavior. We should invite the students' input into the subject of whether the Civil War could have been avoided, of whether the southern states' desire to secede from the Union was legitimate self-determination or a dangerous threat to the very concept of democracy. School yard tensions and even family regroupings are not precisely analogous to the Civil War, of course. But the students' opinions will be refined and strengthened not by avoiding such analogies but by pressing to make them more accurate and appropriate. Insisting that the students tackle important and demonstrably relevant ideas, such as the meaning of justice, can be a tonic. It is one very important reason to be in school. And the students want more of it.

Text-based discussions are also amenable to grappling. For all sorts of reasons, many contemporary high school students read Harper Lee's *To Kill a Mockingbird,* a story of race, guilt, innocence, and courage set in the American South of the 1930s. The story shows the importance of evidence and argument. It portrays raw courage and the toughness of honesty. It is the sort of tale that usually provokes moral outrage and with that outrage the attention and engagement of high school students.

The litany of good questions that can arise is endless. To ponder them is to wrestle with specific and carefully described ideas that are freighted with values. Teachers can catch the heat that arises from the careful discussion of issues such as those raised by *To Kill a Mockingbird* and use it to deepen the talk, to broaden the questions, and to demand that the students use the text to support their arguments. Circling back over familiar ground, asking new sorts of questions about that ground, and looking for every scrap of data are necessary steps in building the habit of thoughtful grappling. A student who grapples is made aware of this complexity. And if there is an explicit assumption on the part of the school and its teachers that this sort of grappling is as worthy as it is complex, the student may get into the habit of the struggle.

When the students stick to a text such as *To Kill a Mockingbird* long enough to understand the abstractions in it, they are likely to apply that understanding to the next text they encounter. The exercise can thus lead a class into many places, with the depth of study growing as the interest deepens. Careful grappling is its own reward; it leads to further grappling.

Fiction is particularly useful in this kind of discussion because it gets the students outside of themselves. It provides a new and unfamiliar setting to play out enduring issues and thus avoids the pressures of the immediate. The sense of suspense in the narrative draws in even those students who do not feel comfortable in moral discussions. History itself is stories, and the line between fiction and fact is a necessarily fuzzy one when it comes to the consideration of moral dilemmas. Questions about who writes history and why, about the role of ideas and of personality in communities, and about the varied and changing nature of government are also subject to debate. In science, there are many prominent moral questions in need of discussion, both on the basis of scientific evidence and on the basis of belief. One of the most important technological questions in our time is clearly "Just because we can do something, should we?" This is a particularly pressing question for adolescents. John F. Kennedy thought the answer was yes when it came to exploring space. The issues of developing and testing nuclear weapons, cloning animals and humans, and reaching children through the Internet, however, may lead to different answers.

One difference between grappling and other forms of learning is that, when the questions become the student's own, so do the answers. When simple curiosity about the birds visiting a winter feeder leads to questions about territory, sharing, cruelty, and the relationship between animals and humans, the process becomes a reality check. What is the evidence that some birds mate for life? That they return to the same feeder? How does this finding connect with other characteristics of birds? Is it real? Does it matter? If it matters, how am I affected? And finally and most important, How should I respond or behave? Should "last year's birds" have precedence over newcomers? Who am I to decide such things?

As adults, we must really be interested in what the students' "answers" are. If they are shallow, if they are biased, the teacher needs to help students develop them further but not necessarily replace them neatly with the teacher's own conclusions. The students may sense the teacher's personal views and be greatly influenced by them. However, they will also see that issues of weight are complex and that there are interpretations about which thoughtful, decent people can differ.

Few issues of value can be persuasively reduced to sharply painted absolutes. Even the dictum "Thou shalt not kill," for example, is a conflicted matter for those in the armed services or those in the part of the criminal justice system charged with carrying out legal executions. Depending on one's definition of when life begins, the issue of killing may arise in connection with abortion. There are few easy answers to central moral concerns. This is why young people must be given practice in grappling with them in as informed and principled a manner as possible.

In addition to providing additional information and offering informed opinion, a third kind of input that students can provide is their skills. Why should the local malls be the only agencies that know how to appreciate responsible teenagers? Besides the ability to do research, students have mathematical, artistic, writing, and speaking skills that can be valued in a complex world. Many high schools now have peer mediation programs, and students are learning much about identifying one another's needs and interests and finding common ground. These skills can be applied to a wider arena: at first in hypothetical role plays and under close supervision, but later with a somewhat more autonomous structure and in real situations, such as student-run businesses that raise money for the poor.

Unfortunately, the sort of grappling described here is all too rare in U.S. high schools. Few teachers have been offered the incentives or provided the support necessary to gain a deep grasp of their subjects. But a good deal of knowledge and authority on the teacher's part are usually required to teach in the interrogatory manner necessary to provoke the students to grapple. The larger the question, the more likely that the students will grow frustrated, at least at first. Only a confident coach can help his or her students move through that frustration to a greater clarity. It is much easier to give a lecture on the three causes of the French Revolution than to question the nature of revolution itself. The conventional metaphor for education is one of delivery, not of constructive, generative provocation. To teach grappling, teachers have to model it, which is difficult to do in a typical high school.

There are other factors as well. Given the sweeping nature of high school curricula—a bit of this and much of that, Cleopatra to Clinton, the history of China in two weeks, all branches of biology in a year—few schools are able to allow the time necessary for students to grapple. As long as the end result of high school is measured in "coverage" and as long as "coverage" is assessed by measuring the student's memory, there will be no time for students' own questions. Inquisitiveness, skepticism, and imagination are rarely priorities for state "curriculum frameworks" or, in all too many cases, for standardized tests. Indeed, the spiraling of ideas, the testing and retesting and testing again of hypotheses, the unpredictability of any one class, the messiness of this kind of inquiry will put the bravest and most effective teachers' students at a certain kind of short-term risk.

Another factor concerns deportment. High schools are such crowded places that certain norms seem only sensible. One is that people should listen to one another talk, which requires that only one person talk at a time. Most often, that person is the teacher, toward whom most students give the greatest respect. In many classrooms, the teacher has to shut a student up in order to open him up—that is, in order to give him the time to digest what is being said by the teacher or by other students.

In a classroom that puts a premium on developing ideas, everybody's hand would be up. No matter how pleased a teacher might be by this level of engagement, by the time it was any one student's turn to speak, any sense of coherence would be lost. Loosening up this structure by working in groups or by tolerating a certain amount of chaos would upset a lot of people. Some would be those students inside the classroom who need a degree of order and predictability to learn or who get intimidated by their classmates' ideas or even by their confidence. Other upset people might well be the folks who walk the school's halls. From such a distance, it is hard to tell the difference between excitement and cheekiness. Sometimes, it's the teacher whose initial convictions about the best kind of learning have been shaken or have put him on the line. He might be "grappling" with finding a new job by next spring.

And finally, many schools are afraid of the political ramifications of any sort of teaching that brings to the surface matters of value, matters that are often controversial and thus threatening. What if Susanna refuses to go to church on Sunday because she's offended by what she learned about abuses in the medieval church? What if Carlos can't sleep because he's upset about a predicted rise in the sun's temperature? What if Derek starts lecturing his parents about their smoking? If students take their education into their own hearts and begin to act according to their new discoveries, the dislocations in their own and their families' lives may well be difficult. The students will inevitably make some mistakes, and the school will be a convenient scapegoat.

Grappling with the tough issues is hard work. No matter how smart they sound, most students are new to the game of dealing with controversy. Recently, we observed a class that was learning about the Bill of Rights by discussing a case that involved downloading pornography, how much privacy a student should expect in school, who should decide what reasonable proof is, who has responsibility for the safety of students, and a host of other issues. One couldn't help but be struck not just by the students' commitment to the discussion but also by their skill at handling complex concepts, at looking at the background of the case, at imagining outcomes had the case been handled differently. One young man had an opinion on nearly every aspect; he was very well spoken and seemed confident and persuasive. Definitely a lawyer and a good one in the making, we thought. At the end of the class, though, he jumped up and, with a big smile, announced, "But what do we know? We're only children."

This young man wasn't undercutting the sophistication that he'd demonstrated so convincingly earlier. Indeed, he was adding to it by admitting that he had more that he needed to think about, more that he needed to learn. His perspective about his own place in life made it seem even more important to let him begin such discussions in school.

Few people in high schools believe that all young people are both capable of this level of work and ready to do it. Thus a self-fulfilling prophecy of lack of interest is at work. In matters such as the recent controversy over a national history curriculum, for example, adults with one perspective argued with adults with another perspective. The questions they argued over are important and enduring ones, such as how the experiences of Native Americans or African slaves or European immigrants should be presented. Much energy was being expended, and all these adults were honorable people trying to portray a complicated legacy in as fair and compelling a way as possible. They were mindful of the students they were teaching, in that they agreed that younger students should have a simpler and more complacent version of history than older ones. Teachers, too, try to design their lessons so carefully and to teach them so skillfully that there won't be any chance that they will misinform, or unnecessarily hurt, their students.

What these concerned adults leave out, however, is the dimension that each learner has to add to the material in order really to carry it in his or her head. There has to be a shred of interest present already on which the talented teacher can build. If the interest is based on a shared racial identity, a shared economic identity, or a shared psychological identity (such as seventh-graders often feel with the rebellious American colonists struggling to get out from under a "mother country"), so be it. Building on these existing interests seems more important than presenting each unit in the recommended number of days.

When the external tests are administered, however, the honest grappling that the teacher has encouraged may end up harming her students. Other teachers may have prepared their students better for the tests by sticking to the prescribed curriculum, which "covered" immigration and railroad regulation in the same number of days. However, by emphasizing accuracy, by which they mean the ability to sort through semi-right clues to get to the all-right answer on a machine-graded test to the exclusion of all other aspects of the material, those teachers (and the principals and parents who are flogging them to get the test scores up) are neglecting an important part of the process.

The material that stays in a student's head only until the test will never make it into his or her outlook. When it is in a student's outlook—when he thinks, for example, of the losses and gains that immigration brought to those who engaged in it, or when she compares the immigration experience with a recent move that her family made—it gains moral importance.

When a student has gotten his juices up in some way, he will think about such material outside of school, argue about it at the dinner table, take a book about it out of the library, choose the topic for his next paper. Accuracy will start to matter, but only if it follows engagement, only if the student has put himself on the line. Only then will he care if he gets his dates right or if he finds himself changing his interpretation of something. He has started to grapple with a question of importance to him, and it may well emerge into a lifelong interest and a lifelong habit.

Few schools place a high value on questioning, even though it is the habit that is most likely to lead to consequential scholarship and responsible adulthood. Schools are such crowded places: crowded not only with restless bodies but with parents' dreams for their children. No wonder so much emphasis is put on order. But order discourages questioning. Surrounded by the disorderliness of too many children, most teachers find themselves waiting for 3 p.m., waiting for Friday, and waiting for vacation all with a longing bordering on obsession, which makes them think in short-run rather than in long-run terms. In such a context, questions look messy and even rude. Besides, the students' own questions will take a lot more time to answer than the teachers' questions will, because the answers to most teachers' questions can be found on page 554 of the textbook. Better, most school systems seem to say, to present a watery diet of philosophical or psychological absolutes as a way to avoid conflict while appearing to attend to students' education in matters of value.

But more and more schoolpeople see things differently. They recognize that for humans the moral is embedded in the intellectual, that thinking hard by grappling in an informed and careful way is the most likely route to a principled and constructive life. The good person has both passion and restraint, respect for evidence and patience when evidence is not readily at hand.

These matters can be deeply embedded in the full academic curriculum. "Moral" or "character" education is neither a discrete curriculum added as an afterthought nor an unreflective activity, such as "community service," that has never been probed for its meaning. Truly moral education is an intellectual undertaking that must infuse the entire school. And it must be led by adults who know things, who themselves are regular grapplers with all the work and messiness and confusion that rich content entails.

DISCUSSION QUESTIONS

1. How does a teacher's concerns about moral or character education influence his or her instruction?
2. Why is grappling an important part of learning?
3. Is confusion a valuable or unavoidable step in the learning process?
4. What can adults do to provide a learning environment that challenges students to grapple?
5. Why is it important for moral education to infuse an entire school?

CHAPTER 13

Creating Creative Minds

ROBERT J. STERNBERG
TODD I. LUBART

FOCUSING QUESTIONS

1. How are intelligence and creativity related?
2. What is the relationship between knowledge and creativity?
3. How are intellectual styles related to creativity?
4. What are the advantages and disadvantages of giving students the responsibility for selecting problems they would like to solve?
5. What distinguishes creative thinking and ordinary thinking?
6. How can the use of ill-structured problems help students to think insightfully?
7. How do the norms of a school's environment influence the development of creativity?

Creativity is not simply inborn. On the contrary, schooling can create creative minds—though it often doesn't. To create creativity, we need to understand the resources on which it draws and to determine how we can help children develop these resources. In particular, we need to know how we can invest in our children's futures by helping them invest in their own creative endeavors.

We propose an "investment theory of creativity."[1] The basic notion underlying our theory is that, when making any kind of investment, including creative investment, people should "buy low and sell high." In other words, the greatest creative contributions can generally be made in areas or with ideas that at a given time are undervalued. Perhaps people in general have not yet realized the importance of certain ideas, and hence there is a potential for making significant advances. The more in favor an idea is, the less potential there is for it to appreciate in value, because the idea is already valued.

A theory of creativity needs to account for how people can generate or recognize undervalued ideas. It also needs to specify who will actually pursue these undervalued ideas rather than join the crowd and make contributions that, while of some value, are unlikely to turn around our existing ways of thinking. Such a theory will enable us and our children to invest in a creative future.[2] As is sometimes said, nothing is as practical as a good theory.

We hold that developing creativity in children—and in adults—involves teaching them to use six resources: intelligence, knowledge, intellectual style, personality, motivation, and environmental context. Consider each of these resources in turn.

INTELLIGENCE

Two main aspects of intelligence are relevant to creativity. These aspects, based on the triarchic theory of human intelligence, are the ability to define and redefine problems and the ability to think insightfully.[3]

Problem Definition and Redefinition

Major creative innovations often involve seeing an old problem in a new way. For example, Albert Einstein redefined the field of physics by proposing the theory of relativity; Jean Piaget redefined the field of cognitive development by conceiving of the child as a scientist; Pablo Picasso redefined the field of art through his cubist perspective on the world.

In order to *re*define a problem, a student has to have the option of defining a problem in the first place. Only rarely do schools give students this luxury. Tests typically pose the problems that students are to solve. And if a student's way of seeing a problem is different from that of the test constructor, the student is simply marked wrong. Similarly, teachers typically structure their classes so that they, not the students, set the problems to be solved. Of course, textbooks work the same way. Even when papers or projects are assigned, teachers often specify the topics. Some teachers, who view themselves as more flexible, allow students to define problems for themselves. These same teachers may then proceed to mark students down when students' definitions of problems do not correspond to their own.

In the "thinking-skills movement," we frequently hear of the need for schools to emphasize more heavily the teaching of problem-solving skills. Educators are then pleased when students do not merely memorize facts but rather use the facts to solve problems. Certainly, there is much to be said for a problem-solving approach to education. But we need to recognize that creative individuals are often most renowned not for solving problems, but for posing them. It is not so much that they have found the "right" answers (often there are none); rather, they have asked the right questions—they recognized significant and substantial problems and chose to address them. One only has to open almost any professional journal to find articles that are the fruit of good problem solving on bad—or at least fairly inconsequential—problems.

If we are to turn schooling around and emphasize creative definition and redefinition of problems, we need to give our students some of the control we teachers typically maintain. Students need to take more responsibility for the problems they choose to solve, and we need to take less. The students will make mistakes and attempt to solve inconsequential or even wrongly posed problems. But they learn from their mistakes, and if we do not give them the opportunity to make mistakes, they will have no mistakes to learn from. Instead of almost always giving children the problems, we more often need to let them find the problems that they are to solve. We need to help them develop their skills in defining and redefining problems, not just in solving them.

Insight Skills

Insight skills are involved when people perceive a high-quality solution to an ill-structured problem to which the solution is not obvious. Being truly creative involves "buying low"—that is, picking up on an idea that is out of favor. But just picking up on any idea that is out of favor is not sufficient. Insight is involved in spotting the *good* ideas. We have proposed a theory of insight whereby insights are of three kinds.[4]

The first kind of insight involves seeing things in a stream of inputs that most people would not see. In other words, in the midst of a stream of mostly irrelevant information, an individual is able to zero in on particularly relevant information for his or her purposes. For example, the insightful reader observes clues to an author's meaning that others may miss. An insightful writer is often one whose observations about human behavior, as revealed through writing, go beyond those of the rest of us.

The second kind of insight involves seeing how to combine disparate pieces of information whose connection is nonobvious and usually elusive. For example, proving mathematical theorems requires seeing how to fit together various axioms and theorems into a coherent proof. Interpreting data from a scientific experiment often involves making sense of seemingly disparate pieces of information.

The third kind of insight involves seeing the nonobvious relevance of old information to a new problem. Creative analogies and metaphors are representative of this kind of insight. For example, the student of history comes to see how understanding events of long ago can help us understand certain events in the present. A scientist might recall a problem from the past that was solved by using a certain methodology and apply this methodology to a current scientific problem.

Problems requiring insightful solution are almost always ill-structured; that is, there are no readily available paths to solution. Rather, much of the difficulty in solving the problem is figuring out what the steps toward solution might be. For example, when James Watson and Francis Crick sought to find the structure of DNA, the nature of the problem was clear. The way in which to solve it was not clear at all.

Problems presented in schools, however, are usually well structured; that is, there is a clear path—or several paths—to a prompt and expedient solution. In standardized tests, for example, there is always a path that guarantees a "correct" solution. The examinee's problem is, in large part, to find that guaranteed path. Similarly, textbook problems are often posed so that there can be an answer key for the teacher that gives the "correct" answers. Problems such as these are unlikely to require insightful thinking. One ends up trying to "psych out" the thought processes of the person who formulated the problem, rather than to generate one's own insightful thought processes.

While not exclusively limited to ill-structured problems, creative innovations tend to address such problems—not the well-structured ones that we typically use in school settings. If we want students to think insightfully, we need to give them opportunities to do so by increasing our use of ill-structured problems that allow insightful thinking. Project work is excellent in this regard, for it requires students not only to solve problems but also to structure the problems for themselves.

KNOWLEDGE

In order to make a creative contribution to a field of knowledge, one must, of course, have knowledge of that field. Without such knowledge, one risks rediscovering what is already known. Without knowledge of the field, it is also difficult for an individual to assess the problems in the field and to judge which are important. Indeed, during the past decade or so, an important emphasis in psychology has been on the importance of knowledge of expertise.

Schools can scarcely be faulted for making insufficient efforts to impart knowledge. Indeed, that seems to be their main function.

Yet we have two reservations about the extent to which the knowledge they impart is likely to lead to creativity.

First, there is a difference between knowledge and usable knowledge. Knowledge can be learned in a way that renders it inert. Knowledge may be stored in the brain, but an individual may nonetheless be unable to use it. For example, almost every college undergraduate who majors in psychology takes a course in statistics as a part of that major. Yet very few undergraduates who have taken statistics are able to use what they have learned in the design and analysis of scientific experiments. (At the secondary level, many physics and chemistry students are unable to use basic algebra when they need to apply it.) Undergraduates in psychology do fine as long as they are given highly structured problems in which it is obvious which statistical technique applies. But they have trouble when they have to figure out which technique to apply and when to apply it. The context in which they acquired their knowledge is so different from the context in which they must use it that their knowledge is simply unavailable.

Our experience with knowledge learned in statistics courses is, we believe, the rule rather than the exception. Students do not generally learn knowledge in a way that renders it useful to them. To the contrary, they are likely to forget much of what they learn soon after they are tested on it. We have all had the experience of studying for an exam and then quickly forgetting what we studied. The information was learned in such a way as to make it useful in the context of a structured exam; once the exam is finished, so is that use of the knowledge.

Our second reservation about the knowledge that schools typically impart is that students are not taught in a way that makes clear to them why the information they are learning is important. Students do much better in learning if they believe that they can use what they learn. Foreign language provides a good example. People who need to use a foreign language learn it. Those who don't need it rarely retain much of it. Unless we show students why what they are learning should matter to them, we cannot expect them to retain what they are taught. Unfortunately, we often don't really know ourselves how students might use what we are teaching them. And if we don't know, how can we expect them to?

We also need to be concerned about the trade-off that can develop between knowledge and flexibility. We have suggested that increased expertise in terms of knowledge in a given domain often comes at the expense of flexibility in that domain.[5] We can become so automatic about the way we do certain things that we lose sight of the possibility of other ways. We can become entrenched and have trouble going beyond our very comfortable perspective on things. Because creativity requires one to view things flexibly, there is a danger that, with increasing knowledge, one will lose creativity by losing the ability to think flexibly about the domain in which one works. We need to recognize that sometimes students see things that we do not see—that they may have insights we have not had (and that initially we may not even recognize as insights). Teachers who have been doing the same thing year after year can become so self-satisfied and happy with the way they do things that they are closed to new ways of doing these things. They are unwilling to "buy low"—to try an idea that is different from those they have favored in the past.

On the one hand, we do not wish to underemphasize the importance of knowledge to creativity. On the other hand, we cannot overemphasize the importance of usable knowledge that does not undermine flexibility. Often we need to adopt the maintenance of flexibility as a goal to be achieved self-consciously. We might go to in-service training sessions, read new kinds of books, learn about a new domain of knowledge, seek to learn from our students, or whatever. If we want students to be creative, we have to model creativity for them, and we won't be able to do that if we seek to turn students' minds into safe-deposit boxes in which to store our assorted and often undigested bits of knowledge.

INTELLECTUAL STYLES

Intellectual styles are the ways in which people choose to use or exploit their intelligence as well as their knowledge. Thus intellectual styles concern not abilities, but how these abilities and the knowledge acquired through them are used in day-to-day interactions with the environment.

Elsewhere, one of the authors has presented details of a theory of intellectual styles based on a notion of "mental self-government."[6] Hence, we need not cover the theory in detail here. The basic idea is that people need to govern themselves mentally and that styles provide them with ways to do so. The ways in which people govern themselves are internal mirrors of the kinds of government we see in the external world.

Creative people are likely to be those with a legislative proclivity. A legislative individual is someone who enjoys formulating problems and creating new systems of rules and new ways of seeing things. Such a person is in contrast to an individual with an executive style: someone who likes implementing the systems, rules, and tasks of others. Both differ from an individual with a judicial style: someone who enjoys evaluating people, things, and rules. Thus the creative person not only has the ability to see things in new ways but likes to do so. The creative person is also likely to have a global—not just a local—perspective on problems. Seeing the forest despite all the trees is the mark of creative endeavor.

PERSONALITY

Creative people seem to share certain personality attributes. Although one can probably be creative in the short term without these attributes, long-term creativity requires most of them. The attributes are tolerance of ambiguity, willingness to surmount obstacles and persevere, willingness to grow, willingness to take risks, and courage of one's convictions.

Tolerance for Ambiguity

In most creative endeavors, there is a period of time during which an individual is groping—trying to figure out what the pieces of the puzzle are, how to put them together, how to relate them to what is already known. During this period, an individual is likely to feel some anxiety—possibly even alarm—because the pieces are not forming themselves into a creative solution to the problem being confronted. Creative individuals need to be able to tolerate such ambiguity and to wait for the pieces to fall into place.

In many schools, most of the assignments students are given are due the next day or within a very short period of time. In such circumstances students cannot develop a tolerance for ambiguity because they cannot spare the time to allow a situation to be ambiguous. If an assignment is due in a day or two, ambiguities need to be resolved quickly. A good way to help students develop a tolerance for ambiguity is to give them more long-term assignments and encourage them to start thinking about the assignments early on so that they can mull over whatever problems they face. Moreover, students need to realize that a period of ambiguity is the rule, not the exception, in creative work and that they should welcome this period as a chance to hatch their ideas, rather than dread it as a time when their ideas are not fully formed.

Willingness to Surmount Obstacles and Persevere

Almost every major creative thinker has surmounted obstacles at one time or another, and the willingness not to be derailed is a crucial element of success. Confronting obstacles is almost a certainty in creative endeavor because most such endeavors threaten some kind of established and entrenched interest. Unless one can learn to face adversity and conquer it, one is unlikely to make a creative contribution to one's field.

We need to learn to think of obstacles and the need to surmount them as part of the game, rather than as outside it. We should not think of obstacles as something only we have, but as something that everyone has. What makes creative people special is not that they have obstacles but how they face them.

Schools can be fairly good proving grounds for learning to surmount obstacles because we face so many of them while we are in school (whether as students or as teachers). But students sometimes leave school with the feeling that society is more likely to get in the way of creativity than to support it. Sometimes they are right, of course. And ultimately, they may have to fight for their ideas, as creative people have done before them. However, training to overcome resistance to new ideas shouldn't be the main contribution of the schools to students' creativity.

Willingness to Grow

When a person has a creative idea and is able to have others accept it, that person may be highly rewarded for the idea. It then becomes difficult to move on to still other ideas. The rewards for staying with the first idea are often great, and it feels comfortable to stick with that idea. At the same time, the person who has had a creative idea often acquires a deep-seated fear that his or her next idea won't be as good as the first one. Indeed, the phenomenon of "statistical" regression toward the mean would suggest that subsequent ideas actually will not be as good—that they will regress toward the mean. This is the same phenomenon that operates when the "rookie of the year" in baseball doesn't play as well in his second year as in his first or when a restaurant that seems outstanding when we first eat there isn't quite as good the second time. In short, there is a fair amount of pressure to stay with what one has and knows. But creativity exhibited over prolonged periods of time requires one to move beyond that first creative idea and even to see problems with what at one time may have seemed a superb idea. While schools often encourage the growth of a student's knowledge, such growth will by no means lead automatically to creativity, in part because schools do not encourage students to take risks with their newly acquired knowledge and abilities.

Willingness to Take Risks

A general principle of investment is that, on the average, greater return entails greater risk. For the most part, schools are environments that are not conducive to risk taking. On the contrary, students are as often as not punished for taking risks. Taking a course in a new area or in an area of weakness is likely to lead to a low grade, which in turn may dim a student's future prospects. Risking an unusual response on an exam or an idiosyncratic approach in a paper is a step likely to be taken only with great trepidation because of the fear that a low or failing grade on a specific assignment may ruin one's chances for a good grade in the course. Moreover, there is usually some safe response that is at least good enough to earn the grade for which one is aiming.

In addition, many teachers are not themselves risk-takers. Teaching is not a profession that is likely to attract the biggest risk-takers, and hence, many teachers may feel threatened by students who take large risks, especially if the teacher perceives those risks to be at his or her expense. Unfortunately, students' unwillingness to take risks derives from their socialization in the schools, which are environments that encourage conformity to societal norms. The result is often stereotyped thinking.

Courage of One's Convictions and Belief in Oneself

There are times in the lives of almost all creative people when they begin to doubt their ideas—and themselves. Their work may not be achieving the recognition it once achieved, or they may not have succeeded in getting recognition in the first place. At these times, it is difficult to maintain a belief in one's ideas or in oneself. It is natural for people to go through peaks and valleys in their creative output, and there are times when creative people worry that their most recent good idea will end up being their final good idea. At such times, one needs to draw upon deep-seated personal resources and to believe in oneself, even when others do not.

Schools do teach some students to believe in themselves: namely, those who consistently receive high grades. But the skills one needs to earn high grades are often quite different from those one needs to be creative. Thus those who go out and set their own course may receive little encouragement, whereas those who play the game and get good grades may develop a confidence in themselves that, though justified, is not necessarily related to their past or potential creative contributions. Those who most need to believe in themselves may be given every reason not to.

MOTIVATION

There is now good evidence to suggest that motivation plays an important part in creative endeavors. Two kinds of motivation are particularly important: intrinsic motivation and the motivation to excel. Both kinds of motivation lead to a focus on tasks rather than on the external rewards that performance of these tasks might generate.

Intrinsic Motivation

Teresa Amabile has conducted and reviewed a number of studies suggesting the importance of intrinsic motivation to creativity.[7] People are much more likely to respond creatively to a task that they enjoy doing for its own sake, rather than a task that they carry out exclusively or even primarily for such extrinsic motivators as grades. Indeed, research suggests that extrinsic rewards undermine intrinsic motivation.[8]

There is little doubt as to the way in which most schools motivate students today: namely, through grades. Grades are the ultimate criterion of one's success in school, and if one's grades are not good, love of one's work is unlikely to be viewed as much compensation. Therefore, many students chart a path in school that is just sufficient to get them an A. (If they put too much effort into a single course, they risk jeopardizing their performance in the other courses they are taking.) Students who once may have performed well for love of an intellectual challenge may come to perform well only to get their next A. Whatever intrinsic motivation children may have had at the start is likely to be drummed out of them by a system that rewards extrinsically, not intrinsically.

Motivation to Excel

Robert White identified as an important source of motivation a desire to achieve competence in one or more of a person's endeavors.[9] In order to be creative in a field, one generally will need to be motivated not only to be competent, but also to excel. The best "investors" are almost always those who put in the work necessary to realize their goals. Success does not just come to them—they work for it.

Schools vary in the extent to which they encourage students to excel. Some schools seem to want nothing more than for all their students to be at some average or "golden mean." Many schools, however, encourage excellence. Unfortunately, it is rare in our experience for the kind of excellence that is encouraged to be *creative* excellence. It may be excellence in grades, which generally does not require great creativity to attain; it may be excellence in sports or in extracurricular activities. There is nothing wrong with excellence of these kinds. Indeed, they are undoubtedly important in today's world. But seeking such excellences does not foster creativity—and may even interfere with it. When a student is simultaneously taking five or six courses, there is not much opportunity to spend the time or to expend the effort needed to be creative in any of them.

ENVIRONMENTAL CONTEXT

Creativity cannot be viewed outside an environmental context. What would be viewed as creative in one context might be viewed as trivial in another. The role of context is relevant to the creative enterprise in at least three different ways: in sparking creative ideas, in encouraging follow-up of these ideas, and in rewarding the ideas and their fruits.

Sparking Creative Ideas

Some environments provide the bases for lots of creative sparks, whereas other environments may provide the basis for none at all. Do schools provide environments for sparking creative ideas? Obviously, the answer to this question is necessarily subjective. Given the discussion above, we would have difficulty saying that they do. Schools provide environments that encourage learning about and dealing with existing concepts rather than inventing new ones. There is a lot of emphasis on memorization and some emphasis on analysis, but there is little emphasis on creative synthesis. Indeed, it is difficult for us to remember more than a handful of tests we ever took in school that encouraged creative thinking. On the contrary, the tests students typically take reward them for spitting back what they have learned—or, at best, analyzing it in a fairly noncreative way.

Encouraging Follow-up of Creative Ideas

Suppose a student has a genuinely creative idea and would like to pursue it within the school setting. Is there any vehicle for such follow-up? Occasionally, students will be allowed to pursue projects that encourage them to develop their creative thinking. But again, spending a great deal of time on such projects puts them at risk in their other courses and in their academic work. It is quite rare that any allowance is made whereby students can be excused from normal requirements in order to pursue a special interest of their own.

Evaluating and Rewarding Creative Ideas

Most teachers would adamantly maintain that, when grading papers, they reward creativity. But, if the experience of other teachers is similar to that of the teachers with whom we have worked, they don't find a great deal of creativity to reward. And we sometimes worry whether they would recognize creativity in student work were they to meet it. Please note that we do not except ourselves from this charge. We have failed more than once to see the value of a student's idea when we first encountered it, only to see that value later on—after the student had decided to pursue some other idea, partly at our urging. Teachers genuinely believe that they reward creativity. But the rewards are few and far between.

Look at any school report card, and assess the skills that the report card values. You will probably not find creativity anywhere on the list. One of us actually analyzed the report cards given to children in several elementary schools. A number of skills were assessed. However, not a single one of the report cards assessed creativity in any field whatsoever.

The creative child might indeed be valued by the teacher, but it would not show up in the pattern of check marks on the report card.

TEACHING FOR CREATIVITY

How can we help develop students' creativity in the classroom? Consider an example. One of us had the opportunity to teach a class of 9- and 10-year-olds in a New York City school. The children ranged fairly widely in abilities and came from various socioeconomic backgrounds. The guest teacher was asked to demonstrate how to "teach for thinking" and decided to do so in the context of teaching about psychology. However, he wanted to impart not merely a set of decontextualized "facts" about the field, but rather the way psychologists think when they develop ideas for creative scientific theory and research.

He didn't tell the students what problem they were going to solve or even offer them suggestions. Rather, he asked each of them to share with the class some aspect of human behavior—their own, their parents', their friends'—that intrigued them and that they would like to understand better. In other words, the students were asked to *define problems* rather than have the teacher do it for them. At first, no one said anything. The children may never have been asked to formulate problems for themselves. But the teacher waited. And then he waited some more (so as not to teach them that, if only they said nothing, he would panic and start to answer his own questions).

Eventually, one student spoke up, and then another, and then another. The ice broken, the children couldn't wait to contribute. Rather than adopting the executive and largely passive style to which they were accustomed, they were adopting a *legislative style* whereby they enjoyed and actively participated in the opportunity to create new ideas. And create ideas they did. Why do parents make children dress up on special occasions? Why do parents sometimes have unreasonable expectations for their children? Why do some siblings fight a lot while others don't? How do we choose our friends?

Because these problems were the children's own problems and not the teacher's, the children were *intrinsically motivated* to seek answers. And they came up with some very perceptive answers indeed. We discussed their ideas and considered criteria for deciding which potential experiment to pursue as a group. The criteria, like the ideas, were the students' own, not the teacher's. And the students considered such factors as *taking risks* in doing experiments, *surmounting obstacles to doing an experiment*, and so on.

The children entered the class with almost no formal knowledge about psychology. But they left it with at least a rudimentary *procedural knowledge* of how psychologists formulate research. The teacher didn't give them the knowledge; they created it for themselves, in an environment that *sparked* and then *rewarded* creative ideas. To be sure, not all of the ideas were creative or even particularly good. But the students were encouraged to give it their best shot, and that's what they did.

The class didn't have time in one 75-minute period to complete the full design of an experiment. However, it did have time to demonstrate that even children can do the kind of creative work that we often reserve until graduate school. We can teach for creativity at any level, in any field. And if we want to improve our children and our nation, this is exactly what we need to do.

Does teaching for creativity actually work? We believe that it does. Moreover, the effectiveness of such teaching has been demonstrated.[10] After five weeks of insight training involving insight problems in language arts, mathematics, science, and social studies, students in grades 4 through 6 displayed significant and substantial improvements (from a pretest to a posttest) over an untrained control group on insight skills and general intelligence. In addition, the training transferred to insight problems of kinds not covered in the course, and a year later, the gains were maintained. These children had improved their creative skills with only a relatively small investment of instructional time.

Those who invest are taught that most obvious of strategies: buy low and sell high. Yet few people manage to do so. They don't know when a given security is really low or when it is really high. We believe that those who work in the schools do not have much better success in fostering creativity. We often don't recognize creativity when we see it. And although most of us believe that we encourage it, our analysis suggests that schools are probably as likely to work against the development of creativity as in its favor. The conventional wisdom is likely correct: schools probably do at least as much to undermine creativity as to support it.

It is important to realize that our theory of creativity is a "confluence" theory: the elements of creativity work together interactively, not alone. The implication for schooling is that addressing just one—or even a few—of the resources we have discussed is not sufficient to induce creative thinking. For example, a school might teach "divergent thinking," encouraging students to see multiple solutions to problems. But children will not suddenly become creative in the absence of an environment that tolerates ambiguity, encourages risk taking, fosters task-focused motivation, and supports the other aspects of creativity that we have discussed.

It is also important to realize that obtaining transfer of training from one domain to another is at least as hard with creative thinking as with critical thinking. If you use trivial problems in your classroom (e.g., "What are unusual uses of a paper clip?"), you are likely to get transfer only to trivial problems outside the classroom. We are not enthusiastic about many so-called tests of creativity, nor about many training programs, because the problems they use are trivial. We would encourage the use of serious problems in a variety of disciplines in order to maximize the transfer of training. Better to ask students to think of unusual ways to solve world problems—or school problems, for that matter—than to ask them to think of unusual ways to use a paper clip!

CONCLUSION

Perhaps the greatest block to the enhancement of creativity is a view of the "ideal student" that does not particularly feature creativity. Paul Torrance used an "Ideal Child Checklist," composed of characteristics that had been found empirically to differentiate highly creative people from less creative people.[11] A total of 264 teachers in the state of New York ranked the items in terms of desirability. The teachers' rankings showed only a moderate relation with the rankings of ten experts on creativity. The teachers supported more strongly than the experts such attributes as popularity, social skills, and acceptance of authority. The teachers disapproved of asking questions, being a good guesser, thinking independently, and risk taking. A replication of this study in Tennessee showed only a weak relation between the views of teachers and those of experts on creativity.[12] Clearly, to engender creativity, first we must value it!

Schools could change. They could let students define problems, rather than almost always doing it for them. They could put more emphasis on ill-structured rather than well-structured problems. They could encourage a legislative rather than (or in addition to) an executive style, by providing assignments that encourage students to see things in new ways. They could teach knowledge for use, rather than for exams; they could emphasize flexibility in using knowledge, rather than mere recall. They could encourage risk taking and other personality attributes associated with creativity, and they could put more emphasis on motivating children intrinsically rather than through grades. Finally, they could reward creativity in all its forms, rather than ignore or even punish it.

But for schools to do these things, it would take a rather fundamental revaluation of what schooling is about. We, at least, would like to see that process start now. Rather than put obstacles in their paths, let's do all that we can to *value* and encourage the creativity of students in our schools.

ENDNOTES

1. Robert J. Sternberg, "A Three-Facet Model of Creativity," in R. J. Sternberg, ed., *The Nature of Creativity* (New York: Cambridge University Press, 1988), pp. 125–47; and Robert J. Sternberg and Todd I. Lubart, "An Investment Theory of Creativity and Its Development," *Human Development*, vol. 34, 1991, pp. 1–31.
2. Herbert J. Walberg, "Creativity and Talent as Learning," in Sternberg, *The Nature of Creativity*, pp. 340–61.
3. Robert J. Sternberg, *Beyond IQ: A Triarchic Theory of Human Intelligence* (New York: Cambridge University Press, 1985); and Sternberg, *The Triarchic Mind: A New Theory of Human Intelligence* (New York: Viking, 1988).
4. Janet E. Davidson and Robert J. Sternberg, "The Role of Insight in Intellectual Giftedness," *Gifted Child Quarterly*, vol. 28, 1984, pp. 58–64; and Robert J. Sternberg and Janet E. Davidson, "The Mind of the Puzzler," *Psychology Today*, June 1982, pp. 37–44.
5. Robert J. Sternberg and Peter A. Frensch, "A Balance-Level Theory of Intelligent Thinking," *Zeitschrift für Pädagogische Psychologie*, vol. 3, 1989, pp. 79–96.
6. Robert J. Sternberg, "Mental Self-Government: A Theory of Intellectual Styles and Their Development," *Human Development*, vol. 31, 1988, pp. 197–224; and "Thinking Styles: Keys to Understanding Student Performance," *Phi Delta Kappan*, January 1990, pp. 366–71.
7. Teresa M. Amabile, *The Social Psychology of Creativity* (New York: Springer-Verlag, 1983).
8. Mark Lepper, David Greene, and Richard Nisbett, "Undermining Children's Intrinsic Interest with Extrinsic Rewards: A Test of the 'Overjustification' Hypothesis," *Journal of Personality and Social Psychology*, vol. 28, 1973, pp. 129–37.
9. Robert White, "Motivation Reconsidered: The Concept of Competence," *Psychological Review*, vol. 66, 1959, pp. 297–323.
10. Davidson and Sternberg, op. cit.
11. E. Paul Torrance, *Role of Evaluation in Creative Thinking* (Minneapolis: Bureau of Educational Research, University of Minnesota, 1964).
12. Bill Kaltsounis, "Middle Tennessee Teachers' Perceptions of Ideal Pupil," *Perceptual and Motor Skills*, vol. 44, 1977, pp. 803–806.

DISCUSSION QUESTIONS

1. How can curriculum workers plan instruction that encourages students to use legislative intellectual styles?
2. In what ways will the curriculum need to be structured to promote creative thinking?
3. What kinds of changes at the school level might be necessary to foster creative thinking?
4. What instructional approaches are most likely to promote creative thinking?
5. What personality attributes do creative people seem to share?

CHAPTER 14

The Cognitive-Developmental Approach to Moral Education

LAWRENCE KOHLBERG

FOCUSING QUESTIONS

1. How does moral education promote the aims of education?
2. What are the levels of moral development?
3. How do moral judgment, content of moral judgment, and moral action differ?
4. How do conventional rules and principles influence moral choice?
5. How do indoctrination and values clarification differ as approaches to moral education?
6. What is the cognitive developmental approach to moral education?

In this chapter, I present an overview of the cognitive-developmental approach to moral education and its research foundations, compare it with other approaches, and report the experimental work my colleagues and I are doing to apply the approach.

MORAL STAGES

The cognitive-developmental approach was fully stated for the first time by John Dewey. The approach is called *cognitive* because it recognizes that moral education, like intellectual education, has its basis in stimulating the *active thinking* of the child about moral issues and decisions. It is called developmental because it sees the aims of moral education as movement through moral stages. According to Dewey:

> The aim of education is growth or *development,* both intellectual and moral. Ethical and psychological principles can aid the school in the *greatest of all the constructions—the building of a free and powerful character.* Only knowledge of the *order and connection of the stages in psychological development can insure this.* Education is the work of *supplying the conditions* which will enable the psychological functions to mature in the freest and fullest manner.[1]

Dewey postulated three levels of moral development: (1) the *pre-moral* or *preconventional* level "of behavior motivated by biological and social impulses with results for morals," (2) the *conventional* level of behavior "in which the individual accepts with little critical reflection the standards of his group," and (3) the *autonomous* level of behavior in which "conduct is guided by the individual thinking and judging for himself whether a purpose is good, and does not accept the standard of his group without reflection."[2]

Dewey's thinking about moral stages was theoretical. Building upon his prior studies of cognitive stages, Jean Piaget made the first effort to define stages of moral reasoning in children through actual interviews and through observations of children (in games with rules).[3] Using this interview material, Piaget defined the levels as follows: (1) the *premoral stage,* where there was no sense of obligation to rules; (2) the *heteronomous stage,* where the right was literal obedience to rules and an equation of obligation with submission to power and punishment (roughly ages four to eight); and (3) the *autonomous stage,* where the purpose and consequences of following rules are considered and obligation is based on reciprocity and exchange (roughly ages eight to twelve).[4]

In 1955, I started to redefine and validate (through longitudinal and cross-cultural study) the Dewey–Piaget levels and stages. The resulting stages are presented in Table 14.1.

We claim to have validated the stages defined in Table 14.1. The notion that stages can be *validated* by longitudinal study implies that stages have definite empirical characteristics.[5] The concept of stages (as used by Piaget and myself) implies the following characteristics:

1. Stages are "structured wholes," or organized systems of thought. Individuals are *consistent* in level of moral judgment.
2. Stages form an *invariant sequence.* Under all conditions except extreme trauma, movement is always forward, never backward. Individuals never skip stages; movement is always to the next stage up.
3. Stages are "hierarchical integrations." Thinking at a higher stage includes or comprehends within it lower-stage thinking. There is a tendency to function at or prefer the highest stage available.

Each of these characteristics has been demonstrated for moral stages. Stages are defined by responses to a set of verbal moral dilemmas classified according to an elaborate scoring scheme. Validating studies include

1. A twenty-year study of fifty Chicago-area boys, middle- and working-class. Initially interviewed at ages ten to sixteen, they have been reinterviewed at three-year intervals thereafter.
2. A small, six-year longitudinal study of Turkish village and city boys of the same age.
3. A variety of other cross-sectional studies in Canada, Britain, Israel, Taiwan, Yucatan, Honduras, and India.

With regard to the structured whole or consistency criterion, we have found that more than 50 percent of an individual's thinking is always at one stage, with the remainder at the next adjacent stage (which he is leaving or which he is moving into).

With regard to invariant sequence, our longitudinal results have been presented in the *American Journal of Orthopsychiatry*

Table 14.1 Definition of Moral Stages

I. Preconventional level

At this level, the child is responsive to cultural rules and labels of good and bad, right or wrong, but interprets these labels either in terms of the physical or the hedonistic consequences of action (punishment, reward, exchange of favors) or in terms of the physical power of those who enunciate the rules and labels. The level is divided into the following two stages:

Stage 1: *The punishment-and-obedience orientation.* The physical consequences of action determine its goodness or badness, regardless of the human meaning or value of these consequences. Avoidance of punishment and unquestioning deference to power are valued in their own right, not in terms of respect for an underlying moral order supported by punishment and authority (the latter being Stage 4).

Stage 2: *The instrumental-relativist orientation.* Right action consists of that which instrumentally satisfies one's own needs and occasionally the needs of others. Human relations are viewed in terms like those of the marketplace. Elements of fairness, of reciprocity, and of equal sharing are present, but they are always interpreted in a physical, pragmatic way. Reciprocity is a matter of "You scratch my back and I'll scratch yours," not of loyalty, gratitude, or justice.

II. Conventional level

At this level, maintaining the expectations of the individual's family, group, or nation is perceived as valuable in its own right, regardless of immediate and obvious consequences. The attitude is not only one of *conformity* to personal expectations and social order, but of loyalty to it, of actively *maintaining,* supporting, and justifying the order, and of identifying with the persons or group involved in it. At this level, there are the following two stages:

Stage 3: *The interpersonal concordance or "good boy-nice girl" orientation.* Good behavior is that which pleases or helps others and is approved by them. There is much conformity to stereotypical images of what is majority or "natural" behavior. Behavior is frequently judged by intention—"he means well" becomes important for the first time. One earns approval by being "nice."

Stage 4: *The "law and order" orientation.* There is orientation toward authority, fixed rules, and the maintenance of the social order. Right behavior consists of doing one's duty, showing respect for authority, and maintaining the given social order for its own sake.

III. Postconventional level

At this level, there is a clear effort to define moral values and principles that have validity and application apart from the authority of the groups or persons holding these principles and apart from the individual's own identification with these groups. This level also has two stages:

Stage 5: *The social-contract, legalistic orientation,* generally with utilitarian overtones. Right action tends to be defined in terms of general individual rights and standards, which have been critically examined and agreed upon by the whole society. There is a clear awareness of the relativism of personal values and opinions and a corresponding emphasis upon procedural rules for reaching consensus. Aside from what is constitutionally and democratically agreed upon, the right is a matter of personal "values" and "opinion." The result is an emphasis upon the "legal point of view," but with an emphasis upon the possibility of changing law in terms of rational considerations of social utility (rather than freezing it in terms of Stage 4 "law and order"). Outside the legal realm, free agreement and contract is the binding element of obligation. This is the "official" morality of the American government and Constitution.

Stage 6: *The universal-ethical-principle orientation.* Right is defined by the decision of conscience in accord with self-chosen *ethical principles* appealing to logical comprehensiveness, universality, and consistency. These principles are abstract and ethical (the Golden Rule, the categorical imperative); they are not concrete moral rules like the Ten Commandments. At heart, these are universal principles of *justice,* of the *reciprocity* and *equality* of human *rights,* and of respect for the dignity of human beings as *individual persons.*

(see endnote 12), and indicate that on every retest individuals either were at the same stage as three years earlier or had moved up. This was true in Turkey as well as in the United States.

With regard to the hierarchical integration criterion, it has been demonstrated that adolescents exposed to written statements at each of the six stages comprehend or correctly put in their own words all statements at or below their own stage but fail to comprehend any statements more than one stage above their own.[6] Some individuals comprehend the next stage above their own; some do not. Adolescents prefer (or rank as best) the highest stage they can comprehend.

To understand moral stages it is important to clarify their relations to stages of logic or intelligence on the one hand and to moral behavior on the other. Maturity of moral judgment is not highly correlated with IQ or verbal intelligence (correlations are only in the 30s, accounting for 10 percent of the variance). Cognitive development, in the stage sense, however, is more important for moral development than such correlations suggest. Piaget has found that after the child learns to speak there are three major stages of reasoning: the intuitive, the concrete operational, and the formal operational. At around age seven, the child enters the stage of concrete logical thought: He can make logical inferences, classify, and handle quantitative relations about concrete things. In adolescence individuals usually enter the stage of formal operations. At this stage they can reason abstractly—i.e., consider all possibilities, form hypotheses, deduce implications from hypotheses, and test them against reality.[7]

Since moral reasoning clearly is reasoning, advanced moral reasoning depends upon advanced logical reasoning; a person's logical stage puts a certain ceiling on the moral stage he can attain. A person whose logical stage is only concrete operational is limited to the preconventional moral stages (Stages 1 and 2). A person whose logical stage is only partially formal operational is limited to the conventional moral stages (Stages 3 and 4). While logical development is necessary for moral development and sets limits to it, most individuals are higher in logical stage than they are in moral stage. As an example, over 50 percent of late adolescents and adults are capable of full formal reasoning, but only 10 percent of these adults (all formal operational) display principled (Stages 5 and 6) moral reasoning.

The moral stages are *structures of moral judgment* or *moral reasoning*. *Structures* of moral judgment must be distinguished from the *content* of moral judgment. As an example, we cite responses to a dilemma used in our various studies to identify moral stage. The dilemma raises the issue of stealing a drug to save a dying woman. The inventor of the drug is selling it for ten times what it costs him to make it. The woman's husband cannot raise the money, and the seller refuses to lower the price or wait for payment. What should the husband do?

The choice endorsed by a subject (steal, don't steal) is called the *content* of his moral judgment in the situation. His reasoning about the choice defines the structure of his moral judgment. This reasoning centers on the following ten universal moral values or issues of concern to persons in these moral dilemmas:

1. Punishment
2. Property
3. Roles and concerns of affection
4. Roles and concerns of authority
5. Law
6. Life
7. Liberty
8. Distributive justice
9. Truth
10. Sex

A moral choice involves choosing between two (or more) of these values as they *conflict* in concrete situations of choice.

The stage or structure of a person's moral judgment defines (1) *what* he finds valuable in each of these moral issues (life, law), i.e., how he defines the value, and (2) *why* he finds it valuable, i.e., the reasons he gives for valuing it. As an example, at Stage 1 life is valued in terms of the power or possessions of the person involved; at Stage 2, for its usefulness in satisfying the needs of the individual in question or others; at Stage 3, in terms of the individual's relations with others and their valuation of him; at Stage 4, in terms of social or religious law. Only at Stages 5 and 6 is each life seen as inherently worthwhile, aside from other considerations.

MORAL JUDGMENT VS. MORAL ACTION

Having clarified the nature of stages of moral *judgment*, we must consider the relation of moral judgment to moral *action*. If logical reasoning is a necessary but not sufficient condition for mature moral judgment, mature moral judgment is a necessary but not sufficient condition for mature moral action. One cannot follow moral principles if one does not understand (or believe in) moral principles. However, one can reason in terms of principles and not live up to these principles. As an example, Richard Krebs and I found that only 15 percent of students showing some principled thinking cheated as compared to 55 percent of conventional subjects and 70 percent of preconventional subjects.[8] Nevertheless, 15 percent of the principled subjects did cheat, suggesting that factors additional to moral judgment are necessary for principled moral reasoning to be translated into "moral action." Partly, these factors include the situation and its pressures. Partly, what happens depends upon the individual's motives and emotions. Partly, what the individual does depends upon a general sense of will, purpose, or "ego strength." As an example of the role of will or ego strength in moral behavior, we may cite the study by Krebs: Slightly more than half of his conventional subjects cheated. These subjects were also divided by a measure of attention/will. Only 26 percent of the "strong-willed" conventional subjects cheated; however, 74 percent of the "weak-willed" subjects cheated.

If maturity of moral reasoning is only one factor in moral behavior, why does the cognitive-developmental approach to moral education focus so heavily upon moral reasoning? For the following reasons:

1. Moral judgment, while only one factor in moral behavior, is the single most important or influential factor yet discovered in moral behavior.
2. While other factors influence moral behavior, moral judgment is the only distinctively *moral* factor in moral behavior. To illustrate, we noted that the Krebs study indicated that "strong-willed" conventional stage subjects resisted cheating more than "weak-willed" subjects. For those at a preconventional level of moral reasoning, however, "will" had an opposite effect. "Strong-willed" Stages 1 and 2 subjects cheated more, not less, than "weak-willed" subjects; i.e., they had the "courage of their (amoral) convictions" that it was worthwhile to cheat. "Will," then, is an important factor in moral behavior, but it is not distinctively moral; it becomes moral only when informed by mature moral judgment.
3. Moral judgment change is long-range or irreversible; a higher stage is never lost. Moral behavior as such is largely situational and reversible or "losable" in new situations.

AIMS OF MORAL AND CIVIC EDUCATION

Moral psychology describes what moral development is, as studied empirically. Moral education must also consider moral philosophy, which strives to tell us what moral development ideally *ought to be*. Psychology finds an invariant sequence of moral stages; moral philosophy must be invoked to answer whether a later stage is a better stage. The "stage" of senescence and death follows the "stage" of adulthood, but that does not mean that senescence and death are better. Our claim that the latest or principled stages of moral reasoning are morally better stages, then, must rest on considerations of moral philosophy.

The tradition of moral philosophy to which we appeal is the liberal or rational tradition, in particular the "formalistic" or "deontological" tradition running from Immanuel Kant to John Rawls.[9] Central to this tradition is the claim that an adequate morality is *principled*—i.e., that it makes judgments in terms of *universal* principles applicable to all mankind. *Principles* are to be distinguished from *rules.* Conventional morality is grounded on rules, primarily "thou shalt nots" such as are represented by the Ten Commandments, prescriptions of kinds of actions. Principles are, rather, universal guides to making a moral decision. An example is Kant's "categorical imperative," formulated in two ways. The first is the maxim of respect for human personality, "Act always toward the other as an end, not as a means." The second is the maxim of universalization, "Choose only as you would be willing to have everyone choose in your situation." Principles like that of Kant state the formal conditions of a moral choice or action. In the dilemma in which a woman is dying because a druggist refuses to release his drug for less than the stated price, the druggist is not acting morally, though he is not violating the ordinary moral rules (he is not actually stealing or murdering). But he is violating principles: He is treating the woman simply as a means to his ends of profit, and he is not choosing as he would wish anyone to choose (if the druggist were in the dying woman's place, he would not want a druggist to choose as he is choosing). Under most circumstances, choice in terms of conventional moral rules and choice in terms of principles coincide. Ordinarily, principles dictate not stealing (avoiding stealing is implied by acting in terms of a regard for others as ends and in terms of what one would want everyone to do). In a situation where stealing is the only means to save a life, however, principles contradict the ordinary rules and would dictate stealing. Unlike rules which are supported by social authority, principles are freely chosen by the individual because of their intrinsic moral validity.[10]

The conception that a moral choice is a choice made in terms of moral principles is related to the claim of liberal moral philosophy that moral principles are ultimately principles of justice. In essence, moral conflicts are conflicts between the claims of persons, and principles for resolving these claims are principles of justice, "for giving each his due." Central to justice are the demands of *liberty, equality,* and *reciprocity.* At every moral stage, there is a concern for justice. The most damning statement a school child can make about a teacher is that "he's not fair." At each higher stage, however, the conception of justice is reorganized. At Stage 1, justice is punishing the bad in terms of "an eye for an eye and a tooth for a tooth." At Stage 2, it is exchanging favors and goods in an equal manner. At Stages 3 and 4, it is treating people as they desire in terms of the conventional rules. At Stage 5, it is recognized that all rules and laws flow from justice, from a social contract between the governors and the governed designed to protect the equal rights of all. At Stage 6, personally chosen moral principles are also principles of justice, the principles any member of a society would choose for that society if he did not know what his position was to be in the society and in which he might be the least advantaged.[11] Principles chosen from this point of view are, first, the maximum liberty compatible with the like liberty of others and, second, no inequalities of goods and respect which are not to the benefit of all, including the least advantaged.

As an example of stage progression in the orientation to justice, we may take judgments about capital punishment.[12] Capital punishment is only firmly rejected at the two principled stages, when the notion of justice as vengeance or retribution is abandoned. At the sixth stage, capital punishment is not condoned even if it may have some useful deterrent effect in promoting law and order. This is because it is not a punishment we would choose for a society if we assumed we had as much chance of being born into the position of a criminal or murderer as being born into the position of a law abider.

Why are decisions based on universal principles of justice better decisions? Because they are decisions on which all moral men could agree. When decisions are based on conventional moral rules, men will disagree, since they adhere to conflicting systems of rules dependent on culture and social position. Throughout history men have killed one another in the name of conflicting moral rules and values, most recently in Vietnam and the Middle East. Truly moral or just resolutions of conflicts require principles which are, or can be, universalizable.

Alternative Approaches

We have given a philosophic rationale for stage advance as the aim of moral education. Given this rationale, the developmental approach to moral education can avoid the problems inherent in the other two major approaches to moral education. The first alternative approach is that of indoctrinative moral education, the preaching and imposition of the rules and values of the teacher and his culture on the child. In America, when this indoctrinative approach has been developed in a systematic manner, it has usually been termed "character education."

Moral values, in the character education approach, are preached or taught in terms of what may be called the "bag of virtues." In the classic studies of character by Hugh Hartshorne and Mark May, the virtues chosen were honesty, service, and self-control.[13] It is easy to get superficial consensus on such a bag of virtues—until one examines in detail the list of virtues involved and the details of their definition. Is the Hartshorne and May bag more adequate than the Boy Scout bag (a Scout should be honest, loyal, reverent, clean, brave, etc.)? When one turns to the details of defining each virtue, one finds equal uncertainty or difficulty in reaching consensus. Does honesty mean one should not steal to save a life? Does it mean that a student should not help another student with his homework?

Character education and other forms of indoctrinative moral education have aimed at teaching universal values (it is assumed that honesty or service is a desirable trait for all men in all societies), but the detailed definitions used are relative; they are defined by the opinions of the teacher and the conventional culture and rest on the authority of the teacher for their justification. In this sense, character education is close to the unreflective valuings by teachers which constitute the hidden curriculum of the school.[14] Because of the current unpopularity of indoctrinative approaches to moral education, a family of approaches called "values clarification" has become appealing to teachers. Values clarification takes the first step implied by a rational approach to moral education: the eliciting of the child's own judgment or opinion about issues or situations in which values conflict, rather than imposing the teacher's opinion on him. Values clarification, however, does not attempt to go further than eliciting awareness of values; it is assumed that becoming more self-aware about one's values is an end in itself. Fundamentally, the definition of the end of values education as self-awareness derives from a belief in ethical relativity held by many value-clarifiers. As stated by Peter Engel, "One must contrast value clarification and value inculcation. Value clarification implies the principle that in the consideration of values there is no single correct answer." Within these premises of "no correct answer," children are to discuss moral dilemmas in such a way as to reveal different values and discuss their value differences with each other. The teacher is to stress that "our values are different," not that one value is more adequate than others. If this program is systematically followed, students will themselves become relativists, believing there is no "right" moral answer. For instance, a student caught cheating might argue that he did nothing wrong, since his own hierarchy of values, which may be different from that of the teacher, made it right for him to cheat.

Like values clarification, the cognitive-developmental approach to moral education stresses open or Socratic peer discussion of value dilemmas. Such discussion, however, has an aim: stimulation of movement to the next stage of moral reasoning. Like values clarification, the developmental approach opposes indoctrination. Stimulation of movement to the next stage of reasoning is not indoctrinative, for the following reasons:

1. Change is in the way of reasoning rather than in the particular beliefs involved.
2. Students in a class are at different stages; the aim is to aid movement of each to the next stage, not convergence on a common pattern.
3. The teacher's own opinion is neither stressed nor invoked as authoritative. It enters in only as one of many opinions, hopefully one of those at a next higher stage.
4. The notion that some judgments are more adequate than others is communicated. Fundamentally, however, this means that the student is encouraged to articulate a position which seems most adequate to him and to judge the adequacy of the reasoning of others.

In addition to having more definite aims than values clarification, the moral development approach restricts value education to that which is moral or, more specifically, to justice. This is for two reasons. First, it is not clear that the whole realm of personal, political, and religious values is a realm which is nonrelative—i.e., in which there are universals and a direction of development. Second, it is not clear that the public school has a right or mandate to develop values in general. In our view, value education in the public schools should be restricted to that which the school has the right and mandate to develop: an awareness of justice, or of the rights of others in our Constitutional system.[15] While the Bill of Rights prohibits the teaching of religious beliefs, or of specific value systems, it does not prohibit the teaching of the awareness of rights and principles of justice fundamental to the Constitution itself.

When moral education is recognized as centered in justice and differentiated from value education or affective education, it becomes apparent that moral and civic education are much the same thing. This equation, taken for granted by the classic philosophers of education from Plato and Aristotle to Dewey, is basic to our claim that a concern for moral education is central to the educational objectives of social studies.

The term *civic education* is used to refer to social studies as more than the study of the facts and concepts of social science, history, and civics. It is education for the analytic understanding, value principles, and motivation necessary for a citizen in a democracy if democracy is to be an effective process. It is political education. Civic or political education means the stimulation of development of more advanced patterns of reasoning about political and social decisions and their implementation directly derivative of broader patterns of moral reasoning. Our studies show that reasoning and decision making about political decisions are directly derivative of broader patterns of moral reasoning and decision making. We have interviewed high school and college students about concrete political situations involving laws to govern open housing, civil disobedience for peace in Vietnam, free press rights to publish what might disturb national order, and distribution of income through taxation. We find that reasoning on these political decisions can be classified according to moral stage and that an individual's stage on political dilemmas is at the same level as on nonpolitical moral dilemmas (euthanasia, violating authority to maintain trust in a family, stealing a drug to save one's dying wife). Turning from reasoning to action, similar findings are obtained. In 1963 a study was made of those who sat in at the University of California, Berkeley, administration building and those who did not in the Free Speech Movement crisis. Of those at Stage 6, 80 percent sat in, believing that principles of free speech were being compromised, and that all efforts to compromise and negotiate with the administration had failed. In contrast, only 15 percent of the conventional (Stage 3 or Stage 4) subjects sat in. (Stage 5 subjects were in between.)[16]

From a psychological side, then, political development is part of moral development. The same is true from the philosophic side. In the *Republic,* Plato sees political education as part of a broader education for moral justice and finds a rationale for such education in terms of universal philosophic principles rather than the demands of a particular society. More recently, Dewey claims the same.

In historical perspective, the United States was the first nation whose government was publicly founded on postconventional principles of justice, rather than upon the authority central to conventional moral reasoning. At the time of our founding, postconventional or principled moral and political reasoning was the possession of the minority, as it still is. Today, as in the time of our founding, the majority of our adults are at the conventional level, particularly the "law and order" (fourth) moral stage. (Every few years the Gallup Poll circulates the Bill of Rights unidentified, and every year it is turned down.) The Founding Fathers intuitively understood this without benefit of our elaborate social science research; they constructed a document designing a government which would maintain principles of justice and the rights of man even though principled men were not the men in power. The machinery included checks and balances, the independent judiciary, and freedom of the press. Most recently, this machinery found its use at Watergate. The tragedy of Richard Nixon, as Harry Truman said long ago, was that he never understood the Constitution (a Stage 5 document), but the Constitution understood Richard Nixon.[17]

Watergate, then, is not some sign of moral decay of the nation, but rather of the fact that understanding and action in support of justice principles are still the possession of a minority of our society. Insofar as there is moral decay, it represents the weakening of conventional morality in the face of social and value conflict today. This can lead the less fortunate adolescent to fixation at the preconventional level, the more fortunate to movement to principles. We find a larger proportion of youths at the principled level today than was the case in their fathers' day, but also a larger proportion at the preconventional level.

Given this state, moral and civic education in the schools becomes a more urgent task. In the high school today, one often hears both preconventional adolescents and those beginning to move beyond convention sounding the same note of disaffection for the school. While our political institutions are in principle Stage 5 (i.e., vehicles for maintaining universal rights through the democratic process), our schools have traditionally been Stage 4 institutions of convention and authority. Today more than ever, democratic schools systematically engaged in civic education are required.

Our approach to moral and civic education relates the study of law and government to the actual creation of a democratic school in which moral dilemmas are discussed and resolved in a manner which will stimulate moral development.

Planned Moral Education

For many years, moral development was held by psychologists to be primarily a result of family upbringing and family conditions. In particular, conditions of affection and authority in the home were believed to be critical, some balance of warmth and firmness being optimal for moral development. This view arises if morality is conceived as an internalization of the arbitrary rules of parents and culture, since such acceptance must be based on affection and respect for parents as authorities rather than on the rational nature of the rules involved.

Studies of family correlates of moral stage development do not support this internalization view of the conditions for moral development. Instead, they suggest that the conditions for moral development in homes and schools are similar and that the conditions are consistent with cognitive-developmental theory. In the cognitive-developmental view, morality is a natural product of a universal human tendency toward empathy or role taking, toward putting oneself in the shoes of other conscious beings. It is also a product of a universal human concern for justice, for reciprocity or equality in the relation of one person to another. As an example, when my son was four, he became a morally principled vegetarian and refused to eat meat, resisting all parental persuasion to increase his protein intake. His reason was "It's bad to kill animals." His moral commitment to vegetarianism was not taught or acquired from parental authority; it was the result of the universal tendency of the young self to project its consciousness and values into other living things, other selves. My son's vegetarianism also involved a sense of justice, revealed when I read him a book about Eskimos in which a real hunting expedition was described. His response was to say, "Daddy, there is one kind of meat I would eat—Eskimo meat. It's all right to eat Eskimos because they eat animals." This natural sense of justice or reciprocity was Stage 1—an eye for an eye, a tooth for a tooth. My son's sense of the value of life was also Stage 1 and involved no differentiation between human personality and physical life. His morality, though Stage 1, was, however, natural and internal. Moral development past Stage 1, then, is not an internalization but the reconstruction of role taking and conceptions of justice toward greater adequacy. These reconstructions occur in order to achieve a better match between the child's own moral structures and the structures of the social and moral situations he confronts. We divide these conditions of match into two kinds: those dealing with moral discussions and communication and those dealing with the total moral environment or atmosphere in which the child lives.

In terms of moral discussion, the important conditions appear to be:

1. Exposure to the next higher stage of reasoning.
2. Exposure to situations posing problems and contradictions for the child's current moral structure, leading to dissatisfaction with his current level.
3. An atmosphere of interchange and dialogue combining the first two conditions, in which conflicting moral views are compared in an open manner.

Studies of families in India and America suggest that morally advanced children have parents at higher stages. Parents expose children to the next higher stage, raising moral issues and engaging in open dialogue or interchange about such issues.[18]

Drawing on this notion of the discussion conditions stimulating advance, Moshe Blatt conducted classroom discussions of conflict-laden hypothetical moral dilemmas with four classes of junior high and high school students for a semester.[19] In each of these classes, students were to be found at three stages. Since the children were not all responding at the same stage, the arguments they used with each other were at different levels. In the course of these discussions among the students, the teacher first supported and clarified those arguments that were one stage above the lowest stage among the children; for example, the teacher supported Stage 3 rather than Stage 2. When it seemed that these arguments were understood by the students, the teacher then challenged that stage, using new situations, and clarified the arguments one stage above the previous one: Stage 4 rather than Stage 3. At the end of the semester, all the students were retested; they showed significant upward change when compared to the controls, and they maintained the change one year later. In the experimental classrooms, from one-fourth to one-half of the students moved up a stage, while there was essentially no change during the course of the experiment in the control group.

Given the Blatt studies showing that moral discussion could raise moral stage, we undertook the next step: to see if teachers could conduct moral discussions in the course of teaching high school social studies with the same results. This step we took in cooperation with Edwin Fenton, who introduced moral dilemmas in his ninth- and eleventh-grade social studies texts. Twenty-four teachers in the Boston and Pittsburgh areas were given some instruction in conducting moral discussions around the dilemmas in the text. About half of the teachers stimulated significant developmental change in their classrooms—upward stage movement of one-quarter to one-half a stage. In control classes using the text but no moral dilemma discussions, the same teachers failed to stimulate any moral change in the students. Moral discussion, then, can be a usable and effective part of the curriculum at any grade level. Working with filmstrip dilemmas produced in cooperation with Guidance Association, second-grade teachers conducted moral discussions yielding a similar amount of moral stage movement.

Moral discussion and curriculum, however, constitute only one portion of the conditions stimulating moral growth. When we turn to analyzing the broader life environment, we turn to a consideration of the *moral atmosphere* of the home, the school, and the broader society. The first basic dimension of social atmosphere is the role-taking opportunities it provides, the extent to which it encourages the child to take the point of view of others. Role taking is related to the amount of social interaction and social communication in which the child engages, as well as to his sense of efficacy in influencing attitudes of others. The second dimension of social atmosphere, more strictly moral, is the level of justice of the environment or institution. The justice structure of an institution refers to the perceived rules or principles for distributing rewards, punishments, responsibilities, and privileges among institutional members. This structure may exist or be perceived at any of our moral stages. As an example, a study of a traditional prison revealed that inmates perceived it as Stage 1, regardless of their own level.[20] Obedience to arbitrary command by power figures and punishment for disobedience were seen as the governing justice norms of the prison. A behavior-modification prison using point rewards for conformity was perceived as a Stage 2 system of instrumental exchange. Inmates at Stage 3 or 4 perceived this institution as more fair than the traditional prison, but not as fair in their own terms.

These and other studies suggest that a higher level of institutional justice is a condition for individual development of a higher sense of justice. Working on these premises, Joseph Hickey, Peter Scharf, and I worked with guards and inmates in a women's prison to create a more just community.[21] A social contract was set up in which guards and inmates each had a vote of one and in which rules were made and conflicts resolved through discussions of fairness and a democratic vote in a community meeting. The program has stimulated moral stage advance in inmates.

Fenton, Ralph Mosher, and I received a grant from the Danforth Foundation (with additional support from the Kennedy Foundation) to make moral education a living matter in two high schools in the Boston area (Cambridge and Brookline) and two in Pittsburgh. The plan had two components. The first was training counselors and social studies and English teachers in conducting moral discussions and making moral discussion an integral part of the curriculum. The second was establishing a just community school within a public high school.

We have stated the theory of the just community high school, postulating that discussing real-life moral situations and actions as issues of fairness and as matters for democratic decision would stimulate advance in both moral reasoning and moral action. A participatory democracy provides more extensive opportunities for role taking and a higher level of perceived institutional justice than does any other social arrangement. Most alternative schools strive to establish a democratic governance, but none we have observed has achieved a vital or viable participatory democracy. Our theory suggested reasons why we might succeed where others failed. First, we felt that democracy had to be a central commitment of a school, rather than a humanitarian frill. Democracy as moral education provides that commitment. Second, democracy in alternative schools often fails because it bores the students. Students prefer to let teachers make decisions about staff, courses, and schedules, rather than to attend lengthy, complicated meetings. Our theory said that the issues a democracy should focus on are issues of morality and fairness. Real issues concerning drugs, stealing, disruptions, and grading are never boring if handled as issues of fairness. Third, our theory told us that if large democratic community meetings were preceded by small-group moral discussion, higher-stage thinking by students would win out in later decisions, avoiding the disasters of mob rule.[22]

We can report that the school based on our theory makes democracy work or function where other schools have failed.

Our Cambridge just community school within the public high school was started after a small summer planning session of volunteer teachers, students, and parents. At the time the school opened in the fall, only a commitment to democracy and a skeleton program of English and social studies had been decided on. The school started with six teachers from the regular school and sixty students, twenty from academic professional homes and twenty from working-class homes. The other twenty were dropouts and troublemakers or petty delinquents in terms of previous record. The usual mistakes and usual chaos of a beginning alternative school ensued. Within a few weeks, however, a successful democratic community process had been established. Rules were made around pressing issues: disturbances, drugs, hooking. A student discipline committee or jury was formed. The resulting rules and enforcement have been relatively effective and reasonable. We do not see reasonable rules as ends in themselves, however, but as vehicles for moral discussion and an emerging sense of community. This sense of community and a resulting morale are perhaps the most immediate signs of success. This sense of community seems to lead to behavior change of a positive sort. An example is a fifteen-year-old student who started as one of the greatest combinations of humor, aggression, light-fingeredness, and hyperactivity I have ever known. From being the principal disturber of all community meetings, he has become an excellent community meeting participant and occasional chairman. He is still more ready to enforce rules for others than to observe them himself, yet his commitment to the school has led to a steady decrease in exotic behavior. In addition, he has become more involved in classes and projects and has begun to listen and ask questions in order to pursue a line of interest.

CONCLUSION

We attribute such behavior change not only to peer pressure and moral discussion but to the sense of community which has emerged from the democratic process in which angry conflicts are resolved through fairness and community decision. This sense of community is reflected in statements of the students to us that there are no cliques—that the blacks and the whites, the professors' sons and the project students, are friends. These statements are supported by observation. Such a sense of community is needed where students in a given classroom range in reading level from fifth grade to college.

There is very little new in anything we are doing. Dewey wanted democratic experimental schools for moral and intellectual development seventy years ago. Perhaps Dewey's time has come.

ENDNOTES

1. John Dewey, "What Psychology Can Do for the Teacher," in Reginald Archambault, ed., *John Dewey on Education: Selected Writings* (New York: Random House, 1964).
2. These levels correspond roughly to our three major levels: the preconventional, the conventional, and the principled. Similar levels were propounded by William McDougall, Leonard Hobhouse, and James Mark Baldwin.
3. Jean Piaget, *The Moral Judgment of the Child,* 2nd ed. (Glencoe, IL: Free Press, 1948).
4. Piaget's stages correspond to our first three stages: Stage 0 (premoral), Stage 1 (heteronomous), and Stage 2 (instrumental reciprocity).
5. Lawrence Kohlberg, "Moral Stages and Moralization: The Cognitive-Developmental Approach," in Thomas Lickona, ed., *Moral Development and Behavior* (New York: Holt, Rinehart and Winston, 1976).
6. James Rest, Elliott Turiel, and Lawrence Kohlberg, "Relations Between Level of Moral Judgment and Preference and Comprehension of the Moral Judgment of Others," *Journal of Personality,* vol. 37, 1969, pp. 225–52; and James Rest, "Comprehension, Preference, and Spontaneous Usage in Moral Judgment," in Lawrence Kohlberg, ed., *Recent Research in Moral Development* (New York: Holt, Rinehart and Winston, 1986).
7. Many adolescents and adults only partially attain the stage of formal operations. They do consider all the actual relations of one thing to another at the same time, but they do not consider all possibilities and form abstract hypotheses. A few do not advance this far, remaining "concrete operational."
8. Richard Krebs and Lawrence Kohlberg, "Moral Judgment and Ego Controls as Determinants of Resistance to Cheating," in Lawrence Kohlberg, ed., *Recent Research.*
9. John Rawls, *A Theory of Justice* (Cambridge, MA: Harvard University Press, 1971).
10. Not all freely chosen values or rules are principles, however. Hitler chose the "rule" "exterminate the enemies of the Aryan race," but such a rule is not a universalizable principle.
11. Rawls, *A Theory of Justice.*
12. Lawrence Kohlberg and Donald Elfenbein, "Development of Moral Reasoning and Attitudes Toward Capital Punishment," *American Journal of Orthopsychiatry,* Summer, 1975.
13. Hugh Hartshorne and Mark May, *Studies in the Nature of Character: Studies in Deceit,* vol. 1; *Studies in Service and Self-Control,* vol. 2; *Studies in Organization of Character,* vol. 3 (New York: Macmillan, 1928–30).
14. As an example of the "hidden curriculum," we may cite a second-grade classroom. My son came home from this classroom one day saying he did not want to be "one of the bad boys." Asked "Who are the bad boys?" he replied, "The ones who don't put their books back and get yelled at."
15. Restriction of deliberate value education to the moral may be clarified by our example of the second-grade teacher who made tidying up of books a matter of moral indoctrination. Tidiness is a value, but it is not a moral value. Cheating is a

moral issue, intrinsically one of fairness. It involves issues of violation of trust and taking advantage. Failing to tidy the room may under certain conditions be an issue of fairness, when it puts an undue burden on others. If it is handled by the teacher as a matter of cooperation among the group in this sense, it is a legitimate focus of deliberate moral education. If it is not, it simply represents the arbitrary imposition of the teacher's values on the child.

16. The differential action of the principled subjects was determined by two things. First, they were more likely to judge it right to violate authority by sitting in. But second, they were also in general more consistent in engaging in political action according to their judgment. Ninety percent of all Stage 6 subjects thought it right to sit in, and all 90 percent lived up to this belief. Among the Stage 4 subjects, 45 percent thought it right to sit in, but only 33 percent lived up to this belief by acting.

17. No public or private word or deed of Nixon ever rose above Stage 4, the "law and order" stage. His last comments in the White House were of wonderment that the Republican Congress could turn on him after so many Stage 2 exchanges of favors in getting them elected.

18. Bindu Parilch, "A Cross-Cultural Study of Parent-child Moral Judgment," unpublished doctoral dissertation, Harvard University, 1975.

19. Moshe Blatt and Lawrence Kohlberg, "Effects of Classroom Discussions upon Children's Level of Moral Judgment," in Lawrence Kohlberg, ed., *Recent Research.*

20. Lawrence Kohlberg, Peter Scharf, and Joseph Hickey, "The Justice Structure of the Prison: A Theory and an Intervention," *The Prison Journal*, Autumn-Winter, 1972.

21. Lawrence Kohlberg, Kelsey Kauffman, Peter Scharf, and Joseph Hickey, *The Just Community Approach to Corrections: A Manual, Part I* (Cambridge, MA: Education Research Foundation, 1973).

22. An example of the need for small-group discussion comes from an alternative school community meeting called because a pair of the students had stolen the school's video-recorder. The resulting majority decision was that the school should buy back the recorder from the culprits through a fence. The teachers could not accept this decision and returned to a more authoritative approach. I believe if the moral reasoning of students urging this solution had been confronted by students at a higher stage, a different decision would have emerged.

DISCUSSION QUESTIONS

1. Should moral and civic education be the responsibility of the schools? Why? Why not?
2. What type of curriculum design lends itself to promoting the aims of moral education?
3. How do the family and norms of school cultures influence children's moral development?
4. What is the role of the social atmosphere in moral education?
5. Should values be infused into the curriculum or explicitly taught? Why? Why not?

CHAPTER 15

A Critical Examination of Character Education

ALFIE KOHN

FOCUSING QUESTIONS

1. What meanings are generally used to describe character education?
2. Why is understanding how individuals behave in context-specific situations relevant to analyzing the assumptions underlying character education programs?
3. In your opinion, is a negative view of human beings an appropriate orientation for creating character education programs? Why? Why not?
4. What essential components would traditional moralist and constructivists suggest for a character education program?
5. What should be the teachers' role in promoting students' moral development?

Were you to stand somewhere in the continental United States and announce, "I'm going to Hawaii," it would be understood that you were heading for those islands in the Pacific that collectively constitute the fiftieth state. Were you to stand in Honolulu and make the same statement, however, you would probably be talking about one specific island in the chain—the big one to your southeast. The word *Hawaii* would seem to have two meanings, a broad one and a narrow one; we depend on context to tell them apart.

The phrase *character education* also has two meanings. In the broad sense, it refers to almost anything that schools might try to provide outside of academics, especially when the purpose is to help children grow into good people. In the narrow sense, it denotes a particular style of moral training, one that reflects particular values as well as particular assumptions about the nature of children and how they learn.

Unfortunately, the two meanings of the term have become blurred, with the narrow version of character education dominating the field to the point that it is frequently mistaken for the broader concept. Thus educators who are keen to support children's social and moral development may turn, by default, to a program with a certain set of methods and a specific agenda that, on reflection, they might very well find objectionable.

My purpose in this chapter is to subject these programs to careful scrutiny and, in so doing, to highlight the possibility that there are other ways to achieve our broader objectives. I address myself not so much to those readers who are avid proponents of character education (in the narrow sense), but to those who simply want to help children become decent human beings and may not have thought carefully about what they are being offered.

Let me get straight to the point. What goes by the name of character education nowadays is, for the most part, a collection of exhortations and extrinsic inducements designed to make children work harder and do what they're told. Even when other values are also promoted—caring or fairness, say—the preferred method of instruction is tantamount to indoctrination. The point is to drill students in specific behaviors, rather than to engage them in deep, critical reflection about certain ways of being. This is the impression one gets from reading articles and books by contemporary proponents of character education, as well as the curriculum materials sold by the leading national programs. The impression is only strengthened by visiting schools that have been singled out for their commitment to character education. To wit:

> A huge, multiethnic elementary school in Southern California uses a framework created by the Jefferson Center for Character Education. Classes that the principal declares "well behaved" are awarded Bonus Bucks, which can eventually be redeemed for an ice cream party. On an enormous wall near the cafeteria, professionally painted Peanuts characters instruct children: "Never talk in line." A visitor is led to a fifth-grade classroom to observe an exemplary lesson on the current character education topic. The teacher is telling students to write down the name of the person they regard as the "toughest worker" in school. The teacher then asks them, "How many of you are going to be tough workers?" (Hands go up.) "Can you be a tough worker at home, too?" (Yes.)

> A small, almost entirely African American school in Chicago uses a framework created by the Character Education Institute. Periodic motivational assemblies are used to "give children a good pep talk," as the principal puts it, and to reinforce the values that determine who will be picked as Student of the Month. Rule number one posted on the wall of a kindergarten room is "We will obey the teachers." Today students in this class are listening to the story of "Lazy Lion," who orders each of the other animals to build him a house, only to find each effort unacceptable. At the end, the teacher drives home the lesson: "Did you ever hear Lion say thank you?" (No.) "Did you ever hear Lion say please?" (No.) "It's good to always say . . . what?" (Please.) The reason for using these words, she points out, is that by doing so we are more likely to get what we want.

> A charter school near Boston has been established specifically to offer an intensive, homegrown character education curriculum to its overwhelmingly white, middle-class student body. At weekly public ceremonies, certain children receive a leaf that will then be hung in the Forest of Virtue. The virtues themselves are "not open to debate," the headmaster insists, since moral precepts in his view enjoy the same status as mathematical truths. In a first-grade classroom, a teacher is observing that "it's very hard to be obedient when you want something. I want you to ask yourself, 'Can I have it—and why not?'" She proceeds to ask the students, "What kinds of things show obedience?" and, after collecting a few suggestions, announces that she's "not going to call on anyone else now. We could go on forever, but we have to have a moment of silence and then a spelling test."

Some of the most popular schoolwide strategies for improving students' character seem dubious at face value. When President Clinton mentioned the importance of character education in his 1996 State of the Union address, the only specific practice he recommended was requiring students to wear uniforms. The premises here are, first, that children's character can be improved by forcing them to dress alike and, second, that if adults object to students' clothing the best solution is not to invite them to reflect together about how this problem might be solved, but instead to compel them all to wear the same thing.

A second strategy, also consistent with the dominant philosophy of character education, is an exercise that might be called "If It's Tuesday, This Must Be Honesty." Here, one value after another is targeted, with each assigned its own day, week, or month. This seriatim approach is unlikely to result in a lasting commitment to any of these values, much less a feeling for how they may be related. Nevertheless, such programs are taken very seriously by some of the same people who are quick to dismiss other educational programs, such as those intended to promote self-esteem, as silly and ineffective.

Then there is the strategy of offering students rewards when they are "caught" being good, an approach favored by right-wing religious groups[1] and orthodox behaviorists but also by leaders of—and curriculum suppliers for—the character education movement.[2] Because of its popularity and because a sizable body of psychological evidence germane to the topic is available, it is worth lingering on this particular practice for a moment.

In general terms, what the evidence suggests is this: the more we reward people for doing something, the more likely they are to lose interest in whatever they had to do to get the reward. Extrinsic motivation, in other words, not only is quite different from intrinsic motivation but actually tends to erode it.[3] This effect has been demonstrated under many different circumstances and with respect to many different attitudes and behaviors. Most relevant to character education is a series of studies showing that individuals who have been rewarded for doing something nice become less likely to think of themselves as caring or helpful people and more likely to attribute their behavior to the reward.

"Extrinsic incentives can, by undermining self-perceived altruism, decrease intrinsic motivation to help others," one group of researchers concluded on the basis of several studies. "A person's kindness, it seems, cannot be bought."[4] The same applies to a person's sense of responsibility, fairness, perseverance, and so on. The lesson a child learns from Skinnerian tactics is that the point of being good is to get rewards. No wonder researchers have found that children who are frequently rewarded—or, in another study, children who receive positive reinforcement for caring, sharing, and helping—are less likely than other children to keep doing those things.[5]

In short, it makes no sense to dangle goodies in front of children for being virtuous. But even worse than rewards are awards—certificates, plaques, trophies, and other tokens of recognition whose numbers have been artificially limited so only a few can get them. When some children are singled out as "winners," the central message that every child learns is this: "Other people are potential obstacles to my success."[6] Thus the likely result of making students beat out their peers for the distinction of being the most virtuous is not only less intrinsic commitment to virtue but also a disruption of relationships and, ironically, of the experience of community that is so vital to the development of children's character.

Unhappily, the problems with character education (in the narrow sense, which is how I'll be using the term unless otherwise indicated) are not restricted to such strategies as enforcing sartorial uniformity, scheduling a value of the week, or offering students a "doggie biscuit" for being good. More deeply troubling are the fundamental assumptions, both explicit and implicit, that inform character education programs. Let us consider five basic questions that might be asked of any such program: At what level are problems addressed? What is the view of human nature? What is the ultimate goal?

Which values are promoted? And, finally, what is the theory of learning?

1. *At what level are problems addressed?* One of the major purveyors of materials in this field, the Jefferson Center for Character Education in Pasadena, California, has produced a video that begins with some arresting images—quite literally. Young people are shown being led away in handcuffs, the point being that crime can be explained on the basis of an "erosion of American core values," as the narrator intones ominously. The idea that social problems can be explained by the fact that traditional virtues are no longer taken seriously is offered by many proponents of character education as though it were just plain common sense.

But if people steal or rape or kill solely because they possess bad values—that is, because of their personal characteristics—the implication is that political and economic realities are irrelevant and need not be addressed. Never mind staggering levels of unemployment in the inner cities or a system in which more and more of the nation's wealth is concentrated in fewer and fewer hands; just place the blame on individuals whose characters are deficient. A key tenet of the "Character Counts!" Coalition, which bills itself as a nonpartisan umbrella group devoid of any political agenda, is the highly debatable proposition that "negative social influences can [be] and usually are overcome by the exercise of free will and character."[7] What is presented as common sense is, in fact, conservative ideology.

Let's put politics aside, though. If a program proceeds by trying to "fix the kids"—as do almost all brands of character education—it ignores the accumulated evidence from the field of social psychology demonstrating that much of how we act and who we are reflects the situations in which we find ourselves. Virtually all the landmark studies in this discipline have been variations on this theme. Set up children in an extended team competition at summer camp, and you will elicit unprecedented levels of aggression. Assign adults to the roles of prisoners or guards in a mock jail, and they will start to become their roles. Move people to a small town, and they will be more likely to rescue a stranger in need. In fact, so common is the tendency to attribute to an individual's personality or character what is actually a function of the social environment that social psychologists have dubbed this the "fundamental attribution error."

A similar lesson comes to us from the movement concerned with Total Quality Management associated with the ideas of the late W. Edwards Deming. At the heart of Deming's teaching is the notion that the "system" of an organization largely determines the results. The problems experienced in a corporation, therefore, are almost always due to systemic flaws, rather than to a lack of effort or ability on the part of individuals in that organization. Thus, if we are troubled by the way students are acting, Deming, along with most social psychologists, would presumably have us transform the structure of the classroom, rather than try to remake the students themselves—precisely the opposite of the character education approach.

2. *What is the view of human nature?* Character education's "fix the kids" orientation follows logically from the belief that kids need fixing. Indeed, the movement seems to be driven by a stunningly dark view of children—and, for that matter, of people in general. A "comprehensive approach [to character education] is based on a somewhat dim view of human nature," acknowledges William Kilpatrick, whose book *Why Johnny Can't Tell Right from Wrong* contains such assertions as "Most behavior problems are the result of sheer 'willfulness' on the part of children."[8]

Despite—or more likely because of—statements like that, Kilpatrick has frequently been invited to speak at character education conferences.[9] But that shouldn't be surprising in light of how many prominent proponents of character education share his views. Edward Wynne says his own work is grounded in a tradition of thought that takes a "somewhat pessimistic view of human nature."[10] The idea of character development "sees children as self-centered," in the opinion of Kevin Ryan, who directs the Center for the Advancement of Ethics and Character at Boston University, as well as heading up the character education network of the Association for Supervision and Curriculum Development.[11] Yet another writer approvingly traces the whole field back to the bleak world view of Thomas Hobbes: it is "an obvious assumption of character education," writes Louis Goldman, that people lack the instinct to work together. Without laws to compel us to get along, "our natural egoism would lead us into 'a condition of warfare one against another.'"[12] This sentiment is echoed by F. Washington Jarvis, headmaster of the Roxbury Latin School in Boston, one of Ryan's favorite examples of what character education should look like in practice. Jarvis sees human nature as "mean, nasty, brutish, selfish, and capable of great cruelty and meanness. We have to hold a mirror up to the students and say, 'This is who you are. Stop it.'"[13]

Even when proponents of character education don't express such sentiments explicitly, they give themselves away by framing their mission as a campaign for self-control. Amitai Etzioni, for example, does not merely include this attribute on a list of good character traits; he *defines* character principally in terms of the capacity "to control impulses and defer gratification."[14] This is noteworthy because the virtue of self-restraint—or at least the decision to give special emphasis to it—has historically been preached by those, from St. Augustine to the present, who see people as basically sinful.

In fact, at least three assumptions seem to be at work when the need for self-control is stressed: (1) we are all at war not only with others but with ourselves, torn between our desires and our reason (or social norms); (2) these desires are fundamentally selfish, aggressive, or otherwise unpleasant; and (3) these desires are very strong, constantly threatening to overpower us if we don't rein them in. Collectively, these statements describe religious dogma, not scientific fact. Indeed, the evidence from several disciplines converges to cast doubt on this sour view of human beings and, instead, supports the idea that it is as "natural" for children to help as to hurt. I will not rehearse that evidence here, partly because I have done so elsewhere at some length.[15] Suffice it to say that even the most hard-headed empiricist might well conclude that the promotion of prosocial values consists to some extent of supporting (rather than restraining or controlling) many facets of the self. Any educator who adopts this more balanced position might think twice before joining an educational movement that is finally inseparable from the doctrine of original sin.

3. *What is the ultimate goal?* It may seem odd even to inquire about someone's reasons for trying to improve children's character. But it is worth mentioning that the whole enterprise—not merely the particular values that are favored—is often animated by a profoundly conservative, if not reactionary, agenda. Character education based on "acculturating students to conventional norms of 'good' behavior . . . resonates with neoconservative concerns for social stability," observed David Purpel.[16] The movement has been described by another critic as a "yearning for some halcyon days of moral niceties and social tranquillity."[17] But it is not merely a *social* order that some are anxious to preserve (or recover): character education is vital, according to one vocal proponent, because "the development of character is the backbone of the economic system" now in place.[18]

Character education, or any kind of education, would look very different if we began with other objectives—if, for example, we were principally concerned with helping children to become active participants in a democratic society (or agents for transforming a society *into* one that is authentically democratic). It would look different if our top priority were to help students to develop into principled and caring members of a community or advocates for social justice. To be sure, these objectives are not inconsistent with the desire to preserve certain traditions, but the point would then be to help children to decide which traditions are worth preserving and why, based on these other considerations. That is not at all the same as endorsing anything that is traditional or making the preservation of tradition our primary concern. In short, we want to ask character education proponents what goals they emphasize—and ponder whether their broad vision is compatible with our own.

4. *Which values?* Should we allow values to be taught in school? The question is about as sensible as asking whether our bodies should be allowed to contain bacteria. Just as humans are teeming with microorganisms, so schools are teeming with values. We can't see the former because they're too small; we don't notice the latter because they're too similar to the values of the culture at large. Whether or not we deliberately adopt a character or moral education program, we are always teaching values. Even people who insist that they are opposed to values in school usually mean that they are opposed to values other than their own.[19]

And that raises the inevitable question: Which values, or whose, should we teach? It has already become a cliché to reply that this question should not trouble us because, while there may be disagreement on certain issues, such as abortion, all of us can agree on a list of basic values that children ought to have. Therefore, schools can vigorously and unapologetically set about teaching all those values.

But not so fast. Look at the way character education programs have been designed and you will discover, alongside such unobjectionable items as "fairness" or "honesty," an emphasis on values that are, again, distinctly conservative—and, to that extent, potentially controversial. To begin with, the famous Protestant work ethic is prominent: children should learn to "work hard and complete their tasks well and promptly, even when they do not want to," says Ryan.[20] Here the Latin question *cui bono?* comes to mind. Who benefits when people are trained not to question the value of what they have been told to do but simply to toil away at it—and to regard this as virtuous?[21] Similarly, when Wynne defines the moral individual as someone who is not only honest but also "diligent, obedient, and patriotic,"[22] readers may find themselves wondering whether these traits really qualify as *moral*—as well as reflecting on the virtues that are missing from this list.

Character education curricula also stress the importance of things like "respect," "responsibility," and "citizenship." But these are slippery terms, frequently used as euphemisms for uncritical deference to authority. Under the headline "The Return of the 'Fourth R'"—referring to "respect, responsibility, or rules"—a news magazine recently described the growing popularity of such practices as requiring uniforms, paddling disobedient students, rewarding those who are compliant, and "throwing disruptive kids out of the classroom."[23] Indeed, William Glasser observed some time ago that many educators "teach thoughtless conformity to school rules and call the conforming child 'responsible.'"[24] I once taught at a high school where the principal frequently exhorted students to "take responsibility." By this he meant specifically that they should turn in their friends who used drugs.

Exhorting students to be "respectful" or rewarding them if they are caught being "good" may likewise mean nothing more than getting them to do whatever the adults demand. Following a lengthy article about character education in the *New York Times Magazine,* a reader mused, "Do you suppose that if Germany had had character education at the time, it would have encouraged children to fight Nazism or to support it?"[25] The more time I spend in schools that are enthusiastically implementing character education programs, the more I am haunted by that question.

In place of the traditional attributes associated with character education, Deborah Meier and Paul Schwarz of the Central Park East Secondary School in New York nominated two core values that a school might try to promote: "empathy and skepticism: the ability to see a situation from the eyes of another and the tendency to wonder about the validity of what we encountered."[26] Anyone who brushes away the question "Which values should be taught?" might speculate on the concrete differences between a school dedicated to turning out students who are empathic and skeptical and a school dedicated to turning out students who are loyal, patriotic, obedient, and so on.

Meanwhile, in place of such personal qualities as punctuality or perseverance, we might emphasize the cultivation of autonomy so that children come to experience themselves as "origins" rather than "pawns," as one researcher put it.[27] We might, in other words, stress self-determination at least as much as self-control. With such an agenda, it would be crucial to give students the chance to participate in making decisions about their learning and about how they want their classroom to be.[28] This stands in sharp contrast to a philosophy of character education like Wynne's, which decrees that "it is specious to talk about student choices" and offers students no real power except for when we give "some students authority over other students (for example, hall guard, class monitor)."[29]

Even with values that are widely shared, a superficial consensus may dissolve when we take a closer look. Educators across the spectrum are concerned about excessive attention to self-interest and are committed to helping students to transcend a preoccupation with their own needs. But how does this concern play out in practice? For some of us, it takes the form of an emphasis on *compassion;* for the dominant character education approach, the alternative value to be stressed is *loyalty,* which is, of course, altogether different.[30] Moreover, as John Dewey remarked at the turn of the century, anyone seriously troubled about rampant individualism among children would promptly target for extinction the "drill and skill" approach to instruction: "The mere absorbing of facts and truths is so exclusively individual an affair that it tends very naturally to pass into selfishness."[31] Yet conservative champions of character education are often among the most outspoken supporters of a model of teaching that emphasizes rote memorization and the sequential acquisition of decontextualized skills.

Or take another example: all of us may say we endorse the idea of "cooperation," but what do we make of the practice of setting groups against one another in a quest for triumph, such that cooperation becomes the means and victory is the end? On the one hand, we might find this even more objectionable than individual competition. (Indeed, we might regard a "We're Number One!" ethic as a reason for schools to undertake something like character education in the first place.) On the other hand, "school-to-school, class-to-class, or row-to-row academic competitions" actually have been endorsed as part of a character education program,[32] along with contests that lead to awards for things like good citizenship.

The point, once again, is that it is entirely appropriate to ask which values a character education program is attempting to foster, notwithstanding the ostensible lack of controversy about a list of core values. It is equally appropriate to put such a discussion in context—specifically, in the context of which values are *currently* promoted in schools. The fact is that schools are already powerful socializers of traditional values—although, as noted above, we may fail to appreciate the extent to which this is true because we have come to take these values for granted. In most schools, for example, students are taught—indeed, compelled—to follow the rules regardless of whether the rules are reasonable and to respect authority regardless of whether that respect has been earned. (This process isn't always successful, of course, but that is a different matter.) Students are led to accept competition as natural and desirable and to see themselves more as discrete individuals than as members of a community. Children in U.S. schools are even expected to begin each day by reciting a loyalty oath to the Fatherland, although we call it by a different name. In short, the question is not whether to adopt the conservative values offered by most character education programs, but whether we want to consolidate the conservative values that are already in place.

5. *What is the theory of learning?* We come now to what may be the most significant, and yet the least remarked on, feature of character education: the way values are taught and the way learning is thought to take place.

> The character education coordinator for the small Chicago elementary school also teaches second grade. In her classroom, where one boy has been forced to sit by himself for the last two weeks ("He's kind of pesty"), she is asking the children to define tolerance. When the teacher gets the specific answers she is fishing for, she exclaims, "Say that again," and writes down only those responses. Later comes the moral: "If somebody doesn't think the way you think, should you turn them off?" (No.)
>
> Down the hall, the first-grade teacher is fishing for answers on a different subject. "When we play games, we try to understand the—what?" (Rules.) A moment later, the children scramble to get into place so she will pick them to tell a visitor their carefully rehearsed stories about conflict resolution. Almost every child's account, narrated with considerable prompting by the teacher, concerns name-calling or some other unpleasant incident that was "correctly" resolved by finding an adult. The teacher never asks the children how they felt about what happened or invites them to reflect on what else might have been done. She wraps up the activity by telling the children, "What we need to do all the time is clarify—make it clear—to the adult what you did."

The schools with character education programs that I have visited are engaged largely in exhortation and directed recitation. At first one might assume that this is due to poor implementation of the programs on the part of individual educators. But the programs themselves—and the theorists who promote them—really do seem to regard teaching as a matter of telling and compelling. For example, the broad-based "Character Counts!" Coalition offers a framework of six core character traits and then asserts that "young people should be specifically and repeatedly told what is expected of them." The leading providers of curriculum materials walk teachers through highly structured lessons in which character-related concepts are described and then students are drilled until they can produce the right answers.

Teachers are encouraged to praise children who respond correctly, and some programs actually include multiple-choice tests to ensure that students have learned their values. For example, here are two sample test questions prepared for teachers by the Character Education Institute, based in San Antonio, Texas: "Having to obey rules and regulations (a) gives everyone the same right to be an individual, (b) forces everyone to do the same thing at all times, (c) prevents persons from expressing their individually [sic]"; and "One reason why parents might not allow their children freedom of choice is (a) children are always happier when they are told what to do and when to do it, (b) parents aren't given a freedom of choice; therefore, children should not be given a choice either, (c) children do not always demonstrate that they are responsible enough to be given a choice." The correct answers, according to the answer key, are (a) and (c), respectively.

The Character Education Institute recommends "engaging the students in discussions," but only discussions of a particular sort: "Since the lessons have been designed to logically guide the students to the right answers, the teacher should allow the students to draw their own conclusions. However, if the students draw the wrong conclusion, the teacher is instructed to tell them why their conclusion is *wrong*."[33]

Students are told what to think and do, not only by their teachers but by highly didactic stories, such as those in the Character Education Institute's "Happy Life" series, which end with characters saying things like "I am glad that I did not cheat," or "Next time I will be helpful," or "I will never be selfish again." Most character education programs also deliver homilies by way of posters and banners and murals displayed throughout the school. Children who do as they are told are presented with all manner of rewards, typically in front of their peers.

Does all of this amount to indoctrination? Absolutely, says Wynne, who declares that "school is and should and must be inherently indoctrinative."[34] Even when character education proponents tiptoe around that word, their model of instruction is clear: good character and values are *instilled in* or *transmitted to* students. We are "planting the ideas of virtue, of good traits in the young," says William Bennett.[35] The virtues or values in question are fully formed and, in the minds of many character education proponents, divinely ordained. The children are—pick your favorite metaphor—so many passive receptacles to be filled, lumps of clay to be molded, pets to be trained, or computers to be programmed.

Thus, when we see Citizen-of-the-Month certificates and "Be a good sport!" posters, when we find teachers assigning preachy stories and principals telling students what to wear, it is important that we understand what is going on. These techniques may appear merely innocuous or gimmicky; they may strike us as evidence of a scattershot, let's-try-anything approach. But the truth is that these are elements of a systematic pedagogical philosophy. They are manifestations of a model that sees children as objects to be manipulated, rather than as learners to be engaged.

Ironically, some people who accept character education without a second thought are quite articulate about the bankruptcy of this model when it comes to teaching academic subjects. Plenty of teachers have abandoned the use of worksheets, textbooks, and lectures that fill children full of disconnected facts and skills. Plenty of administrators are working to create schools where students can actively construct meaning around scientific and historical and literary concepts. Plenty of educators, in short, realize that memorizing right answers and algorithms doesn't help anyone to arrive at a deep understanding of ideas.

And so we are left scratching our heads. Why would all these people, who know that the "transmission" model fails to facilitate intellectual development, uncritically accept the very same model to promote ethical development? How could they understand that mathematical truths cannot be shoved down students' throats, but then participate in a program that essentially tries to shove moral truths down the same throats? In the case of individual educators, the simple answer may be that they missed the connection. Perhaps they just failed to recognize that "a classroom cannot foster the development of autonomy in the intellectual realm while suppressing it in the social and moral realms," as Constance Kamii and her colleagues put it.[36]

In the case of the proponents of character education, I believe the answer to this riddle is quite different. The reason they are promoting techniques that seem strikingly ineffective at fostering autonomy or ethical development is that, as a rule, they are not *trying* to foster autonomy or ethical development. The goal is not to support or facilitate children's social and moral growth, but simply to "demand good behavior from students," in Ryan's words.[37] The idea is to get compliance, to *make* children act the way we want them to.

Indeed, if these are the goals, then the methods make perfect sense—the lectures and pseudodiscussions, the slogans and the stories that conk students on the head with their morals. David Brooks, who heads the Jefferson Center for Character Education, frankly states, "We're in the advertising business." The way you get people to do something, whether it's buying Rice Krispies or becoming trustworthy, is to "encourage conformity through repeated messages"[38] The idea of selling virtues like cereal nearly reaches the point of self-parody in the Jefferson Center's curriculum, which includes the following activity: "There's a new product on the market! It's Considerate Cereal. Eating it can make a person more considerate. Design a label for the box. Tell why someone should buy and eat this cereal. Then list the ingredients."[39]

If "repeated messages" don't work, then you simply force students to conform: "Sometimes compulsion is what is needed to get a habit started," says William Kilpatrick.[40] We may recoil from the word "compulsion," but it is the premise of that sentence that really ought to give us pause. When education is construed as the process of inculcating *habits*—which is to say, unreflective actions—then it scarcely deserves to be called education at all. It is really, as Alan Lockwood saw, an attempt to get "mindless conformity to externally imposed standards of conduct."[41]

Notice how naturally this goal follows from a dark view of human nature. If you begin with the premise that "good conduct is not our natural first choice," then the best you can hope for is "the development of good habits"[42]—that is, a system that gets people to act unthinkingly in the manner that someone else has deemed appropriate. This connection recently became clear to Ann Medlock, whose Giraffe Project was designed to evoke "students' own courage and compassion" in thinking about altruism, but which, in some schools, was being turned into a traditional, authoritarian program in which students were simply told how to act and what to believe. Medlock recalls suddenly realizing what was going on with these educators: "Oh, *I* see where you're coming from. You believe kids are no damn good!"[43]

The character education movement's emphasis on habit, then, is consistent with its view of children. Likewise, its process matches its product. The transmission model, along with the use of rewards and punishments to secure compliance, seems entirely appropriate if the values you are trying to transmit are things like obedience and loyalty and respect for authority. But this approach overlooks an important distinction between product and process. When we argue about which traits to emphasize—compassion or loyalty, cooperation or competition, skepticism or obedience—we are trafficking in value judgments. When we talk about how best to teach these things, however, we are being descriptive rather than just prescriptive. Even if you like the sort of virtues that appear in character education programs, and even if you regard the need to implement those virtues as urgent, the attempt to transmit or instill them dooms the project because that is just not consistent with the best theory and research on how people learn. (Of course, if you have reservations about many of the values that the character educators wish to instill, you may be *relieved* that their favored method is unlikely to be successful.)

I don't wish to be misunderstood. The techniques of character education may succeed in temporarily buying a particular behavior. But they are unlikely to leave children with a *commitment* to that behavior, a reason to continue acting that way in the future. You can turn out automatons who utter the desired words or maybe even "emit" (to use the curious verb favored by behaviorists) the desired actions. But the words and actions are unlikely to continue—much less transfer to new situations—because the child has not been invited to integrate them into his or her value structure. As Dewey observed, "The required beliefs cannot be hammered in; the needed attitudes cannot be plastered on."[44] Yet watch a character education lesson in any part of the country and you will almost surely be observing a strenuous exercise in hammering and plastering.

For traditional moralists, the constructivist approach is a waste of time. If values and traditions and the stories that embody them already exist, then surely "we don't have to reinvent the wheel," remarks Bennett.[45] Likewise an exasperated Wynne: "Must each generation try to completely reinvent society?"[46] The answer is no—and yes. It is not as though everything that now exists must be discarded and entirely new values fashioned from scratch. But the process of learning does indeed require that meaning, ethical or otherwise, be actively invented and reinvented, from the inside out. It requires that children be given the opportunity to make sense of such concepts as fairness or courage, regardless of how long the concepts themselves have been around. Children must be invited to reflect on complex issues, to recast them in light of their own experiences and questions, to figure out for themselves—and with one another—what kind of person one ought to be, which traditions are worth keeping, and how to proceed when two basic values seem to be in conflict.[47]

In this sense, reinvention is necessary if we want to help children to become moral people, as opposed to people who merely do what they are told—or reflexively rebel against what they are told. In fact, as DeVries and Zan add (in a book that offers a useful antidote to traditional character education), "If we want children to resist [peer pressure] and not be victims of others' ideas, we have to educate children to think for themselves about all ideas, including those of adults."[48]

Traditionalists are even more likely to offer another objection to the constructivist approach, one that boils down to a single epithet: *relativism!* If we do anything other than insert moral absolutes in students, if we let them construct their own meanings, then we are saying that anything goes, that morality collapses into personal preferences. Without character education, our schools will just offer programs such as Values Clarification, in which adults are allegedly prohibited from taking a stand.

In response, I would offer several observations. First, the Values Clarification model of moral education, popular in some circles a generation ago, survives today mostly in the polemics of conservatives anxious to justify an indoctrinative approach. Naturally, no statistics are ever cited as to the number of school districts still telling students that any value is as good as any other—assuming the program actually said that in the first place.[49] Second, conservative critics tendentiously try to connect constructivism to relativism, lumping together the work of the late Lawrence Kohlberg with programs like Values Clarification.[50] The truth is that Kohlberg, while opposed to what he called the "bag of virtues" approach to moral education, was not much enamored of Values Clarification either, and he spent a fair amount of time arguing against relativism in general.[51]

If Kohlberg can fairly be criticized, it is for emphasizing moral reasoning, a cognitive process, to the extent that he may have slighted the affective components of morality, such as caring. But the traditionalists are not much for the latter either: caring is seen as an easy or soft virtue (Ryan) that isn't sufficiently "binding or absolute" (Kilpatrick). The objection to constructivism is not that empathy is eclipsed by justice, but that children—or even adults—should not have an active role to play in making decisions and reflecting on how to live. They should be led instead to an uncritical acceptance of ready-made truths. The character educator's job, remember, is to elicit the right answer from students and tell those who see things differently "why their conclusion is *wrong*." Any deviation from this approach is regarded as indistinguishable from full-blown relativism; we must "plant" traditional values in each child or else morality is nothing more than a matter of individual taste. Such either/or thinking, long since discarded by serious moral philosophers,[52] continues to fuel character education and to perpetuate the confusion of education with indoctrination.

To say that students must construct meaning around moral concepts is not to deny that adults have a crucial role to play. The romantic view that children can basically educate themselves so long as grown-ups don't interfere is not taken seriously by any constructivists I know of—certainly not by Dewey, Piaget, Kohlberg, or their followers. Rather, like Values Clarification, this view seems to exist principally as a straw man in the arguments of conservatives. Let there be no question, then: educators, parents, and other adults are desperately needed to offer guidance, to act as models (we hope), to pose challenges that promote moral growth, and to help children to understand the effects of their actions on other people, thereby tapping and nurturing a concern for others that is present in children from a very young age.[53]

Character education rests on three ideological legs: behaviorism, conservatism, and religion. Of these, the third raises the most delicate issues for a critic; it is here that the charge of *ad hominem* argument is most likely to be raised. So let us be clear: it is of no relevance that almost all the leading proponents of character education are devout Catholics. But it is entirely relevant that, in the shadows of their writings, there lurks the assumption that only religion can serve as the foundation for good character. (William Bennett, for example, has flatly asserted that the difference between right and wrong cannot be taught "without reference to religion."[54]) It is appropriate to consider the personal beliefs of these individuals if those beliefs are ensconced in the movement they have defined and directed. What they do on Sundays is their own business, but if they are trying to turn our public schools into Sunday schools, that becomes everybody's business.

Even putting aside the theological underpinnings of the character education movement, the five questions presented in this chapter can help us to describe the natural constituency of that movement. Logically, its supporters should be those who firmly believe that we should focus our efforts on repairing the characters of children, rather than on transforming the environments in which they learn, those who assume the worst about human nature, those who are more committed to preserving than to changing our society, those who favor such values as obedience to authority, and those who define learning as the process of swallowing whole a set of preexisting truths. It stands to reason that readers who recognize themselves in this description would enthusiastically endorse character education in its present form.

The rest of us have a decision to make. Either we define our efforts to promote children's social and moral development as an *alternative* to "character education," thereby ceding that label to the people who have already appropriated it, or we try to *reclaim* the wider meaning of the term by billing what we are doing as a different kind of character education.

The first choice—opting out—seems logical: it strains the language to use a single phrase to describe practices as different as engaging students in reflecting about fairness, on the one hand, and making students dress alike, on the other. It seems foolish to pretend that these are just different versions of the same thing, and thus it may be unreasonable to expect someone with a constructivist or progressive vision to endorse what is now called character education. The problem with abandoning this label, however, is that it holds considerable appeal for politicians and members of the public at large. It will be challenging to explain that "character education" is not synonymous with helping children to grow into good people and, indeed, that the movement associated with the term is a good deal more controversial than it first appears.

The second choice, meanwhile, presents its own set of practical difficulties. Given that the individuals and organizations mentioned in this chapter have succeeded in putting their own stamp on character education, it will not be easy to redefine the phrase so that it can also signify a very different approach. It will not be easy, that is, to organize conferences, publish books and articles, and develop curricular materials that rescue the broad meaning of "character education."

Whether we relinquish or retain the nomenclature, though, it is vital that we work to decouple most of what takes place under the banner of "character education" from the enterprise of helping students become ethically sophisticated decision makers and caring human beings. Wanting young people to turn out that way doesn't require us to adopt traditional character education programs, any more than wanting them to be physically fit requires us to turn schools into Marine boot camps.

What does the alternative look like? Return once more to those five questions: in each case, an answer different from that given by traditional character education will help us to sketch the broad contours of a divergent approach. More specifically, we should probably target certain practices for elimination, add some new ones, and reconfigure still others that already exist. I have already offered a catalogue of examples of what to eliminate, from Skinnerian reinforcers to lesson plans that resemble sermons. As examples of what to add, we might suggest holding regular class meetings in which students can share, plan, decide, and reflect together.[55] We might also provide children with explicit opportunities to practice "perspective taking"—that is, imagining how the world looks from someone else's point of view. Activities that promote an understanding of how others think and feel, that support the impulse to imaginatively reach beyond the self, can provide the same benefits realized by holding democratic class meetings—that is, helping students become more ethical and compassionate while simultaneously fostering intellectual growth.[56]

A good example of an existing practice that might be reconfigured is the use of literature to teach values. In principle, the idea is splendid: it makes perfect sense to select stories that not only help students develop reading skills (and an appreciation for good writing) but also raise moral issues. The trouble is that many programs use simplistic little morality tales in place of rich, complex literature. Naturally, the texts should be developmentally appropriate, but some character educators fail to give children credit for being able to grapple with ambiguity. (Imagine the sort of stories likely to be assigned by someone who maintains that "it is ridiculous to believe children are capable of objectively assessing most of the beliefs and values they must absorb to be effective adults."[57])

Perhaps the concern is not that students will be unable to make sense of challenging literature, but that they will not derive the "correct" moral. This would account for the fact that, even when character education curricula include impressive pieces of writing, the works tend to be used for the purpose of drumming in simple lessons. As Kilpatrick sees it, a story "points to these [characters] and says in effect, 'Act like this; don't act like that.'"[58] This kind of lesson often takes the form of hero worship, with larger-than-life characters—or real historical figures presented with their foibles airbrushed away—held up to students to encourage imitation of their actions.

Rather than employ literature to indoctrinate or induce mere conformity, we can use it to spur reflection. Whether the students are 6-year-olds or 16-year-olds, the discussion of stories should be open ended rather than relentlessly didactic. Teachers who refrain from tightly controlling such conversations are impressed again and again by the levels of meaning students prove capable of exploring and the moral growth that they exhibit in such an environment. Instead of announcing "This man is a hero; do what he did," such teachers may involve the students in *deciding* who (if anyone) is heroic in a given story—or in contemporary culture[59]—and why. They may even invite students to reflect on the larger issue of whether it is desirable to have heroes. (Consider the quality of discussion that might be generated by asking older students to respond to the declaration of playwright Bertolt Brecht: "Unhappy is the land that needs a hero.")

More than specific practices that might be added, subtracted, or changed, a program to help children grow into good people begins with a commitment to change the way classrooms and schools are structured—and this brings us back to the idea of transcending a fix-the-kid approach. Consider the format of classroom discussions. A proponent of character education, invoking such traditional virtues as patience or self-control, might remind students that they must wait to be recognized by the teacher. But what if we invited students to think about the best way to conduct a discussion? Must we raise our hands? Is there another way to avoid having everyone talk at once? How can we be fair to those who aren't as assertive or as fast on their feet? Should the power to decide who can speak always rest with the teacher? Perhaps the problem is not with students who need to be more self-disciplined, but with the whole instructional design that has students waiting to be recognized to answer someone else's questions. And perhaps the real learning comes only when students have the chance to grapple with such issues.

One more example. A proponent of character education says we must make students understand that it is wrong to lie; we need to teach them about the importance of being honest. But why do people lie? Usually because they don't feel safe enough to tell the truth. The real challenge for us as educators is to examine that precept in terms of what is going on in our classrooms, to ask how we and the students together can make sure that even unpleasant truths can be told and heard. Does pursuing this line of inquiry mean that it's acceptable to fib? No. It means that the problem has to be dissected and solved from the inside out. It means behaviors occur in a context that teachers have helped to establish; therefore, teachers have to examine (and consider modifying) that context even at the risk of some discomfort to themselves. In short, if we want to help children grow into compassionate and responsible people, we have to change the way the classroom works and feels, not just the way each separate member of that class acts. Our emphasis should not be on forming individual characters so much as on transforming educational structures.

Happily, programs do exist whose promotion of children's social and moral development is grounded in a commitment to change the culture of schools. The best example of which I am aware is the Child Development Project, an elementary school program designed, implemented, and researched by the Developmental Studies Center in Oakland, California. The CDP's premise is that, by meeting children's needs, we increase the likelihood that they will care about others. Meeting their needs entails, among other things, turning schools into caring communities. The CDP offers the additional advantages of a constructivist vision of learning, a positive view of human nature, a balance of cognitive and affective concerns, and a program that is integrated into all aspects of school life (including the curriculum).[60]

Is the CDP an example of what character education ought to be—or of what ought to replace character education? The answer to that question will depend on tactical, and even semantic, considerations. Far more compelling is the need to reevaluate the practices and premises of contemporary character education. To realize a humane and progressive vision for children's development, we may need to look elsewhere.

ENDNOTES

1. See, for example, Linda Page, "A Conservative Christian View on Values," *School Administrator,* September 1995, p. 22.
2. See, for example, Kevin Ryan, "The Ten Commandments of Character Education," *School Administrator,* September 1995, p. 19; and program materials from the Character Education Institute and the Jefferson Center for Character Education.
3. See Alfie Kohn, *Punished by Rewards: The Trouble with Gold Stars, Incentive Plans, A's, Praise, and Other Bribes* (Boston: Houghton Mifflin, 1993); and Edward L. Deci and Richard M. Ryan, *Intrinsic Motivation and Self-Determination in Human Behavior* (New York: Plenum, 1985).
4. See C. Daniel Batson et al., "Buying Kindness: Effect of an Extrinsic Incentive for Helping on Perceived Altruism," *Personality and Social Psychology Bulletin,* vol. 4, 1978, p. 90; Cathleen L. Smith et al., "Children's Causal Attributions Regarding Help Giving," *Child Development,* vol. 50, 1979, pp. 203–10; and William Edward Upton III, "Altruism, Attribution, and Intrinsic Motivation in the Recruitment of Blood Donors," *Dissertation Abstracts International* 34B, vol. 12, 1974, p. 6260.
5. Richard A. Fabes et al., "Effects of Rewards on Children's Prosocial Motivation: A Socialization Study," *Developmental Psychology,* vol. 25, 1989, pp. 509–15; and Joan Grusec, "Socializing Concern for Others in the Home," *Developmental Psychology,* vol. 27, 1991, pp. 338–42.
6. See Alfie Kohn, *No Contest: The Case Against Competition,* rev. ed. (Boston: Houghton Mifflin, 1992).
7. This statement is taken from an eight-page brochure produced by the "Character Counts!" Coalition, a project of the Josephson Institute of Ethics. Members of the coalition include the American Federation of Teachers, the National Association of Secondary School Principals, the American Red Cross, the YMCA, and many other organizations.
8. William Kilpatrick, *Why Johnny Can't Tell Right from Wrong* (New York: Simon & Schuster, 1992), pp. 96, 249.
9. For example, Kilpatrick was selected in 1995 to keynote the first in a series of summer institutes on character education sponsored by Thomas Lickona.
10. Edward Wynne, "Transmitting Traditional Values in Contemporary Schools," in Larry P. Nucci, ed., *Moral Development and Character Education: A Dialogue* (Berkeley, CA: McCutchan, 1989), p. 25.
11. Kevin Ryan, "In Defense of Character Education," in Nucci, p. 16.
12. Louis Goldman, "Mind, Character, and the Deferral of Gratification," *Educational Forum,* vol. 60, 1996, p. 136. As part of "educational reconstruction," he goes on to say, we must "connect the lower social classes to the middle classes who may provide role models for self-discipline" (p. 139).
13. Jarvis is quoted in Wray Herbert, "The Moral Child," *U.S. News & World Report,* June 3, 1996, p. 58.
14. Amitai Etzioni, *The Spirit of Community: The Reinvention of American Society* (New York: Simon & Schuster, 1993), p. 91.
15. See Alfie Kohn, *The Brighter Side of Human Nature: Altruism and Empathy in Everyday Life* (New York: Basic Books, 1990); and "Caring Kids: The Role of the Schools," *Phi Delta Kappan,* March 1991, pp. 496–506.
16. David E. Purpel, "Moral Education: An Idea Whose Time Has Gone," *The Clearing House,* vol. 64, 1991, p. 311.

17. This description of the character education movement is offered by Alan L. Lockwood in "Character Education: The Ten Percent Solution," *Social Education,* April/May 1991, p. 246. It is a particularly apt characterization of a book like *Why Johnny Can't Tell Right from Wrong,* which invokes an age of "chivalry" and sexual abstinence, a time when moral truths were uncomplicated and unchallenged. The author's tone, however, is not so much wistful about the past as angry about the present: he denounces everything from rock music (which occupies an entire chapter in a book about morality) and feminism to the "multiculturalists" who dare to remove "homosexuality from the universe of moral judgment" (p. 126).

18. Kevin Walsh of the University of Alabama is quoted in Eric N. Berg, "Argument Grows That Teaching of Values Should Rank with Lessons," *New York Times,* January 1, 1992, p. 32.

19. I am reminded of a woman in a Houston audience who heatedly informed me that she doesn't send her child to school "to learn to be nice." That, she declared, would be "social engineering." But a moment later this woman added that her child ought to be "taught to respect authority." Since this would seem to be at least as apposite an example of social engineering, one is led to conclude that the woman's real objection was to the teaching of *particular* topics or values.

20. Kevin Ryan, "Mining the Values in the Curriculum," *Educational Leadership,* November 1993, p. 16.

21. Telling students to "try hard" and "do their best" begs the important questions. *How,* exactly, do they do their best? Surely it is not just a matter of blind effort. And *why* should they do so, particularly if the task is not engaging or meaningful to them, or if it has simply been imposed on them? Research has found that the attitudes students take toward learning are heavily influenced by whether they have been led to attribute their success (or failure) to innate ability, to effort, or to other factors—and that traditional classroom practices such as grading and competition lead them to explain the results in terms of ability (or its absence) and to minimize effort whenever possible. What looks like "laziness" or insufficient perseverance, in other words, often turns out to be a rational decision to avoid challenge; it is rational because this route proves most expedient for performing well or maintaining an image of oneself as smart. These systemic factors, of course, are complex and often threatening for educators to address; it is much easier just to impress on children the importance of doing their best and then blame them for lacking perseverance if they seem not to do so.

22. Edward A. Wynne, "The Great Tradition in Education: Transmitting Moral Values," *Educational Leadership,* December 1985/January 1986, p. 6.

23. Mary Lord, "The Return of the 'Fourth R,'" *U.S. News & World Report,* September 11, 1995, p. 58.

24. William Glasser, *Schools Without Failure* (New York: Harper & Row, 1969), p. 22.

25. Marc Desmond's letter appeared in the *New York Times Magazine,* May 21, 1995, p. 14. The same point was made by Robert Primack, "No Substitute for Critical Thinking: A Response to Wynne," *Educational Leadership,* December 1985/January 1986, p. 12.

26. Deborah Meier and Paul Schwarz, "Central Park East Secondary School," in Michael W. Apple and James A. Beane, eds., *Democratic Schools* (Alexandria, VA: Association for Supervision and Curriculum Development, 1995), pp. 29–30.

27. See Richard de Charms, *Personal Causation: The Internal Affective Determinants of Behavior* (Hillsdale, NJ: Erlbaum, 1983). See also the many publications of Edward Deci and Richard Ryan.

28. See, for example, Alfie Kohn, "Choices for Children: Why and How to Let Students Decide," *Phi Delta Kappan,* September 1993, pp. 8–20; and Child Development Project, *Ways We Want Our Class to Be: Class Meetings That Build Commitment to Kindness and Learning* (Oakland, CA: Developmental Studies Center, 1996).

29. The quotations are from Wynne, "The Great Tradition," p. 9; and Edward A. Wynne and Herbert J. Walberg, "The Complementary Goals of Character Development and Academic Excellence," *Educational Leadership,* December 1985/January 1986, p. 17. William Kilpatrick is equally averse to including students in decision making; he speaks longingly of the days when "schools were unapologetically authoritarian," declaring that "schools can learn a lot from the Army," which is a "hierarchial [sic], authoritarian,

and undemocratic institution" (see *Why Johnny Can't*, p. 228).

30. The sort of compassion I have in mind is akin to what the psychologist Ervin Staub described as a "prosocial orientation" (see his *Positive Social Behavior and Morality*, vols. 1 and 2 [New York: Academic Press, 1978 and 1979])—a generalized inclination to care, share, and help across different situations and with different people, including those we don't know, don't like, and don't look like. Loyally lending a hand to a close friend is one thing; going out of one's way for a stranger is something else.

31. John Dewey, *The School and Society* (Chicago: University of Chicago Press, 1900; reprint, 1990), p. 15.

32. Wynne and Walberg, p. 17. For another endorsement of competition among students, see Kevin Ryan, "In Defense," p. 15.

33. This passage is taken from page 21 of an undated 28-page "Character Education Curriculum" produced by the Character Education Institute. Emphasis in original.

34. Wynne, "Great Tradition," p. 9. Wynne and other figures in the character education movement acknowledge their debt to the French social scientist Emile Durkheim, who believed that "all education is a continuous effort to impose on the child ways of seeing, feeling, and acting which he could not have arrived at spontaneously. . . . We exert pressure upon him in order that he may learn proper consideration for others, respect for customs and conventions, the need for work, etc." (See Durkheim, *The Rules of Sociological Method* [New York: Free Press, 1938], p. 6.)

35. This is from Bennett's introduction to *The Book of Virtues* (New York: Simon & Schuster, 1993), pp. 12–13.

36. Constance Kamii, Faye B. Clark, and Ann Dominick, "The Six National Goals: A Road to Disappointment," *Phi Delta Kappan*, May 1994, p. 677.

37. Kevin Ryan, "Character and Coffee Mugs," *Education Week*, May 17, 1995, p. 48.

38. The second quotation is a reporter's paraphrase of Brooks. Both it and the direct quotation preceding it appear in Philip Cohen, "The Content of Their Character: Educators Find New Ways to Tackle Values and Morality," *ASCD Curriculum Update*, Spring 1995, p. 4.

39. See B. David Brooks, *Young People's Lessons in Character: Student Activity Workbook* (San Diego, CA: Young People's Press, 1996), p. 12.

40. Kilpatrick, p. 231.

41. To advocate this sort of enterprise, he adds, is to "caricature the moral life." See Alan L. Lockwood, "Keeping Them in the Courtyard: A Response to Wynne," *Educational Leadership*, December 1985/January 1986, p. 10.

42. Kilpatrick, p. 97.

43. Personal communication with Ann Medlock, May 1996.

44. John Dewey, *Democracy and Education* (New York: Free Press, 1916; reprint, 1966), p. 11.

45. Bennett, p. 11.

46. Wynne, "Character and Academics," p. 142.

47. For a discussion of how traditional character education fails to offer guidance when values come into conflict, see Lockwood, "Character Education."

48. Rheta DeVries and Betty Zan, *Moral Classrooms, Moral Children: Creating a Constructivist Atmosphere in Early Education* (New York: Teachers College Press, 1994), p. 253.

49. For an argument that critics tend to misrepresent what Values Clarification was about, see James A. Beane, *Affect in the Curriculum* (New York: Teachers College Press, 1990), pp. 104–106.

50. Wynne, for example, refers to the developers of Values Clarification as "popularizers" of Kohlberg's research (see "Character and Academics," p. 141), while Amitai Etzioni, in the course of criticizing Piaget's and Kohlberg's work, asserts that "a typical course on moral reasoning starts with something called 'values clarification'" (see *The Spirit of Community*, p. 98).

51. Kohlberg's model, which holds that people across cultures progress predictably through six stages of successively more sophisticated styles of moral reasoning, is based on the decidedly nonrelativistic premise that the last stages are superior to the first ones. See his *Essays on Moral Development, Vol. 1: The Philosophy of Moral Development* (San Francisco: Harper & Row, 1981), especially the essays titled "Indoctrination versus Relativity in Value Education" and "From Is to *Ought*."

52. See, for example, James S. Fishkin, *Beyond Subjective Morality* (New Haven, CT: Yale University

Press, 1984); and David B. Wong, *Moral Relativity* (Berkeley: University of California Press, 1984).

53. Researchers at the National Institute of Mental Health have summarized the available research as follows: "Even children as young as 2 years old have (a) the cognitive capacity to interpret the physical and psychological states of others, (b) the emotional capacity to effectively experience the other's state, and (c) the behavioral repertoire that permits the possibility of trying to alleviate discomfort in others. These are the capabilities that, we believe, underlie children's caring behavior in the presence of another person's distress. . . . Young children seem to show patterns of moral internalization that are not simply fear based or solely responsive to parental commands. Rather, there are signs that children feel responsible for (as well as connected to and dependent on) others at a very young age." (See Carolyn Zahn-Waxler et al., "Development of Concern for Others," *Developmental Psychology*, vol. 28, 1992, pp. 127, 135. For more on the adult's role in light of these facts, see Kohn, *The Brighter Side*.)

54. "Education Secretary Backs Teaching of Religious Values," *New York Times*, November 12, 1985, p. B-4.

55. For more on class meetings, see Glasser, chaps. 10–12; Thomas Gordon, *T. E.T: Teacher Effectiveness Training* (New York: David McKay Co., 1974), chaps. 8–9; Jane Nelsen, Lynn Lott, and H. Stephen Glenn, *Positive Discipline in the Classroom* (Rocklin, CA: Prima, 1993); and Child Development Project.

56. For more on the theory and research of perspective taking, see Kohn, *The Brighter Side*, chaps. 4–5; for practical classroom activities for promoting perspective-taking skills, see Norma Deitch Feshbach et al., *Learning to Care: Classroom Activities for Social and Affective Development* (Glenview, IL: Scott, Foresman, 1983). While specialists in the field distinguish between perspective taking (imagining what others see, think, or feel) and empathy (*feeling* what others feel), most educators who talk about the importance of helping children to become empathic really seem to be talking about perspective taking.

57. Wynne, "Great Tradition," p. 9.

58. Kilpatrick, p. 141.

59. It is informative to discover whom the proponents of a hero-based approach to character education themselves regard as heroic. For example, William Bennett's nominee for "possibly our greatest living American" is Rush Limbaugh. (See Terry Eastland, "Rush Limbaugh: Talking Back," *American Spectator*, September 1992, p. 23.)

60. See Victor Battistich et al., "The Child Development Project: A Comprehensive Program for the Development of Prosocial Character," in William M. Kurtines and Jacob L. Gewirtz, eds., *Moral Behavior and Development: Advances in Theory, Research, and Applications* (Hillsdale, NJ: Erlbaum, 1989); and Daniel Solomon et al., "Creating a Caring Community: Educational Practices That Promote Children's Prosocial Development," in Fritz K. Oser, Andreas Dick, and Jean-Luc Patry, eds., *Effective and Responsible Teaching* (San Francisco: Jossey-Bass, 1992). For more information about the CDP program or about the research substantiating its effects, write the Developmental Studies Center at 2000 Embarcadero, Suite 305, Oakland, CA 94606.

DISCUSSION QUESTIONS

1. According to the author, how is character education most accurately described?
2. What are the fundamental limitations of current character education program strategies?
3. Why do many educators contest the goals and values that typify character education programs?
4. What divergent approaches would exemplify a program that is different from traditional approaches to moral development?
5. How can reflection be used to enhance students' moral growth?
6. How can classroom norms thwart or facilitate students' moral development?

CHAPTER 16

Limiting Students' School Success and Life Chances: The Impact of Tracking

JEANNIE S. OAKES

FOCUSING QUESTIONS

1. Why has tracking been considered to be a fair educational practice by educators and psychologists?
2. How has tracking affected student outcomes?
3. How do educators tend to justify the practice of tracking?
4. In what ways were criteria used to assign students to tracks?
5. What procedures were used to ensure that parents were informed about tracking and their rights to influence placements?
6. What role did teacher assessment and perception play in assigning students to tracks?

Evidence from two school systems whose ability-grouping and tracking systems were subject to scrutiny in 1993 in conjunction with school desegregation cases demonstrates how grouping practices can create within-school segregation and discrimination against African American and Latino students. In both school systems, tracking created racially unbalanced classes at all three levels—elementary, middle, and senior high, with African American or Latino students consistently overrepresented and white and Asian students consistently underrepresented in low-ability tracks in all subjects. Neither district's placement practices created classrooms with a range of measured student ability and achievement in classrooms sufficiently narrow to be considered homogeneous "ability groups," and African American and Latino students were much less likely than whites or Asians with comparable scores to be placed in high-track courses. These disproportionate lower-track placements worked to disadvantage minority students' achievement outcomes. Whether students began with relatively high or relatively low achievement, those who were placed in lower-level courses showed lesser gains over time than similarly situated students placed in higher-level courses. In both systems, grouping practices created a cycle of restricted opportunities and diminished outcomes and exacerbated differences between African American and Latino and white students.

Since the 1920s, most elementary and secondary schools have tracked their students into separate "ability" groups designed for bright, average, and slow learners and into separate programs for students who are expected to follow different career routes after high school graduation. Tracking has seemed appropriate and fair, given the way psychologists have defined differences in students' intellectual abilities, motivation, and aspirations. Tracking has seemed logical because it supports a nearly century old belief that a crucial job of schools is to ready students for an economy that requires workers with quite different knowledge and skills. According to this logic, demanding academic classes would prepare bright, motivated students heading for jobs that require college degrees, while more rudimentary academic classes and vocational programs would ready less able and less motivated students for less-skilled jobs or for post–high school technical training. With the development early in the 20th century of standardized tests for placement, most people viewed a tracked curriculum with its ability-grouped academic classes as functional, scientific, and democratic—an educationally sound way to accomplish two important tasks: (1) providing students with the education that best suits their abilities and (2) providing the nation with the array of workers it needs.

Despite its widespread legitimacy, there is no question that tracking, the assessment practices that support it, and the differences in educational opportunity that result from it limit many students' schooling opportunities and life chances. These limits affect schoolchildren from all racial, ethnic, and socioeconomic groups. However, schools far more often judge African American and Latino students to have learning deficits and limited potential. Not surprisingly, then, schools place these students disproportionately in low-track, remedial programs.

Educators justify these placements by pointing out that African American and Latino children typically perform less well on commonly accepted assessments of ability and achievement. Moreover, conventional school wisdom holds that low-track, remedial, and special education classes help these students, since they permit teachers to target instruction to the particular learning deficiencies of low-ability students. However, considerable research demonstrates that students do not profit from enrollment in low-track classes; they do not learn as much as comparably skilled students in heterogeneous classes; they have less access than other students to knowledge, engaging learning experiences, and resources.[1] Thus school tracking practices create racially separate programs that provide minority children with restricted educational opportunities and outcomes.

In what follows, I will illustrate these points with evidence from two school systems whose ability grouping and tracking systems have been subject to scrutiny in conjunction with school desegregation cases. The first system, Rockford Public Schools, in Rockford, Illinois (previously under an interim court order), was the target of a liability suit brought by a community group, The People Who Care. Among other complaints, the group charged the school system with within-school segregation through ability grouping and discrimination against the district's nearly 30 percent African American and Latino students. The second system, San Jose Unified School District, in San Jose, California, approached the court hoping to be released from its desegregation order of 1985. The plaintiffs in the San Jose case argued, among other things, that the district had used its ability-grouping system to create within-school segregation and, thereby, circumvented the intent of the court order with regard to its approximately 30 percent Latino student population. I analyzed data about the grouping practices in both these cities, prepared reports for the court, and testified. The San Jose system reached a settlement prior to the formal hearing date. The Rockford system was found liable by the court.

To shed light on the grouping practices in these two systems, I conducted analyses and reported my conclusions about tracking and ability-grouping practices around several questions:

1. Does the school system employ tracking and/or ability grouping? If so, what is the specific nature of these practices?
2. Does the system's use of tracking and/or ability grouping create racially imbalanced classrooms?
3. Does the system's use of these grouping practices reflect sound, consistent, and educationally valid considerations?
4. Are the racial disproportionalities created by the system's ability-grouping practices explained by valid educational considerations?
5. What are the consequences of the system's grouping and tracking practices for the classroom instructional opportunities of Latino children?
6. What are the consequences of the system's grouping and tracking practices for the educational outcomes of Latino children?
7. Does the system have the necessary support and capacity to dismantle racially identifiable tracking and create heterogeneously grouped classrooms?

I addressed these questions with analyses using data specific to the two school systems. These data were gathered from a variety of sources: district and individual school curriculum documents (e.g., curriculum guides, course catalogs, course descriptions, etc.); school plans; computerized student enrollment and achievement data; prior reports prepared by court monitors; and depositions taken from school district employees in the course of the discovery process.[2]

Several analytic methods were applied to these data, all of which had been used in prior published research on tracking and ability grouping. In both systems, I used statistical methods to calculate the achievement range within each track, the distribution of students from various ethnic groups into various tracks, and the probability of placement of students from each ethnic group whose prior achievement "qualified" them for various tracks. In San Jose, but not in Rockford, I was also able to calculate rather precisely the impact of track placement on achievement gains of students with comparable prior achievement. I applied content analysis techniques to district and school curriculum documents in order to classify courses into various track levels, determine placement criteria and processes, and identify curricular goals, course content, and learning opportunities. These documents constitute official district policy statements about the levels and content of the districts' programs and courses, as well as the criteria and procedures by which students enroll in various programs and courses.

The scope of possible analyses was limited, more in Rockford than in San Jose, by a lack of some essential data. Even so, the available data permitted comprehensive analyses of many aspects of the district's grouping practices. They provided a clear picture of tracking and ability grouping in the two systems and enabled me to place the district's practices in light of national research.

PROLIFERATION OF TRACKING

Grouping practices and their effects on minority children were remarkably similar in both systems. Both systems used tracking extensively. At most grade levels and in most academic subject areas at nearly all schools, educators assigned students to classes based on judgments about students' academic abilities. The schools then tailored the curriculum and instruction within classes to the students' perceived ability levels. The districts' tracking systems were not only very comprehensive (in terms of the subject areas and grade levels that are tracked), but also very rigid and stable. That is, the districts tended to place students at the same ability level for classes in a variety of subject areas and to lock students into the same or a lower ability-level placement from year to year.

RACIALLY DISPROPORTIONATE TRACK ENROLLMENTS

In both school systems, tracking had created racially imbalanced classes at all three levels—elementary, middle, and senior high. This imbalance took two forms: (1) white (and Asian, in San Jose) students were consistently overrepresented and African American and Latino students were consistently underrepresented in high-ability classes in all subjects; (2) in contrast, African American or Latino students were consistently overrepresented while white and Asian students were consistently underrepresented in low-ability tracks in all subjects.

INCONSISTENT APPLICATION OF PLACEMENT CRITERIA

The criteria used to assign students to particular tracks were neither clearly specified nor consistently applied. Accordingly, neither district's tracking policies and practices could be construed as the enactment of valid educational purposes; neither did either district present an educational justification for the racial imbalance that results from tracking. Moreover, my analyses demonstrate clearly that neither district's placement practices—practices that result in racially imbalanced tracked classrooms—could be justified by a racially neutral policy of creating classrooms that are distinctly different from one another in terms of students' academic ability or achievement. To the contrary, neither district had enacted ability grouping and tracking in ways that narrow the range of measured student ability and achievement in classrooms sufficiently so that these classrooms can be considered bona fide ability groups.

Both school systems honored parent requests for students' initial track placements and for subsequent changes. This policy undermined the basis of student assignments in either objective measures of students' abilities or more subjective professional judgments. Making matters worse, not all parents were informed about tracking practices or about parents' right to influence their children's placements. Specifically, African American and Latino parents had less access than others to this knowledge.

Additionally, teacher and counselor recommendations at the critical transitions between elementary and middle school and between middle and high school included a formal mechanism to take into account highly subjective judgments about students' personalities, behavior, and motivation. For example, the screening process for gifted programs usually began with a subjective teacher identification of potentially gifted children, who were then referred for formal testing. Such referrals were often based on subjective judgments about behavior, personality, and attitudes.

TRACKS ACTUALLY HETEROGENEOUS GROUPS

The theory of tracking argues that, to facilitate learning, children should be separated into groups so that they may be taught together with peers of similar ability and apart from those with higher or lower abilities. But in both school systems, classes that were supposed to be designated for students at a *particular* ability level actually enrolled students who spanned *a very wide range* of measured ability. These ranges demonstrate dramatically that in both Rockford and San Jose racially imbalanced tracked classes have borne little resemblance to homogeneous ability groups—even though they have been labeled and treated as such by schools. While the mean scores in each of the tracks followed expected patterns—with average achievement score for students in the low track less than average score for students in the standard or accelerated tracks—the extraordinarily broad range of achievement in each of the three tracks makes clear how far these classes are from being homogeneous ability groups. In sum, the district's practices do not represent what tracking advocates would claim is a trustworthy enactment of a "theory" of tracking and ability grouping.

For example, at one Rockford middle school, the range of eighth-grade reading scores in Honors English (31–99 National Percentile [NP]) overlapped considerably with the range in Regular English (1–95 NP), which overlapped considerably with the range in Basic English (1–50 NP). At one of the senior highs, the math scores of tenth graders in the normal progress college prep math track (26–99 NP) overlapped considerably with those in the slow progress college prep courses (1–99), and both overlapped considerably with the scores of those in non–college preparatory classes (1–99). I found similar patterns of large, overlapping ranges of qualifying scores throughout the system.

The same was true in San Jose. For example, sixth graders placed in a low-track mathematics course demonstrated abilities that ranged all the way from rock-bottom Normal Curve Equivalent (NCE) achievement scores of 1 to extraordinarily high scores of 86. Even more striking, sixth graders in standard-track math classes had achievement scores that spanned the entire range, from NCE scores of 1 to 99. And, while sixth graders in accelerated courses had a somewhat more restricted ability range, they too scored all the way from 52 to 99 NCEs. I found similar patterns in a number of other subjects in most middle and senior high school grades.

PLACEMENTS RACIALLY SKEWED BEYOND THE EFFECTS OF ACHIEVEMENT

As a group, African American and Latino students scored lower on achievement tests than whites and Asians in Rockford and San Jose. However, African American and Latino students were much less likely than white or Asian students *with the same test scores* to be placed in accelerated courses. For example, in San Jose, Latino eighth graders with average scores in mathematics were three times less likely than whites with the same scores to be placed in an accelerated math course. Among ninth graders, the results were similar. Latinos scoring between 40 and 49, 50 and 59, and 60 and 69 NCEs were less than half as likely as their white and Asian counterparts to be placed in accelerated tracks. The discrimination is even more striking among the highest scoring students. While only 56 percent of Latinos scoring between 90 and 99 NCEs were placed in accelerated classes, 93 percent of whites and 97 percent of Asians gained admission to these classes.

In Rockford's tracks and class ability levels, the groups of *higher*-track students whose scores fell within a range that would qualify them for participation in either a higher or a lower track (i.e., their scores were the same as students in the lower track) were consistently "whiter" than groups of students whose scores fell within that same range but were placed in the *lower* track. In a number of cases, Rockford's high-track classes included students with exceptionally low scores, but rarely were these students African Americans. Conversely, high-scoring

African Americans were enrolled in low-track classes; again, this was seldom the case for high-scoring whites. For example, in 1987, none of the African American students who scored in the top quartile (75–99 NP) on the California Assessment Program (CAP) reading comprehension test at two of Rockford's large high schools were placed in high-track English, compared with about 40 percent of top-quartile whites who were enrolled in the high track at those schools. In contrast, at three of the system's senior high schools, a small fraction of white students who scored in the bottom quartile (1–25 NP) were in high-track classes, while no similarly low-scoring African Americans were so placed. At two other senior highs, while some top-quartile African Americans were placed in Honors English, many more top-scoring African Americans were in the basic classes. No low-scoring whites were so placed. I found similar patterns in other subjects at the district's high schools.

I found other striking examples of racially skewed placements in Rockford's junior highs. For example, at one, the range of reading comprehension scores among eighth graders enrolled in Basic English classes was from the first to the seventy-second national percentile. Of these, ten students scored above the national average of 50 NP. Six of the highest scoring, above-average students were African American, including the highest achieving student in the class. One other of the above-average students was Latino.

In both San Jose and Rockford, placement practices skewed enrollments in favor of whites over and above that which can be explained by measured achievement.

LOW TRACKS PROVIDING LESS OPPORTUNITY

In both school systems, African American and Latino students in lower-track classes had fewer learning opportunities. Teachers expected less of them and gave them less exposure to curriculum and instruction in essential knowledge and skills. Lower-track classes also provided African American and Latino students with less access to a whole range of resources and opportunities: to highly qualified teachers, to classroom environments conducive to learning, to opportunities to earn extra grade points that could bolster their grade-point averages, and to courses that would qualify them for college entrance and a wide variety of careers as adults.

LOW TRACKS AND LOWER ACHIEVEMENT

Not only did African American and Latino students receive a lower-quality education as a result of tracking in San Jose and Rockford; their academic achievement suffered as well. In Rockford, the initial average achievement gap (i.e., the difference in group mean achievement scores between white and African American and/or white and Latino students on district-administered achievement tests in first grade) did not diminish in higher grades. To the contrary, eleventh graders exhibited gaps somewhat larger than those of first graders. For example, on the 1992 Stanford Achievement Test in reading comprehension, the gap between African American and white first graders was 25 percent; that between African American and white eleventh graders was 30 percent. Undoubtedly more telling, at the time of the seventh-grade test—probably the last point before considerable numbers of lower-achieving minority students drop out of school—the achievement gap between African Americans and whites had grown considerably wider, to 36 percent. A similar pattern was found in students' raw scores in reading comprehension and mathematics for grades 1–6 on the 1992 Stanford Achievement Test. Here, the reading achievement gap between African American and white students was .88 of a standard deviation at first grade and grew to .99 by grade 6. The Latino–white gap grew from .67 to .70 over the same grades. In math, the African American–white gap grew from .87 to 1.01; in contrast, the Latino–white gap dropped from .98 to .79. Clearly, the district's tracked programs failed to close the minority–white gap between average group scores. Neither did these practices correct the overrepresentation of black and Latino-students in the group of lowest-scoring students in the district. For example, in 1992, 37 percent of the first-grade children scoring between the first and the twenty-fifth national percentiles in reading comprehension on the Stanford Achievement Test were African American; at seventh grade, the percentage of African Americans in this low-scoring group had risen to 46 percent, and by grade 11 (following a disproportionately high incidence of dropping out by low-achieving African American students), African American students still made up 35 percent of this group. Neither did student placements in various instructional programs enable minority students to rise into the group of the district's highest achievers. In fact, *the proportion of minority students in the highest-achieving group of students dropped precipitously.* For example, in 1992, 10 percent of the first-grade children scoring between the seventy-fifth and the ninety-ninth national percentiles in reading comprehension on the Stanford Achievement Test were African American; at seventh grade, the percentage of African Americans in this high-scoring group had dropped by half, to only 5 percent (28 in number); this low proportion was also found at grade 11 (even though the actual number of students, 20, was smaller).

Rockford's grouping practices that created racially identifiable classrooms and provided unequal opportunities to learn (with fewer such opportunities provided to minority students) *did not serve a remedial function for minority students.* To the contrary, these practices did not even enable minority students to sustain their position, relative to white students, in the district's achievement hierarchy.

In San Jose, better data permitted me to analyze the impact of track placement on individual students over time. Students who were placed in lower-level courses—disproportionately Latino students—consistently demonstrate lesser gains in achievement over time than their peers placed in high-level courses. For example, among the students with preplacement math achievement between 50 and 59 NCEs, those who were placed in a low-track course began with a mean of 54.4 NCEs, but lost an average of 2.2 NCEs after one year and had lost a total of 1.9 NCEs after three years. Students who scored between 50 and 59 NCEs and were placed in a standard-track course, by contrast, began with a mean of 54.6 NCEs, gained 0.1 NCE after one year, and had gained 3.5 NCEs after three years. The largest gains were experienced by students who were placed in an accelerated course, who began with a mean of 55.4 NCEs, gained 6.5 NCEs after one year, and had gained a total of 9.6 NCEs after three years.

These results are consistent across achievement levels: Whether students began with relatively high or relatively low achievement, those who were placed in lower-level courses showed lesser gains over time than similarly situated students who were placed in higher-level courses.

IN SUM, CONSIDERABLE HARM

The findings from my analyses of San Jose and Rockford support disturbing conclusions about tracking and within-school segregation and discrimination. The districts' tracking systems pervade their schools. The harm that accrues to African Americans and Latinos takes at least three demonstrable forms: (1) unjustifiable, disproportionate, and segregative assignment to low-track classes and exclusion from accelerated classes; (2) inferior opportunities to learn; and (3) lower achievement. In both systems, grouping practices have created a cycle of restricted opportunities and diminished outcomes and have exacerbated differences between African American and Latino and white students. That these districts have not chosen to eliminate grouping practices that so clearly discriminate against their African American and Latino children warrants serious concern and strong remedial action.

IMPLICATIONS FOR REMEDIAL ACTIVITIES AND SCHOOL REFORM

Is it technically possible or politically feasible to abandon these discriminatory practices in San Jose, Rockford, or other school systems that are like them? The two systems are currently charged with making significant progress toward that end.

Both Rockford and San Jose school systems have considerable technical capacity to reform their placement practices so that they teach all children in heterogeneous settings, including the gifted, for part or all of the school day in most or all core academic courses. Conspicuous examples of successful heterogeneous grouping exist currently in San Jose schools. Much of the professional expertise and some of the support structures needed to implement such practices districtwide are already in place. Moreover, in both systems, administrative and teaching staff demonstrate considerable knowledge of the harms of tracking and ample ability to implement educationally sound alternatives.

Furthermore, both districts are situated in a national and state policy environment that encourages the development and use of such alternatives. For example, such national policy groups as the National Governors' Association and federally supported efforts to create national standards in each of the curriculum areas all recommend against tracking. In California, the State Department of Education's major policy documents on the reform of K–12 schooling (*It's Elementary, Caught in the Middle,* and *Second to None*) and the state's subject matter frameworks caution schools about problems with tracking and strongly recommend that they not use it.[3] Similar state-led initiatives promote heterogeneity in Illinois—for example, the state's involvement in middle-school reform and its adoption of the Accelerated Schools model.

However, racially mixed school systems that have tackled this issue around the country have experienced considerable difficulty creating alternatives. Amy Stuart Wells and I are currently studying ten such schools.[4] While each has made considerable progress toward integrated classrooms and a more even distribution of educational opportunities, most have been the target of considerable fear and anger. As with the nation's experiences with between-school segregation, the pursuit of court sanctions against tracking and ability grouping may be critical to ensuring educational equality. However, like that earlier effort, remedies are neither easily specified nor readily accepted.

ENDNOTES

1. For a comprehensive review of the literature, see Jeannie Oakes, Adam Gamoran, and Reba Page, "Curriculum Differentiation: Opportunities, Outcomes, and Meanings," in *Handbook of Research on Education,* ed. Philip Jackson (New York: Macmillan, 1992).
2. These previously unpublished analyses are available in the form of a 1993 report to the court in *The People Who Care* v. *Rockford Board of Education School District no. 205* and in my July 1993 deposition in conjunction with *Jose B. Vasquez* v. *San Jose Unified School District et al.*
3. California State Department of Education, *It's Elementary* (Sacramento: Author, 1993); *Caught in the Middle* (Sacramento: Author, 1988); and *Second to None* (Sacramento: Author, 1991).
4. The study "Beyond Sorting and Stratification: Creating Alternatives to Tracking in Racially Mixed Schools" is sponsored by the Lilly Endowment.

DISCUSSION QUESTIONS

1. What important purposes was tracking designed to fulfill?
2. In your opinion, is tracking (a) a fair practice, (b) a beneficial practice, or (c) a disadvantageous practice? Why?
3. Does research support the practice of tracking? Why? Why not?
4. What educational opportunities are typically provided to students in lower-class tracks?
5. How did lower-track placement affect students' quality of education and student outcomes?
6. What is the relationship among the practice of tracking, in-school segregation, and educational equality?

CHAPTER 17

Disciplining the Mind

VERONICA BOIX MANSILLA
HOWARD GARDNER

FOCUSING QUESTIONS:

1. Compare learning subject matter and disciplinary thinking?
2. What are some limitations of subject matter learning?
3. Describe the four capacities the authors suggest as part of a quality precollegiate education?
4. How is learning history different from doing history?
5. How can teachers "nurture the disciplined mind" of their students?

Students need more than a large information base to understand their ever-changing world. They need to master disciplinary thinking.

The unit on industrialization was almost over, Phillip, a 10th grade world history teacher, began to design the final test. In the past, he had included questions from his weekly quizzes as well as new questions about key events, people, and inventions. This approach had proven comfortable for both him and his students.

But this time he decided to raise the stakes. He wondered whether students' understanding of the process and meaning of industrialization had improved over the last six weeks. Could students explain why industrialization took place? Could they recognize how difficult it is for historians to build an empirically grounded portrait of an unfolding past or draw telling comparisons with today's communications revolution? These goals seemed far more important than the usual litany of names, dates, and locations. Yet Phillip worried that his students would see reflective questions of this kind in the final exam as foul play.

Phillip's dilemma permeates classrooms around the world and across the disciplines. It addresses issues of accountability, the nature of teacher-student interactions, and the rituals of schooling. Most striking, it reveals two colliding views of what it means to understand history, biology, mathematics, or the visual arts. From the conventional standpoint, students learn subject matter. In general, they and their teachers conceive of the educational task as committing to memory large numbers of facts, formulas, and figures. Fixed in textbooks, such facts are taken as uncontroversial, their mastery valued as a sign of cultural literacy.

In sharp contrast with teaching subject matter, an alternative perspective emphasizes teaching disciplines and disciplinary thinking. The goal of this approach is to instill in the young the disposition to interpret the world in the distinctive ways that characterize the thinking of experienced disciplinarians—historians, scientists, mathematicians, and artists. This view entrusts education institutions with the responsibility of disciplining the young mind (Gardner, 1999, 2006; Gardner & Boix Mansilla, 1994).

In our view, Phillip's transition from teaching subject matter to nurturing the disciplined mind is emblematic of a fundamental shift in the way in which educators, policymakers, and the general public conceive of curriculum, instruction, and assessment. Indeed, preparing students to understand the world in which they live today and to brace themselves for the future entails a necessary transformation.

TEACHING SUBJECT MATTER

Most students in most schools today study subject matter. In science, students memorize animal taxonomies, atomic weights, and the organs in the respiratory system. In mathematics, they learn algebraic equations and geometrical proofs by heart so they can plug in the appropriate numbers. In history, they are expected to remember key actors, events, and periods. In the arts, they classify works by artist and school.

Subject-matter learning involves mentally recording such propositions as, "The first Industrial Revolution took place in Britain at the end of the 18th century," "The chemical composition of water is H_2O," and "Picasso's Les Demoiselles d'Avignon is a cubist painting painted in 1907." From a subject-matter perspective, students come to see the subjects of history and science as the collection of dates, actors, facts, and formulas catalogued in textbooks and encountered in rooms 458 and 503, in second and third period.

THE POWER OF INGRAINED IDEAS

Clearly, there is much to admire in an individual who knows a great deal of information. Further, there is an appealing sense of efficiency in subject-matter teaching: Teachers can rapidly present large quantities of information to students and easily test this information. The apparent benefits pale, however, when we consider how the young human mind develops and how best to prepare that mind for the future.

In recent decades, cognitive psychologists have documented a phenomenon of vital importance for anyone interested in education. Although students have little trouble spewing forth information that they have committed to memory, they display great difficulty in applying knowledge and skills to new situations. Youngsters who have studied the solar system are unable to apply what they have learned to explain why it is warm in the summer in the northern hemisphere. When asked to explain how a particular species trait or behavior has emerged, students studying biological evolution revert to pre-Darwinian "intentional" or teleological explanations. Students who are able to define cubism as a successful challenge to 19th-century aesthetic sensibilities naively equate a classical definition of "beautiful" with "good" when visiting a museum. Centuries of accumulated forms of expertise have simply bypassed these young minds despite a decade or more of formal education. Why is this so?

According to cognitive psychologists, early in life children develop powerful intuitive ideas about physical and biological entities, the operations of the human mind, and the properties of an effective narrative or graphic display. Some of these ideas are powerful precursors of sophisticated disciplinary understanding. For example, by age 5, children understand that narratives have beginnings, turning points, and endings and that the succession of events must "make sense" for the story to work, Historians, too, organize their accounts of the past in the form of narratives—intelligible accounts marked by turning points and preferred actors' perspectives.

Unfortunately, not all children's ideas are equally auspicious. Unlike historians, young students prefer simple explanations and clear distinctions between "good" and "mean" actors. They believe that events always result from intentional actions—especially the actions of leaders; they have difficulty understanding unintended consequences. Moreover, students often project contemporary knowledge and values onto the minds of actors in the past, making "presentism" one of the most difficult misconceptions to eradicate.

THE LIMITATIONS OF SUBJECT-MATTER LEARNING

Regrettably, subject-matter learning does not challenge such robust intuitive theories. Indeed, memorization does not even acknowledge the existence of these entrenched ways of making sense of the world. As a result, in subject-matter classrooms, students tend to momentarily retain the information presented, or they reorganize it in oversimplified linear plots. For example, students may record that the steam engine triggered the Industrial Revolution, then farmers rushed to the cities in search of work, then leading businessmen amassed enormous wealth and soon became abusive robber barons. In response, government and labor organized to regulate working conditions.

The plot demonstrates its fragility when students encounter apparent contradictions. Consider, for example, what happens when students learn that organized efforts to defend the rights of working people preceded the popularization of the steam engine. Students who have memorized a plotline—first industrialization, then unrest, then labor unions—cannot assimilate this information. More challenging still, the predisciplinary mind fails to appreciate that aspects of the Industrial Revolution are being recapitulated in the current digital upheavals around the globe.

Subject-matter learning may temporarily increase students' information base, but it leaves them unprepared to shed light on issues that are even slightly novel. A different kind of instruction is in order, one that seeks to discipline the mind.

THE DISCIPLINED MIND

For a historian, a statement such as, "The first Industrial Revolution took place in Britain at the end of the 18th century," is not a fact to remember but rather a contestable claim that stems from deliberate ways to partition the past. It is constructed through close analysis of sources that capture the lives of Britons over centuries of progressive urbanization.

For students, learning to think historically entails understanding that historical accounts are sometimes conflicting and always provisional. Students learn that interpretations of the past are not simply a matter of opinion, nor must one account be "right" and the other "wrong" when differences occur. Rather, the disciplined mind weighs competing accounts through multiple considerations. For instance, a history of the nascent industrial working class will contrast with a history focusing on the captains of industry, Long-term accounts may capture slow population changes, whereas pointed accounts shed better light on the role of individuals and inventions. A disciplinary approach considers the types of sources consulted, such as letters, newsletters, and accounting and demographic records. It also assesses whether conflicting accounts could be integrated into a more comprehensive explanation.

All disciplines embody distinct ways of thinking about the world. Scientists hold theories about the natural world that guide their observations. They make hypotheses, design experiments to test them, revise their views in light of their findings, and make fresh observations. Artists, on the other hand, seek to shed novel light on the object of their attention, depict it with masterful technique, and stretch and provoke themselves and their audiences through deliberate ambiguities in their work.

Of course, it is unreasonable to expect all students to become expert scientists, historians, and artists. Nevertheless, quality precollegiate education should ensure that students become deeply acquainted with a discipline's fundamental perspectives on the world by developing four key capacities (Boix Mansilla & Gardner, 1999).

Capacity 1: Understanding the Purpose of Disciplinary Expertise

Disciplines inform the contexts in which students live. Supply-and-demand principles determine the products that line the shelves of supermarkets; biological interdependence shapes the life of animals and plants at the local park as well as in the rain forest.

Students of history grasp that the purpose of their discipline is to understand past human experience—not to make predictions but to meet the present and the future in informed ways. For example, understanding how novel forms of work accelerated the formation of class consciousness among 18th-century industrial workers prepares students to appreciate the experience of contemporary workers in China, India, or Malaysia. Although students learn to attend to important differences between past and present conditions—contemporary digital calling centers in India bear little resemblance to the early textile factories in Leeds, England—they also understand that rapid urbanization forces these workers, like their predecessors, to juggle economic opportunities with anxiety over challenges to family life and cultural tradition.

Capacity 2: Understanding an Essential Knowledge Base

An essential knowledge base embodies concepts and relations central to the discipline and applicable in multiple contexts. It also equips students with a conceptual blueprint for approaching comparable novel situations. For instance, in a unit on industrialization, students may examine the dynamic interaction between technology and society to decide whether they deem industrialization to be "progress" or "decline." Students can apply this blueprint to technological developments at different points in time, from the printing press, to the sewing machine, to today's Internet.

Capacity 3: Understanding Inquiry Methods

In contrast to naive beliefs or mere information, disciplinary knowledge emerges from a careful process of inquiry and vetting claims. The disciplined mind considers forms of evidence, criteria for validation, and techniques that deliver trustworthy knowledge about the past, nature, society, or works of art.

In our own research, we have found that high school students trained in history recognize the demands of source interpretation, complex causal explanation, and the provisional nature of historical accounts (Boix Mansilla. 2005). However, becoming a better historian does not make students better scientists, artists, or mathematicians—or vice versa. For example, when asked to adjudicate between competing accounts in science—a domain in which they have not been rigorously trained—the same students exhibit a subject-matter approach to inquiry. They view science as a domain in which one simply observes the world and writes down one's conclusions. Conversely, award-winning students in science tend to perceive history as all about dates and facts that one need only "find in sources" and "put together in a story." Cross-disciplinary transfer proves elusive.

Capacity 4: Understanding Forms of Communication

Disciplines communicate their expertise in preferred forms and genres. Historians see narratives as the best fit for their work, whereas scientists opt for data-heavy research reports. The disciplined mind understands these favored genres because it can place them in the broader context of their disciplinary origins. For example, the disciplined scientific mind understands that, unlike Darwin's On the Origin of Species, a biblical account of human creation cannot stand the test of empirical evidence, nor can it aspire to consideration as a scientific claim.

Students develop a disciplined mind when they learn to communicate with the symbol systems and genres of a discipline. In science, students learn how to write (and recognize) a well-crafted scientific report in which clear and testable hypotheses, methodology, results, and discussion are made public for readers to weigh. In history, knowledge about the past is embodied in vivid and well-footnoted narratives as well as in museum exhibits, monuments, and documentary films.

HOW TO NURTURE THE DISCIPLINED MIND

Teachers can help students develop disciplinary competencies in several ways (Gardner, 2006):

- Identify essential topics in the discipline. In our example about industrialization. some topics will address the knowledge base, such as the transformation of production systems and social organization during the Industrial Revolution. Some will address the methods of the discipline, such as understanding conflicting accounts of workers' experiences and worldviews during the early stages of the Industrial Revolution. Some will address the purposes of the discipline, such as understanding how changes in technology lead to changes in ways of thinking both then and now. Some topics will address the forms of communication in the discipline, such as understanding what makes a historical narrative masterful.
- Spend considerable time on these few topics, studying them deeply. By encouraging students to examine multiple perspectives on a topic and study them in depth, teachers help students become young experts in different topic areas.
- Approach the topic in a number of ways. Students may readily approach the social transformations associated with the Industrial Revolution by reading biographies and life stories. Other students may learn through careful analysis of demographic data or interpretation of artworks of the times. Still others may learn better when asked to debate a question like, Did industrialization mean progress? By providing a variety of entry points, teachers not only reach more students but also invite their students to think about important problems in multiple ways—a mental agility that characterizes the disciplined mind.
- Develop performances of understanding. Performances of understanding invite students to think with knowledge in multiple novel situations; they show whether students can actually make use of classroom material once they step outside the door. For example, in the unit on industrialization, teachers may present students with conflicting accounts of workers' experiences in the 1884 planned model industrial town of Pullman in Illinois—a case that students have not yet been coached to examine. In their analysis of the Pullman strike of 1894, some histori-

ans contend that Pullmans model community was a malicious design to exploit workers; other historians believe it was the result of naive paternalism. Teachers might ask students to use what they have learned about historical inquiry to explain how expert historians could disagree. Students with a disciplinary mind in history would understand that they need to examine the conflicting accounts, check the sources used, take into consideration the date of the account, and clarify the historian's perspective. In doing so, students will develop a more informed understanding of historical accounts and will be able to apply their insights in other performances of understanding.

WHAT THE FUTURE REQUIRES

Today, the information revolution and the ubiquity of search engines have rendered having information much less valuable than knowing how to think with information in novel situations. To thrive in contemporary societies, young people must develop the capacity to think like experts. They must also be able to integrate disciplinary perspectives to understand new phenomena in such fields as medicine, bioethics, climate science, and economic development. In doing so, the disciplined mind resists oversimplification and prepares students to embrace the complexity of the modern world.

REFERENCES

Boix Mansilla, V. (2005). Between reproducing and organizing the past; Students' beliefs about the standards of acceptability of historical knowledge. In R. Ashby, P. Gordon, & P. Lee (Eds.), International Review of History Education: Vol. 4 (pp. 98–115). Oxford, UK: Routledge.

Boix Mansilla, V., & Gardner, H. (1999). What are the qualities of understanding? In S. Wiske (Ed.), Teaching for understanding: A practical framework (pp. 161–196). San Francisco: Jossey-Bass.

Gardner, H. (1999). The disciplined mind: What all students should understand. New York: Simon and Schuster.

Gardner, H. (2006). Five minds for the future Boston: Harvard Business School Press.

Gardner, H., & Boix Mansilla, V. (1994). Teaching for understanding in the disciplines and beyond. Teachers College Record, 96(2), 198–218.

DISCUSSION QUESTIONS:

1. Should teachers focus on teaching subject matter or disciplinary thinking? Explain.
2. How would a subject matter learning approach differ from teaching disciplinary thinking?
3. Is it possible to integrate both subject matter teaching and disciplinary thinking into a curriculum? Explain.
4. Should students learn the "basics" before engaging in disciplinary thinking? Explain.
    a. Or is it possible to learn disciplinary thinking without having a firm understanding of "the basics"? Explain.
5. Is it better to use the subject matter or disciplinary thinking approach to teach students 21st century skills? Explain.
6. In this age of accountability and high stakes testing, which educational approach is better? Which is more aligned with the high stakes testing? Explain.

PRO-CON CHART 3

Should special education students be grouped (mainstreamed) into regular education classes?

PRO	CON
1. Schools should be organized so that all students achieve their maximum potential.	**1.** Serving the special education population diminishes resources for students who are most likely to benefit from public schooling.
2. Schools should implement a curriculum that is student-centered and responsive to the students' learning needs.	**2.** Schools should not have to provide an alternative curriculum designed for a small group of special needs students within a regular classroom setting.
3. Students need to work side by side with peers who have different learning needs.	**3.** Legislating to require teachers to fulfill the role of parent, home, and counselor for special education students is unrealistic and unproductive.
4. Teachers must develop a broad-based repertoire of instructional strategies so that they can teach students with different needs and abilities in the same classroom.	**4.** Students who cannot conform to classroom structure and attend to learning tasks will not benefit from regular education instruction.
5. Mainstreaming can improve the social acceptance of special education students.	**5.** Most educators have not been adequately prepared to work with special education students.

CASE STUDY 3

Language and Standardized Testing

East High School in the big city has a large ethnic minority/immigrant population. Most of the immigrant students are placed in English as a Second Language (ESL) classes because of their initial English skill level. At East High School, ESL classes move at a slower pace than mainstream classes and reading selections are often remedial to give students ample time to adapt to their new surroundings.

The ESL language teacher, Fred Davis, drills the students hard, and many become miraculously fluent in a short period of time. To pass out of the ESL classes into the mainstream classes, students must receive 85 percent or higher on the administered English test for ESL students. Many students in ESL find this practice unfair. They claim that their English skill levels surpass those of many of the mainstream students and that they are being unfairly held back in all of their schoolwork because of unfair scoring expectations on one English test. Only students in the mainstream classes are able to take advanced coursework, and ESL students believe that East High is hurting their ultimate potential.

Further, ESL students wishing to continue on to colleges and universities are afraid that they will not be prepared for future tests; that their scores will be adversely affected by their remedial coursework in high school. They also fear that the institutions of higher education will penalize them during the admission process because they were unable to advance into "normal" classes.

1. Is it fair for schools to use standardized testing as the sole measure of ability for determining advancement? Why? Why not? What are other methods that can be used?
2. Should subject tests be administered in a language of the student's choosing?
3. Is it good practice to separate non-English or limited-English immigrant students in all areas of coursework? Should they be integrated into mainstream courses even if their English language ability is limited?
4. How might a teacher handle a class differently if it were integrated with students of different cultural backgrounds? Different academic abilities? Is this beneficial? Why? Why not?
5. How does a cultural knowledge background affect a student's understanding?

PART 4

Curriculum and Instruction

How do curriculum and instruction influence each other? Which instructional strategies are most effective for learners? Why are students' learning experiences still based on highly structured curricula? How can we really know if a school is doing well? What role should standards play in education? In what ways are electronic and information technologies affecting instruction?

In Chapter 18, Benjamin Bloom describes the advantages and disadvantages of conventional instruction, mastery learning, and tutoring. He explains how context variables, including home environments, school learning, and teachers' differential instruction with students, are related to outcomes. In the next chapter, Evans Clinchy focuses on the elusive goal of ensuring equity for all students. Noting that the Civil Rights movement of the 20th century was not wholly successful, he calls for a "new education civil right movement" based on principles adopted by the United Nations.

In Chapter 20, Arthur L. Costa describes a "thought-filled curriculum" in which teachers instruct their students to think critically. Five themes emerge in which students learn how to think and eventually think "big" in order to build a "thought-filled world". In Chapter 21, Geneva Gay highlights a variety of multicultural issues that increasingly influence schools today. She offers a number of ideas that demonstrate the relevance of multiculturalism for professional practice, curriculum development, and closing the achievement gap.

In Chapter 22, David Perkins argues for inclusion of what he call "knowledge arts" in the curriculum. The ability to communicate strategically and effectively, to think critically and creatively, and to apply knowledge to real-world problems can help to enliven teaching and learning. In the last chapter in Part Four, Stanley Pogrow discusses using dramatic methods to teach content to students. "Teaching outrageously", Pogrow argues is efficient and allows the teachers to teach the content in depth. This creative method should be seen as a way to invigorate a teacher's toolbox of instructional strategies.

CHAPTER 18

The Search for Methods of Instruction

Benjamin S. Bloom

FOCUSING QUESTIONS

1. What is the difference between conventional instruction, mastery learning, and tutoring?
2. How does mastery learning influence student achievement?
3. What are the advantages and disadvantages of the mastery learning model and tutoring?
4. In what ways are home environment processes and a student's school learning related?
5. How does tutoring influence student achievement?

Two University of Chicago doctoral students in education, Anania (1982, 1983) and Burke (1984), completed dissertations in which they compared student learning under the following three conditions of instruction:

1. *Conventional.* Students learn the subject matter in a class with about 30 students per teacher. Tests are given periodically for marking the students.
2. *Mastery learning.* Students learn the subject matter in a class with about 30 students per teacher. The instruction is the same as in the conventional class (usually with the same teacher). Formative tests (the same tests used with the conventional group) are given for feedback, followed by corrective procedures and parallel formative tests to determine the extent to which the students have mastered the subject matter.
3. *Tutoring.* Students learn the subject matter with a good tutor for each student (or for two or three students simultaneously). This tutoring instruction is followed periodically by formative tests, feedback-corrective procedures, and parallel formative tests as in the mastery learning classes. It should be pointed out that the need for corrective work under tutoring is very small.

The students were randomly assigned to the three learning conditions, and their initial aptitude test scores, previous achievement in the subject, and initial attitudes and interests in the subject were similar. The amount of time for instruction was the same in all three groups except for the corrective work in the mastery learning and tutoring groups. Burke (1984) and Anania (1982, 1983) replicated the study with four different samples of students at grades 4, 5, and 8 and with two different subject matters, probability and cartography. In each substudy, the instructional treatment was limited to 11 periods of instruction over a three-week block of time.

Most striking were the differences in final achievement measures under the three conditions. Using the standard deviation (sigma) of the control (conventional) class, it was typically found that the average student under tutoring was about two standard deviations above the average of the control class (the average tutored student was above 98 percent of the students in the control class).[1] The average student under mastery learning was about one standard deviation above the average of the control class (the average mastery learning student was above 84 percent of the students in the control class).

The variation of the students' achievement also changed under these learning conditions such that about 90 percent of the tutored students and 70 percent of the mastery learning students attained the level of summative achievement reached by only the highest 20 percent of the students under conventional instructional conditions (see Figure 18.1).

There were corresponding changes in students' time on task in the classroom (65 percent under conventional instruction, 75 percent under Mastery Learning, and 90+ percent under tutoring) and students' attitudes and interests (least positive under conventional instruction and most positive under tutoring). There were great reductions in the relations between prior measures (aptitude or achievement) and the summative achievement measures. Typically, the aptitude-achievement correlations changed from +.60 under conventional to +.35 under mastery learning and +.25 under tutoring. It is recognized that the

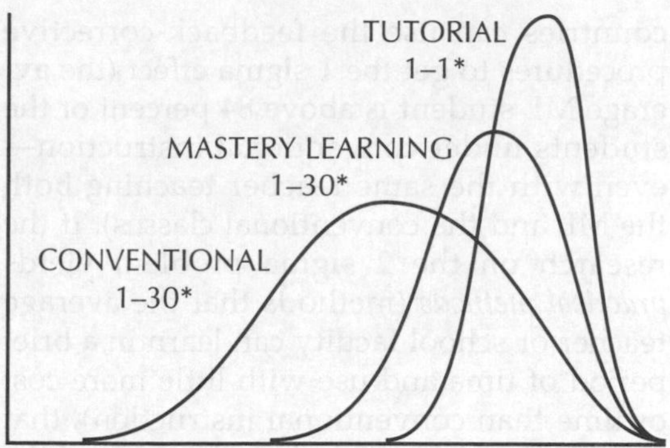

FIGURE 18.1 Achievement Distribution for Students under Conventional, Master Learning, and Tutorial Instruction

correlations for the mastery learning and tutoring groups were so low because of the restricted range of scores under these learning conditions. However, the most striking of the findings is that under the best learning conditions we can devise (tutoring), the average student is 2 sigma above the average control student taught under conventional group methods of instruction.

The tutoring process demonstrates that *most* of the students do have the potential to reach this high level of learning. I believe an important task of research and instruction is to seek ways of accomplishing this under more practical and realistic conditions than one-to-one tutoring, which is too costly for most societies to bear on a large scale. This is the 2 *sigma* problem. Can researchers and teachers devise teaching-learning conditions that will enable the majority of students under *group instruction* to attain levels of achievement that can at present be reached only under good tutoring conditions?

It has taken almost a decade and a half to develop the Mastery Learning (ML) strategy to a point where large numbers of teachers at every level of instruction and in many countries can use the feedback-corrective procedures to get the 1 sigma effect (the average ML student is above 84 percent of the students under conventional instruction—even with the same teacher teaching both the ML and the conventional classes). If the research on the 2 sigma problem yields *practical methods* (methods that the average teacher or school faculty can learn in a brief period of time and use with little more cost or time than conventional instruction), that would be an educational contribution of the greatest magnitude. It would change popular notions about human potential and would have significant effects on what the schools can and should do with the educational years each society requires of its young people.

This chapter is a brief presentation of the work on solutions to the 2 sigma problem. It is hoped that it will interest both educational researchers and teachers in further research and application of these ideas.

THE SEARCH

In a number of articles, my graduate students and I have attempted to contrast alterable educational variables with more stable or static variables (Bloom, 1980). In our treatment of this topic, we summarized the literature on such alterable variables as the *quality of teaching*, the *use of time* by teachers and students, *cognitive* and *affective* entry characteristics of students, *formative testing*, *rate of learning*, and the *home environment*. In each case, we contrasted these alterable variables with the more *stable* variables (e.g., personal characteristics of teachers, intelligence measures, achievement tests for grading purposes, socioeconomic status of the family, etc.) and indicated some of the ways in which the alterable variables influence learning and the processes by which these variables have been altered.

But not all alterable variables are likely to have equal effects on learning. Our research summaries were intended to emphasize the alterable variables that have had the strongest effects on school learning. This search has been aided by the rapid growth of the meta-analysis literature. In this literature, writers have summarized the research literature on a particular set of alterable variables to indicate the effect size between control and experimental groups of students. They have standardized the results in terms of the *difference* between the experimental and control groups divided by the standard deviation of the control group.[2]

In each study, the reviewer also analyzed the effect size under different conditions—level of school, sex of student, school subject, size of sample, and so on. Such reviews are very useful in selecting alterable variables that are most likely to contribute significantly to the 2 sigma solution.

Table 18.1 is adapted from a summary of effect sizes of key variables by Walberg (1984) who, with other co-authors, has contributed greatly to this literature. In Table 18.1 he has listed the selected variables in order of magnitude of effect size. (We have added other variables and indicated the equivalent percentile for each effect size.) Thus, in the first entry, *tutorial instruction,* we have indicated the effect size (2 sigma) and indicated that under tutorial instruction, the average student is above 98 percent of the students under the control teaching conditions. A list of effect size studies appears in the Appendix at the end of this chapter.

In our own attempts to solve the 2 sigma problem we assume that two or three alterable variables must be used that *together* contribute more to the learning than any one of them alone. Because of more than 15 years of experience with ML at different levels of education and in different countries, we have come to rely on ML as one of the possible variables to be combined with selected other variables. ML (the feedback corrective process) under good conditions yields approximately a 1 sigma effect size. We have

TABLE 18.1 Effect of Selected Alterable Variables on Student Achievement

Object of Change Process[a]	*Alterable Variable*	*Effect Size*	*Percentile Equivalent*
D	Tutorial instruction	2.00	98
D	Reinforcement	1.20	
A	Feedback-corrective (ML)	1.00	84
D	Cues and explanations	1.00	
(A)D	Student classroom participation	1.00	
A	Student time on task	1.00[b]	
A	Improved reading/study skills	1.00	
C	Cooperative learning	.80	79
D	Homework (graded)	.80	
D	Classroom morale	.60	73
A	Initial cognitive prerequisites	.60	
C	Home environment intervention	.50[b]	69
D	Peer and cross-age remedial tutoring	.40	66
D	Homework (assigned)	.30	62
D	Higher order questions	.30	
(D)B	New science & math curricula	.30[b]	
D	Teacher expectancy	.30	
C	Peer group influence	.20	58
B	Advance organizes	.20	
	Socioeconomic status (for contrast)	.25	60

Source: This table was adapted from Walberg (1984) by Bloom. See the Appendix for effect size references.

[a]A—Learner; B—Instructional Material; C—Home environment or peer group; D—Teacher.

[b]Averaged or estimated from correlational data or from several effect sizes.

systematically tried other variables which, in combination with ML, might approach the 2 sigma effect size. So far, we have *not* found any two-variable combination that has exceeded the 2 sigma effect. Thus, some of our present research reaches the 2 sigma effect but does not go beyond it.

We have classified the variables in Table 18.1 in terms of the direct object of the change process: (a) the learner; (b) the instructional material; (c) the home environment or peer group; and (d) the teacher and the teaching process.

We have speculated that two variables involving different objects of the change process may, in some instances, be additive, whereas two variables involving the same object of the change process are less likely to be additive (unless they occur at different times in the teaching–learning process). Our research is intended to determine when these rules are true and when they are not. Several of the studies done so far suggest that they may be true. Thus, the ML process (which affects the learner most directly), when combined with changes in the teaching process (which affects the teacher most directly), yields additive results. (See Tenenbaum, 1982, and Mevarech, 1980.) Although we do not believe these two rules are more than *suggestive* at present, future research on this problem will undoubtedly yield a stronger set of generalizations about how the effects of separable variables may be best combined.

In our work so far, we have restricted the search to two or three variables, each of which is likely to have a .5 or greater sigma effect. We suspect that the research, as well as the applications to school situations, would get too complex if more than three alterable variables were used.

In our research with two variables, we have made use of a 2 × 2 randomized design with ML and one other variable. So far we have not done research with three variables. Where possible, we try to replicate the study with at least two subject fields, two levels of schooling, or some combination of subject fields and levels of schooling. We hope that others will take up this 2 sigma search and that some guidelines for the research can be set up to make the combined results more useful and to reduce the time and costs for experimental and demonstration studies.

IMPROVING STUDENT PROCESSING OF CONVENTIONAL INSTRUCTION

In this section, we are concerned with ways in which schools can help students learn more effectively without basically changing the teaching. If students develop good study habits, devote more time to the learning, improve their reading skills, and so on, they will be better able to learn from a particular teacher and course—even though neither the course nor the teacher has undergone a change process.

For example, the ML feedback-corrective approach is addressed primarily to providing students with the cognitive and affective prerequisites for each new learning task. As we have noted before, when the ML procedures are done systematically and well, the school achievement of the average student under ML is approximately 1 sigma (84th percentile) above the average student in the control class, even when both classes are taught by the *same teacher* with much the same instruction and instructional material. We view the ML process as a method of improving the students' learning from the same teaching over a series of learning tasks.

The major changes under the ML process are that more of the students have the cognitive prerequisites for each new learning task, they become more positive about their ability to learn the subject, and they put in more active learning time than do the control students. As we observe the students' learning and the test results in the ML and the conventional class, we note the improvements in the student learning under ML and the lack of such improvement in conventional classes.

One of our University of Chicago doctoral students, Leyton (1983), suggested that one approach to the 2 sigma problem would be to use ML during the advanced course in a sequence, but in addition attempt to *enhance the students' initial cognitive entry prerequisites* at the beginning of the course. Working with high school teachers in Algebra 2 and French 2, Leyton and others developed an initial test of the prerequisites for each of these courses. The procedure in developing the initial test was to take the final examination in the prior course (Algebra 1 or French 1) and have a committee of four to six teachers in the subject independently check each test item that they believed measured an idea or skill that was a necessary prerequisite for the next course in the subject. There was very high agreement on most of the selected items, and discussion among the teachers led to consensus about some of the remaining items.

Two of the classes were helped to review and relearn the specific prerequisites they lacked. This was not done for the students in the other two classes—they spent the time on a more general and informal review of the content taught in the previous course (Algebra 1 or French 1). The method of enhancing the prerequisites was much like the ML feedback-corrective process: the teacher retaught the items that the majority of students had missed, small groups of students helped each other over items that had been missed, and the students reviewed items they were not sure about by referring to the designated pages in the instructional material. The corrective process took about 3 to 4 hours during the first week of the course. After the students completed the corrective process, they were given a parallel test. As a result of the corrective process, most of the students reached the mastery standard (80 percent) on the parallel test given at the end of the first week of the course. In a few cases, students who didn't reach this standard were given further help.

More important was the improved performance of the enhanced classes over the other two classes on the first *formative* test in the advanced course (French 2 or Algebra 2). The two enhanced classes, which had been helped on the initial prerequisites, were approximately .7 sigma higher than the other two classes on the first formative test given at the end of a 2-week period of learning in the advanced course.

When one of the enhanced classes was also provided with ML feedback-corrective procedures over a series of learning tasks, the final result after a 10- to 12-week period of instruction was that this experimental group was approximately 1.6 sigma above the control group on the summative examination. (The average student in the ML plus enhanced initial prerequisites was above 95 percent of the control students on this examination.) There were also attitudinal and other affective differences in students related to these achievement differences. These included positive academic self-concept, greater interest in the subject, and greater desire to learn more in the subject field.

In Leyton's (1983) study, he found that the average effect of initial enhancement of prerequisites alone is about .6 sigma (see differences between conventional and conventional plus enhanced prerequisites and between ML and ML plus enhanced prerequisites in Figure 18.2). That is, we have two processes—*ML* and *initial enhancement of cognitive prerequisites*—that have sizable but separate effects. When they are combined, their separate effects tend to be additive. We believe these two variables are additive because they occur at different times. The enhancement of the initial prerequisites is completed during the first week of the new course, while the ML feedback-corrective process takes place every 2 or 3 weeks during the course, after the initial enhancement.

This solution to the 2 sigma problem is likely to be applicable to sequential courses in most school subjects. (In the United States, over two-thirds of the academic courses in elementary-secondary schools are sequential courses.) This solution, of course, applies most clearly to the second courses in a sequence. It probably will not work as well with the third, fourth, or later courses in a sequence if there has been no earlier use of initial enhancement of prerequisites or ML procedures. We hope these ideas will be further explored in the United States as well as in other countries. We believe this solution is relevant at all levels of education, including elementary-secondary, college, and even the graduate and professional school level.

We also regard this approach as widely applicable within a country because the prerequisites for a particular sequential subject or course are likely to be very similar even though different textbooks and teachers may be involved. Thus, a well-made test of the initial prerequisites for a particular sequential course—Arithmetic 2, French 2, Reading 2, and so on—may with only minor changes apply to other versions of the same course within a particular country. Also, the procedures that work well in enhancing these prerequisites in one school should work equally well in other schools. Further research is needed to establish the sequential courses in which this approach is most effective.

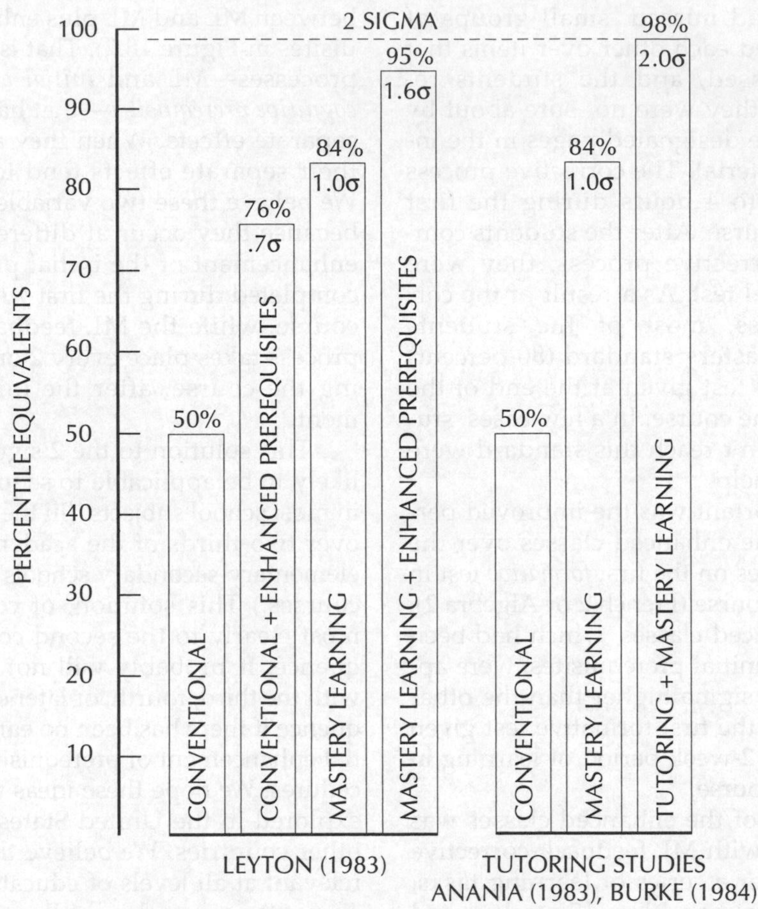

FIGURE 18.2 Average Summative Achievement Scores Under Different Learning Conditions. Comparison of Tutoring Studies, Mastery Learning, and Enhanced Prerequisites

Finally, the time cost of the initial enhancement procedures is limited to the class hours of the course during the first week of the sequential course, while the time or other costs of the ML procedures have usually been very small. We hope that this approach to the 2 sigma problem will be found to be a widely applicable as well as economical solution available to most teachers who wish to improve student learning, student academic self-concept, and student attitudes and interest in the learning.

Our graduate students have written papers on several other approaches for improving student processing of conventional instruction:

1. Help students develop a student support system in which groups of two or three students study together, help each other when they encounter difficulties in the course, help each other review in advance of taking tests, and review their learning periodically. A student support

system that provides support, encouragement and even help when needed can do much to raise the level of learning of the participants. There is evidence that these and other cooperative learning efforts are almost as effective as ML procedures. [Cooperative learning—effect size .80 (79th percentile); Slavin, 1980.]

2. There is evidence that students who take special programs to improve their reading and/or their study and learning methods tend to learn more effectively. Ideally, such special programs should be available at the beginning of each new school level—that is, junior high school, high school, and so on. One would hope that the special programs would be closely related to the academic courses the student is currently taking. [Improved reading/study skills—effect size 1.00 (84th percentile); Pflaum, Walberg, Karegianes, & Rasher, 1980.]

IMPROVE INSTRUCTIONAL MATERIALS AND EDUCATIONAL TECHNOLOGY

In the United States, as well as in most advanced countries in the world, the textbook is an almost universal part of school instruction. There has been much work on the improvement of the textbooks for reading and, to some extent, arithmetic, mathematics, and science subjects. Most of these are in relation to special curricular improvements, which include improvements in the sequential nature of the topics, the attempt to find important ideas or schema that help to interrelate the different parts of the subject, and improvements in the illustrations and exercises in the books. However, as far as we can find, these improvements have not had very significant effects on student achievement unless the teachers were provided with much in-service education for the new curriculum or the new textbook.

My graduate students and I have been intrigued by the possibility that a particular section (or chapter) of the textbook might be better integrated or the parts of the section more closely related to each other. Preorganizers or advance organizers (Ausubel, 1960) have been moderately effective when provided in the textbook or provided by the teacher at the beginning of the new unit of the course. These may be provided in the form of objectives, some ideas about what will be learned in the unit, or a brief discussion of the relation between what has already been learned and what will be learned in the unit. Such advanced organizers (Luiten, Ames, & Ackerson, 1980) appear to have an average effect size on achievement of about .2 sigma. (Incidentally, such advance organizers have about a .4 sigma effect on retention of the learning.) Although this effect is rather consistent, by itself it is not enough to contribute significantly to the 2 sigma effect. It is likely that a *combination* of advance organizers at the beginning of a new topic, further organizational aids during the chapter or unit, and appropriate questions, summaries, or other organizational aids at the end of the unit, may have a substantial effect on the student's learning of that chapter.

Other suggestions for the improvement of instructional materials and educational technology include the following:

1. Some of our students have used computer learning courses, such as the Plato system, which appear to work very well for highly motivated students. We believe that it should be possible to determine whether particular computer courses enable sizable proportions of students to attain the 2 sigma achievement effect. The effectiveness of the computer courses can be determined in terms of the time required, completion rates, student performance on achievement tests, and student retention of the learned material. It is hoped that the more effective computer courses will also have positive

effects on such affective characteristics as academic self-concept, interest in the subject, and desire to learn further with computer learning methods.

2. Although the average effect size for new science and math curricula in the United States is only .3 sigma, some of the new curricula (or textbooks) in these and other subjects may be much more effective than others. We propose a careful search of the new curricula and textbooks to determine which ones are more effective and to determine what characteristics make them more effective than the others.

HOME ENVIRONMENT AND THE PEER GROUP

In this section, we are primarily concerned with the out-of-school support that the student receives from the home or the peer group. We are interested in the ways in which the student's achievement, academic aspirations and goals, and progress in learning are influenced by these types of support. We know that the home environment does have great influence on the pupil's school learning and that this influence is especially effective at the elementary school level or earlier. The peer group's influence is likely to be strongest (both positively or negatively) at the secondary school level.

Home Environment Processes

There have been a large number of studies of the home environment processes that affect the students' school learning. These studies involve interviews and observations directed at determining the relevant interactions between parents and their children. The studies find correlations of +.70 to +.80 between an index of the home environment processes and the children's school achievement.[3] Some of the home environment processes that appear to have high relationships with school achievement include the following:

1. Work habits of the family—the degree of routine in the home management, the emphasis on regularity in the use of space and time, and the priority given to schoolwork over other more pleasurable activities.
2. Academic guidance and support—the availability and quality of the help and encouragement parents give the child for his or her schoolwork and the conditions they provide to support the child's schoolwork.
3. Stimulation in the home—the opportunity provided by the home to explore ideas, events, and the larger environment.
4. Language development—opportunities in the home for the development of correct and effective language usage.
5. Academic aspirations and expectations—the parents' aspirations for the child, the standards they set for the child's school achievement, and their interest in and knowledge of the child's school experiences.

These studies of the home environment processes began with the work of Dave (1963) and Wolf (1964, 1966), and since then have been replicated in other studies done in the United States and other countries (Marjoribanks, 1974; Kalinowski & Sloane, 1981).

These previous studies of the relationship between the home and the children's school achievement suggest a strong effect of the home environment on the school learning of the children, but they do not provide evidence on the extent to which the home environment can be *altered* and the effect of such alteration on changes in the children's school achievement.

A study done in Thailand by Janhom (1983) involved a control group and three experimental groups of parents (and their children). In this study, the most effective treatment of the parents was for the group of parents to meet with a parent educator for about 2 hours twice a month for 6 months. In these meetings, the parents discussed ways in which they could support their children's learning in the school. There was usually an initial presentation made by the parent educator on one of the home environment processes, and then the parents discussed what they did as well as what they hoped to do to support their children's school learning.

Another experimental approach included visits to each home separately by a parent educator twice a month for 6 months. A third experimental approach was that newsletters about the same topics were sent to the home twice a month for 6 months.

The parents of all four groups were observed and interviewed at the beginning and end of the 6-month period using the Dave (1963) interview and observational methods. Although the three experimental approaches show significantly greater changes in the parents' home environment index than the control group, the most effective method was the series of meetings between groups of parents and the parent educator. The changes in the home environment of this group were highly significant when compared with the changes in the other three groups of parents.

The fourth-grade children of all these parents were given a national standardized test on reading and mother tongue as well as arithmetic at the beginning and end of the 6-month period. It was found that the achievement of the children of the meeting group of parents at the end was 1 sigma above that of the control group of children. In comparison, the parent educators' visit to each of the homes every other week had only a .5 sigma effect on the children's school achievement.

Other methods of changing the home environment have been reported by Dolan (1980), Bronfenbrenner (1974), and Kalinowski and Sloane (1981). Again, the most effective approaches to changing the home environment processes result in changes in the children's school achievement. [Home environment—effect size .50 (69th percentile), Iverson & Walberg, 1982.]

The methods of changing the home environments are relatively costly in terms of parent educators meeting with groups of parents over a series of semi-monthly meetings, but the payoff of this approach is likely to be very great. If parents continue to encourage and support each of their children to learn well in school throughout the elementary school years, this should greatly help the children during the years they will attend schools and colleges.

Although such research has not been done as yet, we hope that others will explore an approach to the 2 sigma problem of providing effective parent education combined with the mastery learning method. Because parent support takes place in the home and ML takes place in the school, we expect that these two effects will be additive. The result should be close to a 2 sigma improvement in student learning.

Ideally, if both methods began with first- or second-grade children, one might hope that the combination would result in consistently good learning, at least through the elementary school years, with less and less need for effort expended by the parents or the use of ML procedures in the school.

Peer Group

During the adolescent years, it is likely that the peer group will have considerable influence on the student's activities, behavior, attitudes, and academic expectations. The peer group(s) to which the individual "belongs" also has some effect on the student's high school achievement level as well as further academic aspirations. These effects appear to be greatest in urban settings. Although it is difficult to influence the student's choice of friends and peer groups, the availability in the school of a variety of extracurricular activities and clubs (e.g., athletics, music, science, mathematics, social, etc.) should enable students to be more selective in their peer choices within the school setting. [Peer group influence—effect size .20 (58th percentile); Ide, Haertel, Parkerson, & Walberg, 1981.]

IMPROVEMENT OF TEACHING

When we compare student learning under conventional instruction and tutoring, we note that approximately 20 percent of the students under conventional instruction do about as well as the tutored students (see Figure 18.1). That is, tutoring probably would not enable these top students to do any better than they already do under conventional instruction. In contrast, about 80 percent of the students do poorly under conventional instruction relative to what they might do under tutoring. We have pondered these facts and believe that this in part results from the unequal treatment of students within most classrooms.

Observations of teacher interaction with students in the classroom reveal that teachers frequently direct their teaching and explanations to some students and ignore others. They give much positive reinforcement and encouragement to some students but not to others, and they encourage active participation in the classroom from some students and discourage it from others. The studies find that typically teachers give students in the top third of the class the greatest attention, and students in the bottom third of the class receive the least attention and support. These differences in the interaction between teachers and students provide some students with much greater opportunity and encouragement for learning than is provided for other students in the same classroom (Brophy & Good, 1970).

It is very different in a one-to-one tutoring situation where there is a constant feedback and corrective process between the tutor and the tutee. If the explanation is not understood by the tutee, the tutor soon becomes aware of it and explains it further. There is much reinforcement and encouragement in the tutoring situation, and the tutee must be actively participating in the learning if the tutoring process is to continue. In contrast, there is less feedback from each student in the group situation to the teacher—and frequently the teacher gets most of the feedback on the clarity of his or her explanations, the effect of the reinforcements, and the degree of active involvement in the learning from a *small* number of high-achieving students in the typical class of 30 students.

Teachers are frequently unaware of the fact that they are providing more favorable conditions of learning for some students than they are for other students. Generally, they are under the impression that all students in their classes are given equality of opportunity for learning. One basic assumption of our work on teaching is the belief that when teachers are helped to secure a more accurate picture of their own teaching methods and styles of interaction with their students, they will increasingly be able to provide more favorable learning conditions for more of their students, rather than just for the top fraction of the class.

In some of our research on the 2 sigma problem, we have viewed the task of teaching as providing for more equal treatment of students. We have been trying to give teachers feedback on their differential treatment of students. We attempt to provide teachers with a mirror of what they are now doing and have them develop techniques for equalizing their interactions with the students. These include such techniques as (a) attempting to find something positive and encouraging in each student's response, (b) finding ways of involving more of the students in active engagement in the learning process, (c) securing feedback from a small random sample of students to determine when they comprehend the explanations and illustrations, and

(d) finding ways of supplying additional clarification and illustrations as needed. The major emphasis in this work was *not* to change the teachers' *methods* of instruction, but to have the teacher become more aware of the ways in which he or she could more directly teach to a cross section of the students at each class section.

The first of our studies on improving instruction was done by Nordin (1979, 1980), who found ways of improving the cues and explanations for students as well as increasing the active participation of students.

He found it helpful to meet frequently with the teachers to explain these ideas as well as to observe the teachers and help them determine when they still needed to improve these qualities of the instruction. He also had independent observers noting the frequency with which the experimental teachers were using these ideas well or poorly. Similarly, he had students note the frequency with which they were actively participating in the learning and any problems they had with understanding the ideas or explanations.

In this research he compared student learning under conventional instruction and under enhanced cues (explanations) and participation conditions. During the experiment, observers noted that the student participation and the explanations and directions were positive in about 57 percent of the observations in the control class as compared with about 67 percent in the enhanced cue + participation classes. Students in the control classes noted that the cues and participation were positive for them about 50 percent of the time as compared with about 80 percent of the time for the students in the enhanced cue + participation classes.

In terms of final achievement, the average student in the enhanced cue and participation group was 1.5 sigma higher than the average student in the control classes. (The average student in the enhanced group was above 93 percent of the students in the control classes.) (See Figure 18.3.) Nordin (1979, 1980) also made use of the ML procedures in other classes and found that they worked even better than the enhanced cue + participation procedures. Unfortunately, he did not use the ML in combination with the enhanced cue + participation methods.

In any case, Nordin (1979, 1980) did demonstrate that teachers could be taught ways to be more responsive to most of the students in the class, secure increased participation of the students, and ensure that most of the students understood the explanations and illustrations that the teacher provided. The observers noted that the students in the enhanced participation and cue classes were actively engaged in learning (time on task) about 75 percent of the classroom time, whereas the control students were actively learning only about 57 percent of the time.

In a later study, Tenenbaum (1982) compared control groups, ML groups, and enhanced cues, participation, and reinforcement in combination with ML (CPR + ML). Tenenbaum studied these three methods of teaching with randomly assigned students in two different courses—sixth-grade science and ninth-grade algebra.

Tenenbaum also used student observation of their own classroom processes on cues, participation, and reinforcement. He found that under the CPR + ML, students responded positively about their own participation about 87 percent of the time as contrasted with 68 percent in the control classes.

The results of this study demonstrated large differences between the three methods of instruction, with the final achievement scores of the CPR + ML group about 1.7 sigma above those of the control students (the average student in this group was above 96 percent of the students in the control group). The average student in the ML groups was the usual 1 sigma above the control students (see Figure 18.3).

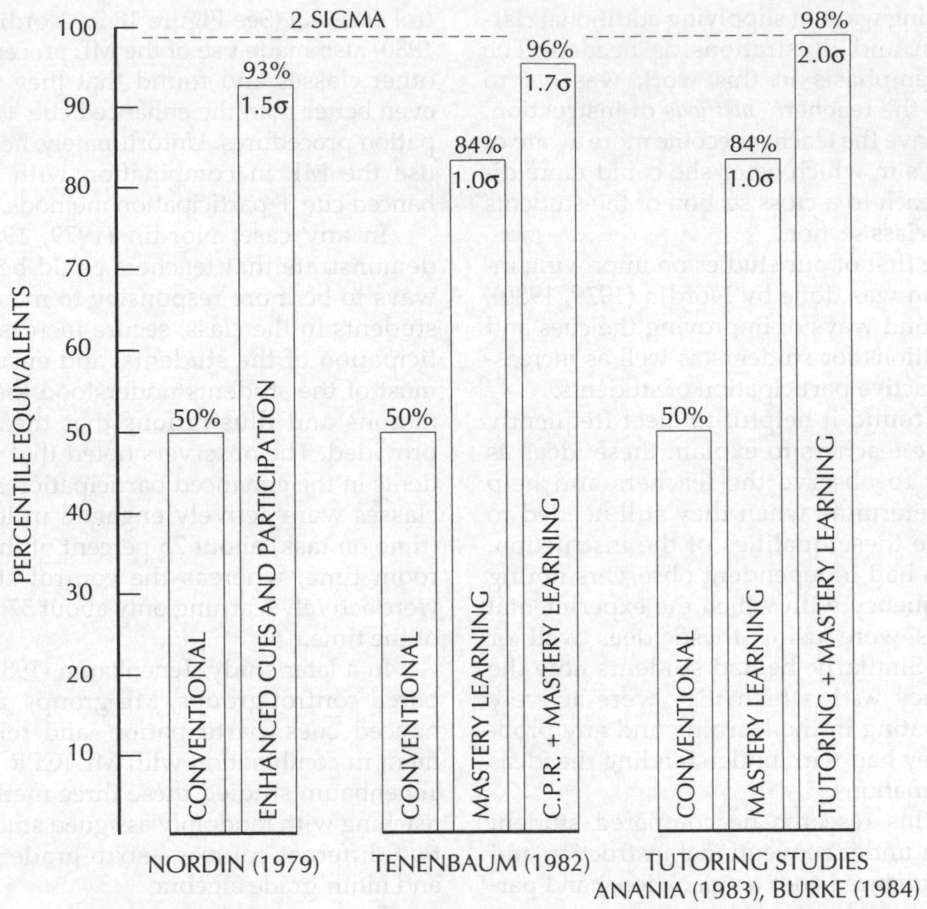

FIGURE 18.3 Average Summative Achievement Scores under Different Learning Conditions: Comparison of tutoring Studies, Mastery Learning, and Enhanced Instructional Methods

We believe that this research makes it clear that teachers in both the Nordin and Tenenbaum studies could (at least temporarily) change their teaching methods to provide more equal treatment of the students in their classes. When this more equal treatment is provided and supplemented with the ML feedback and corrective procedures, the average student approaches the level of learning found under tutoring methods of instruction.

We believe there are a variety of methods of giving feedback to teachers on the extent to which they are providing equality of interaction with their students. The tactic of providing a "mirror" to the teacher of the ways in which he or she is providing cues and explanations and appropriate reinforcement and securing overt as well as covert participation of the students in the learning seems to us to be an excellent approach. This may be in the form of an observer's notes on what the teacher and students did or student observations of their own interactions with the teaching (preferably anonymous, but coded as to whether the students are in the top third, middle third, or bottom third of the class in achievement), such as their understanding of the cues and explanations, the extent of their overt and covert participation, and the amount of reinforcement they are getting. Perhaps a videotape or audiotape recording of the class could serve the same purpose if the teacher were given brief training on ways of summarizing the classroom interaction between the teacher and the students in the class.

It is our hope that when teachers are helped to secure a more accurate picture of their own teaching methods and styles of interaction with their students, they will be better able to provide favorable learning conditions for most of their students.

IMPROVEMENT OF TEACHING OF THE HIGHER MENTAL PROCESSES

Although there is much rote learning in schools through the world, in some of the national curriculum centers in different countries (e.g., Israel, Malaysia, South Korea) I find great emphasis on problem solving, application of principles, analytical skills, and creativity. Such higher mental processes are emphasized because these centers believe that they enable the student to relate his or her learning to the many problems he or she encounters in day-to-day living. These abilities are also stressed because they are retained and used long after the individual has forgotten the detailed specifics of the subject matter taught in the schools. These abilities are regarded as one set of essential characteristics needed to continue learning and to cope with a rapidly changing world. Some curriculum centers believe that these higher mental processes are important because they make learning exciting and constantly new and playful.

In these countries, subjects are taught as methods of inquiry into the nature of science, mathematics, the arts, and the social studies. The subjects are taught as much for the ways of thinking they represent as for their traditional content. Much of this learning makes use of observations, reflections on these observations, experimentation with phenomena, and first-hand data and daily experiences, as well as primary printed sources. All of this is reflected in the materials of instruction, the learning and teaching processes used, and the questions and problems used in the quizzes and formative testing, as well as on the final summative examinations.

In sharp contrast with teachers in some of these other countries, teachers in the United States typically make use of textbooks that rarely pose real problems. These textbooks emphasize specific content to be remembered and give students little opportunity to discover underlying concepts and principles and even less opportunity to attack real problems in the environments in which they live. The teacher-made tests (and standardized tests) are largely tests of remembered information. After the sale of over one million copies of the *Taxonomy of Educational Objectives—Cognitive Domain* (Bloom, Engelhart, Furst, Hill, & Krathwohl, 1956) and over a quarter of a century of use of this domain in preservice and in-service teacher training, it is estimated that over 90 percent of test questions that U.S. public school students are *now* expected to answer deal with little more than information. Our instructional material, our classroom teaching methods, and our testing methods rarely rise above the lowest category of the taxonomy-knowledge.

In the tutoring studies reported at the beginning of this paper, it was found that the tutored students' Higher Mental Process (HMP) achievement was 2.0 sigma above the control students' (see Figure 18.4). (The average tutored student was above 98 percent of the control students on the HMP part of the

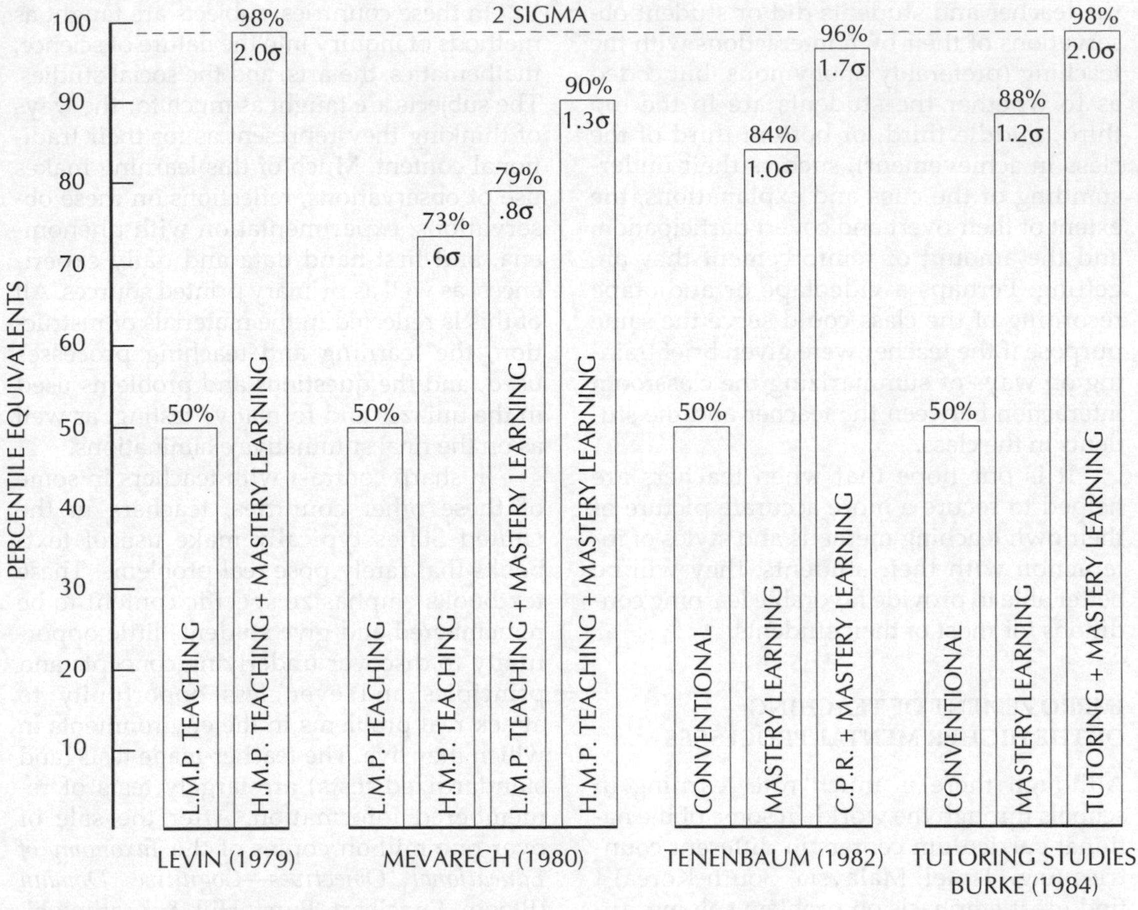

FIGURE 18.4 Average Higher Mental Process Achievement Scores under Different Learning Conditions: Comparison of Tutoring Studies, Mastery Learning, and Higher Mental Process Instructional Methods

summative examination.) It should be noted that in these studies, higher mental process as well as lower mental process questions were included in the formative tests used in the feedback-corrective processes for both the ML and tutored groups. Again, the point is that students can learn the higher mental processes if they become more central in the teaching-learning process.

Several studies have been made in which the researcher was seeking to improve the higher mental processes.

We have already referred to the Tenenbaum (1982) study, which emphasized changing teacher-student interaction. In this study, the cue–participation-reinforcement + mastery learning student group was 1.7 sigma higher than the control students on the higher mental process part of the summative examination. (The average CPR + ML student was above 96 percent of the control students on the higher mental processes.) (See Figure 18.4.)

Another study done by Levin (1979) was directed to improving the higher mental processes by emphasizing the mastery of the lower mental processes and providing learning experiences in which the students applied principles in a variety of different problem situations. On the summative examinations, the students were very high on the knowledge of principles and facts and in their ability to apply the principles in new problem situations. These experimental students were compared with a control group that was taught only the principles (but not their application). On the higher mental processes, the experimental group was 2 sigma above the control students (the average experimental student was above 98 percent of the control students) in the ability to apply the principles to new problem situations.

A third study by Mevarech (1980) was directed at improving the higher mental processes by emphasizing heuristic problem solving and including higher and lower mental process questions in the formative testing and in the feedback-corrective processes. On the higher mental process part of the summative tests, the group using the heuristic methods + ML (HMP Teaching + ML) was 1.3 sigma above the control group (LMP Teaching) taught primarily by learning algorithms—a set of rules and procedures for solving particular math problems (the average student in this experimental group was above 90 percent of the control students).

In all of these studies, attempts to improve higher mental processes included group instruction emphasizing higher mental processes and feedback-corrective processes, which also emphasized higher mental processes. In addition, the tutoring studies included an instructional emphasis on both higher and lower mental processes, as well as the feedback-corrective processes, which included both higher and lower mental processes. It was evident in all of these studies that in the formative feedback and corrective processes the students needed and received more corrective help on the higher mental processes questions and problems than they did on the lower mental process questions.

CONCLUSION

The Anania (1982, 1983) and Burke (1984) studies comparing student learning under one-to-one tutoring, ML, and conventional group instruction began in 1980. As the results of these separate studies at different grade levels and in different school subjects began to emerge, we were astonished at the consistency of the findings as well as the great differences in student cognitive achievement, attitudes, and academic self-concept under tutoring as compared with the group methods of instruction.

For 4 years, the graduate students in my seminars at the University of Chicago and Northwestern University considered various approaches to the search for group methods of instruction that might be as effective as one-to-one tutoring. This chapter reports on the research studies these students completed and some of the other ideas we explored in these seminars.

Although all of us at first thought it was an impossible task, we did agree that if we succeeded in finding *one* solution, there would soon be a great many solutions. In this chapter, I report on six solutions to the 2 sigma problem. In spite of the difficulties, our graduate students found the problem to be very intriguing because the goal was so clear and specific—*find methods of group instruction as effective as one-to-one tutoring.*

Early in the work, it became evident that more than group instruction in the school had to be considered. We also needed to find ways of improving the students' learning processes, the curriculum and instructional materials, as well as the home environmental support of the students' school learning. This chapter is only a preliminary report on what has been accomplished to date, but it should be evident that much can now be done to improve student learning in the schools. However, the search is far from complete. We look for additional solutions to the 2 sigma problem to be reported in the next few years. I hope some of the readers of this chapter will also find this problem challenging.

APPENDIX: EFFECT SIZE REFERENCES

Tutorial Instruction*

Anania, J. (1982). "The Effects of Quality of Instruction on the Cognitive and Affective Learning of Students (doctoral dissertation, University of Chicago, 1981). *Dissertation Abstracts International, 42,* 4269A.

Burke, A. J. (1984). "Students' Potential for Learning Contrasted under Tutorial and Group Approaches to Instruction (doctoral dissertation, University of Chicago, 1983). *Dissertation Abstracts International, 44,* 2025A.

Reinforcement

Lysakowski, R. S., & Walberg, H. J. (1981). "Classroom Reinforcement: A Quantitative Synthesis." *Journal of Educational Research, 75:* 69–77.

Feedback-Corrective, Cues & Explanations, and Student Classroom Participation

Lysakowski, R. S., & Walberg, H. J. (1982). "Instructional Effects of Cues, Participation, and Corrective Feedback: A Quantitative Synthesis." *American Educational Research Journal, 19:* 559–578.

Student Time on Task (in the classroom)

Frederick, W. C., & Walberg, H. J. (1980). "Learning as a Function of Time." *Journal of Educational Research, 73:* 183–194.

Improved Reading/Study Skills

Pflaum, S. W., Walberg, H. J., Karegianes, M. L., & Rasher, S. (1980). "Reading Instruction: A Quantitative Synthesis." *Educational Researcher, 9:* 12–18.

Cooperative Learning

Slavin, R. E. (1980). "Cooperative Learning." *Review of Educational Research, 50:* 315–342.

*Note effect size studies

Home Work (graded) and Home Work (assigned)

Paschal, R., Weinstein, T., & Walberg, H. J. (1984). "Effects of Homework: A Quantitative Synthesis." *Journal of Educational Research, 78:* 97–104.

Classroom Morale

Haertel, G. D., Walberg, H. J., & Haertel, E. H. (1981). "Social-Psychological Environments and Learning: A Quantitative Synthesis." *British Educational Research Journal, 7:* 27–36.

Initial Cognitive Prerequisites*

Leyton, F. S. (1983). "The Extent to Which Group Instruction Supplemented by Mastery of the Initial Cognitive Prerequisites Approximates the Learning Effectiveness of One-to-One Tutorial Instruction (doctoral dissertation, University of Chicago, 1983). *Dissertation Abstracts International, 44,* 974A.

Home Environment Intervention (parental educational program)

Iverson, B. K., & Walberg, H. J. (1982). Home environment and learning: A quantitative synthesis. *Journal of Experimental Education, 50:* 144–151.

Peer & Cross-Age Remedial Tutoring

Cohen, P. A., Kulik, J. A., & Kulik, C. C. (1982). "Educational Outcomes of Tutoring: A Meta-Analysis of Findings." *American Educational Research Journal 19:* 237–248.

Higher Order Questions

Redfield, D. L., & Rousseau, E. W. (1981). "Meta-Analysis of Experimental Research on Teacher Questioning Behavior." *Review of Educational Research, 51:* 235–245.

New Science & Math Curricula and Teacher Expectancy

Walberg, H. J. (1984). "Improving the Productivity of America's Schools." *Educational Leadership, 41:* 8, 19–27.

Peer Group Influence

Ide, J., Haertel, G. D., Parkerson, J. A., & Walberg, H. J. (1981). "Peer-Group Influences on Learning: A Quantitative Synthesis." *Journal of Educational Psychology, 73,* 472–484.

Advance Organizers

Luiten, J., Ames, W., & Ackerson, G. (1980). "A Meta-Analysis of the Effects of Advance Organizers on Learning and Retention." *American Educational Research Journal, 17:* 211–218.

ENDNOTES

1. In giving the percentile equivalent we make use of the normal curve distribution. The control class distributions were approximately normal, although the mastery learning and tutoring groups were highly skewed.

2. $\dfrac{\text{Mean experimental} - \text{Mean control}}{\text{Standard deviation of the control}}$

$= \dfrac{\text{Mex} - \text{Mc}}{\text{Sigma of control}} = \textit{effect size}$

3. When questionnaires rather than interviews and observations have been used, the correlations are somewhat lower, with the average being between +.45 and +.55.

REFERENCES

Anania, J. (1982). "The Effects of Quality of Instruction on the Cognitive and Affective Learning of Students." Doctoral dissertation, University of Chicago, 1981. *Dissertation Abstracts International, 42,* 4269A.

Anania, J. (1983). "The Influence of Instructional Conditions on Student Learning and Achievement." *Evaluation in Education: An International Review Series, 7*(1): 1–92.

Ausubel, D. (1960). "The Use of Advanced Organizers in the Learning and Retention of Meaningful Verbal Material." *Journal of Educational Psychology, 51:* 267–272.

Bloom, B. S. (1980). "The New Direction in Educational Research: Alterable Variables." *Phi Delta Kappan, 61*(6): 382–385.

Bloom, B. S., Engelhart, M. D., Furst, E. J., Hill, W. H., & Krathwohl, D. R. (1956). *Taxonomy of Educational Objectives: Handbook I, Cognitive Domain.* New York: Longman.

Bronfenbrenner, U. (1974). "Is Early Intervention Effective?" In H. J. Leichter, (Ed.), *The Family as Educator.* New York: Teachers College Press.

Brophy, J. E., & Good, T. L. (1970). "Teachers' Communication of Differential Expectations for Children's Classroom Performance: Some Behavioral Data." *Journal of Educational Psychology, 61:* 365–374.

Burke, A. J. (1984). "Students' Potential for Learning Contrasted under Tutorial and Group Approaches to Instruction." Doctoral dissertation, University of Chicago, 1983. *Dissertation Abstracts International, 44,* 2025A.

Dave, R. H. (1963). "The Identification and Measurement of Environment Process Variables that are Related to Educational Achievement." Unpublished doctoral dissertation, University of Chicago.

Dolan, L. J. (1980). "The Affective Correlates of Home Concern and Support, Instructional Quality, and Achievement." Unpublished doctoral dissertation, University of Chicago.

Ide, J., Haertel, G. D., Parkerson, J. A., & Walberg, H. J. (1981). "Peer Group Influences on Learning: A Quantitive Synthesis." *Journal of Educational Psychology, 73:* 472–484.

Iverson, B. K., & Walberg, H. J. (1982). "Home Environment and Learning: A Quantitative Synthesis." *Journal of Experimental Education, 50:* 144–151.

Janhom, S. (1983). "Educating Parents to Educate Their Children." Unpublished doctoral dissertation, University of Chicago.

Kalinowski, A., & Sloane, K. (1981). "The Home Environment and School Achievement." *Studies in Educational Evaluation, 7:* 85–96.

Levin, T. (1979). "Instruction Which Enables Students to Develop Higher Mental Processes." *Evaluation in Education: An International Review Series, 3*(3): 173–220.

Leyton, F. S. (1983). "The Extent to Which Group Instruction Supplemented by Mastery of the Initial Cognitive Prerequisites Approximates the Learning Effectiveness of One-to-One Tutorial Methods." Doctoral dissertation, University of Chicago, 1983. *Dissertation Abstracts International, 44,* 974A.

Luiten, J., Ames, W., & Ackerson, G. (1980). "A Meta-Analysis of the Effects of Advance Organizers on Learning and Retention." *American Educational Research Journal, 17:* 211–218.

Marjoribanks, K. (1974). *Environments for Learning.* London: National Foundation for Educational Research.

Mevarech, Z. R. (1980). "The Role of Teaching-Learning Strategies and Feedback-Corrective Procedures in Developing Higher Cognitive Achievement." Unpublished doctoral dissertation, University of Chicago.

Nordin, A. B. (1979). "The Effects of Different Qualities of Instruction on Selected Cognitive, Affective, and Time Variables." Unpublished doctoral dissertation, University of Chicago.

Nordin, A. B. (1980). "Improving Learning: An Experiment in Rural Primary Schools in Malaysia." *Evaluation in Education: An International Review Series, 4*(2): 143–263.

Pflaum, S. W., Walberg, H. J., Karegianes, M. L., & Rasher, S. (1980). "Reading Instruction: A Quantitative Synthesis." *Educational Researcher, 9:* 12–18.

Slavin, R. E. (1980). "Cooperative Learning." *Review of Educational Research, 50:* 315–342.

Tenenbaum, G. (1982). "A Method of Group Instruction Which Is as Effective as One-to-One Tutorial Instruction." Doctoral dissertation, University of Chicago, 1982. *Dissertation Abstracts International, 43,* 1822A.

Walberg, H. J. (1984). "Improving the Productivity of America's Schools." *Educational Leadership, 41,* 8, 19–27.

Wolf, R. M. (1964). "The Identification and Measurement of Home Environmental Process Variables That Are Related to Intelligence." Unpublished doctoral dissertation, University of Chicago.

Wolf, R. M. (1966). "The Measurement of Environments." In A. Anastasi (Ed.), *Testing Problems in Perspective.* Washington, DC: American Council on Education.

DISCUSSION QUESTIONS

1. Is the mastery learning approach appropriate for all students?
2. How does a teacher's differential interaction with students influence student achievement?
3. How are conditions of learning integrally related to student outcomes?
4. What type of staff development initiatives might be undertaken to provide teachers with an accurate perception of the quality of learning conditions that they provide for their students?
5. How effective are conventional instruction, mastery learning, and tutoring?

CHAPTER 19

Needed: A New Educational Civil Rights Movement

EVANS CLINCHY

FOCUSING QUESTIONS

1. Why was true desegregation never realized?
2. What are steps that can be taken to reduce the segregation problem (especially for inner-city schools)?
3. What are solutions to overcome the inequalities?
4. How is a student harmed by being held back? How is she or he benefited?
5. What are the benefits of "tracking" programs? The pitfalls?
6. What steps can be taken to "level the playing field" of education?
7. What aspects of an education make up a "proper" public education?

Now that the great U.S. post–World War II civil rights movement in education has apparently run its course and appears to be moving backwards, it is time to launch a new educational civil rights movement. Or at least it's time to take the old one in a new and more comprehensive direction for the 21st century.

I think we might all agree that the Supreme Court's 1954 decision in *Brown v. Board of Education* was the single greatest recognition in the 20th century that the parents and children of this country really do have educational rights. In that sense, it was the high-water mark of that century's educational civil rights movement.

The Brown decision made two vitally important points. The first was that the "segregation of children in public schools solely on the basis of race deprives children of the minority group of equal educational opportunities, even though the physical facilities and other 'tangible' factors may be equal." The second and equally important finding was that "where a state has undertaken to provide an opportunity for an education in its public schools, such opportunity is a right which must be made available to all on equal terms."[1]

NOT WHOLLY A SUCCESS

Following the Brown decision and subsequent court decisions, this country embarked on the long effort to desegregate all our public schools and provide all U.S. children of every racial and ethnic group with those "equal educational opportunities." But if we look at what has happened since 1954, we can see all too clearly that that movement has turned out to be only a qualified success. While legal segregation has ended in this country and Southern school districts can no longer run officially segregated schools, many school districts—especially inner-city districts in both the North and the South—are at least as segregated as they were in 1954. Indeed, many districts, such as those in Boston, Chicago, New York, and other major cities, are *more* segregated.[2]

What's more, both federal and state courts are now moving toward declaring that many of our formerly segregated districts have made "good faith"—if unsuccessful—efforts to desegregate and are, therefore, legally "unified" and relieved of any further duty to integrate their schools. These same courts are also declaring that "race-based admissions policies" are unconstitutional and that districts may now return to the policy of racially identifiable neighborhood schools, the very policy that originally caused the de facto segregation of schools in the North.

In addition, we are experiencing an increase in economic segregation throughout our system of public education. Those inner-city schools that house most of our minority children also house large concentrations of our poor children. What's more, the nation's rural schools serve disproportionately large numbers of just plain poor (though mainly nonminority) children.

And all of these schools are still very clearly victims of Jonathan Kozol's "savage inequalities." While suburban school districts may spend $12,000 to $15,000 on every student, city and rural school districts are fortunate if they can raise $7,000 per student, a situation that puts every state in the union except Hawaii in violation of the Brown ruling that requires states to provide public education on equal terms to all children and young people. Urban students and their teachers are all too often housed in ancient, crumbling buildings. Their schools are all too often staffed by poorly trained and underpaid teachers. Classes can be as large as 40 to 45 students and are often supplied with ancient materials and little or no modern electronic equipment. At the same time, there is an inadequate array of community support services to assist the many children and young people and their families who live lives of extreme poverty.

All of this is happening at a time when the United States is not only the richest nation the world has ever seen but also a nation in which the already rich are garnering an ever increasing share of the national wealth while 20 million children still live in poverty. Neither those children nor their parents have adequate health insurance, adequate schools, adequate social services, or adequate jobs. In short, despite the Brown decision, the nation has signally failed to provide anything close to equal educational opportunity to all our children and young people.

MAKING THINGS WORSE

As if all these inequities were not bad enough, we have now embarked on a new national agenda in education that, if it is perhaps not as overtly immoral as segregation, is surely as inhumane, undemocratic, and (many of us devoutly hope and believe) unconstitutional.

This is the Goals 2000 federal agenda that is causing every state except Iowa to impose on all students and all schools a single standardized curriculum that embodies new, "higher," "tougher," "world-class" academic standards.[3]

Many of these new academic standards, according to many of the teachers, principals, and school administrators who must impose them, are hopelessly abstruse, excessively demanding, and quite inappropriate for the age and intellectual development of the children and young people who are forced to attempt to meet them. Indeed, a study conducted by staff members of Midcontinent Research for Education and Learning has estimated that it would take as much as 22 years of schooling for a student to meet all the standards in all the core subject areas that are being mandated by most states.[4]

This attempt to impose on all students a narrow, authoritarian, uniform definition of what it is to be an educated person is being cemented in place in nearly every state by the imposition of new, "tougher," "high-stakes," standardized, pencil-and-paper, most often multiple-choice tests that all students must pass before they can be promoted to the next grade or permitted to graduate from high school. All public schools are now being forced to "align" their curricula with these tests—that is, to teach to and only to the academic orthodoxy that is contained in and thus authorized by the tests.[5]

The National Center for Fair and Open Testing (FairTest) and many testing experts believe that the single, high-stakes tests currently in use are too long, too complicated, and both academically unfair and inaccurate because they often test what has not been studied and pose questions that are well above any student's level of cognitive development. They are also often badly administered and in thousands of cases incorrectly scored. All of these testing malfeasances are causing unjustified anguish for children and parents across the land.[6]

One fact that renders invalid the practice of using any single high-stakes test to determine whether students can be promoted from grade to grade or allowed to graduate from high school is that none of the high-prestige colleges and universities would ever dream of using any single measure to determine whether to admit students. Even though the SAT is used by these institutions, the *New York Times* has pointed out that an institution such as Wesleyan University will "weigh a student's race, ethnicity, home town as well as course selection, athletic prowess, alumni connections, artistic skill, musical talent, writing ability, community service and the quality of the school" from which the student comes. High-prestige colleges and universities want to make sure that their entering classes are "not only academically sound and ethnically and racially diverse but also well-stocked with poets, running backs, activists, politicians, painters, journalists and cellists." And they will often use a variety of criteria in choosing to admit students who have lower test scores than other applicants.[7] The practices of these highly selective institutions clearly spell out the kind of broad, inclusive, and all-encompassing criteria we should be using in assessing the progress of all students as they move from kindergarten through high school.

But to this range of sterling and necessary human endeavors we need to add the full range of technical and mechanical skills, few of which are going to be acquired by going to college. Just as we need poets, running backs, and cellists, we need skilled (and equally well-paid) farmers, carpenters, electricians, plumbers, sheet metal workers, auto mechanics, construction workers, chefs, and so on, and the full range of skilled and even unskilled service industry people. After all, it is these skilled and unskilled workers, many with only a high school education or less, who actually keep the social and economic worlds working.

PUNISHING STUDENTS FOR THE FAILURE OF SCHOOLS

But there is more to this sad story. In an effort to end what the school authorities call "social promotion," policies are being adopted that force students who do not pass the tests to go to summer school and to be "retained" in grade if they still fail to pass the tests. Or take the case of Boston, where students who don't pass the eighth-grade state test are not held back but are instead forced to go to summer school and, if they still fail the test, are then placed in "transition" classes in the ninth grade. This, according to Judith Baker, a veteran Boston high school teacher,

> is the same exact thing as tracking used to be. [The students] are denied electives or creative programs, they take double English and math, and if they fail these, they will probably go into transition 10th-grade and 11th-grade classes. . . . Although there is an attempt to bolster these courses, they are essentially remedial. They create "higher" and "lower" tracks, just by taking the majority of entering ninth-graders into what automatically becomes the school's "lower" track. These "transition" classes throw the entire curriculum sequence off, because they delay until later grades many required courses, and by the time students fulfill their requirements, they will never have had a chance to take an elective, an honors or AP course, anything remotely interesting.
>
> Students are responding by being sullen and bored, by failing (the guidance counselor for grade 9 went home with a stuffed shopping bag full of warning notices), and by other negative behavior. I have heard of no positive behavior, academic or other, associated with the "transition" course.[8]

So what are the utterly expectable results of this wave of so-called school reform? The reformers say that "all children can and now will learn"—if only they and their teachers settle down, work hard, and concentrate on those lessons that will help them raise their test scores. Forget about those "savage inequalities." Success can be achieved solely by hard work and teaching to the standards and the tests.

But there is no secret about who the children and young people are who are going to fail those tests and, indeed, are already failing them all over the country. They are precisely the poor and minority children and young people—especially those with limited proficiency in English—who inhabit those savagely unequal schools. (Madison Park High School, where Judith Baker teaches, has a student body that is made up almost entirely of minority students and students who qualify for federally subsidized lunches.)

Indeed, the latest figures on dropouts in Boston, according to the Massachusetts Advocacy Center, are that over the period 1995–1999, during which the state and local high-stakes testing program was instituted, the annual dropout rate for all students increased by 34 percent. For African Americans, the rate of increase has been 28 percent; for Hispanics, 40 percent; for Asians, 43 percent; and for whites, 37 percent.

NOT GOOD FOR ANYBODY

Now I hasten to add that I am not suggesting that the largely majority and most often suburban students who pass the tests are thereby being supplied with a good and proper education. I steadfastly maintain that the narrow, authoritarian, uniform, "high-standards," academically and politically orthodox definition of what it means to be an educated person is no better for well-to-do, white suburbanites than it is for low-income, inner-city minorities. Indeed, the kind of education that everyone should be getting is precisely the kind of schooling that will produce those poets, running backs, activists, politicians, painters, journalists, and cellists that the elite colleges want and need, as well as the farmers, carpenters, electricians, auto mechanics, and service providers that American society as a whole wants and needs.

So the expected is happening. The poor and minority children and young people who do not pass the tests are being humiliated and labeled as failures. It is interesting to note here that most states, including Massachusetts, are not imposing such tests on students in private schools, thus enabling rich parents to buy their children's way out of any such humiliation. The always unlevel playing field is growing even steeper for the poor and for minorities as each day passes.

And it is not just the students who are being punished. If those poor and minority children in public schools don't pass the tests, their teachers and principals will also be labeled failures and threatened with the loss of their jobs or the takeover of their schools by the state.

As these thousands of poor and minority children and young people continue to fail the tests and to be publicly excoriated as failures, what is going to be their inevitable reaction? As at Madison Park, they will believe the labels certifying them as failures, they will realize what that failure means in terms of their chances in life, and large numbers of them will drop out of school as quickly as they legally—or illegally—can. And if you, as a school administrator, can rid your school of its low-scoring failures, you have hit upon a surefire way to guarantee that the test scores of your school and school district will go up and that your school and district will be considered successes.

A SUSPICIOUS AGENDA

This scenario leads to the dark suspicion that this is precisely what some of the reformers—not all of them, of course—may have had in mind all along. They certainly seem to be seeking to build an increasingly two-tiered system of American society: one tier for the small number of successfully "educated," largely nonminority winners who have succeeded in school and a second tier for the many failures who will be left to serve the needs of the increasingly wealthy successes.

Many of these reformers, having given up on the possibility of building a truly democratic system of public education that can provide a high-quality education for all children, now advocate that we abandon any such attempt and move instead toward a completely privatized system by providing all children with vouchers that can be used to pay at least part of the tuition at private schools. There is also a burgeoning movement to create publicly supported charter schools that parents can choose, schools that are for the most part independent of local school districts and are usually directly responsible to state governments.

Insofar as these charters are and remain genuinely public schools with guaranteed access for all poor and minority students and are not exempted from the standards and tests required of other public schools, they constitute a legitimate choice for both parents and teachers. Unfortunately, many of these charters are being run by profit-making corporations, and in many instances they are not being adequately supervised by the states. Thus charter schools appear to be increasingly serving the nonminority, middle-class portion of the population, including many students whose parents either have been paying or at least could pay for tuition at private schools. (Recall that charter schools tend to be located in urban centers where large numbers of minorities reside; thus statewide figures for charter school attendance can be skewed to make minority enrollments appear proportionally larger than they are.)

WHO IS DOING ALL OF THIS?

This authoritarian, antidemocratic national educational regime of high standards and high-stakes testing is being imposed almost entirely by self-appointed experts with, at best, weak credentials in education—primarily state and local politicians, including governors and state legislators, and state department of education bureaucrats. These are the folks who have attended three national education "summits" called by the National Governors' Association, by foundation officials, and by the CEOs of such leading corporations as IBM. The rallying cry at these gatherings is that the new, viciously competitive, capitalistic world economy requires that any nation that hopes to survive must produce large numbers of technologically adept, well-behaved, mentally skillful workers to staff those multinational corporations and the vast service industries that support not only the corporations but society as a whole.

Over the past several years, this strictly economic argument has been revealed as a deceptive myth, for despite our purported educational woes, the U.S. economy has somehow managed to become the most powerful economic engine in the history of the world. As the eminent social and educational thinker Richard Rothstein has pointed out, when *A Nation at Risk* was published in 1983 the economy appeared to be in big trouble. It was then widely believed that this poor economic performance was the result of the shoddy quality of the nation's public schools. In those days, the unemployment rate (and in many minds the unemployability rate) was over 6 percent, and the school dropout rate was twice that.

Now, in these early years of the new millennium, the unemployment rate is 3.9 percent, and even high school dropouts are finding jobs. The U.S. system of public education, however, is not being credited as one of the chief causes of this economic miracle. Nor have those governors and state legislators, those state department of education bureaucrats, those foundation officials, and those corporate CEOs held another national education summit to announce that their highly touted reform agenda of high standards and high-stakes testing may be totally wrongheaded, educationally damaging, and even economically counterproductive.[9]

BUT NO DEVILS HERE

Now, before I attempt any further exploration of what is going on here, let me be very clear on one point. Despite any and all suspicions to the contrary, I refuse to believe that those governors and legislators, those corporate leaders and foundation executives, the many state bureaucrats, and even those leaders of teacher unions and learned professors in our colleges and universities who support and help implement this arrogant, inhumane agenda are evil people. Nor are they uniformly ultraconservative "right wingers" or "leftist revolutionaries." Indeed, they inhabit every niche of the political spectrum, sharing only the undemocratic, authoritarian belief that they have the right and, indeed, the moral duty to impose their limited and limiting version of educational truth on all children, all young people, all parents, all teachers and other educators, and thus on all public schools throughout the land. I do not doubt that they genuinely believe that what they are advocating is in the best interests of the nation and even in the best interests of the schoolchildren—and especially the poor and minority children—of this country and their parents.

A NEW CIVIL RIGHTS MOVEMENT

But a growing number of parents, older students, teachers, frontline school administrators, school board members, and leading educational thinkers have come to believe that these self-appointed experts could not be more misguided in their efforts to impose what they call school reform on all of our public schools. Indeed, we see this movement as a flagrant and open violation of the basic human educational rights of the citizens of this nation.

By "basic human educational rights," I mean not only the two set forth in the Brown decision but also those contained in the United Nations' Universal Declaration of

Human Rights. Article 26 of that Declaration says first that "everyone has a right to education. Education shall be free [i.e., publicly supported] at least at the elementary and fundamental stages. Technical and professional education shall be made generally available, and higher education shall be equally accessible to all on the basis of merit."

The Declaration then goes on to state the two fundamental rights that have the most relevance to the argument here: "Education shall be directed to the full development of the human personality and to the strengthening of respect for human rights and fundamental freedoms," and "Parents have a prior right to choose the kind of education that shall be given to their children."[10]

Article 26 clearly states that all children have a right to an education that is aimed at the "full development" of the individual human personalities of all children—not just their academic capacities but all their social, political, and artistic capacities as well. The full range of these capacities is what the developmental psychologist Howard Gardner believes are the "multiple intelligences" that all children have: not only the verbal and logico/mathematical intelligences (the only ones usually dealt with in school and tested on the tests), but also the visual, kinetic, musical, naturalistic, social, and personal intelligences—in short, the range of capacities that will produce those poets, running backs, activists, politicians, painters, journalists, and cellists.

BOTH DIVERSITY AND CHOICE

The part of Article 26 that guarantees parental choice recognizes two of the most stubborn and important facts about any truly democratic system of education. The first is that children and young people do not come in any single size, shape, or collection of attributes, capacities, talents, or intelligences. The second fact is a corollary truism: there cannot be any single educational environment that is going to be suitable and appropriate for all children. As Susan Ohanian has put it, "One size fits few."[11]

It is in part because of the broad diversity among children and young people that there is an equivalent diversity of educational philosophies, curricula, and methodologies. At one end of that diverse spectrum are the very conservative, traditional, rigorously academic, "back-to-basics" approaches, such as the Paideia Schools of Mortimer Adler and the Core Knowledge Schools of E. D. Hirsch, Jr. Somewhere in the middle of the spectrum are schools such as those advocating the "continuous progress" of students and those that specialize in particular areas of the conventional curriculum, such as the arts or science and technology. At the other end of the spectrum are the schools that would most likely call themselves progressive—such as Montessori and Waldorf schools, "open" schools, integrated day schools, or microsociety schools. It is from this broad array of educational possibilities that parents have a right to choose the kind of public schooling they believe best fits the individual educational needs of each of their children.

Those of us who reject the new totalitarian educational agenda believe that this right of choice is guaranteed not only by the United Nations Universal Declaration but by the U.S. Constitution through its guarantees of free speech and free assembly. Surely, under those guarantees and under the basic democratic principle that governments may act only with the consent of the governed, parents have the right to specify the kind of public schooling they want their children to have and thus what they wish to have taught to their children in a publicly supported institution called a school. This right of choice is limited only by the First Amendment separation of church and state and by the now watered-down Fourteenth Amendment civil rights decisions that still say that all public schools should be at least as integrated as the school district in which they exist.

BUT NOT JUST PARENTAL CHOICE

It is those two unbending facts—the diversity among our students and the diversity of educational belief and practice—that make educational diversity and choice absolute requirements of any reasonably fair, just, and democratic U.S. education system. And I don't mean just parental choice of the schools their children will go to. Teachers and other professional educators also have the right—called "academic freedom" by college and university professors and guaranteed by the First Amendment—to choose the kind of schooling they wish to practice, since they share with parents that diversity of educational belief. It is this dual right of choice for both parent and professional—along with the right to the full development of each child's personality—that must overrule any state's power to impose a single standardized curriculum and a single high-stakes testing system on all children, all parents, and all professionals.

A DIVERSITY OF STANDARDS AND ASSESSMENTS

Let me also be clear about one more thing. To say that one is against the imposition of a single set of solely academic standards and a single high-stakes, solely academic test—which together add up to the establishment of a single, solely academic intellectual orthodoxy—is not to say that there should be no high educational expectations and no system of public accountability in U.S. public education. Has anyone ever heard of a school that does not propose that its students read and write well and do all appropriate forms of basic arithmetic?

But above and beyond providing these valuable "basics" and quite possibly a commitment to help students develop their capacity for high-level reasoning, it is the task of the parents and the professional staff of each freely chosen public school to decide and spell out in detail what that school conceives its educational mission to be. This would include what its intellectual (rather than academic) standards are, what and how it proposes that teachers should teach and students should learn, and how it proposes to measure its progress toward achieving those desired ends. And if a school decides that a standardized test would be useful, it is, of course, free to use one.

What's more, there is also the basic right of parents operating within such a system of strictly public school choice to opt out of manifestly failing schools and to choose other public schools that they believe will provide the better quality of education they are seeking. This same principle of "free market" public school choice allows teachers to leave failing schools and choose "better" ones. As both parents and teachers abandon failing schools and opt for schools they see as "better," the overall quality of the system is not only likely—but perhaps bound—to improve. At the very least, this is an organizational theory that many people would like to see put to the test.

How then might this new system of U.S. education be organized and operated? After each school selected by both parents and professional staff members has spelled out its educational mission, it is the task and responsibility of the locally elected school board, acting as the agent of state government, to review each school's stated mission and goals to make sure that what the school plans to do falls within the broad limits of democratic belief and practice and the U.S. Constitution. The board would then monitor each school's yearly performance as measured against its stated goals.

It is then the task of the state to monitor the civil rights performance of local school districts and to make sure that every school in every district is equally and adequately funded. And it is the task of the federal government to monitor the civil rights performance of the states and to make sure that the schools of every state are equally and adequately funded. No savage inequalities are permitted anywhere.

NOT A NEW IDEA

It is interesting—but not at all surprising—that what I am proposing here is hardly a new idea. Indeed, back in the latter part of the 19th century, Alfred Russel Wallace, the co-constructor with Charles Darwin of the theory of evolution by natural selection, set forth these ideas in the following fashion:

> In our present society the bulk of the people have no opportunity for the full development of all their powers and capacities. . . . The accumulation of wealth is now mainly effected by the misdirected energy of competing individuals; and the power that wealth so obtained gives them is often used for purposes which are hurtful to the nation. There can be no true individualism, no fair competition, without equality of opportunity for all. This alone is social justice, and by this alone can the best that is in each nation be developed and utilised for the benefit of all its citizens.

"Equality of opportunity," Wallace went on to say,

> is absolute fair play as between man and man in the struggle for existence. It means that all shall have the best education they are capable of receiving; that their faculties shall all be well trained, and their whole nature obtain the fullest moral, intellectual, and physical development. This does not mean that we shall all have the same education, that all shall be made to learn the same things and go through the same training, but that all shall be so trained as to develop fully all that is best in them. It must be an adaptive education, modified in accordance with the peculiar mental and physical nature of the pupils, not a rigid routine applied to all alike, as is too often the case now.[12]

THE PATH TO A NEW MOVEMENT

Now it is unfortunately true that recent federal court decisions, one in Florida and one in Texas, have ruled that those two states have the right to set academic standards and to administer a single high-stakes test to all students in order to determine whether those standards are being met, even though poor and minority students in those states are failing the tests at an alarming rate. This, of course, suggests that, until there is an eventual ruling by the U.S. Supreme Court, all states are free to pursue their present autocratic course.[13]

Concerned parents, teachers, school administrators, and test experts in all the states, refusing to accept these decisions as final, are preparing further challenges to the authoritarian agenda of standards and testing in state legislatures and in state and federal courts all across the land. No court decision is unalterable. After all, it was the Supreme Court's 1896 decision in *Plessy v. Ferguson* that established the doctrine of "separate but equal," which was eventually overturned by the 1954 Brown decision.

It will almost certainly take a new educational civil rights movement, such as the one proposed here, to bring about the kind of just, fair, equal, and truly democratic system of U.S. public education we want and deserve. Let us hope as well that we are not in for another century of continued educational injustice before we set the record straight and achieve that just, fair, and equitable system.

ENDNOTES

1. *Brown v. Board of Education*, 347 U.S. 483 (1954), p. 1.
2. See Gary Orfield and John T. Yun, *Resegregation in American Schools* (Cambridge, MA: Harvard Civil Rights Project, June 1999), for data on increased racial, ethnic, and economic segregation.
3. For more on this movement, see Marion Brady, "The Standards Juggernaut," *Phi Delta Kappan*, May 2000, pp. 649–51; and Susan Ohanian, *One Size Fits Few: The Folly of Educational Standards* (Portsmouth, NH: Heinemann, 1999).
4. Robert J. Marzano and John S. Kendall, *Awash in a Sea of Standards* (Aurora, CO: Midcontinent Research for Education and Learning, 1998).

5. See Gary Natriello and Aaron M. Pallas, *The Development and Impact of High-Stakes Testing* (Cambridge, MA: Harvard Civil Rights Project, November 1999); and Linda McNeil and Angela Valenzuela, "Harmful Effects of the TAAS System of Testing in Texas: Beneath the Accountability Rhetoric," in Mindy Kornhaber, Gary Orfield, and Michal Kurlaendar (Eds.), *Raising Barriers? Inequality and High-Stakes Testing in Public Education* (New York: Century Foundation, 2000).

6. For details, see the newsletters and publications of the National Center for Fair and Open Testing, 342 Broadway, Cambridge, MA 02139; or send e-mail to info@fairtest.org.

7. Jacques Sternberg, "For Gatekeepers at Colleges, a Daunting Task of Sorting," *New York Times*, February 27, 2000, pp. A–1, A–24.

8. Judith Baker, personal e-mail communication, June 12, 1999.

9. Richard Rothstein, "Education and Job Growth," *New York Times*, May 10, 2000, p. A–23.

10. Universal Declaration of Human Rights (Geneva: Office of the United Nations High Commissioner for Human Rights, United Nations Department of Public Information, 1998).

11. Ohanian, *One Size Fits Few*.

12. Harry Clements, *Alfred Russel Wallace: Biologist and Social Reformer* (London: Hutchinson, 1983), pp. 96–98.

13. For the Texas decision, see *G. I. Forum et al. v. Texas Education Agency et al.*, Civil Action No. SA-97-CA-1278EP (www.txwd.uscourts.gov).

DISCUSSION QUESTIONS

1. Do you agree that the civil rights movement in the United States during the last half of the 20th century was not wholly successful? What evidence do you see?
2. Do you agree that the federal government's current policies are making our society less equitable?
3. Can high-stakes testing serve the purpose of ensuring equity in public schooling or is it an obstacle to that end?
4. Should the United Nations Universal Declaration of Human Rights be used to guide education policy in the United States?
5. What kind of "new educational civil rights movement" does the author propose? Do you think it would be successful?

CHAPTER 20

The Thought-Filled Curriculum

Arthur L. Costa

FOCUSING QUESTIONS:

1. How can a thought-filled curriculum promote student learning?
2. How can teachers teach their students to think?
3. How do Costa's five themes encourage thoughtful learning?
4. What tools are necessary to think "skillfully"?
5. What does it mean to think "skillfully"?

Everyone thinks. Keeping five themes in mind will ensure that every learner thinks skillfully.

How do you know that your students need to learn how to think?

When I have posed this question to teachers of all grade levels in countries around the world, teachers have given surprisingly similar and consistent descriptions of their students' thinking:

- They just blurt out answers. They should think before they respond.
- They depend on me for their answers. I wish they would think for themselves.
- They give up so easily on difficult tasks. I'd like them to hang in there.
- They can't seem to work in groups. They must learn to cooperate and work together.
- They don't apply their knowledge. I want them to use what they know in other situations.
- They are afraid to take risks. I'd like them to be more creative, more adventuresome.

Such comments reflect teachers' awareness that to function in school, at work, and in life, students must persist when faced with adversity, solve cognitively complex problems, draw on vast reservoirs of knowledge, and work collaboratively. To strengthen these skills, instruction must become more reflective, complex, and relevant (Commission on the Whole Child, 2007).

Curriculums must become more thought-filled in the sense of enlarging students' capacities to think deeply and creatively.

FIVE THEMES TO SHAPE CURRICULUM

I propose that educators make five themes part of any thought-filled curriculum. These themes provide lenses through which we can shape, organize, and evaluate curriculums.

1. Learning to Think

> Iron rusts from disuse; stagnant water loses its purify and in cold weather becomes frozen; even so does inaction sap the vigor of the mind.
>
> — Leonardo da Vinci

Humans are born with the capacity and inclination to think. Nobody has to "teach us how to think" just as no one teaches us how to move or walk. Moving with precision and style, however, takes much time and coaching. The distinction between awkwardness and grace is obvious to even an undisciplined observer. A superb ballerina, tai chi master, or gymnast needs years of practice, concentration, reflection, and guidance to perform intricate maneuvers on command with seemingly effortless agility.

Like strenuous movement, skillful thinking is hard work. And as with athletics, students need practice, reflection, and coaching to think well. With proper instruction, human thought processes can become more broadly applied, more spontaneously generated, more precisely focused, more complex, and more insightfully divergent.

Unlike athletics, however, thinking is usually idiosyncratic and covert. Awkwardness and agility are not as easily distinguished in thinking as they are in athletics. Definitions of thought processes, strategies for their development, and assessment of the stamina required for increased mastery, therefore, are elusive, as the following classroom interaction illustrates.

After showing a class of 8th graders how the Earth's population is likely to double in the next 50 years, a teacher asks students what could be done to solve the problem of population explosion.

> STUDENT: I don't know.
>
> TEACHER: Well, think about it. We may not have enough food and space. It's a problem we will need to solve.
>
> STUDENT: We could send some people somewhere where they won't need food and space.
>
> TEACHER: Where?
>
> STUDENT: Uh, into space.
>
> TEACHER: Why there?
>
> STUDENT: They won't need to eat our food or live here anymore. (Swartz, Costa, Kallick, Beyer, & Reagan, 2007, p. 9)

Is this student thinking? Yes. Is this student thinking critically, skillfully, and creatively? It seems not.

Teachers who value thinking and habits of mind would ensure that students confront a problem like population expansion with a questioning attitude, arm themselves with attendant data, explore alternatives to the status quo, and predict the consequences of each of those alternatives. A contrasting teaching approach here might bring out strenuous thinking by taking time as a class to gather more information and understand why the problem exists. A teacher might pose such questions as, Where in the world has this problem been encountered and resolved in the past? What alternative solutions might be generated? or, By what humane and just criteria might the consequences of each of those solutions be evaluated?

Although thinking is innate and spontaneous, skillful thinking must be cultivated. One way to enhance such thinking is to get students intrigued by relevant, generative, conceptual knowledge. Cognition and content are inseparable. One cannot think about "nothing," and deep conceptual understanding requires such cognitive skills as comparing, analyzing, applying, translating, and evaluating (Wiggins & McTighe, 1998). Further, the deeper knowledge a learner has, the more analytical, experimental, and creative are that learner's thought processes (Willingham, 2007).

We can catalyze learning to think by making thinking skills explicit. We should use cognitive terminology and label and identify cognitive processes, saying, for example, "So as you're analyzing this problem . . ." (Costa & Marzano, 2001). Teachers should also employ thinking maps and visual tools (Hyerle, 2004) and model problem solving, decision making, and investigating (Swartz et al., 2007).

It is not enough, however, for students to learn thinking and problem-solving skills in teacher-constructed classroom situations. They must also develop the inclination to use productive habits of mind, including persisting, managing impulsivity, thinking flexibly, striving for accuracy, and remaining open to continuous learning—on their own (Costa & Kallick, 2001).

2. Thinking to Learn

Learning is an engagement of the mind that changes the mind.

—Martin Heidegger

Meaning making is not a spectator sport. Knowledge is a constructive process; to really understand something, each learner must create a model or metaphor derived from that learner's personal world. Humans don't get ideas; they make ideas.

Content learning, therefore, should not be viewed as the only aim of instruction. Rather, teachers should select relevant, generative, wondrous content to serve as a vehicle for the joyride of learning. We can equip that vehicle by

- Posing challenging, content embedded questions and problems that tax the imagination and stimulate inquiry.
- Inviting students to assess their own learning.
- Urging students to question their own and others' assumptions.
- Valuing students' viewpoints by maintaining a safe, nonjudgmental classroom atmosphere.

For example, to challenge students to dig deeper into historical perspectives, a teacher might have 5th graders compare and contrast two versions of the story of Pocahontas and John Smith by reading the fictionalized account The Double Life of Pocahontas (Fritz, 1987) and watching the Disney movie Pocahontas. Students could work in groups to take notes about the characters, setting, plot, and events depicted in the movie and to extract details from the text.

The teacher might direct student groups to draw conclusions about the accuracy of historical events after they identify significant patterns in the similarities and differences of the two sources (Reagan, in press). As each group shares its conclusions, the teacher should reinforce the skill of valuing others' viewpoints by reminding all students to paraphrase, clarify, or question what their peers in other groups report, so that they can better understand each group's conclusions rather than judging them. Following the discussion, students might reflect in their journals about skills to keep in mind when striving for accuracy and searching for truth; the value of listening to and empathizing with a speaker; how well they think they listened and empathized in this activity; and situations in school, home, and life that require them to strive for accuracy and listen with understanding and empathy.

3. Thinking Together

Friendship is one mind in two bodies.

—Mencius

Meaning making is not just an individual operation. Learning is a reciprocal process; the individual influences the group's thinking, and the group influences the individual's thinking (Marzano, Pickering, & Pollock, 2001; Vygotsky, 1978). Instructional techniques that encourage group activities help students construct both their own and shared knowledge.

When learners fail to see the interconnections and coherence of divergent views, collaborative thinking falters. If each student fixates on his or her own certainties, each perceives the solution to a problem solely from his or her own viewpoint. Such an egocentric view hinders serious reflection and honest inquiry.

Another purpose of a thought-filled curriculum, therefore, is to build an "ecology of thought"—a network of shared memories and awareness that links community members together (Isaacs, 1999). Collegial interaction is a crucial factor in the intellectual ecology of the school and classroom. Collaboratively individuals can elicit thinking that surpasses individual effort, but such collaboration is difficult because it means temporarily suspending what I, individually, think. It means relaxing our grip on certainties and opening our minds to new perspectives, abiding by and supporting group decisions that are arrived at through deep, respectful listening and dialogue. Learners must come to understand that as they transcend the self and become part of the whole, they will not lose their individuality, only their egocentricity.

Learning to listen with understanding and empathy may be one of the least-taught skills in school, yet it is one of the most powerful skills of intelligent problem solvers (Steil & Bommelje, 2007). Thought-filled curriculums should include instruction in and practice of

- Focusing mental energy on understanding others.
- Summarizing and paraphrasing others' thoughts.
- Empathizing.
- Monitoring clarity in communication.
- Setting aside judgments, solutions, and autobiographical responses.

4. Thinking About Our Own Thinking

> I thank the Lord for the brain he put in my head. Occasionally, I love to just stand to one side and watch how it works.
>
> —Richard Bolles

A broader intent of a thought-filled curriculum is the development of heightened consciousness of our own thinking among both teachers and students. The human species is known as Homo sapiens sapiens, which means "a being that knows its knowing." What distinguishes humans is our capacity for metacognition—the ability to stand back and examine our own thoughts while we engage in them. Although the human brain is capable of generating this reflective consciousness, generally we are not very aware of how we are thinking. Not everyone uses his or her capacity for metacognition equally (Csikszentmihalyi, 1993).

Learning to think begins with recognizing how we are thinking—by listening to ourselves and our own reactions and realizing how our thoughts may encapsulate us. Much of the kind of thinking people practice happens simply by virtue of their embedded habits, not because they closely examine their assumptions, their limited history, or their mental models.

Metacognition involves the whole of us: our emotions, bodily sensations, ideas, beliefs, values, character qualities, and the inferences we generate from interactions with others. When confronted with perplexing, ambiguous situations, skillful thinkers engage in an internal mental dialogue that helps them decide on intelligent actions. We can get students into the habit of such mindful probing by using self-reflective questions like these:

- How can I draw on my past successes to solve this new problem? What do I already know about the problem, and what resources do I have available or need to generate?
- How can I approach this problem flexibly? How might I look at the situation

from a fresh perspective? Am I remaining open to new possibilities?

- How can I make this problem clearer, more precise, and more detailed? Do I need to check out my data sources? How might I break this problem down into its component parts and develop a strategy for approaching each step?
- What do I know or not know? What might I be missing, and what questions do I need to ask?
- What strategies are in my mind now? What values, beliefs, and intentions are influencing my approach? What emotions might be blocking or enhancing my progress?
- How is this problem affecting others? How might we solve it together, and what can I learn from others that would help me become a better problem solver?

Teachers can spur metacognition by directing students to verbalize plans and strategies for solving challenging problems—and by urging students to share their thinking as they monitor their progress, evaluate their strategies, and generate alternative strategies.

5. Thinking Big

I learned to make my mind large, as the universe is large, so that there is room for paradoxes.

—Maxine Hong Kingston

Building a thought-filled curriculum serves the larger agenda of building a more thought-filled world—an interdependent learning community where people continually search for ways to care for one another, learn together, and grow toward greater intelligence. We must deepen student thinking to hasten the arrival of a world community that

- Generates more thoughtful, peaceful approaches to solving problems, rather than resorting to violence to resolve differences.
- Values the diversity of other cultures, races, religions, language systems, time perspectives, and political and economic views.
- Shows greater consciousness of how humans affect Earth's limited resources and how we must live in harmony with our delicate environment.
- Engages in clear and respectful dialogue to resolve misunderstandings.

While designing each lesson, thought-filled teachers focus on this larger vision by asking themselves, Are these learnings essential? How do they contribute to building more thoughtful classrooms, schools, and communities, and a more thoughtful world? Teachers encourage students to "think big" when they lead them to inquire into such moral, ethical, and philosophical questions as, What makes human beings human? What is beauty? What is justice? How can we learn to unite and not divide?

These five themes constitute unfinished tasks for teachers and curriculum designers in building a more thought filled curriculum. As noted computer scientist Alan Kay (1990) stated, "The best way to predict the future is to invent it." If we want a future that is vastly more thoughtful, cooperative, compassionate, and loving, then we have to create it. The future is in our schools and classrooms today.

REFERENCES

Commission on the Whole Child. (2007). The learning compact redefined: A call to action. Alexandria, VA: ASCD.

Costa, A., & Kallick, B. (2001). Discovering and exploring habits of mind Alexandria, VA: ASCD.

Costa, A., & Marzano, R. (2001). Teaching the language of thinking. In A. Costa (Ed.), Developing minds: A resource book for teaching thinking (pp. 379–383). Alexandria, VA: ASCD.

Csikszentmihalyi, M. (1993). Flow: The psychology of optimal experience. New York: Harper and Row.

Fritz, J. (1987). The double life of Pocahontas. New York: Puffin Books.

Hyerle, D. (Ed.). (2004). Student successes with thinking maps. Thousand Oaks, CA: Corwin Press.

Isaacs, W. (1999). Dialogue and the art of thinking together. New York: Currency.

Kay, A. (1990, March). The best way to predict the future is to invent it. Keynote presentation at the annual conference of the Association for Supervision and Curriculum Development, San Francisco, CA.

Marzano, R., Pickering, D., & Pollock, J. (2001). Classroom instruction that worfes. Alexandria, VA: ASCD.

Reagan, R. (in press). Cognitive composition: Thinking based writing. In A. Costa & B. Kallick (Eds.), Habits of mind: Voices from the field. Alexandria, VA: ASCD.

Steil, L. K., & Bommelje, R. (2007). Listening leaders: The ten golden rules to listen, lead and succeed. Edina, MN: Beaver Pond Press.

Swartz, R., Costa, A., Kailick, B., Beyer, B., & Reagan, R. (2007). Thinking based learning. Norwood, MA: Christopher Gordon.

Vygotsky, L. S. (1978). Mind in society: The development of higher psychological processes. Cambridge, MA: Harvard University Press.

Wiggins, G., & McTighe, J. (1998). Understanding by design. Alexandria, VA: ASCD.

Willingham, D. (2007, Summer), Critical thinking: Why is it so hard to teach? American Educator, 9–16.

DISCUSSION QUESTIONS:

1. How can you incorporate the five themes into your own teaching?
2. Do you agree with the author regarding the importance of teaching thinking explicitly? How would this most effectively be translated into classroom practice?
3. How interrelated are the five themes? Are they hierarchical or complementary? Can they be taught concurrently or must they be taught sequentially?
4. How can a thought filled curriculum be integrated into an existing standards based curriculum model?
5. How can we ensure that teachers are equipped with the requisite skills and pedagogy to explicitly teach thinking to their students?

CHAPTER 21

The Importance of Multicultural Education

GENEVA GAY

FOCUSING QUESTIONS

1. How has multiculturalism changed in the United States?
2. How does lack of ethnic, racial, and cultural community harm schools? How does this extend into society?
3. How can multicultural education extend beyond the arts/humanities? Why is this important?
4. What are some steps to incorporating multicultural content into a curriculum?
5. How does cross-referencing subjects aid multicultural learning?
6. How do reality/representation and relevance shape a multicultural curriculum? How do they shape student learning?

Multiculturalism in U.S. schools and society is taking on new dimensions of complexity and practicality as demographics, social conditions, and political circumstances change. Domestic diversity and unprecedented immigration have created a vibrant mixture of cultural, ethnic, linguistic, and experiential plurality.

Effectively managing such diversity in U.S. society and schools is at once a very old and a very new challenge. Benjamin Barber (1992) eloquently makes the point that

> America has always been a tale of peoples trying to be a People, a tale of diversity and plurality in search of unity. Cleavages among [diverse groups] . . . have irked and divided Americans from the start, making unity a civic imperative as well as an elusive challenge. (p. 41)

Accomplishing this end is becoming increasingly important as the 21st century unfolds. People coming from Asia, the Middle East, Latin America, Eastern Europe, and Africa differ greatly from earlier generations of immigrants who came primarily from western and northern Europe. These unfamiliar groups, cultures, traditions, and languages can produce anxieties, hostilities, prejudices, and racist behaviors among those who do not understand the newcomers or who perceive them as threats to their safety and security. These issues have profound implications for developing, at all levels of education, instructional programs and practices that respond positively and constructively to diversity.

A hundred years ago, W. E. B. Du Bois (1994) proposed that the problem of the 20th century was conflict and controversy among racial groups, particularly between African and European Americans. He concluded,

> Between these two worlds [black and white], despite much physical contact and daily intermingling, there is almost no community of intellectual life or point of transference where the thoughts and feelings of one race can come into direct contact and sympathy with the thoughts and feelings of the other. (p. 110)

Although much has changed since Du Bois's declarations, too much has not changed nearly enough. Of course, the color line has become more complex and diverse, and legal barriers against racial intermingling have been dismantled. People from different ethnic, racial, and cultural groups live in close physical proximity. But coexistence does not mean that people create genuine communities in which they know, relate to, and care deeply about one another. The lack of a genuine community of diversity is particularly evident in school curriculums that still do not regularly and systematically include important information and deep study about a wide range of diverse ethnic groups. As disparities in educational opportunities and outcomes among ethnic groups have continued to grow, the resulting achievement gap has reached crisis proportions.

Multicultural education is integral to improving the academic success of students of color and preparing all youths for democratic citizenship in a pluralistic society. Students need to understand how multicultural issues shape the social, political, economic, and cultural fabric of the United States as well as how such issues fundamentally influence their personal lives.

CONCEPTIONS OF MULTICULTURAL EDUCATION

Even though some theorists (Banks & Banks, 2002) have argued that multicultural education is a necessary ingredient of quality education, in actual practice educators most often perceive it either as an addendum prompted by some crisis or as a luxury. Multicultural education has not yet become a central part of the curriculum regularly offered to all students; instead, educators have relegated it primarily to social studies, language arts, and the fine arts and have generally targeted instruction for students of color.

These attitudes distort multicultural education and make it susceptible to sporadic and superficial implementation, if any. Textbooks provide a compelling illustration of such an attitude: The little multicultural content that they offer is often presented in sidebars and special-events sections (Loewen, 1995).

Another obstacle to implementing multicultural education lies with teachers themselves. Many are unconvinced of its worth or its value in developing academic skills and building a unified national community. Even those teachers who are more accepting of multicultural education are nevertheless skeptical about the feasibility of its implementation. "I would do it if I could," they say, "but I don't know how." "Preparing students to meet standards takes up all my time," others point out. "School curriculums are already overburdened. What do I take out to make room for multicultural education?"

A fallacy underlies these conceptions and the instructional behaviors that they generate: the perception of multicultural education as separate content that educators must append to existing curriculums as separate lessons, units, or courses. Quite the contrary is true. Multicultural education is more than content; it includes policy, learning climate, instructional delivery, leadership, and evaluation (see Banks, 1994; Bennett, 2003; Grant & Gomez, 2000). In its comprehensive form, it must be an integral part of everything that happens in the education enterprise, whether it is assessing the academic competencies of students or teaching math, reading, writing, science, social studies, or computer science. Making explicit connections between multicultural education and subject- and skill-based curriculum and instruction is imperative.

It is not pragmatic for K–12 educators to think of multicultural education as a discrete entity, separated from the commonly accepted components of teaching and learning. These conceptions may be fine for higher education, where specialization is the rule. But in K–12 schools, where the education process focuses on teaching eclectic bodies of knowledge and skills, teachers need to use multicultural education to promote such highly valued outcomes as human development, education equality, academic excellence, and democratic citizenship (see Banks & Banks, 2001; Nieto, 2000).

To translate these theoretical conceptions into practice, educators must systematically weave multicultural education into the central core of curriculum, instruction, school leadership, policy making, counseling, classroom climate, and performance assessment. Teachers should use multicultural content, perspectives, and experiences to teach reading, math, science, and social studies.

For example, teachers could demonstrate mathematical concepts, such as less than/greater than, percentages, ratios, and probabilities, using ethnic demographics. Younger children could consider the ethnic and racial distributions in their own classrooms, discussing which group's representation is greater than, less than, or equal to another's. Older students could collect statistics about ethnic distributions on a larger scale and use them to make more sophisticated calculations, such as converting numbers to percentages and displaying ethnic demographics on graphs.

Students need to apply such major academic skills as data analysis, problem solving, comprehension, inquiry, and effective communication as they study multicultural issues and events. For instance, students should not simply memorize facts about major events involving ethnic groups, such as civil rights movements, social justice efforts, and cultural accomplishments. Instead, educators should teach students how to think critically and analytically about these events, propose alternative solutions to social problems, and demonstrate understanding through such forms of communication as poetry, personal correspondence, debate, editorials, and photo essays.

Irvine and Armento (2001) provide specific examples for incorporating multicultural education into planning language arts, math, science, and social studies lessons for elementary and middle school students and connecting these lessons to general curriculum standards. One set of lessons demonstrates how to use Navajo rugs to explain the geometric concepts of perimeter and area and to teach students how to calculate the areas of squares, rectangles, triangles, and parallelograms.

These suggestions indicate that teachers need to use systematic decision-making approaches to accomplish multicultural curriculum integration. In practice, this means developing intentional and orderly processes for including multicultural content. The decision-making process might involve the following steps:

- Creating learning goals and objectives that incorporate multicultural aspects, such as "Developing students' ability to write persuasively about social justice concerns."
- Using a frequency matrix to ensure that the teacher includes a wide variety of ethnic groups in a wide variety of ways

in curriculum materials and instructional activities.

- Introducing different ethnic groups and their contributions on a rotating basis.
- Including several examples from different ethnic experiences to explain subject matter concepts, facts, and skills.
- Showing how multicultural content, goals, and activities intersect with subject-specific curricular standards.

Virtually all aspects of multicultural education are interdisciplinary. As such, they cannot be adequately understood through a single discipline. For example, teaching students about the causes, expressions, and consequences of racism and how to combat racism requires the application of information and techniques from such disciplines as history, economics, sociology, psychology, mathematics, literature, science, art, politics, music, and health care. Theoretical scholarship already affirms this interdisciplinary need; now, teachers need to model good curricular and instructional practice in elementary and secondary classrooms. Putting this principle into practice will elevate multicultural education from impulse, disciplinary isolation, and simplistic and haphazard guesswork to a level of significance, complexity, and connectedness across disciplines.

MULTICULTURALISM AND CURRICULUM DEVELOPMENT

How can teachers establish linkages between multicultural education and the disciplines and subject matter content taught in schools? One approach is to filter multicultural education through two categories of curriculum development: reality/representation and relevance.

Reality/Representation

A persistent concern of curriculum development in all subjects is helping students understand the realities of the social condition and how they came to be, as well as adequately representing those realities. Historically, curriculum designers have been more exclusive than inclusive of the wide range of ethnic and cultural diversity that exists within society. In their haste to promote harmony and avoid controversy and conflict, they gloss over social problems and the realities of ethnic and racial identities, romanticize racial relations, and ignore the challenges of poverty and urban living in favor of middle-class and suburban experiences. The reality is distorted and the representations incomplete (Loewen, 1995).

An inescapable reality is that diverse ethnic, racial, and cultural groups and individuals have made contributions to every area of human endeavor and to all aspects of U.S. history, life, and culture. When students study food resources in the United States, for example, they often learn about production and distribution by large-scale agribusiness and processing corporations. The curriculum virtually ignores the contributions of the many ethnically diverse people involved in planting and harvesting vegetables and fruits (with the Mexican and Mexican American farm labor unionization movement a possible exception). School curriculums that incorporate comprehensive multicultural education do not perpetuate these exclusions. Instead, they teach students the reality—how large corporations and the food industry are directly connected to the migrant workers who harvest vegetables and pick fruits. If we are going to tell the true story of the United States, multicultural education must be a central feature in its telling.

School curriculums need to reverse these trends by also including equitable representations of diversity. For example, the study of American literature, art, and music should include the contributions of males and females from different ethnic groups in all genres and in different expressive styles. Thus, the study of jazz would examine various forms and techniques produced not just by African

Americans but also by Asian, European, and Latino Americans.

Moreover, educators should represent ethnically diverse individuals and groups in all strata of human accomplishment instead of typecasting particular groups as dependent and helpless victims who make limited contributions of significance. Even under the most oppressive conditions, diverse groups in the United States have been creative, activist, and productive on broad scales. The way in which Japanese Americans handled their internment during World War II provides an excellent example. Although schools must not overlook or minimize the atrocities this group endured, students should also learn how interned Japanese Americans led dignified lives under the most undignified circumstances, elevating their humanity above their circumstances. The curriculum should include both issues.

Relevance

Many ethnically diverse students do not find schooling exciting or inviting; they often feel unwelcome, insignificant, and alienated. Too much of what is taught has no immediate value to these students. It does not reflect who they are. Yet most educators will agree that learning is more interesting and easier to accomplish when it has personal meaning for students.

Students from different ethnic groups are more likely to be interested and engaged in learning situations that occur in familiar and friendly frameworks than in those occurring in strange and hostile ones. A key factor in establishing educational relevance for these students is cultural similarity and responsiveness (see Bruner, 1996; Hollins, 1996; Wlodkowski & Ginsberg, 1995). For example, immigrant Vietnamese, Jamaican, and Mexican students who were members of majority populations in their home countries initially may have difficulty understanding what it means to be members of minority groups in the United States. Students who come from education environments that encourage active participatory learning will not be intellectually stimulated by passive instruction that involves lecturing and completing worksheets. Many students of color are bombarded with irrelevant learning experiences, which dampen their academic interest, engagement, and achievement. Multicultural education mediates these situations by teaching content about the cultures and contributions of many ethnic groups and by using a variety of teaching techniques that are culturally responsive to different ethnic learning styles.

Using a variety of strategies may seem a tall order in a classroom that includes students from many different ethnic groups. Research indicates, however, that several ethnic groups share some learning style attributes (Shade, 1989). Teachers need to understand the distinguishing characteristics of different learning styles and use the instructional techniques best suited to each style. In this scenario, teachers would provide alternative teaching techniques for clusters of students instead of for individual students. In any given lesson, the teacher might offer three or four ways for students to learn, helping to equalize learning advantages and disadvantages among the different ethnic groups in the classroom.

Scholars are producing powerful descriptions of culturally relevant teaching for multiethnic students and its effects on achievement. Lipka and Mohatt (1998) describe how a group of teachers, working closely with Native Alaskan (Yup'ik) elders, made school structure, climate, curriculum, and instruction more reflective of and meaningful to students from the community. For ten years, the teachers translated, adapted, and embedded Yup'ik cultural knowledge in math, literacy, and science curriculums. The elders served as resources and quality-control monitors of traditional knowledge, and they provided the inspiration and moral strength for the teachers to persist in their efforts to center the schooling of Yup'ik students around the students' own cultural orientations. In math, for instance, the teachers now habitually make connections among the Yup'ik numeration system, body measurements, simple and complex computations, geometry, pattern designs, and tessellations.

Similar attributes apply to the work of such scholars as Moses and Cobb (2001), Lee (1993), and Boykin and Bailey (2000), who are studying the effects of culturally relevant curriculum and instruction on the school performance of African American students. Moses and his colleagues are making higher-order math knowledge accessible to African American middle school students by teaching this material through the students' own cultural orientations and experiences. To teach algebra, they emphasize the experiences and familiar environments of urban and rural low-income students, many of whom are at high risk for academic failure. A key feature of their approach is making students conscious of how algebraic principles and formulas operate in their daily lives and getting students to understand how to explain these connections in nonalgebraic language before converting this knowledge into the technical notations and calculations of algebra. Students previously considered by some teachers as incapable of learning algebra are performing at high levels—better, in fact, than many of their advantaged peers.

Evidence increasingly indicates that multicultural education makes schooling more relevant and effective for Latino American, Native American, Asian American, and Native Hawaiian students as well (see McCarty, 2002; Moll, Amanti, Neff, & Gonzalez, 1992; Park, Goodwin, & Lee, 2001; Tharp & Gallimore, 1988). Students perform more successfully at all levels when there is greater congruence between their cultural backgrounds and such school experiences as task interest, effort, academic achievement, and feelings of personal efficacy or social accountability.

As the challenge to better educate underachieving students intensifies and diversity among student populations expands, the need for multicultural education grows exponentially. Multicultural education maybe the solution to problems that currently appear insolvable: closing the achievement gap; genuinely not leaving any children behind academically; revitalizing faith and trust in the promises of democracy, equality, and justice; building education systems that reflect the diverse cultural, ethnic, racial, and social contributions that forge society; and providing better opportunities for all students.

Multicultural education is crucial. Classroom teachers and educators must answer its clarion call to provide students from all ethnic groups with the education they deserve.

REFERENCES

Banks, J. A. (1994). *Multiethnic Education: Theory and Practice* (3rd ed.). Boston: Allyn and Bacon.

Banks, J. A., & Banks, C. A. M. (Eds.). (2001). *Multicultural Education: Issues and Perspectives* (4th ed.). Boston: Allyn and Bacon.

Banks, J. A., & Banks, C. A. M. (Eds.). (2002). *Handbook of Research on Multicultural Education* (2nd ed.). San Francisco: Jossey-Bass.

Barber, B. R. (1992). *An Aristocracy of Everyone: The Politics of Education and the Future of America.* New York: Oxford University Press.

Bennett, C. I. (2003). *Comprehensive Multicultural Education: Theory and Practice.* Boston: Allyn and Bacon.

Boykin, A. W., & Bailey, C. T. (2000). "The Role of Cultural Factors in School Relevant Cognitive Functioning: Synthesis of Findings on Cultural Context, Cultural Orientations, and Individual Differences." (ERIC Document Reproduction Service No. ED 441 880).

Bruner, J. (1996). *The Culture of Education.* Cambridge, MA: Harvard University Press.

Du Bois, W. E. B. (1994). *The Souls of Black Folk.* New York: Gramercy Books.

Grant, C. A., & Gomez, M. L. (Eds.). (2000). *Making School Multicultural: Campus and*

Classroom (2nd ed.). Upper Saddle River, NJ: Merrill/Prentice-Hall.

Hollins, E. R. (1996). *Culture in School Learning: Revealing the Deep Meaning*. Mahwah, NJ: Erlbaum.

Irvine, J. J., & Armento, B. J. (Eds.). (2001). *Culturally Responsive Teaching: Lesson Planning for Elementary and Middle Grades*. New York: McGraw-Hill.

Lee, C. (1993). "Signifying as a Scaffold to Literary Interpretation: The Pedagogical Implications of a Form of African American Discourse" (NCTE Research Report No. 26). Urbana, IL: National Council of Teachers of English.

Lipka, J., & Mohatt, G. V. (1998). *Transforming the Culture of Schools: Yup'ik Eskimo Examples*. Mahwah, NJ: Erlbaum.

Loewen, J. W. (1995). *Lies My Teacher Told Me: Everything Your American History Textbook Got Wrong*. New York: New Press.

McCarty, T. L. (2002). *A Place to Be Navajo: Rough Rock and the Struggle for Self-Determination in Indigenous Schooling*. Mahwah, NJ: Erlbaum.

Moll, L. C., Amanti, C., Neff, D., & Gonzalez, N. (1992). "Funds of Knowledge for Teaching: Using a Qualitative Approach to Connect Homes and Classrooms." *Theory into Practice, 31*(1): 132–141.

Moses, R. P., & Cobb, C. E., Jr. (2001). *Radical Equations: Math Literacy and Civil Rights*. Boston: Beacon Press.

Nieto, S. (2000). *Affirming Diversity: The Sociopolitical Context of Multicultural Education* (3rd ed.). New York: Longman.

Park, C. C., Goodwin, A. L., & Lee, S. J. (Eds.). (2001). *Research on the Education of Asian and Pacific Americans*. Greenwich, CT: Information Age Publishers.

Shade, B. J. (Ed.). (1989). *Culture, Style, and the Educative Process*. Springfield, IL: Charles C. Thomas.

Tharp, R. G., & Gallimore, R. (1988). *Rousing Minds to Life: Teaching, Learning, and Schooling in Social Context*. Cambridge, UK: Cambridge University Press.

Wlodkowski, R. J., & Ginsberg, M. B. (1995). *Diversity and Motivation: Culturally Responsive Teaching*. San Francisco: Jossey-Bass.

DISCUSSION QUESTIONS

1. What issues related to multiculturalism have emerged in your school in recent years?
2. Do you agree with the author's claim that many teachers remain unconvinced that multicultural education has value?
3. What would be needed to bring theoretical concepts of multiculturalism into practice? Would this be of benefit to students? How?
4. How should considerations of multiculturalism influence the process of curriculum development?
5. Would a greater emphasis on multiculturalism help close the achievement gap? Why or why not?

CHAPTER 22

Knowledge Alive

DAVID PERKINS

FOCUSING QUESTIONS

1. How are knowledge arts used in society? How does this translate to schools?
2. How do schools fail to transmit the knowledge arts between subjects?
3. What are the ways listed by which a teacher can make knowledge visible? How does this relate to student understanding?
4. How can a teacher provide a culture of learning?

Perhaps the broadest and most basic question for educators—before matters of method, testing, or grading—is "What should we teach?" And perhaps the most basic answer is "knowledge." Knowledge in the broad sense—facts, ideas, and skills—provides the mainstay of the school curriculum from kindergarten through college.

But then there's the question of what you do with knowledge. Education has always been more generous about exposing learners to large volumes of knowledge than about teaching them the diverse skills involved in handling knowledge well—the knowledge arts.

The knowledge arts include communicating strategically, insightfully, and effectively; thinking critically and creatively; and putting school knowledge to work in what educators sometimes humbly call the "real world." The knowledge arts bundle together deep reading, compelling writing, strong problem solving and decision making, and the strategic and spirited self-management of learning itself, within and across the disciplines.

We need to put the knowledge arts on the table—to celebrate them for the depth and power they provide and for the ways they make knowledge meaningful. And we need to worry about their neglect.

THE KNOWLEDGE ARTS IN SOCIETY

To get a picture of how the knowledge arts work in schools, let's start with the bigger picture of how they work in society. We can tell the broad story of knowledge in four chapters, starting with creating it and moving on to communicating it, organizing it, and acting on it.

People create knowledge in various ways. Scientists examine the sky or the sea or quarks or viruses; historians puzzle over ancient documents and artifacts; pollsters survey public opinion; engineers design and test prototypes; newspaper reporters investigate political dogfights; police officers comb for evidence about crimes. Then we communicate that knowledge in various ways: through writing and reading; mathematical equations, maps, and diagrams; news broadcasts; electronic mailing lists; and works of art. We organize knowledge in various ways for ready access (notes, concept maps, Web sites) or for particular purposes, judgments, plans, and decisions (the court's verdict, the advertising campaign, the blueprints for a new building). And eventually, we act on all this knowledge: We carry out the judgment, erect the building, or launch the mission.

Of course, the story of knowledge in the form of these four chapters is far too linear. Creating, communicating, organizing, and acting on knowledge mix with one another in complex and generative ways. However, the four chapters provide a rough and ready overview.

THE KNOWLEDGE ARTS IN SCHOOL: A REPORT CARD

Keeping the four chapters in mind, how well does schooling develop the knowledge arts of learners? The report card for business-as-usual schooling would look like this:

Creating knowledge: D
Communicating knowledge: B
Organizing knowledge: C
Acting on knowledge: D

The first D reflects the fact that in typical schools, investigative, inquiry-oriented activities in which learners create knowledge are sparse. Of course, such activities occur here and there—for instance, in some kinds of science learning—but even then they often entail simply going through the motions of a laboratory experiment rather than genuinely wrestling with ideas.

Acting on knowledge also earns a D. We rarely ask students to do much with their learning outside school—except homework, of course. As a result, knowledge tends to become passive or inert. In both academic and practical contexts, learners fail to connect what they have learned to new situations or to act effectively on that knowledge (Bransford, Franks, Vye, & Sherwood, 1989). Students may memorize key information about biology for the science test but never ponder what that knowledge says about personal health care or public health issues.

Problems of transfer of learning have long plagued education (Bransford & Schwartz, 1999; Detterman & Sternberg, 1992; Perkins & Salomon, 1988). Typical schooling does not even encourage students to carry their knowledge from one classroom to another. Science instructors often complain that the math from math class somehow evaporates in the science room. History instructors grumble that some cognitive Bermuda Triangle in the corridor between the English and history classrooms has sucked away students' knowledge of writing.

Conventional education probably does best at communicating knowledge, so why does it rate only a B in this area? On the receptive side of communication, although learners spend a great deal of time loading up on knowledge, schools do not typically teach them to do so strategically. Many young readers can decode competently but have never learned to ask themselves what they are reading for, to monitor their reading as they go, to assess themselves afterward, and to fill in what they missed. The productive side of communication includes not only writing but also artistic expression, presentations, multimedia work, and so on. These areas, except for the mechanics of writing, typically receive little time or guidance.

Further, some schools direct dogged attention to skill and content learning in a narrow sense, with the unsettling consequence that skills become ritualized into mere recipes to follow (Perkins, 1992). For instance, students who know how to add, subtract, multiply, and divide can become quite confused about how to apply these operations to story problems, and they often fall back on limited keyword strategies, such as "all together means add." Students learn what they are supposed to say in class without really understanding it. Science educator Marcia Linn amusingly noted what one student made of a Newtonian principle of motion: "Objects in motion remain in motion in the classroom, but come to rest on the playground" (2002).

Organizing knowledge also receives little attention in typical schools—thus, the grade of C. In most school settings, strategic guidance in this skill appears only during review sessions or around such products as essays. Yet learning logs, concept mapping, debates, group presentations, and many other activities can dramatically expand students' skills in organizing knowledge.

At this point, dedicated educators will object: "My kids are deeply engaged in inquiry-oriented science learning!" "My students keep learning journals and review their learning every week!" "We stage a debate after every unit!" "Teams of youngsters are out there in the community investigating local history!" Good. These undertakings certainly cultivate the knowledge arts and deserve kudos when and where they occur. But we need to ask, How often is this kind of teaching and learning happening, and how well? Between the oases of glory stretch deserts of neglect.

BRINGING KNOWLEDGE TO LIFE

What does it look like to enliven teaching and learning through the knowledge arts? The following examples come from the work of my colleagues at Project Zero of the Harvard Graduate School of Education (www.pz.harvard.edu).

Making Thinking Visible

One way to advance the knowledge arts is to use thinking routines (Ritchhart, 2002) to make students' thinking visible, thus increasing their awareness of what goes into creating, communicating, organizing, and acting on knowledge.

For instance, Shari Tishman (2002) explored a simple way to make certain kinds of thinking visible by asking two key questions: "What's going on here?" and "What do you see that makes you say so?" She adapted this approach from a procedure for thoughtfully examining works of visual art (Housen, Yenawine, & Arenas, 1991), but learners can apply these questions to many different objects—for example, a short poem or a satellite photograph of a hurricane. Or a history instructor might show a historical artifact, like a crossbow, accompanied by the slightly tweaked questions "How does this work?" and "What do you see that makes you think so?"

Tina Grotzer and I have developed inquiry-oriented activities that engage students in communicating about the complex causal models that can often make science concepts difficult to understand—models that involve such invisible features as electrons, causal loops, and simultaneous cause and effect (Grotzer, 2003; Perkins & Grotzer, 2000). For instance, fourth graders studying electrical circuits compare different ideas about what the current does. Does it start at the battery and fill the circuit, as when a hot-water radiator system is turned on for the first time, and then continue to cycle? Or does the current of electrons move all at once, like a bicycle chain? Young learners lean toward the first idea, but the second is more scientifically accurate. The following discussion shows how the teacher can help students make visible their thinking about the scientific explanation of electrical flow (Grotzer, 2000):

TEACHER: Let's compare how cause and effect works in these two different kinds of cyclic models. In the cyclic sequential model [as in the radiator system analogy], what makes the electrons move?

STUDENT 1: They want to get out of the battery because of all the electrons so they go onto the wire.

TEACHER: And then what happens?

STUDENT 2: They go along the wire till they get to the bulb and that makes the bulb light up.

TEACHER: Why do the electrons move in the cyclic simultaneous model [as in the bicycle chain analogy]?

STUDENT 1: The electrons push the one in front but at the same time they are pushed by the one behind them. So everything moves at the same time.

TEACHER: Yes, each electron repels the next one but is repelled by the one behind it. It's both a cause and an effect at the same time. The whole thing turns like the chain on a bicycle. What causes the bulb to light?

STUDENT 3: When the electrons start to flow.

Grotzer's research shows that conversations like this one, along with simple experiments and activities, can make causal thinking visible and lead to higher levels of understanding.

Teaching for Understanding

Understanding is one of the most cherished goals of education. Teaching for understanding can bring knowledge to life by requiring students to manipulate knowledge in various ways. For instance, understanding a historical event means going beyond the facts to explain it, explore the remote causes, discuss the incident as different people might see it from their own perspectives, and skeptically critique what various sources say.

A number of years ago, several colleagues and I developed the Teaching for Understanding framework, which centers on the idea of performances of understanding (Blythe & Associates, 1998; Gardner, 1999; Perkins & Blythe, 1994). Here are two examples of classrooms using this framework, drawn from Wiske (1998).

Joan Soble employed the Teaching for Understanding framework to organize and deliver an introductory writing course for at-risk ninth graders—students whom she described as "perpetually overwhelmed." The students engaged in a wide range of understanding performances, including work with collages as preparation for writing; keeping and critically reviewing portfolios; and setting and pursuing goals individually, using a form that listed writing skills they wanted to improve, from sentence structure to revision practices to aspects of self-management. Thus, these students worked directly on the knowledge art of writing, learning how to practice it with more skill, confidence, and flair. Soble's approach also helped students with another knowledge art: the thoughtful management of their own learning.

Lois Hetland's seventh-grade class examined fundamental questions about Colonial America throughout the year. Some questions concerned the land: How does land shape human culture? How do people think about the land? How do people change the land? Another line of questioning concerned historical truth: How do we find out the truth about things that happened long ago or far away? How do we see through bias in sources? There throughlines, as Hetland called them, provided abiding points of reference for the learners. Discussing the same throughlines in connection with topic after topic helped students to develop not only a deeper understanding of Colonial America but also important knowledge arts: the ins and outs of historical inquiry and the management of their own learning through sustained questioning.

Such practices engage students in various mixes of the four broad activities identified earlier—creating, communicating, organizing, and acting on knowledge—in ways linked to the disciplines. Moreover, research has revealed something quite striking: Students who participate in Teaching for Understanding classrooms display shifts in their attitudes toward understanding. Compared with other students, they think of understanding in a more dynamic and exploratory way, rather than as a collection of facts and skills (Wiske, 1998). This stance toward understanding amounts to a knowledge art that equips students for deeper learning.

Creating a Culture of Learning

The knowledge arts—like any art—are more than skills: They involve passion, energy, and commitment (Tishman, Perkins, & Jay, 1995). Teachers promote the knowledge arts when they strive to establish a classroom culture of inquiry and excitement.

Ritchhart (2002) describes an algebra teacher who began the first day of school by displaying a mathematical puzzle problem from the newspaper, noting that a student had brought it in, saying that he loved little problems, and encouraging students to provide other puzzle problems throughout the year. Then he wrote on the chalkboard an elaborate arithmetic computation drawn from an episode in *The Phantom Tollbooth*, asking students to work out the answer and commenting that he had better figure it out himself. Inevitably, students came up with a variety of answers. The teacher gave his own answer but warned that he didn't think it was correct. He challenged students to find the right answer.

Through these actions and others like them—informal, welcoming, and inquiring—this teacher signaled that the coming school year would bring knowledge alive.

THE SECOND CURRICULUM

One natural reaction to these examples—and others from ingenious teachers across the world—is that they simply illustrate good teaching methods. They show ways of teaching content that enhance student engagement and make knowledge more meaningful.

True enough, but the knowledge arts are more than just tools for teachers to teach with; they encompass ideas, skills, and attitudes for learners to learn—a second curriculum. Thinking of the knowledge arts in this way creates new responsibilities for educators. As teachers teach science, history, or literature, they should be able to specify what skills of inquiry, strategies of communication, methods of organization, and ranges of application they are striving to develop in students; how they are spending time doing so; and how they are exciting students' interest and providing serious guidance. Without such an account, the second curriculum does not exist in any substantive sense.

The bad news: All this amounts to one more agenda in an era in which educators must prepare students for high-stakes tests that often emphasize *having* knowledge far more than *doing* something with it. The good news: The second curriculum is not just an add-on to the first. Instead, it's a meld, a fusion, an infiltration designed to bring knowledge to life and keep it alive. Taking the second curriculum seriously will not only equip students with knowledge-handling skills they need but also deepen and broaden their mastery of the first curriculum.

Behind the second curriculum is a simple idea: Education is not just about acquiring knowledge, but also about learning how to do significant things with what you know. It's not about dead knowledge, but about bringing knowledge to life. To educate for today and tomorrow, every school and every classroom should teach the knowledge arts seriously and well.

REFERENCES

Blythe, T., & Associates. (1998). *The Teaching for Understanding Guide*. San Francisco: Jossey-Bass.

Bransford, J. D., Franks, J. J., Vye, N. J., & Sherwood, R. D. (1989). "New Approaches to Instruction: Because Wisdom Can't Be Told."

In S. Vosniadou & A. Ortony (Eds.), *Similarity and Analogical Reasoning* (pp. 470–497). New York: Cambridge University Press.

Bransford, J. D., & Schwartz, D. L. (1999). "Rethinking Transfer: A Simple Proposal with Interesting Implications." In A. Iran-Nejad & P. D. Pearson (Eds.), *Review of Research in Education* (Vol. 24, pp. 61–101). Washington, DC: American Educational Research Association.

Detterman, D., & Sternberg, R. (Eds.). (1992). *Transfer on Trial.* Norwood, NJ: Ablex.

Gardner, H. (1999). *The Disciplined Mind.* New York: Simon and Schuster.

Grotzer, T. A. (2000, April). *How Conceptual Leaps in Understanding the Nature of Causality Can Limit Learning: An Example from Electrical Circuits.* Paper presented at the annual conference of the American Educational Research Association, New Orleans, LA.

Grotzer, T. A. (2003). "Learning to Understand the Forms of Causality Implicit in Scientific Explanations." *Studies in Science Education, 39:* 1–74.

Housen, A., Yenawine, P., & Arenas, A. (1991). *Visual Thinking Curriculum.* (Unpublished but used for research purposes). New York: Museum of Modern Art.

Linn, M. (2002, May). *The Role of Customization of Innovative Science Curricula: Implications for Design, Practice, and Professional Development.* Symposium at the annual meeting of the National Association for Research in Science Teaching, New Orleans, LA.

Perkins, D. N. (1992). *Smart Schools: From Training Memories to Educating Minds.* New York: Free Press.

Perkins, D. N., & Blythe, T. (1994). "Putting Understanding Up Front." *Educational Leadership, 51*(5): 4–7.

Perkins, D. N., & Grotzer, T. A. (2000, April). *Models and Moves: Focusing on Dimensions of Causal Complexity to Achieve Deeper Scientific Understanding.* Paper presented at the annual conference of the American Educational Research Association, New Orleans, LA.

Perkins, D. N., & Salomon, G. (1988). "Teaching for Transfer." *Educational Leadership, 46*(1), 22–32.

Ritchhart, R. (2002). *Intellectual Character: What It Is, Why It Matters, and How to Get It.* San Francisco: Jossey-Bass.

Tishman, S. (2002). "Artful Reasoning." In T. Grotzer, L. Howick, S. Tishman, & D. Wise, (Eds.), *Art Works for Schools.* Lincoln, MA: DeCordova Museum and Sculpture Park.

Tishman, S., Perkins, D. N., & Jay, E. (1995). *The Thinking Classroom.* Boston: Allyn and Bacon.

Wiske, M. S. (Ed.). (1998). *Teaching for Understanding: Linking Research with Practice.* San Francisco: Jossey-Bass.

DISCUSSION QUESTIONS

1. What types of learning does the author include in the category "knowledge arts"?
2. Why does the author give schools low grades in the teaching of knowledge arts?
3. What suggestions are offered for enlivening teaching and learning?
4. Do the suggestions offered make you think differently about what goes on in your own classroom or school?
5. Which of the suggested changes would be easiest to make and which would be most difficult?

CHAPTER 23

Teaching Content Outrageously

STANLEY POGROW

FOCUSING QUESTIONS:

1. How is outrageous instruction different from traditional instruction?
2. Identify the key characteristics of an outrageous lesson.
3. Describe the advantages of teaching outrageously.
4. How can teachers become comfortable with teaching outrageously?

A little craziness really does help. The techniques of Outrageous Instruction not only will fascinate students, they will lead students to learn any content more deeply.

What do you do when students are bored? How do you explain content that seems too abstract for most students to understand? You could rely on the old standby: "You need to learn it because it's on the test." You could make the lesson "authentic" and tell students, "You'll understand why this is important when you're older." But the best solution is to convert those lessons into learning experiences that are so fascinating that students cannot help but be drawn into them and hang onto every word and gesture. That is, you can teach the same content outrageously.

Outrageous Instruction links teaching specific objectives to students' sense of imagination and how they view the world. The techniques of Outrageous Instruction make it possible to draw all students deeply into any content. These techniques work on even the oldest and most jaded students who are the most resistant to learning, particularly learning that requires thought and active participation.

These techniques evolved from my work with teachers in the Higher Order Thinking Skills (HOTS) and Supermath programs (Pogrow, 1990, 2004, 2005). These programs used imaginative alternative contexts for teaching content and for developing both basic and problem-solving skills.

In Outrageous Instruction, the teacher uses a dramatic, humorous, and suspenseful storyline to create an imaginary context in which the need for the content objective is critical to solving a problem of interest to students. When the storyline taps into students' sense of imagination and self, it is then "Creatively Authentic." The creatively authentic lesson or unit then becomes the primary method for teaching that content objective. This is a departure from traditional uses of dramatic techniques in education, which tend to focus on self-expression for its own sake, for learning about theater, or for the reinforcement or enrichment of content already learned.

The best way to understand Outrageous Instruction is to observe a lesson. Meet "Dwight."

DWIGHT'S OUTRAGEOUS LESSON

I had observed Dwight's high school sophomore class several times. It was a difficult class to teach because the majority did not like to participate and some delighted in being unruly. Most students looked bored, a group I came to think of as "loungers." Whenever Dwight tried to teach new content, 15 minutes were lost to student groans, excuses, requests for pencils, requests to go to the bathroom, and so on. Sound familiar?

Dwight was getting frustrated with teaching this class, but he agreed to develop an outrageous lesson and use it to teach a critical learning objective.

The lesson begins. When the students finally are settled, a supervisor announces that Dwight is homesick, but there will be a special guest who will make them an exciting offer.

Dwight then comes in disguised with a huge, bushy, white beard and an Amish-style black hat. He is dressed in overalls and carries a real tree stump. He emphatically puts the tree stump on the floor and announces in a booming voice:

> I am a master salesman and have heard that all of you in this room have wonderful social skills and would make great salespeople. I am here as part of a national search to find the next generation of salespeople to sell a new, exciting line of products, the next great product, a complete line of stumps!

By now, the students have recognized Dwight and are starting to titter a bit, though they are also curious. Dwight continues:

> I see that you are skeptical about the importance and sales potential of stumps. Well, let me tell you all the things that you can do with stumps, and I am sure that in five minutes you are all going to want to know how to find out where you can buy one.

Dwight then talks like a TV car salesman for five minutes. He gives a confident, nonstop monologue about all the benefits of having a stump. He gives about a dozen reasons why everyone would want a stump; each reason is more outrageous than the one before.

> Suppose you come home and have a terrible itch on your back. What can you do? Why, you can rub your back against the stump. You come home and it's cold and your heater is not working, what can you do? You can burn part of your stump for warmth. For you guys, having a stump is a symbol of manliness. Women look up to a man with a stump. Suppose you come home and find that someone has stolen all of your furniture—you can sit on your stump.
>
> You can even serve food on your stump. And after you have eaten a wonderful meal, when you look in the kitchen for a toothpick, there are none, and you suddenly remember that you forgot to buy more, what to do? Break off a splinter from your stump and, voilá, you have a toothpick.

Of course, Dwight is just getting started. He continues:

> And in addition to all the ways that I have just described in which a stump can enrich your life, there is more, much more. If, you have a problem, you can confide in your stump, tell it your deepest fears and concerns—it will always listen and never argue with you.

> If you do not have enough closet or shelf space at home, you can hang your socks or jewelry on your stump.

Dwight goes on and on about many other uses for stumps, occasionally pounding the stump on the floor for emphasis.

The students laugh politely or give skeptical looks. Above all, they are enjoying the moment and wondering where things are going and why their teacher is acting this way.

Lesson interruptus. Why, indeed, is Dwight acting this way? More important, what is he teaching? At this point, the reader may be as puzzled as the students. You probably cannot even guess the content area. The important thing at this point is that the students are engaged, attentive, and, above all, curious.

Lesson continued. After five to 10 minutes of nonstop selling, Dwight finally pauses and says, "I know that all of you now realize that you cannot live without having a tree stump and that all of you want one." Of course, even though the students are having a great time, no one wants to buy one. Nonplussed, Dwight continues:

> Unfortunately, I cannot sell you this stump, as it is my last one until I get my next shipment. However, I have an even better opportunity for you right now, as I am looking to hire one of you to be on my sales team. I want to see which of you can be a great salesperson like myself. This is a chance of a lifetime for a great career.

Dwight then picks up a shopping bag and pulls out a series of common objects, such as a comb, a large piece of cardboard, and so on. He gives one object to the first person in each row. He then directs each row to form a team and take 10 minutes to come up with as many reasons as they can for why someone should buy their object. Each team must elect a spokesperson to present their ideas and to convince the rest of the class to buy their product.

The students quickly transition into groups. To my amazement, the loungers start taking leadership in the group discussions. Indeed, the loungers become the group spokespeople.

After 10 minutes of preparation, each team does a three- to five-minute presentation. The presentations are imaginative, and the former loungers deliver highly creative soliloquies that mimic the tone of Dwight's presentation. I am amazed at the volume, variety, and creativity of the presentations because I suspect that, for some of these students, this is the first time they've volunteered all semester.

After the last presentation, Dwight says, "Before I announce the winner, I want everyone to write down the ideas that your team just presented for why someone should buy your product." The students quickly shift modes and start writing. There is no whining or wasted time; the students are eager to capture their team's ideas on paper.

Dwight then has one student from each team read their list of ideas. The students read in a very confident tone. There is none of the typical reluctance to share what they wrote. Dwight announces that not only are all the groups worthy of being hired as salespeople, he is going to give everyone a salesperson award.

In the last five minutes of the class, Dwight tells his students that they have just done something else that is very important: They have just written excellent persuasive essays. He notes that writing a persuasive essay is one of the district's major requirements for promotion. Dwight gives them a definition of a persuasive essay and a few characteristics of such writing. He notes that most students have trouble writing such essays, which was why, he is so impressed with the writing they have done and how easy it was for them to do so.

Dwight ends the lesson by saying in a very puzzled tone:

> Hmmm. . . . I don't understand why you found it so easy to write a persuasive essay when most students have so much trouble doing so. I wonder if the reason is something that you can use to continue to develop your essays. Let's try to figure that out in tomorrow's lesson.

WHAT CAN BE LEARNED FROM DWIGHT'S LESSON?

This lesson demonstrates the latent talent, ability, and creativity that reside within our most academically resistant students. That so many of the loungers quickly met the challenge is a tribute to Dwight's imaginative approach. However, it also raises the question of why we don't make a greater effort to create such alternative, dramatic approaches. What is clear is that, when teachers apply their imagination to teaching, students will apply their imagination to learning.

Why choose this lesson to teach outrageously? Dwight knew that if he taught this critical first lesson on writing a persuasive essay conventionally, students would have tuned him out, and little would have been accomplished no matter how hard he tried to convince them that the topic is important. Indeed, I subsequently observed other classrooms in the district in which teachers were trying to get students to write acceptable persuasive essays—for the fifth time—with little apparent success. I also attended some staff meetings at other schools and at district headquarters, where everyone was complaining about how hard it is to get students to write reasonable persuasive essays.

The ease and enthusiasm with which Dwight's students began to write creative persuasive essays demonstrates that many "problems" in teaching and learning are often the result of the failure of teachers and curriculum designers to be imaginative, weird, and bold.

Characteristics of Outrageous Instruction. Dwight's lesson illustrates many of the key characteristics of an outrageous lesson. He used the invented storyline (training them to become salespeople), and it is only in the last five minutes of the lesson that he reveals the true learning objective. Judging from the reaction of the students, his storyline and context were creatively authentic, which made deeper forms of learning possible.

The lesson also illustrates that the goal of Outrageous Instruction is to use highly dramatic methods as the primary method for teaching critical content. In other words, Dwight's lesson is not reinforcing or enriching a lesson on writing. Instead of using a dramatic approach to enrich conventional instruction, he is teaching in an enriched fashion from the beginning.

Another unique aspect of Outrageous Instruction is how role playing is used. Instead of the teacher organizing and directing the roles that students play—a process that takes a great deal of time and effort—the teacher plays the role. It is the teacher's performance that efficiently changes the teaching-learning dynamic, and that produces the surprise and suspense that captivates students. Students have no idea what is going to happen next or even that they are, in fact, learning.

Clearly, Dwight's lesson is highly original and masterful. However, it is not the extemporaneous work of a master teacher. He developed the lesson by applying the specific lesson-planning technique used to generate outrageous lessons, found in Pogrow (2008). This planning technique is generalizable to any content area and objective, and it guides the creative process. In addition, Dwight was not a master teacher, or even an experienced one. Rather, he was a typical, good, student teacher who was not particularly extroverted. In other words, any teacher can employ the techniques of Outrageous Instruction.

ADVANTAGES OF OUTRAGEOUS INSTRUCTION

Outrageous Instruction uses dramatic technique as a tool for teaching and learning. It is not only highly effective, it is also highly efficient. This may seem counterintuitive. How can Outrageous Instruction be efficient when it requires significant class time to set up the dramatic context? This time is more than made up by the reduced amount of time needed to maintain discipline, organize activity transitions, and get students' attention. So instead of being able to organize only one or two transitions per period in conventional instruction, outrageous lessons often have seamless multiple transitions, from listening to the teacher, to reading, to writing, to reflecting. Therefore, the cumulative effect is that students learn the content more quickly. Generating student suspense and curiosity are the most efficient ways to increase and deepen learning.

In addition, an outrageous lesson speeds up and deepens learning not only for that specific objective, but also for the subsequent related lessons. As a result, Outrageous Instruction is valuable even during this era of standards-based accountability.

Of course, teaching outrageously every day is not practical or necessary. A little bit goes a long way. Even one or two such lessons are enough to have a major effect on student learning and attitudes. Such a lesson serves as an ongoing reference point. Even if this is the only outrageous lesson in an extended unit on persuasive writing, Dwight can continue to refer to the process as salesmanship and can continue to point out to students how good they are at it.

Teachers should prioritize converting a lesson (or unit) into an outrageous one when they know that it is a critical lesson that will not interest students, when it is content that students will find inaccessible, or when the teacher cares deeply about the objective and wants students to become engrossed in it.

GETTING STARTED

Clearly, developing and teaching an outrageous lesson the first time is a leap of faith. Will I be able to make the techniques work? Will I look foolish? Will I lose control of my class?

Outrageous Instruction is so far removed from one's comfort zone and conventional practice and the dynamics are so different than what occurs in the everyday classroom that it is akin to the first time you walked into a classroom to teach. Stepping back into that zone of uncertainty can be viewed either as something fearful or as an exciting opportunity to expand one's toolbox. Indeed, when I first started training teachers to develop outrageous lessons, I was not sure what they would come up with, and I was constantly amazed by how original and creative their lessons were. What always started with reluctance, misgivings, and a sense of "that is not me" led invariably to those teachers feeling exhilarated by the results. All teachers have an untapped creativity that, when unleashed, produces amazing results. All it takes is a willingness to try.

I have never seen a teacher lose control of a class during an outrageous lesson—even when the lesson required the teacher to hide under a desk, to spend large parts of the period not looking at the class, or to run in and out of the room. It turns out that suspense is the most underused technique for maintaining classroom control. Indeed, the best form of classroom control and discipline is to surprise and fascinate students. Rather than viewing their teacher as foolish, students react to outrageous lessons as a sign that their teacher cares so much about their learning that he or she is willing to go the extra mile—which in turn leads to increased mutual respect and opens new lines of communication.

However, planning Outrageous Instruction requires a willingness to adopt a different mindset for that given lesson or unit—a mindset that is almost the opposite of that for a conventional lesson. Teachers must embrace being imaginative, playful, and weird—three traits not typically associated with professional practice—and be willing to take a creative risk. In return, they will discover unexpected, and welcome, changes in student behavior and attitude. A teacher does not have to be an extrovert or a jokester to be dramatic. Indeed, many of the top Hollywood stars are introverts in real life. The real personality key for teaching an outrageous lesson is the attitude that I will do anything to help my students learn.

Getting started as individuals. The best way for teachers to get started developing outrageous lessons is to form a study and development group with peers. Teachers can brainstorm with each other and push each other to continually add creative and humorous elements to their planned lessons. The initial goal should be for each member to present one such lesson a semester. Over time, teachers will develop a portfolio of such lessons. In addition, because students will encounter more such experiences in different classes, student attitudes toward learning will change. Principals can stimulate such development by having awards for the most outrageous lesson.

Getting started as a profession. We need to recognize that teaching with imaginative and suspenseful storylines that link content to students' sense of fantasy is more effective than conventional teaching in many situations, and the rules for both types of teaching are almost opposite.

We need to expand the definition of "master teacher" to refer to someone who can apply the best of both conventional and outrageous teaching—that is, someone who can teach by direction and also use fantasy and imagination to create suspenseful curiosity. A master teacher should be able to switch between the two modes of teaching and do a great job at both. At the very least, all student teachers should be required to teach at least one outrageous lesson.

SUMMARY

Student boredom and superficial learning are epidemics in American education. While we have made great progress as a profession in how to employ scientific principles of psychology to teaching and learning, we have made little progress in how not to bore students. We have not made progress in linking instruction to students' sense of imagination, nor have we recognized that imagination is fundamental to the psychological and cultural characteristics of young adults. The resultant boredom and uninspired instruction is a major cause of dropping out for both students and teachers.

Outrageous Instruction enables teachers to add a new technique to their toolbox that totally reshapes the teaching process. The techniques provide a practical way for teachers, either individually or schoolwide, to realize the ideal that inspired them to become teachers: the vision of inspiring students. While external forces increasingly dictate what we have to teach, there is no reason to let them determine how we teach. There is no rationale in this age of ubiquitous entertainment on demand and You Tube exhibitionism why education should remain rooted solely in literal and simplistic presentation of content. Teaching some objectives outrageously is a critical tool for school improvement and for making teaching and learning exhilarating—even for seemingly prosaic content. Outrageous Instruction melds imaginative and dramatic teaching with the pragmatics of meeting standards.

There is a wellspring of untapped creative potential and imagination in both students and teachers that can be harnessed to the more effective teaching of key content objectives. But the teacher must be willing to create a Monty Python moment, that is, something completely different. Outrageous Instruction provides a practical way for teachers who are willing to extend their comfort zone to revitalize their instruction and stimulate student learning—and to have a ball doing so.

REFERENCES

Pogrow, Stanley. "Challenging At-Risk Students: Findings from the HOTS Program." Phi Delta Kappan 71 (January 1990): 389–397.

Pogrow, Stanley. "Supermath: An Alternative Approach to Improving Math Performance in Grades 4 Through 9." Phi Delta Kappan 86 (December 2004): 297–303.

Pogrow, Stanley. "HOTS Revisited: A Thinking Development Approach to Reducing the Learning Gap After Grade 3." Phi Delta Kappan 87 (September 2005): 64–75.

Pogrow, Stanley. Teaching Content Outrageously: How to Captivate and Accelerate the Learning of All Students in Grades 4–12. San Francisco: Jossey-Bass, 2008.

DISCUSSION QUESTIONS

1. Imagine a context when you might teach outrageously in your own classroom. Describe how you would transform your lesson to an outrageous one.
2. The author does not recommend teaching outrageously every day. Do you agree with this? Explain.
3. How important is it to engage your students? What methods or strategies do you use already to engage your students?
4. How is teaching outrageously related to intrinsic and extrinsic motivation? Do you believe the students in this article were more intrinsically or extrinsically motivated due to participating in this outrageous lesson?
5. Do you have to be a master teacher to teach outrageously? Explain.

PRO-CON CHART 4

Should academic content standards be used in place of curriculum guides?

PRO	CON
1. Content standards ensure high expectations for every student in every classroom.	**1.** Raising expectations will hurt students who are already not achieving by making a difficult challenge impossible.
2. Standards make public what all students should know and be able to do.	**2.** Curriculum guides and textbooks are public documents that already exist and serve the same purpose.
3. Standards ensure that important content is not overlooked and that students are exposed to new content at each grade.	**3.** Teachers need flexibility when covering content to meet the needs of diverse groups of students who may be at different stages in their development.
4. Standards focus teaching, student work, and assessment on the knowledge and skills that are most important for success in life.	**4.** Students need to learn how to be responsible for their own learning, because no one really knows what knowledge and skills will be most important in the future.
5. Standards can reduce the wide variability in the quality of curriculum, instruction, and assessment that exists from one classroom to another.	**5.** Teachers deserve to be treated as professionals who employ academic freedom to help students to construct knowledge that is personally meaningful.
6. Rubrics and scoring guides that describe the specific criteria that must be met at each level of achievement help to communicate what students should know to both students and parents.	**6.** Standards are really nothing but a smokescreen for one-shot, high-stakes tests.

CASE STUDY 4

An Advocate for Longer School Days

Jack Pierce, curriculum coordinator of Ipsid Elementary District, handed a written proposal to the superintendent, Dick Bosio, which suggested that the district lengthen the school day by forty minutes beginning in the fall. Pierce cited research to support his claim that academic learning time is the most important variable associated with student learning for most types of learners. He also reported research that showed significant relationships between increased academic time and gains in student achievement. While explaining his rationale for increasing the length of the school day, Pierce said he felt confident that overall the district would demonstrate an increase in students' Iowa Test of Basic Skills scores. He suggested that this change would probably satisfy the public that Ipsid was promoting excellence in education.

Pierce emphasized that since time spent on relevant academic tasks is measurable, the district would be able to show that better test scores were the result of the increased academic instruction. Furthermore, he said that increased instructional time was advisable according to the research on teaching that emphasized student outcomes.

The Ipsid superintendent listened closely to Pierce's proposal. He had some concerns, but decided that Pierce had analyzed almost all the critical factors. Noting some of the considerations that might need to be addressed, Bosio thought to himself that because engaged time was equivalent to time devoted to actual work, asking teachers to stay a little longer each day would not be an issue. Bosio turned to Pierce and said, "I think this is a good idea. Go ahead and implement this change."

1. Assume you are Bosio and discuss how you would implement an extension of your school's instructional day by forty minutes.
2. Do you think that student achievement is directly correlated with academic engaged time? Why? Why not?
3. Based on your experience, what factors other than time on task influence student outcomes?
4. In what ways does the use of different instructional models influence student outcomes?
5. What alternatives might be considered to promote student outcomes, instead of lengthening the school day?
6. What is the relationship among content, quality of teaching, academic engaged time, and student outcomes?
7. How do subject matter content and social atmosphere of the classroom affect academic engaged time?

PART FIVE

Curriculum and Supervision

How do developments and curriculum influence each other? What are the issues changing our views of supervision and leadership? How would new conceptions of supervision influence practice and professional programs of preparation?

In Chapter 24, Thomas Sergiovanni describes how conceptions of school leadership practice would be reconceived if the politics of division were replaced with the politics of virtue. He explores how the role of the principal as steward differs from perceptions of transformational leadership. He also claims that students as well as teachers will be able to embrace the concept of civic virtue. In the next chapter, Harry Wong, Ted Britton, and Tom Gasner point out that induction of new teachers in the United States is either entirely lacking or not well structures, typically involving support from a single mentor. The authors describe more systematic approaches to induction that other countries have adopted.

In Chapter 26, Edward Pajak describes how various models of clinical supervision are linked to the concept of psychological style. He explains why and how clinical supervisors can better communicate by applying approaches that coincide with teachers' psychological types. Pajak also suggests that supervisors should strive to work with teachers in ways that are consistent with how teachers are expected to work with students by celebrating diversity and responding to that diversity in ways that enhance learning for all. In the next chapter in Part Five, Frank Levy and Richard Murnane suggest that teachers can be thought of as managers of students and classrooms who can benefit from four lessons learned at IBM, where technology has been used successfully to improve the quality of professional development.

In Chapter 28, W. James Popham discusses the importance of identifying the instructional sensitivity of assessments. He defines instructional sensitivity as how closely a student's performance on an assessment reflects what they learned. Popham contends that instructional sensitivity is important when assessments are used in accountability and describes how the instructional sensitivity of an assessment can be evaluated. In the final chapter of Part Five, Daniel Duke describes the importance of identifying previously well performing schools that have begun to "slip". Duke identifies issues including budget cuts, state and federal mandates, increase in at risk students, and loss of staff which can affect school performance. Likewise, he cites factors such as increases in class size and ineffective professional development that can lead to the school decline.

CHAPTER 24

The Politics of Virtue: A New Framework for School Leadership

THOMAS J. SERGIOVANNI

FOCUSING QUESTIONS

1. What is the politics of virtue?
2. In what ways are the politics of virtue and the democratic legacy related?
3. How would practice emanating from a pluralistic conception of politics influence school leadership?
4. What are the basic principles of formal organization theories?
5. If the politics of division were replaced with the politics of virtue, how would conceptions of leadership need to be redefined?
6. In what ways does the role of the principal as steward differ from current conceptions of school leadership?
7. What are the similarities and differences between conceptions of stewardship and transformational leadership?

Margaret Mead once remarked, "Never doubt that a small group of thoughtful, committed citizens can change the world; indeed, it's the only thing that ever has." Her thought suggests that perhaps there is something to the 1,000 points of light theory of change. Is it possible to rally enough small groups of thoughtful and committed citizens to create the kind of schools we want? I think so, if we are willing to change the way politics is thought about in schools.

Rarely does a day go by without the media telling us still another story about divisions, hostilities, factions, and other symptoms of disconnectedness in schools. Teachers disagreeing over methods; parents bickering with teachers over discipline problems; board members squabbling over curriculum issues; administrators complaining about encroachments on their prerogatives; everyone disagreeing on sex education; and students, feeling pretty much left out of it all, making it difficult for everyone in the school by tediously trading their compliance and goodwill for things that they want. This mixture of issues and this mixture of stakeholders, all competing for advantage, resembles a game of bartering where self-interest is the motivator and individual actors engage in the hard play of the politics of division. The purpose of this game is to win more for yourself than you have to give back in return. Allison (1969) summarizes the game of *politics of division* as follows:

> Actions emerge neither as the calculated choice of a unified group nor as a formal summary of a leader's preferences. Rather the context of shared power but separate judgment concerning important choices determines that politics is the mechanism of choice. Note the environment in which the game is played: inordinate uncertainty about what must be done, the necessity that something be done and crucial consequences of whatever is done. These features force responsible men to become active players. The *pace of the game*—hundreds of issues, numerous games, and multiple channels—compels players to fight to "get others' attention," to make them "see the facts," to assure that they "take the time to think seriously about the broader issue." The *structure of the game*—power shared by individuals with separate responsibilities—validates each player's feeling that "others don't see my problem," and "others must be persuaded to look at the issue from a less parochial perspective." The *rules of the game*—he who hesitates loses his chance to play at that point, and he who is uncertain about his recommendation is overpowered by others who are sure—pressures players to come down on the side of a 51–49 issue and play. The *rewards of the game*—effectiveness, i.e., impact on outcomes, as the immediate measure of performance—encourage hard play. (p. 710)

The politics of division is a consequence of applying formal organization theories of governance, management, and leadership to schools. At root, these theories assume that human nature is motivated by self-interest and that leadership requires the bartering of need fulfillment for compliance. Would things be different if we applied community theories instead? Communities, too, "play the game" of politics. But it is a different game. It is a game of politics more like that envisioned by James Madison, Alexander Hamilton, John Jay, Thomas Jefferson, and other American Founders and enshrined in such sacred documents as the Declaration of Independence, the Constitution of the United States, and the amendments to that Constitution that represent a bill of rights and a bill of responsibilities for all Americans. It is a game called the *politics of virtue*—a politics motivated by shared commitment to the common good and guided by protections that ensure the rights and responsibilities of individuals.

CIVIC VIRTUE

Is it possible to replace the politics of division with a politics of virtue? I think so, if we are willing to replace the values that have been borrowed from the world of formal organizations with traditional democratic values that encourage a commitment to civic virtue. This would entail development and use of different theories of human nature and leadership. For example, the rational choice theories of human nature we now use will need to be replaced with a normative and moral theory of human nature. And the executive images of leadership that we now rely on will need to be replaced with collegial images aimed at problem solving and ministering.

Creating a politics of virtue requires that we renew commitments to the democratic legacy that gave birth to our country. This is the legacy that can provide the foundation for leadership in schools. The American Founders had in mind the creation of a covenantal polity within which "The body is one but has many members. There can be unity with diversity. . . . The great challenge was to create a political body that brought people together and created a 'we' but still enabled people to separate themselves and recognize and respect one another's individualities. This remains the great challenge for all modern democracies" (Elshtain, 1994, p. 9). The cultivation of commitment to civic virtue is a key part of this challenge.

During the debate over passing the Constitution of 1787, America was faced with a choice between two conceptions of politics: *republican* and *pluralist*. In republican politics, civic virtue was considered to be the cornerstone principle—the prerequisite for the newly proposed government to work. Civic virtue was embodied in the willingness of citizens to subordinate their own private interests to the general good (e.g., see Sunstein, 1993) and was therefore the basis for creating a politics of virtue. This politics of virtue emphasized self-rule by the people, but not the imposition of their private preferences on the new government. Instead, preferences were to be developed and shaped by the people themselves for the benefit of the common good.

Haefele (1993) believes that it is easier to provide examples of how civic virtue is expressed than to try to define it with precision. In his words:

> It is fashionable nowadays for both the left and the right to decry the loss of civic virtue; the left on such issues as industry rape of the environment and the right because of the loss of patriotism. Both sides are undoubtedly right, as civic virtue belongs to no single party or creed. It is simply a quality of caring about public purposes and public destinations. Sometimes the public purpose is chosen over private purposes. A young Israeli economist investigating a Kibbutz came across the following case. The Kibbutz had money to spend. The alternatives were a TV antenna and TV sets for everyone or a community meeting hall. The economist found that everyone preferred the TV option but that, when they voted, they unanimously chose the meeting hall. Call it enlightened self-interest, a community preference or something else, it is civic virtue in action. (p. 211)

When the republican conception of politics is applied to schools, both the unique shared values that define individual schools as communities and our common democratic principles and conceptions of goodness that provide the basis for defining civic virtue are important.

The pluralist conception of politics differs from the republican. Without the unifying power of civic virtue, factions are strengthened and the politics of division reigns. In the ideal, the challenge of this politics is to play people and events in a way that the self-interests of individuals and factions are mediated in some orderly manner. "Under the pluralist conception, people come to the political process with preselected interests that they seek to promote through political conflict and compromise" (Sunstein, 1993, p. 176). Deliberate governmental processes of conflict resolution and compromise, of checks and balances, are needed in the pluralist view because preferences are not shaped by the people themselves as they strive to control self-interests that happen to dominate at the time.

Civic virtue was important to both Federalists, who supported the proposed Constitution, and Anti-Federalists, who opposed the Constitution, though it was the centerpiece of Anti-Federalist thinking. The Anti-Federalists favored decentralization in the form of democracy tempered by a commitment to the common good. The Federalists, by contrast, acknowledged the importance of civic virtue, but felt the pull of pluralistic politics was too strong for the embodiment of virtue to be left to chance. They proposed a representative rather than a direct form of government that would be guided by the principles of a formal constitution that specified a series of governmental checks and balances to control factionalism and self-interest.

Both the positions of the Federalists and the Anti-Federalists have roles to play in the governance of schools. In small communities, for example, the politics of virtue expressed within a direct democracy that is guided by *citizen* devotion to the public good seems to make the most sense. Small schools and small schools within schools would be examples of such communities. They would be governed by autonomous school councils that are responsible for both educational policy and site-based management—both ends and means. This approach to governance represents a significant departure from present policies that allow principals, parents, and teachers in local schools to decide how they will do things, but not what they will do. The decisions that local school councils make would be guided by shared values and beliefs that parents, teachers, and students develop together. Schools, in this image, would not function as markets where self-interests reign or bureaucracies where entrenched rule systems reign, but as morally based direct democracies within which parents, teachers, and students, guided by civic virtue, make the best decisions possible for learning.

At the school district level, by contrast, the position of the Federalists might make the most sense. A representative form of government spearheaded by elected school boards, guided by an explicit constitution that contains the protections and freedoms needed to enable individual school communities to function both responsibly and autonomously, would be the model. School communities would have to abide by certain school district regulations regarding safety, due process, equity, fiscal procedures, and a few basic academic standards. But, beyond these, schools would be free to decide for themselves not only their management processes, but their policy structures as well. They would be responsible for deciding their own educational purposes, educational programs, scheduling and ways of operating, and means to demonstrate to the school district and to the public that they are functioning responsibly. Accountability in such a system would be both responsive to each school's purposes and, in light of those purposes, to tough standards of proof.

How can schools be held accountable for different standards? First, we will need to create standards for standards. Then we will be able to assess whether the standards that individual schools set for themselves are good ones. Once standards are accepted, each school is then assessed on its own terms. Here is how such a strategy would work: Schools make promises to the people; the promises must be good ones; school boards and states hold schools accountable for keeping their promises.

THE RATIONAL CHOICE QUESTION

Formal organization theories of human nature can be traced back to a few principles that are at the center of classical economic theory. Prime among them is the *utility function,* which is believed to explain all consumer behavior. The reasoning behind this belief is as follows. Humans are by their nature selfish. They are driven by a desire to maximize their self-interests and thus continually calculate the costs and benefits of their actions. They choose courses of action that either make them winners (they get a desired payoff) or keep them from losing (they avoid penalties). So dominant is this view and so pervasive is the concept of utility function that emotions such as love, loyalty, obligation, sense of duty, belief in goodness, commitment to a cause, and a desire to help make things better are thought to count very little in determining the courses of actions that humans choose. This view of human nature comprises a model of economics called *rational choice theory.*

Rational choice theory, expressed simply as "What gets rewarded gets done," undergirds much of the thinking in schools about how to motivate teachers to perform, how to introduce school improvement initiatives in schools, how to motivate people to accept change, and how to motivate students to learn and to behave. By emphasizing self-interest, rational choice theory discourages the development of civic virtue.

Two additional motivational rules need to be recognized if we are to have a more complete picture of human nature: "What is *rewarding* gets done," and "What people value and believe in gets done." Both rules compel people to perform, improve, change, and meet their commitments from within, even if doing so requires that self-interest be sacrificed. Both rules address the intrinsic and moral nature of human nature. Both rules are essential to the cultivation of civic virtue.

IS CIVIC VIRTUE FOR STUDENTS, TOO?

Some readers might concede that perhaps we should move away from a rational choice view of motivation. Perhaps we should acknowledge the capacity of parents and teachers to respond less in terms of their self-interest and more in terms of what they believe is right and good. But what about students? Can they too respond to the call of virtue?

Children and young adults in schools have different needs and different dispositions. They function developmentally at different levels of moral reasoning than do adults. But the evidence is clear that students from kindergarten to grade 12 have the capacity to understand what civic virtue is and to respond to it in ways that are consistent with their own levels of maturation.

Reissman (1993) and several other teachers in New York City's District 25, for example, have been working with elementary school children (even first and second graders) on developing "bills of responsibilities." The bills are designed to teach the meaning of civic virtue and to introduce students to sources of authority that are more morally based than the usual behavioristic ways to get students to do things. Key is the emphasis on reciprocal responsibilities—a critical ingredient in community building. Communities of mind, for example, evolve from commitments to standards that apply to everyone in the school, not just to students. Thus, if students must be respectful, so must parents, teachers, principals, and everyone else who is a member of the school community or who visits the school.

Events at the Harmony School in Bloomington, Indiana, illustrate civic virtue in action (Panasonic Foundation, Inc., 1994). A well-known sculptor had removed his limestone rhinoceros from its place in front of an art gallery in Bloomington to keep it from being vandalized. The kindergarten through twelfth grade students at the Harmony School launched a campaign to return the rhino to Bloomington. They raised $6,000 and purchased the rhino, which now stands in front of the school for the entire community to enjoy.

One year Harmony High School students decided that, instead of the traditional field trip to Chicago, they would go to Quincy, Illinois, where the Mississippi floods had devastated the city. One of the students explained, "They have plenty of food, and plenty of relief supplies, but they don't have anybody to help get life in order." Harmony students helped by clearing mud, garbage, and debris from the streets and by planting flowers and shrubs. Many similar stories, I know, are coming to your mind as you read about and think about the events at Harmony.

Harmony School is private, and Bloomington, Indiana, is hardly downtown Kansas City, Miami, or San Antonio. But students everywhere are pretty much the same. They have the capacity to care. They want to be called to be good, and they know the difference between right and wrong. The fact is that students, too, under the right conditions, not only will be responsive to the calls of civic virtue, but they need to be responsive if they are to develop into the kinds of adults that we want them to be.

NEW LEADERSHIP IMAGES

Replacing the politics of division with a politics of virtue requires a redefined leadership. Civic virtue is encouraged when leadership aims to develop a web of moral obligations that administrators, teachers, parents, and even students must accept. One part of this obligation is to share in the responsibility for exercising leadership. Another part of this obligation is to share in the responsibility for ensuring that leadership, whatever its source, is successful. In this redefinition, teachers continue to be responsible for providing leadership in classrooms. But students, too, have a moral obligation to help make things work. They, too, provide leadership where they can and try as best they can to make the teacher's leadership effective. Similarly, administrators, parents, and teachers would accept responsibility together for the provision and the success of leadership.

Key to leadership in a democracy is the concept of social contract. Heifetz (1994) notes, "In part, democracy requires that average citizens become aware that they are indeed the principals, and that those upon whom they confer power are the agents. They have also to bear the risks, the costs, and the fruits of shared responsibility and civic participation" (p. 61).

It is through morally held role responsibilities that we can understand school administration as a profession in its more traditional sense. School administration is bound not just to standards of technical competence, but to standards of public obligation as well (Bellah et al., 1985, p. 290). The primacy of public obligation leads us to the roots of school leadership—stewardship defined as a commitment to administer to the needs of the school by serving its purposes, by serving those who struggle to embody these purposes, and by acting as a guardian to protect the institutional integrity of the school.

Principals function as stewards by providing for the overseeing and caring of their schools. As stewards, they are not so much managers or executives but administrators. According to Webster, to "manage" means to handle, to control, to make submissive, to direct an organization. "Superintend," in turn, means attending to, giving attention to, having oversight over what is intended. It means, in other words, supervision. As supervisor, the principal acts in loco parentis in relationship to students, ensuring that all is well for them. And as supervisor the principal acts as steward, guarding and protecting the school's purposes and structures.

Supervision in communities implies accountability, but not in the tough, inspectoral sense suggested by factory images of inspection and control. Instead, it implies an accountability embedded in tough and tender caring. Principals care enough about the school, the values and purposes that undergird it, the students who are being served, the parents whom they represent, and the teachers upon whom they depend that they will do whatever they can to protect school values and purposes, on the one hand, and to enable their accomplishment on the other.

In a recent interview, Deborah Meier, then co-director of the celebrated Central Park East Secondary School in New York City, was asked, "What is the role of the principal in an effective school?" (Scherer, 1995). Her response shows how the various ministerial roles of the principal are brought together by supervision understood as an expression of stewardship:

> Someone has to keep an eye on the whole and alert everyone when parts need close- or long-range attention. A principal's job is to

put forth to the staff an agenda. The staff may or may not agree, but they have an opportunity to discuss it. I'll say, "Listen, I've been around class after class, and I notice this, don't notice this, we made a commitment to be accountable for one another, but I didn't see anybody visiting anybody else's class. . . ." Paul [Schwartz, Meier's co-director] and I also read all the teachers' assessments of students. Once we noticed that the 9th and the 10th grade math teachers often said the kids didn't seem to have an aptitude for math. We asked the math staff, "How can these kids do nicely in 7th and 8th grade, and then seem inept in 9th and 10th? Are we fooling ourselves in 7th and 8th, or are we fooling ourselves in 9th and 10th? Because they are the same kids." (p. 7)

Meier and Schwartz both practiced leadership that is idea based. The source of authority that they appealed to are the values that are central to the school and the commitments that everyone has made to them. And because of this, their supervisory responsibilities do not compromise democratic principles, dampen teacher empowerment, or get in the way of community building. Both directors were committed to creating a staff-run school with high standards—one where staff must know each other, be familiar with each other's work, and know how the school operates. As Meier (1992) explained,

> Decisions are made as close to each teacher's own classroom setting as possible, although all decisions are ultimately the responsibility of the whole staff. The decisions are not merely on minor matters—length of classes or the number of field trips. The teachers collectively decide on content, pedagogy, and assessment as well. They teach what they think matters . . . governance is simple. There are virtually no permanent standing committees. Finally, we work together to develop assessment systems for our students, their families, ourselves, and the broader public. Systems that represent our values and beliefs in as direct a manner as possible. (p. 607)

This process of shared decision making is not institutionalized into a formal system, but is embedded in the daily interactions of everyone working together.

In stewardship the legitimacy of leadership comes in part from the virtuous responsibilities associated with the principal's role and in part from the principal's obligation to function as the head follower of the school's moral compact. In exercising these responsibilities and obligations, it is not enough to make the right moves for just any purpose or just any vision. The noted historian and leadership theorist James MacGregor Burns (1978) pointed out that purposes and visions should be socially useful, should serve the common good, should meet the needs of followers, and should elevate followers to a higher moral level. He calls this kind of leadership *transformational*.

Many business writers and their imitators in educational administration have secularized this original definition of transformational leadership to make it more suitable to the values of formal organizations. They "conceive of transformation, not in Burns's sense of elevating the moral functioning of a polity, but in the sense of inspiration, intellectual stimulation, and personal considerations . . . ; or altering the basic normative principles that guide an institution . . . ." (Heifetz, 1994, pp. 228–229; see also Bass, 1985, and Hargrove, 1989). This revisionist concept of transformational leadership might be alright for managers and CEOs in business organizations. But when it comes to the kind of leadership that they want for their children's schools, few businesspersons are likely to prefer the corporate definition over Burns's original definition.

When principals practice leadership as stewardship, they commit themselves to building, serving, caring for, and protecting the school and its purposes. They commit themselves to helping others to face problems and to make progress in getting problems solved. Leadership as stewardship asks a great deal of leaders and followers alike. It calls both to higher levels of commitment. It calls both to higher levels of goodness. It calls both to higher levels of effort. And it calls both to higher levels of accountability. Leadership as stewardship is the *sine qua non* for cultivating civic virtue. Civic virtue can help to transform individual stakeholders into members of a community who share common commitments and who feel a moral obligation to help each other to embody those commitments.

ENDNOTE

This Chapter is drawn from *Leadership for the School-house: How Is It Different? Why Is It Important?* San francisco: Jossey-Bass. 1996

REFERENCES

Allison, G. T. (1969). "Conceptual Models and the Cuban Missile Crisis." *American Political Science Review, 63* (3): 689–718.

Bass, B. M. (1985). *Leadership and Performance beyond Expectations.* New York: Free Press.

Bellah, R. N., and others. (1985). *Habits of the Heart: Individualism and Commitment in American Life.* New York: HarperCollins.

Burns, J. M. (1978). *Leadership.* New York: HarperCollins.

Elshtain, J. B. (1994). "Democracy and the Politics of Difference." *Responsive Community, 4* (2): 9–20.

Haefele, E. T. (1993). "What Constitutes the American Republic?" In S. L. Elkin and K. E. Soltan (eds.), *A New Constitutionalism.* Chicago: University of Chicago Press: 207–233.

Hargrove, E. C. (1989). "Two Conceptions of Institutional Leadership. In B. D. Jones (ed.), *Leadership and Politics: New Perspectives in Political Science.* Lawrence: University of Kansas Press.

Heifetz, R. (1994). *Leadership without Easy Answers.* Cambridge, MA: Harvard University Press.

Meier, D. (1992). "Reinventing Teaching." *Teacher's College Record, 93* (4): 594–609.

Panasonic Foundation. (1994). *Panasonic Partnership Program.* A newsletter of the Panasonic Foundation, 4 (1).

Reissman, R. (1993). "A Bill of Responsibilities." *Educational Leadership, 51* (4): 86–87.

Samuelson, P. (1947). *Foundations of Economic Analysis.* Cambridge, MA: Harvard University Press.

Scherer, M. (1995). "On Schools Where Students Want to Be: A Conversation with Deborah Meier." *Educational Leadership, 52* (1): 4–8.

Sunstein, C. R. (1993). "The Enduring Legacy of Republicanism." In S. L. Elkin and K. E. Soltan (eds.), *A New Constitutionalism.* Chicago: University of Chicago Press: 174–207.

van Mannen, M. (1991). *The Tact of Teaching: The Meaning of Pedagogical Thoughtfulness.* Albany: State University of New York Press.

DISCUSSION QUESTIONS

1. What is the relationship between the politics of division and the application of formal organization theories of governance, management, and leadership in schools?
2. What are the implications of applying the politics of virtue to the practice of school leadership?
3. What are the disadvantages of applying rational choice theory to change initiatives and student motivation?
4. What evidence is there to support the belief that students of all ages have the capacity to understand and support civic virtue?
5. Why are the concepts of social contract and obligation key to the practice of leadership in a democracy?
6. In your opinion, is the notion of school leadership based on the politics of virtue a (a) practical, (b) feasible, or (c) desirable idea? Why? Why not?

CHAPTER 25

What the World Can Teach Us about New Teacher Induction

HARRY K. WONG
TED BRITTON
TOM GANSER

FOCUSING QUESTIONS

1. What are some new teacher induction techniques?
2. How does extended teacher assistance training shape a new teacher's experience? What are the benefits?
3. How does teacher induction aid in teacher retention?
4. How can teacher induction aid seasoned teachers (those that have been teaching over 5 years)? The administration? The community?
5. What are some ways to combat isolation/alienation in U.S. schools? What are ways that teachers, administration, and community can do this?

An effective teacher is perhaps the most important factor in producing consistently high levels of student achievement.[1] Thus the profession must see to it that teachers are continually learning throughout their careers, and that process begins with those newest to the profession. A new teacher induction program can acculturate newcomers to the idea that professional learning must be a lifelong pursuit.

A book edited by Ted Britton, Lynn Paine, David Pimm, and Senta Raizen provides a more detailed look at how five countries—Switzerland, Japan, France, New Zealand, and China (Shanghai)—acculturate their new teachers, specifically their science and mathematics teachers, and shape their entry into the profession.[2] In this chapter, we share a brief summary of the findings reported in that volume.

The five countries studied provide well-funded support that reaches all beginning teachers, incorporates multiple sources of assistance, typically lasts at least two years, and goes beyond the imparting of mere survival skills. For example, in Switzerland, new teachers are involved in practice groups, in which they network to learn effective problem solving. In Shanghai, new teachers join lesson-preparation and teaching-research groups. New teachers in New Zealand take part in a 25-year-old Advice and Guidance program that extends for 2 years. Lesson study groups are the mode in Japan, while in France, new teachers work for an extended time with groups of peers who share experiences, practices, tools, and professional language.

Before we go into more detail about these programs, a basic definition of induction is in order. *Induction* is a highly organized and comprehensive form of staff development, involving many people and components, that typically continues as a sustained process for the first 2 to 5 years of a teacher's career. Mentoring is often a component of the induction process.

The exponential growth in the number of induction programs in the United States attests to the value that staff developers and other school leaders ascribe to them. Educational leaders have eagerly adapted their approaches to induction to reflect the many changes in the teaching profession.[3] But induction programs are a global phenomenon, and here we offer to U.S. leaders a summary of the best practices of the international programs reported by Britton and his colleagues.

SWITZERLAND

In the Swiss system, teachers are assumed to be lifelong learners. From the start, beginning teachers are viewed as professionals, and induction focuses on the development of the person as well as on the development of the professional.

Induction begins during student teaching as teams of three students network with one another. It continues for beginning teachers in practice groups of about half a dozen teachers and is carried forward in mutual classroom observations between beginning teachers and experienced teachers. Thus induction moves seamlessly from a teacher's preservice days to novice teaching to continuing professional learning.

The Swiss philosophy explicitly rejects a deficit model of induction, which assumes that new teachers lack training and competence and thus need mentors. Instead, several cantons provide a carefully crafted array of induction experiences for new teachers, including:

- *Practice groups.* These are a form of structured, facilitated networking that supports beginning teachers from different schools as they learn to be effective solvers of practical problems.
- *Standortbestimmung.* Practice groups generally conclude with a group Standortbestimmung—a form of self-evaluation of the first year of teaching that reflects the Swiss concern with developing the whole person as well as the teacher.
- *Counseling.* Counseling is generally available for all teachers, but a greater number of beginning teachers take part. It can grow out of the practice groups and can involve one-on-one mentoring of classroom practice. In some cantons, counseling is mandatory for beginning teachers.
- *Courses.* Course offerings range from obligatory courses to voluntary courses available on a regular basis to impulse courses, which are put together on short notice to meet a short-term need.

These practices are supported with training for practice-group leaders, counselors, and mentors.

A professional team heads the whole set of induction activities and is in charge of the practice-group leaders. These leaders, all active teachers themselves, are the key to the quality of the practice groups and other components of induction, such as classroom visits and individual counseling. These individuals are relieved of some of their teaching duties to make time for their responsibilities as practice-group leaders. They also receive additional pay and are themselves supported by the central team. The group leaders are trained to carry out their responsibilities and take part in a wide range of professional development offerings to increase their competence as leaders.

CHINA (SHANGHAI)

The teaching culture in Shanghai features research groups and collective lesson planning. It is a culture in which all teachers learn to engage in joint work to support their teaching and their personal learning, as well as the learning of their pupils. The induction process is designed to help bring new teachers into this culture.

There is an impressive array of learning opportunities at both the school and the district level; among them:

- Welcoming ceremonies at the school
- District-level workshops and courses
- District-organized teaching competitions
- District-provided mentoring
- A district hot line for new teachers that connects them with subject specialists
- District awards for outstanding novice/mentor work
- Half-day training sessions at colleges of education and in schools for most weeks for the first year of teaching
- Peer observation, both in and outside of school
- Public, or open, lessons, with debriefing and discussion of the lesson afterwards
- Report lessons, in which a new teacher is observed and given comments, criticisms, and suggestions
- Talk lessons, in which a teacher (new or experienced) talks through a lesson and provides justification for its design, but does not actually teach it
- Inquiry projects and action research carried out by new teachers, with support from those on the school or district teaching research section or induction staff
- District- or school-developed handbooks for new teachers and mentors
- End-of-year celebrations of teachers' work and collaboration

In keeping with the collective and collaborative focus of the teaching culture in Shanghai, a number of other critical components play a role in the induction process for new teachers.

Lesson-Preparation Groups

The heart of the professional learning culture is the lesson-preparation group. These groups engage new and veteran teachers in discussing and analyzing the lessons they are teaching.

Teaching-Research Groups

A beginning teacher is also a member of a teaching-research group, which provides a forum for the discussion of teaching techniques. Each teacher, new or experienced, must observe at least eight lessons a semester, and most teachers observe more. It is very common for teachers to enter others' classrooms and to engage in discussion about mutually observed teaching. These conversations help new teachers acquire the language and adopt the norms of public conversation about teaching, and that conversation becomes a natural part of the fabric of any teacher's professional life.

Teaching Competitions

Districts organize teaching competitions with the goal of motivating new teachers and encouraging the serious study of and preparation for teaching. The competitions also identify and honor outstanding accomplishment. Lessons are videotaped so that the district can compile an archive for future use. Teaching thus becomes community property, not owned privately by one teacher, but shared by all.

NEW ZEALAND

In New Zealand, the induction phase is called the Advice and Guidance (AG) program. The AG program is seen as the initial phase of the lifelong professional development of teachers. Every beginning teacher is released from 20 percent of work time to participate in the program.

Teachers and school-level administrators are willing to invest in the effort to support beginning teachers partly because schools are required to provide an AG program. Provisionally registered teachers must document the AG support they received during their first 2 years when they apply for a permanent certificate. But many of those who provide support for new teachers view their assistance as a commitment to the teaching profession.

The National Ministry of Education also provides limited regional resources for professional development services to beginning teachers. Regional meetings, which attract teachers from different schools, provide for the free exchange of induction experiences among a wide variety of participants. Although there is a national handbook outlining the goals of the AG program, the extent, nature, and quality of the local programs vary widely.

At the local school, an administrator or a staff member is typically the coordinator of the AG program. The people involved most directly in supporting beginning teachers are typically the AG coordinator, department heads, "buddy teachers," and, to a lesser extent, all other school staff members. In schools that have more than one beginning teacher, the AG coordinator convenes all the beginning teachers every 2 weeks throughout most of the year. Observation of teaching is a key activity in school-level induction programs and comes in several varieties. As in Switzerland, facilitated peer support is an important induction strategy.

Ted Britton explains that one reason New Zealand was chosen as a subject for study was the contrast it offered to countries that place a great deal of the responsibility for assisting beginning teachers on a single mentor or on just a couple of people. (He was alluding to the United States.) Indeed, we were struck by the variety of the sources of support in New Zealand and by how the schools make use of a range of induction activities. Throughout the education system in New Zealand, there is a universal commitment to supporting beginning teachers.

JAPAN

Teaching in Japan is regarded as a high-status occupation, a dignified profession. New teachers have a reduced teaching load and are assigned guiding teachers. The guiding teacher is the key to success in the Japanese system.

In-School Teacher Education

In their first year, all new teachers typically teach two or more demonstration lessons, which are viewed by prefectural administrators, the guiding teacher, the school principal or assistant principal, and other teachers in the school. The demonstration, or "study teaching," lesson, a traditional Japanese method for improving teaching, is a formal public lesson, which is observed and then subjected to critique by colleagues.

James Stigler and James Hiebert view these lessons and their subsequent public analysis as the core activity of in-school teacher education.[4] To prepare for their public lessons, the new teachers write and rewrite their lesson plans, practice teaching the lesson with one of their classes, and modify the lesson with the help of a guiding teacher. They might even call teachers from neighboring schools, whom they know from their university or prefectural classes, and seek their help and advice.

In Japan, as in Shanghai, teaching is viewed as a public activity, open to scrutiny by many. The induction process welcomes beginners into that open practice and provides beginning teachers with many regular opportunities to observe their peers, their guiding teachers, and other teachers in their school, as well as those in other schools. No special arrangements need to be made, for schools and teaching are organized to allow for such open observations. Indeed, the method is so universal that all teachers have experienced it, and all seem to see its wisdom and believe in its efficacy. The most critical factor is that it is the lesson that is criticized, not the teacher.

New teachers are also required to submit a culminating "action research" project based on a classroom lesson they would like to investigate. This project is usually about 30–40 pages in length and is handed in to the prefectural education office (though no formal feedback on it is provided). These projects are accumulated in the prefectural inservice offices and are available for other teachers to use.

Japanese teachers do not have their own, isolated offices. Rather, teams or even an entire staff occupy one large room with individual desks and the accompanying equipment and supplies. Thus a new teacher receives help from many teachers, since most veteran teachers believe it is their responsibility to help new teachers become successful.

Out-of-School Teacher Education

Most out-of-school activity occurs under the guidance of a city or prefectural inservice center. Such a center is usually housed in a rather large building, is well staffed with specialists in most disciplines, and is dedicated to the inservice development of local teachers.

Induction is only the first phase of a teacher's professional learning. All Japanese teachers must participate in sponsored inservice programs 5, 10, and 20 years after their induction program has been completed.

FRANCE

To become a certified secondary teacher in France, one must successfully pass a highly competitive national recruitment examination, both oral and written. A new teacher is referred to as a *stagiaire*, which translates roughly as someone who is undertaking a stage of development or formation.

A pedagogical advisor, appointed by a regional pedagogical inspector, is provided for all secondary school stagiaires. When new teachers need advice, the advisors give it, but the teachers are encouraged to proceed on their own. Stagiaires observe one another's classes on numerous occasions.

All new teachers are required to attend off-campus sessions several days per week at the nearest Institut Universitaire de Formation des Maîtres (IUFM), an institution created in 1991 specifically to handle teacher education and development. The main goal of the IUFM is to increase both the intellectual status of teacher education and the professionalism of teachers.

At the IUFM, groups of stagiaires meet, and their work is directed by their *formateur*, an experienced teacher educator who teaches in the classroom part time and is employed part time by the IUFM. *Formation*, which translates roughly as development or shaping, is the process a new teacher undergoes to become a member of the teaching profession, and the formateur is the person who provides formative experiences. A typical day for a new teacher might include:

- Preparing several lessons, teaching the lessons, and marking the pupils' homework
- Tutoring a smaller group of pupils
- Observing the pedagogical advisor teach and discussing features of the lesson
- Observing, participating in, and discussing lessons taught by a teacher in a different school in the same town
- Working on aspects of teaching for a day and a half at the IUFM

A professional *memoir*, written under the guidance of a memoir tutor, is required of every new teacher. The memoir is a report on some detailed exploratory work relating to some aspect of teaching practice or to an academic issue. It can be done either individually or by a pair of stagiaires.

The compulsory learning opportunities for stagiaires are varied. In France, first-year teaching and learning about teaching take place in a number of settings, and a certain amount of flexibility is required, as stagiaires move between institutional settings. The French view working with different teachers as ideal for formation, because these experiences bring the stagiaires into contact with a considerable number of different people in varied roles: the formateurs, the pedagogical advisors; the school staff in different schools, including administrators and teachers of various subjects; the memoir tutor; different groups of pupils; parents; and possibly the regional pedagogical inspectors.

Stagiaires can come to think of the group with which they work at the IUFM as a "tribe," a group of same-subject teachers working together in their joint area of specialization. And the notion of tribe is an important one. Various things support the integrity of a tribe: shared experience, shared practices, shared tools, and shared language.

To an outsider, this process might look like induction that ends after the first year of teaching. But the French view it as simply part of teacher formation; it is the method by which the system takes in new members.

APPLICATION TO U.S. SCHOOLS

Although the approaches to the induction of new teachers in these five countries differ from one another, they do have three major similarities that can provide useful ideas for staff developers responsible for induction programs in the United States. First, the induction approaches are highly structured, comprehensive, rigorous, and seriously monitored. There are well-defined roles for staff developers, administrators, and instructors, mentors, or formateurs.

In contrast, the professional development programs in the United States are often sporadic, incoherent, and poorly aligned, and they lack adequate follow-up.[5] The amount of time devoted to professional development in a given area is most commonly about 1 day during the year for any given teacher.[6]

Second, the induction programs of the five countries focus on professional learning and on the growth and professionalism of teachers. They achieve these ends through an organized, sustained professional development system that employs a variety of methods. These countries all consider their induction programs to be one phase or a single part of a total lifelong professional learning process.

In contrast, in more than 30 states, the nearly universal U.S. practice seems remarkably narrow: mentoring predominates, and often there is little more.[7] In many schools, one-on-one mentoring is the dominant or even the sole strategy for supporting new teachers, and it often lacks real structure and relies on the willingness of the veteran teacher and the new teacher to seek each other out. Many mentors are assigned to respond to new teachers' need for day-to-day survival tips, and so they function primarily as a safety net for the new teachers.

Third, collaboration is a strength of each of these five induction programs. Collaborative group work is understood, fostered, and accepted as a part of the teaching culture in all five countries surveyed. Experiences, practices, tools, and language are shared among teachers. And it is the function of the induction phase to engender this sense of group identity in new teachers and to help experienced teachers begin treating them as colleagues.

In contrast, isolation is the common thread and complaint among new teachers in U.S. schools. New teachers want more than a job. They want to experience success. They want to contribute to a group. They want to make a difference. Thus collegial interchange, not isolation, must become the norm for U.S. teachers.[8]

Indeed, the most successful U.S. induction programs go beyond mentoring.[9] They are structured, sustained, intensive professional development programs that allow new teachers to observe others, to be observed by others, and to be part of networks or study groups, in which all teachers share with one another and learn to respect one another's work. Michael Garet and his colleagues confirmed this finding when they showed that teachers learn more in teacher networks and study groups than with mentoring.[10]

In their examination of over 30 new teacher induction programs in the United States, Annette Breaux and Harry Wong also found the inevitable presence of a leader.[11] These leaders have created organized and comprehensive induction programs that stress collaboration and professional growth. Teacher induction programs that rely on networking and collaboration can be found in such places as the Flowing Wells Schools in Tucson, Arizona (the Institute for Teacher Renewal and Growth); the Lafourche Parish Schools in Lafourche, Louisiana (the Framework for Inducting, Retaining, and Supporting Teachers program); and the Dallas Public Schools in Dallas, Texas (New Teacher Initiatives: New Teacher Support and Development Programs and Services).

The district staff developer and the building principal are the keys to establishing the commitment to teacher improvement and student achievement. But the bottom line remains: Good teachers make the difference. Districts that provide structured, sustained induction, training, and support for their teachers achieve what every school district seeks to achieve—improved student learning through improved professional learning.

ENDNOTES

1. Eric A. Hanushek, John F. Kain, and Steven G. Rivkin, "Why Public Schools Lose Teachers," Working Paper 8599, National Bureau of Economic Research (Cambridge, Mass., 2001); and Aubrey Wang et al., *Preparing Teachers around the World* (Princeton, N.J.: Educational Testing Service, 2003), available at *www.ets.org/research/pic.*
2. Edward Britton et al., eds., *Comprehensive Teacher Induction: Systems for Early Career Learning* (Dordrecht, Netherlands: Kluwer Academic Publishers and WestEd, 2003), available at *www.WestEd.org.*
3. Tom Ganser, "The New Teacher Mentors: Four Trends That Are Changing the Look of Mentoring Programs for New Teachers," *American School Board Journal*, December 2002, pp. 25–27; and Tom Ganser, "Sharing a Cup of Coffee Is Only a Beginning," *Journal of Staff Development*, Fall 2002, pp. 28–32.
4. James Stigler and James Hiebert, *The Teaching Gap* (New York: Free Press, 1999).
5. Wang et al., *Preparing Teachers.*
6. Basmat Parsad, Laurie Lewis, and Elizabeth Farris, *Teacher Preparation and Professional Development, 2000* (Washington, D.C.: National Center for Education Statistics, 2001).
7. Edward Britton et al., "More Swimming, Less Sinking. Perspectives from Abroad on U.S. Teacher Induction," paper prepared for the National Commission on Mathematics and Science Teaching in the 21st Century, San Francisco, 2000.

8. Harry K. Wong, "Collaborating with Colleagues to Improve Student Learning," Eisenhower National Clearinghouse, ENC Focus, vol. 11, no. 6, 2003, available at *www.enc.org/features/focus*; and "Induction Programs That Keep Working," in Marge Scherer, ed., *Keeping Good Teachers* (Alexandria, Va.: Association for Supervision and Curriculum Development, 2003), chap. 5, available at *www.newteacher.com*—click on "Published Papers."

9. Annette L. Breaux and Harry K. Wong, *New Teacher Induction: How To Train, Support, and Retain New Teachers* (Mountain View, Calif.: Harry K. Wong Publications, 2003).

10. Michael Garet, "What Makes Professional Development Effective?" *American Educational Research*, Winter 2001, pp. 915–946.

11. Breaux and Wong, *New Teacher Induction*.

DISCUSSION QUESTIONS

1. What kind of professional support did you receive when you first became a teacher? Was this support adequate?
2. Is the support that beginning teachers receive today any better than the support that you received?
3. Which country's induction program described in this chapter sounds most appealing to you?
4. Which induction practices do you think are least likely to be adopted in the United States? Why?
5. What changes in induction practices would be of most benefit to teachers in the United States?

CHAPTER 26

Clinical Supervision and Psychological Functions

Edward F. Pajak

FOCUSING QUESTIONS

1. What is clinical supervision, and how has it evolved over time?
2. What are psychological functions?
3. How do psychological functions influence communication styles?
4. What are the implications of psychological functions for the practice of clinical supervision?
5. How can supervisor–teacher relationships be improved?

Clinical supervision of instruction has a fairly long history in the United States, stretching back more than three decades. The seminal work began with Morris Cogan (1973) and Robert Goldhammer (1969) at Harvard University in the 1960s and continued later at the University of Pittsburgh. Since its inception, scholars have commented and elaborated on the fundamental clinical cycle at great length and from a wide variety of perspectives. So many volumes and articles have been published about clinical supervision over the years, in fact, that fresh insights and refinements may seem improbable at this point. This article asserts, on the contrary, that the theory of psychological functions introduced by Carl Jung (1971) and popularized by others (Briggs & Myers, 1977; Keirsey, 1998) can bring some conceptual clarity to the field of clinical supervision and also serve as a guide to practitioners when communicating with teachers.

Because the number of authors who have written about clinical supervision during recent decades is so very large, a complete account of every perspective is well beyond the scope of this article. The most prominent approaches, however, have been classified according to certain shared qualities into four families (see Figure 26.1). These four families of clinical supervision emerged chronologically in approximately the order in which they are listed (Pajak, 2000). The *original clinical* models of Goldhammer (1969) and Cogan (1973), which appeared in the late

Original clinical models	The models proposed by Goldhammer, Mosher and Purpet, and Cogan offer an electric blending of empirical, phenomenological, behavioral, and developmental perspectives. These models emphasize the importance of collegial relations between supervisors and teachers, cooperative discovery of meaning, and development of individually unique teaching styles.
Humanistic–artistic models	The perspectives of Blumberg and Eisner are based on existential and aesthetic principles. These models forsake step-by-step procedures and emphasize open interpersonal relations and personal intuition, artistry, and idiosyncrasy. Supervisors are encouraged to help teachers to understand the expressive and artistic richness of teaching.
Technical–didactic models	The work of Acheson and Gall, Hunter, and Joyce and Showers draws on process–product and effective teaching research. These models emphasize techniques of observation and feedback that reinforce certain effective behaviors or predetermined models of teaching to which teachers attempt to conform.
Developmental–reflective models	The models of Glickman; Costa and Garmston; Schon; Zeichner and Liston; Garman; Smyth and Retallick; Bowers and Flinders; and Waite are senstive to individual difference and the organizational, social, political, and cultural contexts of teaching. These models call for supervisors to encourage reflection among teachers, foster professional growth, discover context-specific principles of practice, and promote justice and equity.

FIGURE 26.1 Four Families of Clinical Supervision
Source: Pajak (2000).

1960s and early 1970s, for example, were followed during the mid- to late-1970s by what may be described as the *humanistic–artistic* models of Blumberg (1974) and Eisner (1979). In turn, the *technical–didactic* models advocated by Acheson and Gall (1980) and Hunter (1984) gained ascendancy in the early to mid-1980s and were followed by the *developmental–reflective* models. The latter category arose during the mid-1980s and continued proliferating through the 1990s; it includes models proposed by Glickman (1985), Costa and Garmston (1994), and Zeichner and Liston (1996), among others (Garman, 1986; Waite, 1995). These four families of clinical supervision and the models comprising them differ greatly in the purposes toward which they strive, their relative emphasis on objectivity versus subjectivity, the type of data collected and the procedures for recording it, the number and series of steps or stages involved, the degree of control exercised by the supervisor versus the teacher, and the nature and structure of pre- and postobservation conferences (Pajak, 2000).

What could possibly be the source of so many divergent perspectives on what is essentially a straightforward process involving a preobservation conference, a classroom observation, and a postobservation conference? How can such a multiplicity of models that differ among themselves in fundamental ways conceivably coexist and retain adherents among theorists and school practitioners? More practically, how can anyone sort through this profusion of advice and reasonably decide which version of clinical supervision may actually be appropriate for oneself or for any given situation? A number of supervision scholars have recently suggested that concepts derived from the psychology of Carl Jung may offer a promising perspective for answering these and other questions related to the supervision of instruction (Champagne & Hogan, 1995; Garmston, Lipton, & Kaiser, 1998; Hawthorne & Hoffman, 1998; Norris, 1991; Oja & Reiman, 1998; Shapiro & Blumberg, 1998).

JUNG'S PSYCHOLOGICAL FUNCTIONS

Among many other important discoveries related to conscious and unconscious mental processes, Jung (1971) proposed that people exhibit four psychological functions with respect to their perceptions. Two of these functions, intuition (N) and sensing (S), characterize the way that we gather data about and perceive reality, while another two functions, thinking (T) and feeling (F), refer to the ways that we appraise or judge the reality that is perceived. Although gathering data and making judgments about perceptions are obviously central issues for clinical supervision, Champagne and Hogan (1995) appear to be alone in having applied Jung's formulations to the field in a thorough and systematic way. (Their book includes a useful assessment instrument for determining psychological type and function and speculates about the effect that these mental processes have on both teaching and supervision.) The concept of psychological functions already productively informs other areas of study, including learning styles (Silver, Strong, & Perini, 1997), leadership (Fitzgerald & Kirby, 1997), and organizational dynamics (Hirsch & Kummerow, 1998), all of which have clear relevance for understanding classrooms and schools. It seems worthwhile, therefore, to further explore the implications of Jung's formulations for clinical supervision.

According to Jung (1971), people who draw primarily on *intuition* to collect data and perceive reality prefer exploring and discussing ideas and theories, untried possibilities, and what is new. They easily become bored with specifics, details, data, and facts that are unrelated to concepts. Intuitive people tend to think and communicate with spontaneous leaps of intuition and may omit or neglect details. In contrast, those who draw on the *sensing* function to gather data and perceive reality prefer focusing on what is real, concrete, and tangible in the here and now. They tend to be more concerned with facts and data than with theory and abstractions. Sensing people think and communicate carefully and accurately, referring to and emphasizing facts and details, but may miss seeing the *gestalt*, or big picture.

People who favor *thinking* over feeling when making judgments about the reality that they perceive prefer using evidence, analysis, and logic. They are more concerned with being rational than with empathy, emotions, and values. Thinking types communicate in an orderly and linear manner, emphasizing if–then and cause–effect linkages. On the other hand, those who prefer using *feeling* to guide their judgments do so on the basis of empathy, warmth, personal convictions, and a consistent value system that underlies all their decision processes. They are more interested in people, emotions, and harmony than in logic, analysis, or attaining impersonal goals. Feeling people communicate by expressing personal likes and dislikes, as well as feelings about what is good versus bad and right versus wrong.

Jung (1971) compared the four functions to the points on a compass and suggested that their interplay was just as indispensable as this navigational device for psychological

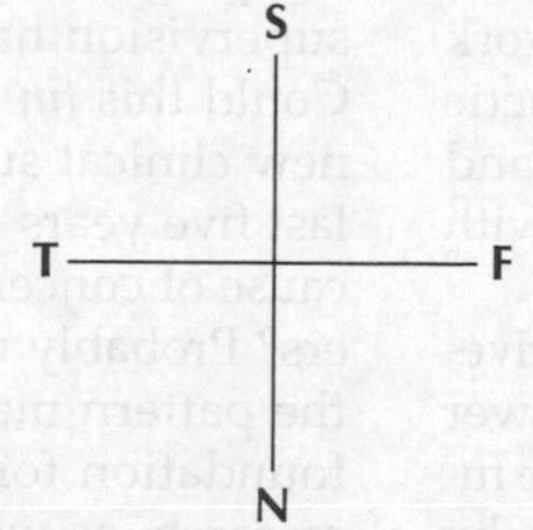

FIGURE 26.2 The Four Functions as Compass Points and the Resulting Combinations Related to Clinical Supervision Families

orientation and discovery. Displaying the functions in a compasslike configuration (see Figure 26.2) highlights the manner in which the two psychological processes of getting information and making decisions interact, resulting in four possible function pairs: sensory–thinking (S–T), sensory–feeling (S–F), intuitive–thinking (N–T), and intuitive–feeling (N–F). These four combinations (bracketed by parentheses in the quadrants illustrated in Figure 26.2) have distinctive effects on how individuals relate to the world. They also appear to correspond well with the four families of clinical supervision described earlier.

People characterized by an intuitive–thinking (N–T) function pair, for example, are concerned with competence and tend to concentrate on the future, ideas, and possibilities. They are guided by theoretical concepts and work by testing hypotheses. N–Ts are likely to consider the big picture and are distressed by what they view as incorrect or faulty principles. This worldview most closely parallels the original clinical models, particularly those of Goldhammer (1969) and Cogan (1973).

In comparison, those individuals who display a sensory–feeling (S–F) combination primarily want to be helpful to others. They focus attention on the present and facts, but are most concerned with people. S–Fs want to provide support and are guided by a sense of service. They work by meeting people's needs and are troubled by conflict and disagreements. An S–F orientation, in turn, would seem to most closely resemble the humanistic–artistic family of models represented by Blumberg (1974) and Eisner (1979).

People possessing a sensory–thinking (S–T) orientation mainly strive to be efficient.

They focus on the present and facts and attend closely to current reality. They prefer to follow established policies and procedures and believe that their work and the work of others is facilitated by having such processes and structures in place. S–Ts want to see results produced and are annoyed when work is done incorrectly. The technical–didactic models of Acheson and Gall (1980) and Hunter (1984) appear to match up well with this perspective.

Finally, people who possess an intuitive-feeling (N–F) combination seek to empower others and are strongly concerned with the future, people, and possibilities. Guided by ideals that they believe are worthy, N–Fs work by expressing and acting on their values. These individuals seek to promote growth and are troubled when values are absent or are viewed as incorrect. The developmental–reflective models, represented by a range of contemporary authors, would seem to be associated with the N–F viewpoint.

Applying the concept of psychological functions in this way illustrates how the four clinical supervision families are related and complement one another despite their obvious differences. Rather than solely expressing the *Zeitgeist* of the decade when it emerged or the worldview of particular authors, each family of models may be viewed as expressing a logic that is complete only in relation to the other three families. Chronologically, the intuitive–thinking qualities of the original clinical supervision models that emerged in the 1960s were mirrored by their psychological opposite, the sensory–feeling orientation of the humanistic–artistic models in the 1970s, following what could be conceived as a sort of Hegelian thesis–antithesis dialectic (Friedrich, 1954). The tension between them was then resolved by a synthesis of the two, which incorporated the sensing and thinking functions of each and resulted in the technical–didactic models that were prominent in the 1980s. This synthesis became a new thesis, in turn, giving rise to its own antithesis, the N–F-oriented developmental–reflective models of the 1990s. This final grouping, thus, rounded out the range of psychological possibilities.

Does this mean that the potential for developing entirely new approaches to clinical supervision has been exhausted? Probably. Could this *fin de siecle* explain the dearth of new clinical supervision models during the last five years or so? Perhaps. Should it be a cause of concern for theorists and practitioners? Probably not. Rather, this completion of the pattern may provide an unprecedented foundation for further theory building and research, as well as a basis for more precise and successful practice.

THE COMMUNICATION WHEEL

Thompson (2000) has recently adapted and applied Jung's concept of psychological functions to the purpose of better understanding and improving communication within organizations. He notes that communication is effective only when information and understanding are passed along accurately from a sender to a receiver. Problems are likely to arise when individuals or groups encode or decode messages differently while trying to communicate with one another. Not all communication problems can be traced to differences in psychological type, he cautions, but communication preferences do serve as filters that influence our perceptions. These perceptions ultimately become the realities to which we all respond.

Of particular relevance and interest to theorists and practitioners of clinical supervision is Thompson's (2000) assertion that attending to psychological functions can enhance the quality of interaction between coaches (i.e., supervisors) and their clients within all types of organizations. He proposes that the functions (S, N, T, and F) can be thought of as four languages that people use when communicating. Thompson further hypothesizes the existence of eight

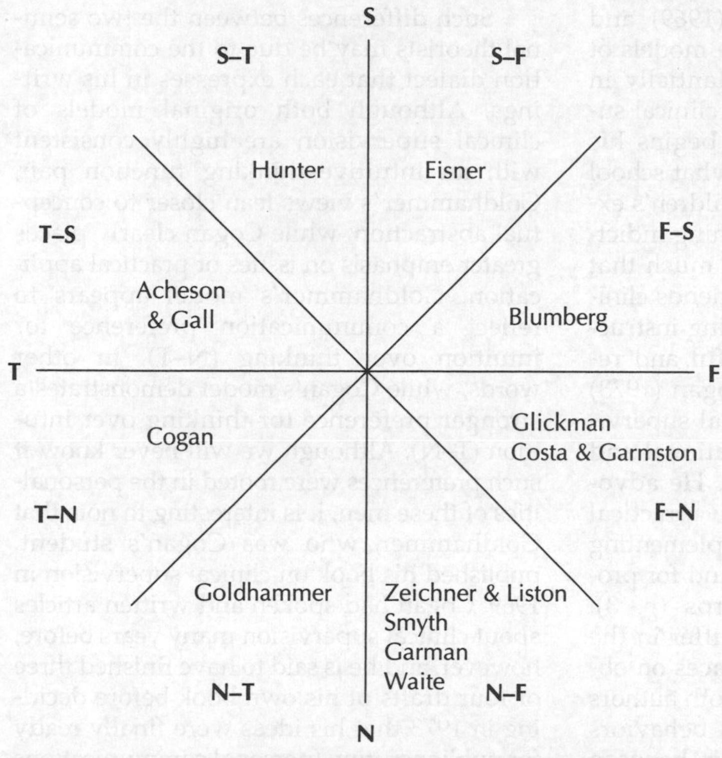

FIGURE 26.3 Models of Clinical Supervision as Communication Dialects

communication dialects (T–N, N–T, S–T, T–S, S–F, F–S, N–F, and F–N), which are determined by whether an individual usually relies more heavily on his or her dominant or auxiliary function. Everyone can use both, but people tend to rely more heavily on their dominant function during times of stress. Drawing on this finer differentiation, the relationship among the various models of clinical supervision can be depicted in terms of these eight communication dialects, as in Figure 26.3.

Communication works best, Thompson (2000) suggests, when both parties speak the same primary language. If they differ, one or the other must adjust or else communication will break down. On the other hand, the better an individual can approximate the language and dialect of others, the more communication should improve. Understanding how psychological type affects communication can be useful for diagnosing causes of communication problems, both interpersonally and in groups. Possible solutions to existing problems can be identified and potential problems in supervisory situations may be avoided entirely by anticipating communication difficulties in advance. In any case, listening for cues about the communication preferences of other people is obviously the key.

By aligning the models of clinical supervision with the function-based communication dialects, fine conceptual distinctions among the models that fall within the various families can be explained (see Figure 26.3). Despite many similarities between the perspectives of Goldhammer (1969) and Cogan (1973), for example, these models of clinical supervision differ substantially in their respective justifications for clinical supervision. Goldhammer (1969) begins his book by "generating images of what school can be like, particularly in the children's experience" (p. 1). He offers a scathing indictment of the meaninglessness of much that occurs in classrooms and recommends clinical supervision as a way of making instruction more consciously purposeful and responsive to students' needs. Cogan (1973) grounds his argument for clinical supervision, in contrast, along organizational and professional development lines. He advocates clinical supervision as a practical means for "disseminating and implementing new practices" more effectively and for professionalizing the teaching corps (p. 3). Cogan and Goldhammer also differ in the relative importance that each places on objective versus subjective issues. Both authors are concerned with observable behaviors and meanings and the relationship between them as expressed in the teacher's unique teaching style. Cogan (1973) urges supervisors to focus attention primarily on teacher behaviors, however, arguing that a change in style will naturally follow if behavior changes: "The proper domain of the clinical supervisor is the classroom behavior of the teacher. That is, the proper subject of supervision is the teacher's classroom behavior, not the teacher as a person" (p. 58). Goldhammer (1969), on the other hand, advocates consideration of how supervisory processes affect the teacher's "ideas and feelings about himself," beyond "substantive technical learning" (p. 133). Supervisors themselves are advised by Goldhammer (1969) to submit their own behavior to "reflexive examination" during the postconference analysis stage (p. 337), intriguingly anticipating the reflective practice associated with the adjacent N–F perspective (see Figure 26.3).

Such differences between the two seminal theorists may be due to the communication dialect that each expresses in his writings. Although both original models of clinical supervision are highly consistent with an intuitive–thinking function pair, Goldhammer's views lean closer to conceptual abstraction, while Cogan clearly places greater emphasis on issues of practical application. Goldhammer's model appears to reflect a communication preference for intuition over thinking (N–T), in other words, while Cogan's model demonstrates a stronger preference for thinking over intuition (T–N). Although we will never know if such preferences were rooted in the personalities of these men, it is interesting to note that Goldhammer, who was Cogan's student, published his book on clinical supervision in 1969. Cogan had spoken and written articles about clinical supervision many years before, however, and he is said to have finished three or four drafts of his own book before deciding in 1973 that his ideas were finally ready for public scrutiny (personal communications with Robert H. Anderson and David W. Champagne). Even then, he referred to his work rather tentatively as a "rationale," apparently anticipating further refinement.

Moving to the technical–didactic family, the approaches to clinical supervision advocated both by Acheson and Gall and by Hunter plainly give voice to a sensory–thinking (S–T) combination (see Figure 26.3). Yet the former carry objective analysis to an extreme. Where Goldhammer had five stages and Cogan had eight phases, Acheson and Gall (1980) propose no less than *thirty-two* discrete behavioral techniques for classroom observation and conferencing, indicating an exceptionally heavy reliance on the thinking function. They contrast their *techniques* with competing texts, noting that other authors "have emphasized theory and research on clinical supervision. Our book is practical in intent. We emphasize the techniques of clinical supervision, the 'nuts and bolts' of how to work with teachers to help them improve their classroom teaching" (p. xiii).

In comparison, Hunter (1984) draws heavily on her personal experience to inform practice and is concerned with obtaining a complete and accurate record, through "script-taping" of everything that is said and done in the classroom by teachers and students. While every bit as linear and rational as Acheson and Gall's approach, Hunter's version requires the clinical supervisor to directly experience and record sensory input, unmediated and unimpeded by observation instruments or mechanical devices. A major advantage of script-taping, she notes, is that "the observer can quickly 'swing' focus from one part of the group to another (something not possible for a camera). This enables an observer to scan and record many parts of the room almost simultaneously" (pp. 185–186). Thus, although both models express an S–T preference, Acheson and Gall place greater emphasis on the thinking function (T–S), whereas Hunter emphasizes sensing (S–T) more heavily.

Blumberg's (1974) model of clinical supervision is highly sensing as well, but, coupled with a dominant feeling function, the primary focus is on people and the quality of their interpersonal relations. As typifies an F–S function pair, Blumberg's model of clinical supervision is built on the assumption that much of the difficulty that teachers and supervisors face in working together stems from behavioral conflicts that originate in the organizational context of schools. Blumberg (1974) advises supervisors to concentrate on issues of trust, affection, and influence that he believes create psychological barriers between teachers and supervisors. He suggests that three conditions must be in place for instructional supervision to be successful: "the teacher must want help, the supervisor must have the resources to provide the kind of help required or know where the resources may be found, and the interpersonal relationships between a teacher and supervisor must enable the two to give and receive in a mutually satisfactory way" (p. 18).

Along with Blumberg, Eisner (1979) eschews following a step-by-step formula, as would be expected of any S–F combination. But Eisner is considerably less concerned with improving interpersonal relations. By relying on personal sensitivities and experiences, Eisner proposes that an instructional supervisor can become the major instrument through which the classroom and its context are perceived and understood. He views clinical supervisors ideally as "connoisseurs" who perceive what is important yet subtle in classroom behavior and who can eloquently describe its essential expressive value. This esthetic aspect of Eisner's (1979) model suggests an affinity with the N–F function pairing, but a closer reading of the process that he outlines indicates a very strong emphasis on visual, auditory, and kinaesthetic sensing accompanied by the subjective feeling function (S–F dialect). That is, a combination of heightened sensing and feeling are critical for informing an artistic appreciation of the teaching act:

> By artistic I mean using an approach to supervision that relies on the sensitivity, perceptivity, and knowledge of the supervisor as a way of appreciating the significant subtleties occurring in the classroom, and that exploits the expressive, poetic, and often metaphorical potential of language to convey to teachers or to others whose decisions affect what goes on in schools, what has been observed. (p. 59)

Finally, the developmental and reflective models, respectively, appear to represent the F–N and N–F communication dialects, as depicted in Figure 32.3. Costa and Garmston's (1994) and Glickman's (1985) versions of clinical supervision place a high premium on both feeling and intuition (F–N), with a focus on facilitating the cognitive growth and decision-making ability of teachers through empathetic understanding and flexible response to teachers' current levels of functioning. Both aim to influence the way that teachers mentally process information and strongly favor abstract over concrete thinking as a goal to pursue. They concentrate primarily on the matter of how supervisors can guide teachers toward conscious understanding and control of their actions in the individual classroom, as well as when working collectively, to attain desirable learning outcomes for students. For example, Glickman (1985) defines "the key to successful schools as instructional supervision that fosters teacher development by promoting greater abstraction, commitment and collective action" (p. 381). Similarly, Costa and Garmston (1994) explain that "cognitive coaching enhances the intellectual capacities of teachers, which in turn produces greater intellectual achievement in students" (p. 6). A major goal of cognitive coaching is "enhancing growth toward *holonomy*," which they define as "individuals acting *autonomously* while simultaneously acting *interdependently* with the group" (p. 3).

Advocates of reflective practice, such as Zeichner and Liston (1987), Garman (1986), Waite (1995), and Smyth (1985), also seek to influence cognitive processes, but their position more closely approximates the value-driven N–F orientation. Accordingly, these authors urge supervisors and teachers to question the hierarchical nature of interpersonal relationships in schools, to raise issues of gender, race, and culture to conscious levels, and to challenge the knowledge embodied in the books, curriculum, lessons, and examinations that are part of schooling. Teachers and supervisors are encouraged to consider those aspects of classrooms and schools (including their own professional identities) that disempower other educators and debilitate students. This potential transformation of schooling is to be fueled by collaborative inquiry and guided by the moral principles of justice and equity.

DISCUSSION AND IMPLICATIONS

Choosing the proper communication style when working with teachers has been a perennial concern in the clinical supervision literature. Although general consensus exists that the process of selecting a communication style should include consideration of the needs of teachers, experts conflict substantively in the specific advice that they offer on this point. Goldhammer (1969), writing from an intuitive–thinking point of view, for example, cautions supervisors to refrain from being overly direct when working with inexperienced teachers lest these teachers become dependent on the supervisor and fail to develop a personal teaching identity. He advises that experienced veterans can more easily tolerate a supervisor's forthrightness and assimilate into their teaching repertoire what seems appropriate to them, without feeling unduly pressured or intimidated. In contrast, Hunter (1984), writing from a sensing–thinking perspective, asserts that a direct communication style is exactly the tonic for inducting newcomers into the teaching profession, because novices are inexperienced and sorely need the expert advice that a supervisor can readily provide. Collaborative communication, she believes, should be reserved for teachers who possess the experience and expertise to engage in dialogue with the supervisor on a more equal footing.

Which of these rationales is correct? Each view seems sound and plausible until the other is considered, because both positions are consistent within their own internal logic. Yet each remains diametrically opposed to the other. Rather than quibble about the *right* way and the *wrong* way to treat teachers with varying levels of experience and expertise on the basis of general principles, an understanding of psychological functions and communication dialects allows us to accept *both—and* a range of other alternatives that may be appropriate under different sets of circumstances. Instead of stereotyping beginning teachers and experienced teachers as being all alike, a *functional* perspective on clinical supervision enables us to see that each situation is defined by the psychological processes of the individuals who happen to be involved in the teacher–supervisor relationship. While this insight greatly complicates things for both supervision theorists and practitioners, it also promises a refinement of our understanding and an improvement of our chances for success by moving us beyond the *direct* versus *indirect* communication controversy.

The application of psychological functions to clinical supervision sheds light on another contemporary issue, as well: shaping the content of communication with teachers on the basis of the hierarchical goals that a supervisor hopes to accomplish. Several authors, all writing from a developmental–reflective perspective, have independently recommended that a supervisor's practice should be guided by whether the object is to improve a teacher's technical competence, conceptual understanding, or sensitivity to issues of an ethical nature (e.g., Grimmett, 1989; Zeichner & Liston, 1996). In each instance, a preference for goals favoring moral sensitivity over technical competence is explicitly stated. A view of clinical supervision that considers psychological functions suggests that this hierarchical device is essentially arbitrary, except from the perspective of those who favor intuition and feeling as ways of perceiving and evaluating reality. A supervisor with a sensing–thinking preference, in contrast, is likely to consider an idealistic and well-intentioned teacher who lacks the skills needed to help students to learn as more problematic than a motivated and technically proficient teacher who expresses little concern for principles of social justice. A view informed by psychological functions suggests, as well, that in addition to technical (S–T), conceptual (N–T), and moral (N–F) considerations, a relational (S–F) dimension of growth is also possible, desirable, and seriously worth considering as an outcome of instruction and supervision. Without questioning the value of moral commitment or more abstract thinking, in other words, the legitimacy and importance of development along other lines for students, teachers, and supervisors become evident.

The major implication of psychological functions for practice, however, is that clinical supervisors ought to interact with teachers in the manner through which the teachers, themselves, learn best. Wiles (2001) reported preliminary findings that Florida teachers who were nominated by their superintendents as "the best" differ from other teachers on a learning styles inventory based on Jung's psychological functions and other measures. The teachers who were nominated as exemplary "tend to be more flexible, more experimental, and more student-centered than the regular population of teachers in Florida" (p. 7). Yet much of what supervisors do, say, and think when they interact with teachers, consciously or unconsciously, is typically determined by their own psychological preferences for perceiving and judging. Indeed, Goldhammer (1969) very clearly anticipated this very point. Until supervisors become conscious of their own preferences and more sensitive to those of teachers, they will inadvertently tend to favor, reward, and reinforce teachers who behave, speak, and think as they do, while misunderstanding and failing to communicate with teachers who differ from themselves.

The bases of a true collegial relationship include trust and a willingness to share and understand personal meanings, understandings, and frames of reference. Clinical supervision should provide support for teachers with an aim toward increasing professional responsibility and openness and the capacity for self-analysis and self-direction. By attending carefully to psychological functions, clinical supervisors can recognize and build on existing strengths. Instead of calling attention to deficits and shortcomings, supervisors can open alternative paths for teachers to reach their professional goals. Teachers can be helped to perfect their uniquely personal teaching styles and also round out their repertoires by developing styles that reflect other modes of thinking. Clinical supervisors should initially be willing to accept each teacher's unique style and enter into dialogue with the assumption that the teacher is professionally competent, even though the two of them may experience and respond to the world very differently. Indeed, tracking teachers according to the supervisor's subjective judgments of their ability is as indefensible as the placing of students into different curriculum tracks according to the teacher's perceptions of their academic aptitude.

Clinical supervisors, no less than teachers, should make a deliberate effort to honor and legitimate perspectives and strategies that are not harmonious with their own preferred tendencies for perceiving and judging reality. That is to say, clinical supervisors should strive to work with teachers in ways that are consistent with how teachers are expected to work with students—by celebrating diversity and responding to that diversity in ways that enhance learning for all.

REFERENCES

Acheson, K. A., & Gall, M. D. (1980). *Techniques in the Clinical Supervision of Teachers* (White Plains, NY: Longman).

Blumberg, A. (1974). *Supervisors and Teachers: A Private Cold War* (Berkeley, CA: McCutchan).

Briggs, K. A., & Myers, I. B. (1977). *Myers–Briggs Type Indicator* (Palo Alto, CA: Consulting Psychologists Press).

Champagne, D. W., & Hogan, R. C. (1995). *Consultant Supervision: Theory and Skill Development*, 3rd Ed. (Wheaton, IL: CH Publications).

Cogan, M. L. (1973). *Clinical Supervision* (Boston: Houghton Mifflin).

Costa, A. L., & Garmston, R. J. (1994). *Cognitive Coaching: A Foundation for Renaissance Schools* (Norwood, MA: Christopher–Gordon).

Eisner, E. W. (1979). *The Educational Imagination: On the Design and Evaluation of Educational Programs* (New York: Macmillan).

Fitzgerald, C., & Kirby, L. (Eds.) (1997). *Developing Leaders: Research and Applications in Psychological Type and Leadership Development* (Palo Alto, CA: Davies–Black).

Friedrich, C. J. (1954). *The Philosophy of Hegel* (New York: Random House).

Garman, N. B. (1986). Reflection, the Heart of Clinical Supervision: A Modern Rationale for Practice. *Journal of Curriculum and Supervision*, *2*(1), 1–24.

Garmston, R. J., Lipton, L. E., & Kaiser, K. (1998). The Psychology of Supervision. In Gerald R. Firth and Edward F. Pajak (Eds.), *Handbook of Research on School Supervision*, pp. 242–286. (New York: Simon & Schuster Macmillan).

Glickman, C. D. (1985). *Supervision of Instruction: A Developmental Approach* (Boston: Allyn and Bacon).

Goldhammer, R. (1969). *Clinical Supervision: Special Methods for the Supervision of Teachers* (New York: Holt, Rinehart & Winston).

Hawthorne, R. D., & Hoffman, N. E. (1998). Supervision in Non-Teaching Professions. In Gerald R. Firth and Edward F. Pajak (Eds.), *Handbook of Research on School Supervision*, pp. 555–580 (New York: Simon & Schuster Macmillan).

Hirsch, S. K., & Kummerow, J. M. (1998). *Introduction to Type in Organizations* (Palo Alto, CA: Consulting Psychologists Press).

Hunter, M. (1984). Knowing, Teaching, and Supervising. In. P. L. Holford (Ed.), *Using What We Know about Teaching* (Alexandria, VA: Association for Supervision and Curriculum Development).

Jung, C. G. (1971). *Psychological Types*. A revision by R. F. C. Hull of the translation by H. G. Baynes. (Princeton, NJ: Princeton University Press).

Keirsey, D. (1998). *Please Understand Me II: Temperament, Character, Intelligence* (Del Mar, CA: Prometheus Nemesis).

Norris, C. J. (1991). Supervising with Style. *Theory Into Practice*, *30* (Spring 1991), 129–133.

Oja, S. N., & Reiman, A. J. (1998). Supervision for Teacher Development across the Career Span.

In Gerald R. Firth and Edward F. Pajak (Eds.), *Handbook of Research on School Supervision*, pp. 463–487 (New York: Simon & Schuster Macmillan).

Pajak, E. F. (2000). *Approaches to Clinical Supervision: Alternatives for Improving Instruction*, 2nd Ed. (Norwood, MA: Christopher–Gordon).

Shapiro, A. S., & Blumberg, A. (1998). Social Dimensions of Supervision. In Gerald R. Firth and Edward F. Pajak (Eds.), *Handbook of Research on School Supervision*, pp. 1055–1084 (New York: Simon & Schuster Macmillan).

Silver, H., Strong, R., & Perini, M. (1997). Integrating Learning Styles and Multiple Intelligences, *Educational Leadership, 55* (September), 22–27.

Smyth, J. W. (1985). Developing a Critical Practice of Clinical Supervision. *Journal of Curriculum Studies, 17* (January–March), 1–15.

Thompson, H. L. (2000). *Introduction to the Communication Wheel* (Watkinsville, GA: Wormhole Publishing).

Waite, D. (1995). *Rethinking Instructional Supervision: Notes on Its Language and Culture* (Washington, DC: Falmer Press).

Wiles, J. (2001). Some of Our Best Teachers. *Wingspan, 13* (March), 4–9.

Zeichner, K. M., & Liston, D. P. (1987). Teaching Student Teachers to Reflect. *Harvard Educational Review, 57* (February), 23–48.

Zeichner, K. M., & Liston, D. P. (1996). *Reflective Teaching: An Introduction* (Mahwah, NJ: Erlbaum).

DISCUSSION QUESTIONS

1. How effective and how collegial have your experiences been with clinical supervision?
2. In your experience, do teachers tend to exhibit the various psychological types described?
3. How could a principal or peer coach apply the concept of psychological functions when working with a teacher?
4. Would understanding and use of psychological types make clinical supervision more collegial? Why or why not?
5. Would understanding and use of psychological types make clinical supervision more effective? Why or why not?

CHAPTER 27

A Role for Technology in Professional Development? Lessons from IBM

FRANK LEVY
RICHARD J. MURNANE

FOCUSING QUESTIONS

1. In what ways can professional development be altered to become more useful? What challenges are faced in making such changes?
2. What is an educator?
3. How can technology aid in training educators?
4. How can corporate training techniques translate to educator training in schools?
5. How does follow-up enhance the training process?
6. In what way can technology be implemented to enhance training programs?

Standards-based accountability systems challenge American educators to accomplish something that has never been done in the nation's history: teaching all children to master a demanding set of skills. The challenge makes sense today because technological changes and outsourcing have left American workers who lack strong skills unable to earn a decent living wage. However, the magnitude of the challenge is frequently underestimated. Working harder will not by itself allow American educators to meet this challenge. Indeed, most already work so hard that burnout is a continual danger. Instead, educators need to learn how to work together more effectively.

Professional development, the primary strategy for improving the effectiveness of educators, has not worked well. As Mike Schmoker has pointed out, too often professional development consists of workshops led by an outside speaker, with little or no follow-up.[1] These efforts do not change how well teachers teach or how effectively children learn. Nor do they improve the quality of administrators' leadership.

One response to the professional development challenge has been to make greater use of technology. Initiatives that use the Internet in professional development include TeachScape, LessonLab, and the Center for Online Professional Education. What role should technology play in professional development? Can it substitute for face-to-face meetings that are expensive and hard to schedule? Can it make face-to-face meetings more valuable? Does it change how meeting time should be spent and require new skills of those who facilitate these meetings?

In this chapter, we describe how IBM answered these questions in the process of revamping its training program for new managers. We then consider how the IBM experience can inform efforts to improve professional development for educators. At this point, readers may well ask, What can educators learn from a profit-making company engaged in a business so different from teaching children? Our answer has three parts.

First, for reasons we explain below, the challenges IBM managers face have much in common with those educators face. We want to be clear that we are using the term *educators* to include teachers as well as school administrators. We see teachers as "managers" in that they are responsible for the well-being and development of a large number of children. In the differentiated staffing models that many school reformers advocate, experienced teachers also serve as mentors and supervisors for beginning teachers.[2] Second, as a technology-based company, IBM has significant expertise in developing and implementing new ways to use computer networks in its training programs. Third, because IBM operates in an extremely competitive industry, it has both a great incentive to design efficient training programs and the freedom to do so.

WHAT INFORMATION TECHNOLOGY CAN AND CANNOT DO

Computers excel at conveying information. Because using information lies at the center of teachers' and administrators' jobs, it makes intuitive sense that networked computers could be valuable in improving the effectiveness of teachers and administrators. Indeed, we believe this is true. Networked computers can improve teachers' and administrators' access to a wide range of potentially useful information, including patterns in student test scores, ideas for lesson plans, and school district rules and strategies for dealing with disruptive students.

Yet, for information to be useful, it needs to be interpreted in context. Suppose in the course of conversation, a friend speaks the word *bill*. How do we interpret it? As a person's first name? As the front end of a duck? As a piece of legislation? As a request for payment? As a piece of currency? The answer depends on the context of the conversation. The same is true for much of the information teachers and administrators receive. Seeing an Internet video of a teacher explaining to third-graders how to write topic sentences may spark useful ideas. However, only by talking with fellow teachers about the strengths and limitations of the lesson and about what happened when each teacher tried it in her or his own classroom will the information result in constructive changes in instruction.

Similarly, accessing the district's network to read the policy for dealing with disruptive students may provide some guidance in dealing with a particular student. However, the rules alone will not be sufficient to tell a teacher or administrator what to do. She will need to learn how to find out why the student misbehaved and the consequences of that misbehavior for the rest of the class. She will have to deal with her own emotions in this situation. Educators learn to do this by practicing and receiving constructive feedback. Computer simulations can be useful in creating opportunities for practice, but they cannot provide the intense learning experiences that discussions of specific cases, role-playing, and other face-to-face activities can.

It follows that designing professional development efforts to improve the skills of educators requires an understanding of what ideas can be conveyed adequately by text and video—and consequently can be transmitted electronically—and what ideas and skills need to be learned through face-to-face interactions. This is the question IBM faced.

THE GENESIS OF BASIC BLUE

Strong management training is part of the IBM tradition. Formerly, novice managers went to the company headquarters in Armonk, New York, for New Managers School, a week of polished lectures on IBM policies and practices. Participants found the week stimulating and worthwhile. Their positive responses reflected the week's content—but also its timing. Managers arrived 4–6 months after their appointment. Their initial experiences had made them well aware of what they did not know. Unfortunately, the timing also meant that they faced their first months of managing with relatively few resources.

During the 1990s, changes at IBM put the New Managers School under pressure not unlike that now placed on U.S. schools. Lou Gerstner, the new chairman hired to turn the company around, soon developed an ambitious training agenda. He wanted IBM managers to learn how to manage in a different way, to become more active in coaching—developing and supporting the skills of the people who reported to them. He knew that managing by following rules would not work in a rapidly changing business environment.

As IBM's management development team faced its new challenge, its options were bounded by two extremes. It could have expanded the face-to-face professional development time in Armonk from one week to, say, three weeks. But tight training budgets ruled out this option immediately.

Alternatively, the team could have put all the relevant material into text, stored it on CDs or on Web pages, and instructed new managers to read it (videos were ruled out because new managers in many locations lacked high-speed connections). We have already seen one objection to this option: The team knew that the skills needed to manage effectively could not be learned by reading text alone. A second objection would have been a lack of accountability. Like teachers, new managers face a stream of daily problems that require immediate attention. Simply giving these managers access to written information was no guarantee they would read the material, much less understand it.

The new training program steered between these extremes. The team responsible for revamping new manager training recognized that much of the material presented in New Managers School was essential rules: IBM's policies governing promotions, leaves, and other aspects of employment. While rules are open to interpretation, their basic substance could be conveyed in text, provided the text was easily accessible and a new manager was given incentives to read it. At the same time, many of the skills needed to manage effectively were too complex to be conveyed in text. They would have to be learned through direct interactions, but even here the proper text could complement face-to-face interactions by defining coaching and similar concepts.

The resulting program, dubbed Basic Blue, was introduced in 1999. It extends through three phases over a full year and covers several times as much material as the earlier New Managers School. The first phase takes about two hours a week over a period of 6 months to complete. All the Phase 1 work is done with text-based training materials downloaded from IBM's intranet site.

Each new manager is placed in a training cohort of 75 individuals who are collectively assigned a Lotus Learning Space, a Web-based collaborative learning tool that allows cohort members to correspond as they tackle the online material. To get new managers' attention, the first two program modules, to be completed in 30 days, cover "keep out of jail" topics, including business conduct and sexual harassment. Each module contains one or more Management Quick Views, short summaries of best-practice strategies for such commonly occurring tasks as running a meeting, conducting an employee evaluation, and coaching an employee. Management Quick Views also contain links to more detailed information. Each module ends with a brief multiple-choice test of mastery to be completed online and sent electronically to an IBM site for scoring. The test is "open book," and a new manager may take it as often as necessary to achieve a passing score. Scores are returned electronically in a few hours.

Several of the modules contain text-based simulations, short cases in which the new manager chooses among alternative responses at several steps of a personal interaction. One simulation explores strategies for coaching a team member who is not performing well in a new position. The simulations contain links to relevant online material and provide instant reactions to the selected responses. In terms of learning by doing, the simulations fall well short of group role-playing and discussion, but they do stimulate thinking about applying IBM policies to situations managers face frequently.

To ensure that managers actually read these modules, the Basic Blue team designed two-way information flows. The same software that scores new managers' tests keeps the management development team informed of the managers' progress. This tracking is crucial. Often, the time new managers budget for online work is taken up dealing with clients' questions instead. Managers who don't keep up receive e-mails and sometimes follow-up phone calls urging them to get back on schedule.

The reward for completing Phase 1 is admission to Phase 2, the week spent at the IBM Learning Center in Armonk. For that week, each cohort is divided into three groups of 25 new managers. Throughout the week, the work of each group is facilitated by an experienced IBM manager who knows the pressures IBM managers face and has learned how to facilitate intense discussions. The facilitator leads the group through a variety of interactive tasks to help them become more aware of their strengths and limitations as managers and to experiment with strategies for improvement. He assures the participants that their performances during the week will not be graded and that reports will not be sent to their managers. In the words of one facilitator, this is a week to "discuss the undiscussable."

REALLOCATING HUMAN EFFORT

There is more to describe about Basic Blue, but it is useful to take a step back to see how computers complement the face-to-face interactions. In designing Basic Blue, IBM's management development team used Web-based technology in five ways:

1. To convey text-based training materials, including company policies and tips on managing the IBM way.
2. To keep track of new managers' progress in studying these materials.
3. To create virtual collaboration forums in which new managers in the same training cohort could discuss training materials and tests.

4. To provide hypertext links to fully documented company policies, providing greater detail than the training course materials.
5. To provide interactive text-based simulations that offer new managers opportunities to apply IBM policies to specific management challenges, such as evaluating and coaching staff members who report directly to them.

TEACHING COMPLEX COMMUNICATION SKILLS

The week at Armonk begins with an exploration of different managerial styles—a topic as complex as, say, teaching strategies, for which text descriptions only scratch the surface. For this reason, much of the teaching and learning comes through role-playing followed by discussion. In one role-playing exercise, Carol Dorsey, a new IBM manager from Atlanta, demonstrated coercion by demanding that an angry employee who might have brought a gun to work (played by another new manager) give her his security badge and leave the building. Carol's performance was compelling, in part, because she had faced a similar situation as a new manager for another company. The other class members watched in rapt silence as the skit unfolded. Their expressions made it clear that they were watching a dress rehearsal of something they could actually face. As the first day at Armonk progresses, the group uses role-playing and discussion to explore other management styles in the context of completing various tasks, such as setting a pace or democratically eliciting team members' views.

The group returns to the subject of management styles later in the week when discussing detailed cases in which it is not clear which management styles are appropriate. The managers identify with the problems—among them a rancorous interaction between an IBM project manager and a client and an employee who might have an alcohol problem. Increasingly, the managers begin to explore how they can elicit information—verbal and nonverbal—that might reveal early signs of trouble. The managers also begin to mention policies they studied in Phase 1. The discussions are sometimes heated, in part because the managers are revisiting decisions they made on their own jobs.

In the middle of the week, the facilitator leads the new managers through assessments of their own management styles, using information that they, their managers, their colleagues, and the people they supervise provided during Phase 1. Because the group has now spent several days examining management styles, understanding one's own tendencies takes on greater importance. Equally important is understanding how others see you and translating this knowledge into ideas for managing more effectively.

FROM KNOWLEDGE TO ACTION

In management as in teaching, behavior change rarely occurs without follow-up. For this reason, one of the final activities in the week requires the new managers to construct "individual development plans" and "organizational action plans." These are detailed descriptions of concrete steps they will take to translate the week's lessons into improvements in their own managing and into enhancements in their team's skills. The new managers share their plans with one another, swapping ideas for improving them.

The individual and organizational plans are a natural transition into Phase 3 of Basic Blue. One part of Phase 3 is another round of online learning, similar to Phase 1. New managers work to develop their skills in such areas as creating strong teams, networking, and making mobile management work. While some of these topics are mandatory, others reflect learning commitments managers made in their individual development plans.

In addition, as part of Phase 3, each new manager is required to schedule meetings with both his or her supervisor and the members of the team he or she leads. In the meeting with team members, the new manager explains the goals for the group and his or her plans to realize these goals. The meeting between the new manager and his or her boss, which takes place 90 days after completion of Phase 2, serves to review progress toward the individual and organizational goals. Completion of this work starts the clock counting down to the next round of professional development, a process of ongoing structured learning that continues as long as the manager is with IBM.

MAKING BASIC BLUE WORK

Face-to-face debate, discussion, and role-playing are central to Basic Blue. However, computers complement these expensive activities by helping participants to learn text-based information outside of class. In the process of making this hybrid model work, the IBM design team learned four lessons.

1. *Know the audience and the curriculum.* To design training that would help new managers to pursue IBM's goals effectively, the team responsible for creating Basic Blue had to understand the problems new managers encountered in trying to manage the "IBM way" as Lou Gerstner had defined it, the skills and knowledge the managers needed to solve these problems, and what aspects of the appropriate curriculum new managers could learn by reading Web-based text and which parts required face-to-face interactions.
2. *Get the right mix of teaching skills.* The content of the curriculum dictated the requirements for instructors. The team had first thought that Basic Blue could use the instructors who had lectured in the New Managers School. It soon learned otherwise: Facilitating rich discussions of management issues required different skills from those needed to lecture about company policies. In Basic Blue, the facilitator needed to know how to guide intense discussions among very different people who worked in a variety of settings. Instead of searching for experts on particular company policies, the management development team recruited individuals who had IBM management experience and were interested in spending two years working with new managers. It then helped the interested managers to strengthen their facilitation skills.
3. *Get the technology right.* Basic Blue was designed for new IBM managers all over the world, many of whom access the Web via telephone modems rather than high-speed fiber-optic cables. Faced with this problem, the management development team could have placed the curriculum on CDs, but it rejected this approach because frequent curriculum revisions would be required in response to both weaknesses identified by program participants and changes in company policies—the subject of much of the online curriculum. The Web-based approach made it possible to give all users immediate access to curriculum revisions. The team also learned that the technology had to include the ability to track student progress.
4. *Create the right incentives.* When the management development team launched Basic Blue, it assumed a good curriculum and the chance to come to Armonk would be incentive enough for new managers to devote two hours each week to completing the learning tasks. It soon learned that job pressures caused many new managers to fall behind. The team adopted a variety of tactics to keep the new managers working at the Phase 1 tasks, including using the tracking system

to trigger e-mails and telephone calls to spur on lagging managers.

Incentives are also required in Phase 3, when knowledge is turned into performance. The Basic Blue curriculum focuses directly on the skills managers need to manage effectively. But even the best training can be ineffective as people, confronted with the stress of their jobs, fall back into familiar habits. The requirement to design an individual development plan and an organizational action plan is intended to focus the new manager's attention on concrete goals and the steps needed to reach them. The required Phase 3 meetings with supervisors and team members make visible the commitments of Basic Blue participants to translate new learning into new behavior.

FROM IBM TO THE CLASSROOM

In many respects, the work of teachers and administrators is very different from that of IBM managers. For example, K–12 educators are responsible for helping all clients (children) succeed, not just those who can pay the bill. However, despite many differences between the work educators and IBM managers do, the lessons from IBM shed light on opportunities for improving professional development for educators.

Before turning to the applicability of these lessons, let's consider some of the factors that hinder the creation of effective professional development for teachers and administrators. One is a lack of time. For most teachers and administrators, the school day is filled with pressing responsibilities to children. It is difficult in most schools to find opportunities for teachers to watch one another work with children and then to work collaboratively to improve instruction.

A second problem is a lack of capacity. Under the pressure of standards-based education reforms, schools are introducing new curricula, especially in mathematics, that require instructional methods quite different from the ones teachers are familiar with. Many schools lack resource people who know a new curriculum well and can demonstrate how to teach it effectively.

A third problem is the information deluge. Educators do their work in highly regulated environments. They need to follow a variety of policies and rules—for example, how to place and teach English-language learners, how to create Individualized Education Programs for learning-disabled students, and what disciplinary steps they may take with a misbehaving student. The policies and rules that govern educators' work often change. As a result, considerable time that could be devoted to improving instruction is spent listening to descriptions of new rules and policies. With this context in mind, we turn to the lessons from IBM.

1. *Know the audience and the curriculum.* In many school districts, teachers and administrators spend much of the first days back at school after the summer vacation listening to descriptions of new policies. This is typically not an effective use of time, both because educators don't remember what they hear and because the limited time together has more valuable uses. Posting the new information on a Web site and asking educators to answer questions online about the new policies would free up professional development time. The obligation to respond to the online questionnaire would also help educators to learn where to look for the information when they need it.

   Just as IBM used collaborative learning tools to help busy new managers communicate with their peers, these same tools can enable educators to share ideas and information about curriculum and teaching strategies. Technology can also allow teachers to view from home demonstrations of the teaching of new curricula or videos of a colleague teaching a particular topic. By themselves, these activities will not result in improved instruction. However, they can provide busy educators with ideas and bring up questions that will catalyze focused conversations about how to improve instruction. In other words, technology can increase the effectiveness of the time educators spend in face-to-face interactions. However, technology cannot substitute for the development of face-to-face learning communities.

2. *Get the right mix of teaching skills.* Just as IBM learned that the lecturers in its New Managers School could not function effectively as facilitators of intense conversations among new managers in Basic Blue, schools that change the format of professional development are likely to confront the same problem. Consider the consequences of changing the format of beginning-of-the-year professional development.

   In preparation for the first day back to work, school principals are asked to read online the district's new policy for evaluating teachers' instructional strengths and weaknesses, watch a 30-minute video of a teacher providing mathematics instruction, write an evaluation of the instruction following the new guidelines, and submit this evaluation electronically. Then on the first morning back to work, principals meet in small groups, read one another's evaluations, watch segments of the video, and then discuss the evaluations that they wrote. The goal of the session is to use the advice of their colleagues to revise their evaluations. After lunch, the principals role-play the meeting they would have with the teacher in the video, explaining the points in the evaluation and helping the teacher develop a plan to improve the weak aspects of his or her instruction. It seems unlikely that many central office officials accustomed to explaining the district's teacher evaluation policies each August would know how to effectively facilitate the intense face-to-face interactions that the new format would produce.

3. *Get the technology right.* Whether it is software to provide school-based educators with information on student test results, videos of classroom instruction, or descriptions of state learning standards, most busy K–12 educators will use the electronic tools only if the technology works reliably on the computer they typically use, most often their home computer. Many efforts to use technology for training fall by the wayside because insufficient attention is paid to ensuring that members of the learning community using computers of different vintages and running different operating systems can access the relevant information reliably.

4. *Create the right incentives.* Most K–12 educators want to improve their skills, just as new managers at IBM do. However, like the new IBM managers, teachers are often sidetracked by unexpected demands of jobs and families. As a result, investments in professional development will result in improved teaching and learning only if time is set aside in the school schedule for the face-to-face interactions necessary for improving instruction. Just as critical are incentives for educators to prepare for the face-to-face sessions and to translate the professional development initiatives into instructional change. Getting the incentives right is not easy. However, facing the incentive problem is just as important when working with educators as it is when working with IBM managers.

SUMMING UP

The four lessons that the developers of Basic Blue learned are not new to K–12 educators or to groups developing online professional development tools for an audience of educators.

However, they are easy to forget, especially given the pressures to improve instruction rapidly and the difficulty of creating time in the school schedule for educators to work together on improving instruction.

The lure of substituting technology for face-to-face interactions can be great. Realizing that these same lessons held for IBM, a company with enormous technical expertise and with the resources to apply technology intensively to solve its training problems, may help K–12 educators to remember their importance. Keeping in mind what computers are good at and what they are not good at will be critical to using technology in ways that will help K–12 educators meet the unprecedented challenge of preparing all students to meet high learning standards.

ENDNOTES

1. Michael Schmoker, *Phi Beta Kappan*, February 2004, pp. 424–432.
2. See, for example, Vivian Troen and Katherine C. Boles, *Who's Teaching Your Children?* (New Haven, CT: Yale University Press, 2003).

DISCUSSION QUESTIONS

1. **Are you convinced that technology can be a useful tool for improving professional development opportunities for teachers?**
2. **What advantages or disadvantages arise from thinking of teachers as "managers"?**
3. **What are the author's specific recommendations for improving professional development in schools?**
4. **Can models developed in the business world translate successfully to the world of education?**
5. **What would have to change in your school to make the approach to professional development, described in this chapter, work successfully?**

CHAPTER 28

Instructional Insensitivity of Tests: Accountability's Dire Drawback

W. JAMES POPHAM

FOCUSING QUESTIONS

1. Describe what is meant by instructional sensitivity.
2. What role do judgmental evidence and empirical evidence play in determining instructional sensitivity of assessments?
3. Identify and describe the four dimensions used to evaluate an assessment.
4. Why is it important to evaluate the instructional insensitivity of an assessment?
5. Who should be involved in evaluating the instructional sensitivity of an assessment? Explain.

ABSTRACT

If we plan to use tests for purposes of accountability, we need to know that they measure traits that can be influenced by instruction. Mr. Popham offers a model procedure for judging our tests.

LARGE-SCALE accountability tests have become increasingly important. They influence the deliberations of policy makers and affect the day-by-day behaviors of teachers in their classrooms. The premise underlying the use of these accountability tests is that students' test scores will indicate the quality of instruction those students have received. If students score well on accountability tests, we conclude that those students have been well taught.

Conversely, if students score poorly on accountability tests, we believe that those students have been poorly taught.

Furthermore, advocates of these tests make two assumptions: 1) that teachers who realize they are going to be judged by their students' test scores will try to do a better instructional job and 2) that higher-level authorities can take action to bolster the quality of instruction in schools or districts where test results indicate ineffective instruction is taking place. For either of these assumptions to make sense, the accountability tests being employed must actually be able to determine the effect of instruction on students' test scores. However, all but a few of the accountability tests now having such a profound impact on our nation's schools are instructionally insensitive. That is, they are patently unsuitable for use in any sensible educational accountability program.

INSTRUCTIONAL SENSITIVITY

A test's instructional sensitivity represents the degree to which students' performances on that test accurately reflect the quality of the instruction that was provided specifically to promote students' mastery of whatever is being assessed. In other words, an instructionally sensitive test would be capable of distinguishing between strong and weak instruction by allowing us to validly conclude that a set of students' high test scores are meaningfully, but not exclusively, attributable to effective instruction. Similarly, such a test would allow us to accurately infer that a set of students' low test scores are meaningfully, but not exclusively, attributable to ineffective instruction. In contrast, an instructionally insensitive test would not allow us to distinguish accurately between strong and weak instruction.

Students' performances on most of the accountability tests currently used are more heavily influenced by the students' socioeconomic status (SES) than by the quality of teachers' instructional efforts. That is, such instructionally insensitive accountability tests tend to measure the SES composition of a school's student body rather than the effectiveness with which the school's students have been taught.

Instructionally insensitive tests render untenable the assumptions underlying a test-based strategy for educational accountability. How can the prospect of annual accountability testing ever motivate educators to improve their instruction once they've realized that better instruction will not lead to higher test scores? How can officials accurately intervene to improve instruction on the basis of low test scores if those low scores really aren't a consequence of ineffective instruction?

There is ample evidence that, instead of improving instructional quality, ill-conceived accountability programs can seriously diminish it. Teachers too often engage in a curricular reductionism and give scant, if any, instructional attention to content not assessed by accountability tests. Too often teachers impose excessive test-preparation drills on their students and thereby extinguish the genuine joy those students should experience as they learn. And too often, we hear of teachers or administrators disingenuously portraying students' test scores as improved when, in fact, no actual improvement has taken place.

Yet, while the distinction between instructionally sensitive and insensitive accountability tests may be readily understandable and the classroom consequences of using instructionally insensitive accountability tests are all too apparent, it accomplishes little when educators complain, even profusely, about policy makers' reliance on the wrong kinds of accountability tests. Educators who simply carp about accountability tests are usually seen as individuals eager to escape evaluation. Only when we can convincingly demonstrate that an accountability program is relying on instructionally insensitive tests will we be able to remedy the current absurdity. Clearly, we need a credible procedure to determine the instructional sensitivity of a given accountability test.

This article describes the main features of a practical procedure for ascertaining the instructional sensitivity of any test, whether it is already in use or is under development. Because the instructional sensitivity of an accountability system's tests is the dominant determinant of whether that system helps or harms students, this approach should be used widely. Although the chief ingredients of the approach are described here, devils hide in details, and thus, a more detailed description of the procedures is available from wpopham@ucla.edu or at www.ioxassessment.com.

GATHERING EVIDENCE

There are two main categories of evidence for determining the instructional sensitivity of an accountability test: judgmental evidence and empirical evidence. Judgmental evidence can be collected by using panels of trained judges to rate specified attributes of a test. Empirical evidence can be provided by students' actual test scores, but these test scores must be collected under specific conditions—for instance, by comparing differences between the test scores of "taught" and "untaught" students.

"Whether" the instructional sensitivity of a test is determined by reliance on judgmental evidence alone, empirical evidence alone, or a combination of both, instructional sensitivity should be conceived of as a continuum rather than a dichotomy. Rarely will one encounter an accountability test that is totally sensitive or insensitive to instruction. The task facing anyone who wishes to determine an accountability test's instructional sensitivity is to arrive at a defensible estimate of where that test falls on such a continuum.

For practical reasons, the chief evidence to be routinely gathered about a test should be judgmental, not empirical. If resources permit, empirical studies should be used to confirm the extent to which judgmental data are accurate. But in today's busy world of education, the collection of even judgmental evidence regarding instructional sensitivity would be an improvement. The assembly of confirmatory empirical evidence is desirable but not absolutely necessary when embarking on an appraisal of an accountability test's instructional sensitivity. A number of key test-appraisal procedures currently rely only on judgment-based approaches, for instance, studies focused on content-related evidence of validity are based on judges' reviews of a test's items.

There is nothing sacrosanct about the kinds of judgmental evidence for appraising instructional sensitivity or how to go about assembling such evidence. One practical method is to create panels of 15 to 20 curriculum specialists and teachers who are knowledgeable about the content. If the results of an instructional sensitivity review are to be released to the public, it is sensible to include several noneducators as panelists for the sake of credibility.

After receiving ample orientation and training, panelists would use 10-point scales to rate the tests on four evaluative dimensions. For each evaluative dimension, panelists would be given a rubric that contains sufficient explanatory information and, as necessary, previously judged exemplars so that all panelists would use similar evaluative perspectives.

Panelists could use a variety of procedures for their tasks. But most likely their procedures would be similar to either the iterative models that have been commonly employed in setting standards for the past couple of decades or the judgmental methods used in recent years to ascertain the alignment between a state's accountability tests and the content standards those tests are ostensibly assessing. In both of those approaches, panelists typically make individual judgments and then share them with the entire panel. After that, an open discussion of panelists' judgments occurs, followed by another set of individual judgments. As many iterations of this procedure are carried out as are necessary for the group to reach a consensus. Another method uses the average of the panelists' final ratings as the overall judgment.

The four evaluative dimensions that should be used are 1) the number of curricular aims assessed, 2) the clarity of assessment targets, 3) the number of items per assessed curricular aim, and 4) the instructional sensitivity of items. As noted above, panelists would be given sufficient information to allow them to rate each dimension on a 10-point scale. Then the four separate ratings would be combined to arrive at an overall rating of a test's instructional sensitivity. Those who are designing an instructional sensitivity review need to determine whether to assign equal weight to each of the four dimensions or to assign different weights to each dimension.

NUMBER OF CURRICULAR AIMS ASSESSED

Experience makes it all too clear that teachers cannot realistically focus their instruction on large numbers of curricular aims. In many states, lengthy lists of officially approved curricular aims often oblige teachers to guess about what will be assessed on a given year's accountability tests. More often than not, there are far too many "official" curricular aims to be tested in the available testing time (or, in truth, to be taught in the available teaching time). After a few years of guessing incorrectly, many teachers simply abandon any reliance on the state's sanctioned curricular aims. If an accountability test is to be genuinely sensitive to the impact of instruction, all teachers should be pursuing the same curricular aims, not teacher-divined subsets of those aims.

Clearly, therefore, one evaluative dimension to be considered when determining an accountability test's instructional sensitivity should be the number of curricular aims assessed by the test. Note that there is no reference here to the worth of those curricular aims. Obviously, the worth of a set of curricular aims is extremely important, but the appraisal of that worth should be a separate, albeit indispensable, activity. A test's instructional sensitivity is not dependent on the grandeur of the curricular aims being measured.

To evaluate the number of curricular aims assessed, it is necessary to deal with those curricular aims at a grain size (that is, degree of breadth) that meshes with teachers' day-to-day or week-to-week instructional decisions. Evaluators must be wary of aims that are too large. If the grain size of a curricular aim is so large that it prevents a teacher from devising activities sensibly targeted toward that curricular aim, then the curricular aim's grain size is too broad. For example, some states have very general sets of "content standards," such as "measurement" or "algebra" in mathematics. This grain size is much too large for panelists to make sense of when using this evaluative dimension. Instead, a panelist's focus needs to be on the smaller curricular aims typically subsumed by more general standards. These smaller curricular aims are often labeled "benchmarks," "indicators," "objectives," or something similar.

The rubric for this evaluative dimension should be organized around a definition in which higher ratings would be given to a set of curricular aims whose numbers would be regarded by teachers as easily addressed in the instructional time available. In other words, if teachers have enough instructional time to teach students to achieve all of the curricular aims to be assessed, panelists would give the highest ratings. In contrast, lower ratings would be given to sets of curricular aims regarded as too numerous to teach in the available instructional time, because teachers would be uncertain about which of the aims would be assessed on a given year's accountability test.

CLARITY OF ASSESSMENT TARGETS

The second evaluative dimension revolves around the degree to which teachers understand what they are supposed to be teaching. If teachers have only a murky idea of what constitutes the knowledge or skills they are supposed to be teaching—as exemplified by what's measured on an accountability test—then those teachers will often end up teaching the wrong things. Thus an instructionally sensitive accountability test should be accompanied by descriptive information that describes not only the types of items eligible to be used on the test but, more important, the essence of the skills or knowledge the test will be measuring. If teachers have a clear understanding of what's to be measured, then their instructional efforts can be directed toward those skills and bodies of knowledge rather than toward specific test items. A test consisting of items that measure instructional targets that teachers understand is surely more apt to accurately measure the degree to which those targets have been hit.

The manner in which an accountability test describes what it's supposed to be measuring can, of course, vary considerably. Sometimes state officials supply no descriptive information beyond the curricular aims themselves. In other instances, a state's educational authorities provide explicit assessment descriptions intended to let the state's teachers know what's to be measured by the state's accountability tests. And, of course, there are many other ways of describing what's to be assessed by an accountability test. Thus, in carrying out a judgmental appraisal of an accountability test's descriptive clarity, the material under review should be whatever descriptive information is readily available to teachers. If this turns out to be only the state's official curricular aims, then that's the information to be used when panelists render their judgments about this second dimension of instructional sensitivity. If a state's tests have more detailed assessment descriptions, then this is the information to use. The descriptive information to be reviewed by panelists must be routinely accessible to teachers, not hidden in the often fugitive technical reports associated with an accountability test.

The rubric for this evaluative dimension should emphasize the teachers' likely understanding of the nature of the skills and knowledge to be assessed. Higher ratings would be supplied when panelists believe teachers can readily comprehend what's to be assessed well enough to design appropriate instructional activities.

Ideally, before ratings on this evaluative dimension are collected, a separate data-gathering activity would be carried out in which a half-dozen or so teachers are first given copies of whatever materials are routinely available that describe the accountability test's assessment targets, are asked to read them carefully, and then are directed to put that descriptive information away. Next, in their own words and without reference to the previously read descriptive material, the teachers would be asked to write, independently, what they understood to be the essence of each skill or body of knowledge to be assessed. The degree to which such independently written descriptions are homogeneous would then be supplied to the panelists before they render a judgment. This information would supply panelists with an idea of just how much ambiguity appears to be present in the test's descriptive materials. Although not necessary, this optional activity would clearly strengthen the conclusions reached by the panel.

ITEMS PER ASSESSED CURRICULAR AIM

The third evaluative dimension on which an accountability test's instructional sensitivity can be judged deals with whether there are enough items on a test to allow teachers (as well as students and students' parents) to determine if each assessed curricular aim has been satisfactorily achieved. The rationale for this evaluative factor is straightforward. If teachers can't tell which parts of their instruction are working and which parts aren't, they'll be unable to improve ineffectual instructional segments for future students. Moreover, if there are too few items to determine a student's status with respect to, say, a specific skill in mathematics, then a student (or the student's parents) can't tell whether additional instruction appears to be needed on that skill. Similarly, if teachers are given meaningful information regarding their incoming students' skills and knowledge at the beginning of a school year, then more appropriately tailored instruction can be provided for those new students. Although not strictly related to a test's instructional sensitivity, the reporting of students' status on each curricular aim can transform an instructionally sensitive test into one that is also instructionally supportive.

The number of items necessary to arrive at a reasonably accurate estimate of a student's mastery of a particular assessed skill or body of knowledge depends, of course, on the curricular aim being measured. Broad curricular aims require more items than do narrower ones. Thus the number of items on a given test might vary for the different curricular aims to be measured. Panelists need to make their ratings on this evaluative dimension by reviewing the general pattern of a test's distribution of items per assessed curricular aim after taking into consideration the particular outcomes being assessed.

The rubric to appraise this evaluative dimension should take into account the number and representativeness of the sets of items being used. Panelists would first be asked to review any materials describing what the test is supposed to measure, then consider the degree to which a designated collection of items satisfactorily provides an estimate of a test-taker's achievement. High ratings would reflect both excellent content representativeness and sufficient numbers of items. In other words, to get a high rating on this evaluative dimension, there would need to be enough items to assess a given skill or body of knowledge, and those items would need to satisfactorily sample the key components of the skill or knowledge being measured. Low ratings would be based on too few items, insufficient representativeness of the items, or both.

ITEM SENSITIVITY

The fourth and final evaluative dimension is the degree to which the items on the test are judged to be sensitive to instructional impact. The panelists must either be able to render judgments themselves on a substantial number of actual items from the test or have access to item-by-item judgments rendered by others. In either scenario, the item reviewers must make judgments, one item at a time, about a sufficiently large number of actual items so that a defensible conclusion can be drawn about the instructional sensitivity of a test. Sometimes, because of test-security considerations, these judgments may be made in controlled situations by individuals other than the regular panelists. Ideally, the panelists would personally review a test's items one at a time.

There are three aspects of this evaluative dimension that, in concert, can allow panelists to arrive at a rating of a test's item sensitivity. First, three separate judgments need to be rendered about each item. These judgments might take the form of Yes, No, or Not Sure and would be made in response to three questions:

1. *SES influence.* Would a student's likelihood of responding correctly to this item be determined mostly by the socioeconomic status of the student's family?
2. *Inherited academic aptitudes.* Would a student's likelihood of responding

correctly to this item be determined mostly by the student's innate verbal, quantitative, or spatial aptitudes?

3. *Responsiveness to instruction.* If a teacher has provided reasonably effective instruction related to what's measured by this item, is it likely that a substantial majority of the teacher's students will respond correctly to the item?

An instructionally sensitive item should receive a flock of No responses for the first two questions and a great many Yes responses for the third question. For each item, then, the reviewers' judgments indicating the degree to which the item is instructionally sensitive would be reported on all three of these questions. Then the panel would use the per-item data to arrive at a judgment on the test as a whole.

It should be noted that many current accountability tests, especially those constructed along traditional psychometric lines, contain numerous items closely linked to students' SES or to their inherited academic aptitudes. This occurs because the mission of traditional achievement tests is to permit comparisons among test-takers' scores. In order for those comparisons to work properly, however, there must be a reasonable degree of score spread in students' tests scores. That is, students' test results must be meaningfully different so that fine-grained contrasts between test-takers are possible. Because students' SES and inherited academic aptitudes are both widely dispersed variables, and ones that do not change rapidly, test items linked to either of these variables efficiently spread out students' test scores. Accordingly, builders of traditional achievement tests often end up putting a considerable number of such items into their tests, including those tests used for accountability purposes.

To the extent that accountability tests measure what students bring to school rather than what they are taught there, the tests will be less sensitive to instruction. It is true, of course, that SES and inherited academic aptitudes are themselves substantially interrelated. However, by asking panelists to recognize that either of those variables, if pervasively present in an accountability test, will contaminate the test's ability to gauge instructional quality, we have a reasonable chance to isolate the magnitude of such contaminants.

INSTRUCTIONAL SENSITIVITY REVIEWS

The vast majority of today's educational accountability tests are fundamentally insensitive to instructional quality. If these tests cannot indicate whether students' scores are affected by the quality of a teacher's instruction, then they prevent well-intentioned accountability programs from accomplishing what their architects had hoped. If educators find that the quality of their instructional efforts is being determined by students' scores on accountability tests that are inherently incapable of detecting effective instruction, they should take steps to review the tests' instructional sensitivity. The judgmental procedures set forth here provide the framework for a practical process for carrying out such a review.

If the review of an accountability test reveals it to be substantially sensitive to instruction, then it is likely that other test-influenced elements of the accountability program are acceptable. However, if a review indicates that an accountability program's tests are instructionally insensitive, then two courses of action seem warranted. First, there should be a serious attempt made to replace the instructionally insensitive tests with those that are sensitive to instruction. If that replacement effort fails, it is imperative to inform the public, and especially education policy makers, that the accountability tests being used are unable to detect successful instruction even if it is present. In that case it is particularly important to involve noneducators as review panelists so that the public does not see the instructional sensitivity review as the educators' attempt to escape accountability. Parents and members of the business community can be readily trained to function effectively as members of an instructional sensitivity panel.

An evaluation of the instructional sensitivity of the nation's accountability tests is long overdue. We must discover whether the key data-gathering tools of the accountability movement have been claiming to do something they simply cannot pull off.

DISCUSSION QUESTIONS

1. With the emphasis on high stakes testing, how important is it to determine the instructional sensitivity of an assessment?
2. How important is it that teachers be involved in the evaluation of assessments? Explain.
3. If a test is determined to be instructionally insensitive what should the course of action be?
4. Can the four dimension of evaluation be modified to examine classroom made tests and assessments? Explain how evaluation of teacher-made assessments might look?
5. Do you agree with the authors about the importance of including non-educators in the evaluation process? Explain.

CHAPTER 29

Diagnosing School Decline

DANIEL L. DUKE

FOCUSING QUESTIONS

1. What are some signs that a school is in decline?
2. What factors lead to school decline?
3. How can school decline be counteracted?
4. How is a school in decline different from a chronically low-performing school?
5. What is the purpose in identifying schools that are in decline?

When we run a fever, we suspect that something is wrong with our bodies—a virus perhaps or a bacterial infection. The elevated temperature is a symptom of a deeper problem, though left untreated it can become a cause for additional problems. Such is the case with scores on standardized tests. If test scores start to drop, that may be an indication of deeper problems. Left unaddressed, declining test scores can become the cause of other problems, both for individual students and for entire schools.

Researchers know a great deal about how to improve schools, but they have spent less time trying to understand what causes schools to decline in the first place.[1] One probable reason for the scarcity of research is the reluctance of declining schools to place themselves under the microscope. Here I argue that knowing the possible causes of school decline, especially an initial drop in performance, is critical for educators who want to intervene early. Failing to nip student achievement problems in the bud can set into motion a dangerous downward spiral in which every downturn triggers new problems and accelerates the school's rate of decline.[2]

Of course, some low-performing schools do not experience decline, because they have never performed well. My focus here is on schools that once were characterized by adequate or even good performance but have begun to slip. A number of these schools have participated over the past four years in the University of Virginia's School Turnaround Specialist Program (STSP). This unique outreach program combines the talents of experienced educators and faculty members from the Curry School of Education and the Darden Graduate School of Business

Administration. The goal is to train principals to be school turnaround specialists and to support them in their efforts to reverse a downward trend in school performance.

As research director for the STSP, I have spent the past four years working with a team of researchers to understand the circumstances that confront these school turnaround specialists and to discover how they deal with them. This knowledge, combined with what we know from previous investigations of school decline, has led us to identify a number of potential indicators of school decline. By attending to these indicators when they first surface, educators are more likely to prevent a school from slipping into a self-perpetuating downward spiral.

The approach I take here may best be characterized as a challenge-and-response analysis. Schools face challenges from time to time. Among the challenges associated with school decline, I want to focus on four that are common: serious budget cuts, new state and federal mandates, the loss of key personnel, and an influx of at-risk students.[3] Strictly speaking, these challenges do not cause schools to decline, but decline is a consequence of failing to address these challenges effectively. In medicine, specialists in iatrogenic medicine study medical problems created or exacerbated by improper medical practice. Education needs an equivalent enterprise devoted to examining the academic problems created or exacerbated by inadequate educational practice.

Problems in addressing challenges can be found at the levels of the individual, the group, and the school. Individual teachers may fail to recognize when particular students need help, or they may prescribe a "treatment" that actually makes matters worse. Groups of educators may invest more energy in diverting blame for low performance than in correcting problems, thereby delaying much-needed reforms. School leaders may fail to recognize systemic issues that undermine a school's ability to raise achievement. In some cases, these failures are ones of omission. Nothing is done to address a challenge. In other cases, the problem is a failure of commission. Actions are taken, but they are inadequate or inappropriate.

Here I want to identify 11 early indicators of school decline that are associated with inadequate and inappropriate responses to the aforementioned quartet of challenges.[4] I should note that these challenges sometimes travel in packs. New mandates, for example, may cause some veteran educators to retire or seek other employment. An influx of at-risk students without an increase in funding may have the effect of reducing resources.

Undifferentiated assistance. One indicator of school decline is the absence of systematic efforts to identify the learning problems and knowledge deficits of struggling students who have not been placed on an IEP (individualized education program). Instead of providing assistance that targets each student's specific issues, the school assigns all students judged to be in academic difficulty to a common supplementary program or intervention. Help takes the form of repetition and extended practice. Some students, however, may require assistance that targets particular learning problems, such as problems with decoding, comprehension, sequencing, and information processing. Repetition and extended practice are of little benefit to these students.

Another problem with generic interventions is that students may be compelled to cover material that they already understand, as well as material that they do not understand. Valuable time is wasted, and the risk of students' becoming bored increases. Furthermore, if students receive assistance at the same time that their classmates are moving ahead in the curriculum, the initial problem is compounded because the struggling students fall further behind.

Inadequate monitoring of progress. One reason why assistance may be undifferentiated is the absence of efforts to systematically monitor student progress in learning required content. All states, in order to comply with their own accountability mandates as well as the federal No Child Left Behind (NCLB) Act, test students annually on state curriculum standards. Teachers are provided with pacing guides in many school systems to ensure that they cover all of the curriculum requirements for which their students are responsible. In an effort to cover this content, however, some teachers feel that they cannot take time to carefully assess student progress on a regular basis. As a consequence, students may go weeks or even months without grasping key concepts and skills. In certain subjects, such as mathematics, the result can be disastrous.

Schools that have successfully combated decline often discover efficient ways to monitor student progress and provide differentiated assistance. Training in classroom assessment and the use of periodic benchmark testing aligned to state curriculum standards enable teachers to spot student deficits and provide timely and targeted assistance. Waiting until students take end-of-year standardized tests to identify learning deficits is a sure prescription for performance problems.

Unadjusted daily schedule. Another reason that students may not receive timely and targeted assistance is the inflexibility of the daily school schedule. In order to address content-related problems and skill deficits, teachers need to work with students during times other than regular class periods. It is typically of little value for students to receive help while their classmates are moving forward with new material. Low-performing schools that have turned around often modify the daily schedule in ways that provide struggling students with extended learning time. Sometimes these schools offer double-block classes in core subjects like language arts and mathematics so that low-achieving students can receive an additional period of instruction during the regular school day. In other cases, the school day is lengthened on certain days to provide students who need help with supplementary instruction.

A modified schedule also makes it possible for teachers working as a team to meet during the regular school day. Meetings allow for collaborative planning, curriculum alignment, professional development, and discussions of students experiencing problems. Schedules that do not facilitate teacher collaboration increase the likelihood of communication and coordination problems, thereby contributing to school decline.

Alignment problems. In the wake of pressure for greater accountability, states have adopted curriculum standards and standardized tests based on these standards. Students stand the best chance of mastering the standards and performing well on the state tests when their teachers align class content with state standards and tests. A decline in student achievement may reflect the fact that teachers are neglecting required content.

One indicator of instructional neglect can be found in an analysis of student answers on standardized tests. Results on state tests often can be broken down by specific curriculum standards. When student errors are randomly distributed, the problem may be traceable to variations in how individual students prepared for the tests. When lots of students miss the same questions, however, the fault probably lies with alignment problems and teachers' failure to cover or adequately explain certain subject matter.

Alignment is not just a matter of individual teachers making adjustments in content to reflect curriculum standards. Teachers at the same grade level, as well as across grade levels, need to review their content to make certain that 1) students at the same grade level are exposed to the mandated curriculum and 2) students at one grade level learn the content necessary to succeed at the next grade level. When teachers do not meet on a regular basis to review their coverage of curriculum standards and analyze student progress, the prospects for school decline increase.

Ineffective staff development. Some form of staff development is available to teachers in practically every school, but the mere availability of such training is no guarantee of instructional effectiveness. Schools that begin to decline are frequently the recipients of one-shot inservice programs and staff development that is only tangentially related to core academic concerns. When teachers complain about irrelevant workshops and useless staff development, school leaders need to take heed.

The most worthwhile staff development opportunities are often associated with a sustained focus on a key aspect of the required curriculum, such as literacy. Teachers benefit from learning how to use a new textbook, refine classroom assessment skills, improve classroom management, and detect learning problems. Using the same consultant or trainer over an extended period can provide continuity and avoid the confusion and mixed messages that often attend sporadic staff development involving multiple providers.

Lost focus. One of the first signs of school decline may be the loss of a clear academic focus. Discussions with school personnel may reveal a lack of clarity regarding priorities. If everything seems to be a priority, the concentration of time and resources on critical elements of the school program is apt to be inadequate. Lack of focus makes it difficult to provide effective staff development and targeted assistance for struggling students.

While it may be "politically correct" in public schools to act as if all subject matter and all aspects of schooling were of equal importance, the hard, cold fact is that some subjects and teaching functions are more important than others when dealing with a drop in student achievement. When we studied declining schools that participated in our program at the University of Virginia, we discovered that every school had substantial numbers of students with reading problems. Improving instruction and assistance in reading needed to be a top priority in these schools. Students' success in every other subject, including mathematics, depended on their ability to read and comprehend written material. To have chosen any focus other than reading and literacy would have made little sense.

Another focus in many low-performing schools must be student attendance. It is difficult for students to master essential content when they are not in school. The lack of a well-coordinated initiative to address student absenteeism can be another early indicator of school decline.

Lack of leadership. Leadership is synonymous with focus and direction.[5] Leaders are expected to see that priorities are identified and addressed. More than just a set of skills or traits, leadership is a perception, a perception that one or more individuals grasp what must be done in order to achieve the mission at hand.[6] The first individual to whom people look for leadership in schools is the principal. Key members of school faculties can also play important leadership roles.

Not surprisingly, declining schools frequently are characterized by a lack of leadership. An effective principal or veteran teacher may have retired or been reassigned. The replacement is not perceived to have the competence, commitment, or clarity of purpose of the one who departed. Teachers begin to feel adrift without a rudder. Where once there was a shared understanding of what needed to be done, now there is disagreement. Confusion displaces consensus.

The critical role of leadership in arresting school decline was driven home to me last year when my colleagues and I searched for examples of low-performing schools where teachers took the initiative and spontaneously organized themselves to turn their school around. We combed the literature on school turnarounds and even placed an advertisement in Education Week. We were unable to locate a single example. It would seem that there is no substitute for capable leaders when it comes to reversing a downward slide in performance.

Hasty hiring. One aspect of the school turnaround process where capable leaders make their impact felt is hiring. Many of our most successful turnaround specialists had to replace staff members during their first year or two. In some cases, individuals left of their own accord. In other instances, principals had to document deficiencies and initiate an employment termination process. When it came to new hires, however, our principals did not panic, nor did they settle for questionable replacements.

It is tempting for principals in declining schools to approach the hiring process fatalistically. They assume that highly qualified educators are unlikely to want to work in a troubled school. Consequently, they rush to judgment and select individuals about whom they have reservations. Declining schools need topnotch teachers if they are to combat falling test scores. Settling for "warm bodies" is likely to compound rather than resolve academic problems. Successful turnaround specialists find that retaining a long-term substitute and continuing to search for a qualified teacher is preferable to hiring someone who is unlikely to make a positive impact on student achievement.

Increased class size. Even highly qualified teachers may have difficulty when class sizes are allowed to increase to the point where it is difficult to maintain order and provide targeted assistance. Large classes are especially problematic when the classes involve critical academic subjects such as reading, language arts, and mathematics. Some states and school systems have mandated maximum class sizes for early elementary grades, clearly a step in the right direction. Few states and school systems, however, have taken similar action with regard to middle and high school courses that enroll large percentages of at-risk students.

A declining school is apt to lose some students as parents take advantage of the provisions in NCLB that permit transfers from a low-performing school. Quite often the students who are withdrawn from these schools are high-achieving students, not the struggling students who presumably would most benefit from a change. As a result, the proportion of low-achieving students may climb in a declining school. If this occurs, it is especially important for class sizes to remain as low as possible.

Overreliance on untrained helpers. No declining school wants to be caught without programs to help struggling students. Simply offering assistance programs, however, is no guarantee of success, especially when these programs rely heavily on volunteers, teacher aides, and other individuals who may lack the expertise to recognize learning problems and provide effective help.

Schools that have successfully turned around tend to place the responsibility for assisting struggling students into the hands of qualified teachers and specialists. Supplementary programs are evaluated regularly to determine whether they are making a difference in academic achievement. Ineffective programs are either improved or eliminated.

More rules and harsher punishments. Decreases in student achievement often are accompanied by increases in student behavior problems. Such problems rob struggling students of precious instructional time as teachers are compelled to devote more energy to maintaining order and dealing with discipline. Confronted with rising behavior problems, declining schools often rely on promulgating more rules and harsher punishments. This prescription can backfire. Teachers may find themselves devoting even more time to enforcing rules and monitoring punishments. Less time is available for instruction, assistance, and building relationships with students. Meanwhile, students chafe under greater restrictions and a more punitive climate. Some rules and punishments may be necessary, but they are no substitute for caring and concern.

FOREWARNED IS FOREARMED

The purpose of identifying characteristics of declining schools is to give educators some tangible indicators for which to be on the alert. Early intervention can prevent a precipitous slide. Many of the schools in the School Turnaround Specialist Program have experienced the benefits of early intervention. A major reason for their success is the fact that principals recognized the initial signs of decline. They also understood what needed to be done to address these concerns.

Of course, the 11 indicators I've identified here do not constitute an exhaustive list. There are no doubt a number of more subtle indicators of decline, including certain shared beliefs and aspects of school culture. For example, I suspect that teachers in declining schools are more likely to give up on struggling students and less likely to hold themselves to high standards of professional practice. These 11 indicators should be regarded as no more than a starting place for diagnosing school decline. Educators can refine and expand this list so that improvements can be made in the early detection and reversal of school decline.

ENDNOTES

1. Daniel L. Duke, "Understanding School Decline," unpublished manuscript, Partnership for Leaders in Education, Charlottesville, Virginia, 2007; and idem, "What We Know and Don't Know About Improving Low-Performing Schools," Phi Delta Kappan, June 2006, pp. 729–34.

2. Daniel L. Duke and Jon S. Cohen, "Do Public Schools Have a Future? A Case Study of Retrenchment and Its Implications," The Urban Review, vol. 15, 1983, pp. 89–105.

3. Duke, "Understanding School Decline."

4. The research from which the indicators of school decline are drawn includes the following: Daniel L. Duke, "Keys to Sustaining Successful School Turnarounds," ERS Spectrum, Fall 2006, pp. 21–35; idem, "Understanding School Decline"; Daniel L. Duke et al., Liftoff: Launching the School Turnaround Process in 10 Virginia Schools (Charlottesville, Va.: Partnership for Leaders in Education, 2005); and Daniel L. Duke et al., "How Comparable Are the Perceived Challenges Facing Principals of Low-Performing Schools?," International Studies in Educational Administration, vol. 35, no. 1, 2007, pp. 3–21.

5. Michael Fullan, Leading in a Culture of Change (San Francisco: Jossey-Bass, 2001).

6. Daniel L. Duke, "The Aesthetics of Leadership," Educational Administration Quarterly, Winter 1986, pp. 7–27.

DISCUSSION QUESTIONS

1. What role can teachers play in identifying and combating school decline?
2. Is it possible to turnaround a school without the strong leadership of a principal? Explain.
3. The author identifies ineffective staff development as a factor contributing to school decline. What type of staff development do you find beneficial? How should it be delivered effectively?
4. According to Duke, behavior issues often accompany declines in school performance and this hampers effective instruction. How should behavior issues be addressed?
5. The author identifies a variety of factors in diagnosing school decline. Which factor do you believe is the most influential in leading to school decline? Explain.
6. Should the approach to improve a declining school and a chronically low performing school be the same? Explain.

PRO-CON CHART 5

Should the person who helps teachers improve instruction also evaluate their performance?

PRO	CON
1. The threat of evaluation can stimulate reluctant teachers to improve.	**1.** Supervision requires an environment where new skills can be safely practiced without threat.
2. Evaluation is simply the final step in an extended period of formative supervisory feedback.	**2.** Supervision and evaluation, like formative and summative-assessment, are entirely separate categories of thought and practice.
3. Trust and honesty are built by people working closely together over a long period of time.	**3.** The threat of evaluation irrevocably eliminates trust and makes open communication impossible.
4. The relationship between supervisor and teacher is very similar to the relationship between teacher and student.	**4.** Supervisors should always treat teachers as professional colleagues, not as subordinates who know less than they do.
5. The person who has been working with a teacher all year long is best qualified to make a judgment about whether the teacher's employment should continue.	**5.** The person who has been working with a teacher all year long in a helping relationship cannot be relied on to provide an objective judgment of performance.

CASE STUDY 5

A Principal Works for Inclusion

Imagine you are the principal at Northmore High School, in a small, rural town. Northmore's surrounding population is fairly homogenous, as is the student body. The school counselor has approached you concerning a number of students who are mildly handicapped or have special needs and who have recently become targets of unwelcoming comments in the hallways and schoolyard. The comments come from a specific group of students who participate on various athletic teams.

It is a basic concern of yours that all students feel welcomed at the school and do not have to be subjected to behavior or remarks that make them uncomfortable.

1. Do you approach the teachers first and discuss how to deal with the issue in the classroom?
2. How should the teachers approach the subject in the classroom to establish a healthy relationship among all students?
3. What programs can you present in the school to make the environment more accepting: clubs, peer and outside discussion groups, films, classroom discussions, parent-teacher conferences, guest speakers, etc.?
4. Is it better to work with outside groups to provide a forum for discussion that puts the issue in a larger community or national context? To what extent should the issue be put in a larger sociological perspective, and to what extent should it be dealt with locally?
5. Should the coaches of the respective athletic teams be notified so that they can announce that they will suspend the athletes or limit playing time if there is another occurrence?
6. Is it better to inform parents in writing about their children's misbehavior and warn them that another incident could lead to suspension or worse?
7. To what extent, if at all, should the school district's attorney be consulted? Are the incidents a legal matter?

PART SIX

Curriculum and Policy

In Part Six, the relationship between policy and curriculum is considered. What are the implications of current demographic trends for curriculum? How are issues of diversity, homosexuality, educational equity, and practice-based assessment influencing the curriculum? Does academic tracking help or hinder the pursuit of equitable student learning outcomes? How are school reform and restructuring efforts affecting the curriculum, and what policy alternatives are available?

In Chapter 30, Harold Hodgkinson identifies key demographic changes that are influencing educational policy and offers recommendations for teachers who work with diverse students in their classrooms. His ideas include practices such as valuing all students, understanding student backgrounds, helping new students get settled, paying close attention to students who are eligible for free or reduced-price lunches, and emphasizing that students are all Americans, regardless of their differences. In Chapter 31, Andy Hargreaves and Dennis Shirley examine the educational policies of Finland, England, Canada, and the grassroots movement in the United States. Through their examination they identify principles of improvement required for educational policy reform.

In Chapter 32, Carl Glickman argues that singe models, structures, methods, and systems of education should be avoided. A diversity of approaches is preferable, he contends as long as every school and district is held responsible for providing an education for all students that increases their choices for exercising their rights to life, liberty, and the pursuit of happiness. In Chapter 33, Linda Darling-Hammond and Laura McCloskey compare the curricula and assessment methods of the United States and other internationally competitive countries. In countries such as Finland, teachers play an active role in assessment development and local assessments are used to inform and influence the national standards. Other high performing countries use portfolio based assessments and school-based tasks compared to the standardized tests the United States uses under No Child Left Behind.

In Chapter 34, Larry Cuban describes how the public's goals for education have structured school time in this country. Additionally, Cuban identifies proposals put forth over the

past quarter century to extend school time and factors that have prevented the success of extended school time reform. He also examines how the belief that college for all has affected policymakers' attitudes towards school time. In the concluding chapter in Part Six, Allan Ornstein examines how his thinking on education, equality, and equity has changed over the span of his career, especially in light of current events, policies, and social trends that seem to signal growing inequality in American society. He challenges educators to ask whether and how schools can serve as equalizers of differences.

CHAPTER 30

Educational Demographics: What Teachers Should Know

HAROLD HODGKINSON

FOCUSING QUESTIONS

1. What key demographic trends are affecting educational policy today?
2. How can teachers use demographics in their daily practice?
3. How will changes in the racial and age composition of the U.S. population influence education in coming years?
4. What different worldviews will students be bringing to classrooms?
5. What are some things teachers can do to help students to adjust to school?

Teachers are, unfortunately, rarely invited to participate in policy discussions affecting their schools—either by local or state boards of education or by various legislative bodies, from state legislatures to the United States Congress. Over the last two decades, the field of demographics has become vitally important to education policymakers at all levels. What are the key demographics affecting educational policy? How can teachers make good use of demographics in their daily practice?

KEY DEMOGRAPHICS

Nothing is distributed evenly across the United States. Not race, not religion, not age, not fertility, not wealth, and certainly not access to higher education. For example, only five states will have a 20 percent (or more) increase in school enrollments; most states will have smaller increases and about nine states will have declines. "Tidal Wave II," as former U.S. Secretary of Education Richard Riley likes to call the new increases in enrollments, is a statistical fiction for the vast majority of states.

But what will happen where you work? That depends on your state and your location. About one-quarter of Americans live in big cities, half live in suburbs, and a quarter live in small towns or rural areas. If you live in a central city in the eastern half of the country, you can expect almost no enrollment increases and some decreases. Those who can flee to the suburbs.

The inner suburban ring (where there is nothing between you and the city limits) will see a major increase in student diversity—more minorities, more immigrants, more students learning English as a second language (ESL), and more students from poverty. Teaching in an inner suburb will increasingly resemble teaching in an inner city. The second suburban ring (with one suburb between you and the city) will see some expansion in student enrollments, especially as you reach the beltway, which used to contain growth—like a belt—but is now the jumping-off place for growth. In these areas, parents do not commute to the central city; they live in one suburb and work in another.

Finally, enrollments in small towns or rural areas will be flat. But these places will have increasingly large percentages of elderly people. Older residents tend to "age in place," and whereas the young move away, some elderly do seek out small-town life.

Inner cities in the West tend to be economically flexible and porous, whereas those in the East and Midwest rigidly segregate low-income people in the cities. Racial and economic segregation are almost the same thing in the East and Midwest, which have the 10 most racially segregated cities in the nation; none of the 10 most racially segregated cities is in the South.

Consider another kind of diversity: the percentage of youth who by age 19 have graduated from high school and have been admitted to a college. Attaining this status is, of course, the American Dream. Some states have 65 percent of their 19-year-olds in this category, whereas others have 25 to 30 percent—a range that is far greater than any differences in scores between the United States and other nations.

One form of diversity that affects every teacher is transiency. Although about 3 million children are born each year, up to 40 million Americans move in that same time period, making mobility far more important than births in explaining population changes. Many teachers have 22 students in the fall and 22 in the following spring, but 20 out of the 22 are different students. Hospitals in these regions spend most of their time taking case histories from strangers. Each Sunday, ministers preach to congregations, a third of whose members are new. Transiency also relates to crime—knowing your neighbor will prevent you from stealing his lawnmower.

In addition, the states with the lowest rates of high school graduation and college admissions are the five most transient states in the United States. Most migration occurs within the same state, but about 6 to 8 million people move to another state each year. People in the New England, Middle Atlantic, and Midwestern states are moving to the Southeast and Southwest. In addition, a million immigrants each year are settling mainly in California, Texas, and Florida.

RACE FACTS

The nature of race is changing. Fact one: About 65 percent of America's population growth in the next two decades will be "minority," particularly from Hispanic and Asian immigrants. These groups have higher fertility rates than Caucasians, whose fertility level is too low to even replace the current population.

Fact two: The 2000 Census allows you to check as many race boxes as you wish. As a result, Tiger Woods, who is a "Cablinasian," will be able to check Caucasian, Black, Indian, and Asian. But how do we score his four checks? Does he count as four people? Is each check mark exactly one-quarter of Tiger? Can he be counted as white for housing surveys and black for civil rights actions?

Fact three: Three million black Hispanics in the United States, mostly dark-skinned Spanish speakers from the Caribbean, have checked black on the census form because Hispanic is not a race. Although race is vitally important politically, economically, and historically, it remains scientific nonsense—Office of Management and Budget Directive 15, the guide for the census for more than 20 years, states that the racial categories in the census have no scientific validity.

Fact four: At least 40 percent of all Americans have had some racial mixing in the last three generations—including President Bill Clinton and Martin Luther King, Jr.—but only 2 to 4 percent will admit it on Census 2000. The blurring of racial identity will grow rapidly; however, children of Asian and Hispanic immigrants are marrying out of their parents' heritage at rates between 30 to 60 percent. In the 1900 immigration wave, an Italian's marriage to a German was called miscegenation, and the families would not speak to each other. Today, only 15 percent of European Americans are married to a spouse from the same country of origin, and we laugh about this outdated notion. Soon, Asians and Hispanics may do the same.

Diversity is increasingly unevenly distributed. In fact, the 65 percent increase in diverse populations will be absorbed by only about 230 of our 3,068 counties; California, Texas, and Florida will get about three-fifths of the increase. Remember that more than half of our entire population lives in only nine states—those three, plus New York, Pennsylvania, Ohio, Illinois, Michigan, and New Jersey—yet only California, Texas, and Florida are growing so quickly; the other six seem to be "wealthy but tired." Forty-one states compete for the other half of the population. Although we talk of "minority majorities," this phenomenon is only possible in a handful of counties. Whites will become a minority of the U.S. population around 2050, and you will have retired before then.

But the blurring of racial lines suggests the declining importance of race, and many people are lobbying for race data to be excluded from the next census because it tells many things that are not accurate. Most poor children in the United States are white, but a higher percentage of black and Hispanic kids are poor. Being black is no longer a universal handicap; over one-quarter of black households have a higher income than the white average, and rates of blacks who go to college and own homes continue to grow. But poverty is a universal handicap. If you have poor kids of diverse ethnicities as well as middle-class minorities in your classes, you know exactly what I mean.

Racial desegregation has not led to economic equality. Twenty percent of U.S. kids are below the poverty line today—exactly the same percentage as 15 years ago—even though most of the nation is less segregated and wealthier. This poverty rate is inexcusable in the wealthiest nation on earth. It is time to do what Kentucky has done—build an economic "floor" under every child in the state to equalize the investment in each child's education. That is economic desegregation, and many states are doing it. Our new understanding of the importance of children's preschool years has led many states to mandate a preschool program for all poverty-level children in the state, another attempt to equalize investment in every child and economically desegregate.

AN AGING POPULATION

We grow old. Although immigration and high minority fertility stall the trend, the U.S. population is steadily getting older, as are populations in other developed or industrialized nations. Census 2000 added an extra box for the state-your-age question because 57,000 Americans are now over 100 years of age, and 1.4 million are in their 90s. President Clinton, born in 1946 (a leading-edge baby boomer), will be 65 in 2011. By then, 65 will not be considered old—today, geriatrics defines middle age as 50 through 75 and old age as 75 and older. Of the baby boomers, born between 1946 and 1964, one in four will live past 85. Today, only one household in four has a child in the public schools.

President and Mrs. Clinton now have an empty nest, since their daughter graduated from college and moved out. The question for schools: Will baby boomers (70 million of them) maintain their interest in public schools after their kids have left the educational system? Will they vote for bond issues for someone else's children? Or for raises for teachers to benefit someone else's children? The answer is key to the future of public school finance. Already, many school board meetings are dominated by today's much smaller group of citizens ages 65 and older who wish to be removed from the public school tax rolls. And remember the mantra from demographics to politics: As you get older, you vote more often. How will we convince seniors that their Social Security and Medicare trust funds will be replenished by today's high school students when they join the work force?

DIFFERENCES IN WORLDVIEWS

A final issue for teachers concerns the switch from race to national origin. This new category will tell much more about students and their parents. Knowing that students and parents are Hispanic tells very little—15 percent of California's Hispanics do not even speak Spanish. Knowing that they are Cuban or Panamanian tells lots more. The following is a collection of important differences in how people see the world.

- *The sense of time.* Americans believe in the future as if it were a religion (except Californians, who seem to live in the eternal now). Many immigrants have a sophisticated sense of the past that puts us all to shame. Yet teachers usually motivate students on the grounds of a brighter future—when consistency with the past might be a better motivator for some students.
- *The sense of family.* Whereas most Americans are only aware of their nuclear family (parents plus their children), some Americans are from extended families—for them, a loan to buy a house might come from an uncle; a medical problem might be solved by an aunt. The extended family provides comfort, stability, and many services that the U.S. government typically provides.
- *The sense of hierarchy.* America is as "flat" as you can get on this score, but many newcomers are from rigidly structured societies in which children (and women) are considered inferior beings. Thus, the child enters school having been told by parents that teachers are authority figures. To show respect, they look at the floor when the teacher addresses them. Most teachers see this behavior as evasive and prefer students to look them straight in the eye, indicating honesty, trust, and interest in the class.

In many seminars, students are encouraged to disagree with their teachers to show their individuality. But in many nations and cultures, such behavior is called "putting yourself forward," often a major sin. Asian, Hispanic, and Native American kids seldom leap into the air, fists extended, saying "Yes! I'm wonderful!" Indeed, at one high school graduation I attended, the valedictorian downplayed her own talent and hard work, declaring that the award belonged to her entire family and that her family should be on the stage with her (they later joined her there). This behavior was not excessive modesty: The young lady truly believed that the honor was her family's achievement, not just her own.

DEMOGRAPHIC TIPS FOR TEACHERS

Some simple actions can help teachers work with the diverse students in their classrooms.

- If a student is presented in records as "Hispanic," make sure you know what country that student's family is from, what language the family uses at home, and whether the parents also speak English and how well. If parents speak only Spanish and you speak none, try to get a colleague who is bilingual to be on the line during your first phone call home.

- If a student won't look you in the eye during the first week of school, don't make a big deal of it in front of the class. Take a minute to ask the student about it privately.
- Find out as soon as possible which of your students is new to the area and may need some help in getting settled. If half your students (or fellow teachers) are new in town, be prepared for some problems. Transiency often brings out the worst in people at any age.
- Even though students may choose to sit with their racial or ethnic groups in the cafeteria or in other informal settings, your classroom must value all students. Rather than "color blind," your goal should be "culture fair."
- Pay particular attention to your students who are eligible for free or reduced-price lunches—they may need extra help and may not get enough to eat on weekends. (There should be no "Title I pullout program" that identifies low-income students in your classroom.)
- If you have lots of diversity in your classroom, try to use as many different visual presentations as possible. Pictures can often convey meaning when words do not.
- Some students may be genuinely confused about their ethnic ancestry. Several state courts have indicated that it is illegal to force a child to choose between the mother's and father's backgrounds. Although it's a sensitive issue, you can communicate clearly to your class that you value all children and that you expect them to do their best. The important thing is the understanding that we are all Americans, regardless of our backgrounds.
- Make a list of student successes for any ethnic group in your school, whether in your class or not. It's the perfect defense against the student who says, "You just don't understand! No one from [country x] can do [math/English/science]."
- Some students may be the responsibility of grandparents—more than 1 million public school students are. If so, make sure that the grandparents get the same level of attention that you give to biological parents—they may need even more help.

THE IMPORTANCE OF DEMOGRAPHICS

We have only scratched the surface regarding the impact of demographics on education and on the president of the classroom—the teacher. All of these demographic changes are coming soon to a classroom near you.

DISCUSSION QUESTIONS

1. Which demographic changes are likely to have the greatest impact on your classroom or school?
2. Which demographic changes are likely to have the greatest impact on the United States as a whole?
3. Should newcomers to the United States be expected to adjust quickly to American culture?
4. Why is it important for teachers to be sensitive to student differences?
5. What implications do changes in demographics have for curriculum and instruction?

CHAPTER 31

Beyond Standardization: Powerful New Principles for Improvement

ANDY HARGREAVES
DENNIS SHIRLEY

FOCUSING QUESTIONS

1. Explain the integration between education and economic policy in Finland.
2. How has Ontario, Canada reformed its highly standardized educational system?
3. Describe the successes and limitations of the networking program undertaken in England.
4. What types of grassroots programs are influencing education reform in the United States?
5. Describe the principles of improvement that emerge from examining the educational policies of Finland, Canada, and England in addition to the grassroots movement in the United States.

A new phase of reforms promises to move us past standards and accountability and into an era that allows greater creativity, flexibility, inclusiveness, and inspiration.

We are entering an age of post-standardization. Improvement in terms of tested achievement has reached a plateau. The curriculum is shrinking, classroom creativity is disappearing, and dropout rates are frozen. Top-down prescriptions without support and encouragement at the grassroots and local level are exhausted. If you find that you are in the midst of another grueling year of trying to meet Adequate Yearly Progress (AYP) targets, if you dread teaching the standardized literacy program that your district has adopted, and if your classroom coaches and mentors have turned into curriculum compliance officers, then "post-standardization" might sound like more academic argot coined by ivory-tower intellectuals. But hold on! Especially when we look beyond the American context, signs are emerging that the era of market competitiveness between schools in delivering standardized curriculum and teaching practices is on its last legs.

High-stakes and high-pressure standardization, where short-term gains in measurable results have been demanded at any price, have turned many U.S. schools not into learning-enriched environments, but into enervating "Enrons of educational change."[1] When policy makers turn up the heat; define reading, writing, and math as core subjects to be tested; and threaten to close struggling schools that can't make AYP and to disperse their pupils, educators respond—and with a vengeance! They slash social studies at the same time the country is internationally isolated; they skimp on science when there is unprecedented global competition for technological breakthroughs; and they decimate the arts, foreign languages, and physical education with the prospect that America's next generation will be uncouth, uncultured, and unfit.

And what has the U.S. gained from its obsession with raising test scores? Although more time has been spent on language arts and math since 2001, this has come at the cost of reducing time for such subjects as science, history, and the arts.[2] NAEP reading scores for 4th and 8th graders have remained flat for more than a decade. Math scores show more encouraging signs of progress, especially for pupils in the bottom 10th percentile, so here we have the proverbial silver lining in the dark clouds.[3] But U.S. teachers have suffered mightily through the nation's new policies, and they resent it. Only 15% indicate on surveys that the No Child Left Behind Act is improving local education,[4] indicating a loss of faith in the government's ability to galvanize the very people who care the most about educating this nation's children.

Confronted by data on the limits of existing strategies and challenged by the economic need for increased innovation and creativity, a new shift in education reform is upon us. This is already evident in recent developments in Finland, Canada, England, and the United States. Beside and beyond standardization, each of the alternatives outlined here contains different theories of action, of how and what to change, and carries different consequences—though all, to some degree, wed proposals for future change with traces and legacies from the past.

FINNISHING SCHOOLS

In January 2007, with colleagues Gabor Halasz and Beatriz Pont, one of us undertook an investigative inquiry for the Organisation for Economic Co-operation and Development (OECD) into the relationship between leadership and school improvement in one of the world's highest performing education systems and economies: Finland.

At the core of Finland's success and sustainability is its capacity to reconcile, harmonize, and integrate elements that have divided other developed economies and societies—a prosperous, high-performing economy and a decent, socially just society. While the knowledge economy has weakened the welfare state in many other societies, a strong welfare state is a central part of the Finnish narrative that supports and sustains a successful economy.

The contrast with Anglo-Saxon countries, where material wealth has been gained at the expense of increasing social division and also at the cost of children's well-being, could not be more striking. The U.K. and U.S. rank dead last and next to last, respectively, on the UNICEF 2007 survey on children's well-being, while Finland ranks near the top.[5]

The Finnish education system is at the center of this successful integration that, in less than a half-century, has transformed Finland from a rural backwater into a high-tech economic powerhouse.[6] Respondents interviewed by the OECD team indicated that Finns are driven by a common and articulately expressed social vision that connects a creative and prosperous future to the people's sense of themselves as having a creative history and common social identity.

Technological creativity and competitiveness connect the Finns to their past in a unitary narrative of lifelong learning and societal development. This occurs within a strong welfare state that supports education and the economy. Schooling is free as a universal right from well-funded early childhood education through higher education—including free school meals and all necessary resources, equipment, and musical instruments. Science and technology are high priorities. Almost 3% of GDP is allocated to scientific and technological development, and a national committee that includes leading corporate executives and university presidents, and is chaired by the prime minister, steers and integrates economic and educational strategy.[7] Yet Finland also boasts the highest number of composers per capita in the world.[8]

This educational and economic integration occurs in a society that values children, education, and social welfare. Finland's high school graduates rank teaching as their most desired occupation. As a result, entry into teaching is demanding and highly competitive, with teaching applicants having only a 10% chance of acceptance.[9]

In Finland, the state steers but does not prescribe in detail the national curriculum. Trusted teams of highly qualified teachers write much of the curriculum at the local level, adjusting it to the students they know best. In schools characterized by an uncanny calmness, teachers exercise their sense of professional and social responsibility to care especially for children at the bottom, so as to lift them to the level of the rest. Individual assistants are available for children who struggle, special educational support is provided for those with more serious difficulties, and school teams including teachers, administrators, welfare workers, and the school nurse meet regularly to discuss and support children in danger of falling behind.

By law, Finnish principals must have been teachers themselves and most continue to teach at least two hours per week. By remaining tethered to the daily details of teaching and interacting with children, principals enjoy credibility among their teachers and overcome the traditional divide between administrators and teachers.

How is it, school principals in Finland were asked, that they could still teach as well as lead in their high-performing education system on the leading edge of the global economy? "Because," one said, "unlike the Anglo-Saxon countries, we do not have to spend our time responding to long, long lists of government initiatives that come from the top."

Of course, there are dramatic differences between Finland and the U.S. For example, Finland has only four million people and little ethnic diversity; the U.S. has more than 300 million people and extraordinary cultural and linguistic diversity. We cannot duplicate Finland, but we also should not dismiss it.

Finland contains essential lessons for societies that aspire, educationally and economically, to be successful and sustainable knowledge societies, societies that go beyond an age of low-skill standardization. Building a future by wedding it to the past; fostering strong connections between education and economic development without sacrificing culture and creativity; raising standards by lifting the many rather than pushing a privileged few; developing a highly qualified profession that brings about improvement through commitment, trust, cooperation, and responsibility; and sharing responsibility for all of our children's futures, not just those in our own schools or classes—these are just some of the signs about possible lessons to be learned from Finland's exceptional educational and economic achievements.

CAN-DO CANADA

If Finland seems too far away geographically, demographically, and politically to offer lessons for educational improvement to the United States, then let's move closer to home—into Canada. In the latter half of the 1990s and beyond, the Canadian province of Ontario was the epitome of standardization. Its conservative agenda of diminished resources and reductions in teachers' preparation time, high-stakes tests linked to graduation, and accelerating reform requirements exacted high costs on teaching and learning. Research one of us conducted in six secondary schools exposed the pernicious impact of its policies.[10] Teachers complained of "too many changes, too fast," "too much, too quickly," "just so much, so soon," to an extent that was overwhelming. Having to take shortcuts meant teachers did not always feel they could do their best work. "What a waste of my intelligence, creativity, and leadership potential!" one teacher concluded. Ontario's education system was about as far removed from the needs of a fast-paced new knowledge economy as a country could get.

This changed in 2003 when the Liberal Party replaced the Progressive Conservative government. Appointing a well-published education policy scholar in the education ministry's most senior position, and being formally advised by international change consultant Michael Fullan, the province wedded a continuing commitment to test-based educational accountability with initiatives that built capacity for improvement and provided professional support.[11]

A Literacy and Numeracy Secretariat has driven instructional improvement by using teams of consultants and coaches supported by quality materials and by avoiding the worst excesses of the overly-prescriptive models that characterized literacy strategies in the U.K. and U.S.[12] Though provincial targets are fixed, schools and districts are also encouraged to commit to and set their own goals.

Within this framework of high aspirations, building professional capacity is emphasized. The province has allocated $5 million to teacher unions to spend on professional development, successful practices are networked across schools, and underperforming schools are encouraged (not compelled) to seek assistance from government support teams and higher performing peers.

As with other alternatives, this reform strategy also has imperfections. For instance, the measurement-driven emphasis on literacy and math seems to be a politically expedient (if slightly modified) import from England more than an educationally necessary improvement strategy, given Ontario's already strikingly high performance in literacy on international tests.[13] But these limitations could be remedied by widening the reform focus, developing professionally shared rather than politically imposed targets, and testing sample populations rather than administering a complete census for accountability purposes.

Notwithstanding these limitations, Ontario's theory of action offers many lessons. Intelligent accountability, increased investment, heightened trust, and strengthened professional networking provide a noteworthy contrast to policies endorsed south of the border that cut funding, pit teachers and schools against one another, and reduce teacher professionalism to the hurried implementation of policy makers' ever-changing mandates.

ENGLAND'S EDGE

Across the Atlantic is one of America's closest policy partners, Britain. We recently evaluated a major project in England involving more than 300 secondary schools that had experienced a dip in measured performance over one or two years. These schools were networked with one another, provided with technical assistance in interpreting achievement results, given access to support from mentor schools, and offered a modest discretionary budget to spend in anyway they chose, provided it addressed the goals of improvement.[14] Participating schools also had a practitioner-generated menu of proven strategies for short-, medium-, and long-term improvement.

The initial results of the project were remarkable. More than two-thirds of these networked schools improved at double the rate of the national average over one or two years, and they entirely avoided the characteristic top-down mandates and prescriptions that typified English educational reforms before this point.

In this high-trust culture of schools helping schools and the strong supporting the weak, teachers and administrators praised the flexible budgeting that focused on improvement, applauded the network's conferences for their inspirational input and practical assistance, and greatly appreciated the availability (rather than forced imposition) of mentor schools and principals who shared practical strategies and advice.

Schools were especially successful in improving in the short term, stimulated by the menu of short-term strategies provided by experienced colleagues. Teachers and schools excitedly implemented and exchanged short-term change strategies, such as providing students with test-taking strategies, paying past students to mentor existing ones, feeding students with bananas and water before examinations, bringing in examiners and university teachers to share their grading criteria with students, collecting mobile phone numbers to contact students who did not show up on exam days, introducing motivational speakers for such vulnerable groups as working-class boys in old mill towns, providing web-based support for home learning, and so on.

Such short-term strategies do not bring about deeper transformations of teaching and learning, but they do give instant lifts in measured attainment—and in ways that largely avoid the unethical manipulation of test-score improvement in regimes of standardization (e.g., selecting only higher-performing students, narrowing the curriculum, or teaching only to the test). Useful in their own right, these strategies have even greater value when they are confidence-building levers that assist more challenging long-term improvements.

But this approach also has limitations. Strategies are "so gimmicky and great," as one principal put it, that they do not challenge or encourage teachers to question and revise their existing approaches to teaching and learning. The rush to raise achievement injects teachers with an addictive "high" of short-term success. The result is a somewhat hyperactive culture of change that can be exhilarating but also draining and distracting.

The project's successful short-term strategies, therefore, seem to serve less like levers to longer-term transformation than like lids upon it. In part, this is because the project—successful as it is—remains embedded in a wider national policy culture of short-term funding and proposal cycles, pressure for quick turnarounds and instant results, proliferation of multiple initiatives, and language that emphasizes moving students into the right achievement cells. Educators talk about "targeting" the right groups, "pushing" students harder, "moving" them up, "raising aspirations," "holding people down," and "getting a grip" on where youngsters are.

Yet, despite this limitation, the success of hightrust networks, school-to-school collaboration, discretionary budgeting, and a combination of proven insider experience with powerful outside-in evidence, points to a potential for an even greater transformation still to be unleashed. This alternative theory of action holds great promise if it can be separated from the surrounding context of bureaucratic accountability and wedded instead to higher-level professional and peer-driven principles of accountability. The English example suggests that it is the "peer factor" more than the "fear factor" that offers our best hope for raising achievement further.

GROWING THE GRASSROOTS IN AMERICA

American educators who teach poor and working-class children can only look with envy at the broad social safety net enjoyed by children and youth in other western nations, where educators are not expected to achieve everything by themselves. Rather than learn from other nations about policies that increase economic performance and social cohesion, reduce income disparities, and expand educational access for all, American policy makers have endorsed the untested and ideologically driven strategy of more markets, more privatization, and more pupil testing as the path to academic achievement.

Yet policy makers are not the only shapers of public education. One of the more inspiring recent developments in the U.S. has been the emergence of community and youth organizing as drivers of change and creators of "civic capacity" in urban education.[15] For years, these local initiatives were bit players in school reform. Symbolic language about "parent involvement" rarely went beyond one-on-one deals between individual parents and the educators who served their children.[16] Larger efforts to organize parents indicated that they were usually divided among themselves, incapable of galvanizing anything beyond episodic protests, and sidestepped in the push for standardization and control. Moreover, this pattern of fragmented and fractious engagement has occurred within a new context of "diminished democracy," in which fewer Americans participate in the traditional forms of civic life and prefer large voluntary associations that represent their interests but do not bring them into deliberative processes in the public sphere.[17]

Yet perhaps the tide is starting to turn. A new wave of community and youth organizing, supported by such powerful funders as the Ford, Hazen, Mott, and Gates foundations, is helping to get us beyond the "deep reforms with shallow roots" that Michael Usdan and Larry Cuban decried as endemic patterns in American change efforts.[18] In New York City, the Community Collaborative to Improve District 9 Schools in the South Bronx developed a teacher support program with that city's public schools that reduced teacher attrition from 28% to 6.5% in targeted schools in a single year.[19] In Philadelphia, high school activists with Youth United for Change exposed the way by which one of the only three secondary schools in the city that achieved AYP did so: by having teachers coach students on test items and by posting answers to anticipated test questions on walls where tests were administered.[20] In Chicago, the Logan Square Neighborhood Association and other community groups have created a Grow Your Own teacher preparatory program linked with area universities to prepare poor and working-class parents to become certified teachers.[21]

In these and other cases, community and youth organizers have moved beyond 1960s-style protest politics to conduct research with university allies, create and lead charter schools, provide professional development for teachers, and educate parents in how to combine data analyses of pupil achievement with in-class observations of teaching and learning.

Earlier work by one of us has documented efforts by the Industrial Areas Foundation in Texas to turn around struggling urban schools in the 1990s—efforts that developed a network of roughly 150 Alliance Schools that linked schools with faith-based institutions and community organizations, although these promising efforts fell on hard times as new accountability systems led principals to view working with parents as a distraction from the quest for AYP.[22]

Yet Oakes and Rogers in Los Angeles have described how UCLA faculty provided crucial expertise to community and youth organizing groups that has ranged from high-level legal representation to the day-to-day politics of improving large urban high schools.[23]

We do not yet know whether these diverse efforts will be sustainable. But if government does not meet its obligations, then activist parents and communities must become the prime movers of educational change. The emerging educational activism of grassroots America indicates that powerful reform efforts need not all begin with governments or guiding coalitions that come from the top. Instead, with the support of foundations and other organizations, these reforms can unleash the immense commitment and capacity locked up in our children's homes and communities.

CONCLUSION

When we put together what we can learn from the Finns, the Canadians, and the Brits, as well as from the grassroots activism of ordinary Americans, we begin to see the evolution of powerful new principles of improvement. These are different from the principles of markets, standardization, and the quick but fleeting turnarounds that have dominated U.S. reform efforts for more than a decade—the same strategies now being abandoned by other nations. These new principles suggest that:

- A compelling, inclusive, and inspirational vision for economic, social, and educational development that offers people more individual choice is in the best American traditions of freedom and justice, appeals to public spiritedness, and includes financial responsibility for the development of others.
- Learning and achievement priorities should follow the vision, which means much more than narrowing numerical achievement gaps in tested basics. We must attend to the basics but also move far beyond them. Creativity and innovation for the knowledge economy, cosmopolitan identity and global engagement in an age of insecurity, environmental awareness if we are to avert a planetary catastrophe, physical fitness for all to turn back the epidemic of obesity, and cultivation of the arts and humanities that enrich our spirit and develop our responsibility toward others—these are the learning priorities of a sustainable knowledge society. Americans need a more enriching and engaging curriculum for all, not to replace the basics, but to bolster and move us beyond them.
- This kind of powerful learning calls for high-quality teaching. But high-performing countries elsewhere do not create and keep quality teachers by using the market to manipulate the calculus of teachers' pay. Rather, good and smart people are called to teaching and kept in the profession by an inspiring and inclusive social vision to which the society subscribes and for which it accords high status.
- Trust, cooperation, and responsibility create the collegiality and shared, committed, professional learning that improve classroom effectiveness and raise standards with students. Shared targets rather than externally arbitrary AYP keeps pushing teachers to higher and higher levels of performance. Such strong professional learning communities depend on inspirational and more widely distributed leadership, rather than fleeting and heroic turnarounds that rely on single individuals. At a time of extraordinary demographic turnover in school and school leadership, the time is ripe for America to undertake significant investment in developing and renewing its next generation of leaders.
- Data can inform and enhance teacher decisions and interventions, but they should never "drive" instruction. Teaching

entails gathering information from a variety of sources; and some valuable teacher traits have more in common with the skilled thespian who responds instantly to a demanding and vocal audience and with the doctor who combines evidence and intuition to diagnose a patient than with the civil engineer who relies on scientific data to design roads, bridges, or tunnels. Evidence collected by teachers that enables schools to compare themselves to similar schools and that stresses how schools and teachers make a difference to the students they serve is a more fair and instructive guide to improvement than are the crude data which are too often used to rank and shame struggling schools.

- The evidence from almost everywhere else points to how much teachers and schools can learn from being networked with peers and how achievement gaps can be narrowed by systems that encourage and support strong schools to help their weaker counterparts. It would make immense sense for Americans to reallocate resources to peer learning and to systems of teachers helping teachers and schools helping schools.
- Governments are often pushed into politically popular though educationally ineffective strategies for change because they feel they must pander to parental nostalgia for schools as they remember them. Treating parents as customers and clients, as recipients of services, or as targets of external interventions only intensifies this sense of defensive nostalgia. But the activist element in American communities demonstrates what can be achieved when parents and communities are engaged and empowered to advocate for and help improve the quality of education for some of the nation's poorest children. Great value can be added to educational investment through parallel investment in parent and community development. Educators cannot be expected to do everything themselves.

A bigger and better vision; a bolder view of enriching and engaging learning; the inspiration, support, and professional discretion that will attract and retain the very best teachers; a national strategy that will develop and renew the leadership that can build and constantly improve strong professional learning communities; intelligent accountability that monitors standards and improves every child's instruction; ambitious, professionally shared targets rather than politically arbitrary ones; support for school networks where good practices can be exchanged and the strong can help the weak; and recasting parents and communities as actively engaged partners rather than as consumers, recipients, or targets of government strategies and services—these are the international and instructive lessons for education reform if the United States does not want to fall even further behind its international competitors.

Now is the time for U.S. education to learn from other nations about the most productive ways forward. There is no good reason why the wealthiest nation in the world should be ashamed about investing in all of its children and their futures. That is the true challenge that all Americans who care about their nation's future must now face.

ENDNOTES

1. Andy Hargreaves and Dean Fink, Sustainable Leadership (San Francisco: Jossey-Bass, 2005).
2. Center on Education Policy, Choices, Changes, and Challenges: Curriculum and Instruction in the NCLB Era (Washington, D.C.: Center on Education Policy, 2007).
3. Jihyun Lee, Wendy S. Grigg, and Gloria S. Dion, The Nation's Report Card: Mathematics 2007, NCES 2007–494 (Washington, D.C.: National Center for Education Statistics, Institute of Education Sciences, U.S. Department of Education, 2007).

4. Jean Johnson, Ana Maria Arumi, and Amber Ott, Issue Number 3: Is Support for Standards and Testing Fading? Reality Check 2006 (New York: Public Agenda, 2006).

5. UNICEF, Child Poverty in Perspective: An Overview of Child Well-Being in Rich Countries, Innocenti Report Card 7 (Florence: UNICEF Innocenti Research Centre, 2007).

6. Erkki Aho, Kari Pitkänen, & Pasy Sahlberg, Policy Development and Reform Principles of Basic and Secondary Education in Finland Since 1968, Education Working Paper Series Number 2 (Washington, D.C.: World Bank, 2006).

7. Manuel Castells and Pekka Himanen, The Information Society and the Welfare State: The Finnish Model (New York: Oxford University Press, 2004).

8. W. Norton Grubb, "Dynamic Inequality and Intervention: Lessons from a Small Country," Phi Delta Kappan, October 2007, pp. 105–14.

9. Pasi Sahlberg, "Education Reform for Raising Economic Competitiveness," Journal of Educational Change, December 2006, pp. 259–87; Idem, "Education Policies for Raising Student Learning: The Finnish Approach," Journal of Education Policy, March 2007, pp. 147–71; and Aho, Pitkanen, and Sahlberg, op. cit.

10. Andy Hargreaves, Teaching in the Knowledge Society: Education in the Age of Anxiety (New York: Teachers College Press, 2003); and Andy Hargreaves and Ivor Goodson, eds., "Change over Time," special issue of Educational Administration Quarterly, February 2006.

11. Michael Fullan, Turnaround Leadership (San Francisco: Jossey-Bass, 2007); and Land Sharratt and Michael Fullan, "Accomplishing Districtwide Reform," Journal of School Leadership, 2006, pp. 583–95.

12. Betty Achinstein and Rodney T. Ogawa, "(In)Fidelity: What the Resistance of New Teachers Reveals About Professional Principles and Prescriptive Educational Policies," Harvard Educational Review, Spring 2006, pp. 30–63.

13. Hargreaves and Fink, op. cit.

14. Andy Hargreaves et al., The Long and Short of School Improvement: Final Evaluation of the Raising Achievement Transforming Learning Programme of the Specialist Schools and Academies Trust (London: Specialist Schools and Academies Trust, 2007).

15. Clarence N. Stone et al., Building Civic Capacity: The Politics of Reforming Urban Schools (Lawrence: University Press of Kansas, 2001).

16. Dennis Shirley, Community Organizing for Urban School Reform (Austin: University of Texas Press, 1997).

17. Theda Skocpol, Diminished Democracy: From Membership to Management in American Civic Life (Norman: University of Oklahoma Press, 2004).

18. Michael D. Usdan and Larry Cuban, Powerful Reforms with Shallow Roots: Improving America's Urban Schools (New York: Teachers College Press, 2003).

19. Academy for Educational Development, Lead Teacher Report: Second Year Report Submitted to the Community Collaborative to Improve Bronx Schools (Washington, D.C.: Academy for Educational Development, 2006).

20. Seema Shah and Kavitha Mediratta, "Negotiating Reform: Young People's Leadership in the Educational Arena," New Directions in Youth Development, April 2008, pp. 43–59.

21. Mark R. Warren, "Communities and Schools: A New View of Urban Education Reform," Harvard Educational Review, Summer 2005, pp. 133–73.

22. Dennis Shirley, Community Organizing; idem, Valley Interfaith and School Reform: Organizing for Power in South Texas (Austin: University of Texas Press, 2002); and Dennis Shirley and Michael Evans, "Community Organizing and No Child Left Behind," in Marion Orr, ed., Transforming the City: Community Organizing and the Challenge of Political Change (Lawrence: University Press of Kansas, 2007), pp. 109–33.

23. Jeannie Oakes, John Rogers, and Martin Lipton, Learning Power: Organizing for Education and Justice (New York: Teachers College Press, 2006).

DISCUSSION QUESTIONS

1. Finland is very different from the United States demographically and geographically. Is it possible to adopt or adapt any of the policies of their educational system? Explain.
2. Which of the different country's policies do you believe are most practical and feasible for implementation in the United States? Explain.
3. According to the authors, "Americans have endorsed the untested and ideologically driven strategy of more markets, more privatization, and more pupil testing as the path to academic achievement" (p. 140). Do you agree with this statement? Explain.
4. What role do you believe grassroots activism will play in reforming the educational policy in the United States?
5. Using what we know from other countries how can quality teachers be recruited and retained?

CHAPTER 32

Dichotomizing Educational Reform

CARL D. GLICKMAN

FOCUSING QUESTIONS

1. What principles should guide education in the United States?
2. What are some examples of what the author calls ideological absolutes?
3. To what extent does ideological conflict contribute to pedagogical pain?
4. What does it mean to be an educated person in a democracy?
5. Is it possible to find common ground in the issues facing public education today?

I did not lightly take pen in hand (yes, I still use a pen) in writing this chapter. I have devoted my entire professional life to working with colleagues to create, establish, and sustain public schools that are driven by collaboration, personalization, and active and participatory student learning.[1] And I will continue to do so, as I personally believe such is the best way to prepare all students for the intellectual, social, and aesthetic life of a democracy.

Yet, even in the fervor of my beliefs, I still see other concepts of education that generate degrees of uncertainty in me. My memories of my own best teachers are revealing. Most taught in highly interactive ways, but one grand elder taught from behind a podium in a huge auditorium and engaged in little interaction with students. He was perhaps my greatest teacher. Such discrepancies don't change the strength of my own beliefs; they simply remind me that the viable possibilities of educating students well are broad indeed.

Ultimately, an American education must stand on a foundation that is wider than the beliefs of any one individual or any one group. It should encourage, respect, and support any conceptions—no matter how diametrically opposed to one's own—that are willing to be tested openly and freely. Furthermore, it should involve the willing and nondiscriminatory participation of all students, parents, and educators. That is what should be at the core of an American education. But with the "winner take all" wars being fought today, I am seriously concerned about the future of our students and of our public schools and about the vitality of a better democracy.

IDEOLOGICAL ABSOLUTES

The either/or debates about standards versus no standards, intrinsic versus extrinsic motivation, core versus multicultural knowledge, direct instruction versus constructivist learning, and phonics versus whole language are symptomatic of ideologies that attempt to crush one another and leave only one solution standing. Whether the ideology is education anchored in traditional, behaviorist authority or progressive, inquiry-based learning, the stance toward the final outcome is the same. One group possesses the truth, and the other side is demonized as a pack of extremists: scary, evil persons. Articles and books present educators and the public with a forced choice that unfortunately disregards reality and endangers the very concept of an American education.[2]

Let me illustrate the incompleteness of ideological absolutes with one of today's most emotional issues, the relationship of race to socioeconomic achievement. One side of this debate argues that America is the land of opportunity, where freedom rings, where anyone—regardless of race, religion, gender, or class—can work hard and rise to a position of authority, success, and accomplishment. The other side argues that America is a hegemonic system, protecting the ruling class and extant privilege while keeping the poor, the dispossessed, and people of color stifled, oppressed, and marginalized. Well, which side of this debate is correct? The answer to that question has important implications for what our society needs to change in terms of practices, programs, and the targeting of resources. But the truth is that both contradictory realities have compelling evidence and must be used together to figure out what needs to be done next.

Consider the economic component of this debate. Seymour Martin Lipset compares the United States with other Western industrialized nations.[3] Since the post–Civil War era, America has been the wealthiest country, with a steady rise in living standards and unparalleled social and economic advances for the poor and working class. Yet the income of the poorest fifth of this nation continues to *decline* relative to that of other Americans.

The African American scholar Henry Louis Gates, Jr., takes on this same dichotomy in reference to race. He observes that, since 1967, the number of middle-class African American families has quadrupled. Since 1973 the top 100 African American businesses have moved from sales of $473 million to $11.7 billion. In 1970 "only one in ten blacks had attended college; today one in three has." He then goes on to discuss the continuous wrenching poverty of a third of African Americans today and concludes: "We need something we don't have: a way of speaking about black poverty that doesn't falsify the reality of black advancement, a way of speaking about black advancement that doesn't distort the enduring realities of black poverty. I'd venture that a lot depends on whether we get it."[4]

In truth, America has been one of the leading countries of opportunity for disenfranchised persons and, at the same time, a country of the greatest economic stratification between the luxury of the wealthiest and the wretched conditions of the poorest.[5] In essence, the beliefs of Ayn Rand and Pete Seeger are both correct. To speak only of one side and ignore the other is to create disbelief in most ordinary citizens, who know firsthand of counterexamples to any single view. And this is what I believe to be the danger of ideological truth in education. Many educators in classrooms and schools feel that they have become pawns in the reformers' and policy makers' propaganda game that insists there is a single best way to change the system of American schools.

IDEOLOGY IN EDUCATION

The attacks by E. D. Hirsch, Jr., against progressive education and the equally strident attacks by others such as Alfie Kohn against traditional education are wonderful examples of this either/or ideological stance. Hirsch argues that a common core of knowledge is essential for all students, if they are to succeed in mainstream society. Without a common framework of spoken and written English, historical and cultural references, and direct instruction, marginalized and poor children are deprived of the education that wealthier children pick up automatically from their parents and peers. Thus there is the need to rid our schools of the overwhelming "permissive" practices of activity-based education and to use tests of common knowledge to ensure that all children are acquiring the "cultural capital" needed for success in later life. Kohn in turn speaks against standards, core knowledge, and tests and says that children, regardless of their circumstances, are innately curious and that teachers should explore the topics that intrigue them to open up new freedoms and possibilities. Each proponent has his version of "truth." Each sees little validity in any research supporting the methods that oppose his ideology. Again, the reality is that education is composed of many complexities that defeat any singular truth of how the world can and should work.

For example, might it be that both Hirsch and Kohn have valid perspectives? Focusing on core knowledge that students themselves might not choose but that gives them access to a society in which they might possibly change the current balance of power, wealth, and control seems quite reasonable. Using the curiosity of students to learn multiple histories and cultures and to explore a variety of intelligences in an intensely involving way also seems quite reasonable. It is important that schools be joyful and engaging places. Yet is all learning intrinsically or extrinsically motivated? Most would say it's both—we learn for the joy of it, but some of the most useful learning has taken place because others, not we ourselves, demanded that we do it, do it well, and do it until we got it right.

The polemics surrounding standards versus no standards do not account for complex realities. Are external standards bad or good? Might they be both? Might we have state standards and assessments for most (but not all) public schools in the same state? Some states have standards and assessments that have been well received by educators and the public—not seen as heavy-handed, intrusive, or unfair. Many states have standards and assessments that are volatile in makeup, format, pressure, and consequences.

The standards polarization—again, only one side can win—has come about because people have applied the term "standards" to all systems as if they were identical. However, Maine's standards are quite different from Virginia's. Elements of standards systems can be quite good, such as using disaggregated data to focus on the progress of all students, equalizing funding for poor students and communities, and targeting additional resources. Some states grant variances allowing schools and districts to develop their own assessments. And yes, there are cases in which it is good that standards can be used to close and reorganize schools that have done a disservice to students and parents. Standards systems can be demeaning and harmful—when they equate education with narrowly derived assessments and tests. They can also be tremendously positive in challenging schools and communities to leave no student behind.[6] We need to acknowledge simultaneous realities if we are to educate all students better than before.

PEDAGOGICAL PAIN

The "single-truth" wars have created much pain among teachers and school leaders who are swept into the battles. When whole language gained currency as "the" way to teach reading, teachers using phonics were lambasted, swept aside, and made to feel that they were evil, archaic, fascist practitioners of an indefensible method. Recently, the opposing force has "won" in states led by California and Texas. They have blamed whole language and invented spelling for declining literacy in America. Now teachers of whole language are made to feel abandoned and rejected as "feel-good," self-esteem–promoting contributors to the demise of basic skills.

These periodic surges and countersurges occur because one set of believers ignores any possible merits of the other side. Isn't it possible that many highly literate and culturally diverse people—people that you and I both know—were taught how to read mainly by decoding, phonics, and grammatical rules? Isn't it equally obvious that many highly literate and culturally diverse people have learned to read through literacy immersion, writing workshops, and experiential learning? Why is it so difficult to accept that an open mind about possibilities in education should be seen as a virtue rather than a liability?

Cooperative versus competitive learning is another such brawl. Cooperation is a key aspect of how one learns with and from others, and it undergirds much of community, civic, and business life. Research exists that demonstrates the power of structured team activities for academic and social development. Yet humans, as part of the animal kingdom, are also moved to learn by traits that have helped them to survive: dominance, power, and the need to test oneself against others. Cooperation and competition are not different versions of humanity; they are different dimensions of the same humanity. And thus there is evidence that both cooperation and competition bring out high performance in individuals.

The overarching debate about progressive, learner-centered schools versus teacher-centered, direct-instruction schools will be my last venture into the foolishness of single truths. This debate simplifies and silences the cultural and family values that Lisa Delpit so eloquently writes about in *Other People's Children.*[7] Asking students to conform to certain manners, expecting them to learn what adults determine is important for them, being didactic in instruction, and using "call and response" methods have resulted in great success for teachers and leaders such as Marva Collins, Jaime Escalante, and Lorraine Monroe and for a number of school programs.[8] Regardless of what one personally believes about the atmosphere of such classrooms and schools, students and parents in these settings see such didactic methods as expressions of teachers' love, care, and cultural solidarity.[9] The teachers are proud to demand that their students learn, and they go to almost any length to see that their students can compete with other students.

Yet progressive classrooms and schools that are activity- or project-centered and that cultivate imagination, problem solving, responsibility, and a variety of intellectual pursuits have, in the hands of the most dedicated teachers, also attained incredible success for students. Educators such as Eliot Wigginton, Deborah Meier, George Wood, Gloria Ladson-Billings, Sonia Nieto, and Jabari Mahiri have shown the power of inquiry-centered, progressive learning.

My point is *not* that all methods, techniques, curricula, and structures are of equal worth or that the attitude "anything goes" is acceptable. My point is that, when a group of students and parents choose to be with a group of educators dedicated to a particular philosophy and way of learning, the results for students can be awesome. No one group should have the presumption or power to tell another group that only its way is the right way. Instead, in accordance with publicly determined purposes and criteria, we should be seeking, testing, and developing research-based alternative conceptions and practices of successful education. Kenneth Wilson, a Nobel laureate in physics, remarked about the need to test a multitude of educational approaches through longitudinal research and self-correction to find out what works well, what can be adapted, and what should be discarded.[10] The idea is not to prove that one way is the only way but instead to allow for different conceptions of education to flourish in the marketplace of public education.

RELIGION IN AMERICA AND AN EDUCATED AMERICAN

Of all Western nations, America is the country with the highest percentage of citizens actively involved in religious and spiritual practices.[11] Why? Because it has no official state religion and no divine story behind its creation. Those countries that do have histories of such official state religion—a one way to believe for all—tend to have lower percentages of citizen involvement in religious practice. This example suggests why we must avoid a single governmental (local, state, or national) conception of education. The analogy with religion ends at a certain point, as the U.S. government needs to remain neutral and not use public funds to promote any particular set of religious beliefs. But government must use public funds to support a public education consistent with democratic ideals.[12] And the best way for doing so is to create a system of state schools that promote various publicly determined conceptions of an educated American.

Public education can be defined in several overlapping ways. Public education is funded by taxpayers, it is an education for the public, it is open and without cost to students and parents, it is compulsory, it is governed by public authority, it is nonprofit, and it always *should be* nondiscriminatory and nonrepressive of students and parents.[13] It is public because it serves a common good: the education of students to have choices of "life, liberty, and the pursuit of happiness" and to acknowledge those choices for others.

Within these definitions of public, American education is always an experiment—one hopes a thoughtful one—that must constantly test ways to further realize the hopes and aspirations of all the nation's people. Whenever one truth stamps out all others—whether it be through one system of tests, one approach to curriculum, one conception of knowledge, a single method of instruction, or a uniform structure for all public schools—democracy itself and education for a democracy are subverted.

In first proposing the need for common schools, Horace Mann wrote in the 1840s that public schools would be the great equalizers of human conditions, the balance wheel of the social machinery. Poverty would disappear and with it the discord between the haves and the have-nots; life for all people would be longer, better, and happier. The common school would be free, for poor and rich alike, as good as any private school, and nonsectarian. (The common school was not to be a school for common people but rather a school common to all people.) And the pedagogy of the common or free school would stress the "self-discipline of individuals, self-control, and self-governance." The issue for Mann was that the educated person was to have a free, deliberate choice between obedience and anarchy.[14]

Another view of the educated person in a democracy was shaped by the Lockean sympathies of early American thought. The educated person would be the one who renounced self-indulgence, practiced restraint, and saw the virtue of frugality and labor. In this view, one would work not for what one could accumulate but in order to focus the human mind and body.

Jefferson's concept of the educated person was the farmer—a person who lived apart from others; pursued his own curiosity about science, philosophy, and art after a long day of self-sustaining chores; and then determined those times that he should participate in neighborhood and community affairs. The farmer's life was a combination of aloneness, individuality, and self-learning with minimal but significant civic responsibility.

W. E. B. Du Bois, referring to the need for African American children to learn, saw public education as giving "our children the fairness of a start which will equip them with such an array of facts and such an attitude toward truth that they can have a real chance to judge what the world is and what its greater minds have thought it might be."[15]

Education might also be defined as making a good neighbor—one who cares for and respects others, who takes care of his or her own family needs, and who contributes to the welfare of others.[16] Such a person would possess a respect for other people and an understanding of life conditions locally, nationally, and internationally; the ability to communicate with diverse others; analytic and problem-solving skills; and the competence to choose what to do with one's own life in economic, social, recreational, and aesthetic pursuits. Does one need three years of high school or college-level preparatory mathematics to develop these attributes? Does one need to learn French? How about Chinese? What level of mastery does one need in the various disciplines? Is it better to study discrete subjects or an integrated curriculum with applications to the world outside of school? The question here is, What knowledge, skills, and understandings are needed to be a good neighbor and citizen?

In a high school curriculum controlled by college admission requirements, there are expected core courses, and good scores on the SAT or ACT have become essential measures of an educated American. Whether going to college or not, most students will not use most of what they are required to learn, whether mathematics or history or language or science. Is it still essential? Again, says who? Dare I ask the unspeakable: Can one be a good neighbor and a wise and productive citizen without going to college?

Is the purpose of public education to train a highly skilled work force to support American corporations? If so, the definition of a well-educated American as a good worker will place a great deal of emphasis on technology. But again, who should determine what is a well-educated person? For example, the Waldorf schools in America have children work with natural materials for the first three to five years of schooling.[17] Children work only with wood, clay, water, and paint, on long, painstaking projects for several years before the technological world becomes a source of their learning—no televisions, no phones, no computers in early childhood and primary classrooms. The prime emphasis is on imagination and work in an all-natural environment. Are these students educated less well than others? According to what criteria?

To be blunt, any single truth or concept of an educated American will be fraught with contradictions. The real danger of any one reform effort, such as a standards movement that relies on a single test, is the promotion of a single definition of the well-educated citizen as a college graduate who is technologically prepared to lead a successful economic life. The idea that an educated citizen might not want to make vast sums of money or work in a corporation but instead might seek success in quietness, resistance, or even detachment from corporate/college-controlled work, has eroded in America. Even to mention the idea that education is not mostly about jobs or money but about choosing how to live one's life among others is to be seen as a romantic, a throwback to another time.

My point is not to convince others of any one definition of a well-educated person but to share the need for varied conceptions of education, conceptions that must be in conformance with "public" criteria and equally based on data about student accomplishments and successes.

WHAT DO WE DO?

As a reformer who advocates the progressive tradition and assists schools in keeping it alive, I do not seek a common ground for public education—an eclectic "all things of equal merit" ground—but instead wish to move beyond that to a higher ground that incorporates complexity and competing conceptions. A higher ground where contradictory truths must be part and parcel of American democracy. We need an education system that supports multiple conceptions of an educated American, that subjects all such conceptions to the scrutiny of research and public accountability, and that fixes all actions of classrooms and schools within the boundaries of equity. American students and schools lose each time one "truth" gains currency and suppresses competing notions of public education.

So let me end by stating that, in my experience with schools, education reformers, policy makers, legislators, corporate persons, community activists, and citizens at large, I have found people of astonishingly good will and passionate intent who labor in the light of controversy about what our schools need or deserve. They are accused by their opponents of being self-indulgent conspirators with sinister motives, but most of them, or at least those that I know, are not. However, many of those who are most influential or powerful are singularly convinced that theirs is the true way to improve education and that all other ways are false, bad, and corrupt.

We need to realize that, most often, life does not contain single truths but instead is about predicaments, competing views, and apparent conflicts. The public school system must value and allow multiple conceptions of education that students, parents, and faculty members can choose from—some purebreds, some hybrids, and some yet to be known, but all devoted to students and their pursuit of the American Dream.

We must fight against any single model, structure, method, or system of education. We must expand the freedom of schools to test new concepts of standards, assessments, and accountability. Ultimately, we must hold every school and district responsible for whether it has provided an education for all children that can be documented to increase choices of "life, liberty, and the pursuit of happiness." *That* is an American education.

ENDNOTES

1. Carl D. Glickman, *Revolutionizing America's Schools* (San Francisco: Jossey–Bass, 1998).
2. See E. D. Hirsch, Jr., The Schools We Need and Why We Don't Have Them (New York: Doubleday, 1996); Alfie Kohn, The Schools Our Children Deserve (Boston: Houghton Mifflin, 1999); Susan Ohanian, One Size Fits Few: The Folly of Educational Standards (Portsmouth, NH: Heinemann, 1999); and I. de Pommereau, "Tougher High School Standards Signal Greater Demands on Students," Christian Science Monitor, 16 June 1996, p. 12, 1-C.
3. Seymour Martin Lipset, *American Exceptionalism: A Double-Edged Sword* (New York: Norton, 1996).
4. Henry Louis Gates, Jr., and Cornel West, *The Future of the Race* (New York: Random House, 1996), pp. 19, 38.
5. Jim Myers, "Notes on the Murder of Thirty of My Neighbors," *Atlantic*, March 2000, pp. 72–88.
6. Chris Gallagher, "A Seat at the Table: Teachers Reclaiming Assessment Through Rethinking Accountability," *Phi Delta Kappan*, March 2000, pp. 502–7.
7. Lisa Delpit, *Other People's Children: Cultural Conflict in the Classroom* (New York: New Press, 1995).
8. See, for example, such schools as P.S. 161 in New York, KIPP Academies in Texas and New York, and the Frederick Douglass Middle School in New York.
9. Samuel Casey Carter, *No Excuses: Seven Principals of Low-Income Schools Who Set the Standards for High Achievement* (Washington, DC: Heritage Foundation, 1999); and Jacqueline Jordan

Irvine, "Seeing with the Cultural Eye: Different Perspectives of African American Teachers and Researchers," DeWitt Wallace–Reader's Digest Distinguished Lecture presented at the annual meeting of the American Educational Research Association, New Orleans, April 2000.

10. Kenneth Wilson and Bennett Daviss, *Redesigning Education* (New York: Teachers College Press, 1994).

11. Lipset, op. cit.; and Warren A. Nord, *Religion and American Education: Rethinking a National Dilemma* (Chapel Hill: University of North Carolina Press, 1995).

12. John Dayton and Carl D. Glickman, "Curriculum Change and Implementation: Democratic Imperatives," *Peabody Journal of Education*, vol. 9, no. 4, 1994, pp. 62–86; Benjamin R. Barber, *An Aristocracy of Everyone: The Politics of Education and the Future of America* (New York: Ballantine, 1992); and Amy Gutmann, *Democratic Education* (Princeton, NJ: Princeton University Press, 1987).

13. Gutmann, op. cit.

14. Lawrence A. Cremin, *The Transformation of the School: Progressivism in American Education 1876–1957* (New York: Random House, 1964), pp. 3–11.

15. W. E. B. Du Bois, "The Freedom to Learn," in Philip S. Foner, ed., *W. E. B. Du Bois Speaks* (New York: Pathfinder, 1970), pp. 230–31.

16. George H. Wood, *A Time to Learn* (New York: Dutton, 1998).

17. Todd Oppenheimer, "Schooling the Imagination," *Atlantic*, September 1999, pp. 71–83.

DISCUSSION QUESTIONS

1. Does the United States live up to its reputation as the land of opportunity? Does public education live up to its reputation for providing a ladder to success for groups that are not part of the mainstream culture?
2. Are educational decisions made more often on the basis of good intentions, ideology, or results? Which is the criterion that is most appropriate for guiding practice?
3. What essential knowledge and skills should an educated person in a democracy possess?
4. Given the heated debates about education that are prevalent today, is it possible to make decisions about public education in a civil and responsible manner?
5. Would increasing the number of charter schools or the opportunities for school choice have the effect of undermining or reinforcing the principles of democracy?

CHAPTER 33

Assessment for Learning Around the World: What Would It Mean to Be Internationally Competitive?

LINDA DARLING-HAMMOND
LAURA MCCLOSKEY

FOCUSING QUESTIONS

1. Compare the curriculum of the United States with the curriculum of highly ranked nations.
2. Compare assessment methods in the United States with that of other highly ranked nations.
3. How do curricula and assessment differ based on country size? Explain.
4. Internationally, what role do teachers play in the development of assessments?
5. Compared with the United States, what role do assessments play in school rankings and the development of curriculum?

High-performing nations integrate curriculum, instruction, and assessment to improve both teaching and learning.

Since the release of A Nation at Risk, the U.S. has launched a set of wide-ranging reforms with the intention of better preparing all children for the higher educational demands of life and work in the 21st century. All 50 states have developed standards for learning and tests to evaluate student progress. No Child Left Behind reinforced using test-based accountability to raise achievement, yet the U.S. has fallen further behind on international assessments of student learning since the law was passed in 2001.

On the Program in International Student Assessment (PISA) tests in 2006, the U.S. ranked 35th among the top 40 countries in mathematics and 31st in science, a decline in both raw scores and rankings from three years earlier.[1] (Reading scores were not reported, because of editing problems with the U.S. test.) Furthermore, in each disciplinary area tested, U.S. students scored lowest on the problem-solving items. The U.S. also had a much wider achievement gap than the most highly ranked jurisdictions, such as Finland, Canada, Australia, New Zealand, Hong Kong, Korea, and Japan.

Policy discussions in Washington often refer to these rankings when emphasizing the need to create more "internationally competitive" standards by benchmarking expectations in the U.S. to those in high-performing nations. Typically, this means looking at topics that are taught at various grade levels in various countries. These analyses reveal that higher-achieving countries teach fewer topics more deeply each year; focus more on reasoning skills and applications of knowledge, rather than mere coverage; and have a more thoughtful sequence of expectations based on developmental learning progressions within and across domains.[2]

However, we must examine how these topics are taught and assessed—so that we understand how other countries' education systems shape what students actually learn and can do. European and Asian nations that have steeply improved student learning have focused explicitly on creating curriculum guidance and assessments that focus on the so-called 21st-century skills: the abilities to find and organize information to solve problems, frame and conduct investigations, analyze and synthesize data, apply learning to new situations, self-monitor and improve one's own learning and performance, communicate well in multiple forms, work in teams, and learn independently.

Curriculum differences are reinforced by sharp divergence between the forms of testing used in the U.S. and those used in higher-achieving countries. Whereas U.S. tests rely primarily on multiple-choice items that evaluate recall and recognition of discrete facts, most high-achieving countries rely largely on open-ended items that require students to analyze, apply knowledge, and write extensively. Furthermore, these nations' growing emphasis on project-based, inquiry-oriented learning has led to an increasing prominence for school-based tasks, which include research projects, science investigations, development of products, and reports or presentations about these efforts. These assessments, which are incorporated into the overall examination scoring system, influence the day-to-day work of teaching and learning, focusing it on the development of higher-order skills and use of knowledge to solve problems.

Smaller countries often have a system of national standards that are sometimes—though not always—accompanied by national tests in the upper grades. Top-ranking Finland uses local assessments almost exclusively in order to evaluate its national standards and manages a voluntary national assessment at only one grade level. Larger nations—like Canada, Australia, and China—have state- or provincial-level standards, and their assessment systems are typically a blend of state and local assessments. Managing assessment at the state rather than national level, where it remains relatively close to the schools, turns out to be an important way of enabling strong teacher participation and ensuring high-quality local assessments that can be moderated to ensure consistency in scoring.

In many cases, local assessments complement centralized "on-demand" tests, constituting up to 50% of the final examination score. Tasks are mapped to the standards or syllabus for the subject and are selected because they represent critical skills, topics, and concepts. They are often outlined in the curriculum guide, but they are generally designed, administered, and scored locally, based on common specifications and evaluation criteria. Whether locally or centrally developed, decisions about when to undertake these tasks are made at the classroom level, so they are used when appropriate for students' learning process and teachers can get information and provide feedback as needed, something that traditional standardized tests cannot do. In addition, as teachers use and evaluate these tasks, they become more knowledgeable about both the standards and how to teach to them and about their students' learning needs. Thus the process improves the quality of teaching and learning.

Like the behind-the-wheel test given for all new drivers in the U.S., these performance assessments evaluate what students can actually do, not just what they know. The road test not only reveals some important things about drivers' skills, preparation for the test also helps improve those skills as novice drivers practice to get better. In the same way, performance assessments set a standard toward which everyone must work. The task and the standards are not secret, so teachers and students know what skills they need to develop and how they will need to be demonstrated.

Finally, these countries do not use their examination systems to rank or punish schools or to deny diplomas to students. Following the problems that resulted from the Thatcher government's use of test based school rankings, which caused a narrowing of the curriculum and widespread exclusions of students from school,[3] several countries enacted legislation precluding the use of test results for school rankings. High school examinations provide information for higher education, vocational training, and employment, and students often choose areas in which they will be examined, as a means of demonstrating their qualifications. Because the systems are focused on using information for curriculum improvement, rather than sanctions, governments can set higher standards and work with schools to achieve them, rather than devising tests and setting cut scores at a minimal level to avoid dysfunctional side effects.

Many states in the U.S.—including Connecticut, Kentucky, Maine, Nebraska, New Hampshire, New Jersey, New York, Rhode Island, Vermont, and Wyoming—have developed and used state and local performance assessments as part of their testing systems. Indeed, the National Science Foundation provided millions of dollars for states to develop such hands-on science and math assessments as part of its Systemic Initiative in the 1990s, and prototypes exist all over the country. Studies have found that using such assessments has improved teaching quality and increased student achievement, especially on tasks that require complex reasoning and problem solving.[4] However, these assessments have been difficult to sustain, especially under NCLB's annual testing requirements, because the policy community has little understanding about how systems of assessment for learning might be constructed and managed at scale.

The U.S. can learn a great deal by examining the assessment systems of several high-achieving education systems: two of the highest-achieving Scandinavian nations—Finland and Sweden—plus a group of English-speaking jurisdictions that have some shared approaches to assessment, as well as some interesting variations—Australia, Hong Kong, and the United Kingdom. In particular, we can learn from how assessments in those nations are linked to curriculum and integrated into the instructional process to shape and improve learning for students and teachers alike.

FINLAND AND SWEDEN

Finland has been a poster child for school improvement since it rapidly climbed to the top of international rankings after emerging from the Soviet Union's shadow. Finland now ranks first among all OECD nations on the PISA assessments in mathematics, science, and reading. Finland attributes these gains to intensive investments in teacher education—all teachers receive three years of high-quality graduate-level preparation completely at state expense—plus major overhaul of the curriculum and assessment system. Most teachers now hold master's degrees in both their content and in education, and their preparation is aimed at learning to teach diverse learners—including special needs students—for deep understanding. Preparation includes a strong focus on how to use formative performance assessments in the service of student learning.[5] Sweden also invests heavily in state-funded graduate teacher education for all teachers and relies on a highly trained teaching force to implement its curriculum and assessment system.

Over 40 years, both Finland and Sweden have shifted from highly centralized systems emphasizing external testing to more localized systems using multiple forms of assessments. Around 1970, Sweden abolished its nationally administered exit exam that ranked upper secondary students and placed them in higher education programs.[6] Finland followed suit, and both nations stopped tracking students into different streams by their test scores, offering a common core curriculum to all students. These changes were intended to equalize educational outcomes and provide more open access to higher education.[7]

Although it may seem counterintuitive to Americans accustomed to external testing as a means of accountability, Finland's leaders point to its use of school-based, student-centered, open-ended tasks embedded in the curriculum as an important reason for the nation's extraordinary success on international exams.[8] Policy makers decided that if they invested in very skillful teachers, they could allow local schools more autonomy to decide what and how to teach—a reaction against the highly centralized system they sought to overhaul. Finland's national core curriculum is a much leaner document, reduced from hundreds of pages of highly specific prescriptions to descriptions of a small number of skills and core concepts each year. (For example, about 10 pages describe the full set of math standards for all grades.) This guides teachers in collectively developing local curricula and assessments that encourage students to be active learners who can find, analyze, and use information to solve problems in novel situations.

Finland has no external standardized tests to rank students or schools. Finnish education authorities periodically evaluate school-level samples of student performance, generally at the end of the 2nd and 9th grades, to inform curriculum decisions and school investments. Local educators design and manage all other assessments. The national core curriculum provides teachers with recommended assessment criteria for specific grades in each subject and for the final assessment of student progress each year.[9] Schools then use those guidelines to craft more detailed learning outcomes and curricula at each school, along with approaches to assessing curriculum benchmarks.

The national standards emphasize that the main purpose of assessing students is to guide and encourage students' own reflection and self-assessment. Consequently, ongoing feedback from the teacher is very important. Teachers give students formative and summative reports both through verbal feedback and on a numerical scale reflecting the students' levels of performance in relation to curriculum objectives. The teachers' reports must be based on multiple forms of assessment, not only exams.

Finland uses assessments to cultivate students' active learning skills by asking open-ended questions and helping students address these problems. In a Finnish classroom, teachers rarely stand at the front of a classroom lecturing students for 50 minutes. Instead, students are generally engaged in independent or group projects, often choosing tasks to work on and setting their own targets with teachers, who serve as coaches.[10] The cultivation of independence and active learning encourages students to develop analytical thinking, problem-solving, and metacognitive skills.

Before attending university, most Finnish students take a voluntary matriculation exam that asks students to apply problem-solving, analytic, and writing skills.[11] Teachers use official guidelines to grade matriculation exams locally, and samples of the grades are re-examined by professional raters hired by the Matriculation Exam Board.

Similarly, Sweden implements its nationally outlined and locally implemented curriculum with multiple assessments managed at the school level. Each school adapts a national curriculum and subjectmatter syllabi to local conditions.[12] Teachers design and score school-based assessments based on objectives outlined in each syllabus, and they assign grades based on syllabus goals and national assessment criteria. They are expected to meet with every student and parent each term to discuss the student's learning and social development, and they use a number of diagnostic materials to assess students' learning in Swedish, Swedish as a second language, English, and mathematics in relation to goals set by the syllabi.[13]

Schools offer nationally approved examinations in these same subjects in 9th grade and in the upper secondary years, where additional subject exams are available.[14] Teachers work with university faculty to design the tasks and questions, and they weight information from these exams, their own assessments, and classroom work to assign a grade reflecting how well students have met the objectives of the syllabus.[15] Regional education officials and schools provide time for teachers to calibrate their grading practices to minimize variation across the schools and across the region.[16] Toward the end of their upper secondary schooling, Swedish students receive a final grade or "learning certificate" in each area that acts as a compilation of all of these sources of evidence, including projects completed by the student as well as grades awarded for courses.

AUSTRALIA, THE UNITED KINGDOM, AND HONG KONG

Unlike such smaller countries as Finland and Sweden that have national curricula, in the much larger Australia each state has its own curriculum and assessment system. Australia's only national assessment is a periodic, matrix-sample-based assessment, similar to the National Assessment of Educational Progress in the U.S. In most Australian states, local school-based performance assessment is a well-developed part of the system. In some cases, states have also centralized assessment with performance components. The two highest-achieving states, Queensland and Victoria, have the most highly developed systems of local performance assessment. Victoria, which uses a blended model of centralized and school-based assessment, also generally performs well on national and international tests.

Queensland, Australia. Queensland has had no external assessment system for 40 years. All assessments became school-based when the traditional "post-colonial" examination system was eliminated in the early 1970s, about the same time as in Finland and Sweden. Teachers develop, administer, and score school-based assessments in relation to the national curriculum guidelines and state syllabi (also developed by teachers). Panels that include teachers from other schools and university professors also moderate the assessments.

The syllabi spell out a few key concepts and skills to be learned in each course and the projects or activities (including minimum assessment requirements) that students should engage in. Each school designs its program to fit the needs and experiences of its own students, choosing specific texts and topics with this in mind. At year's end, teachers use a five-point grading scale to grade each portfolio of student work, which includes specific assessment tasks. To calibrate these grades, teachers assemble a selection of portfolios from each grade level—one from each of the five score levels, plus borderline cases—and send these to a regional panel for moderation. A panel of five teachers rescores the portfolios and confers about whether the grade is warranted. A state panel also looks at portfolios across schools. Based on these moderation processes, the school is instructed to adjust grades so they are comparable to others.

Queensland's "New Basics" and "Rich Tasks" approach to assessment, which began in 2003, offers extended, multidisciplinary tasks developed centrally but used when teachers determine the time is right and they can be integrated with locally oriented curricula. They are "specific activities that students undertake that have real-world value and use, and through which students are able to display their grasp and use of important ideas and skills."[17] Rich Tasks are defined as:

> a culminating performance or demonstration or product that is purposeful and models a life role. It presents substantive, real problems to solve and engages learners in forms of pragmatic social action that have real value in the world. The problems require identification, analysis, and resolution, and require students to analyze, theorize, and engage intellectually with the world. As well as having this connectedness to the world beyond the classroom, the tasks are also rich in their application: they represent an educational outcome of demonstrable and substantial intellectual and educational value. And, to be truly rich, a task must be transdisciplinary. Transdisciplinary learnings draw upon practices and skills across disciplines while retaining the integrity of each individual discipline.

The science and ethics task summarized on the left illustrates these traits.

A bank of these tasks now exists across grade levels, along with scoring rubrics and moderation processes by which the quality of the tasks, the student work, and the scoring can be evaluated. Research indicates the system has supported school improvement. Studies have found stronger student engagement in learning in schools using the Rich Tasks. On traditional tests, New Basics students scored about the same as students in the traditional program, but they performed notably better on assessments designed to gauge higher-order thinking.

The Singapore government has employed the developers of the Queensland system to focus its new school improvement strategies on performance assessments. High-scoring Hong Kong has also begun to expand its already ambitious school-based assessment system in collaboration with Queensland assessment developers.

Victoria, Australia. In Victoria, a mixed system of centralized and decentralized assessment combines school-based assessment practices with a set of state exams. Guided by the Victoria Essential Learning Standards, the AIM assessment program indicates how well students' literacy and numeracy skills are developing at grades 3, 5, 7, and 9. Assessment tasks include extended open-ended writing tasks, as well as some multiple-choice responses.

The Victoria Curriculum and Assessment Authority (VCAA) establishes courses in a wide range of studies, develops external examinations, and ensures the quality of the school-assessed component of the Victoria

Certification of Education. VCAA conceptualizes assessment as "of," "for," and "as" learning. Teachers, along with university faculty, develop assessments, and all prior year assessments are public in order to make the standards and means of measuring them as transparent as possible. Before students take the external examinations, teachers and academics take the exams themselves, as if they were students. The external subject-specific examinations, given in grades 11 and 12, include written, oral, and performance elements scored by classroom teachers.

In addition, at least 50% of the total examination score consists of classroom-based tasks given throughout the school year. Teachers design these required assignments and assessments—lab experiments and investigations on central topics, as well as research papers and presentations. These classroom tasks ensure that students have the kind of learning opportunities that prepare them for assessments, that they are getting feedback to improve, and that they will be prepared to succeed not only on these very challenging tests but in college and in life, where they will have to apply knowledge in these ways.

An example of how this blended assessment system works can be seen in the interplay between an item from the Victoria, Australia, biology test and the classroom-based tasks also evaluated for the examination score. The open-ended item describes a particular virus and how it operates, then asks students to design a drug to kill the virus and explain how the drug operates (the multipage written answer is to include diagrams), and then asks students to design and describe an experiment to test the drug. In preparation for this on-demand test, students taking biology will have been assessed on six pieces of work during the school year covering specific outcomes in the syllabus. For example, they will have conducted "practical tasks," such as using a microscope to study plant and animal cells by preparing slides of cells, staining them, and comparing them in a variety of ways, resulting in a written product with visual elements. They also will have completed and presented a research report on characteristics of pathogenic organisms and mechanisms by which organisms can defend against disease. These tasks link directly to the expectations that students will encounter on the external examination but go well beyond what that examination can measure in terms of how students can apply their knowledge.

The tasks are graded according to criteria set out in the syllabus. The quality of the tasks assigned by teachers, work done by students, and the appropriateness of the grades and feedback given to students are audited through an inspection system, and schools receive feedback on all of these elements. In addition, the VCAA uses statistical moderation to ensure that the same assessment standards are applied to students across schools. External exams are used as the basis for this moderation, which adjusts the level and spread of each school's assessments of its students to match the level and spread of the same students' scores on the common external test score. The result is a rich curriculum for students with extensive teacher participation and a comparable means for examining student learning.

United Kingdom. As in Victoria, assessments in Great Britain use a combination of external and school-based tasks based on the national curriculum and course syllabi. Throughout die school years, classroom-based tasks scored by teachers are used to evaluate student achievement of curriculum goals. At age 7, students take open-ended, nationally developed assessments in English and math that are scored by teachers in the school; at age 11, similar tests in English, math, and science are marked externally. At age 14, there was once a set of national exams to supplement teacher-created and administered assessments. Those external exams were abolished in October 2008, leaving only the teacher-developed assessments.[18]

While not mandatory, most students take a set of exams at year 11 (age 16) to achieve their General Certificate of Secondary Education (GCSE). Students may take as many single-subject or combined-subject assessments as they like, and they choose which ones they will take based on their interests and areas of expertise. Most GCSE items are essay questions. The math exam includes questions that ask students to show the reasoning behind their answers, and foreign language exams require oral presentations. About 25% to 30% of the final examination score is based on coursework and assessments developed and graded by teachers. In many subjects, students also complete a project worked on in class that is specified in the syllabus.

Wales and Northern Ireland allow students to participate in the GCSE exams at the high school level on a voluntary basis, but both broke from the more centralized system introduced in England under the Thatcher administration (later modified during the Blair administration as described above) and opted to abolish national exams.[19] Much like Finland and Sweden, Welsh schools during the primary years have a national school curriculum supported by teacher-created, administered, and scored assessments.[20] Northern Ireland, which has recently climbed significantly in international rankings, especially in literacy, is implementing "Assessment for Learning." This approach emphasizes locally developed, administered, and scored assessments and focuses, as in Finland, on students and teachers setting goals and success criteria together, teachers asking open-ended questions and students explaining their reasoning, teachers providing feedback during formative assessment sessions, and students engaging in self-assessment and reflection on their learning. Optional externally graded assessments also focus on how students reason, think, and problem solve.[21]

Hong Kong. In collaboration with educators from Australia, the UK, and other nations, Hong Kong's assessment system is evolving from a highly centralized examination system to one that increasingly emphasizes school-based, formative assessments that expect students to analyze issues and solve problems. The government has decided to gradually replace the Hong Kong Certificate of Education Examinations, which most students sit for at the end of their five-year secondary education, with a new diploma that will feature school-based assessments. In addition, the Territory-wide System Assessment (TSA), which assesses lower-grade student performance in Chinese, English, and mathematics, is developing an online bank of assessment tasks to enable schools to assess students and receive feedback on their performance on their own timeframes. The formal TSA assessments, which include both written and oral components, occur at primary grades 3 and 6 and secondary grade 3 (the equivalent of 9th grade in the U.S.).

As outlined in Hong Kong's "Learning to Learn" reform plan, the goal of the reforms isto shape curriculum and instruction around critical thinking, problem solving, self-management skills, and collaboration. A particular concern is to develop metacognitive thinking skills, so that students may themselves identify strengths and areas needing additional work.[22] By 2007, curriculum and assessment guides were published for four core subjects and 20 elective subjects, and assessments in the first two subjects—Chinese language and English language—were revised. These became criterion-referenced, performance-based assessments featuring not only the kinds of essays previously used on the exams, but also new speaking and listening components, the composition of written papers testing integrated skills, and a school-based component that factors into the examination score. Although existing assessments already use open-ended responses, the proportion of such responses will increase in the revised assessments.

As they do with existing assessments, teachers develop the new assessments with the participation of higher education faculty, and teachers who are trained as assessors score them. Tests are allocated randomly to scorers, and essay responses are typically rated by two independent scorers.[23] Results of the new school-based assessments are statistically moderated to ensure comparability within the province. The assessments are internationally benchmarked, through the evaluation of sample student papers, to peg results to those in other countries.

CONCLUSION

The design and use of standards, curricula, and assessments in high-achieving nations around the world are significantly different from the way tests are designed and used in the U.S. Most testing in the U.S. emphasizes externally developed, machine-scored instruments that enter and leave the school in secret, offering little opportunity for teacher engagement with the evaluation of standards and little opportunity for student production of analyses, solutions, or ideas.

By contrast, assessment abroad involves teachers in developing and scoring intellectually challenging performance tasks that are embedded in and guide instruction, providing grist for feedback, student self-evaluation, and learning. The integration of curriculum, assessment, and instruction in a well-developed teaching and learning system creates the foundation for much more equitable and productive outcomes. Teachers and students come to understand the standards deeply, and they work continuously on activities and projects that develop skills as they are applied in the real world, as well as on the examinations themselves.

The tasks common in these assessment systems reflect what people increasingly need to know to succeed in today's knowledge-based economy: the abilities to find, analyze, and use information to solve real problems; to write and speak clearly and persuasively; to defend ideas; and to design and manage projects. While U.S. accountability efforts have focused on achieving higher test scores, they have not yet developed the kind of teaching and learning systems that could develop widespread capacity for significantly greater learning. A new vision for assessment will be critical to this goal—and to the possibilities of success for our children in today's and tomorrow's world.

Linda Darling-Hammond is the Charles E. DuCommun professor of education at Stanford University. Laura McCloskey is a doctoral student in the Stanford University School of Education.

SWEDISH ASSESSMENTS

Swedish assessments use open-ended, authentic tasks asking students to demonstrate content knowledge and analytic skills in grappling with real-world problems. This sample question from a 5th-grade exam asks students (aged 11–12) to think through a problem that they might have in their own lives:

> Carl bikes home from school at four o'clock, it takes about a quarter of an hour. In the evening, he's going back to school because the class is having a party. The party starts at 6 o'clock. Before the class party starts, Carl has to eat dinner. When he comes home, his grandmother calls, who is also his neighbor. She wants him to bring in her post before he bikes over to the class party. She also wants him to take her dog for a walk, then to come in and have a chat. What does Carl have time to do before the party begins? Write and describe below how you have reasoned.[1]

Upper secondary exams also frame challenging questions in real-world terms, with

1. Astrid Petterson, The National Tests and National Assessment in Sweden (Stockholm: PRIM gruppen, 2008), www.prim.su.se/artiktar/pdf/Sw_test_ICME.pdf.

the expectation that students will show their work and reasoning. For example:

> In 1976, Lena had a monthly salary of 6,000 kr. By 1984, her salary had risen to 9,000 kr. In current prices, her salary had risen by 50%. How large was the percent change in fixed prices? In 1976, the Consumer Price Index (CPI) was 382; in 1984, it was 818.[2]

> Students who experience a steady diet of such challenging assignments, which require thoughtful reasoning and the ability to communicate their thinking, are well-prepared for the kinds of problem solving required in the real world.

SCIENCE AND ETHICS CONFER

Students must identify, explore, and make judgments about a biotechnological process to which there are ethical dimensions. Students identify scientific techniques used, as well as significant recent contributions to the field. They will also research frameworks of ethical principles for coming to terms with an identified ethical issue or question. Using this information, they prepare preconference materials for an international conference that will feature selected speakers who are leading lights in their respective fields.

In order to do this, students must choose and explore an area of biotechnology where ethical issues are under consideration and undertake laboratory activities that help them understand some of the laboratory practices. This enables them to:

A. Provide a written explanation of the fundamental technological differences in some of the techniques used, or of potential use, in this area (included in the preconference package for delegates who are not necessarily experts in this area).

B. Consider the range of ethical issues raised in regard to this area's purposes and actions, as well as scientific techniques and principles, and present a deep analysis of an ethical issue about which there is a debate in terms of an ethical framework.

C. Select six real-life people who have made relevant contributions to this area and write a 150–200 word precis about each one indicating his or her contribution, as well as a letter of invitation to one of them.

This assessment measures research and analytic skills; laboratory practices; understanding biological and chemical structures and systems, nomenclature and notations; organizing, arranging, sifting through, and making sense of ideas; communicating using formal correspondence; précis writing with a purpose; understanding ethical issues and principles; time management, and much more.

2. Max A. Eckstein and Harold J. Noah, Secondary School Examinations: International Perspectives on Policies and Practice (New Haven, Conn.: Yale University Press, 1993), pp. 270–72.

ENDNOTES

1. Institute for Education Sciences, Highlights from PISA2006: Performance of U.S. 15-Year-Old Students in Science and Mathematics Literacy in an International Context (Washington, D.C.: U.S. Department of Education, 2007), http://nces.ed.gov/surveys/pisa/index.asp.

2. See for example, William H. Schmidt, Hsing Chi Wang, and Curtis McKnight, "Curriculum Coherence: An Examination of U.S. Mathematics and Science Content Standards from an International Perspective," Journal of Curriculum Studies, vol. 37, 2005, pp. 525–59; Gilbert A. Valverde and William H. Schmidt, "Greater Expectations: Learning from Other Nations in the Quest for 'World-Class Standards' in U.S. School Mathematics and Science," Journal of Curriculum Studies, vol. 32, 2000, pp. 651–87; and Peter Fensham, "Progression in School Science Curriculum: A Rational Prospect or a Chimera?" Research in Science Education, vol. 24, 1994, pp. 76–82.

3. Elle Rustique-Forrester, "Accountability and the Pressures to Exclude: A Cautionary Tale from England," Education Policy Analysis Archives, 2005, http://epaa.asu.edu/epaa/vl3n26/.
4. For a summary, see Linda Darling-Hammond and E. Rustique-Forrester, "The Consequences of Student Testing for Teaching and Teacher Quality," in Joan Herman and Edward Haertel, eds., The Uses and Misuses of Data in Accountability Testing (Maiden, Mass.: Blackwell, 2005), pp. 289–319.
5. Reijo Laukkanen, "Finnish Strategy for High-Level Education for All," in N. C. Soguel and P. Jaccard, eds., Governance and Performance of Education Systems (Springer, 2008), p. 319. See also Friedrich Buchberger and Irina Buchberger, "Problem Solving Capacity of a Teacher Education System as a Condition of Success? An Analysis of the 'Finnish Case,'" in F. Buchberger and S. Berghammer, eds., Education Policy Analysis in a Comparative Perspective (Linz: Trauner, 2003), pp. 222–37.
6. European Commission, Directorate-General for Education and Culture, Eurybase: The Information Database on Education Systems in Europe, The Education System in Sweden, 2006/2007 (Brussells: Eurydice, 2007).
7. Max A. Eckstein and Harold J. Noah, Secondary School Examinations: International Perspectives on Policies and Practice (New Haven, Conn.: Yale University Press, 1993), p. 84.
8. Finnish National Board of Education, "Background for Finnish PISA Success," 12 November 2007, www.oph.fi/english/SubPage.asp?parxi=447,65535,77331; and Jari Lavonen. "Reasons Behind Finnish Students' Success in the PISA Scientific Literacy Assessment," (Helsinki: University of Helsinki, 2008), www.oph.fi/info/fenlandinpisastudies/conference2008/science_results_and_reasons.pdf
9. Finnish National Board of Education, "Basic Education," 10 June 2009, www.oph.fi/english/page.asp?path=447,4699,4847.
10. Salla Korpela, "The Finnish School—A Source of Skills and Well-Being: A Day at Stromberg Lower Comprehensive School," December 2004, http://virtual.finland.fi/netacomm/news/showarticle.asp?intNWSAID=30625.
11. The Finnish Matriculation Examination, 2008, www.ylioppilastutkinto.fi/en/index.html.
12. Swedish National Agency for Education, "The Swedish School System: Compulsory School," 2005, www.skolverket.se/sb/d/354/a/959.
13. Eckstein and Noah, op. cit., pp. 83–84; Qualifications and Curriculum Authority, "Sweden: Assessment Arrangements," 2008, www.inca. org. uk/690.html; and Sharon O'Donnell, International Review of Curriculum and Assessment Framework: Comparative Tables and Factual Summaries, 2004 (London: Qualifications and Curriculum Authority, National Foundation for Educational Research, December 2004), p. 23, www.inca.org.uk/pdf/comparative.pdf.
14. Swedish National Agency for Education, op. cit.
15. Eckstein and Noah, op. cit.; and O'Donnell, op. cit.
16. Eckstein and Noah, op. cit., p. 230.
17. New Basics Branch, New Basics: The Why, What, How and When of Rich Tasks (Brisbane: Queensland Department of Education, 2001), http://education.qld.gov.au/corporate/newbasics/pdis/richtasksbklet.pdf.
18. Qualifications and Curriculum Authority, "England: Assessment Arrangements," 2008, www.inca.org.uk/england-assessment-mainstream.html.
19. Jeff Archer, "Wales Eliminates National Exams for Many Students," Education Week, 19 December 2006, www.edweek.org/ew/articles/2006/12/20/16wales.h26.html?qs=Wales.
20. Welsh Assembly Government, "Primary (3–11),"2008, http://old.accac.org.uk/eng/content.php?cID = 5; idem, "Secondary (11–16)," 2008, http://oldaccac.org.uk/eng/content.php?cID=6.
21. Council for the Curriculum Examinations and Assessment, "Curriculum, Key Stage 3, Post-Primary Assessment," 2008, www.ccea.org.uk, search on tide.
22. Jacqueline Kin-Sang Chan, Kerry J. Kennedy, Flora Wai-Ming Yu, and Ping-Kwan Fok, "Assessment Policy in Hong Kong: Implementation Issues for New Forms of Assessment," paper presented at the 32nd annual conference of the International Association for Educational Assessment, Singapore, 2006, www.iaea.info/papers.aspx?id=68.
23. Mark Dowling, "Examining the Exams," no date, www.hkeaa.edu.hk.

DISCUSSION QUESTIONS

1. Curriculum and assessments vary internationally. Why do you believe some nations are more successful in educating their students than others?
2. The authors describe the educational systems of different countries. Which system's methods do you most agree with? Explain.
3. Other high performing countries use the results of assessments to inform and influence curricular decisions. In the wake of No Child Left Behind and the increased emphasis on accountability, do you believe assessments results should be used punitively to "grade" schools.
4. The United States focuses on multiple choice assessments while other high-achieving countries assess their students using open-ended, school-based tasks, and portfolios. What is the feasibility of adopting these assessment methods in the United States?
5. Some other high achieving countries such as Finland use local assessments to test their national standards. Do you believe this is an effective way to evaluate student progress? Explain.

CHAPTER 34

Perennial Reform: Fixing School Time

LARRY CUBAN

FOCUSING QUESTIONS

1. Compare the different proposals to extend academic learning time over the past quarter century.
2. Why haven't school reform efforts to extend academic learning time been successful?
3. How have the public's goals for education shaped the structure of schools in this country?
4. Compare the views of policy makers and teachers towards school time reform.
5. How has the belief that college is for everyone affected policy makers' attitudes towards school time?

ABSTRACT

Education critics often call for longer school days and years. But there is little research to support such demands and several reasons why little will change.

In the past quarter century, reformers have repeatedly urged schools to fix their use of time, even though it is a solution that is least connected to what happens in classrooms or what Americans want from public schools. Since A Nation at Risk in 1983, Prisoners of Time in 1994, and the latest blue-ribbon recommendations in Tough Choices, Tough Times in 2007, both how much time and how well students spend it in school has been criticized no end.[2]

Business and civil leaders have been critical because they see U.S. students stuck in the middle ranks on international tests. These leaders believe that the longer school year in Asia and Europe is linked to those foreign students scoring far higher than U.S. students on those tests.

Employers criticize the amount of time students spend in school because they wonder whether the limited days and hours spent in classes are sufficient to produce the skills that employees need to work in a globally competitive economy. Employers also wonder whether our comparatively short school year will teach the essential workplace behaviors of punctuality, regular attendance, meeting deadlines, and following rules.

Parents criticize school schedules because they want schools to be open when they go to work in the morning and to remain open until they pick up their children before dinner.

Professors criticize policy makers for allotting so little time for teachers to gain new knowledge and skills during the school day. Other researchers want both policy makers and practitioners to distinguish between requiring more time in school and academic learning time, academic jargon for those hours and minutes where teachers engage students in learning content and skills or, in more jargon, time on task.[3]

Finally, cyberschool champions criticize school schedules because they think it's quaint to have students sitting at desks in a building with hundreds of other students for 180 days when a revolution in communication devices allows children to learn the formal curriculum in many places, not just in school buildings. Distance learning advocates, joined by those who see cyberschools as the future, want children and youths to spend hardly any time in K-12 schools.[4]

TIME OPTIONS

Presidential commissions, parents, academics, and employers have proposed the same solutions, again and again, for fixing the time students spend in school: Add more days to the annual school calendar. Change to year-round schools. Add instructional time to the daily schedule. Extend the school day.

What has happened to each proposal in the past quarter century?

Longer School Year. Recommendations for a longer school year (from 180 to 220 days) came from A Nation at Risk (1983) and Prisoners schools was made possible of Time (1994) plus scores of other commissions and experts. In 2008, by the generous support of foundation-funded report, A Stagnant Nation: Why American Students Are Still at Risk, found that the 180-day school year was intact across the nation and only Massachusetts had started a pilot program to help districts lengthen the school year. The same report gave a grade of F to states for failing to significantly expand student learning time.[5]

Year-Round Schools. Ending the summer break is another way to maximize student time in school. There is a homespun myth, treated as fact, that the annual school calendar, with three months off for both teachers and students, is based on the rhythm of 19th-century farm life, which dictated when school was in session. Thus, planting and harvesting chores accounted for long summer breaks, an artifact of agrarian America. Not so.

Actually, summer vacations grew out of early 20th-century urban middle-class parents (and later lobbyists for camps and the tourist industry) pressing school boards to release children to be with their families for four to eight weeks or more. By the 1960s, however, policy maker and parent concerns about students losing ground academically during the vacation months—in academic language, "summer loss"—gained support for year-round schooling. Cost savings also attracted those who saw facilities being used 12 months a year rather than being shuttered during the summer.

Nonetheless, although year-round schools were established as early as 1906 in Gary, Indiana, calendar innovations have had a hard time entering most schools. Districts with year-round schools still work within the 180-day year but distribute the time more evenly (e.g., 45 days in session, 15 days off) rather than having a long break between June and September. As of 2006, nearly 3,000 of the nation's 90,000 public schools enrolled more than 2.1 million students on a year-round calendar. That's less than 5% of all students attending public schools, and almost half of the year-round schools are in California. In most cases, school boards adopted year-round schools because increased enrollments led to crowded facilities, most often in minority and poor communities—not concerns over "summer loss."[6]

Adding Instructional Time to the School Day. Many researchers and reformers have pointed out that the 6½-hour school day has so many interruptions, so many distractions that teachers have less than five hours of genuine instruction time. Advocates for more instructional time have tried to stretch the actual amount of instructional time available to teachers to a seven-hour day (or 5½ hours of time for time-on-task learning) or have tried to redistribute the existing secondary school schedule into 90-minute blocks rather than the traditional 50-minute periods. Since A Nation at Risk, this recommendation for more instructional time has resulted only in an anemic 10 more minutes per day when elementary school students study core academic subjects.[7]

Block scheduling in public secondary schools (60- to 90-minute periods for a subject that meets different days of the week) was started in the 1960s to promote instructional innovations. Various modified schedules have spread slowly, except in a few states where block schedules multiplied rapidly. In the past decade, an explosion of interest in small high schools has led many traditional urban comprehensive high schools of 1,500 or more students to convert to smaller high schools of 300 to 400 students, sometimes with all of those smaller schools housed within the original large building, sometimes as separate schools located elsewhere in the district. In many of these small high schools, modified schedules with instructional periods of an hour or more have found a friendly home. Block schedules rearrange existing allotted time for instruction; they do not add instructional time to the school day.[8]

Extended School Day. In the past half century, as the economy has changed and families increasingly have both (or single) parents working, schools have been pressed to take on childcare responsibilities, such as tutoring and homework supervision before and after school. Many elementary schools open at 7 a.m. for parents to drop off children and have after-school programs that close at 6 p.m. PDK/Gallup polls since the early 1980s show increased support for these before-and after-school programs. Instead of the familiar half-day program for 5-year-olds, all-day kindergartens (and prekindergartens for 4-year-olds) have spread swiftly in the past two decades, especially in low-income neighborhoods. Innovative urban schools, such as the for-profit Edison Inc. and KIPP (Knowledge Is Power Program), run longer school days. The latter routinely opens at 7:30 a.m. and closes at 5 p.m. and also schedules biweekly Saturday classes and three weeks of school during the summer.[9]

If reformers want a success story in fixing school time, they can look to extending the school day, although it's arguable how many of those changes occurred because of reformers' arguments and actions and how many from economic and social changes in family structure and the desire to chase a higher standard of living.

Cybereducation. And what about those public school haters and cheer-leading technological enthusiasts who see fixing time in school as a wasted effort when online schooling and distance learning can replace formal schooling? In the 1960s and 1970s, Ivan Illich and other school critics called for dismantling public schools and ending formal schooling. They argued that schools squelched natural learning, confused school-based education with learning, and turned children into obedient students and adults rather than curious and independent lifelong learners. Communication and instructional technologies were in their infancy then, and thinkers such as Illich had few alternatives to offer families who opted out.[10]

Much of that ire directed at formal public schooling still exists, but now technology has made it possible for students to learn outside school buildings. Sharing common ground in this debate are deeply religious families who want to avoid secular influences in schools, highly educated parents who fear the stifling effects of school rules and text-bound instruction, and rural parents who simply want their children to have access to knowledge unavailable in their local schools. These advocates seek home schooling, distance learning, and cyber schools.[11]

Slight increases in home schooling may occur—say from 1.1 million in 2003 to 2 to 3 million by the end of the decade, with the slight uptick in numbers due to both the availability of technology and a broader menu of choices for parents. Still, this represents less than 3% of public school students. Even though cheerleaders for distance learning have predicted wholesale changes in conventional site-based schools for decades, such changes will occur at the periphery, not the center, because most parents will continue to send their children to public schools.[12]

Even the most enthusiastic advocates for cyberschools and distance education recognize that replacing public schools is, at best, unlikely. The foreseeable future will still have 50 million children and youths crossing the schoolhouse door each weekday morning.

3 REASONS

Reformers have spent decades trotting out the same recipes for fixing the time problem in school. For all the hoopla and all of the endorsements from highly influential business and political elites, their mighty efforts have produced minuscule results. Why is that?

Cost is the usual suspect. Covering additional teacher salaries and other expenses runs high. Minnesota provides one example: shifting from 175 to 200 days of instruction cost districts an estimated $750 million a year, a large but not insurmountable price to pay.[13] But costs for extending the school day for instruction and childcare are far less onerous.

Even more attractive than adding days to the calendar, however, is the claim that switching to a year-round school will save dollars. So, while there are costs involved in lengthening the school calendar, cost is not the tipping point in explaining why so few proposals to fix school time are successful.

I offer two other reasons why fixing school time is so hard.

Research showing achievement gains due to more time in school are sparse; the few studies most often displayed are contested.

Late 20th-century policy makers seriously underestimated the powerful tug that conservative, noneconomic goals (e.g., citizenship, character formation) have on parents, taxpayers, and voters. When they argued that America needed to add time to the school calendar in order to better prepare workers for global competition, they were out of step with the American public's desires for schools.

SKIMPY RESEARCH

In the past quarter century of tinkering with the school calendar, cultural changes, political decisions, or strong parental concerns trumped research every time. Moreover, the longitudinal and rigorous research on time in school was—and is—skimpy. The studies that exist are challenged repeatedly for being weakly designed. For example, analysts examining research on year-round schools have reported that most of the studies have serious design flaws and, at best, show slight positive gains in student achievement—except for students from low-income families, for whom gains were sturdier. As one report concluded: "[N]o truly trustworthy studies have been done on modified school calendars that can serve as the basis for sound policy decisions." Policy talk about year-round schools has easily outstripped results.[14]

Proving that time in school is the crucial variable in raising academic achievement is difficult because so many other variables must be considered—the local context itself, available resources, teacher quality, administrative leadership, socioeconomic and cultural background of students and their families, and what is taught. But the lack of careful research has seldom stopped reform-driven decision makers from pursuing their agendas.

CONFLICTING SCHOOL GOALS

If the evidence suggests that, at best, a longer school year or day or restructured schedules do not seem to make the key difference in student achievement, then I need to ask: What problem are reformers trying to solve by adding more school time?

The short answer is that for the past quarter century—A Nation at Risk (1983) is a suitable marker—policy elites have redefined a national economic problem into an educational problem. Since the late 1970s, influential civic, business, and media leaders have sold Americans the story that lousy schools are the reason why inflation surged, unemployment remained high, incomes seldom rose, and cheaper and better foreign products flooded U.S. stores. Public schools have failed to produce a strong, postindustrial labor force, thus leading to a weaker, less competitive U.S. economy. U.S. policy elites have used lagging scores on international tests as telling evidence that schools graduate less knowledgeable, less skilled high school graduates—especially those from minority and poor schools who will be heavily represented in the mid-21st century workforce—than competitor nations with lower-paid workforces who produce high-quality products.

Microsoft founder Bill Gates made the same point about U.S. high schools.

> In district after district across the country, wealthy white kids are taught Algebra II, while low-income minority kids are taught how to balance a checkbook. This is an economic disaster. In the international competition to have the best supply of workers who can communicate clearly, analyze information, and solve complex problems, the United States is falling behind. We have one of the highest high school dropout rates in the industrialized world.[15]

And here, in a nutshell, is the second reason why those highly touted reforms aimed at lengthening the school year and instructional day have disappointed policy makers. By blaming schools, contemporary civic and business elites have reduced the multiple goals Americans expect of their public schools to a single one: prepare youths to work in a globally competitive economy. This has been a mistake because Americans historically have expected more from their public schools. Let me explore the geography of this error.

For nearly three decades, influential groups have called for higher academic standards, accountability for student outcomes, more homework, more testing, and, of course, more time in school. Many of their recommendations have been adopted. By 2008, U.S. schools had a federally driven system of state-designed standards anchored in increased testing, results-driven accountability, and demands for students to spend more time in school. After all, reformers reasoned, the students of foreign competitors were attending school more days in the year and longer hours each day, even on weekends, and their test scores ranked them higher than the U.S.

Even though this simplistic causal reasoning has been questioned many times by researchers who examined education and work performance in Japan, Korea, Singapore, Germany, and other nations, "common sense" observations by powerful elites swept away such questions. So the U.S.'s declining global economic competitiveness had been spun into a time-in-school problem.[16]

But convincing evidence drawn from research that more time in school would lead to a stronger economy, less inequalities in family income, and that elusive edge in global competitiveness—much less a higher rank in international tests—remains missing in action.

THE PUBLIC'S GOALS FOR EDUCATION

Business and civic elites have succeeded at least twice in the past century in making the growth of a strong economy the primary aim of U.S. schools, but other goals have had an enormous and enduring impact on schooling, both in the past and now. These goals embrace core American values that have been like second-hand Roses, shabby and discarded clothes hidden in the back of the closet and occasionally trotted out for show during graduation. Yet since the origins of tax-supported public schools in the early 19th century, these goals have been built into the very structures of schools so much so that, looking back from 2008, we hardly notice them.[17]

Time-based reforms have had trouble entering schools because other goals have had—and continue to have—clout with parents and taxpayers. Opinion polls, for example, display again and again what parents, voters, and taxpayers want schools to achieve. One recent poll identified the public's goals for public schools. The top five were to:

- Prepare people to become responsible citizens;
- Help people become economically sufficient;
- Ensure a basic level of quality among schools;
- Promote cultural unity among all Americans;
- Improve social conditions for people.

Tied for sixth and seventh were goals to:

- Enhance people's happiness and enrich their lives; and
- Dispel inequities in education among certain schools and certain groups.[18]

To reach those goals, a democratic society expects schools to produce adults who are engaged in their communities, enlightened employers, and hard-working employees who have acquired and practiced particular values that sustain its way of life. Dominant American social, political, and economic values pervade family, school, workplace, and community: Act independently, accept personal responsibility for actions, work hard and complete a job well, and be fair, that is, willing to be judged by standards applied to others as long as the standards are applied equitably.[19]

These norms show up in school rules and classroom practices in every school. School is the one institutional agent between the family, the workplace, and voting booth or jury room responsible for instilling those norms in children's behavior. School is the agent for turning 4-year-olds into respectful students engaged in their communities, a goal that the public perceives as more significant than preparing children and youths for college and the labor market. In elite decision makers' eagerness to link schools to a growing economy, they either overlooked the powerful daily practices of schooling or neglected to consider seriously these other goals. In doing so, they erred. The consequences of that error in judgment can be seen in the fleeting attention that policy recommendations for adding more time in school received before being shelved.

TEACHING IN A DEMOCRACY

Public schools were established before industrialization, and they expanded rapidly as factories and mills spread.

Those times appear foreign to readers today. For example, in the late 19th century, calling public schools "factory-like" was not an epithet hurled at educators or supporters of public schools as it has been in the U.S. since the 1960s.[20] In fact, describing a public school as an assembly-line factory or a productive cotton mill was considered a compliment to forward-looking educators wh sought to make schools modern through greater efficiency in teaching and learning by copying the successes of wealthy industrialists. Progressive reformers praised schools for being like industrial plants in creating large, efficient, age-graded schools that standardized curriculum while absorbing millions of urban migrants and foreign immigrants. As a leading progressive put it:

> Our schools are, in a sense, factories in which the raw products (children) are to be shaped and fashioned into products to meet the various demands of life. . . . It is the business of the school to build its pupils to the specifications [of manufacturers].[21]

Progressive reformers saw mills, factories, and corporations as models for transforming the inefficient one-room schoolhouse in which students of different ages received fitful, incomplete instruction from one teacher into the far more efficient graded school where each teacher taught students a standardized curriculum each year. First established in Boston in 1848 and spreading swiftly in urban districts, the graded school became the dominant way of organizing a school by 1900. By the 1920s, schools exemplified the height of industrial efficiency because each building had separate classrooms with their own teachers. The principal and teachers expected children of the same age to cover the same content and learn skills by the end of the school year and perform satisfactorily on tests in order to be promoted to the next grade.[22]

Superintendents saw the age-graded school as a modern version of schooling well adapted to an emerging corporate-dominated industrial society where punctuality, dependability, and obedience were prized behaviors. As a St. Louis superintendent said in 1871:

> The first requisite of the school is Order: each pupil must be taught first and foremost to conform his behavior to a general standard. . . . The pupil must have his lessons ready at the appointed time, must rise at the tap of the bell, move to the line, return; in short, go through all of the evolutions with equal precision.

Recognition and fame went to educators who achieved such order in their schools.[23]

But the farm-driven seasonal nature of rural one-room schoolhouses was incompatible with the explosive growth of cities and an emerging industrial society. In the early 20th century, progressive reformers championed compulsory attendance laws while extending the abbreviated rural-driven short hours and days into a longer school day and year. Reformers wanted to increase the school's influence over children's attitudes and behavior, especially in cities where wave after wave of European immigrants settled. Seeking higher productivity in organization, teaching, and learning at the least cost, reformers broadened the school's mission by providing medical, social, recreational, and psychological services at schools. These progressive reformers believed schools should teach society's norms to both children and their families and also educate the whole child so that the entire government, economy, and society would change for the better. So, when reformers spoke about "factory-like schools" a century ago, they wanted educators to copy models of success; they were not scolding them. That changed, however, by the late 20th century.

As the U.S. shifted from a manufacturing-based economy to a post-industrial information-based economy, few policy makers reckoned with this history of schooling. Few influential decision makers view schools as agents of *both* stability and change. Few educational opinion makers recognize that the conservative public still expects schools to instill in children dominant American norms of being independent and being held accountable for one's actions, doing work well and efficiently, and treating others equitably to ensure that when students graduate they will practice these values as adults. And, yes, the public still expects schools to strengthen the economy by ensuring that graduates have the necessary skills to be productive employees in an ever-changing, highly competitive, and increasingly global workplace. But that is just one of many competing expectations for schools.

Thus far, I have focused mostly on how policy makers and reform-minded civic and business elites have not only defined economic problems as educational ones that can be fixed by more time spent in schools but also neglected the powerful hold that socialization goals have on parents' and taxpayers' expectations. Now, I want to switch from the world of reform-driven policy makers and elites to teachers and students because each group views school time differently from their respective perch. Teacher and student perspectives on time in school have little influence in policy makers' decision making. Although the daily actions of teachers and students don't influence policy makers, they do matter in explaining why reformers have had such paltry results in trying to fix school time.

DIFFERING VIEWS OF TIME IN SCHOOL

For civic and business leaders, media executives, school boards, superintendents, mayors, state legislators, governors, U.S. representatives, and the President (what I call "policy elites"), electoral and budget cycles become the timeframe within which they think and act. Every year, budgets must be prepared and, every two or four years, officials run for office and voters decide who should represent them and whether they should support bond referenda and tax levies. Because appointed and elected policy makers are influential with the media, they need to assure the public during campaigns that slogans and stump speeches were more than talk. Sometimes, words do become action when elected decision makers, for example, convert a comprehensive high school into a cluster of small high schools, initiate 1:1 laptop programs, and extend the school day. This is the world of policy makers.

The primary tools policy makers use to adopt and implement decisions, however, are limited and blunt—closer to a hammer than a scalpel. They use exhortation, press conferences, political bargaining, incentives, and sanctions to formulate and adopt decisions. (Note, however, that policy makers rarely implement decisions; administrators and practitioners put policies into practice.) Policy makers want broad social, political, economic, and organizational goals adopted as policies, and then they want to move educators, through encouragement, incentives, and penalties, to implement those policies in schools and classrooms that they seldom, if ever, enter.

The world of teachers differs from that of policy makers. For teachers, the time-driven budget and electoral cycles that shape policy matter little for their classrooms, except when such policies carry consequences for how and what teachers should teach, such as accountability measures that assume teachers and students are slackers and need to work harder. In these instances, teachers become classroom gatekeepers in deciding how much of a policy they will put into practice and under what conditions.

What matters most to teachers are student responses to daily lessons, weekly tests, monthly units, and the connections they build over time in classrooms, corridors, during lunch, and before and after school. Those personal connections become the compost of learning. Those connections account for former students pointing to particular teachers who made a difference in their lives. Teacher tools, unlike policy maker tools, are unconnected to organizational power or media influence. Teachers use their personalities, knowledge, experience, and skills in building relationships with groups of students and providing individual help. Teachers believe there is never enough time in the daily schedule to finish a lesson, explain a point, or listen to a student. Administrative intrusions gobble up valuable instructional time that could go to students. In class, then, both teachers and students are clock watchers, albeit for different reasons.[24]

Students view time differently as well. For a fraction of students from middle and low-income families turned off by school requirements and expectations, spending time in classrooms listening to teachers, answering questions, and doing homework is torture; the hands of the clock seldom move fast enough for them. The notion of extending the school day and school year for them—or continuing on to college and four more years of reading texts and sitting in classrooms—is not a reform to be implemented but a punishment to be endured. Such students look for creative shortcuts to skip classes, exit the school as early as they can, and find jobs or enter the military once they graduate.

Most students, however, march from class to class until they hear "Pomp and Circumstance." But a high school diploma, graduates have come to realize, is not enough in the 21st-century labor market.

COLLEGE FOR EVERYONE

In the name of equity and being responsive to employers' needs, most urban districts have converted particular comprehensive high schools into clusters of small college-prep academies where low-income minority students take Advanced Placement courses, write research papers, and compete to get into colleges and universities. Here, then, is the quiet, unheralded, and unforeseen victory of reformers bent on fixing time in school. They have succeeded unintentionally in stretching K-12 into preK-16 public schooling, not just for middle- and upper-middle class students, but for everyone.

As it has been for decades for most suburban middle- and upper-middle class white and minority families, now it has become a fact, an indisputable truth converted into a sacred mission for upwardly mobile poor families: A high school diploma and a bachelor's degree are passports to high-paying jobs and the American Dream.

For families who already expect their sons and daughters to attend competitive colleges, stress begins early. Getting into the best preschools and elementary and secondary schools and investing in an array of activities to build attractive résumés for college admission officers to evaluate become primary tasks. For such families and children, there is never enough time for homework, Advanced Placement courses, music, soccer, drama, dance, and assorted after-school activities. For high-achieving, stressed-out students already expecting at least four more years of school after high school graduation, reform proposals urging a longer school year and an extended day often strike an unpleasant note. Angst and fretfulness become familiar clothes to don every morning as students grind out 4s and 5s on Advanced Placement exams, play sports, and compile just the right record that will get them into just the right school.[25]

For decades, pressure on students to use every minute of school to prepare for college has been strongest in middle- and upper-middle-class suburbs. What has changed in the past few decades is the spread of the belief that everyone, including low-income minority students, should go to college.

To summarize, for decades, policy elites have disregarded teacher and student perspectives on time in school. Especially now when all students are expected to enter college, children, youths, and teachers experience time in school differently than policy makers who seek a longer school day and school year. Such varied perceptions about time are heavily influenced by the socialization goals of schooling, age-graded structures, socioeconomic status of families, and historical experience. And policy makers often ignore these perceptions and reveal their tone-deafness and myopia in persistently trying to fix time in schools.

Policy elites need to parse fully this variation in perceptions because extended time in school remains a high priority to reform-driven policy makers and civic and business leaders anxious about U.S. performance on international tests and fearful of falling behind in global economic competitiveness. The crude policy solutions of more days in the year and longer school days do not even begin to touch the deeper truth that what has to improve is the quality of "academic learning time." If policy makers could open their ears and eyes to student and teacher perceptions of time, they would learn that the secular Holy Grail is decreasing interruption of instruction, encouraging richer intellectual and personal connections between teachers and students, and increasing classroom time for ambitious teaching and active, engaged learning. So far, no such luck.

CONCLUSION

These three reasons—cost, lackluster research, and the importance of conservative social goals to U.S. taxpayers and voters—explain why proposals to fix time in U.S. schools have failed to take hold.

Policy elites know research studies proving the worth of year-round schools or lengthened school days are in short supply. Even if an occasional study supported the change, the school year is unlikely to go much beyond 180 days. Policy elites know school goals go far beyond simply preparing graduates for college and for employability in a knowledge-based economy. And policy elites know they must show courage in their pursuit of improving failing U.S. schools by forcing students to go to school just as long as their peers in India, China, Japan, and Korea. That courage shows up symbolically, playing well in the media and in proposals to fix time in schools, but it seldom alters calendars.

While cost is a factor, it is the stability of schooling structures and the importance of socializing the young into the values of the immediate community and larger society that have defeated policy-driven efforts to alter time in school over the past quarter century. Like the larger public, I am unconvinced that requiring students and teachers to spend more time in school each day and every year will be better for them. How that time is spent in learning before, during, and after school is far more important than decision makers counting the minutes, hours, and days students spend each year getting schooled. That being said, I have little doubt that state and federal blue-ribbon commissions will continue to make proposals about lengthening time in school. Those proposals will make headlines, but they will not result in serious, sustained attention to what really matters—improving the quality of the time that teachers and students spend with one another in and out of classrooms.

ENDNOTES

1. I wish to thank Selma Wassermann for her most helpful comments and suggestions on the penultimate draft and Bruce Smith for inviting me to do this special report.

2. National Commission on Excellence in Education, A Nation at Risk (Washington, D.C.: U.S. Government Printing Office, 1983); National Education Commission on Time and Learning, Prisoners of Time (Washington, D.C.: U.S. Government Printing Office, 1994); New Commission on the Skills of the American Work Force, Tough Times or Tough Choices (San Francisco: Jossey-Bass, 2006).

3. David Berliner, "What's All the Fuss About Instructional Time?" in Miriam Ben-Peretz and Rainer Bromme, eds., The Nature of Time in Schools: Theoretical Concepts, Practitioner Perceptions (New York: Teachers College Press, 1990).

4. See, for example, North Central Regional Educational Laboratory, "E-Learning Policy Implications for K-12 Educators and Decision

Makers," 2001, www.ncrel.org/policy/pubs/html/pivol11/apr2002d.htm.

5. Strong American Schools, A Stagnant Nation: Why American Students Are Still at Risk (Washington, D.C., 2008), pp. 3–4.

6. Joel Weiss and Robert Brown, "Telling Tales Over Time: Constructing and Deconstructing the School Calendar," Teachers College Record, 2003, pp. 1720–57; Shaun P. Johnson and Terry E. Spradlin, "Alternatives to the Traditional School-Year Calendar," Education Policy Brief, Center for Evaluation & Education Policy, Spring 2007, p. 3; for a description of the "Gary Plan" of year-round schooling, see Ronald Cohen, Children of the Mill: Schooling and Society in Gary, Indiana, 1906–1960 (Bloomington: Indiana University Press, 1990).

7. Strong American Schools, op. cit., p. 4.

8. Robert Canady and Michael Rettig, Block Scheduling: A Catalyst for Change in High Schools (Larchmont, N.Y.: Eye on Education, 1995); personal communication from Michael Rettig, 28 April 2008.

9. Lowell C. Rose and Alec M. Gallup, "38th Annual Phi Delta Kappa/Gallup Poll of the Public's Attitudes Toward the Public Schools," Phi Delta Kappan, September 2006; Sarah Huyvaert, Time Is of the Essence: Learning in School (Boston: Allyn & Bacon, 1998), pp. 59–67; for KIPP, see: www.kipp.org/01/whatisakipp-school.cfm.

10. Ivan Illich, Deschooling Society (New York: Harper & Row, 1971).

11. For a politically conservative view on home schooling and its history, see Isabel Lyman, "Home Schooling: Back to the Future?" Cato Institute Policy Analysis No. 294, 7 January 1998, www.cato.org/pubs/pas/pa-294.html. Beginning nearly a decade ago, state- and district-funded cyber schools, such as Florida Virtual School, provide courses for homeschoolers, parents who want more learning options for their children, and students in isolated rural areas who lack access to advanced high school courses. Florida Virtual School served over 50,000 students in 2006–07 and expects to reach 100,000 in 2009. See www.flvs.net.

12. For predictions from the 1990s and current ones for distance learning and students' use of the Internet, see "Predictions Database" in Elon University's "Imagining the Internet," www.elon.edu/predictions/q13.aspx. For an astute analysis of distance learning, see Clayton M. Christensen and Michael B. Horn, "How Do We Transform Our Schools?" Education Next, Summer 2008, www.hoover.org/publications/ednext/18575969.html. For the 2003 figure on home-schooled children, see "Fast Facts" from National Center for Education Statistics, http://nces.ed.gov/fastfacts/display.asp?id=65.

13. The Minnesota example comes from Elena Silva, "On the Clock: Rethinking the Way Schools Use Time," Education Sector Reports, January 2007, p. 8; for cost savings in year-round schools, see Nasser Daneshvary and Terrence M. Clauretie, "Efficiency and Costs in Education: Year-Round Versus Traditional Schedules," Economics of Education Review, 2001, pp. 279–87.

14. Shaun P. Johnson and Terry E. Spradlin, op. cit., p. 5; Harris Cooper, et al., "The Effects of Modified School Calendars on Student Achievement and on School and Community Attitudes," Review of Educational Research, Spring 2003, pp. 1–52.

15. Bill Gates, "What Is Wrong with America's High Schools?" Los Angeles Times, 3 March 2005, p. B11.

16. One of the better summaries of how schools had become the central problem to the future of the nation in the 1980s can be found in Chester E. Finn, Jr., We Must Take Charge: Our Schools and Our Future (New York: Free Press, 1991); also see Diane Ravitch, "The Test of Time," Education Next, Spring 2003, www.educationnext.org/20032/32.html; and, in the same issue, see a reprint of Albert Shanker's retrospective (9 May 1993) on A Nation at Risk report. For analyses of other countries compared to the U.S., see Norton Grubb and Marvin Lazerson, The Education Gospel: The Economic Power of Schooling (Cambridge: Harvard University Press, 2004), pp. 170–72.

17. John Goodlad, A Place Called School (New York: McGraw-Hill, 1984); and David Labaree, "Public Goods, Private Goods: The American Struggle over Educational Goals," American Educational Research Journal, Spring 1997, pp. 39–81.

18. Lowell C. Rose and Alec M. Gallup, "The 32nd Annual Phi Delta Kappa/Gallup Poll of the Public's Attitudes Toward the Public Schools," Phi Delta Kappan, September 2000, p. 47.

19. There are other personal values, such as honesty, trustworthiness, etc., that are highly prized and reinforced by teachers and school policies, but I will focus on the obvious societal values embedded in the structures and processes of tax-supported schooling. See Robert Dreeben, On What Is Learned in School (Reading, Mass.: Addison-Wesley, 1968); Steven Brint, Mary C. Contreras, and Michael T. Matthews, "Socialization Messages in Primary Schools: An Organizational Analysis," Sociology of Education, July 2001, pp. 157–80; and Philip Jackson, Life in Classrooms (New York: Holt, Rinehart, and Winston, 1968).
20. For examples of the pejorative use of "factory-like schools," see, Samuel Bowles and Herbert Gintis, Schooling in Capitalist America: Educational Reform and the Contradictions of Economic Life (New York: Basic Books, 1976); and Joel Spring, "Education as a Form of Social Control," in Clarence Karier, Paul Violas, and Joel Spring, eds., Roots of Crisis: American Education in the 20th Century (Chicago: Rand McNally, 1973), pp. 30–39.
21. Quote cited in Raymond Callahan, Education and the Cult of Efficiency (Chicago: University of Chicago Press, 1962), p. 152. It comes from Stanford Professor Ellwood P. Cubberley in his textbook, Public School Administration, written in 1916.
22. David L. Angus, Jeffrey E. Mirel, and Maris A. Vinovskis, "Historical Development of Age-Stratification in Schooling," Teachers College Record, Winter 1988, pp. 211–36.
23. David B. Tyack, The One Best System: A History of American Urban Education (Cambridge: Harvard University Press, 1974), p. 43.
24. Marty Swaim and Stephen Swaim, Teacher Time: Why Teacher Workload and School Management Matter to Each Student in Our Public Schools (Arlington, Va.: Redbud Books, 1999); Claudia Meek, "Classroom Crisis: It's About Time," Phi Delta Kappan, April 2003, pp. 592–95; and National Center for Education Statistics, Time Spent Teaching Core Academic Subjects in Elementary Schools (Washington, D.C.: National Center for Education Statistics, 1997).
25. Although aware of anxiety-stressed teenagers, I was surprised by an article that described students in an affluent high school being required to eat lunch because they skipped eating in order to take another Advanced Placement class. See Winnie Hu, "Too Busy to Eat, Students Get a New Required Course: Lunch," New York Times, 24 May 2008, pp. A1, A11.

The crude policy solutions of more days in the year and longer school days do not even begin to touch the deeper truth that we have to improve the quality of "academic learning time."

Cost is not the tipping point in explaining why so few proposals to fix school time are successful. Time-based reforms have had trouble entering schools because other goals have had—and continue to have—clout with parents and taxpayers.

DISCUSSION QUESTIONS

1. Do you believe the current school calendar needs to be modified to meet the needs of your students? Explain.
2. Which of the options to extend learning time do you believe is the most practical and suitable? Explain.
3. The author identifies three reasons which have prevented school time reform for gaining any traction: cost, limited research, and powerful, conservative, noneconomic goals. Which of these do you feel best explains why policy makers have been unsuccessful in implementing school time reform?
4. According to the author, there is a disconnect between policy makers and students and teachers in regards to school time reform. What is the best way to bridge this gap? Explain.
5. With the increased emphasis on college access for everyone, what can policy makers and schools do to prepare students for postsecondary education?

CHAPTER 35

Global Inequality and Instability

ALLAN ORNSTEIN AND JASON ORNSTEIN

FOCUSING QUESTIONS

1. What global issues are often not discussed in American classrooms?
2. How is the world's population changing?
3. What does it mean for nations to be caught in a "poverty trap"?
4. What are some of the competing theories on how to solve issues of global poverty?

Some 150 years ago, Herbert Spencer, in his famous essay, asked, "What knowledge is most worth?" for the survival of the individual and society. Spencer's original question about the worth of subject matter is more relevant today because of the increased complexity of society and globalization. Actually, the question dates back to the ancient Greeks, when Plato and Aristotle questioned the values of knowlepdge in relation to citizenship and government affairs.

The Founding Fathers articulated similar concerns about education for citizenship and democracy, for the common people to reflect critically on political and social issues and to acquire knowledge of history to avoid the mistakes of the past and to make wise choices in the selection of government leaders. In the final analysis, it was Thomas Jefferson who had great faith in educating the common citizen (what he called the yeoman farmer) as a means of promoting democracy, for it was "The people (who) are the ultimate guardians of their own liberty." It is the kings and queens, the nobility and elite classes that could not be trusted to promote the interests of the ordinary people.

Among American educators, there is a rich history on the question of citizenship and democracy, and for students learning how to reflect on issues and problem solved, as opposed to an education that promotes training and indoctrination. Horace Mann, John Dewey and Alfred Whitehead, and more contemporary thinkers such as Lawrence German, Ralph Tyler and John Goodlad, although diverse in their education philosophy, all understand that democracy is not the average people electing leaders. It is average people with education to think intelligently on crucial issues and problems and to elect the best leaders who could deal with the issues and problems.

The early reconstructionists (George Counts and Harold Rugg) and curriculum theorists (Harold Alberty and Nelson Bossing), the midentury problem-centered proponents (Florence Stratemeyer and B.O. Smith), activity-centered proponents (H. H. Giles and J. Lloyd Trump), and discipline-centered theorists (Harry Broudy and Phil Phenix), as well as current cultural pedagogists (Michael Apple and Henry Givoux) all understood the need to examine economic and social problems, "moral choices," and "controversial issues" in social studies, civics, and history courses, as well as to raise questions and challenge the textbook and teacher.

Despite all this theory for the last one hundred years, textbooks and teacher talk continue to dominate the classroom, while students play passive role. Rarely do we find students engaged in critical thinking as problem solving, discussing controversial issues, much less examining events as themes that criticize our nations or its leaders. The focus is on facts or what conservative educators refer to as "essential knowledge," "base knowledge," or "in depth knowledge." The issue with regard to social studies, civics or history is not whether to teach it, but what to teach and how to interpret historical events, given the concerns of nationalism, pluralism, and globalism. Here I am referring curriculum issues dealing not only with knowledge and skills but also involving American virtues and values, patriotism and assimilation and historical standards and analysis of problems and policies facing the nation and world—how Americans perceive the world and how the world perceives the United States.

Allow me some discussion on global issues for example, that are rarely, if ever, mentioned in American classrooms, nonetheless, the issues have both direct and indirect influences on our society now and in the future and how the world perceives us.

GLOBAL POVERTY

Consider that the United States represents 4 percent of the world's population but consumes 25 percent of the world's resources. Once we leave the Anglo world (U.S., England, Canada, Australia, and New Zealand), the wealthiest 1 percent of the people have gobbled up more than 50 percent of the remaining world's income and 75 percent of the assets for the last 2,000 years, whereas the poorest 50 percent have received less than 1.5 percent. Now consider that there are some 2 to 3 billion people marginally existing on either $1 or $2 a day, and 1.5 to 2 billion people earning between $2 and $3.50 a day, and the number is growing because of the "population bomb."[1]

THE CHANGING GLOBAL VILLAGE

Many critics take great pride in holding a mirror in front of us to show only the cruel side of America. I cannot fathom, and only fear to think of, a world without the United States. Without this land, there would be no asylum for the wretched poor, little hope for the masses from distant places to escape their oppression and misery, and the world would be possessed by one or more of the great evils—Nazism, Japanese imperialism, Stalinism, and/or Maoism. I would not exist nor my children; my ancestors would most likely be buried in some mass grave at Belostock (the most violent Russian pogrom),[2] and the others at Auschwitz, and most of the civilized world would be "subject people" or puppets of some foreign political order. Sadly, however, many Americans take our human rights and our blessings for granted. We tend to be ignorant of the history that molded America, lacking the barest concept of hopes and dreams of millions of early immigrants, many who were illiterate or semiilliterate peasants and laborers, making the perilous journey, often on unseaworthy and fever-ridden "coffinships." The spirit of freedom that has guided the American political and social order, the country that welcomes the wretched of the earth and provides asylum for refugees, is an America that our own youth take for granted and/or fail to appreciate.

Today, I write from the perspective of a third-generation American, proud and thankful that I am an American. Had Europe been a different place, I might have spoken a different language and had a different set of experiences and relationships. To this extent, I am a citizen of an ideal land because of the cruelty and hatred of other lands that my ancestors were fortunate to escape with three or four bundles on their backs. As uneducated peasants, they never read Plato, Locke, or Rousseau nor the writings of Jefferson and Madison, but they understood that America was an asylum for the oppressed, regardless of their background. The other immigrants from other places also understood, and were foreign observers, like de Tocqueville and Lord Bryce eyewitnessed and translated into magical words, and what artists such as Irving Berlin, George Gershwin, and Rogers and Hammerstein have put to music in Broadway hits.

Had my ancestors not understood the story of America, I would have no story to tell, no existence—one out of a million whose ancestors were reduced to nothingness by plunder and war in Europe. In fact, many of us reading this article would have no existence had their ancestors not made the long, treacherous journey across the ocean that once took several months. I don't think modern multiculturalists or speakers of immigrants, including Nathan Glazer, Oscar Handlin, Michael Novak, or Ben Wattenberg, could say what I just said with any more appreciation, conviction, or passion toward America and our way of life.[3]

I also write as a global citizen who feels that human beings are 99 percent alike in terms of DNA and human characteristics, a map of eighty thousand genes in every human cell. Yet, it is the 1 percent of differences (usually based on race or color) that humans focus on. As a recent resident of New York City, with the greatest percentage of first- and second-generation immigrants than any other American city (more than 75 percent), I am aware of the world's diverse population. In a two-to-three-block stretch in parts of Manhattan, Queens, Brooklyn, and the Bronx, some forty to fifty different languages are spoken. You cannot find that type of diversity anywhere in the world; in fact, New York is a microcosm of the world, inhabited by many who have escaped from the third world.

THE SHRINKING WHITE WORLD

Given the shrinking white world we live in—from 13 percent in 2000, to 9 percent by 2010, and to 5 percent by midcentury—there is need to understand, respect and get along with people of color. The fertility rate in Southeast Asia is 7.8 children per female; the average fertility rate of the whites is 1.7 children per female, which illustrates the reason for the world decline of the white population.[4] This decline is most pronounced in Europe, which had a 2000 white population of 727 million and is projected ("medium rate") by 2050 to be 603 million. This unprecedented drop represents a loss of 17 percent, which has serious and economic implications. The "low" (most likely) projection puts Europe's population at 556 million, a loss of 24 percent. If the birthrate remains this low, the European union will have a shortfall of 20 million workers by 2030 and possibly 40 million by 2050, putting a huge strain on pension plans, health care, and the workforce.

No European country today is managing its population. Through births, with rates commonly at 1.2 to 1.4 for most countries,[5] the demographic trends in Europe represent one reason why these nations are willing to take in a large number of Middle Eastern and Asian Moslems and black African immigrants.[6] The problem with this policy is that it results in a surge of uneducated and low-wage earners who depress the overall labor market for European workers (similar to what is happening in our own southern border-states because of illegal immigration). The growth of Moslem and Arab immigrants in Western Europe is so dramatic that by the end of this century Europe may become Euro-Arabic, a form of Pan-Arabism or Islamic expansion. Given the ultraconservative and extremist segment of the Moslem world, both anti-Western and intent on disrupting Western societies, these population trends are considered alarming by many policy makers in Europe and the United States.

White population in Western and technological countries continue to shrink and populations of color in poor countries continue to accelerate (the fastest growing in Africa). For example, the Congo population will increase from 49.1 million in 1998 to 160.3 million in 2050 (a 226 percent change); Ethiopia from 59.7 million to 169.5 million (a 184 percent change); Ghana from 19.1 to 51.8 million (a 170 percent change); and Uganda from 20.6 million to 64.9 million (a 216 percent change).[7] All the old legacies of "separate" and "unequal" in the United States and "colonization" and "white supremacy" abroad are viewed as self-destructive in nature. Although the health and vitality of America depends on technology and efficiency, they also assume a good political and economic relationship with Africa, Asia, and Latin America—the non-Western world, people of color—as well as people of races and ethnic groups getting along in our own country.

Although the United States is the only Western country (along with Australia and Canada) expected to grow in population in the next several decades, by 2050 the majority (white) populace in the United States will be in the minority population, and the minority (blacks, Hispanic Americans, and Asian Americans) will be the majority.[8] Put in different terms, about 65 percent of the U.S. population growth in the next fifty years will be "minority," particularly Hispanic and Asian, because of immigration trends and fertility rates. In fact, from 2000 on, the Hispanic population will increase twice as fast as the black population because of Hispanic population trends (whereas blacks have no comparable immigration pool). Thus, by 2010 there will be more Hispanic students than black students in U.S. schools.[9] By 2050, the Hispanic population is expected to represent 25 percent of the U.S. population, then estimated to be 400 million. Most of this population growth will take place in ten states (with the main shift in California, Texas, Florida, and the New York–New Jersey metropolitan area).

Although the world population is expected to increase at 75 to 80 million a year, we are now aware of a shrinking white world. The world is becoming more urban. As of 2007, there were some 425 cities worldwide that had 1 million or more residents, compared to one hundred years ago when there were none. Moreover, by 2025, as many as 75 to 80 percent of the world's urban population (projected to be more than 6 billion urban dwellers) will live in mega cities of 25 million or more, in the cities of developing countries such as Beijing, Mumbai, Cairo, Kolkata, Dhaka, Jakarta, Lagos, Mexico City, and Sao Paolo[10]—freewheeling places of outrageous contrasts, with wealth (less than 1 percent) coexisting with abject poverty(about 90 percent) and the remaining working in middle-class populations. Even among high-growth countries such as China and India, the vast majority of the populaces have watched fellow citizens gain the benefits of prosperity. In rural parts of these countries, where more than 50 to 60 percent of the people live, the overwhelming number struggle for the subsistence. Hundreds of millions of Chinese and Indians still survive in less than $1 a day; more than half of the Chinese and nearly half of the Indians (mostly women) are illiterate. All those microchip designers and engineers we hear about, although numberin in the millions, represent a small percentage of the population.

HIGH-TECH VERSUS LOW-TECH NATIONS

The cell phones, Internet, and cable TV that we are accustomed to are apparitions to the population of poverty. A world of color is growing rapidly, and so is the gulf where danger resides. Put simply, the low-tech/disconnected world could overwhelm the high-tech/connected world. So long as these poor remain docile, they remain visible to us, and we remain unaware and unconcerned about billions of people running through heaps of garbage and sleeping in the streets, places where the majority of children drop out of school by sixth or seventh grade and are called "street children," "beggars," and "no hopers." Our education system is divorced from this global reality, yet this world (the third world) may weigh down the world we know—what most of us call the Western world, or industrialized world.

Despite the world increasingly speaking English and drinking Coca-Cola, most of the inhabitants in developing areas of the world are rural immigrants and urban refugees within their own countries, many living in streets, drinking poisonous contaminated water sip by sip, people adrift and yearning for a better life and a little dignity. These poor and wretched people are the new proletariat—possessed by a growing dislike, jealousy, and even hatred toward Western values. These are the same kinds of people Europeans, and to a much lesser extent Americans, have exploited through colonization and capitalism.

Third-world nations are now trying to pull themselves into the world market by selling their agricultural products, only to come up against the rich nations' insistence on subsidizing their own farmers, creating rock-bottom prices. Poor people around the world, often farmers, are unable to compete on a global basis and continue to struggle on a daily basis. The developed world's (or G-8 nations') annual $320 billion in farm subsidies dwarfed its $75 billion in assistance to the undeveloped world. A 1 percent increase in Africa's share of world exports would amount to $70 billion a year, almost three times the amount ($25 billion) provided in aid in 2005.[11]

This "rigged game" of keeping agribusiness afloat in wealthy nations fuels poverty and is sowing great hostility toward the United States, as it is viewed as the principle architect of the world economic order. (Actually, the United States spent $19 billion in annual subsidies to American farmers, as compared to the more than $60 billion spent by the European Union.) In short, poor nations are unable to expand their agriculture markets, which would shift hundreds of billions of dollars from the rich to poor nations of the world. By rich countries imposing tariffs and eliminating the farm competition of poor countries, they have added to both malnutrition, as well as illegal immigration to Europe and a movement of rural poor to third-world cities—increasing worldwide, urban squalor and sowing the seeds of radicalism and anti-Western movements.

This is an obscure but serious trend: billions of people, about two-thirds of a growing world population, are squashed by a new kind of economic imperialism and resenting the United States. These masses represent an evitable force with a reason to rebel and bring down our way of life—not by invading armies but through social breakdown, health problems and viruses, rebellion from mountains and jungles, as well as overpopulated cities, nuclear terrorism, and/or cyber warfare. Conservatives might argue that the world knows us much better than we know the world. They would also argue that globalization will eventually lead to a trickle-down economic benefit that over time will help the poor and make production more efficient and less expensive. Such an argument is rooted in the idea of a free-market economy, whereby consumer demand and efficient production win the day for capitalists while benefiting the masses with lower consumer prices. Let me say it in a different way. The U.S. economic output represents 38 percent of the world's gross domestic product. When we hiccup the rest of the world hears the echo. Who we trade with and what goods we buy or consume, and from where, affect the world's standard of living, especially within undeveloped nations, where the populace subsists on a daily basis.

Depending on the benchmarks we employ, about seventy-five to one hundred countries are caught in a "poverty trap." A term used by Columbia University's Jeffrey Sachs to describe a combination of poor geography, poor infrastructure, poor health care, and limited educational resouces[12] and, if I may add, poor transportation links, a shortage of skilled labor, and nonexistent credit. Moreover "dirty" money and money laundering, as well as the smuggling and trafficking of people and goods, make up half the economies of the nations in Africa, the Middle East, and Latin America.[13] About the only thing holding the world's poor populace together is their government, and we are forced to support corrupt leaders and dictators and hope these governments can restrain the extremist part of the population that wants to cripple the West. These impoverished people today are to some extent the people we once called barbarians, who brought down Rome. The world has not changed much in the last one thousand years, at least not when it comes to counting powerful people and powerless people, except maybe the scales are more lopsided and there are more people in the world willing to storm and sack the place where all roads lead (no longer Rome, now Washington, D.C.).

Is foreign aid the answer? Will money solve the "poverty trap"? Sachs believes that if the rich countries increased their annual foreign-aid budgets to between $135 and $195 billion for the next decade, extreme poverty in the world would be eliminated. Conservative critics would argue that Sachs needs a reality check—that political, social, and cultural conditions prevent economic improvement in the foreseeable future. Even if oil or other resources were discovered in these countries, political and business corruption would prevent the vast majority of the populace from receiving benefits. The money would wind up in the hands of a tiny group of families or politicians, nothing more than a mirror of history of most third-world, poor nations. Sometimes it is European businessmen protecting their investments, sometimes it is homegrown mercenaries or rebels, and sometimes it is government officials or the country's ruling class hatching plots and stealing the riches from the country's oil fields. Typical cases where political corruption, family conflict, or mercenaries steal or squander oil revenues or prevent oil production are countries like Azerbaijan, Kazakhstan, the Congo, Nigeria, Sudan, and Yemen.

Given our wealth and resources, and our belief in the rule of law, how do we prepare our children and their children for this age of uncertainty, for what endures around the world? And for what might be? American students are unaware of the global village and often feel they are on top of the heap, but all around us there are ghettos and genocide, starvation and malnourishment, sickly and starving people living amid rampant political waste, fraud, and corruption, a pending global apocalypse. Do American teenagers who visit Nike and Reebok outlet stores, or who shop at J. Crew and the Gap, understand the thousands of foreign factories, many American, taking advantage of low wages and lax child labor laws in the pursuit of profits?

Do you think that the millions of U.S. teenagers who listen to the repugnant lyrics of Eminem and other hip-hop sounds,[14] coupled with photographs of multiracial sex acts or a sadomasochistic culture on VH1 or MTV, can make the leap and listen to the sounds and cries of the poor a world away from them? Do Americans understand that we are no longer the source of "cool"? That our movies, music, and art no longer win friends but make enemies? In the past (and even today), Americans have been unable to make the leap to the other side of the tracks, one or two miles away, to understand what sociologists have called the "invisible poor." How are Americans expected to make the global leap to better understand the world around them, when 60 percent of college-age Americans do not know where the United Nations headquarters are located and cannot find Iraq on the map?[15]

THE GROWING PROLETARIAT

The world's poor are a forgotten people; few people know or care to know their plight. This is the way it has been since Moses parted the sea and Jesus walked the earth preaching to the poor. About 40 million third-world people are infected with HIV; 300 to 500 million people are infected with malaria every year; 20 million children in third-world countries die of starvation each year, while another 800 million people suffer daily from malnourishment and hunger; and 50 percent of the world's population lives on no more than two dollars a day.[16] Ironically, in ten years , between 1987 and 1998, poverty (defined by the World Bank) increased 20 percent in Latin America, 40 percent in South Asia, and 50 percent in Africa. In Eastern Europe and Central Asia, it has increased more than 1000 percent. In twenty third-world countries (ten in Africa), the life expectancy is expected to dip below forty years. In sub-Saharan Africa, children under the age of five die at twenty-two times the rate of children in industrialized countries and also twice the rate of entire developing world.[17] According to economist and professor Gregory Clark of the University of California-Davis, living standards in almost half of Africa have fallen below hunter-gatherer times and 40 percent below the living standard of eighteenth-century England.[18]

An angry urban proletariat is growing around the world as poor populations—namely, hundreds of millions of rural migrants—flood to grimy overpopulated urban areas. There, they are assaulted by what is perceived as Western culture: luxury cars, nightclubs, sex and drugs, porno movies, gangs, and prostitution. Their daily existence is plagued by electric blackouts, unsanitary drinking water, overflowing sewage, and an assortment of five killer diseases—tuberculosis, typhoid, malaria, measles, and AIDS—annually killing some 54 million people worldwide.[19] It is not uncommon for more than half of this new proletariat to live on rooftops, in street alleys, and on the outskirts of the cities by garbage dumps.

This is the way of the world, the real world that Americans do not understand or know, given the paradox of American prosperity. The result is that many of these people find salvation in revolution and guerilla warfare, and still others in religion that offers eternal hope for a better life, including extreme and fanatical groups that preach U.S. hatred. Many of the nations in the developing worlds are going to unravel, not all at once, but in piecemeal fashion. As we try to assist these countries and buy off their political leaders, it will be the challenge of modernity itself (and with it comes Western culture) that will make so many of these people more bellicose toward the United States.

Dealing with global poverty is essential if democracy is to continue to prosper; otherwise, the growing world poor may tip the scale and its weight may eventually bring down our way of life. The people of third-world countries are not burning the American flag or effigies of President Obama, nor are they rioting in the streets on a regular basis. Their anger toward the West and rich nations is loosely articulated because these people, for the greater part, are working and struggling on a daily basis to exist and do not have time to take part in demonstrations. The third-world people we do see demonstrating on CNN are riveting to the American audience partially because of their anger toward the United States, partially because of their zeal, and partially because they seem to exist in another world so different from ours. For the most part, the world's poor believe, or are led to believe, that the United States is the cause of their squalor and misery, that their government cannot function efficiently because of U.S. dependence. In their need to lash out at someone, to vent their subsistence existence, they are recruits for various anti-American movements, including totalitarian and religious extremists.

The old elite, the wealthy in third-world countries, the one percenters, live a life walled off from the masses who are poor and who have migrated from rural shanty towns to urban squalor, where children die from starvation and disease, a world ripe with catastrophe that has lost much of its meaning to wealthy nations. By 2015, more than fifty cities in developing countries will have populations of 5 to 10 million in which the poor have no land, no business, no machines, no tangibles asset to create wealth—only the labor or sweat on their backs to offer, presently at a minimum wage for twelve to fourteen hours of work per day.

It is in these places, the rotting cities or urban garbage heaps of the world, where a new proletariat is being created—one in which the present governments are unable to provide basic necessities. Although some of these governments have been celebrated in the West and in the United States as pro-American or "democratic," this new and growing proletariat sees their government as corrupt, elected by ballot-rigging, or overrun by military coups, and supported by U.S. dollars, which get diverted to the pockets of the politicians and military at the expense of the inhabitants. The paradox is that, as government authority is weakened or overthrown, the people of the third world are being organized by regional, guerilla, or religious parties at the expense of national, progressive or secular ones.[20]

The governments in power must contend with, and in some cases to survive work with or actually support, those with extreme religious beliefs, terrorist ambitions, and left-wing political ideologies. In the mean time, the third-world proletariat grows larger—fostered by increasing poverty, illiteracy, and birthrates—and it is fueled by anti-American and anti-Western sentiments, which are easy to induce because of the growing gap between the rich and poor in the world, between the West and the third world, between modern-day rationalism and medieval irrationalism. For the greater part, the third-world cities are severely dysfunctional places, consisting of crumbling infrastructure, urban decay, drugs, and disease—and getting worse. It is happening slowly enough to avoid public sensitivity and sudden catastrophe, but it is happening in front of our eyes. Anyone who wishes to deal with a dose of reality can read about it in the *New York Times*, the UNESCO reports, sometimes in *Time* or *Newsweek*, or see it live on CNN or Fox news. You are not going to read about it in school textbooks, and very few teachers seem to have the interest or time to discuss these problems in class simply because the curriculum doesn't allow time for it and most teachers themselves are ignorant of this part of the world.

According to the sociologist Hernando de Soto, Marx was right in claiming that capitalism strips workers of their assets, except their labor. They are unable to accumulate capital legally because they don't own property or other tangible assets, such as businesses that create capital and permit people to accumulate wealth. So the market is restricted, mobility is inhibited, and wealth is limited to those who control the property and other tangible assets.[21] The only way for the poor in these countries to accumulate money is to deal in drugs, arms, sex trafficking, or some other black-market product or become a corrupt government bureaucrat and provide some service for a fee.[22]

Democracy and free trade, the globalization of the world, means in blunt terms tha the West is dominating third-world countries. The reason is that there is no legal avenue for the poor population in third-world countries to acquire assets (or education) and break from their misery and squalor on a scale sufficiently large to reverse worldwide growing poverty. Government officials in these countries are rarely held accountable; the powerful few—landowners, top military echelons and drug lords—continue to plunder the country and keep the poor in "chains," a metaphor originally described by Marx and Lenin. Modern-day smugglers and traffickers fleece and menace governments by trading military equipment, engaging in sex trade, and smuggling heroin or weapons of mass destruction. In short, world corruption and criminal behaviors are rampant among the powerful and no so powerful aspiring to break from poverty within most developing and undeveloped countries. Greed is not an American invention, but rather part of human condition. Adam Smith's theory of profit was read by more than Americans and our English cousins, and a lot more people around the world saw Michael Douglas's movie *Wall Street*, which glorified money and materialism.

Educators claim that the key to alleviating poverty is through education; sociologists claim that the key is to limit population growth; and business people claim that the key is industry, technology and free trade. Neo-Marxists (including de Soto) have a different spin, and it has some historical validity to it. They would like to redistribute the poverty, factories, businesses, and machines to the poor so they can accumulate capital—in short, so they can buy into the capitalistic system, instead of relying only in their labor, which amounts to continuous exploitation. The validity to the argument is that, in the Western world, this is how Australia and Canada were settled. People searched out and were able to acquire land for free by squatting on and settling it. The American government permitted its immigrants to acquire large tracts of farmland for free or for a few dollars, and the English nobility sold ninety-nine-year leases for low rent on many rural estates to the "common folk."

POSTMODERN REALITY

What do we tell American students so they wake up to world reality? How do we explain all the anti-American sentiments seen on cable television? How do our future citizens learn to deal with world anger—millions and billions of people driven by poverty, famine, and backbreaking labor? Even in boomtowns, the poor vent their anger at the West, and it becomes increasingly obvious in the media. Textbooks in American schools are currently censored and sanitized—and rarely reflect the political and economic realities of the world. Given different interpretations of that world, and that historical facts are little more than biases of the political left or right, how and what should American teachers do to prepare their students for globalization?

The ice cap is melting, the air we breathe is polluted, our energy resources are being depleted, drinking water is in short supply, sexual slavery and AIDS are facts of life, the worldwide landscape had been continuously plundered, and third-world business captains and politicians are often corrupt and drain off resources from their nations. Ask yourself how U.S. textbooks and teachers sanitize these issues, or the way they interpret "facts," and then ask what makes for a sound education. How do we prepare the next generation of Americans for what they will inherit? Indeed, the third world is growing in population and surrounding us! We are no longer able to live in a vacuum or on an island; 9/11 shattered our protective layer.

How much of a divide between "haves and "have-nots" can the world tolerate without insatiability? What role does the United States play? Should it be the world's policeman and moral compass? Based on whose values? Should the American president decide who is qualified to possess nuclear weapons? Why India? Why not Iran? Can our nation afford to remain isolationist, distant, or indifferent? How much of our resources should we share with the third-world populations? How much money should the average American give up to hopefully gain friends or converts abroad? What can educators do to prepare students, the next generation, for the world of 2050 and beyond in which it is estimated that the world population will reach about 10 billion? Can people living in a tent in the desert or on a mountaintop, distant from modern civilization, be expected to understand why Americans jets have invaded their sky?

I wish I could end on a positive note and fill your hearts and minds with Cinderella stories about how education reform will save the day around the world. Personally, I believe the gaps (in terms of productivity and wealth) between rich and poor nations have grown too wide, and the political/economic leadership within poor nations are too corrupt for "average people" or working people to accumulate sufficient income or assets to modify their social/economic mobility on any large scale. Poor people in poor nations have always lived a life characterized by limited education and subsistence economic levels. This is how economic elite groups, businesses and banking interests (less than 1 percent) have kept the "masses" in check for the last 7,000 years. The labels have changed over the centuries—slaves, serfs, peasants, farmers, factory workers, government bureaucrats, etc.—but the common people and workers of the world are still pushing stones uphill, as in the age of the pharaohs.

There has been vast inequality of income and wealth throughout the ages, and very few people have cared and those who have cared often been labeled as misfits: Jacobians, nihilists, radicals, anarchists, communists, etc. Here in the United States, a few "populists" now talk about growing inequality and how it has accelerated in the last five years due to recent tax policies that favor the rich. But around the world, the vast majority—billions of people—remain stone deaf about the nature of poverty and the growing inequality between rich and poor. For every cent of improvement produced by education, the birthrate of the world's poor moves us backward twice the amount. Sorry to go against the tide of popular opinion: Only a political revolution can make a difference, not education.

ENDNOTES

1. Allan C. Ornstein, *Class Counts* Education, Inequality and The Shrinking Middle Class (Lanham, MD: Rowman & Littlefield, 2007)
2. Here I feel the presence of Yevgeni Yevuschenko, who saw himself and his ancestors "persecuted, spat on, and slandered" for centuries in Europe and wrote about Belostock and Babiyar (mass murderer and mass grave): "I'm every old man executed here, as I am every child murdered," he wrote.
3. Nathan Glazer, *We Are All Multiculturalists Now* (Cambridge, MA: Harvard University Press, 1997); Oscar Handlin, The Newcomers (Garden City, NY: Doubleday, 1959); Michael Novak; *The Unmeltable Ethics,* rev. ed. (New Brunswick, NJ: Transaction Publishers, 1996); Theodore Caplow, Louis Hicks, and Ben J. Wattenberg, *The First Measured Century: An Illustrated Guide to Trends in America, 1900–2000* (Washington, DC: AEI Press, 2000).
4. David E. Sanger, "In Leading Nations, A population Bust?" *New York Times,* January 1, 2000, 8; Harold Hodgkinson, "The Demographics of Diversity," *Principle* (September 1998): 23–24.
5. Elisabeth Rosenthal, "European Union's Plunging Birthrates Spread Eastward," *New York Times,* September 4, 2006.
6. Ben J. Wattenberg, "Burying the Big Population Story," *International Herald Tribune,* May 18, 2001, 9.
7. Leslie Gaton, "Report on Staes." *New York Times,* January 1, 2000, 8.
8. "Fastest Growing Countries," *New York Times,* January 1, 2000, 8.
9. Between 2000 and 2010, the Hispanic population should increase by 9 million compared to the black population increase of 3.9 million.

10. Roger Cohen, "Cities: Audis and Cell Phones, Poverty and Fear," *New York Times,* January 1, 2000; Wattenberg, "Burying Big Population Story." If we add 80 million per year until 2025, the total approximates 8 billion people. Eighty percent of 8 billion is 6.4 billion; 75 percent is 6 billion.

11. Edmund L. Andrews and James Kanter, "Poor Nations Are Still Waiting," *New York Times,* July 4, 2006; Elizabeth Becker, "Poorer Countries Pull Out of Talks Over World Trade," *New York Times,* September 15, 2003; "The Rigged Game," *New York Times,* July 26, 2003; and Juliane von Reppert-Bismark, "How Trade Barriers Keep Africans Adrift," *Wall Street Journal,* December 27, 2006. The G-8 nations, the most industrialized, are Canada, England, France, Germany, Italy, Japan, Russia and the United States.

12. Keith Bradsher, "Ending Tariffs Is Only the Start," *New York Times,* February 28, 2006; John Zarocostas, "2007 Seen as a Potentially Defining Year," *New York Times,* December 27, 2006.

13. Jeffery D. Sachs, *The End of Poverty: Economic Possibilities for Our Time* (New York: Penguin, 2005).

14. Despite his crude slurs about women, gays and minorities, and despite his fantasies that promote murder, rape, and incest, including a defense in the Columbine killers, and his overall offensive lyrics, Eminem has won numerous Grammy Awards from the Academy of Recording Arts and Sciences. Some people believe that a nation's greatness is measured not only by its economic and military power but also by its artistic achievement or what might be called the "quality" of its civilization. Put into report-card terms, I would rate American hard rock and metal music "A" for free expression and shocking bourgeoisie and "F" for its visual themes and portrayal of American life and values. I suspect a good number of younger folks and jet-setting swingers would argue that I'm merely part of the older establishment and my views are humdrum and no longer relevant.

15. Allan C. Ornstein, *Teaching and Schooling in America: Pre and Post September 11* (Boston Allyn and Bacon, 2005); Charles Passy, "War of the Worlds," *New York Times,* March 26, 2006.

16. Based on 1998 World Bank data, "Poverty and Globalization," Center for Global Studies Conference, St John's University, April 16, 2001; Allan Ornstein, "Curriculum Trends Revisited," in *Contemporary Issues in Curriculum,* 2nd ed., ed. A.C. Ornstein and L. Behar-Hornstein, 265–276 (Boston: Allyn and Bacon, 1999); Virginia Postrel, "The Poverty Puzzle," *New York Times Book Review,* March 19, 2006. Also see Howard W. French, "Whistling Past the Global Graveyard," *New York Times,* July 14, 2002.

17. 1998 World Bank data; "Poverty and Globalization," Center for Global Studies Conference; Postrel, "The Poverty Puzzle"; French, "Whistling Past the Global Graveyard"; and Michael Wines, "Malnutrition Is Cheating Its Survivors, and Africa's Future," *New York Times,* July 14, 2002.

18. Gregory Clark, *A Farewell to Alms:A Brief Economic History of the World* (Princeton, NJ: Princeton University Press, 2007).

19. Stephanie Flanders, "In the Shadow of AIDS, A world of Other Problems," *New York Times,* June 24, 2001; Robert D. Kaplan, "A Nation's High Price for Success," *New York Times,* March 19, 2000, 15.

20. Todd S. Purdum, *A time of Our Choosing: America's War in Iraq* (New York: Times Books, 2004).

21. See Stephen Graubard, *Command of Office* (New York: Basic Books, 2005).

22. Hernando de Soto, *The Mystery of Capital: Why Capitalism Triumphs in the West and Fails Everywhere Else* (New York: Basic Books, 2001).

DISCUSSION QUESTIONS

1. How do global issues and changes in the world's population affect the world?
2. Why do you think the global issues outlined in this article are rarely taught in American classrooms?
3. The authors state, "For every cent of improvement produced by education, the birthrate of the world's poor moves us backward twice the amount." Explain what you think is meant by this.
4. How do you think the global issues outlined in this article can be best solved? Explain.

PRO-CON CHART 6

Should parental choice be a major consideration in determining where students attend school?

PRO	CON
1. The public school system is a monolithic structure that fosters middle-class conformity.	**1.** School choice will promote a dual-class educational system—schools for the rich and schools for the poor.
2. Public schooling perpetuates the existing power structure, including the subordinating effects of class, caste, and gender.	**2.** Parental choice will breed intolerance for diversity and will further religious, racial, and socioeconomic isolation.
3. The reduced quality of public education necessitates that parents be given options in order to locate better learning environments.	**3.** Transporting students out of neighborhoods is costly for school districts and is time-consuming for students.
4. Increasing choices means expanding educational opportunities for low-income and minority students.	**4.** Choice may not increase equity. In fact, it may lead to further segregation of low-income and minority students.
5. Competitive schools should stimulate statewide efforts to implement school reform.	**5.** Choice is not a solution for securing adequate funding, upgrading teachers' pedagogical skills, or reforming education.

CASE STUDY 6

School Board Debates Bilingual Education Program

"There can be no debate," demanded school board member Ricardo Del Rotberg. "Public education monies should be used for educating students in English only. Bilingual education is poor use of the community's tax dollars." Following this fiery opening statement, people in the gallery sat momentarily stunned. The entire community knew that this school year was sure to be contentious. No one doubted that the school board members were deeply divided over the issue of providing bilingual education to immigrant children.

After a long silence, board member Evita Ellmano moved toward the microphone. She reminded the board that the number of immigrant children attending district schools was increasing dramatically each year. She cited research showing that children who were given several years of instruction in their native language learned English faster and were successful academically. Ellmano also read results from the district's test scores, which demonstrated that students for whom English was not the dominant language lagged significantly behind other students academically. Del Rotberg retorted that it was his belief that multilingual education is an ill-founded practice that seeks to instill pride in students with low self-esteem. He also suggested that the school board lobby for legislation declaring English to be the nation's official language.

School board president Sarah Turner could no longer remain silent. She reminded board members that schools are obligated to help all students to live up to their fullest potential and to provide an education in their native language. Turner remarked that schools must embrace and value the traditions and cultures of all students. Moreover, she commented that bilingual education had become a target for people who opposed immigration. Finally, she stated that all teachers should be competent enough to teach their subject matter in at least one foreign language. Immediately, the teachers in the audience roared with protest. Turner pounded her gavel for nearly 8 minutes to restore order. Meanwhile, several security personnel came to the meeting room to encourage calmness.

Consider the following questions:

1. What information should be obtained to clarify the facts reflective of both positions?
2. What members of the community should become involved in discussions related to bilingual education programs?
3. Should teachers be expected to retool their pedagogical skills and learn to teach their subject matter in a foreign language? Why? Why not?
4. Are there programmatic alternatives to providing bilingual education to immigrant children?
5. Do schools have a responsibility in maintaining the ethnic culture of immigrant children?

Credits

This page constitutes a continuation of the copyright page.

Chapter 1 Allan C. Ornstein, "Philosophy as a Basis for Curriculum Decisions," *The High School Journal*, Vol. 74, December–January 1991, pp. 102–109. Reprinted from *The High School Journal*, Vol. 74, No. 2, December/January 1991. Copyright © 1991 by the University of North Carolina Press. Used by permission of *The High School Journal* and the University of North Carolina Press. All rights reserved.

Chapter 2 Ronald S. Brandt and Ralph W. Tyler, "Goals and Objectives," in *Fundamental Curriculum Decisions*, ASCD Yearbook, 1983, pp. 40–51. Reprinted with the permission of the Association for Supervision and Curriculum Development. Copyright © 1983 by the Association for Supervision and Curriculum Development. All rights reserved. The Association for Supervision and Curriculum Development is a worldwide community of educators advocating sound policies and sharing best practices to achieve the success of each learner. To learn more, visit ASCD at www.ascd.org.

Chapter 3 Peter McLaren, "A Pedagogy of Possibility: Reflecting Upon Paulo Freire's Politics of Education," *Educational Researcher*, Vol. 28, March 1999, pp. 49–54, 56. Reprinted with permission of *Educational Researcher*. Copyright © 1999 by *Educational Researcher*. All rights reserved.

Chapter 4 Maxine Greene, "Art and Imagination: Overcoming a Desperate Stasis," *Phi Delta Kappan*, Vol. 76, January 1995, pp. 378–382. Originally entitled, "Art and Imagination: Reclaiming a Sense of Possibility." Reprinted with permission of the author and *Phi Delta Kappan*. Copyright © 1995 by *Phi Delta Kappan*. All rights reserved.

Chapter 5 Phillip C. Schlechty, "No Community Left Behind," *Phi Delta Kappan*, *89*(8), April 2008, pp. 552–559. Reprinted with permission of the author and *Phi Delta Kappan*. Copyright 2008 by *Phi Delta Kappan*. All rights reserved.

Chapter 6 Nel Noddings, "Teaching Themes of Care," *Phi Delta Kappan*, Vol. 76, May 1995, pp. 675–679. Reprinted with permission of the author and *Phi Delta Kappan*. Copyright © 1995 by *Phi Delta Kappan*. All rights reserved.

Chapter 7 Parker J. Palmer, "The Heart of a Teacher: Identity and Integrity in Teaching," *Change*, Vol. 29, November–December 1997, pp. 14–21. Reprinted with permission of author and *Change*. Copyright © 1997 by Parker J. Palmer. All rights reserved.

Chapter 8 Allan C. Ornstein, "Critical Issues in Teaching." Printed with permission of the author. Copyright © 2001 by Allan C. Ornstein. All rights reserved.

Chapter 9 Herbert J. Walberg, "Productive Teachers: Assessing the Knowledge Base," *Phi Delta Kappan*, February 1990, pp. 470–478. Reprinted with permission of the author and *Phi Delta Kappan*. Copyright © 1990 by *Phi Delta Kappan*. All rights reserved.

Chapter 10 Edward F. Pajak, Elaine Stotko, and Frank Masci, "Honoring Diverse Styles of Beginning Teachers." Printed with permission of authors. Copyright 2007 by Edward F. Pajak. All rights reserved.

Chapter 11 Linda Darling-Hammond, "Keeping Good Teachers," *Educational Leadership*, May 2003, pp. 7–13. Reprinted with permission of the author.

Chapter 12 Theodore R. Sizer and Nancy Faust Sizer, "Grappling," *Phi Delta Kappan*, Vol. 81, November 1999, pp. 184–190. Reprinted with permission of the authors and *Phi Delta Kappan*. Copyright © 1999 by *Phi Delta Kappan*. All rights reserved.

Chapter 13 Robert J. Sternberg and Todd I. Lubart, "Creating Creative Minds," *Phi Delta Kappan*, Vol. 21, April 1991, pp. 608–614. Reprinted with permission of authors and *Phi Delta Kappan*. Copyright © 1991 by *Phi Delta Kappan*. All rights reserved.

Chapter 14 Lawrence Kohlberg, "The Cognitive—Developmental Approach to Moral Education," *Phi Delta Kappan*, Vol. 56, June 1975, pp. 670–677. Reprinted with permission of *Phi Delta Kappan*. Copyright © 1975 by the *Phi Delta Kappan*. All rights reserved. Table 1, Definition of Moral Stages in "The Claim to Moral Adequacy of a Highest Stage of Moral Judgment," reprinted with permission of the *Journal of Philosophy*, Vol. 70, October 1973, pp. 631–632. Copyright by the *Journal of Philosophy*. All rights reserved.

Chapter 15 Alfie Kohn, "A Critical Examination of Character Education," *Phi Delta Kappan*, Vol. 78, February 1997, pp. 428–439. Originally entitled, "How Not to Teach Values: A Look at Character Education." Copyright © 1997 by Alfie Kohn. Reprinted from *Phi Delta Kappan* with author's permission. All rights reserved.

Chapter 16 Jeannie S. Oakes, "Limiting Students' School Success and Life Chances: The Impact of Tracking," *Teachers College Record*, Vol. 96, Summer 1995, pp. 681–690. Originally entitled, "Two Cities: Tracking and Within School Segregation." Reprinted with permission of the author and Teachers College Record. Copyright © 1995 by *Teachers College Press.* Columbia University. All rights reserved.

Chapter 17 Veronica Boix Mansilla and Howard Gardner, "Disciplining the Mind," *Educational Leadership*, *65*(5) February 2008, pp. 14–19. Reprinted with permission of ASCD. Copyright by ASCD. All rights reserved. Learn more about ASCD at www.ascd.org.

Chapter 18 Benjamin S. Bloom, "The Search for Methods of Instruction," *Educational Researcher,* Vol. 13, June/July 1984, pp. 4–16. Originally entitled, "The 2 Sigma Problem: The Search for Methods of Group Instruction as Effective as One-to-One Tutoring." Reprinted with permission of *Educational Researcher.* Copyright © 1984 by *Educational Researcher.* All rights reserved.

Chapter 19 Evans Clinchy, "Needed: A New Educational Civil Rights Movement," *Phi Delta Kappan*, Vol. 82, March 2001, pp. 493–498. Reprinted with permission of the author.

Chapter 20 Arthur L. Costa, "The Thought-Filled Curriculum," *Educational Leadership, 65*(5), February 2008, pp. 20–24. Reprinted with permission of ASCD. Copyright 2003 by ASCD. All rights reserved. Learn more about ASCD at www.ascd.org.

Chapter 21 Geneva Gay, "The Importance of Multicultural Education," *Educational Leadership,* December/January 2003/2004, pp. 30–35. Reprinted with permission of author.

Chapter 22 David Perkins, "Knowledge Alive," *Educational Leadership*, September 2004, pp. 14–18. Reprinted with permission of the author.

Chapter 23 Stanley Pogrow, "Teaching Content Outrageously," *Phi Delta Kappan, 95*(5), January 2009, pp. 379–383. Reprinted with permission of the author and *Phi Delta Kappan.* Copyright 2008 by *Phi Delta Kappan.* All rights reserved.

Chapter 24 Thomas J. Sergiovanni, "The Politics of Virtue: A New Framework for School Leadership," *The School Community Journal*, Vol. 5, Fall/Winter 1995, pp. 13–22. Originally entitled "The Politics of Virtue: A New Compact for Leadership in Schools." Reprinted with permission from *The School Community Journal.* Copyright © 1995 by *The School Community Journal.* All rights reserved.

Chapter 25 Harry K. Wong, Ted Britton, and Tom Ganser, "What the World Can Teach Us About New Teacher Induction," *Phi Delta Kappan*, January 2005, pp. 379–384. Reprinted with permission of the authors.

Chapter 26 Edward F. Pajak, "Clinical Supervision and Psychological Functions: A New Direction for Theory and Practice," *Journal of Curriculum and Supervision*, Vol. 17, Spring 2002, pp. 187–205. Reprinted with permission of the author. Copyright © 2001 by Edward F. Pajak. All rights reserved.

Chapter 27 Frank Levy and Richard J. Murnane, "A Role for Technology in Professional Development? Lessons from IBM," *Phi Delta Kappan,* June 2004, pp. 728–734. Used with permission of Richard J. Murnane and Frank Levy.

Chapter 28 James Popham, "Instructional Insensitivity of Tests: Accountability's Dire Drawback," *Phi Delta Kappan, 89* (2), October 2007, pp. 146–150+155. Reprinted with permission of author and *Phi Delta Kappan.* Copyright 2004 by *Phi Delta Kappan.* All rights reserved.

Chapter 29 Daniel L. Duke, "Diagnosing School Decline," *Phi Delta Kappan, 89* (9), May 2008, pp. 667–671. Reprinted with permission of author and *Phi Delta Kappan.* Copyright 2008 by *Phi Delta Kappan.* All rights reserved.

Chapter 30 Harold L. Hodgkinson, "Educational Demographics: What Teachers Should Know," *Educational Leadership*, Vol. 58, December 2000, pp. 6–11. Reprinted with permission of the Association for Supervision and Curriculum Development. Copyright © 2000 by the Association for Supervision and Curriculum Development. All rights reserved. The Association for Supervision and Curriculum Development is a worldwide community of educators advocating sound policies and sharing best practices to achieve the success of each learner. To learn more, visit ASCD at www.ascd.org.

Chapter 31 Andy Hargreaves and Dennis Shirley, "Beyond Standardization: Powerful New Principles for Improvement," *Phi Delta Kappan,* October 2008, pp. 135–143. Copyright 2008 by *Phi Delta Kappan.* All rights reserved.

Chapter 32 Carl D. Glickman, "Dichotomizing School Reform: Why No One Wins and America Loses," *Phi Delta Kappan,* Vol. 83, October 2001, pp. 147–152. Reprinted with permission of the author and *Phi Delta Kappan.* Copyright © 2001 by the *Phi Delta Kappan.* All rights reserved.

Chapter 33 Linda Darling-Hammond and Laura McCloskey, "Assessment Around the World: What

Would It Mean to Be Internationally Competitive?," *Phi Delta Kappan, 90* (4), December 2008, pp. 263–272. Reprinted with permission of author and *Phi Delta Kappan*.

Chapter 34 Larry Cuban "The Perennial Reform: Fixing School Time," *Phi Delta Kappan, 90* (4), December 2008, pp. 240–250. Reprinted with permission of author and *Phi Delta Kappan*.

Chapter 35 Allan C. Ornstein and Jason Ornstein, "Poverty, Global Inequality, and Instability." Printed with permission of the authors.

Name Index

E

F

G

L

M

N

O

P

Y

Z

Subject Index

W

Y